American Experiences

Readings in American History

American Experiences

Readings in American History

Fourth Edition

∎

Randy Roberts

Purdue University

∎

James S. Olson

Sam Houston State University

An imprint of Addison Wesley Longman, Inc.

New York • Reading, Massachusetts • Menlo Park, California • Harlow, England
Don Mills, Ontario • Sydney • Mexico City • Madrid • Amsterdam

Executive Editor: Pam Gordon
Development Manager: Betty Slack
Senior Marketing Manager: Sue Westmoreland
Full Service Project Coordination, Text Design, and Electronic Page Makeup: Interactive
  Composition Corporation
Cover Designer: Kay Petronio
Cover Illustration: PhotoDisc, © 1997
Art Studio: Interactive Composition Corporation
Photo Researcher: Leslie Coopersmith
Production Manager: Eric Jorgensen
Manufacturing Manager: Hilda Koparanian
Printer and Binder: Maple-Vail Book Manufacturing Group
Cover Printer: Phoenix ColorCorp.

For permission to use copyrighted material, grateful acknowledgment is made to the copyright holders on p. 367, which are hereby made part of this copyright page

Library of Congress Cataloging-in-Publication Data

American experiences : readings in American history / [edited by]
  Randy Roberts, James S. Olson. — 4th ed.
    p.   cm.
  Includes bibliographical references.
  ISBN 0-321-01030-2 (v. 1). — ISBN 0-321-01031-0 (v. 2)
  1. United States—History.   I. Roberts, Randy, 1951–   .
II. Olson, James Stuart, 1946–   .
E178.6.A395   1997
973—dc21   97-34459
                                                  CIP

ISBN 0-321-01030-2

  5678910—MV—00

To Our Families

Contents

Preface

American History instructors enjoy talking about the grand sweep of the American past. Many note the development of unique traditions such as the American political tradition and the American diplomatic tradition. They employ the article *the* so often that they depict history as a seamless garment and Americans as all cut from the same fabric. Nothing could be further from the truth. America is a diverse country, and its population is the most ethnically varied in the world—white and black, Indian and Chicano, rich and poor, male and female. No single tradition can encompass this variety. *American Experiences* shows the complexity and richness of the nation's past by focusing on the people—how they coped with, adjusted to, or rebelled against America. The readings examine these people as they worked and played, fought and made love, lived and died.

We designed *American Experiences* as a supplement to the standard textbooks used in college survey classes in American History. Unlike other readers, it covers ground not usually found in textbooks. For example, instead of a discussion of the political impact of the Populist movement, it explores the *Wizard of Oz* as a Populist parable. In short, it presents different slants on standard and not-so-standard topics.

We have tested each essay in classrooms so that *American Experiences* reflects not only our interest in social history but also student interests in American history in general. We have selected essays that are readable, interesting, and that illustrate important aspects of America's past. For example, to show the nature of the class system in the South and to introduce the topic of southern values, we selected one essay on gambling and horse racing in the Old South and another on gouging matches in the southern backcountry. As an introduction to the conventional and medical view of women in the late nineteenth century, we selected an essay about Lizzie Borden. Each essay, then, serves at least two purposes: to tell a particular story well, and to help illuminate the social or political landscape of America.

This reader presents a balanced picture of the experiences of Americans. The characters in these volumes are not exclusively white males from the Northeast, whose eyes are continually focused on Boston, New York, and Washington. Although their stories are certainly important, so too are the stories of blacks adjusting with dignity to a barbarous labor system, Chicanos coming to terms with Anglo society, and women striving for increased opportunities in a society restricted by gender. We have looked at all of these stories and, in doing so, we have assumed that Americans express themselves in a variety of ways, through work, sex, and games, as well as politics and diplomacy.

During the past three years, we have solicited a variety of opinions, from colleagues and students, about the selections for *American Experiences*. Based on that feedback, we have made a number of changes in the fourth edition, always with the intent of selecting articles that undergraduate students will find interesting and informative. The new articles for the first volume of this edition are

- Marcus Rediker, "'Under the Banner of King Death': The Social World of the Anglo-American Pirates, 1716 to 1726"
- "Establishing a Government, 1789" from Forrest McDonald, *The Presidency of George Washington*
- John Mack Faragher, "'But a Common Man': Daniel Boone"
- Susan G. Davis, "'Making Night Hideous': Christmas Revelry and Public Order in Nineteenth-Century Philadelphia"
- William A. DeGregorio, "'The Choice': The Jackson-Dickinson Duel"
- Paul Andrew Hutton, "The Alamo: An American Epic"
- Maury Klien, "From Utopia to Mill Town"

New articles in Volume Two include

- Peter Stevens and Marian Eide, "The First Chapter of Children's Rights"
- Donald Worster, "The Black Blizzards Roll In"
- Roger J. Spiller, "My Guns: A Memoir of the Second World War"
- Ernest Sharpe, Jr., "The Man Who Changed His Skin"
- Matthew Dallek, "Liberalism Overthrown"

Each volume of *American Experiences* is divided into standard chronological and topical parts. Each part is introduced by a brief discussion of the major themes of the period or topic. In turn, each individual selection is preceded by a short discussion of how it fits into the part's general theme. We employed this method to give students some guidance through the complexity of American experience. At the conclusion of each selection is a series of study questions and a brief bibliographic essay. These are intended to further the usefulness of *American Experiences* for students as well as teachers.

We would like to thank our reviewers, who read the manuscript carefully and provided many valuable suggestions.

Terry Bilhartz, Sam Houston State University
Ronald H. Fritze, Lamar University
Beatriz B. Hardy, Coastal Carolina University
Marc S. Maltby, Owensboro Community College
Ronald E. Mickel, University of Wisconsin-Eau Claire
Judith A. Parsons, Sul Ross State University
Max Reichard, Delgado Community College
Thomas R. Turner, Bridgewater State College
Charles Zelden, Nova Southeastern University

Randy Roberts
James S. Olson

Part One

NEW ENGLAND LIFE

John Winthrop, the first governor of the Puritan settlement of Massachusetts Bay, was charged with a sense of mission. He and his Puritan followers braved the North Atlantic to establish a society in which the will of God would be observed completely. Aboard the flagship *Arbella* in April 1630, Winthrop explained their "errand into the wilderness." They were a unique people, for they had been given "a special commission" by God, and "He looks to have it strictly observed in every article." By working together, defeating selfishness, and keeping the Lord foremost in their thoughts, they would help create a kingdom of God on earth and blaze a trail for the future of all people. As Winthrop said, "Wee shall be as a City upon a Hill, the eies of all people are upon us."

The Puritans' Lord was a stern master, and their religion was as uncompromising as the cold rocky shores of New England. At the heart of Puritanism was the doctrine of predestination. Since humanity was too sinful to deserve salvation, God simply gave the gift of salvation to select individuals, while condemning the rest to eternal damnation. There was nothing an individual could do to alter this decision. Nor could an individual ever know absolutely if he or she was saved or damned.

The ultimate mystery of predestination created an underlying tension in Puritan society. Puritans searched constantly for some sign that they had received God's gift of salvation. In their diaries, they scrutinized their actions and thoughts, examining their lives for evidence of the sin that was inherent in all people. Puritans believed that sin could be as passive as an envious thought or as active as a violent deed. Occasionally, however, they found reason for hope.

The Puritans' deep religious belief influenced every aspect of their lives. They believed that God and the devil intervened constantly in daily affairs. The devil lurked in the New England forests and the Indian tribes, and stood ready to claim those with

weak hearts and bodies. In addition, God punished those who disobeyed His laws. A bolt of lightning or debilitating disease might very well be a sign of God's disfavor. The epidemic diseases that devastated the Indians were, in the Puritan mind, afflictions imposed by God.

Nevertheless, the Puritans should not be viewed as one-dimensional people. Their sins, excesses, and great accomplishments were the actions of humans. The following selections of essays present the world of the Puritans at its best and worst. The common thread in these essays is the Puritans' commitment to their religion and the way in which they used that religion to interpret and determine the course of their lives. Ultimately, the history of American Puritanism is the unfolding of a religious idea.

Not all of New England was Puritan, however. As the northern colonies matured, many people moved away from the stern religion of the earliest settlers. Some were more recent immigrants who had never followed the Puritan faith; others were children or grandchildren of Puritans in whose hearts the fire of faith did not burn as strongly. Certainly Boston and Massachusetts Bay retained something of its Puritan heritage, but its economic position in the British empire also exerted a powerful influence. By the eighteenth century, images of zealous Puritans and shrewd Yankees mixed to form the popular conception of the New Englander. If Sunday remained God's day, trade and commerce ruled the rest of the week. Tied to England and the West Indies by economic bonds, Boston—like Philadelphia and Charles Town—became part of the Atlantic community.

"GOD...WOULD DESTROY THEM, AND GIVE THEIR COUNTRY TO ANOTHER PEOPLE..."

Alfred W. Crosby

In 1616 or 1617, several years before the Pilgrims and later the Puritans ever arrived in Massachusetts, the local Indians suffered from catastrophic epidemics of disease, probably from a malignant form of typhus left behind by some sick Europeans whose ships anchored temporarily along the coast as a refuge from bad weather. The Indians had no immunities. They had been separated geographically from the European and Asian landmasses for thousands of years, leaving them unprepared for the variety of diseases the Europeans brought—typhus, bubonic plague, smallpox, chicken pox, mumps, measles, influenza, diphtheria, and a host of other maladies. Europeans, with their dense urban populations and wide variety of domesticated animals, had already accumulated the necessary immunities. But the illnesses spread like a wildfire through the Indian villages, devastating whole tribes and whole regions, depopulating the area as Indians either died or fled. European germs were far more important than European weapons in explaining how so few conquered so many in the New World.

Indians found the plagues profoundly disturbing—a series of events inconsistent with their worldview. For them, disease was simply a manifestation of spiritual imbalances, which could be cured by medicine men who understood the balances of nature and the human psyche. When their own healers failed to stem the plagues, the Indians lost not only their lives but their faith and vision as well. Puritans interpreted the plague as the punishment of God. Indian idolatry could not be tolerated, and since they would not repent, God poured out his wrath upon them. In the process of destroying the Indians, God also gave "their country to another people"—the Puritans.

In December of 1620, a group of English dissenters who "knew they were pilgrimes," in the words of William Bradford, stepped ashore on the southern coast of Massachusetts at the site of the Wampanoag Indian village of Pawtuxet. The village was empty, abandoned long enough for the grasses and weeds to have taken over the cornfields, but not long enough for the trees to have returned. The Pilgrims occupied the lonely place and called it Plymouth.

It was pestilence that had cleared the way for this tiny foothold in New England, and the shadow of death would be a major factor in giving the settlement form and substance in the months ahead.

New England Indians and European fishermen and traders had been in intermittent contact for a century, and it was inevitable that more than otter skins, beaver pelts, knives, and kettles would be exchanged. Disease was among the commodities, and in this trade the Indians would come off second best. Europe, with ancient contact by land and new ones by sea with the chief disease communities of the world, and with her relatively dense populations of often hungry and always filthy people, had all the advantages of her disadvantages: an arsenal of diseases.

Europe was in the midst of a golden age for infectious disease organisms, an era ushered in by the Black Death in the fourteenth century. To such old regulars as smallpox and consumption were added such new, or newly recognized, diseases as plague, typhus, and syphilis. Bubonic plague, the greatest killer of them all, smoldered continually and broke out periodically in consuming epidemics. Early in 1617 southeast gales drove whales ashore in the Netherlands. The fearful thought them a portent of plague, and

"God . . . Would Destroy Them, and Give Their Country to Another People . . ." by Alfred W. Crosby in *American Heritage* 29 (October/November 1978), pp. 39–43. Reprinted by permission of *American Heritage Magazine,* a division of Forbes Inc., © Forbes Inc., 1978.

sure enough, by August the plague was general throughout the land. London had full-scale epidemics of that killer in 1603 and again in 1625, and the plague—or something very like it—soon made its presence felt among the Indians of the Northeast coast of America. Innocent of immunity or experience, the Indians were helpless.

As Indian tempers rose, respect for Europeans fell in the second decade of the seventeenth century, particularly after the kidnaping of Indians for purposes of slavery began. Sometime in that period, a French ship was wrecked on the shores of Massachusetts, and some of the crew escaped alive. Possibly, in retaliation for a recent kidnaping raid by whites, the Indians eventually killed all but three or four, whom they reduced to slavery. According to what the Indians told the Pilgrims, one of these captives, angry and helpless, had struck at his captors with words, telling them that "God was angry with them for their wickedness, and would destroy them, and give their country to another people, that should not live as beasts as they did but should be clothed. . . ." The Indians laughed at him, saying that they were so numerous that the white man's god could not kill them. He answered "that though they were never so many, God had many ways to destroy them that they knew not." Within a year or so an epidemic struck the coast of New England, devastating the tribes like an autumnal nor'easter raking leaves from the trees.

When did this pestilence first appear in New England? Probably no earlier than 1616 and no later than 1617, and it lasted until at least 1619. What vessel brought it? It is improbable that we will ever know. What was the disease? Another difficult question. We know it lasted through winters, which suggests that it wasn't a mosquito-borne disease, like yellow fever. We know that the few Europeans who actually saw its victims did not identify it as smallpox, measles, mumps, chicken pox, or any of Europe's common diseases, which they certainly would have recognized. We know it spread along the coast no farther southwest than Narragansett Bay, nor farther northeast than the Kennebec River or possibly Penobscot

Bay, nor did it penetrate inland more than twenty or thirty miles. The narrow geographical limitations of the epidemic suggest that the disease was not one of the breath-borne maladies, like smallpox or measles, which normally surge across vast areas. A flea- or louse-borne disease like typhus or plague seems more likely.

We know that the disease produced spots on its victim's skins; and we know by hearsay that some Englishmen in New England at the peak of the epidemic slept in huts with dead and dying Indians, but that not one of these whites fell ill or even so much as "felt their heads to ache while they stayed there." Spots certainly suggest typhus. The Europeans' freedom from infection suggests some disease so common in Europe that they all had acquired immunity to it at home, or that they didn't stay around long enough to get a proper dose of the disease—or that the account is in part or whole false.

Most of the seventeenth-century chroniclers called the disease the plague. "Plague" was and is a word often used to mean any pestilence, but these chroniclers often called it "*the* plague." Captain Thomas Dermer, one of the few Europeans actually to see Indians who were freshly recovering from the experience, called their infection in 1619 "the Plague, for wee might perceive the sores of some that had escaped, who described the spots of such as usually died."

Plague is certainly capable of doing what this pestilence did, and Europeans certainly knew it well enough to recognize it by sight or description. And it is true that plague was well established in Western Europe in the early years of the seventeenth century. Like some kinds of typhus, it is a disease carried by rats and their attendant vermin, rats which swarmed in the holds of the sailing vessels of that era. The disease travels readily by ship, as the European colonists in America knew. Many Britons fell ill and died on the vessels of the Third Supply sailing to Virginia in 1609, and a rumor was that one of the vessels had plague on board. In the 1660's, during London's last great siege of plague, Virginians fled from their ports for fear of the disease coming across on the ships from England.

Fear was justified because ship rats were coming across and establishing beachheads in America. Captain John Smith tells us that they already numbered in the thousands in Jamestown in 1609, when the rats almost starved out the colony by eating its stores of food. They were present and prospering in New England by at least the 1660's, and probably a great deal earlier. It is likely that they found living in the layered bark walls of the Indian wigwams warm and comfortable, and the Indian food-storage practices and eating habits conducive to good diet. Once the rats were established, the transfer of their plague-ridden fleas to the Indians would have been almost automatic and perhaps not even noticed by the new hosts. Body lice were even more common among New England Indians than among white settlers, and the natives commonly passed the time by picking lice and killing them between their teeth.

It is disturbing, though, to those who diagnose the pestilence as plague, that Dermer described its chief signs as sores and spots, rather than the terrible buboes or boils of the groin and armpits that are impossible to overlook in typical victims of the plague. And it is even more odd that the plague-infected fleas did not establish themselves and their bacilli permanently among the wild rodents of New England, as they did in those of the western United States at the end of the nineteenth century. A diagnosis of typhus is tempting, but the historian is reluctant to contradict first-hand witnesses.

Whether plague or typhus, the disease went through the Indians like fire. Almost all the seventeenth-century writers say it killed nine of ten and even nineteen of twenty of the Indians it touched—an incredible mortality rate. But if it was, indeed, plague, it could well have killed that proportion. In the fourteenth century, plague killed one-third of all the people in Europe and a much higher percentage than that in many towns and districts. Further, the Indians knew nothing of the principle of contagion and had an ancient custom of visiting the sick, jamming into extremely hot little huts with them, assuring maximum dispersal of the illness. Their methods of treating illness, which usually featured a stay in a sweatbox, followed by immersion in the nearest cold pond or river, would have been a dreadful trauma for a person with a high fever, and a fine way to encourage pneumonic complications. Consider, too, that the epidemic could not have failed to disrupt food-procurement patterns, as women lay too ill to tend the corn and the men too weak to hunt. Starvation often gleans what epidemic disease has missed. Consider, finally, that after the Indians realized the full extent of the disease, some of them, at least, ran away and left the sick and convalescent to die of neglect. In short, one does not necessarily have to accept a 90 per cent death rate for a given village or area in order to accept a 90 percent depopulation rate.

It is undeniable that the pestilence largely emptied the Indian villages of coastal New England by 1619. That year, Thomas Dermer found "ancient plantations, not long since populous, now utterly void; in other places a remnant remains, but not free of sickness."

In 1621 a party of Pilgrims went to visit Massasoit, the most powerful Wampanoag sachem, at his summer quarters on a river about fifteen miles from Plymouth. They saw the remnants of many villages and former Indian cornfields along both sides of the river grown up in weeds higher than a man's head: "Thousands of men have lived there, which died in a great plague not long since: and pity it was and is to see so many goodly fields, and so well seated, without men to dress and manure the same."

Near Boston Bay, Thomas Morton saw even more vivid indications of the plague: "For in a place where many inhabited, there hath been but one left alive, to tell what became of the rest, the living being (as it seemed) not able to bury the dead, they were left for Crowes, kites and vermin to prey upon. And the bones and skulls upon the severall places of their habitations, made such a spectacle after my coming into those partes, that as I travailed in that Forrest, nere the Massachusets, it seemed to mee a new found Golgotha."

What destroyed Indian bodies also undermined Indian religion—the Indian's entire view of the universe and of himself. Disease was always considered a manifestation of spiritual influences, and the power of the powwows (medicine men) to direct and cure disease was central to the Indian religion. Later in the century we hear of powwows being hounded, punished, and even killed for failing to produce promised cures. What was the impact when hundreds, even thousands, died under the hands of leaders whose chief distinction was their ability to cure? Many of the powwows themselves, in constant contact with the sick they sought to cure, must have died. What was the impact of this final and irrevocable defeat of these priestly physicians?

What seemed cosmically appalling to the Indians was interpreted as clear proof of God's love by the Pilgrims—a divine intercession that revealed itself from the beginning. They had planned to settle in the Hudson River area or thereabouts, but the master of the *Mayflower* deposited them on the coast of New England. His inability or refusal to take them where they wanted to go proved a bit of luck—"God outshoots Satan oftentimes in his own bow"—for the lands about the Hudson's mouth, though more attractive because more fertile than Plymouth's, were "then abounding with a multitude of pernicious savages. . . ." God had directed the Pilgrims to a coast His plague had cleared of such savages: "whereby he made way for the carrying of his good purpose in promulgating his gospel. . . ." There were no Indians at Plymouth and none for eight or ten miles, and yet it had recently been a village of Wampanoags who had, over the years, cut away the tough climax growth of forest to plant corn. When the weak and hungry Colonists went out to plant in the following spring, all they had to do was to clear out the weeds. Death, it seemed obvious, was God's handyman and the Pilgrim's friend.

The wind of pestilence did more than merely clear a safe place for the Pilgrims to settle; in the long run, it enabled that settlement not only to survive, but to take root and, in the end, to prosper with a minimum of native resistance. The natives of coastal Massachusetts were fewer in

Tisquantum ("Squanto") taught the Pilgrims how
to plant and grow corn.

number than in a very long time, possibly than in
several thousand years, but there were still quite
enough of them to wipe out the few Europeans
from the *Mayflower,* and they had reason to hate
whites. In addition to kidnapings, Europeans—
English, the Indians told Dermer—recently had
lured a number of Wampanoags on board their
ship and had then "made great slaughter of them
with their murderers (small ship's cannon). . . ."
When a party of Pilgrims visited the next tribe to
the south, the Nausets, in 1621, they met an old
woman who broke "forth into great passion,
weeping and crying excessively." She had lost
three of her sons to kidnapers, and now was without comfort in her old age. A Wampanoag said
that the Nausets had killed three English interlop-
ers in the summer of 1620.

Half the English at Plymouth died of malnutri-
tion, exhaustion, and exposure that first winter.
Indian anger and Indian power could have made
Plymouth one of the lost colonies, like the one
Columbus left behind on La Española in 1493 or
Sir Walter Raleigh's Roanoke colony of the 1580's.

At some time during this low ebb of Pilgrim
history the powwows gathered in the fastnesses
of a swamp, where, for three days, they "did curse
and execrate" the newcomers to destroy them or
drive them away. It almost worked: at times the
number of English healthy enough to offer any
real help to the sick and, if necessary, any real resistance to attackers was as low as six or seven.
But in the end the Indian's gods failed, and the
English survived, "having borne this affliction
with much patience, being upheld by the Lord."

What held the Indians back from physical attack? They had the strength and motive, and
bloody precedent had been set by both whites and
Indians. The answer must be fear. The coastal Indians may have been second only to the Pilgrims
in New England as believers in the power of the
white man's god. A visitor to Plymouth in 1621
wrote that the plague had sapped Wampanoag
courage, as well as the tribe's numbers: "their
countenance is dejected, and they seem as a people affrighted." They were coming to the English
settlement in great numbers every day, "and might
in one hour have made a dispatch of us, yet such a
fear was upon them, as that they never offered us
the least injury in word or deed."

Direct relations between the Wampanoags and
the Pilgrims began in March of 1621, approximately three months after the English arrival. An
Indian walked out of the woods and through the
fields and into Plymouth. He was Samoset, who
spoke some English, having learned it from English fishermen on the coast of Maine. He asked for
beer, and received "strong water," biscuit, butter,
cheese, pudding, and a piece of duck. It was he
who told the Pilgrims the old Indian name for their
village and explained what had happened to its
original inhabitants. A few days later he returned
with the individual whom the Pilgrims would
soon rank as "a special instrument sent of God for
their good beyond their expectation." The man
was Squanto, a Pawtuxet who had been kidnaped,
had escaped in Spain, and had lived in Cornhill,
London, before making his way back to America.

An hour later the sachem, Massasoit, walked in with a train of sixty men. If he had come to fight, he could have swept Plymouth out of existence, but he came in peace, and what amounts to a nonaggression and mutual defense pact was soon agreed upon—the Treaty of Plymouth. Massasoit, wrote Edward Winslow in his first-person account of that day in March, "hath a potent adversary, the Narrohigansets (Narragansets), that are at war with him, against whom he thinks we may be some strength to him, for our peeces are terrible unto them."

In the eyes of the native people of New England, the whites possessed a greater potency, a greater mana, than any Indian people. Nothing could be more immediately impressive than firearms, which made clouds of smoke and a sound like the nearest of thunderclaps and killed at a distance of many paces. And what could seem more logical but to see a similarity between the muskets and cannon, which reached out invisibly and tore bodies, and the plague, which reached out invisibly and corrupted bodies? In the 1580's, Indians in the vicinity of Roanoke had blamed the epidemic then raging on "invisible bullets" that the whites could shoot any distance desired; and it is quite likely that Massasoit and his followers had a similar interpretation of their experience with epidemic disease. No wonder the mighty sachem literally trembled as he sat beside the governor of Plymouth that day in March of 1621.

The following year, the Pilgrims learned that Squanto, taking advantage of his position as go-between for the Indians and English, had been telling the former that he had such control over the latter that he could persuade them to unleash the plague again, if he wished. He tried to use this claim of immense power to persuade the Wampanoags to shift their allegiance from Massasoit to himself. It was a game which nearly cost the schemer his life, and he had to spend the rest of his days living with the Pilgrims.

He told the Indians that the plague was buried under the storehouse in Plymouth, where, interestingly enough, the Pilgrims did have something buried: their reserve kegs of gunpowder. He told

the Wampanoags that the English could send the plague forth to destroy whomever they wished, while not stirring a foot from home. When, in May of 1622, the Pilgrims dug up some of the gunpowder kegs, another Wampanoag, understandably disturbed, asked the English if they did, indeed, have the plague at their beck and call. The answer he got was as honest a one as could be expected from a seventeenth-century Christian: "No; but the God of the English has it in store, and could send it at his pleasure, to the destruction of his or our enemies." Not long after, Massasoit asked Governor William Bradford if "he would let out the plague to destroy the Sachem, and his men, who were his enemies, promising that he himself, and all his posterity, would be their everlasting friends, so great an opinion he had of the English."

Those enemies were the Narragansets, whose presence was the greatest immediate threat to Plymouth, and whose fear of the Englishmen's power was Plymouth's (and the Wampanoags') best shield. In the late fall of 1621 Canonicus, the Narragansets' greatest sachem, sent a bundle of arrows wrapped in a snakeskin to Squanto at Plymouth. Squanto was not present when they arrived, for which the messenger who brought the bundle was visibly thankful, and he departed "with all expedition." When Squanto returned and examined Canonicus' package, he explained that it signified a threat and a challenge to the new colony. The governor, who as a European of the Reformation era knew as much of threat and challenge as any Indian, stuffed the skin with gunpowder and shot, and sent it back to Canonicus. The great and terrible sachem refused to accept it, would not touch the powder and shot, nor suffer the bundle to remain in Narraganset country. The sinister package, "having been posted from place to place a long time, at length came whole back again." The plague perhaps had taught the Indian the principle of contagion.

Disease, real and imagined, remained a crucial element in English-Indian relations for at least the next two years, and seemingly always to the advantage of the English. In 1622 and 1623 the Pilgrims were still so incompetent at living in

America that only the abundance of shellfish and corn obtained from the Indians kept them from starvation: a dangerous situation, because by then the Indians' fear of and respect for the whites were declining. As one Pilgrim chronicler put it, the Indians "began again to cast forth many insulting speeches, glorying in our weakness, and giving out how easy it would be ere long to cut us off. Now also Massassowat [Massasoit] seemed to frown on us, and neither came or sent to us as formerly." A letter arrived from Jamestown far to the south in Virginia telling of how the Indians had risen there, killing hundreds of the colonists. In the summer of 1622 a band of ne'er-do-well English settled at Wessagusset (Weymouth), not far from Plymouth, and after begging food from the impoverished Pilgrims, set about stealing it from the Indians. That fall Squanto, the almost indispensable man in the Pilgrims' dealings with the Indians, fell ill on a trip to collect corn from the natives. After fever and nosebleeds he died, asking the governor to pray for him "that he might go to the Englishman's God in heaven. . . ."

The Indians, apparently with the Massachusetts tribe in the lead, began to plot to exterminate the Wessagusset settlement. They were less intolerant of the Plymouth than the Wessagusset people, but their plan was to destroy the Pilgrims, as well, for fear that the latter would take revenge for the murder of any English. The scheme never got beyond the talking stage. Why weren't the Indians able to organize themselves and take the action they planned? Pilgrims collecting corn from the Massachusetts in the latter part of 1622 learned of a "great sickness" among them "not unlike the plague, if not the same." Soon after, Wampanoag women bringing corn to Plymouth were struck with a "great sickness," and the English were obliged to carry much of the corn home on their own backs.

Disease or, at least, bodily malfunction most dramatically affected New England history in 1623 when Massasoit developed a massive case of constipation. In March the news arrived in Plymouth that Massasoit was close to death and that a Dutch vessel had grounded on the sands right in front of his current home. The English knew of the Indian custom that any and all friends must visit the ill, especially the very ill, and they also wanted to meet with the stranded Dutch; so a small party set out from Plymouth for the sachem's sickbed. The Pilgrims found the Dutch afloat and gone, and Massasoit's dwelling jammed to bursting with well-wishers and powwows "making such a hellish noise, as it distempered us that were well, and therefore unlike to ease him that was sick."

Edward Winslow undertook the sachem's case and managed to get between his teeth "a confection of many comfortable conserves, on the point of my knife. . . ." He then washed out his patient's mouth, put him on a light diet, and soon his bowels were functioning again. The Englishman had, with the simplest of Hippocratic remedies, apparently saved the life of the most powerful man in the immediate environs of Plymouth. For the next day or so Winslow was kept busy going from one to another of the sachem's sick or allegedly sick followers, doling out smidgens of his confection and receiving "many joyful thanks." In an era which was, for the Indians, one of almost incomprehensible mortality, Winslow had succeeded where all the powwows had failed in thwarting the influences drawing Massasoit toward death. The English could not only persuade a profoundly malevolent god to kill, but also *not* to kill.

The most important immediate product of Massasoit's recovery was his gratitude. He revealed the details of the Indian plot against Wessagusset and Plymouth, a plot involving most of the larger tribes within two or three days' travel of Plymouth, and even the Indians of Capawack (Martha's Vineyard). He said he had been asked to join when he was sick, but had refused for himself and his people. The Pilgrims probably had already heard rumors of the plot, and the sachem's story was confirmed by Phineas Pratt, one of the ne'er-do-wells from Wessagusset, who made his way by fleetness of foot and luck through hostile Indians to Plymouth.

Captain Miles Standish sailed to Boston Bay with a small group of armed men, tiny in number but gigantic in the power the Indians thought they possessed. They killed five or so of the alleged leaders of the plot and returned home with the head of one of them. The remnants of the Wessagusset colony were swept together and brought to Plymouth, where in time most of them made the decision to go back to Europe as hands on the vessels fishing along the Maine coast. The Indian head was set up at Plymouth fort as a visual aid to Indian education.

The Indian plan to wipe out the white colonies fell to pieces. Members of the several tribes within striking distance of Plymouth "forsook their houses, running to and fro like men distracted, living in swamps and other desert places, and so brought manifold diseases amongst themselves, whereof very many are dead. . . ." Ianough, sachem of the Massachusets, said "the God of the English was offended with them, and would destroy them in his anger. . . ." The Pilgrims noted smugly that the mortality rate among their opponents was, indeed, high, and "neither is there any likelihood it will easily cease; because through fear they set little or no corn, which is the staff of life, and without which they cannot long preserve health and strength."

By 1622 or so the very last cases of the plague had occurred in New England—if indeed these were examples of plague and not of misdiagnosis —and the only remains of the great pestilence were disarticulating bones lost in fallen walls of rotting bark that had once been homes. But it had done its work. In 1625 the Pilgrims, for the first time, raised enough corn to fill their own stomachs *and* trade with the Indians. The Pilgrims had survived and were getting stronger, thanks more to biology than religion, despite Pilgrim preconceptions, but Thomas Morton nevertheless was reminded of a line from Exodus: "By little and little (saith God of old to his people) will I drive them out from before thee; till thou be increased, and inherit the land."

STUDY QUESTIONS

1. Why does Crosby think typhus was one of the diseases that struck the Indians? What other disease might have been responsible for the epidemics?

2. How were the Pilgrims viewed by their Indian neighbors?

3. How did Indians react when their own healers could not cure the diseases?

4. How did the Pilgrims regard the Indians of New England?

5. Who was Samoset? Squanto? Massasoit?

6. What Indian practices actually made the epidemics worse?

7. Why did the Indian plan to wipe out the Pilgrim settlement fail to materialize?

BIBLIOGRAPHY

Gary B. Nash surveys early Indian-colonist relations in *Red, White, and Black,* 3d ed. (1992). On long-term consequences of the conquest of America, see Alfred W. Crosby, *The Columbian Exchange: Biological and Cultural Consequences of 1492* (1972). Also see Crosby's *Biological Imperialism* (1990). For specific descriptions of Indian-European relations in New England, see Alden T. Vaughn, *New England Frontier: Puritans and Indians* (1965); Neal Salisbury, *Manitou and Providence: Indians, Europeans, and the Making of New England* (1982); and Francis Jennings, *The Invasion of America: Indians, Colonialism, and the Cant of Conquest* (1975).

THE PURITANS AND SEX

Edmund S. Morgan

During the 1920s, as many Americans challenged nineteenth-century social norms and moved toward greater sexual freedom, historians often blamed their Puritan fore-fathers for the restrictive elements they saw in their own society. For them, the Puritans were narrow-minded bigots who were intent on banning all that was natural, joyful, and refreshing in society. H. L. Mencken best captured this attitude by defining Puritanism as "the haunting fear that someone, somewhere, may be happy."

This stereotype of Puritans as humorless and sexually repressed has maintained a firm hold on the popular historical imagination. Reay Tannahill, in her book *Sex in History,* refers to the "dour moral standards" of Puritans. However, the Puritans were not as inhibited as popularly believed. As Edmund S. Morgan demonstrates, the Puritans were intensely religious people who nevertheless understood that humans were often morally weak. Indeed, they "showed none of the blind zeal or narrow-minded bigotry which is too often supposed to have been characteristic of them. The more one learns about these people, the less do they appear to have resembled the sad and sour portraits which their . . . critics have drawn of them."

Henry Adams once observed that Americans have "ostentatiously ignored" sex. He could think of only two American writers who touched upon the subject with any degree of boldness—Walt Whitman and Bret Harte. Since the time when Adams made this penetrating observation, American writers have been making up for lost time in a way that would make Bret Harte, if not Whitman, blush. And yet there is still more truth than falsehood in Adams's statement. Americans, by comparison with Europeans or Asiatics, are squeamish when confronted with the facts of life. My purpose is not to account for this squeamishness, but simply to point out that the Puritans, those bogeymen of the modern intellectual, are not responsible for it.

At the outset, consider the Puritans' attitude toward marriage and the role of sex in marriage. The popular assumption might be that the Puritans frowned on marriage and tried to hush up the physical aspect of it as much as possible, but listen to what they themselves had to say. Samuel Willard, minister of the Old South Church in the latter part of the seventeenth century and author of the most complete textbook of Puritan divinity, more than once expressed his horror at "that Popish conceit of the Excellency of Virginity." Another minister, John Cotton, wrote that

Women are Creatures without which there is no comfortable Living for man: it is true of them what is wont to be said of Governments, That bad ones are better than none: They are a sort of Blasphemers then who dispise and decry them, and call them a necessary Evil, for they are a necessary Good.

These sentiments did not arise from an interpretation of marriage as a spiritual partnership, in which sexual intercourse was a minor or inciden-

"The Puritans and Sex" by Edmund S. Morgan in *New England Quarterly*, XV, December 1942, pp. 591–607. Reprinted by permission.

tal matter. Cotton gave his opinion of "Platonic love" when he recalled the case of

one who immediately upon marriage, without ever approaching the Nuptial Bed, *indented with the* Bride, *that by mutual consent they might both live such a life, and according did sequestring themselves according to the custom of those times, from the rest of mankind, and afterwards from one another too, in their retired Cells, giving themselves up to a Contemplative life; and this is recorded as an instance of no little or ordinary Vertue; but I must be pardoned in it, if I can account it no other than an effort of blind zeal, for they are the dictates of a blind mind they follow therein, and not of that Holy Spirit, which saith It is not good that man should be alone.*

Here is as healthy an attitude as one could hope to find anywhere. Cotton certainly cannot be accused of ignoring human nature. Nor was he an isolated example among the Puritans. Another minister stated plainly that "the Use of the Marriage Bed" is "founded in mans Nature," and that consequently any withdrawal from sexual intercourse upon the part of husband or wife "Denies all reliefe in Wedlock vnto Human necessity: and sends it for supply vnto Beastiality when God gives not the gift of Continency." In other words, sexual intercourse was a human necessity and marriage the only proper supply for it. These were the views of the New England clergy, the acknowledged leaders of the community, the most Puritanical of the Puritans. As proof that their congregations concurred with them, one may cite the case in which the members of the First Church of Boston expelled James Mattock because, among other offenses, "he denied Coniugall fellowship vnto his wife for the space of 2 years together vpon pretense of taking Revenge upon himself for his abusing of her before marryage." So strongly did the Puritans insist upon the sexual character of marriage that one New Englander considered himself slandered when it was reported, "that he Brock his deceased wife's hart with Greife, that he wold be absent from her 3 weeks together when he was at home, and wold never come nere her and such Like."

There was just one limitation which the Puritans placed upon sexual relations in marriage: sex must not interfere with religion. Man's chief end was to glorify God, and all earthly delights must promote that end, not hinder it. Love for a wife was carried too far when it led a man to neglect his God:

. . . sometimes a man hath a good affection to Religion, but the love of his wife carries him away, a man may bee so transported to his wife, that hee dare not bee forward in Religion, lest hee displease his wife, and so the wife, lest shee displease her husband, and this is an inordinate love, when it exceeds measure.

Sexual pleasures, in this respect, were treated like other kinds of pleasure. On a day of fast, when all comforts were supposed to be foregone in behalf of religious contemplation, not only were tasty food and drink to be abandoned but sexual intercourse, too. On other occasions, when food, drink, and recreation were allowable, sexual intercourse was allowable too, though of course only between persons who were married to each other. The Puritans were not ascetics; they never wished to prevent the enjoyment of earthly delights. They merely demanded that the pleasures of the flesh be subordinated to the greater glory of God: husband and wife must not become "so transported with affection, that they look at no higher end than marriage it self." "Let such as have wives," said the ministers, "look at them not for their own ends, but to be fitted for God's service, and bring them nearer to God."

Toward sexual intercourse outside marriage the Puritans were as frankly hostile as they were favorable to it in marriage. They passed laws to punish adultery with death, and fornication with whipping. Yet they had no misconceptions as to the capacity of human beings to obey such laws. Although the laws were commands of God, it was only natural—since the fall of Adam—for human beings to break them. Breaches must be punished lest the community suffer the wrath of God, but no offense, sexual or otherwise, could be occasion for surprise or for hushed tones of voice. How calmly the inhabitants of seventeenth-century New England could contemplate rape or attempted rape is evident in the following testimony offered before the Middlesex County Court of Massachusetts:

The examination of Edward Wire taken the 7th of October and alsoe Zachery Johnson. who sayeth that Edward Wires mayd being sent into the towne about busenes meeting with a man that dogd hir from about Joseph Kettles house to goody marches. She came into William Johnsones and desired Zachery Johnson to goe home with her for that the man dogd hir. accordingly he went with her and being then as far as Samuell Phips his house the man over tooke them. which man caled himselfe by the name of peter grant would have led the mayd but she oposed itt three times: and coming to Edward Wires house the said grant would have kist hir but she refused itt: wire being at prayer grant dragd the mayd between the said wiers and Nathanill frothinghams house. hee then flung the mayd downe in the street and got atop hir; Johnson seeing it hee caled vppon the fellow to be sivill and not abuse the mayd then Edward wire came forth and ran to the said grant and took hold of him asking him what he did to his mayd, the said grant asked whether she was his wife for he did nothing to his wife: the said grant swearing he would be the death of the said wire. when he came of the mayd; he swore he would bring ten men to pul down his house and soe ran away and they followed him as far as good(y) phipses house where they mett with John Terry and George Chin with clubs in there hands and soe they went away together. Zachy Johnson going to Constable Heamans, and wire going home. there came John Terry to his house to ask for beer and grant was in the streete but afterward departed into the town, both Johnson and Wire both aferme that when grant was vppon the mayd she cryed out severall times.

Deborah hadlocke being examined sayth that she mett with the man that cals himselfe peeter grant about good prichards that he dogd hir and followed hir to hir masters and there threw hir downe and lay vppon hir but had not the use of hir body but swore several others that he would ly with hir and gett hir with child before she got home.

Grant being present denys all saying he was drunk and did not know what de did.

The Puritans became inured to sexual offenses, because there were so many. The impression which one gets from reading the records of seventeenth-century New England courts is that illicit sexual intercourse was fairly common. The testimony given in cases of fornication and adultery—by far the most numerous class of criminal cases in the records—suggests that many of the early New Englanders possessed a high degree of virility and very few inhibitions. Besides the case of Peter Grant, take the testimony of Elizabeth Knight about the manner of Richard Nevars's advances toward her:

The last publique day of Thanksgiving (in the year 1674) in the evening as I was milking Richard Nevars came to me, and offered me abuse in putting his hand, under my coates, but I turning aside with much adoe, saved my self, and when I was settled to milking he agen took me by the shoulder and pulled me backward almost, but I clapped one hand on the Ground and held fast the Cows teatt with the other hand, and cryed out, and then came to mee Jonathan Abbot one of my Masters Servants, whome the said Never asked wherefore he came, the said Abbot said to look after you, what you doe unto the Maid, but the said Never bid Abbot goe about his businesse but I bade the lad to stay.

One reason for the abundance of sexual offenses was the number of men in the colonies who were unable to gratify their sexual desires in marriage. Many of the first settlers had wives in England. They had come to the new world to make a fortune, expecting either to bring their families after them or to return to England with some of the riches of America. Although these man left their wives behind, they brought their sexual appetites with them; and in spite of laws which required them to return to their families, they continued to stay, and more continued to arrive, as indictments against them throughout the seventeenth century clearly indicate.

Servants formed another group of men, and of women too, who could not ordinarily find supply for human necessity within the bounds of marriage. Most servants lived in the homes of their masters and could not marry without their consent, a consent which was not likely to be given unless the prospective husband or wife also belonged to the master's household. This situation will be better understood if it is recalled that most servants at this time were engaged by contract for a stated period. They were, in the language of the time, "covenant servants," who had agreed to stay with their masters for a number of years in return for a specified recompense, such as transportation to New England or education in some trade (the latter, of course, were known more specifically as apprentices). Even hired servants who worked for wages were usually single, for as soon as a man had enough money to buy or build a house of his own and to get married, he would set up in farming or trade for himself. It must be emphasized, however, that anyone who was not in business for himself was necessarily a servant. The economic organization of seventeenth-century New England had no place for the independent proletarian workman with a family of his own. All production was carried on in the household by the master of the family and his servants, so that most men were either servants or masters of servants; and the former, of course, were more numerous than the latter. Probably most of the inhabitants of Puritan New England could remember a time when they had been servants.

Theoretically no servant had a right to a private life. His time, day or night, belonged to his master, and both religion and law required that he obey his master scrupulously. But neither religion nor law could restrain the sexual impulses of youth, and if those impulses could not be expressed in marriage, they had to be given vent outside marriage. Servants had little difficulty in finding the occasions. Though they might be kept at work all day, it was easy enough to slip away at night. Once out of the house, there were several ways of meeting with a maid. The simplest way was to go to her bedchamber, if she was so fortunate as to have a private one of her own. Thus, Jock, Mr. Solomon Phipps's Negro man, confessed in court

that on the sixteenth day of May 1682, in the morning, betweene 12 and one of the clock, he did force open the back doores of the House of Laurence Hammond in Charlestowne, and came into the House, and went up into the garret to Marie the Negro.

He doth likewise acknowledge that one night the last week he forced into the House the same way, and went up to the Negro Woman Marie and that the like he hath done at severall other times before.

Joshua Fletcher took a more romantic way of visiting his lady:

Joshua Fletcher . . . doth confesse and acknowledge that three severall nights, after bedtime, he went into Mr Fiskes Dwelling house at Chelmsford, at an open window by a ladder that he brought with him. the said windo opening into a chamber, whose was the lodging place of Gresill Juell servant to mr. Fiske. and there he kept company with the said mayd. she sometimes having her cloathes on, and one time he found her in her bed.

Sometimes a maidservant might entertain callers in the parlor while the family were sleeping up-

stairs. John Knight described what was perhaps a common experience for masters. The crying of his child awakened him in the middle of the night, and he called to his maid, one Sarah Crouch, who was supposed to be sleeping with the child. Receiving no answer, he arose and

went downe the stayres, and at the stair foot, the latch of doore was pulled in. I called severall times and at the last said if shee would not open the dore, I would breake it open, and when she opened the doore shee was all undressed and Sarah Largin with her undressed, also the said Sarah went out of doores and Dropped some of her clothes as shee went out. I enquired of Sarah Crouch what men they were, which was with them. Shee made mee no answer for some space of time, but at last shee told me Peeter Brigs was with them, I asked her whether Thomas Jones was not there, but shee would give mee no answer.

In the temperate climate of New England it was not always necessary to seek out a maid at her home. Rachel Smith was seduced in an open field "about nine of the clock at night, being darke, neither moone nor starrs shineing." She was walking through the field when she met a man who

asked her where shee lived, and what her name was and shee told him. and then shee asked his name, and he told her Saijing that he was old Good-man Shepards man. Also shee saith he gave her strong liquors, and told her that it was not the first time he had been with maydes after his master was in bed.

Sometimes, of course, it was not necessary for a servant to go outside his master's house in order to satisfy his sexual urges. Many cases of fornication are on record between servants living in the same house. Even where servants had no private bedroom, even where the whole family slept in a single room, it was not impossible to make love. In fact many love affairs must have had their consummation upon a bed in which other people

Punishments were often designed not to reform, but to deter others from committing the same offense. This woodcut shows one of the humiliating punishments used in both the Old and New Worlds.

were sleeping. Take for example the case of Sarah Lepingwell. When Sarah was brought into court for having an illegitimate child, she related that one night when her master's brother, Thomas Hawes, was visiting the family, she went to bed early. Later, after Hawes had gone to bed, he called to her to get him a pipe of tobacco. After refusing for some time,

at the last I arose and did lite his pipe and cam and lay doune one my one bead and smoaked about half the pip and siting vp in my bead to give him his pip my bead being a trundell bead at the sid of his bead he reached beyond the pip and Cauth me by the wrist and pulled me on the side of his bead but I biding him let me goe he bid me hold my peas the folks wold here me

and if it be replyed come why did you not call out I Ansar I was posesed with fear of my mastar least my master shold think I did it only to bring a scandall on his brothar and thinking thay wold all beare witnes agaynst me but the thing is true that he did then begete me with child at that tim and the Child is Thomas Hauses and noe mans but his.

In his defense Hawes offered the testimony of another man who was sleeping "on the same side of the bed," but the jury nevertheless accepted Sarah's story.

The fact that Sarah was intimidated by her master's brother suggests that maidservants may have been subject to sexual abuse by their masters. The records show that sometimes masters did take advantage of their position to force unwanted attentions upon their female servants. The case of Elizabeth Dickerman is a good example. She complained to the Middlesex County Court,

against master John Harris senior for profiring abus to her by way of forsing her to be naught with him: . . . he has tould her that if she tould her dame: what cariag he did show to her shee had as good be hanged and shee replyed then shee would run away and he sayd run the way is befor you: . . . she says if she should liwe ther shee shall be in fear of her lif.

The court accepted Elizabeth's complaint and ordered her master to be whipped twenty stripes.

So numerous did cases of fornication and adultery become in seventeenth-century New England that the problem of caring for the children of extra-marital unions was a serious one. The Puritans solved it, but in such a way as to increase rather than decrease the temptation to sin. In 1668 the General Court of Massachusetts ordered:

that where any man is legally convicted to be the Father of a Bastard childe, he shall be at the care and charge to maintain and bring up the same, by such assistance of the Mother as nature requireth, and as the Court from time to time (according to circumstances) shall see meet to Order: and in case the Father of a Bastard, by confession or other manifest proof, upon trial of the case, do not appear to the Courts satisfaction, then the Man charged by the Woman to be the Father, shee holding constant in it, (especially being put upon the real discovery of the truth of it in the time of her Travail) shall be the reputed Father, and accordingly be liable to the charge of maintenance as aforesaid (though not to other punishment) notwithstanding his denial, unless the circumstances of the case and pleas be such, on the behalf of the man charged, as that the Court that have the cognizance thereon shall see reason to acquit him, and otherwise dispose of the Childe and education thereof.

As a result of this law a girl could give way to temptation without the fear of having to care for an illegitimate child by herself. Furthermore, she could, by a little simple lying, spare her lover the expense of supporting the child. When Elizabeth Wells bore a child, less than a year after this statute was passed, she laid it to James Tufts, her master's son. Goodman Tufts affirmed that Andrew Robinson, servant to Goodman Dexter, was the real father, and he brought the following testimony as evidence:

Wee Elizabeth Jefts aged 15 ears and Mary tufts age 14 ears doe testyfie that their being one at our hous sumtime the last winter who sayed that thear was a new law made concerning bastards that If aney man wear aqused with a bastard and the woman which had aqused him did stand vnto it in her labor that he should bee the reputed father of it and should mayntaine it. Elizabeth Wells hearing of the sayd law she sayed vnto vs that If shee should bee with Child shee would bee sure to lay it vn to won who was rich enough abell to mayntayne it wheather it wear his or no and shee farder sayed Elizabeth Jefts would not you doe so likewise If it weare your case and I sayed no by no means for right must tacke place: and the sayd Elizabeith wells sayed If it wear my Caus I think I should doe so.

A tragic unsigned letter that somehow found its way into the files of the Middlesex County Court gives more direct evidence of the practice which Elizabeth Wells professed:

der loue i remember my loue to you hoping your welfar and i hop to imbras the but now i rit to you to let you nowe that i am a child by you and i wil ether kil it or lay it to an other and you shal have no blame at al for i haue had *many children and none have none of them . . .* [i.e., *none of their fathers is supporting any of them.*]

In face of the wholesale violation of the sexual codes to which all these cases give testimony, the

Puritans could not maintain the severe penalties which their laws provided. Although cases of adultery occurred every year, the death penalty is not known to have been applied more than three times. The usual punishment was a whipping or a fine, or both, and perhaps a branding, combined with a symbolical execution in the form of standing on the gallows for an hour with a rope about the neck. Fornication met with a lighter whipping or a lighter fine, while rape was treated in the same way as adultery. Though the Puritans established a code of laws which demanded perfection—which demanded, in other words, strict obedience to the will of God, they nevertheless knew that frail human beings could never live up to the code. When fornication, adultery, rape, or even buggery and sodomy appeared, they were not surprised, nor were they so severe with the offenders as their codes of law would lead one to believe. Sodomy, to be sure, they usually punished with death; but rape, adultery, and fornication they regarded as pardonable human weaknesses, all the more likely to appear in a religious community, where the normal course of sin was stopped by wholesome laws. Governor Bradford, in recounting the details of an epidemic of sexual misdemeanors in Plymouth, wrote resignedly:

it may be in this case as it is with waters when their streames are stopped or damned up, when they gett passage they flow with more violence, and make more noys and disturbance, then when they are suffered to rune quietly in their owne chanels. So wickednes being here more stopped by strict laws, and the same more nerly looked unto, so as it cannot rune in a comone road of liberty as it would, and is inclined, it searches every wher, and at last breaks out wher it getts vente.

The estimate of human capacities here expressed led the Puritans not only to deal leniently with sexual offenses but also to take every precaution to prevent such offenses, rather than wait for the necessity of punishment. One precaution was to see that children got married as soon as possible. The wrong way to promote virtue, the Puritans thought, was to "ensnare" children in vows of virginity, as the Catholics did. As a result of such vows, children, "not being able to contain," would be guilty of "unnatural pollutions, and other filthy practices in secret: and too oft of horrid Murthers of the fruit of their bodies," said Thomas Cobbett. The way to avoid fornication and perversion was for parents to provide suitable husbands and wives for their children:

Lot was to blame that looked not out seasonably for some fit matches for his two daughters, which had formerly minded marriage (witness the contract between them and two men in Sodom, *called therfore for his Sons in Law, which had married his daughters, Gen. 19.14.) for they seeing no man like to come into them in a conjugall way . . . then they plotted that incestuous course, whereby their Father was so highly dishonoured.*

As marriage was the way to prevent fornication, successful marriage was the way to prevent adultery. The Puritans did not wait for adultery to appear; instead, they took every means possible to make husbands and wives live together and respect each other. If a husband deserted his wife and remained within the jurisdiction of a Puritan government, he was promptly sent back to her. Where the wife had been left in England, the offense did not always come to light until the wayward husband had committed fornication or bigamy, and of course there must have been many offenses which never came to light. But where both husband and wife lived in New England, neither had much chance of leaving the other without being returned by order of the county court at its next sitting. When John Smith of Medfield left his wife and went to live with Patience Rawlins, he was sent home poorer by ten pounds and richer by thirty stripes. Similarly Mary Drury, who deserted her husband on the pretense that he was impotent, failed to convince the court that he actually was so, and had to return to him as well as to pay a fine of five pounds. The wife of Phillip Pointing received lighter treatment: when the court thought that she had overstayed her leave in Boston, they simply ordered her "to depart the Towne and goe to Tanton to her husband." The courts, moreover, were not satisfied with mere cohabitation; they insisted that it be peaceful cohabitation. Husbands and wives were forbidden by law to strike one another, and the law was enforced on numerous occasions. But the courts did not stop there. Henry Flood was required to give bond for good behavior because he had abused his wife simply by "ill words calling her whore and cursing of her." The wife of Christopher Collins was presented for railing at her husband and calling him "Gurley gutted divill." Apparently in this case the court thought that Mistress Collins was right, for although the fact was proved by two witnesses, she was discharged. On another occasion the court favored the husband: Jacob Pudeator, fined for striking and kicking his wife, had the sentence moderated when the court was informed that she was a woman "of great provocation."

Wherever there was strong suspicion that an illicit relation might arise between two persons, the authorities removed the temptation by forbidding the two to come together. As early as November, 1630, the Court of Assistants of Massachusetts prohibited a Mr. Clark from "cohabitacion and frequent keepeing company with Mrs. Freeman, vnder paine of such punishment as the Court shall thinke meete to inflict." Mr. Clark and Mr. Freeman were both bound "in XX£ apeece that Mr. Clearke shall make his personall appearance att the nexte Court to be holden in March nexte, and in the meane tyme to carry himselfe in good behaviour towards all people and espetially towards Mrs. Freeman, concerneing whome there is stronge suspicion of incontinency." Forty-five years later the Suffolk County Court took the same kind of measure to protect the husbands of Dorchester from the temptations offered by the daughter of Robert Spurr. Spurr was presented by the grand jury

for entertaining persons at his house at unseasonable times both by day and night to the

greife of theire wives and Relations & The Court having heard what was alleaged and testified against him do Sentence him to bee admonish't and to pay Fees of Court and charge him upon his perill not to entertain any married men to keepe company with his daughter especially James Minott and Joseph Belcher.

In like manner Walter Hickson was forbidden to keep company with Mary Bedwell, "And if at any time hereafter hee bee taken in company of the saide Mary Bedwell without other company to bee forthwith apprehended by the Constable and to be whip't with ten stripes." Elizabeth Wheeler and Joanna Peirce were admonished "for theire disorderly carriage in the house of Thomas Watts being married women and founde sitting in other mens Laps with theire Armes about theire Necks." How little confidence the Puritans had in human nature is even more clearly displayed by another case, in which Edmond Maddock and his wife were brought to court "to answere to all such matters as shalbe objected against them concerning Haarkwoody and Ezekiell Euerells being at their house at unseasonable tyme of the night and her being up with them after her husband was gone to bed." Haarkwoody and Everell had been found "by the Constable Henry Bridghame about tenn of the Clock at night sitting by the fyre at the house of Edmond Maddocks with his wyfe a suspicious weoman her husband being on sleepe [*sic*] on the bedd." A similar distrust of human ability to resist temptation is evident in the following order of the Connecticut Particular Court:

James Hallet is to returne from the Correction house to his master Barclyt, who is to keepe him to hard labor, and course dyet during the pleasure of the Court provided that Barclet is first to remove his daughter from his family, before the sayd James enter therein.

These precautions, as we have already seen, did not eliminate fornication, adultery, or other sexual offenses, but they doubtless reduced the number from what it would otherwise have been.

In sum, the Puritan attitude toward sex, though directed by a belief in absolute, God-given moral values, never neglected human nature. The rules of conduct which the Puritans regarded as divinely ordained had been formulated for men, not for angels and not for beasts. God had created mankind in two sexes; He had ordained marriage as desirable for all, and sexual intercourse as essential to marriage. On the other hand, He had forbidden sexual intercourse outside of marriage. These were the moral principles which the Puritans sought to enforce in New England. But in their enforcement they took cognizance of human nature. They knew well enough that human beings since the fall of Adam were incapable of obeying perfectly the laws of God. Consequently, in the endeavor to enforce those laws they treated offenders with patience and understanding, and concentrated their efforts on prevention more than on punishment. The result was not a society in which most of us would care to live, for the methods of prevention often caused serious interference with personal liberty. It must nevertheless be admitted that in matters of sex the Puritans showed none of the blind zeal or narrow-minded bigotry which is too often supposed to have been characteristic of them. The more one learns about these people, the less do they appear to have resembled the sad and sour portraits which their modern critics have drawn of them.

STUDY QUESTIONS

1. What limitations did Puritans place on sexual relations within marriage?

2. What was the Puritans' attitude toward sexual relations outside marriage?

3. What unique sexual problems did servants in Puritan society face?

4. How did the Puritan view of human nature govern their attitudes toward illicit sexual relations?

5. How did Puritans try to prevent fornication and adultery?

BIBLIOGRAPHY

Historians have only recently begun to explore the significance of attitudes toward sex. On a popular level, Reay Tannahill, *Sex in History* (1980) and Gay Talese, *Thy Neighbor's Wife* (1980) examine changing attitudes toward the subject. More scholarly examinations of early American sexual attitudes include Laurel Ulrich, *Good Wives: Image and Reality in the Lives of Women in Northern New England, 1650–1750* (1982); Ellen K. Rothman, "Sex and Self-Control; Middle-Class Courtship in America, 1770–1870," *Journal of Social History* (1982); Linda Hyman, "The Greek Slave by Hiram Powers: High Art as Popular Culture," *Art Journal* (1976); and Lyle Koehler, *A Search for Power: "The Weaker Sex" in Seventeenth-Century New England* (1974). Puritan theology, on the other hand, has been richly studied. The books by Perry Miller and Edmund Morgan are the best starting point. Miller's ideas are presented clearly in *Errand into the Wilderness* (1956). Equally valuable is Morgan's *Puritan Dilemma: The Story of John Winthrop* (1958).

THE WITCHES OF SALEM VILLAGE

Kai T. Erikson

Most of the "facts" of the Salem witchcraft trials and executions are known. The trouble started during the cold winter of 1691–1692. By the end of the summer, nineteen people were adjudged to be witches and hanged. One other person, Giles Cory, refused to plead innocent or guilty. Because of his refusal, he was to be placed between two boards. Heavy stones were to be piled on the top board until a plea was given. Giles was slowly crushed to death; his last words were "more weight." His death brought the total executions to twenty.

What is difficult to determine is the reason why the trials ever took place. Certainly the belief in witchcraft was nearly universal in seventeenth-century New England, and perhaps a few of the people executed had even practiced witchcraft. But the vast majority had been as innocent as Sarah Good, whose last words to her minister were, "I am no more a witch than you are a wizard, and if you take away my life, God will give you blood to drink."

For almost a century, historians have debated the cause of the outbreak of the witchcraft hysteria. Many have blamed the girls who set the dreadful events into motion. Others have stressed the community conflicts within Salem and the general social and religious tensions created by an expanding society and declining religiosity. One historian has even claimed the real problem was the actual existence of witches.

Kai T. Erikson sides with the historians who stress the social conflict in Puritan society. In his thought-provoking examination of the events, he describes a society that had lost its bearing and that looked toward the future with fear and anxiety.

The witchcraft hysteria that began in Salem Village (a town some miles away from Salem itself) is probably the best known episode of Massachusetts history and has been described in a number of careful works. In the pages which follow, then, the story will be sketched in rather briefly: readers interested in a fuller account of those unusual events are urged to consult *The Devil in Massachusetts* by Marion L. Starkey, a book that captures all the grim drama of the period without losing any of its merit as a scholarly work.

Between the end of the Quaker persecutions in 1665 and the beginning of the Salem witchcraft outbreak in 1692, the colony had experienced some very trying days. To begin with, the political outlines of the commonwealth had been subject to sudden, often violent, shifts, and the people of the colony were quite uncertain about their own future. The King's decrees during the Quaker troubles had provoked only minor changes in the actual structure of the Puritan state, but they had introduced a note of apprehension and alarm which did not disappear for thirty years; and no sooner had Charles warned the Massachusetts authorities of his new interest in their affairs than he dispatched four commissioners to the Bay to look after his remote dominions and make sure that his occasional orders were being enforced. From that moment, New England feared the worst. The sermons of the period were full of dreadful prophecies about the future of the Bay, and as New England moved through the 1670's and 1680's the catalogue of political calamities grew steadily longer and more serious. In 1670, for example, a series of harsh arguments occurred between groups of magistrates and clergymen, threatening the alliance which had been the very cornerstone of the New England Way. In 1675 a brutal and costly war broke out with a confederacy of Indian tribes led

Kai T. Erickson, from *Wayward Puritans: A Study in the Sociology of Deviance.* Copyright © 1966 by Allyn and Bacon. Reprinted/adapted by permission.

by a wily chief called King Philip. In 1676 Charles II began to review the claims of other persons to lands within the jurisdiction of Massachusetts, and it became increasingly clear that the old charter might be revoked altogether. In 1679 Charles specifically ordered Massachusetts to permit the establishment of an Anglican church in Boston, and in 1684 the people of the Bay had become so pessimistic about the fate of the colony that several towns simply neglected to send Deputies to the General Court. The sense of impending doom reached its peak in 1686. To begin with, the charter which had given the colony its only legal protection for over half a century was vacated by a stroke of the royal pen, and in addition the King sent a Royal Governor to represent his interests in the Bay who was both an Anglican and a man actively hostile to the larger goals of New England. For the moment, it looked as if the holy experiment was over: not only had the settlers lost title to the very land they were standing on, but they ran the very real risk of witnessing the final collapse of the congregational churches they had built at so great a cost.

The settlers were eventually rescued from the catastrophes of 1686, but their margin of escape had been extremely narrow and highly tentative. In 1689 news began to filter into the Bay that William of Orange had landed in England to challenge the House of Stuart, and hopes ran high throughout the colony; but before the people of the Bay knew the outcome of this contest in England, a Boston mob suddenly rose in protest and placed the Royal Governor in chains. Luckily for Massachusetts, William's forces were successful in England and the Boston insurrection was seen as little more than a premature celebration in honor of the new King. Yet for all the furor, little had changed. At the time of the witchcraft hysteria, agents of Massachusetts were at work in London trying to convince William to restore the old charter, or at least to issue a new one giving Massachusetts all the advantages it had enjoyed in the past, but everyone knew that the colony would never again operate under the same autonomy. As the people of the Bay waited to hear about the future of their settlement, then, their anxiety was understandably high.

Throughout this period of political crisis, an even darker cloud was threatening the colony, and this had to do with the fact that a good deal of angry dissension was spreading among the saints themselves. In a colony that depended on a high degree of harmony and group feeling, the courts were picking their way through a maze of land disputes and personal feuds, a complicated tangle of litigations and suits. Moreover, the earnest attempts at unanimity that had characterized the politics of Winthrop's era were now replaced by something closely resembling open party bickering. When John Josselyn visited Boston in 1668, for instance, he observed that the people were "savagely factious" in their relations with one another and acted more out of jealousy and greed than any sense of religious purpose. And the sermons of the day chose even stronger language to describe the decline in morality which seemed to darken the prospects of New England. The spirit of brotherhood which the original settlers had counted on so heavily had lately diffused into an atmosphere of commercial competition, political contention, and personal bad feeling.

Thus the political architecture which had been fashioned so carefully by the first generation and the spiritual consensus which had been defended so energetically by the second were both disappearing. At the time of the Salem witchcraft mania, most of the familiar landmarks of the New England Way had become blurred by changes in the historical climate, like signposts obscured in a storm, and the people of the Bay no longer knew how to assess what the past had amounted to or what the future promised. Massachusetts had become, in Alan Heimert's words, "a society no longer able to judge itself with any certainty."

In 1670, the House of Deputies took note of the confusion and fear which was beginning to spread over the country and prepared a brief inventory of the troubles facing the Bay:

Declension from the primitive foundation work, innovation in doctrine and worship, opinion and practice, an invasion of the rights, liberties and privileges of churches, an usurpation of a lordly and prelatical power over God's heritage, a subversion of the gospel order, and all this with a dangerous tendency to the utter devastation of these churches, turning the pleasant gardens of Christ into a wilderness, and the inevitable and total extirpation of the principles and pillars of the congregational way; these are the leaven, the corrupting gangrene, the infecting spreading plague, the provoking image of jealousy set up before the Lord, the accursed thing which hath provoked divine wrath, and doth further threaten destruction.

The tone of this resolution gives us an excellent index to the mood of the time. For the next twenty years, New England turned more and more to the notion that the settlers must expect God to turn upon them in wrath because the colony had lost its original fervor and sense of mission. The motif introduced in this resolution runs like a recurrent theme through the thinking of the period: the settlers who had carved a commonwealth out of the wilderness and had planted "the pleasant gardens of Christ" in its place were about to return to the wilderness. But there is an important shift of imagery here, for the wilderness they had once mastered was one of thick underbrush and wild animals, dangerous seasons and marauding Indians, while the wilderness which awaited them contained an entirely different sort of peril. "The Wilderness thro' which are passing to the Promised Land," Cotton Mather wrote in a volume describing the state of New England at the time of the witchcraft difficulties, "is all over fill'd with Fiery flying serpents. . . . All our way to Heaven, lies by the Dens of Lions, and the Mounts of Leopards; there are incredible Droves of Devils in our way." We will return to discussion of this wilderness theme at the conclusion of the chapter, but for the moment it is important to note that Massachusetts had lost much of its concern for institutions and policies and had begun to seek some vision of its future by looking into a ghostly, invisible world.

It was while the people of the colony were preoccupied with these matters that the witches decided to strike.

I

No one really knows how the witchcraft hysteria began, but it originated in the home of the Reverend Samuel Parris, minister of the local church. In early 1692, several girls from the neighborhood began to spend their afternoons in the Parris' kitchen with a slave named Tituba, and it was not long before a mysterious sorority of girls, aged between nine and twenty, became regular visitors to the parsonage. We can only speculate what was going on behind the kitchen door, but we know that Tituba had been brought to Massachusetts from Barbados and enjoyed a reputation in the neighborhood for her skills in the magic arts. As the girls grew closer together, a remarkable change seemed to come over them: perhaps it is not true, as someone later reported, that they went out into the forest to celebrate their own version of a black mass, but it is apparent that they began to live in a state of high tension and shared secrets with one another which were hardly becoming to quiet Puritan maidens.

Before the end of winter, the two youngest girls in the group succumbed to the shrill pitch of their amusements and began to exhibit a most unusual malady. They would scream unaccountably, fall into grotesque convulsions, and sometimes scamper along on their hands and knees making noises like the barking of a dog. No sooner had word gone around about this extraordinary affliction than it began to spread like a contagious disease. All over the community young girls were groveling on the ground in a panic of fear and excitement, and while some of the less credulous townspeople were tempted to reach for their belts in the hopes of strapping a little modesty into them, the rest could only stand by in helpless horror as the girls suffered their torments.

The town's one physician did what he could to stem the epidemic, but he soon exhausted his meagre store of remedies and was forced to conclude that the problem lay outside the province of medicine. The devil had come to Salem Village, he announced; the girls were bewitched. At this disturbing news, ministers from many of the neighboring parishes came to consult with their colleague and offer what advice they might. Among the first to arrive was a thoughtful clergyman named Deodat Lawson, and he had been in town no more than a few hours when he happened upon a frightening exhibition of the devil's handiwork. "In the beginning of the evening," he later recounted of his first day in the village,

I went to give Mr. Parris a visit. When I was there, his kinswoman, Abigail Williams, (about 12 years of age,) had a grievous fit; she was at first hurried with violence to and fro in the room, (though Mrs. Ingersoll endeavored to hold her,) sometimes making as if she would fly, stretching up her arms as high as she could, and crying "whish, whish, whish!" several times. . . . After that, she run to the fire, and began to throw fire brands about the house; and run against the back, as if she would run up the chimney, and, as they said, she had attempted to go into the fire in other fits.

Faced by such clear-cut evidence, the ministers quickly agreed that Satan's new challenge would have to be met with vigorous action, and this meant that the afflicted girls would have to identify the witches who were harassing them.

It is hard to guess what the girls were experiencing during those early days of the commotion. They attracted attention everywhere they went and exercised a degree of power over the adult community which would have been exhilarating under the sanest of circumstances. But whatever else was going on in those young minds, the thought seems to have gradually occurred to the girls that they were indeed bewitched, and after they had been coaxed over and over again to name their tormentors, they finally singled out three women in the village and accused them of witchcraft.

Three better candidates could not have been found if all the gossips in New England had met to make the nominations. The first, understandably, was Tituba herself, a woman who had grown up among the rich colors and imaginative legends of Barbados and who was probably acquainted with some form of voodoo. The second, Sarah Good, was a proper hag of a witch if Salem Village had ever seen one. With a pipe clenched in her leathery face she wandered around the countryside neglecting her children and begging from others, and on more than one occasion the old crone had been overheard muttering threats against her neighbors when she was in an unusually sour humor. Sarah Osburne, the third suspect, had a higher social standing than either of her alleged accomplices, but she had been involved in a local scandal a year or two earlier when a man moved into her house some months before becoming her husband.

A preliminary hearing was set at once to decide whether the three accused women should be held for trial. The girls were ushered to the front row of the meeting house, where they took full advantage of the space afforded them by rolling around in apparent agony whenever some personal fancy (or the invisible agents of the devil) provoked them to it. It was a remarkable show. Strange creatures flew about the room pecking at the girls or taunting them from the rafters, and it was immediately obvious to everyone that the women on trial were responsible for all the disorder and suffering. When Sarah Good and Sarah Osburne were called to the stand and asked why they sent these spectres to torment the girls, they were too appalled to say much in their defense. But when Tituba took the stand she had a ready answer. A lifetime spent in bondage is poor training for standing up before a bench of magistrates, and anyway Tituba was an excitable woman who had breathed the warmer winds of the Caribbean and knew things about magic her crusty old judges would never learn. Whatever the reason, Tituba gave her audience one of the most exuberant confessions ever recorded in a New England courtroom. She spoke of the crea-

tures who inhabit the invisible world, the dark rituals which bind them together in the service of Satan; and before she had ended her astonishing recital she had convinced everyone in Salem Village that the problem was far worse than they had dared imagine. For Tituba not only implicated Sarah Good and Sarah Osburne in her own confession but announced that many other people in the colony were engaged in the devil's conspiracy against the Bay.

So the hearing that was supposed to bring a speedy end to the affair only stirred up a hidden hornet's nest, and now the girls were urged to identify other suspects and locate new sources of trouble. Already the girls had become more than unfortunate victims: in the eyes of the community they were diviners, prophets, oracles, mediums, for only they could see the terrible spectres swarming over the countryside and tell what persons had sent them on their evil errands. As they became caught up in the enthusiasm of their new work, then, the girls began to reach into every corner of the community in a search for likely suspects. Martha Corey was an upstanding woman in the village whose main mistake was to snort incredulously at the girls' behavior. Dorcas Good, five years old, was a daughter of the accused Sarah. Rebecca Nurse was a saintly old woman who had been bedridden at the time of the earlier hearings. Mary Esty and Sarah Cloyce were Rebecca's younger sisters, themselves accused when they rose in energetic defense of the older woman. And so it went—John Proctor, Giles Corey, Abigail Hobbs, Bridgit Bishop, Sarah Wild, Susanna Martin, Dorcas Hoar, the Reverend George Burroughs: as winter turned into spring the list of suspects grew to enormous length and the Salem jail was choked with people awaiting trial. We know nothing about conditions of life in prison, but it is easy to imagine the tensions which must have echoed within those grey walls. Some of the prisoners had cried out against their relatives and friends in a desperate effort to divert attention from themselves, others were witless persons with scarcely a clue as to what had happened to them, and a few (very few, as it turned

The English witchcraft executions first started in the sixteenth century and peaked by the mid-seventeenth century. It wasn't until the late seventeenth century that Massachusetts Bay began its witchcraft executions.

out) were accepting their lot with quiet dignity. If we imagine Sarah Good sitting next to Rebecca Nurse and lighting her rancid pipe or Tituba sharing views on supernatural phenomena with the Reverend George Burroughs, we may have a rough picture of life in those crowded quarters.

By this time the hysteria had spread well beyond the confines of Salem Village, and as it grew in scope so did the appetites of the young girls. They now began to accuse persons they had never seen from places they had never visited (in the course of which some absurd mistakes were made), yet their word was so little questioned that it was ordinarily warrant enough to put respected people in chains.

From as far away as Charlestown, Nathaniel Cary heard that his wife had been accused of witchcraft and immediately traveled with her to Salem "to see if the afflicted did know her." The two of them sat through an entire day of hearings, after which Cary reported:

I observed that the afflicted were two girls of about ten years old, and about two or three others, of about eighteen. . . . The prisoners were called in one by one, and as they came in were cried out of. . . . The prisoner was placed about seven or eight feet from the Justices, and the accusers between the Justices and them; the prisoner was ordered to stand right before the Justices, with an officer appointed to hold each hand, lest they should therewith afflict them, and the prisoner's eyes must be constantly on the Justices; for if they looked on the afflicted, they would either fall into their fits, or cry out of being hurt by them. . . . Then the Justices said to the accusers, "which of you will go and touch the prisoner at the bar?" Then the most coura-

geous would adventure, but before they had made three steps would ordinarily fall down as in a fit. The Justices ordered that they should be taken up and carried to the prisoner, that she might touch them; and as soon as they were touched by the accused, the Justices would say "they are well," before I could discern any alteration. . . . Thus far I was only as a spectator, my wife also was there part of the time, but no notice taken of her by the afflicted, except once or twice they came to her and asked her name.

After this sorry performance the Carys retired to the local inn for dinner, but no sooner had they taken seats than a group of afflicted girls burst into the room and "began to tumble about like swine" at Mrs. Cary's feet, accusing her of being the cause of their miseries. Remarkably, the magistrates happened to be sitting in the adjoining room—"waiting for this," Cary later decided—and an impromptu hearing took place on the spot.

Being brought before the Justices, her chief accusers were two girls. My wife declared to the Justices that she never had any knowledge of them before that day; she was forced to stand with her arms stretched out. I did request that I might hold one of her hands, but it was denied me; then she desired me to wipe the tears from her eyes, and the sweat from her face, which I did; then she desired she might lean herself on me, saying she should faint. Justice Hathorne replied, she had strength enough to torment those persons, and she should have strength enough to stand. I speaking something against their cruel proceedings, they commanded me to be silent, or else I should be turned out of the room. An Indian . . . was also brought in to be one of her accusers: being come in, he now (when before the Justices) fell down and tumbled about like a hog, but said nothing. The Justices asked the girls, "who afflicted the Indian?", they answered "she" (meaning my wife). . . . The Justices ordered her to touch him, in order of his cure . . . but the Indian took hold of her in a barbarous manner; then his

hand was taken off, and her hand put on his, and the cure was quickly wrought. . . . Then her mittimus was writ.

For another example of how the hearings were going, we might listen for a moment to the examination of Mrs. John Proctor. This record was taken down by the Reverend Samuel Parris himself, and the notes in parentheses are his. Ann Putnam and Abigail Williams were two of the most energetic of the young accusers.

JUSTICE: Ann Putnam, doth this woman hurt you?

PUTNAM: Yes, sir, a good many times. (Then the accused looked upon them and they fell into fits.)

JUSTICE: She does not bring the book to you, does she?

PUTNAM: Yes, sir, often, and saith she hath made her maid set her hand to it.

JUSTICE: Abigail Williams, does this woman hurt you?

WILLIAMS: Yes, sir, often.

JUSTICE: Does she bring the book to you?

WILLIAMS: Yes.

JUSTICE: What would she have you do with it?

WILLIAMS: To write in it and I shall be well.

PUTNAM TO MRS. PROCTOR: Did you not tell me that your maid had written?

MRS. PROCTOR: Dear child, it is not so. There is another judgment, dear child. (Then Abigail and Ann had fits. By and by they cried out, "look you, there is Goody Proctor upon the beam." By and by both of them cried out of Goodman Proctor himself, and said he was a wizard. Immediately, many, if not all of the bewitched, had grievous fits.)

JUSTICE: Ann Putnam, who hurt you?

PUTNAM: Goodman Proctor and his wife too. (Some of the afflicted cried, "there is Proctor going to take up Mrs. Pope's feet—and her feet were immediately taken up.)

JUSTICE: *What do you say Goodman Proctor to these things?*

PROCTOR: *I know not. I am innocent.*

WILLIAMS: *There is Goodman Proctor going to Mrs. Pope (and immediately said Pope fell into a fit).*

JUSTICE: *You see, the Devil will deceive you. The children could see what you was going to do before the woman was hurt. I would advise you to repentance, for the devil is bringing you out.*

This was the kind of evidence the magistrates were collecting in readiness for the trials; and it was none too soon, for the prisons were crowded with suspects. In June the newly arrived Governor of the Bay, Sir William Phips, appointed a special court of Oyer and Terminer to hear the growing number of witchcraft cases pending, and the new bench went immediately to work. Before the month was over, six women had been hanged from the gallows in Salem. And still the accused poured in.

As the court settled down to business, however, a note of uncertainty began to flicker across the minds of several thoughtful persons in the colony. To begin with, the net of accusation was beginning to spread out in wider arcs, reaching not only across the surface of the country but up the social ladder as well, so that a number of influential people were now among those in the overflowing prisons. Nathaniel Cary was an important citizen of Charlestown, and other men of equal rank (including the almost legendary Captain John Alden) were being caught up in the widening circle of panic and fear. Slowly but surely, a faint glimmer of skepticism was introduced into the situation; and while it was not to assert a modifying influence on the behavior of the court for some time to come, this new voice had become a part of the turbulent New England climate of 1692.

Meantime, the girls continued to exercise their extraordinary powers. Between sessions of the court, they were invited to visit the town of Andover and help the local inhabitants flush out whatever witches might still remain at large among them. Handicapped as they were by not knowing anyone in town, the girls nonetheless managed to identify more than fifty witches in the space of a few hours. Forty warrants were signed on the spot, and the arrest total only stopped at that number because the local Justice of the Peace simply laid down his pen and refused to go on with the frightening charade any longer—at which point, predictably, he became a suspect himself.

Yet the judges worked hard to keep pace with their young representatives in the field. In early August five persons went to the gallows in Salem. A month later fifteen more were tried and condemned, of which eight were hung promptly and the others spared because they were presumably ready to confess their sins and turn state's evidence. Nineteen people had been executed, seven more condemned, and one pressed to death under a pile of rocks for standing mute at his trial. At least two more persons had died in prison, bringing the number of deaths to twenty-two. And in all that time, not one suspect brought before the court had been acquitted.

At the end of this strenuous period of justice, the whole witchcraft mania began to fade. For one thing, the people of the Bay had been shocked into a mood of sober reflection by the deaths of so many persons. For another, the afflicted girls had obviously not learned very much from their experience in Andover and were beginning to display an ambition which far exceeded their credit. It was bad enough that they should accuse the likes of John Alden and Nathaniel Cary, but when they brought up the name of Samuel Willard, who doubled as pastor of Boston's First Church and President of Harvard College, the magistrates flatly told them they were mistaken. Not long afterwards, a brazen finger was pointed directly at the executive mansion in Boston, where Lady Phips awaited her husband's return from an expedition to Canada, and one tradition even has it that Cotton Mather's mother was eventually accused.

This was enough to stretch even a Puritan's boundless credulity. One by one the leading men of the Bay began to reconsider the whole question and ask aloud whether the evidence accepted in witchcraft hearings was really suited to the emergency at hand. It was obvious that people were being condemned on the testimony of a few excited girls, and responsible minds in the community were troubled by the thought that the girls' excitement may have been poorly diagnosed in the first place. Suppose the girls were directly possessed by the devil and not touched by intermediate witches? Suppose they were simply out of their wits altogether? Suppose, in fact, they were lying? In any of these events the rules of evidence used in court would have to be reviewed—and quickly.

Deciding what kinds of evidence were admissible in witchcraft cases was a thorny business at best. When the court of Oyer and Terminer had first met, a few ground rules had been established to govern the unusual situation which did not entirely conform to ordinary Puritan standards of trial procedure. In the first place, the scriptural rule that two eye-witnesses were necessary for conviction in capital cases was modified to read that any two witnesses were sufficient even if they were testifying about different events—on the interesting ground that witchcraft was a "habitual" crime. That is, if one witness testified that he had seen Susanna Martin bewitch a horse in 1660 and another testified that she had broken uninvited into his dreams twenty years later, then both were witnesses to the same general offense. More important, however, the court accepted as an operating principle the old idea that Satan could not assume the shape of an innocent person, which meant in effect that any spectres floating into view which resembled one of the defendants must be acting under his direct instruction. If an afflicted young girl "saw" John Proctor's image crouched on the window sill with a wicked expression on his face, for example, there could be no question that Proctor himself had placed it there, for the devil could not borrow that disguise without the permission of its owner. During an early hearing,

one of the defendants had been asked: "How comes your appearance to hurt these [girls]?" "How do I know," she had answered testily. "He that appeared in the shape of Samuel, a glorified saint, may appear in anyone's shape." Now this was no idle retort, for every man who read his Bible knew that the Witch of Endor had once caused the image of Samuel to appear before Saul, and this scriptural evidence that the devil might indeed be able to impersonate an innocent person proved a difficult matter for the court to handle. Had the defendant been able to win her point, the whole machinery of the court might have fallen in pieces at the magistrates' feet; for if the dreadful spectres haunting the girls were no more than free-lance apparitions sent out by the devil, then the court would have no prosecution case at all.

All in all, five separate kinds of evidence had been admitted by the court during its first round of hearings. First were trials by test, of which repeating the Lord's Prayer, a feat presumed impossible for witches to perform, and curing fits by touch were the most often used. Second was the testimony of persons who attributed their own misfortunes to the sorcery of a neighbor on trial. Third were physical marks like warts, moles, scars, or any other imperfection through which the devil might have sucked his gruesome quota of blood. Fourth was spectral evidence, of the sort just noted; and fifth were the confessions of the accused themselves.

Now it was completely obvious to the men who began to review the court's proceedings that the first three types of evidence were quite inconclusive. After all, anyone might make a mistake reciting the Lord's Prayer, particularly if the floor was covered with screaming, convulsive girls, and it did not make much sense to execute a person because he had spiteful neighbors or a mark upon his body. By those standards, half the people in Massachusetts might qualify for the gallows. This left spectral evidence and confessions. As for the latter, the court could hardly maintain that any real attention had been given to that form of evidence, since none of the executed witches had confessed and none of the many confessors had been executed.

Far from establishing guilt, a well-phrased and tear-fully delivered confession was clearly the best guarantee against hanging. So the case lay with spectral evidence, and legal opinion in the Bay was slowly leaning toward the theory that this form of evidence, too, was worthless.

In October, Governor Phips took note of the growing doubts by dismissing the special court of Oyer and Terminer and releasing several suspects from prison. The tide had begun to turn, but still there were 150 persons in custody and some 200 others who had been accused.

In December, finally, Phips appointed a new session of the Superior Court of Judicature to try the remaining suspects, and this time the magistrates were agreed that spectral evidence would be admitted only in marginal cases. Fifty-two persons were brought to trial during the next month, and of these, forty-nine were immediately acquitted. Three others were condemned ("two of which," a contemporary observer noted, "were the most senseless and ignorant creatures that could be found"), and in addition death warrants were signed for five persons who had been condemned earlier. Governor Phips responded to these carefully reasoned judgments by signing reprieves for all eight of the defendants anyway, and at this, the court began to empty the jails as fast as it could hear cases. Finally Phips ended the costly procedure by discharging every prisoner in the colony and issuing a general pardon to all persons still under suspicion.

The witchcraft hysteria had been completely checked within a year of the day it first appeared in Salem Village.

II

Historically, there is nothing unique in the fact that Massachusetts Bay should have put people on trial for witchcraft. As the historian Kittredge has pointed out, the whole story should be seen "not as an abnormal outbreak of fanaticism, not as an isolated tragedy, but as a mere incident, a brief and transitory episode in the biography of a terrible, but perfectly natural, superstition."

The idea of witchcraft, of course, is as old as history; but the concept of a malevolent witch who makes a compact with Satan and rejects God did not appear in Europe until the middle of the fourteenth century and does not seem to have made a serious impression on England until well into the sixteenth. The most comprehensive study of English witchcraft, for example, opens with the year 1558, the first year of Elizabeth's reign, and gives only passing attention to events occurring before that date.

In many ways, witchcraft was brought into England on the same current of change that introduced the Protestant Reformation, and it continued to draw nourishment from the intermittent religious quarrels which broke out during the next century and a half. Perhaps no other form of crime in history has been a better index to social disruption and change, for outbreaks of witchcraft mania have generally taken place in societies which are experiencing a shift of religious focus—societies, we would say, confronting a relocation of boundaries. Throughout the Elizabethan and early Stuart periods, at any rate, while England was trying to establish a national church and to anchor it in the middle of the violent tides which were sweeping over the rest of Europe, increasing attention was devoted to the subject. Elizabeth herself introduced legislation to clarify the laws of dealing with witchcraft, and James I, before becoming King of England, wrote a text book on demonology which became a standard reference for years to come.

But it was during the Civil Wars in England that the witchcraft hysteria struck with full force. Many hundreds, probably thousands of witches were burned or hung between the time the Civil Wars began and Oliver Cromwell emerged as the strong man of the Commonwealth, and no sooner had the mania subsided in England than it broke out all over again in Scotland during the first days of the Restoration. Every important crisis during those years seemed to be punctuated by a rash of witchcraft cases. England did not record its last execution for witchcraft until 1712, but the urgent witch hunts of the Civil War period were never repeated.

With this background in mind, we should not be surprised that New England, too, should experience a moment of panic; but it is rather curious that this moment should have arrived so late in the century.

During the troubled years in England when countless witches were burned at the stake or hung from the gallows, Massachusetts Bay showed but mild concern over the whole matter. In 1647 a witch was executed in Connecticut, and one year later another woman met the same fate in Massachusetts. In 1651 the General Court took note of the witchcraft crisis in England and published an almost laconic order that "a day of humiliation" be observed throughout the Bay, but beyond this, the waves of excitement which were sweeping over the mother country seemed not to reach across the Atlantic at all. There was no shortage of accusations, to be sure, no shortage of the kind of gossip which in other days would send good men and women to their lonely grave, but the magistrates of the colony did not act as if a state of emergency was at hand and thus did not declare a crime wave to be in motion. In 1672, for example, a curious man named John Broadstreet was presented to the Essex County Court for "having familiarity with the devil," yet when he admitted the charge the court was so little impressed that he was fined for telling a lie. And in 1674, when Christopher Brown came before the same court to testify that he had been dealing with Satan, the magistrates flatly dismissed him on the grounds that his confession seemed "inconsistent with truth."

So New England remained relatively calm during the worst of the troubles in England, yet suddenly erupted into a terrible violence long after England lay exhausted from its earlier exertions.

In many important respects, 1692 marked the end of the Puritan experiment in Massachusetts, not only because the original charter had been revoked or because a Royal Governor had been chosen by the King or even because the old political order had collapsed in a tired heap. The Puritan experiment ended in 1692, rather, because the sense of mission which had sustained it from the beginning no longer existed in any recognizable form, and thus the people of the Bay were left with few stable points of reference to help them remember who they were. When they looked back on their own history, the settlers had to conclude that the trajectory of the past pointed in quite a different direction than the one they now found themselves taking: they were no longer participants in a great adventure, no longer residents of a "city upon a hill," no longer members of that special revolutionary elite who were destined to bend the course of history according to God's own word. They were only themselves, living alone in a remote corner of the world, and this seemed a modest end for a crusade which had begun with such high expectations.

In the first place, as we have seen, the people of the colony had always pictured themselves as actors in an international movement, yet by the end of the century they had lost many of their most meaningful contacts with the rest of the world. The Puritan movement in England had scattered into a number of separate sects, each of which had been gradually absorbed into the freer climate of a new regime, and elsewhere in Europe the Protestant Reformation had lost much of its momentum without achieving half the goals set for it. And as a result, the colonists had lost touch with the background against which they had learned to assess their own stature and to survey their own place in the world.

In the second place, the original settlers had measured their achievements on a yardstick which no longer seemed to have the same sharp relevance. New England had been built by people who believed that God personally supervised every flicker of life on earth according to a plan beyond human comprehension, and in undertaking the expedition to America they were placing themselves entirely in God's hands. These were men whose doctrine prepared them to accept defeat gracefully, whose sense of piety depended upon an occasional moment of failure, hardship, even tragedy. Yet by the end of the century, the Puritan planters could look around them and count an impressive number of accomplishments.

Here was no record of erratic providence; here was a record of solid human enterprise, and with this realization, as Daniel Boorstin suggests, the settlers moved from a "sense of mystery" to a "consciousness of mastery," from a helpless reliance on fate to a firm confidence in their own abilities. This shift helped clear the way for the appearance of the shrewd, practical, self-reliant Yankee as a figure in American history, but in the meantime it left the third generation of settlers with no clear definition of the status they held as the chosen children of God.

In the third place, Massachusetts had been founded as a lonely pocket of civilization in the midst of a howling wilderness, and as we have seen, this idea remained one of the most important themes of Puritan imagery long after the underbrush had been cut away and the wild animals killed. The settlers had lost sight of their local frontiers, not only in the sense that colonization had spread beyond the Berkshires into what is now upper state New York, but also in the sense that the wilderness which had held the community together by pressing in on it from all sides was disappearing. The original settlers had landed in a wilderness full of "wild beasts and wilder men"; yet sixty years later, sitting many miles from the nearest frontier in the prosperous seaboard town of Boston, Cotton Mather and other survivors of the old order still imagined that they were living in a wilderness—a territory they had explored as thoroughly as any frontiersmen. But the character of this wilderness was unlike anything the first settlers had ever seen, for its dense forests had become a jungle of mythical beasts and its skies were thick with flying spirits. In a sense, the Puritan community had helped mark its location in space by keeping close watch on the wilderness surrounding it on all sides; and now that the visible traces of that wilderness had receded out of sight, the settlers invented a new one by finding the shapes of the forest in the middle of the community itself.

And as the wilderness took on this new character, it seemed that even the devil had given up his more familiar disguises. He no longer lurked in the underbrush, for most of it had been cut away; he no longer assumed the shape of hostile Indians, for most of them had retreated inland for the moment; he no longer sent waves of heretics to trouble the Bay, for most of them lived quietly under the protection of toleration; he no longer appeared in the armies of the Counter-Reformation, for the old battlefields were still and too far away to excite the imagination. But his presence was felt everywhere, and when the colonists began to look for his new hiding places they found him crouched in the very heart of the Puritan colony. Quite literally, the people of the Bay began to see ghosts, and soon the boundaries of the New England Way closed in on a space full of demons and incubi, spectres and evil spirits, as the settlers tried to find a new sense of their own identity among the landmarks of a strange, invisible world. Cotton Mather, who knew every disguise in the devil's wardrobe, offered a frightening catalogue of the devil's attempts to destroy New England.

I believe, there never was a poor Plantation, more pursued by the wrath of the Devil, than our poor New-England. . . . It was a rousing alarm to the Devil, when a great Company of English Protestants and Puritans, came to erect Evangelical Churches, in a corner of the world, where he had reign'd without control for many ages; and it is a vexing Eye-sore to the Devil, that our Lord Christ should be known, and own'd and preached in this howling wilderness. Wherefore he has left no Stone unturned, that so he might undermine his Plantation, and force us out of our Country. First, the Indian Powawes, used all their Sorceries to molest the first Planters here; but God said unto them, Touch them not! Then, Seducing spirits came to root in this Vineyard, but God so rated them off, that they have not prevail'd much farther than the edges of our Land. After this, we have had a continual blast upon some of our principle Grain, annually diminishing a vast part of our ordinary Food. Herewithal, wasting Sicknesses, especially Burning and Mortal Agues, have Shot the Arrows of Death in at our Windows. Next, we have had many Adversaries of our own Language, who have been perpetually assaying to deprive us of those English Liberties, in the encouragement whereof these Territories have been settled. As if this had not been enough; the Tawnies among whom we came have watered our Soil with the Blood of many Hundreds of Inhabitants. . . . Besides all which, now at last the Devils are (if I may so speak) in Person come down upon us with such a Wrath, as is justly much, and will quickly be more, the Astonishment of the World.

And this last adventure of the devil has a quality all its own.

Wherefore the Devil is now making one Attempt more upon us; an Attempt more Difficult, more Surprising, more snarl'd with unintelligible Circumstances than any that we have hitherto Encountered. . . . An Army of Devils is horribly broke in upon the place which is the center, and after a sort, the First-born of our

English Settlements: and the Houses of the Good People there are fill'd with the doleful shrieks of their Children and Servants, Tormented by Invisible Hands, with Tortures altogether preternatural.

The witchcraft hysteria occupied but a brief moment in the history of the Bay. The first actors to take part in it were a group of excited girls and a few of the less savory figures who drifted around the edges of the community, but the speed with which the other people of the Bay gathered to witness the encounter and accept an active role in it, not to mention the quality of the other persons who were eventually drawn into this vortex of activity, serves as an index to the gravity of the issues involved. For a few years, at least, the settlers of Massachusetts were alone in the world, bewildered by the loss of their old destiny but not yet aware of their new one, and during this fateful interval they tried to discover some image of themselves by listening to a chorus of voices which whispered to them from the depths of an invisible wilderness.

STUDY QUESTIONS

1. What were the social, political, and religious problems that confronted New England in the late seventeenth century? How were these problems related to the outbreak of the witchcraft hysteria in Salem?

2. What were the major types of evidence used in a witchcraft trial? What were the unique problems involved in the use of spectral evidence?

3. What role did the Puritan ministers play in the witchcraft episode?

4. What did the Puritan concept of wilderness entail? How have attitudes toward the wilderness changed over the years?

5. What did the transition from "Puritan" to "Yankee" involve? How did the character of the New Englander change during the seventeenth and eighteenth centuries?

BIBLIOGRAPHY

The Salem witchcraft episode is the single most studied event in colonial history. Certainly the drama of the event accounts for much of the scholarly interest. However, of equal importance is the fact that the documentation produced by the trials provides the historian with a comprehensive view of Salem society. For students interested in these sources, Paul Boyer and Stephen Nissenbaum, eds., *The Salem Witchcraft Papers: Verbatim Transcripts of the Legal Documents of the Salem witchcraft Outbreak of 1692,* three volumes (1977), is the best starting place. The same two authors collected an anthology of primary documents in *Witchcraft at Salem Village* (1972). The collections include relevant maps, church records, deeds, wills, and petitions. The first important history of the events is Charles W. Upham, *Salem Witchcraft,* two volumes (1867), which emphasizes the strains in Salem society. Marion Starkey, *The Devil in Massachusetts* (1949) is a highly readable account of the episode. More scholarly are Chadwick Hansen, *Witchcraft at Salem* (1969) and Paul Boyer and Stephen Nissenbaum, *Salem Possessed: The Social Origins of Witchcraft* (1974). The most recent study, John P. Demos, *Entertaining Satan: Witchcraft and the Culture of Early New England* (1982) combines scholarship with narrative grace. A number of important books have been published on European witchcraft. The best are Keith Thomas, *Religion and the Decline of Magic* (1971); Alan Macfarlane, *Witchcraft in Tudor and Stuart England: A Regional and Comparative Study* (1970); H. C. Erik Midelfort, *Witch Hunting in Southwestern Germany, 1562–1684: The Social and Intellectual Foundation* (1972); E. William Monter, *Witchcraft in France and Switzerland: The Borderlands during the Reformation* (1976); and Julio Caro Baroja, *The World of the Witches* (1964).

"UNDER THE BANNER OF KING DEATH": THE SOCIAL WORLD OF THE ANGLO-AMERICAN PIRATES, 1716 TO 1726

Marcus Rediker

We tend to think of Puritans as ascetics who rejected material goods, yet nothing could be further from the truth. It is true Puritans were opposed to luxury and gluttony, but they had no problem with the creature comforts earned by "honeste industrie" and the pursuit of a "godly calling." Puritans realized early on, however, that New England's rocky soil meant many in the community would not be pursuing their "calling," nor earning disposable income, as grain farmers. Nevertheless, forests and grasslands were plentiful in New England, and by the late 1600s processing lumber, raising livestock, and building ships anchored a healthy regional economy that enabled Puritans to become major players in the mercantile networks of the Atlantic basin. In what became known as the "triangular trade," New England merchants exchanged lumber, cattle, and rum for slaves and manufactured goods in all three of the major trading areas on the Atlantic rim—the Gold Coast of Africa, London, and the West Indies.

New England's success in the "triangular trade" during the seventeenth and eighteenth centuries would not have been possible without the direct or implicit protection of an assertive and expansive mother England and her Royal Navy. American merchants from all regions were grateful for the protection and grew increasingly patriotic when British military power saved the colonies from foreign invasion during the era's numerous intercontinental conflicts. Still, membership in a mercantile empire automatically involved colonists directly in England's wars with European rivals France and Spain, making American merchants the target not only of the navies of opposing powers, but of privateers attacking British trade networks and colonial outposts while the Royal Navy was busy elsewhere. Of course, some American sea captains used periods of warfare as an excuse to become pirates themselves and raid enemy shipping.

Marcus Rediker's "Under the Banner of King Death" picks up the tale of the Atlantic pirates just as England and her American colonies were emerging scarred but victorious from twenty-five years of warfare with France and Spain, warfare sparked by England's "Glorious Revolution" (1688). In the Treaty of Utrecht (1713), which ended the conflict, the combatants made a peace that lasted for a generation and gave England commercial and colonial supremacy in the Atlantic basin. Yet, ironically, the end of war made the pirate threat to the British empire's Atlantic commerce temporarily worse, as disaffected and embittered British sailors mustered out of the peace-time fleet and turned to privateering as an easy way to use their naval skills for profit as well as revenge against cruel masters.

Ten years of pursuit by the Royal Navy, along with trials and public mass hangings in the port cities of the American colonies, finally crushed the pirate threat. But, as Rediker shows, this tale of warfare on the high seas in only part of the story. He demonstrates that pirate crews were as much a part of the Atlantic mercantile world as Puritan merchants and British men-of-war. Moreover, pirate crews were just as jealously protective of their "rights"—and just as skeptical of despotic royal authority—as the British Parliamentarians and American colonists who ousted the Catholic absolutist James II and his colonial officers in the Revolution of 1688. Rediker's pirates, of course, mostly opted out of leading a traditional life under the post-revolutionary British government. Yet, as you read Rediker's article, keep in mind that the social code of the pirates' shadow world had much in common with the strident anti-authoritarianism of American colonists, and that communities of disaffected sailors extended to all of the major port cities of the British empire in the 1700s, including those like Boston and New York which would become hotbeds of rebellion during America's revolutionary era.

Writing to the Board of Trade in 1724, Governor Alexander Spotswood of Virginia lamented his lack of "some safe opportunity to get home" to London. He insisted that he would travel only in a well-armed man-of-war.

Your Lordships will easily conceive my Meaning when you reflect on the Vigorous part I've acted to suppress Pirates: and if those barbarous Wretches can be moved to cut off the Nose & Ears of a Master for but correcting his own Sailors, what inhuman treatment must I expect, should I fall within their power, who have been markt as the principle object of their vengeance, for cutting off their arch Pirate Thatch [Teach, also known as Blackbeard], with all his grand Designs, & making so many of their Fraternity to swing in the open air of Virginia.

Spotswood knew these pirates well. He had authorized the expedition that returned to Virginia boasting Blackbeard's head as a trophy. He had done his share to see that many pirates swung on Virginia gallows. He knew that pirates had a fondness for revenge, that they often punished ship captains for "correcting" their crews, and that a kind of "fraternity" prevailed among them. He had good reason to fear them.

The Anglo-American pirates active between 1716 and 1726 occupied a grand position in the long history of a robbery at sea. Their numbers, near five thousand, were extraordinary, and their plunderings were exceptional in both volume and value. Spotswood and other officials and merchants produced a plentiful body of written testimony on pirates and their ways, but historians, though long fascinated by sea-rovers, have not

Blackbeard (Edward Teach) was killed in 1718 by a royal navy ship.

used this material to full advantage. This essay explores the social and cultural dimensions of piracy, focusing on pirates' experience, the organization of their ships, and their social relations and consciousness, with observations on the social and economic context of the crime and its culture. Piracy represented crime on a massive scale—crime as a way of life voluntarily chosen, for the most part, by large numbers of men and directly challenging the ways of the society from which the pirates excepted themselves. The main intent of this essay is to see how piracy looked from the inside and to examine the kinds of social order that pirates forged beyond the reach of traditional authority. Beneath the Jolly Roger, "the

Marcus Rediker, "'Under the Banner of King Death': The Social World of Anglo-American Pirates, 1716 to 1726," *William and Mary Quarterly*, 3d Ser., 38, (April, 1981) pp. 203–227. Reprinted by permission of the Omohundro Institute of Early American History and Culture.

banner of King Death," a new social world took shape once pirates had, as one of them put it, "the choice in themselves."

Contemporary estimates of the pirate population during the period under consideration placed the number between one and two thousand at any one time. This range seems generally accurate. From records that describe the activities of pirate ships and from reports or projections of crew sizes, it appears that eighteen to twenty-four hundred Anglo-American pirates were active between 1716 and 1718, fifteen hundred to two thousand between 1719 and 1722, and one thousand to fifteen hundred declining to fewer than two hundred between 1723 and 1726. In the only estimate we have from the other side of the law, a band of pirates in 1716 claimed that there were "30 Company of them," or roughly twenty-four hundred men, around the world. In all, some forty-five to fifty-five hundred men went, as they called it, "upon the account."

These sea-robbers followed lucrative trade and, like their predecessors, sought bases for their depredations in the Caribbean Sea and the Indian Ocean. The Bahama Islands, no longer defended or governed by the crown, began in 1716 to attract pirates by the hundreds. By 1718 a torrent of complaints moved George I to commission Woodes Rogers to lead an expedition to bring the islands under control. Rogers's efforts largely succeeded, and pirates scattered to the unpeopled inlets of the Carolinas and to Africa. They had frequented African shores as early as 1691; by 1718, Madagascar served as both an entrepôt for booty and as a spot for temporary settlement. At the mouth of the Sierra Leone River on Africa's western coast pirates stopped off for "whoring and drinking" and to unload goods. Theaters of operation among pirates shifted, however, according to the policing designs of the Royal Navy. Pirates favored the Caribbean because of its shallow waters and numerous unsettled cays, but generally, as one pirate noted, these rovers were "dispers't into several parts of the World." Sea-robbers sought and usually found bases near major trade routes, as distant as possible from the powers of the state.

Almost all pirates had labored as merchant seamen, Royal Navy sailors, or privateersmen. The vast majority came from captured merchantmen as volunteers, for reasons suggested by Dr. Samuel Johnson's observation that "no man will be a sailor who has contrivance enough to get himself into a jail; for being in a ship is being in jail with the chance of being drowned.

. . . A man in jail has more room, better food, and commonly better company." Merchant seamen got a hard, close look at death: disease and accidents were commonplace in their occupation, rations were often meager, and discipline was brutal. Each ship was "a little kingdom" whose captain held a near-absolute power which he often abused. Peacetime wages for sailors were consistently low between 1643 and 1797; fraud and irregularities in the distribution of pay were general. A prime purpose of eighteenth-century maritime laws was "to assure a ready supply of cheap, docile labor." Merchant seamen also had to contend with impressment as practiced by the Royal Navy.

Some pirates had served in the navy where conditions aboard ship were no less harsh. Food supplies often ran short, wages were low, mortality was high, discipline severe, and desertion consequently chronic. As one officer reported, the navy had trouble fighting pirates because the king's ship were "so much disabled by sickness, death, and desertion of their seamen." In 1722 the crown sent the *Weymouth* and the *Swallow* in search of a pirate convoy. Royal surgeon John Atkins, noting that merchant seamen were frequently pressed, underlined precisely what these sailors had to fear when he recorded that the "*Weymouth,* who brought out of *England* a Compliment [*sic*] of 240 Men," had "at the end of the Voyage 280 dead upon her Books." Epidemics, consumption, and scurvy raged on royal ships, and the men were "caught in a machine from which there was no escape, bar desertion, incapacitation, or death."

Pirates who had served on privateering vessels knew well that this employment was far less onerous than on merchant or naval ships: food was usually more plentiful, the pay considerably higher, and the work shifts generally shorter. Even so, owing to rigid discipline and to other grievances, mutinies were not uncommon. On Woodes Rogers's spectacularly successful privateering expedition of 1708–1711, Peter Clark was thrown into irons for wishing himself "aboard a Pirate" and saying that "he should be glad that an Enemy, who could over-power us, was a-long-side of us."

Whether from the merchant service, the navy, or the privateering enterprise, pirates necessarily came from seafaring employments. Piracy emphatically was not an option open to landlubbers since sea-robbers "entertain'd so contemptible a Notion of Landmen." Men who became pirates were grimly familiar with the rigors of life at sea and with a single-sex community of work.

Ages are known for 117 pirates active between 1716 and 1726. The range was seventeen to fifty years, the mean 27.4, and the median 27; the twenty-to-twenty-four and the twenty-five-to-twenty-nine age categories had the highest concentrations, with 39 and 37 men respectively. Significantly, 59.3 percent were aged twenty-five or older. Given the high mortality rates within the occupations from which pirates came, these ages were advanced. Though evidence is sketchy, most pirates seem not to have been bound to land and home by familial ties or obligations. Wives and children are rarely mentioned in the records of trials of pirates, and pirate vessels, to forestall desertion, often would "take no Married Man." Almost without exception, pirates came from the lowest social classes. They were, as a royal official condescendingly observed, "desperate Rogues" who could have little hope in life ashore. These traits served as bases of unity when men of the sea decided, in search of something better, to become pirates.

These characteristics had a vital bearing on the ways pirates organized their daily activities. Contemporaries who claimed that pirates had "no regular command among them" mistook a different social order—different from the ordering of merchant, naval, and privateering vessels—for disorder. This social order, articulated in the organization of the pirate ship, was conceived and deliberately constructed by the pirates themselves. Its hallmark was a rough, improvised, but effective egalitarianism that placed authority in the collective hands of the crew.

A striking uniformity of rules and customs prevailed aboard pirate ships, each of which functioned under the terms of written articles, a compact drawn up at the beginning of a voyage or upon election of a new captain, and agreed to by the crew. By these articles crews allocated authority, distributed plunder, and enforced discipline. These arrangements made the captain the creature of his crew. Demanding someone both bold of temper and skilled in navigation, the men elected their captain. They gave him few privileges: he "or any other Officer is allowed no more [food] than another man, nay, the Captain cannot keep his Cabbin to himself." A merchant captain held captive by pirates noted with displeasure that crew members slept on the ship wherever they pleased, "the Captain himself not being allowed a Bed." The crew granted the captain unquestioned authority "in fighting, chasing, or being chased," but "in all other Matters whatsoever" he was "governed by a Majority." As the majority elected, so it could depose. Captains were snatched from their positions for cowardice, cruelty, or refusing "to take and plunder English Vessels." One captain incurred the class-conscious wrath of his crew for being too "Gentleman-like." Occasionally, a despotic captain was summarily executed. As pirate Francis Kennedy explained, most sea-robbers, "having suffered formerly from the ill-treatment of their officers, provided carefully against any such evil" once they arranged their own command.

To prevent the misuse of authority, countervailing powers were designated for the quartermaster, who was elected to protect "the Interest of the Crew." His tasks were to adjudicate minor disputes, distribute food and money, and in some instances to lead attacks on prize vessels. He served as a "civil Magistrate" and dispensed necessaries "with an Equality to them all." The quartermaster often became the captain of a captured ship when the captor was overcrowded or divided by discord. This containment of authority within a dual executive was a distinctive feature of social organization among pirates.

The decisions that had the greatest bearing on the welfare of the crew were generally reserved to the council, a body usually including every man on the ship. The council determined such matters as where the best prizes could be taken and how disruptive dissension was to be resolved. Some crews continually used the council, "carrying every thing by a majority of votes"; others set up the council as a court. The decisions made by this body constituted the highest authority on a pirate ship: even the boldest captain dared not challenge a council's mandate.

The distribution of plunder was regulated explicitly by the ship's articles, which allocated booty according to skills and duties. Captain and quartermaster received between one and one-half and two shares; gunners, boatswains, mates, carpenters, and doctors, one and one-quarter or one and one-half; all others got one share each. This pay system represented a radical departure from practices in the merchant service, Royal Navy, or privateering. It leveled an elaborate hierarchy of pay ranks and decisively reduced the disparity between the top and bottom of the scale. Indeed, this must have been one of the most egalitarian plans for the disposition of resources to be found anywhere in the early eighteenth century. The scheme indicates that pirates did not consider themselves wage laborers but rather risk-sharing partners. If, as a noted historian of piracy, Philip Gosse, has suggested, "the pick of all seamen were pirates," the equitable distribution of plunder and the conception of the partnership may be understood as the work of men who valued and respected the skills of their comrades. But not all booty was dispensed this way. A portion went into a "common fund" to provide for the men who sustained injury of lasting effect. The loss of eyesight or any appendage merited compensation. By this welfare system pirates attempted to guard against debilities caused by accidents, to protect skills, and to promote loyalty within the group.

The articles also regulated discipline aboard ship, though "discipline" is perhaps a misnomer for a rule system that left large ranges of behavior uncontrolled. Less arbitrary than that of the merchant service and less codified than that of the navy, discipline among pirates always depended on a collective sense of transgression. Many misdeeds were accorded "what Punishment the Captain and Majority of the Company shall think fit," and it is noteworthy that pirates did not often resort to the whip. Their discipline, if no less severe in certain cases, was generally tolerant of behavior that provoked punishment in other maritime occupations. Three major methods of discipline were employed, all conditioned by the fact that pirate ships were crowded: an average crew numbered near eighty on a 250-ton vessel. The articles of Bartholomew Roberts's ship revealed one tactic for maintaining order: "No striking one another on board, but every Man's Quarrels to be ended on Shore at Sword and Pistol." Antagonists were to fight a duel with pistols, but if both their first shots missed, then with swords, and the first to draw blood was declared the victor. By taking such conflicts off the ship (and symbolically off the sea), this practice promoted harmony in the crowded quarters below decks. The ideal of harmony was also reflected when, in an often-used disciplinary action, pirates made a crew member the "Governor of an Island." Men who were incorrigibly disruptive or who transgressed important rules were marooned. For defrauding his mates by taking more than a proper share of plunder, for deserting or malingering during battle, for keeping secrets from the crew, or for stealing, a pirate risked being deposited "where he was sure to encounter Hardships." The ultimate method of maintaining order was execution. This penalty was exacted for bringing on board "a Boy or a Woman" or for meddling with a "prudent Woman" on a prize ship, but was most commonly invoked to punish a captain who abused his authority.

Some crews attempted to circumvent disciplinary problems by taking "no Body against their Wills." By the same logic, they would keep no unwilling person. The confession of pirate Edward

Davis in 1718 indicates that oaths of honor were used to cement the loyalty of new members: "at first the old Pirates were a little shy of the new ones, . . . yet in a short time the *New Men* being sworn to be faithful, and not to cheat the Company to the Value of a *Piece of Eight,* they all consulted and acted together with great unanimity, and no distinction was made between *Old* and *New*." Yet for all their efforts to blunt the cutting edge of authority and to maintain harmony and cohesion, conflict could not always be contained. Occasionally, upon election of a new captain, men who favored other leadership drew up new articles and sailed away from their former mates. The social organization constructed by pirates, although flexible, was unable to accommodate severe, sustained conflict. The egalitarian and collective exercise of authority by pirates had both negative and positive effects. Although it produced a chronic instability, it also guaranteed continuity: the very process by which new crews were established helped to ensure a social uniformity and, as we shall see, a consciousness of kind among pirates.

One important mechanism in this continuity can be seen by charting the connections among pirate crews. The accompanying diagram [Figure 4.1, see p. 44], arranged according to vessel captaincy, demonstrates that by splintering, by sailing in consorts, or by other associations, roughly thirty-six hundred pirates—more than 70 percent of all those active between 1716 and 1726—fit into two main lines of genealogical descent. Captain Benjamin Hornigold and the pirate rendezvous in the Bahamas stood at the origin of an intricate lineage that ended with the hanging of John Phillips's crew in June 1724. The second line, spawned in the chance meeting of the lately mutinous crews of George Lowther and Edward Low in 1722, culminated in the executions of William Fly and his men in July 1726. It was primarily within and through this network that the social organization of the pirate ship took on its significance, transmitting and preserving customs and meanings, and helping to structure and perpetuate the pirates' social world.

Pirates constructed that world in defiant contradistinction to the ways of the world they left behind, in particular to its salient figures of power, the merchant captain and the royal official, and to the system of authority those figures represented and enforced. When eight pirates were tried in Boston in 1718, merchant captain Thomas Checkley told of the capture of his ship by pirates who "pretended," he said, "to be Robbin Hoods Men." Eric Hobsbawm has defined social banditry as a "universal and virtually unchanging phenomenon," an "endemic peasant protest against oppression and poverty: a cry for vengeance on the rich and the oppressors." Its goal is "a traditional world in which men are justly dealt with, not a new and perfect world"; Hobsbawm calls its advocates "revolutionary traditionalists." Pirates, of course, were not peasants, but they fit Hobsbawm's formulation in every other respect. Of special importance was their "cry for vengeance."

Spotswood told no more than the simple truth when he expressed his fear of pirate vengeance, for the very names of pirate ships made the same threat. Edward Teach, whom Spotswood's men cut off, called his vessel *Queen Anne's Revenge*; other notorious craft were Stede Bonnet's *Revenge* and John Cole's *New York Revenge's Revenge*. The foremost target of vengeance was the merchant captain. Frequently, "in a far distant latitude," as one seaman put it, "unlimited power, bad views, ill nature and ill principles all concur[red]" in a ship's commander. This was a man "past all restraint," who often made life miserable for his crew. Spotswood also noted how pirates avenged the captains "correcting" of his sailors. In 1722, merchant captains Isham Randolph, Constantine Cane, and William Halladay petitioned Spotswood "in behalf of themselves and other Masters of Ships" for "some certain method. . . for punishing mutinous & disobedient Seamen." They explained that captains faced great danger "in case of meeting with Pyrates, where we are sure to suffer all the tortures w[hi]ch such an abandoned crew can invent, upon the least intimation of our Striking any of our men."

Upon seizing a merchantman, pirates often administered the "Distribution of Justice," "enquiring

Connections among Anglo-American Pirate Crews, 1714 to 1726

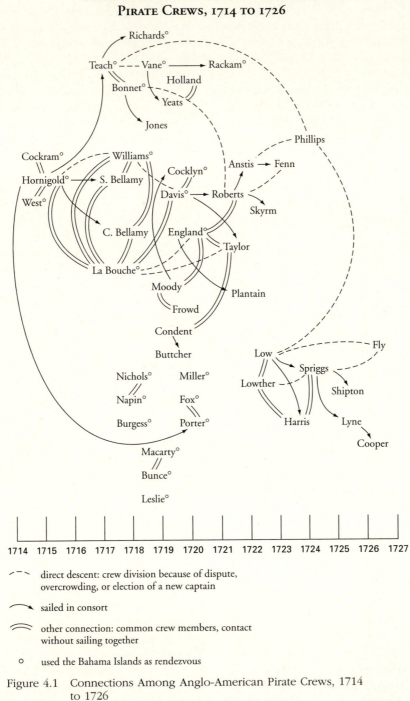

— — —   direct descent: crew division because of dispute,
overcrowding, or election of a new captain

⌒→   sailed in consort

⌒⌒   other connection: common crew members, contact
without sailing together

○   used the Bahama Islands as rendezvous

Figure 4.1   Connections Among Anglo-American Pirate Crews, 1714
to 1726

into the Manner of the Commander's Behaviour to their Men, and those, against whom Complaint was made" were "whipp'd and pickled." In 1724, merchant captain Richard Hawkins described another form of retribution, a torture known as the "Sweat": "Between decks they stick Candles round the Mizen-Mast, and about twenty-five men surround it with Points of Swords, Penknives, Compasses, Forks, Etc. in each of their hands: *Culprit* enters the Circle; the Violin plays a merry Jig; and he must run for about ten Minutes, while each man runs his Instrument into his Posteriors." Many captured captains were "barbarously used," and some were summarily executed. Pirate Philip Lyne carried this vengeance to its bloodiest extremity, confessing when apprehended in 1726 that "during the time of his Piracy" he "had killed 37 Masters of Vessels."

Still, the punishment of captains was not indiscriminate, for a captain who had been "an honest Fellow that never abused any Sailors" was often rewarded by pirates. The best description of pirates' notions of justice comes from merchant captain William Snelgrave's account of his capture in 1719. On April 1, Snelgrave's ship was seized by Thomas Cocklyn's crew of rovers at the mouth of the Sierra Leone River. Cocklyn was soon joined by men captained by Oliver LaBouche and Howell Davis, and Snelgrave spent the next thirty days among two hundred forty pirates.

The capture was effected when twelve pirates in a small boat came alongside Snelgrave's ship, which was manned by forty-five sailors. Snelgrave ordered his crew to arms; though they refused, the pirate quartermaster, infuriated by the command, drew a pistol. He then, Snelgrave testified, "with the but-end endeavoured to beat out my Brains," until "some of my People. . . cried out aloud 'For God sake don't kill our Captain, for we never were with a better Man.'" The quartermaster, Snelgrave noted, "told me, 'my Life was safe provided none of my People complained against me.' I replied, 'I was sure none of them could.'"

Snelgrave was taken to Cocklyn, who told him, "I am sorry you have met with bad usage after Quarter given, but 'tis the Fortune of War sometimes. . . . [I]f you tell the truth, and your Men make no Complaints against you, you shall be kindly used." Howell Davis, commander of the largest of the pirate ships, reprimanded Cocklyn's men for their roughness and, by Snelgrave's account, expressed himself "ashamed to hear how I had been used by them. That they should remember their reasons for going a pirating were to revenge themselves on base Merchants and cruel commanders of Ships. . . . [N]o one of my People, even those that had entered with them gave me the least ill-character. . . . [I]t was plain they loved me."

Snelgrave's character proved so respectable that the pirates proposed to give him a captured ship with full cargo and to sell the goods for him. Then they would capture a Portuguese slaver, sell the slaves, and give the proceeds to Snelgrave so that he could "return with a large sum of Money to London, and bid the Merchants defiance." The proposal was "unanimously approved" by the pirates, but fearing a charge of complicity, Snelgrave hesitated to accept it. Davis then interceded, saying that he favored "allowing every Body to go to the Devil in their own way" and that he knew that Snelgrave feared for "his Reputation." The refusal was graciously accepted, Snelgrave claiming that "the Tide being turned, they were as kind to me, as they had been at first severe."

Snelgrave related another revealing episode. While he remained in pirate hands, a decrepit schooner belonging to the Royal African Company sailed into the Sierra Leone and was taken by his captors. Simon Jones, a member of Cocklyn's crew, urged his mates to burn the ship since he had been poorly treated while in the company's employ. The pirates were about to do so when another of them, James Stubbs, protested that such action would only "serve the Company's interests" since the ship was worth but little. He also pointed out that "the poor People that now belong to her, and have been on so long a voyage, will lose their Wages, which I am sure is Three times the Value of the Vessel." The pirates concurred and returned the ship to its crew, who "came safe home to England in it."

Captain Snelgrave also returned to England soon after this incident, but eleven of his seamen remained behind as pirates.

Snelgrave seems to have been an exceptionally decent captain. Pirates like Howell Davis claimed that abusive treatment by masters of merchantmen contributed mightily to their willingness to become sea-robbers. John Archer, whose career as a pirate dated from 1718 when he sailed with Edward Teach, uttered a final protest before his execution in 1724: "I could wish that Masters of Vessels would not use their Men with so much Severity, as many of them do, which exposes us to great Temptations." William Fly, facing the gallows for murder and piracy in 1726, angrily said, "I can't charge myself,—I shan't own myself Guilty of any Murder,—Our Captain and his Mate used us Barbarously. We poor Men can't have Justice done us. There is nothing said to our Commanders, let them never so much abuse us, and use us like Dogs." To pirates revenge was justice; punishment was meted out to barbarous captains, as befitted the captains' crimes.

Sea-robbers who fell into the hands of the state received the full force of penalties for crimes against property. The official view of piracy as crime was outlined in 1718 by Vice-Admiralty Judge Nicholas Trott in his charge to the jury in the trial of Stede Bonnet and thirty-three members of his crew at Charleston, South Carolina. Declaring that "the Sea was given by God for the use of Men, and is subject to Dominion and Property, as well as the Land," Trott observed of the accused that "the Law of Nations never granted to them a Power to change the Right of Property." Pirates on trial were denied benefit of clergy, were "called *Hostis Humani Generis,* with whom neither Faith nor Oath" were to be kept, and were regarded as "*Brutes,* and *Beasts of Prey*." Turning from the jury to the accused, Trott circumspectly surmised that "no further Good or Benefit can be expected from you but by the Example of your Deaths."

The insistence on obtaining this final benefit locked royal officials and pirates into a system of reciprocal terrorism. As royal authorities offered bounties for captured pirates, so too did pirates "offer any price" for certain officials. In Virginia in 1720 one of six pirates facing the gallows "called for a Bottle of Wine, and taking a Glass of it, he Drank Damnation to the Governour and Confusion to the Colony, which the rest pledged." Not to be outdone, Governor Spotswood thought it "necessary for the greater Terrour to hang up four of them in Chains." Pirates demonstrated disdain for state authority when George I extended general pardons for piracy in 1717 and 1718. Some accepted the grace but refused to reform; others "seem'd to slight it," and the most defiant "used the King's Proclamation with great contempt, and tore it into pieces." One pirate crew downed its punch proclaiming. "Curse the King and all the Higher Powers." The social relations of piracy were marked by vigorous, often violent, antipathy toward traditional authority.

At the Charleston trial over which Trott presided, Richard Allen, attorney general of South Carolina, told the jury that "pirates prey upon all Mankind, their own Species and Fellow-Creatures without Distinction of Nations or Religions." Allen was mistaken in one significant point: pirates did not prey on one another. Rather, they consistently expressed in numerous and subtle ways a highly developed consciousness of kind. Here we turn from the external social relations of piracy to the internal, in order to examine this consciousness of kind—in a sense, a strategy for survival—and the collectivistic ethos it expressed.

Pirates showed recurrent willingness to join forces at sea and in port. In April 1719, when Howell Davis and crew sailed into the Sierra Leone River, the pirates captained by Thomas Cocklyn were wary until they saw on the approaching ship "her Black Flag," then "immediately they were easy in their minds, and a little time after" the crews "saluted one another with their Cannon." Other crews exchanged similar greetings and, like Davis and Cocklyn who combined their powers, frequently invoked an unwritten code of hospitality to forge spontaneous alliances.

This communitarian urge was perhaps most evident in the pirate strongholds of Madagascar and Sierra Leone. Sea-robbers occasionally chose more sedentary lifeways on various thinly populated islands, and they contributed a notorious number of men to the community of logwood cutters at the Bay of Campeachy in the Gulf of Mexico. In 1718 a royal official complained of a "nest of pirates" in the Bahamas "who already esteem themselves a community, and to have one common interest."

To perpetuate such community it was necessary to minimize conflict not only on each ship but also among separate bands of pirates. Indeed, one of the strongest indicators of consciousness of kind lies in the manifest absence of discord between different pirate crews. To some extent this was even a transnational matter: French and Anglo-American pirates usually cooperated peaceably, only occasionally exchanging cannon fire. Anglo-American crews consistently refused to attack one another.

In no way was the pirate sense of fraternity, which Spotswood and others noted, more forcefully expressed than in the threats and acts of revenge taken by pirates. Theirs was truly a case of hanging together or being hanged separately. In April 1717, the pirate ship *Whidah* was wrecked near Boston. Most of its crew perished; the survivors were jailed. In July, Thomas Fox, a Boston ship captain, was taken by pirates who "Questioned him whether anything was done to the Pyrates in Boston Goall," promising "that if the Prisoners Suffered they would Kill every Body they took belonging to New England." Shortly after this incident, Teach's sea-rovers captured a merchant vessel and, "because she belonged to Boston, [Teach] alledging the People of Boston had hanged some of the Pirates, so burnt her." Teach declared that all Boston ships deserved a similar fate. Charles Vane, reputedly a most fearsome pirate, "would give no quarter to the Bermudians" and punished them and "cut away their masts upon account of one Thomas Brown who was (some time) detain'd in these Islands upon suspicion of piracy." Brown apparently had plans to sail as Vane's consort until foiled by his capture.

In September 1720, pirates captained by Bartholomew Roberts "openly and in the daytime burnt and destroyed . . . vessels in the Road of Basseterre [St. Kitts] and had the audaciousness to insult H. M. Fort," avenging the execution of "their comrades at Nevis." Roberts then sent word to the governor that "they would Come and Burn the Town [Sandy Point] about his Ears for hanging the Pyrates there." In 1721, Spotswood relayed information to the Council of Trade and Plantations that Roberts "said he expected to be joined by another ship and would then visit Virginia, and avenge the pirates who have been executed here." The credibility of the threat was confirmed by the unanimous resolution of the Virginia Executive Council that "the Country be put into an immediate posture of Defense." Lookouts and beacons were quickly provided, and communications with neighboring colonies effected. "Near 60 Cannon," Spotswood later reported, were "mounted on sundry Substantial Batteries."

In 1723 pirate captain Francis Spriggs vowed to find a Captain Moore "and put him to death for being the cause of the death of [pirate] Lowther," and, shortly after, similarly pledged to go "in quest of Captain Solgard," who had overpowered a pirate ship commanded by Charles Harris. In January 1724, Lieutenant Governor Charles Hope of Bermuda wrote to the Board of Trade that he found it difficult to procure trial evidence against pirates because residents "feared that this very execution wou'd make our vessels fare the worse for it, when they happen'd to fall into pirate hands."

Pirates also affirmed their unity symbolically. Some evidence indicates that sea-robbers may have had a sense of belonging to a separate, in some manner exclusive, speech community. Philip Ashton, who spent sixteen months among pirates in 1722, noted that "according to the Pirates usual Custom, and *in their proper Dialect*, asked me, If I would sign their Articles." Many sources suggest that cursing, swearing, and blaspheming may have been defining traits of this style of speech. For example, near the Sierra Leone River a British official named Plunkett pretended to cooperate with, but then attacked, the pirates with Bartholomew Roberts. Plunkett was captured, and Roberts

upon the first sight of Plunkett swore at him like any Devil, for his Irish Impudence in daring to resist him. Old Plunkett, finding he had got into bad Company, fell a swearing and cursing as fast or faster than Roberts; which made the rest of the Pirates laugh heartily, desiring Roberts to sit down and hold his Peace, for he had no Share in the Pallaver with Plunkett at all. So that by meer Dint of Cursing and Damning, Old Plunkett . . . sav'd his life.

Admittedly we can see only outlines here, but it appears that the symbolic connectedness, the consciousness of kind, extended into the domain of language.

Certainly the best known symbol of piracy is the flag, the Jolly Roger. Less known and appreciated is the fact that the flag was very widely used: no fewer, and probably a great many more, than two thousand five hundred men sailed under it. So general an adoption indicates an advanced state of group identification. The Jolly Roger was described as a "black Ensign, in the Middle of which is a large white Skeleton with a Dart in one hand striking a bleeding Heart, and in the other an Hour Glass." Although there was considerable variation in particulars among these flags, there was also a general uniformity of chosen images. The flag background was black, adorned with white representational figures. The most common symbol was the human skull, or "death's head," sometimes isolated but more frequently the most prominent feature of an entire skeleton. Other recurring items were a weapon—cutlass, sword, or dart—and an hour glass.

The flag was intended to terrify the pirates' prey, but its triad of interlocking symbols— death, violence, limited time—simultaneously pointed to meaningful parts of the seaman's experience, and eloquently bespoke the pirates' own consciousness of themselves as preyed upon in turn. Pirates seized the symbol of mortality from ship captains who used the skull "as a

marginal sign in their logs to indicate the record of a death." Seamen who became pirates escaped from one closed system only to find themselves encased in another. But as pirates—and only as pirates—these men were able to fight back beneath the somber colors of "King Death" against those captains, merchants, and officials who waved banners of authority. Moreover, pirates self-righteously perceived their situation and the excesses of these powerful figures through a collectivistic ethos that had been forged in the struggles for survival.

The self-righteousness of pirates was strongly linked to the "traditional world in which men are justly dealt with," as described by Hobsbawm. It found expression in their social rules, their egalitarian social organization, and their notions of revenge and justice. By walking "to the Gallows without a Tear," by calling themselves "Honest Men" and "Gentlemen," and by speaking self-servingly but proudly of their "Conscience" and "Honor," pirates flaunted their certitude. When, in 1720, ruling groups concluded that "nothing but force will subdue them," many pirates responded by intensifying their commitment. It was observed of Edward Low's crew in 1724 that they "swear, with the most direful Imprecations, that if ever they should find themselves overpower'd they would immediately blow their ship up rather than suffer themselves to be hang'd like Dogs." These sea-robbers would not "do Jolly Roger the Disgrace to be struck."

This consciousness of kind among pirates manifested itself in an elaborate social code. Through rule, custom, and symbol the code prescribed specific behavioral standards intended to preserve the social world that pirates built for themselves. As the examples of revenge reveal, royal officials recognized the threat of the pirates' alternative order. Some authorities feared that pirates might "set up a sort of Commonwealth"—a correct designation—in uninhabited regions, since "no Power in those Parts of the World could have been able to dispute it with them." But the consciousness of kind never took national shape, and piracy was soon suppressed. We now turn to the general social and economic context of the crime and its culture.

Contemporary observers seem to have attributed the rise of piracy to the demobilizing of the Royal Navy at the end of the War of the Spanish Succession. A group of Virginia merchants, for instance, wrote to the Admiralty in 1713, setting forth "the apprehensions they have of Pyrates molesting their trade in the time of Peace." The navy plunged from 49,860 men at the end of the war to 13,475 just two years later, and only by 1740 did it increase to as many as 30,000 again. At the same time, the expiration of privateering licenses—bills of marque—added to the number of seamen loose and looking for work in the port cities of the empire. Such underemployment contributed significantly to the rise of piracy, but it is not a sufficient explanation since, as already noted, the vast majority of those who became pirates were working in the merchant service at the moment of their joining. The surplus of labor at the end of the war had jarring social effects. It produced an immediate contraction of wages; merchant seamen who made 45–50 shillings per month in 1708 made only half that amount in 1713. It provoked greater competition for seafaring jobs, favorable to the hiring of older, more experienced seamen. And it would, over time, affect the social conditions and relations of life at sea, cutting back material benefits and hardening discipline. War years, despite their dangers, provided seafarers with tangible benefits. The Anglo-American seamen of 1713 had performed wartime labor for twenty of the previous twenty-five years, and for eleven years consecutively. But conditions did not worsen immediately after the war. As Ralph Davis explains, "the years 1713–1715 saw—as did immediate post-war years throughout the eighteenth century—the shifting of heaped-up surpluses of colonial goods, the movement of great quantities of English goods to colonial and other markets, and a general filling in of stocks of imported goods which had been allowed to run down." This small-scale boom gave employment to some of the seamen who had been dropped from naval rolls. But by late 1715, a slump in trade

began, to last into the 1730s. All of these difficulties were exacerbated by the century-long trend in which "life on board [a merchant] ship was carried on amid a discipline which grew harsher with the passage of time." Many seamen knew that things had once been different and, for many, decisively better.

By 1726, the menace of piracy had been effectively suppressed by governmental action. Circumstantial factors do not account for its demise. The number of men in the Royal Navy did increase from 6,298 in 1725 to 16,872 in 1726, and again to 20,697 in 1727. This increase probably had some bearing on the declining numbers of sea-robbers. Yet some 20,000 sailors had been in the navy in 1719 and 1720, years when pirates were numerous. In addition, seafaring wages only twice rose above 24–25 shillings per month between 1713 and the mid-1730s: there were temporary increases to 30 shillings in 1718 and 1727. Conditions of life at sea probably did not change appreciably until war broke out in 1739.

The pardons offered to pirates in 1717 and 1718 largely failed to rid the sea of robbers. Since the graces specified that only crimes committed at certain times and in particular regions would be forgiven, many pirates saw enormous latitude for official trickery and refused to surrender. Moreover, accepting and abiding by the rules of the pardon would have meant for most men a return to the dismal conditions they had escaped. Their tactic failing, royal officials intensified the naval campaign against piracy—with great and gruesome effect. Corpses dangled in chains in British ports around the world "as a Spectacle for the Warning of others." No fewer than four hundred, and probably five to six hundred, Anglo-American pirates were executed between 1716 and 1726. The campaign to cleanse the seas was supported by clergymen, royal officials, and publicists who sought through sermons, proclamations, pamphlets and the newspaper press to create an image of the pirate that would legitimate his extermination. Piracy had always depended in some measure on the rumors and tales of its successes, especially among seamen and dealers in stolen cargo. In 1722 and 1723, after a spate of hangings and verbal chastisements, the pirate population began to decline. By 1726, only a handful of the fraternity remained.

Finally, pirates themselves unwittingly took a hand in their own destruction. From the outset, theirs had been a fragile social group. They produced nothing and were economically parasitic on the mercantile system. And they were widely dispersed, virtually without geographic boundaries. Try as they might, they were unable to create reliable mechanisms through which they could either replenish their ranks or mobilize their collective strength. These deficiencies of social organization made them, in the long run, easy prey.

We see in the end that the pirate was, perhaps above all else, and unremarkable man caught in harsh, often deadly circumstances. Wealth he surely desired, but a strong social logic informed both his motivation and his behavior. Emerging from lower-class backgrounds and maritime employments, and loosed from familial bonds, pirates developed common symbols and standards of conduct. They forged spontaneous alliances, refused to fight each other, swore to avenge injury to their own kind, and even retired to pirate communities. They erected their own ideal of justice, insisted upon an egalitarian, if unstable, form of social organization, and defined themselves against other social groups and types. So, too, did they perceive many of their activities as ethical and justified, not unlike the eighteenth-century crowds described by Edward Thompson. But pirates, experienced as cooperative seafaring laborers and no longer disciplined by law, were both familiar with the workings of an international market economy and little affected by the uncertainties of economic change. Perhaps their dual relationship to the mode of production as free wage laborers and members of a criminal subculture gave pirates the perspective and resources to fight back against brutal and unjust authority, and to construct a new social order where King Death would not reign supreme. This was probably a contradictory pursuit: for many, piracy, as strategy of survival, was ill-fated.

Piracy, in the end, offers us an extraordinary opportunity. Here we can see how a sizeable group of Anglo-Americans—poor men in canvas jackets and tarred breeches—constructed a social world where they had "the choice in themselves." Theirs was truly a culture of masterless men: Pirates were as far removed from traditional authority as any men could be in the early eighteenth century. Beyond the church, beyond the family, beyond disciplinary labor, and using the sea to distance themselves from the powers of the state, they carried out a strange experiment. The social constellation of piracy, in particular the complex consciousness and egalitarian impulses that developed once the shackles were off, might provide valuable clarification of more general social and cultural patterns among the laboring poor. Here we can see aspirations and achievements that under normal circumstances would have been heavily muted, if not rendered imperceptible, by the power relationships of everyday life.

STUDY QUESTIONS

1. Why did many sailors find piracy an appealing substitute for more legitimate employment?

2. What social class were most pirates drawn from and why does Rediker think this is important?

3. How did self-governance in the pirate communities compare with the exercise of authority on British men-of-war or merchant vessels? What function did the "ship's articles" and the "council" serve?

4. What treatment did captured ship masters receive, and how did pirates determine punishment for such captives?

5. What were the usual symbols on the "Jolly Roger," and what did they mean to the pirates and their prey?

6. What conditions after the end of the War of the Spanish Succession contributed to an increase in piracy in the Atlantic?

BIBLIOGRAPHY

Marcus Rediker expands on his own story here in *Between the Devil and Deep Blue Sea: Merchant Seamen, Pirates, and the Anglo-American Maritime World, 1700–1750* (1989). Good sources for the history of piracy include Hugh F. Rankin, *The Golden Age of Piracy* (1969); Neville Williams, *Captains Outrageous: Seven Centuries of Piracy* (1961); and the popular history by Patrick Pringle, *Jolly Roger* (1953). The best recent study of the New England economy in the Puritan era is Stephen Innes, *Creating the Commonwealth: The Economic Culture of Puritan New England* (1995). For a larger portrait of the American colonial economy in general, see John J. McCusker and Russell R. Menard, *The Economy of British North America, 1607–1789,* rev. ed. (1991); and for the American colonial economy in an imperial context see Michael Kammen, *Empire and Interest: The American Colonies and the Politics of Mercantilism* (1970); also Richard R. Johnson, *Adjustment to Empire: The New England Colonies, 1675–1715* (1981); and finally Ian K. Steele, *The English Atlantic, 1675–1740: Communication and Community* (1986). On the social order of American port cities in the decades before the American Revolution, see Gary B. Nash, *The Urban Crucible: Social Change, Political Consciousness, and the Origins of the Revolution* (1979).

Part Two

SOUTHERN LIFE

The Southern colonies differed markedly from the New England colonies. Colonial Virginia, for example, never enjoyed the remarkable demographic stability of colonial Massachusetts Bay. Most of the people who traveled to Virginia during the seventeenth century were young, unmarried male servants—indeed, before 1640 males outnumbered females by a ratio of 6 to 1. In addition, the humid lowlands of the Chesapeake fostered high mortality rates. During the seventeenth century, the average life expectancy for Chesapeake males was about forty-three, and for females it was even lower. Only 50 percent of the children born in the region lived past the age of twenty, and many of the survivors suffered illnesses that left them too weak for strenuous labor.

The most obvious result of this demographic nightmare was a severe labor shortage. English immigration to the South simply did not satisfy the labor needs. As a result, colonial planters began to import black Africans as early as 1619. The question of whether these unwilling emigrants were chattel slaves or free servants fulfilling an indentureship remained in doubt for some years, but certainly by 1700 white planters had developed the institution of slavery. This peculiar institution was far more than an economic arrangement; it had a psychological effect on everyone who lived close to its dominion.

More than demographics and slavery separated the Southern colonies from the New England colonies. The first settlers who landed in Jamestown were not concerned with the impurities in the Anglican Church. Instead, they worried about their own economic futures. Most longed to become wealthy—and the faster the better. They were worldly men in search of worldly success. The majority readily accepted

not only the Anglican Church but also the English class structure. Their goal was to move up the pyramid, not to level it.

With very few exceptions, their dreams of easy prosperity vanished before the hardships of Southern existence. Indians, swamps, diseases, and backbreaking labor were formidable foes. Men who possessed stronger bodies, quicker minds, or larger bank accounts advanced by buying land and growing tobacco. Their society was brutally competitive and early success was no guarantee of lasting success. But by the 1650s a real colonial aristocracy had begun to emerge. The great Chesapeake families—the Byrds, Carters, Masons, and Burwells—commenced their domination of society and politics.

Without losing their competitive urges, the leaders of the major families began to cooperate to preserve and perpetuate their wealth and status. They intermarried, awarded themselves military titles, and dominated the colonial assemblies throughout the South. By the eighteenth century such bodies as Virginia's House of Burgesses began to resemble a gathering of cousins. Not surprisingly, as the gentry consolidated its control over all aspects of colonial society, it became increasingly more difficult for the ordinary man to rise into the ruling class. This development, however, created few problems. Not many people in the colonial South questioned deferential attitudes.

Reading 5

ENGLISHMEN AND AFRICANS

Winthrop Jordan

The institution of chattel slavery developed gradually in the British seaboard colonies. The first Africans landed in Virginia in 1619, but over the next forty years relatively few others followed. By 1660 only about fifteen hundred blacks lived in Virginia, and their status was unclear. White planters regarded some as slaves, others as indentured servants. But as the black population grew after 1660 and the demand for a steady labor force became critical, white planters adopted the institution of chattel slavery.

Planters masked the economic foundations of slavery with a rhetoric that emphasized humanitarianism and Christianity. As Winthrop D. Jordan emphasizes in his National Book Award-winning study, *White Over Black: American Attitudes Toward the Negro, 1550–1812,* from their first meeting, Englishmen viewed Africans as a strange and disturbing people. The Africans' color, religion, and social behavior upset Englishmen. This early form of prejudice laid the intellectual groundwork for later justifications of slavery.

The institution of slavery influenced the development of the entire South and left deep psychological scars both on whites and blacks. In the following essay Jordan discusses the initial English attitude toward Africans.

When the Atlantic nations of Europe began expanding overseas in the sixteenth century, Portugal led the way to Africa and to the east while Spain founded a great empire in America. It was not until the reign of Queen Elizabeth that Englishmen came to realize that overseas exploration and plantations could bring home wealth, power, glory, and fascinating information. By the early years of the seventeenth century Englishmen had developed a taste for empire and for tales of adventure and discovery. More than is usual in human affairs, one man, the great chronicler Richard Hakluyt, had roused enthusiasm for western planting and had stirred the nation with his monumental compilation, *The Principal Navigations, Voyages, Traffiques and Discoveries of the English Nation.* Here was a work to widen a people's horizons. Its exhilarating accounts of voyages to all quarters of the globe constituted a national hymn, a scientific treatise, a sermon, and an adventure story.

English voyagers did not touch upon the shores of West Africa until after 1550, nearly a century after Prince Henry the Navigator had mounted the sustained Portuguese thrust southward for a water passage to the Orient. Usually Englishmen came to Africa to trade goods *with* the natives. The earliest English descriptions of West Africa were written by adventurous traders, men who had no special interest in converting the natives or, except for the famous Hawkins voyages in the 1560s, in otherwise laying hands on them. Extensive English participation in the slave trade did not develop until well into the seventeenth century. Initially English contact with Africans did not take place primarily in a context which prejudged the Negro as a slave, at least not as a slave of Englishmen. Rather, Englishmen met Africans merely as another sort of men.

Englishmen found the peoples of Africa very different from themselves. "Negroes" looked different to Englishmen; their religion was un-Christian; their manner of living was anything but English; they seemed to be a particularly libidinous sort of people. All these clusters of perceptions were related to each other, though they may be spread apart for inspection, and they were related also to the circumstances of contact in Africa, to previously accumulated traditions concerning that strange and distant continent, and to certain special qualities of English society on the eve of its expansion into the New World.

The Blackness Without

For Englishmen, the most arresting characteristic of the newly discovered African was his color. Travelers rarely failed to comment upon it; indeed when describing Africans they frequently began with complexion and then moved on to dress (or, as they saw, lack of it) and manners. At Cape Verde, "These people are all blacke, and are called Negroes, without any apparell, saving before their privities." Robert Baker's narrative poem recounting his two voyages to the West African coast in 1562 and 1563 introduced the people he saw with these engaging lines:

> *And entering in [a river], we see*
> *a number of blacke soules,*
> *Whose likelinesse seem'd men to be,*
> *but all as blacke as coles.*
> *Their Captain comes to me*
> *as naked as my naile,*
> *Not having witte or honestie*
> *to cover once his taile.*

Englishmen actually described Negroes as *black*—an exaggerated term which in itself suggests that the Negro's complexion had powerful impact upon their perceptions. Even the peoples of northern Africa seemed so dark that Englishmen tended to call them "black" and let further refinements go by the board. In Shakespeare's day, the Moors, including Othello, were commonly portrayed as pitchy black and the terms *Moor* and *Negro* were used almost interchangeably. With curious inconsistency, however, Englishmen recognized that Africans south of the Sahara were not at all the same people as the much more familiar Moors. Sometimes they referred to West Africans as "black Moors" to distinguish them from the peoples of North Africa.

The powerful impact which the Negro's color made upon Englishmen must have been partly owing to suddenness of contact. Though the Bible as well as the arts and literature of antiquity and the Middle Ages offered some slight introduction to the "Ethiope," England's immediate acquaintance with "black"-skinned peoples came with relative rapidity. People much darker than Englishmen were not entirely unfamiliar, but really "black" men were virtually unknown except as vaguely referred to in the hazy literature about the sub-Sahara which had filtered down from antiquity. Native West Africans probably first appeared in London in 1554; in that year five "Negroes," as one trader reported, were taken to England, "kept till they could speake the language," and then brought back again "to be a helpe to Englishmen" who were engaged in trade with Africans on the coast. Hakluyt's later discussion of these Africans suggests that these "black Moors" were a novelty to Englishmen. In this respect the English experience was markedly different from that of the Spanish and Portuguese who for centuries had been in close contact with North Africa and had actually been invaded and subjected by people both darker and more "highly civilized" than themselves. The impact of the Negro's color was the more powerful upon Englishmen, moreover, because England's principal contact with Africans came in West Africa and the Congo, which meant that one of the lightest-skinned of the earth's peoples suddenly came face to face with one of the darkest.

In England perhaps more than in southern Europe, the concept of blackness was loaded with intense meaning. Long before they found that some men were black, Englishmen found in the idea of blackness a way of expressing some of their most ingrained values. No other color except white conveyed so much emotional impact. As described by the *Oxford English Dictionary,* the meaning of *black* before the sixteenth century included, "Deeply stained with dirt; soiled, dirty, foul. . . . Having dark or deadly purposes, malignant; pertaining to or involving death, deadly; baneful, disastrous, sinister. . . . Foul, iniquitous, atrocious, horrible, wicked. . . . Indicating disgrace, censure, liability to punishment, etc." Black was an emotionally partisan color, the handmaid and symbol of baseness and evil, a sign of danger and repulsion.

Embedded in the concept of blackness was its direct opposite—whiteness. No other colors so clearly implied opposition, "beinge coloures utterlye contrary":

Everye white will have its blacke,
And every sweete its sowre.

White and black connoted purity and filthiness, virginity and sin, virtue and baseness, beauty and ugliness, beneficence and evil, God and the devil. Whiteness, moreover, carried a special significance for Elizabethan Englishmen: it was, particularly when complemented by red, the color of perfect human beauty, especially *female* beauty. This ideal was already centuries old in Elizabeth's time, and their fair Queen was its very embodiment: her cheeks were "roses in a bed of lillies." (Elizabeth was naturally pale but like many ladies then and since she freshened her "lillies" at the cosmetic table.) An adoring nation knew precisely what a beautiful Queen looked like.

Her cheeke, her chinne, her neck, her
*   nose,*
This was a lillye, that was a rose;
Her bosome, sleeke as Paris plaster,
Held upp twoo bowles of Alabaster.

By contrast, the Negro was ugly, by reason of his color and also his "horrid Curles" and "disfigured" lips and nose. A century later blackness still required apology: one of the earliest attempts to delineate the West African as a heroic character, the popular story *Oroonoko* (1688), presented Negroes as capable of blushing and turning pale. It was important, if incalculably so, that English discovery of black Africans came at a time when the accepted English standard of ideal beauty was a fair complexion of rose and white. Negroes seemed the very picture of perverse negation.

From the first, however, many English observers displayed a certain sophistication about the Negro's color. Despite an ethnocentric tendency to find blackness repulsive, many writers were fully aware that Africans themselves might have different tastes. As early as 1621 one writer told of the "Jetty coloured" Negroes, "Who in their native beauty most delight,/And in contempt doe paint the Divell white"; this assertion became almost a commonplace. Many accounts of Africa reported explicitly that the Negro's preference in colors was inverse to the European's. Even the Negro's features were conceded to be appealing to Negroes.

The Causes of Complexion

Black human beings were not only startling but extremely puzzling. The complexion of Africans posed problems about its nature, especially its permanence and utility, its cause and origin, and its significance. Although these were rather separate questions, there was a pronounced tendency among Englishmen and other Europeans to formulate the problem in terms of causation alone. If the cause of human blackness could be explained, then its nature and significance would follow.

Not that the problem was completely novel. The ancient Greeks had touched upon it. The story of Phaëton's driving the chariot sun wildly through the heavens apparently served as an explanation for the Ethiopian's blackness even before written records, and traces of this ancient fable were still drifting about during the seventeenth century. Ptolemy had made the important suggestion that the Negro's blackness and woolly hair were caused by exposure to the hot sun and had pointed out that people in northern climates

were white and those in temperate areas an intermediate color. Before the sixteenth century, though, the question of the Negro's color can hardly be said to have drawn the attention of Englishmen or indeed of Europeans generally.

The discovery of West Africa and the development of Negro slavery made the question far more urgent. The range of possible answers was rigidly restricted, however, by the virtually universal assumption, dictated by church and Scripture, that all mankind stemmed from a single source. Indeed it is impossible fully to understand the various efforts at explaining the Negro's complexion without bearing in mind the strength of the tradition which in 1614 made the chronicler, the Reverend Samuel Purchas, proclaim vehemently: "the tawney Moore, blacke Negro, duskie Libyan, ash-coloured Indian, olive-coloured American, should with the whiter European become one *sheep-fold,* under *one great Sheepheard* . . . without any more distinction of Colour, Nation, Language, Sexe, Condition, all may bee *One* in him that is One . . . . "

In general, the most satisfactory answer to the problem was some sort of reference to the action of the sun, whether the sun was assumed to have scorched the skin, drawn the bile, or blackened the blood. People living on the line had obviously been getting too much of it; after all, even Englishmen were darkened by a little exposure. How much more, then, with the Negroes who were "so scorched and vexed with the heat of the sunne, that in many places they curse it when it riseth." This association of the Negro's color with the sun became a commonplace in Elizabethan literature; as Shakespeare's Prince of Morocco apologized, "Mislike me not for my complexion,/The shadow'd livery of the burnish'd sun,/To whom I am a neighbour and near bred."

Unfortunately this theory ran headlong into a stubborn fact of nature which simply could not be overridden: if the equatorial inhabitants of Africa were blackened by the sun, why not the people living on the same line in America? Logic required them to be the same color. Yet by the middle of the sixteenth century it was becoming perfectly apparent that the Indians living in the hottest regions of the New World could by no stretch of the imagination be described as black. They were "olive" or "tawny," and moreover they had long hair rather than the curious "wool" of Negroes. Clearly the method of accounting for human complexion by latitude just did not work. The worst of it was that the formula did not seem altogether wrong, since it was apparent that in general men in hot climates tended to be darker than in cold ones.

Another difficulty with the climatic explanation of skin color arose as lengthening experience provided more knowledge about Negroes. If the heat of the sun caused the Negro's blackness, then his removal to cold northerly countries ought to result in his losing it; even if he did not himself surrender his peculiar color, surely his descendants must. By mid-seventeenth century it was becoming increasingly apparent that this expectation was ill founded: Negroes in Europe and northern America were simply not whitening up very noticeably.

From the beginning, in fact, some Englishmen were certain that the Negro's blackness was permanent and innate and that no amount of cold was going to alter it. There was good authority in Jeremiah 13:23; "Can the Ethiopian change his skin/or the leopard his spots?" Elizabethan dramatists used the stock expression "to wash in Ethiop white" as indicating sheer impossibility. In 1578 a voyager and speculative geographer, George Best, announced that the blackness of Negroes "proceedeth of some naturall infection of the first inhabitants of that country, and so all the whole progenie of them descended, are still polluted with the same blot of infection." An essayist in 1695 declared firmly, "A negroe will always be a negroe, carry him to Greenland, give him chalk, feed and manage him never so many ways."

There was an alternative to the naturalistic explanations of the Negro's blackness. Some writers felt that God's curse on Ham (Cham), or upon his son Canaan, and all their descendants was entirely sufficient to account for the color of Negroes. This could be an appealing explanation,

especially for men like George Best who wished to stress the "natural infection" of blackness and for those who hoped to incorporate the Negro's complexion securely within the accepted history of mankind. The original story in Genesis 9 and 10 was that after the Flood, Ham had looked upon his father's "nakedness" as Noah lay drunk in the tent, but the other two sons, Shem and Japheth, had covered their father without looking upon him; when Noah awoke he cursed Canaan, son of Ham, saying that he would be a "servant of servants" unto his brothers. Given this text, the question becomes why a tale which logically implied slavery but absolutely nothing about skin color should have become a popular explanation of the Negro's blackness. The matter is puzzling, but probably, over the very long run, the story was supported by the ancient association of heat with sensuality and by the fact that some sub-Saharan Africans had been enslaved by Europeans since ancient times. In addition, the extraordinary persistence of the tale in the face of centuries of constant refutation was probably sustained by a feeling that blackness could scarcely be anything *but* a curse and by the common need to confirm the facts of nature by specific reference to Scripture. In contrast to the climatic theory, God's curse provided a satisfying purposiveness which the sun's scorching heat could not match until the eighteenth century.

In the long run, of course, the Negro's color attained greatest significance not as a scientific problem but as a social fact. Englishmen found blackness in human beings a peculiar and important point of difference. The African's color set him radically *apart* from Englishmen. But then, distant Africa had been known to Christians for ages as a land of men radically different in religion.

Defective Religion

While distinctive appearance set Africans apart in a novel way, their religious condition distinguished them in a more familiar manner. Englishmen and Christians everywhere were sufficiently acquainted with the concept of heathenism that they confronted its living representatives without puzzlement. Certainly the rather sudden discovery that the world was teeming with heathen people made for heightened vividness and urgency in a long-standing problem; but it was the fact that this problem was already well formulated long before contact with Africa which proved important in shaping English reaction to the Negro's defective religious condition.

In one sense heathenism was less a "problem" for Christians than an exercise in self-definition: the heathen condition defined by negation the proper Christian life. In another sense, the presence of heathenism in the world constituted an imperative to intensification of religious commitment. From its origin Christianity was a universalist, proselytizing religion, and the sacred and secular histories of Christianity made manifest the necessity of bringing non-Christians into the fold. For Englishmen, then, the heathenism of Negroes was at once a counter-image of their own religion and a summons to eradicate an important distinction between the two peoples. Yet the interaction of these two facets of the concept of heathenism made for a peculiar difficulty: On the one hand, to act upon the felt necessity of converting Africans would have been to eradicate the point of distinction which Englishmen found most familiar and most readily comprehensible. Yet if they did not act upon this necessity, continued heathenism among Negroes would remain an unwelcome reminder to Englishmen that they were not meeting their obligations to their own faith—nor to the benighted Negroes. Englishmen resolved this implicit dilemma by doing nothing.

Considering the strength of the Christian tradition, it is almost startling that Englishmen failed to respond to the discovery of heathenism in Africa with at least the rudiments of a campaign for conversion. Although the impulse to spread Christianity seems to have been weaker in Englishmen than, say, in the Catholic Portuguese, it cannot be said that Englishmen were indifferent to the obligation imposed upon them by the overseas discoveries of the sixteenth century. While they were badly out of practice at the business of conversion

(again in contrast to the Portuguese) and while they had never before been faced with the practical difficulties involved in Christianizing entire continents, they nonetheless were able to contemplate with equanimity and even eagerness the prospect of converting the heathen. Indeed they went so far as to conclude that converting the natives in America was sufficiently important to demand English settlement there. As it turned out, the well-publicized English program for converting Indians produced very meager results, but the avowed intentions certainly were genuine. It was in marked contrast, therefore, that Englishmen did not avow similar intentions concerning Africans until the late eighteenth century. Fully as much as with skin color, though less consciously, Englishmen distinguished between the heathenisms of Indians and of Negroes.

It is not easy to account for the distinction which Englishmen made. On the basis of the travelers' reports there was no reason for Englishmen to suppose Indians inherently superior to Negroes as candidates for conversion. But America was not Africa. Englishmen contemplated settling in America, where voyagers had established the King's claim and where supposedly the climate was temperate; in contrast, Englishmen did not envision settlement in Africa, which had quickly gained notoriety as a graveyard for Europeans and where the Portuguese had been first on the scene. Certainly these very different circumstances meant that Englishmen confronted Negroes and Indians in radically different social contexts and that Englishmen would find it far easier to contemplate converting Indians than Negroes. Yet it remains difficult to see why Negroes were not included, at least as a secondary target. The fact that English contact with Africans so frequently occurred in a context of slave dealing does not entirely explain the omission of Negroes, since in that same context the Portuguese and Spanish did sometimes attempt to minister to the souls of Africans and since Englishmen in America enslaved Indians when good occasion arose. Given these circumstances, it is hard to escape the conclusion that the distinction which

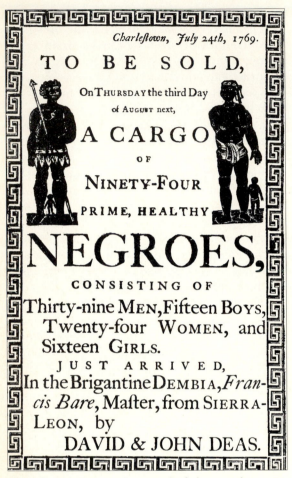

Charleſtown, July 24th, 1769.

TO BE SOLD,

On THURSDAY the third Day
of AUGUST next,

A CARGO

OF

NINETY-FOUR

PRIME, HEALTHY

NEGROES,

CONSISTING OF

Thirty-nine MEN, Fifteen BOYS,
Twenty-four WOMEN, and
Sixteen GIRLS.

JUST ARRIVED,

In the Brigantine DEMBIA, *Francis Bare*, Maſter, from SIERRA-
LEON, by

DAVID & JOHN DEAS.

A notice announcing the arrival of slaves to be
sold at an auction in Charleston, South Carolina.

tact with Africa, Protestant Christianity was an important element in English patriotism; especially during the struggle against Spain the Elizabethan's special Christianity was interwoven into his conception of his own nationality, and he was therefore inclined to regard the Negroes' lack of true religion as part of theirs. Being a Christian was not merely a matter of subscribing to certain doctrines; it was a quality inherent in oneself and in one's society. It was interconnected with all the other attributes of normal and proper men: as one of the earliest English travelers described Africans, they were "a people of beastly living, without a God, lawe, religion, or common wealth"—which was to say that Negroes were not Englishmen. Far from isolating African heathenism as a separate characteristic, English travelers sometimes linked it explicitly with blackness and savagery.

Savage Behavior

The condition of savagery—the failure to be civilized—set Negroes apart from Englishmen in an ill-defined but crucial fashion. Africans were *different* from Englishmen in so many ways: in their clothing, housing, farming, warfare, language, government, morals, and (not least important) in their table manners. To judge from the comments of voyagers, Englishmen had an unquenchable thirst for the details of savage life. Englishmen were, indeed, enormously curious about their rapidly expanding world, and it is scarcely surprising that they should have taken an interest in reports about cosmetic mutilation, polygamy, infanticide, ritual murder, and the like. In addition, reports about "savages" began arriving at a time when Englishmen very much needed to be able to translate their apprehensive interest in an uncontrollable world out of medieval religious terms. The discovery of savages overseas enabled them to make this translation easily, to move from miracles to verifiable monstrosities, from heaven to earth.

As with skin color, English reporting of African customs was partly an exercise in self-inspection by means of comparison. The neces-

Englishmen made as to conversion was at least in some small measure modeled after the difference they saw in skin color.

The most important aspect of English reaction to African heathenism was that Englishmen evidently did not regard it as separable from the Negro's other attributes. Heathenism was treated not so much as a specifically religious defect but as one manifestation of a general refusal to measure up to proper standards, as a failure to be English or even civilized. There was every reason for Englishmen to fuse the various attributes they found in Africans. During the first century of English con-

sity of continuously measuring African practices with an English yardstick of course tended to emphasize the differences between the two groups, but it also made for heightened sensitivity to instances of similarity. Thus the Englishman's ethnocentrism tended to distort his perception of African culture in two opposite directions. While it led him to emphasize differences and to condemn deviations from the English norm, it led him also to seek out similarities. Particularly, Englishmen were inclined to see the structures of African societies as analogous to their own, complete with kings, counselors, gentlemen, and the baser sort. Here especially they found Africans like themselves, partly because they knew no other way to describe any society and partly because there was actually good basis for such a view of the social organization of West African communities.

Despite the fascination and self-instruction Englishmen derived from discussing the savage behavior of Africans, they never felt that savagery was as important a quality in Africans as it was in the American Indians. As was the case with heathenism, contrasting social contexts played an important role in shaping the English response to savagery in the two peoples. Inevitably, the savagery of the Indians assumed a special significance in the minds of those actively engaged in a program of planting civilization in the American wilderness. The case with the African was different; the English errand into Africa was not a new or a perfect community but a business trip. No hope was entertained for civilizing the Negro's steaming continent, and Englishmen therefore lacked compelling reason to develop a program for remodeling the African natives.

From the beginning, also, the importance of the Negro's savagery was muted by the Negro's color. Englishmen could go a long way toward expressing their sense of being different from Africans merely by calling them "black." By contrast, the aboriginals in America did not have the appearance of being radically distinct from Europeans except in religion and savage behavior. English voyages placed much less emphasis upon the Indian's color than upon the Negro's, and they never permitted the Indian's physiognomy to distract their attention from what they regarded as his essential quality, his savagery.

It would be a mistake, however, to slight the importance of what was seen as the African's savagery, since it fascinated Englishmen from the very first. English observers in West Africa were sometimes so profoundly impressed by the Negro's behavior that they resorted to a powerful metaphor with which to express their own sense of difference from him. They knew perfectly well that Negroes were men, yet they frequently described the Africans as "brutish" or "bestial" or "beastly." The supposed hideous tortures, cannibalism, rapacious warfare, revolting diet (and so forth page after page) seemed somehow to place the Negro among the beasts. The eventual circumstances of the Englishman's contact with Africans served to strengthen this feeling. *Slave* traders in Africa necessarily handled Negroes the same way men in England handled beasts, herding and examining and buying, as with any other animals which were products of commerce.

The Apes of Africa

If Negroes were likened to beasts, there was in Africa a beast which was likened to men. It was a strange and eventually tragic happenstance of nature that Africa was the habitat of the animal which in appearance most resembles man. The animal called "orang-outang" by contemporaries (actually the chimpanzee) was native to those parts of western Africa where the early slave trade was heavily concentrated. Though Englishmen were acquainted (for the most part vicariously) with monkeys and baboons, they were unfamiliar with tail-less apes who walked about like men. Accordingly, it happened that Englishmen were introduced to the anthropoid apes and to Negroes at the same time and in the same place. The startlingly human appearance and movements of the "ape"—a generic term though often used as a synonym for the "orang-outang"—aroused some curious speculations.

In large measure these speculations derived from traditions which had been accumulating in Western culture since ancient times. Medieval books on animals contained rosters of strange creatures who in one way or another seemed disturbingly to resemble men. There were the *simia* and the *cynocephali* and the *satyri* and the others, all variously described and related to one another, all jumbled in a characteristic blend of ancient reports and medieval morality. The confusion was not easily nor rapidly dispelled, and many of the traditions established by this literature were very much alive during the seventeenth century.

The section on apes in Edward Topsell's *Historie of Foure-Footed Beastes* (1607) serves to illustrate how certain seemingly trivial traditions and associations persisted in such form that they were bound to affect the way in which Englishmen would perceive the inhabitants of Africa. Above all, according to Topsell, "apes" were venerous. The red apes were "so venerous that they will ravish their Women." Baboons were "as lustful and venerous as goats"; a baboon which had been "brought to the French king . . . above all loved the companie of women, and young maidens; his genitall member was greater than might match the quantity of his other parts." Pictures of two varieties of apes, a "Satyre" and an Ægopithecus," graphically emphasize the "virile member."

In addition to stressing the "lustful disposition" of the ape kind, Topsell's compilation contained suggestions concerning the character of simian facial features. "Men that have low and flat nostrils," readers were told in the section on apes, "are Libidinous as Apes that attempt women. . . ." There also seemed to be some connection between apes and devils. In a not altogether successful attempt to distinguish the "Satyre-apes" from the mythical creatures of that name, Topsell straightened everything out by explaining that it was "probable, that Devils take not any dænomination or shape from Satyres, but rather the Apes themselves from Devils whome they resemble, for there are many things common to the Satyre-apes and devilish Satyres." Association of apes and/or satyrs with devils was common in England: the

inner logic of this association derived from uneasiness concerning the ape's "indecent likenesse and imitation of man"; it revolved around evil and sexual sin; and, rather tenuously, it connected apes with blackness.

Given this tradition and the coincidence of contact, it was virtually inevitable that Englishmen should discern similarity between the manlike beasts and the beastlike men of Africa. A few commentators went so far as to suggest that Negroes had sprung from the generation of apekind or that apes were themselves the offspring of Negroes and some unknown African beast. These contentions were squarely in line with the ancient tradition that Africa was a land "bringing dailie foorth newe monsters" because, as Aristotle himself had suggested, many different species came into proximity at the scarce watering places. Jean Bodin, the famous sixteenth-century French political theorist, summarized this wisdom of the ages with the categorical remark that "promiscuous coition of men and animals took place, wherefore the regions of Africa produced for us so many monsters." Despite all these monsters out of Africa, the notion that Negroes stemmed from beasts in a literal sense was not widely believed. It simply floated about, available, later, for anyone who wanted it.

Far more common and persistent was the notion that there sometimes occurred "a beastly copulation or conjuncture" between apes and Negroes, and especially that apes were inclined wantonly to attack Negro women. The very explicit idea that apes assaulted female human beings was not new; Africans were merely being asked to demonstrate what Europeans had known for centuries. As late as the 1730s a well-traveled, well-educated, and intelligent naval surgeon, John Atkins, was not at all certain that the stories were false: "At some Places the *Negroes* have been suspected of Bestiality with them [apes and monkeys], and by the Boldness and Affection they are known under some Circumstances to express to our Females; the Ignorance and Stupidity on the other side, to guide or control Lust; but more from the near resemblance [of apes] . . . to the Human Species would tempt one to suspect the Fact."

By the time Atkins addressed himself to this evidently fascinating problem, some of the confusion arising from the resemblance of apes to men had been dispelled. In 1699 the web of legend and unverified fact was disentangled by Edward Tyson, whose comparative study of a young "orang-outang" was a masterwork of critical scientific investigation. Throughout his dissection of the chimpanzee, Tyson meticulously compared the animal with human beings in every anatomical detail, and he established beyond question both the close relationship and the non-identity of ape and man. Here was a step forward; the question of the ape's proper place in nature was now grounded upon much firmer knowledge of the facts. Despite their scientific importance, Tyson's conclusions did nothing to weaken the vigorous tradition which linked the Negro with the ape. The supposed affinity between apes and men had as frequently been expressed in sexual as in anatomical terms, and his findings did not effectively rule out the possibility of unnatural sexual unions. Tyson himself remarked that organs were especially given to venery.

The sexual association of apes with Negroes had an inner logic which kept it alive: sexual union seemed to prove a certain affinity without going so far as to indicate actual identity—which was what Englishmen really thought was the case. By forging a sexual link between Negroes and apes, furthermore, Englishmen were able to give vent to their feeling that Negroes were a lewd, lascivious, and wanton people.

Libidinous Men

Undertones of sexuality run throughout many English accounts of West Africa. To liken Africans—any human beings—to beasts was to stress the animal within the man. Indeed the sexual connotations embodied in the terms *bestial* and *beastly* were considerably stronger in Elizabethan English than they are today, and when the Elizabethan traveler pinned these epithets upon the behavior of Africans he was more frequently registering a sense of sexual shock than describing swinish manners.

Lecherousness among Africans was at times for Englishmen merely another attribute which one would expect to find among heathen, savage, beastlike men. One commentator's remarks made evident how closely interrelated all these attributes were in the minds of Englishmen: "They have no knowledge of God . . . they are very greedie eaters, and no lesse drinkers, and very lecherous, and theevish, and much addicted to uncleanenesse: one man hath as many wives as hee is able to keepe and maintaine." Sexuality was what one expected of savages.

Clearly, however, the association of Africans with potent sexuality represented more than an incidental appendage to the concept of savagery. Long before the first English contact with West Africa, the inhabitants of virtually the entire continent stood confirmed in European literature as lustful and venerous. About 1526 Leo Africanus (a Spanish Moroccan Moor converted to Christianity) supplied an influential description of the little-known lands of "Barbary," "Libya," "Numedia," and "Land of Negroes"; and Leo was as explicit as he was imaginative. In the English translation (1600) readers were informed concerning the "Negroes" that "there is no Nation under Heaven more prone to Venery." Leo disclosed that "the Negroes . . . leade a beastly kind of life, being utterly destitute of the use of reason, of dexteritie of wit, and of all arts. Yea, they so behave themselves, as if they had continually lived in a Forrest among wild beasts. They have great swarmes of Harlots among them; whereupon a man may easily conjecture their manner of living." Nor was Leo Africanus the only scholar to elaborate upon the ancient classical sources concerning Africa. In a highly eclectic work first published in 1566, Jean Bodin sifted the writings of ancient authorities and concluded that heat and lust went hand in hand and that "in Ethiopia . . . the race of men is very keen and lustful." Bodin announced in a thoroughly characteristic sentence, "Ptolemy reported that on account of southern sensuality Venus

chiefly is worshiped in Africa and that the constellation of Scorpion, which pertains to the pu-
denda, dominates that continent."

Depiction of the Negro as a lustful creature
was not radically new, therefore, when Englishmen first met Africans face to face. Seizing upon
and reconfirming these long-standing and apparently common notions, Elizabethan travelers and
literati dwelt explicitly with ease upon the espe-
cial sexuality of Africans. Othello's embraces
were "the gross clasps of a lascivious Moor." Francis Bacon's *New Atlantis* (1624) referred to "an
holy hermit" who "desired to see the Spirit of Fornication; and there appeared to him a little foul
ugly Æthiop." Negro men, reported a seventeenth-
century traveler, sported "large Propagators." In
1623 Richard Jobson, a sympathetic observer, reported that Mandingo men were "furnisht with
such members as are after a sort burthensome
unto them." Another commentator thought Negroes "very lustful and impudent, especially,
when they come to hide their nakedness, (for a
Negroes hiding his Members, their extraordinary
greatness) is a token of their Lust, and therefore
much troubled with the Pox." By the eighteenth
century a report on the sexual aggressiveness of
African women was virtually required of European commentators. By then, of course, with
many Englishmen actively participating in the
slave trade, there were pressures making for descriptions of "hot constitution'd Ladies" possessed
of a "temper hot and lascivious, making no scruple to prostitute themselves to the *Europeans* for
a very slender profit, so great is their inclination
to white men."

While the animus underlying these and similar
remarks becomes sufficiently obvious once Englishmen began active participation in the slave
trade, it is less easy to see why Englishmen should
have fastened upon Negroes a pronounced sexuality virtually upon first sight. The ancient notions
distilled by Bodin and Leo Africanus must have
helped pattern initial English perceptions. Yet
clearly there was something in English culture
working in this direction. It is certain that the pre-
sumption of powerful sexuality in black men was

far from being an incidental or casual association
in the minds of Englishmen. How very deeply this
association operated is obvious in *Othello*, a
drama which loses most of its power and several
of its central points if it is read with the assumption that because the black man was the hero English audiences were indifferent to his blackness.
Shakespeare was writing both *about* and *to* his
countrymen's feelings concerning physical distinctions between peoples; the play is shot
through with the language of blackness and sex.
Iago goes out of his way to talk about his own motives: "I hate the Moor,/And it is thought abroad
that twixt my sheets/He has done my office."
Later, he becomes more direct, "For that I do suspect the lusty Moor hath leaped into my seat." It
was upon this so obviously absurd suspicion that
Iago based his resolve to "turn her virtue into
pitch." Such was his success, of course, that Othello finally rushes off "to furnish me with some
means of death for the fair devil." With this con-
torted denomination of Desdemona, Othello unwittingly revealed how deeply Iago's promptings
about Desdemona's "own clime, complexion, and
degree" had eaten into his consciousness. Othello
was driven into accepting the premise that the
physical distinction *matters:* "For she had eyes,"
he has to reassure himself, "and chose me." Then,
as his suspicions give way to certainty, he equates
her character with his own complexion:

Her name, that was as fresh,
  As Dian's visage, is now begrim'd and black
  As mine own face.

This important aspect of Iago's triumph over
the noble Moor was a subtly inverted reflection of
the propositions which Iago, hidden in darkness,
worked upon the fair lady's father. No one knew
better than Iago how to play upon hidden strings
of emotion. Not content with the straight-forward
crudity that "your daughter and the Moor are now
making the beast with two backs," Iago told the
agitated Brabantio that "an old black ram/Is tup-
ping your white ewe" and alluded politely to
"your daughter cover'd with a Barbary horse." This

was not merely the language of (as we say) a "dirty" mind: it was the integrated imagery of blackness and whiteness, of Africa, of the sexuality of beasts and the bestiality of sex. And of course Iago was entirely successful in persuading Brabantio, who had initially welcomed Othello into his house, that the marriage was "against all rules of nature." Eventually Brabantio came to demand of Othello what could have brought a girl "so tender, fair, and happy"

To incur a general mock
Run from her guardage to the sooty bosom
Of such a thing as thou.

Altogether a curious way for a senator to address a successful general.

These and similar remarks in the play *Othello* suggest that Shakespeare and his audiences were not totally indifferent to the sexual union of "black" men and "white" women. Shakespeare did not condemn such union; rather, he played upon an inner theme of black and white sexuality, showing how the poisonous mind of a white man perverted and destroyed the noblest of loves by means of bringing to the surface (from the darkness, whence Iago spoke) the lurking shadows of animal sex to assault the whiteness of chastity. Never did "dirty" words more dramatically "blacken" a "fair" name. At the play's climax,

standing stunned by the realization that the wife he has murdered was innocent, Othello groans to Emilia, "Twas I that killed her"; and Emilia responds with a torrent of condemnation: "O! the more angel she,/And you the blacker devil." Of Desdemona: "She was too fond of her filthy bargain." To Othello: "O gull! O dolt!/As ignorant as dirt!" Shakespeare's genius lay precisely in juxtaposing these two pairs: inner blackness and inner whiteness. The drama meant little if his audiences had felt no response to this cross-inversion and to the deeply turbulent double meaning of black *over* white.

It required a very great dramatist to expose some of the more inward biocultural values which led—or drove—Englishmen to accept readily the notion that Negroes were peculiarly sexual men. Probably these values and the ancient reputation of Africa upon which they built were of primary importance in determining the response of Englishmen to Africans. Whatever the importance of biologic elements in these values—whatever the effects of long northern nights, of living in a cool climate, of possessing light-colored bodies which excreted contrasting lumps of darkness—these values by Shakespeare's time were interlocked with English history and culture and, more immediately, with the circumstances of contact with Africans and the social upheaval of Tudor England.

STUDY QUESTIONS

1. How might the sixteenth-century define "black"? How did their concept of blackness influence their attitude toward Africans?

2. What different theories were advanced to explain the reasons why Africans were black? What do these theories indicate about the attitude of the English toward the Africans?

3. How did Africans' behavior and customs reinforce English prejudice?

4. How did Englishmen interpret African sexual behavior? Did their interpretation strengthen or weaken their prejudice toward Africans?

5. How did the formation of prejudice lead to the development of slavery?

BIBLIOGRAPHY

Historians have written more about slavery than any other aspect of Southern life. Those interested in the origins of slavery should read Winthrop Jordan, *White Over Black: American Attitudes Toward the Negro, 1550–1812* (1968); David B. Davis, *The Problem of Slavery in Western Culture* (1966); and Oscar and Mary Handlin, *"The Origins of the Southern Labor System,"* William and Mary Quarterly, 3rd Ser., 7 (1950). To gauge the severity of slavery in the United States, historians have taken a comparative approach. Frank Tannenbaum, *Slave and Citizen: The Negro in the Americas* (1947), began the debate over theory and practice of slavery. Other important studies in this field are H. S. Klein, *Slavery in the Americas: A Comparative Study of Virginia and Cuba* (1967); Carl N. Degler, *Neither Black nor White: Slavery and Race Relations in Brazil and the United States* (1971); and Philip D. Curtin, *The Atlantic Slave Trade: A Census* (1969).

Reading 6

TREATMENT OF THE SLAVES

Alexander Falconbridge

The first African slaves were seized by the Portuguese to supply labor for their Brazilian sugar plantations. Late in the seventeenth century, after tobacco and sugar plantations were well established in North America, the Caribbean, and Brazil, the English created the Royal African Company. From that time until its demise in the nineteenth century, the slave trade was dominated by the British. It was, in the words of one European trader, "a dreadful business." Perhaps one-fourth of the slaves never survived the trip to the New World. Because perhaps 10 million slaves were taken from Africa to all the colonies in the Western Hemisphere between 1600 and 1830, it can safely be assumed that 2.5 million of them died along the way.

There were three stages to the enslavement of Africans. First, the slaves were captured by other Africans. Second, the African captors transported the newly acquired slaves from the interior of their countries to coastal exchange posts where European traders purchased them with rum, cotton cloth, guns, gunpowder, cowrie shells, brass rings, and pig iron. Finally, there was the third stage, the "Middle Passage" across the Atlantic to the New World. Hundreds of slaves were crowded into the dark, damp holds of slave ships for months at a time, with little exercise, subsistence diets, and no sanitary facilities. The mortality rate from flu, dysentery, pleurisy, pneumonia, and smallpox was devastating.

As soon as the wretched Africans, purchased at the fairs, fall into the hands of the black traders, they experience an earnest[1] of those dreadful sufferings which they are doomed in future to undergo. And there is not the least room to doubt, but that even before they can reach the fairs, great numbers perish from cruel usage, want of food, travelling through inhospitable deserts, and so forth. They are brought from the places where they are purchased . . . in canoes; at the bottom of which they lie, having their hands tied with a kind of willow twigs, and a strict watch is kept over them. Their usage in other respects, during the time of the passage, which generally lasts several days, is equally cruel. Their allowance of food is so scanty that it is barely sufficient to support nature. They are, besides, much exposed to the violent rains which frequently fall here, being covered only with mats that afford but a slight defence; and as there is usually water at the bottom of the canoes, from their leaking, they are scarcely ever dry.

Nor do these unhappy beings, after they become the property of the Europeans (from whom, as a more civilized people, more humanity might naturally be expected), find their situation in the least amended. Their treatment is not less rigorous. The men negroes, on being brought aboard the ship, are immediately fastened together, two and two, by hand-cuffs on their wrists, and by irons rivetted on their legs. They are then sent down between the decks and placed in an apartment partitioned off for that purpose. The women likewise are placed in a separate apartment between decks, but without being ironed. And an adjoining room, on the same deck, is besides appointed for the boys. Thus are they all placed in different apartments.

But at the same time, they are frequently stowed so close, as to admit of not other posture than lying on their sides. Neither will the height between decks, unless directly under the grating, permit them the indulgence of an erect posture; especially where there are platforms, which is generally the case. These platforms are a kind of shelf, about eight or nine feet in breadth, extending from the side of the ship towards the centre. They are placed nearly midway between the decks, at the distance of two or three feet from each deck. Upon these the negroes are stowed in the same manner as they are on the deck underneath.

In each of the apartments are placed three or four large buckets, of a conical form, being near two feet in diameter at the bottom, and only one foot at the top, and in depth about twenty-eight inches; to which, when necessary, the negroes have recourse. It often happens, that those who are placed at a distance from the buckets, in endeavouring to get to them, tumble over their companions, in consequence of their being shackled. These accidents, although unavoidable, are productive of continual quarrels, in which some of them are always bruised. In this distressed situation, unable to proceed, and prevented from getting to the tubs, they desist from the attempt; and, as the necessities of nature are not to be repelled, ease themselves as they lie. This becomes a fresh source of boils and disturbances, and tends to render the condition of the poor captive wretches still more uncomfortable. The nuisance arising from these circumstances, is not unfrequently increased by the tubs being much too small for the purpose intended, and their being usually emptied but once every day. The rule for doing this, however, varies in different ships, according to the attention paid to the health and convenience of the slaves by the captain.

About eight o'clock in the morning the negroes are generally brought upon deck. Their irons being examined, a long chain, which is locked to a ring-bolt, fixed in the deck, is run through the rings of the shackles of the men, and then locked to another, ring-bolt, fixed also in the deck. By this means fifty or sixty, and sometimes

---

[1]*Foretaste.*

Alexander Falconbridge, "Treatment of the Slaves," *An Account of the Slave Trade on the Coast of Africa.* London: 1788.

more, are fastened to one chain, in order to prevent them from rising, or endeavouring to escape. If the weather proves favourable, they are permitted to remain in that situation till four or five in the afternoon, when they are disengaged from the chain, and sent down.

The diet of the negroes, while on board, consists chiefly of horse-beans, boiled to the consistence of a pulp; of boiled yams and rice, and sometimes of a small quantity of beef or pork. The latter are frequently taken from the provisions laid in for the sailors. They sometimes make use of a sauce, composed of palm-oil, mixed with flour, water, and pepper, which the sailors call slabber-sauce. Yams are the favourite food of the Eboe, or Bight negroes; and rice or corn, of those from the Gold and Windward Coasts, each preferring the produce of their native soil.

In their own country, the negroes in general live on animal food and fish, with roots, yams, and Indian corn. The horse-beans and rice, with which they are fed aboard ship, are chiefly taken from Europe. The latter, indeed, is sometimes purchased on the coast, being far superior to any other.

The Gold Coast negroes scarcely ever refuse any food that is offered them, and they generally eat larger quantities of whatever is placed before them, than any other species of negroes, whom they likewise excel in strength of body and mind. Most of the slaves have such an aversion to the horse-beans that unless they are narrowly watched, when fed upon deck, they will throw them overboard, or in each other's faces when they quarrel.

They are commonly fed twice a day, about eight o'clock in the morning and four in the afternoon. In most ships they are only fed with their own food once a day. Their food is served up to them in tubs, about the size of a small water bucket. They are placed round these tubs in companies of ten to each tub, out of which they feed themselves with wooden spoons. These they soon lose, and when they are not allowed others, they feed themselves with their hands. In favourable weather they are fed upon deck, but in bad weather their food is given them below. Num-

berless quarrels take place among them during their meals; more especially when they are put upon short allowance, which frequently happens, if the passage from the coast of Guinea to the West-India islands, proves of unusual length. In that case, the weak are obliged to be content with a very scanty portion. Their allowance of water is about half a pint each at every meal. It is handed round in a bucket and given to each negroe in a pannekin; a small utensil with a strait handle, somewhat similar to a sauceboat. However, when the ships approach the islands with a favourable breeze, they are no longer restricted.

Upon the negroes refusing to take sustenance, I have seen coals of fire, glowing hot, put on a shovel, and placed so near their lips, as to scorch and burn them. And this has been accompanied with threats, of forcing them to swallow the coals, if they any longer persisted in refusing to eat. These means have generally had the desired effect. I have also been credibly informed, that a certain captain in the slave trade, poured melted lead on such of the negroes as obstinately refused their food.

Exercise being deemed necessary for the preservation of their health, they are sometimes obliged to dance, when the weather will permit their coming on deck. If they go about it reluctantly, or do not move with agility, they are flogged; a person standing by them all the time with a cat-ó-nine-tails in his hand for that purpose. Their musick, upon these occasions, consists of a drum, sometimes with only one head, and when that is worn out, they do not scruple to make use of the bottom of one of the tubs before described. The poor wretches are frequently compelled to sing also; but when they do so, their songs are generally, as may naturally be expected, melancholy lamentations of their exile from their native country.

The women are furnished with beads for the purpose of affording them some diversion. But this end is generally defeated by the squabbles which are occasioned, in consequence of their stealing them from each other.

On board some ships, the common sailors are allowed to have intercourse with such of the

European slave traders built compounds on the African coast. Each compound served a different European company.

black women whose consent they can procure. And some of them have been known to take the inconstancy of their paramours so much to heart, as to leap overboard and drown themselves. The officers are permitted to indulge their passions among them at pleasure and sometimes are guilty of such brutal excesses as disgrace human nature.

The hardships and inconveniences suffered by the negroes during the passage are scarcely to be enumerated or conceived. They are far more violently affected by the sea-sickness than the Europeans. It frequently terminates in death, especially among the women. But the exclusion of the fresh air is among the most intolerable. For the purpose of admitting this needful refreshment, most of the ships in the slave-trade are provided, between the decks, with five or six air-ports on each side of the ship, of about six inches in length, and four in breadth; in addition to which, some few ships, but not one in twenty, have what they denominate

wind-sails. But whenever the sea is rough, and the rain heavy, it becomes necessary to shut these, and every other conveyance by which the air is admitted. The fresh air being thus excluded, the negroes rooms very soon grow intolerably hot. The confined air, rendered noxious by the effluvia exhaled from their bodies and by being repeatedly breathed, soon produces fevers and fluxes, which generally carries off great numbers of them.

During the voyages I made, I was frequently a witness to the fatal effects of this exclusion of the fresh air. I will give one instance, as it serves to convey some idea, though a very faint one, of the sufferings of those unhappy beings whom we wantonly drag from their native country and doom to perpetual labour and captivity. Some wet and blowing weather having occasioned the portholes to be shut, and the grating to be covered, fluxes and fevers among the negroes ensued. While they were in this situation, my profession requiring it, I frequently went down among them, till at length their apartments became so extremely hot, as to be only sufferable for a very short time. But the excessive heat was not the only thing that rendered their situation intolerable. The deck, that is, the floor of their rooms, was so covered with the blood and mucus which had proceeded from them in consequence of the flux, that it resembled a slaughter-house. It is not in the power of the human imagination to picture to itself a situation more dreadful or disgusting. Numbers of the slaves having fainted, they were carried upon deck, where several of them died, and the rest were, with great difficulty, restored. It had nearly proved fatal to me also. The climate was too warm to admit the wearing of any clothing but a shirt, and that I had pulled off before I went down; notwithstanding which, by only continuing among them for about a quarter of an hour, I was so overcome with the heat, stench, and foul air that I had nearly fainted; and it was not without assistance that I soon after fell sick of the same disorder, from which I did not recover for several months.

A circumstance of this kind, sometimes repeatedly happens in the course of a voyage; and often to a greater degree than what was just been described; particularly when the slaves are much crowded, which was not the case at that time, the ship having more than a hundred short of the number she was to have taken in.

This devastation, great as it was, some few years ago was greatly exceeded on board a Liverpool ship. I shall particularize the circumstances of it, as a more glaring instance of an insatiable thirst for gain, or of less attention to the lives and happiness even of that despised and oppressed race of mortals, the fable inhabitants of Africa, perhaps was never exceeded; though indeed several similar instances have been known.

This ship, though a much smaller ship than that in which the event I have just mentioned happened, took on board at Bonny, at least six hundred negroes; but according to the information of the black traders, from whom I received the intelligence immediately after the ship failed, they

amounted to near seven hundred. By purchasing so great a number, the slaves were so crowded, that they were even obliged to lie one upon another. This occasioned such a mortality among them, that, without meeting with unusual bad weather, or having a longer voyage than common, nearly one half of them died before the ship arrived in the West Indies.

That the publick may be able to form some idea of the almost incredible small space into which so large a number of negroes were crammed, the following particulars of this ship are given. According to Liverpool custom she measured 235 tons. Her width across the beam, 25 feet. Length between the decks, 92 feet, which was divided into four rooms, thus:

Store room, in which there were not any negroes placed	<u>15 feet</u>
Negroes' rooms:	
men's room	about 45 feet
women's ditto	about 10 feet
boys' ditto	about 22 feet
Total room for negroes	<u>77 feet</u>

Exclusive of the platform before described, from 8 to 9 feet in breadth, and equal in length to that of the rooms.

It may be worthy of remark, that the ships in this trade, are usually fitted out to receive only one third women negroes, or perhaps a smaller number, which the dimensions of the room allotted for them, above given, plainly shew, but in a great disproportion.

One would naturally suppose, that an attention to their own interest, would prompt the owners of the Guinea ships not to suffer the captains to take on board a greater number of negroes than the ship would allow room sufficient for them to lie with ease to themselves, or, at least, without rubbing against each other. However that may be, a more striking instance than the above, of avarice, completely and deservedly disappointed, was surely never displayed; for there is little room to doubt, but that in consequence of the expected premium usually allowed to the captains, of 61 per cent sterling on the produce of the negroes, this vessel was so thronged as to occasion such a heavy loss.

The place allotted for the sick negroes is under the half deck, where they lie on the bare planks. By this means, those who are emaciated, frequently have their skin, and even their flesh, entirely rubbed off, by the motion of the ship, from the prominent parts of the shoulders, elbows, and hips, so as to render the bones in those parts quite bare. And some of them, by constantly lying in the blood and mucus, that had flowed from those afflicted with the flux, and which, as before observed, is generally so violent as to prevent their being kept clean, have their flesh much sooner rubbed off, than those who have only to contend with the mere friction of the ship. The excruciating pain which the poor sufferers feel from being obliged to continue in such a dreadful situation, frequently for several weeks, in case they happen to live so long, is not to be conceived or described. Few, indeed, are ever able to withstand the fatal effects of it. The utmost skill of the surgeon is here ineffectual. If plaisters be applied, they are soon displaced by the friction of the ship; and when bandages are used, the negroes very soon take them off, and appropriate them to other purposes.

The surgeon, upon going between decks, in the morning, to examine the situation of the slaves, frequently finds several dead; and among the men, sometimes a dead and living negro fastened by their irons together. When this is the case, they are brought upon the deck, and being laid in the grating, the living negroe is disengaged, and the dead one is thrown overboard.

It may not be improper here to remark, that the surgeons employed in the Guinea trade are generally driven to engage in so disagreeable an employ by the confined state of their finances. An exertion of the greatest skill and attention could afford the diseased negroes little relief, so long as the causes of their diseases, namely, the breathing of a putrid atmosphere, and wallowing in their own excrements, remain. When once the fever and dysentery get to any height at sea, a cure is scarcely ever effected.

Almost the only means by which the surgeon can render himself useful to the slaves is by seeing that their food is properly cooked and distributed among them. It is true, when they arrive near the markets for which they are destined, care is taken to polish them for sale, by an application of the lunar caustic to such as are afflicted with the yaws. This, however, affords but a temporary relief, as the disease most assuredly breaks out, whenever the patient is put upon a vegetable diet.

It has been asserted, in favour of the captains in this trade, that the sick slaves are usually fed from their tables. The great number generally ill at a time, proves the falsity of such an assertion. Were even a captain disposed to do this, how could he feed half the slaves in the ship from his own table? For it is well known, that more than half are often sick at a time. Two or three perhaps may be fed.

The loss of slaves, through mortality arising from the causes just mentioned, is frequently very considerable. In the voyage lately referred to (not the Liverpool ship before-mentioned) one hundred and five, out of three hundred and eighty, died in the passage. A proportion seemingly very great, but by no means uncommon. One half, sometimes two thirds, and even beyond that, have been known to perish. Before we left Bonny River, no less than fifteen died of fevers and dysenteries occasioned by their confinement. On the Windward Coast, where slaves are procured more slowly, very few die, in proportion to the numbers which die at Bonny, and at Old and New Calabar, where they are obtained much faster; the latter being of a more delicate make and habit.

The havock made among the seamen engaged in this destructive commerce will be noticed in another part; and will be found to make no inconsiderable addition to the unnecessary waste of life just represented.

As very few of the negroes can so far brook the loss of their liberty and the hardships they endure as to bear them with any degree of patience, they are ever upon the watch to take advantage of the least negligence in their oppressors. Insurrections are frequently the consequence; which are seldom suppressed without much bloodshed. Sometimes these are successful, and the whole ship's company is cut off. They are likewise always ready to seize every opportunity for committing some act of desperation to free themselves from their miserable state; and not withstanding the restraints under which they are laid, they often succeed.

While a ship, to which I belonged, lay in a Bonny River, one evening, a short time before our departure, a lot of negroes, consisting of about ten, was brought on board; when one of them, in a favourable moment, forced his way through the net-work on the larboard side of the vessel, jumped overboard, and was supposed to have been devoured by the sharks.

During the time we were there, fifteen negroes belonging to a vessel from Liverpool, found means to throw themselves into the river; very few were saved; and the residue fell a sacrifice to the sharks. A similar instance took place in a French ship while we lay there.

Circumstances of this kind are very frequent. On the coast of Angola, at the River Ambris, the following incident happened: During the time of our residing on shore, we erected a tent to shelter ourselves from the weather. After having been there several weeks and being unable to purchase the number of slaves we wanted, through the opposition of another English slave vessel, we determined to leave the place. The night before our departure, the tent was struck; which was no sooner perceived by some of the negroe women on board, than it was considered as a prelude to our sailing; and about eighteen of them, when they were sent between decks, threw themselves into the sea through one of the gun ports; the ship carrying guns between decks. They were all of them, however, excepting one, soon picked up; and that which was missing, was, not long after, taken about a mile from the shore.

I once knew a negroe woman, too sensible of her woes, who pined for a considerable time, and was taken ill of a fever and dysentery; when declaring it to be her determination to die, she refused all food and medical aid, and, in about a fort-

night after, expired. On being thrown overboard, her body was instantly torn to pieces by the sharks.

The following circumstance also came within my knowledge. A young female negroe, falling into a desponding way, it was judged necessary, in order to attempt her recovery, to send her on shore, to the hut of one of the black traders. Elevated with the prospect of regaining her liberty by this unexpected step, she soon recovered her usual cheerfulness; but hearing, by accident, that it was intended to take her on board the ship again, the poor young creature hung herself.

. . . I saw a middle aged stout woman, who had been brought down from a fair the preceding day, chained to the post of a black trader's door, in a state of furious insanity. On board a ship in Bonny River, I saw a young negroe women chained to the deck, who had lost her senses, soon after she was purchased and taken on board. In a former voyage, on board a ship to which I belonged, we were obliged to confine a female negroe, of about twenty-three years of age, on her becoming a lunatic. She was afterwards sold during one of her lucid intervals.

One morning, upon examining the place allotted for the sick negroes, I perceived that one of them, who was so emaciated as scarcely to be able to walk, was missing, and was convinced that he must have gone overboard in the night, probably to put a more expeditious period to his sufferings. And, to conclude on this subject, I could not help being sensibly affected, on a former voyage, at observing with what apparent eagerness a black woman seized some dirt from off an African yam, and put it into her mouth; seeming to rejoice at the opportunity of possessing some of her native earth.

From these instances I think it may be clearly deduced, that the unhappy Africans are not bereft of the finer feelings but have a strong attachment to their native country, together with a just sense of the value of liberty. And the situation of the miserable beings above described, more forcibly urge the necessity of abolishing a trade which is the source of such evils, than the most eloquent harangue or persuasive arguments could do.

STUDY QUESTIONS

1. What was Falconbridge's general opinion about the morality of the slave trade? Did he feel guilty about the role he played in the traffic?

2. What was the greatest threat to the health of the slaves on the slave ship?

3. Why did the slave traders bring the slaves up on deck periodically and have them dance?

4. Describe the general living arrangements among the Africans being transported across the Atlantic Ocean.

5. Why was disease so rampant on the slave ships?

BIBLIOGRAPHY

For general histories of the Atlantic slave trade, see Phillip D. Curtin, *The Atlantic Slave Trade: A Census* (1969); Basil Davidson, *Black Mother: The Years of the African Slave Trade* (1961); Daniel Mannix and Malcolm Cowley, *Black Cargoes: A History of the Atlantic Slave Trade, 1518–1865* (1962); James Pope-Hennessey, *Sin of the Fathers: A Study of the Atlantic Slave Trade, 1441–1807* (1968); and James A. Rawley, *The Transatlantic Slave Trade* (1981). For the impact of the slave trade on regional politics and society in West Africa, see David Birmingham, *Trade and Conflict in Angola, 1483–1790* (1966); K. Y. Daaku, *Trade and Politics on the Gold Coast, 1600–1720: A Study of the African Reaction to European Trade* (1970); and Karl Polanyi, *Dahomey and the Slave Trade* (1966). The best study of the Royal African Company is Kenneth Davies, *The Royal African Company* (1957). For the death rate among slaves being transported to the New World, see Raymond L. Cohn and Richard A. Jensen, "Mortality Rates and the Slave Trade," *Essays in Economic and Business History* (1981), and Phillip D. Curtin, "Epidemiology and the Slave Trade," *Political Science Quarterly* (June 1968).

HORSES AND GENTLEMEN

T. H. Breen

Traditional lines between history and the social sciences, and history and the humanities have largely melted in the past generation. Historians have employed sociological, psychological, and anthropological theories and techniques to better uncover the richness of the past. In the following essay, T. H. Breen demonstrates in an exciting and provocative fashion the uses of anthropological techniques for the historian. Breen particularly was influenced by the ground-breaking work of anthropologist Clifford Geertz, who used cockfighting as a text for interpreting Balinese society. In "Notes on the Balinese Cockfight," Geertz writes, "In the cockfight . . . the Balinese forms and discovers his temperament and his society's temper at the same time."

Breen is interested in the temperament of the aristocratic Virginian and the temper of his society. In horse racing, a passion for the wealthy of Virginia, he hoped to expose the core values of colonial society. As he illustrates, horse racing involved more than simply wagering money, creating excitement, and aping English aristocratic manners: "By promoting horse racing the great planters legitimized the cultural values which racing symbolized—materialism, individualism, and competitiveness. . . . The wild sprint down the dirt track served the interests of Virginia's gentlemen better than they imagined."

In the fall of 1686 Durand of Dauphiné, a French Huguenot, visited the capital of colonial Virginia. Durand regularly recorded in a journal what he saw and heard, providing one of the few firsthand accounts of late seventeenth-century Virginia society that has survived to the present day. When he arrived in Jamestown the House of Burgesses was in session. "I saw there fine-looking men," he noted, "sitting in judgment booted and with belted sword." But to Durand's surprise, several of these Virginia gentlemen "started gambling" soon after dinner, and it was not until midnight that one of the players noticed the Frenchman patiently waiting for the contest to end. The Virginian—obviously a veteran of long nights at the gaming table—advised Durand to go to bed. "'For,' said he, 'it is quite possible that we shall be here all night,' and in truth I found them still playing the next morning."

The event Durand witnessed was not unusual. In late seventeenth- and early eighteenth-century Virginia, gentlemen spent a good deal of time gambling. During this period, in fact, competitive gaming involving high stakes became a distinguishing characteristic of gentry culture. Whenever the great planters congregated, someone inevitably produced a deck of cards, a pair of dice, or a backgammon board; and quarter-horse racing was a regular event throughout the colony. Indeed, these men hazarded money and tobacco on almost any proposition in which there was an element of chance. Robert Beverley, a member of one of Virginia's most prominent families, made a wager "with the gentlemen of the country" that if he could produce seven hundred gallons of wine on his own plantation, they would pay him the handsome sum of one thousand guineas. Another leading planter offered six-to-one odds that

T.H. Breen, "Horses and Gentlemen: The Cultural Significance of Gambling among the Gentry of Virginia" *William and Mary Quarterly,* 3d Ser., 34, (April 1977) pp.239–257. Reprinted by permission of the author and the Omohundro Institute of Early American History and Culture.

Alexander Spotswood could not procure a commission as the colony's governor. And in 1671 one disgruntled gentleman asked a court of law to award him his winnings from a bet concerning "a Servant maid." The case of this suspect-sounding wager—unfortunately not described in greater detail—dragged on until the colony's highest court ordered the loser to pay the victor a thousand pounds of tobacco.

The great planters' passion for gambling, especially on quarter-horse racing, coincided with a period of far-reaching social change in Virginia. Before the mid-1680s constant political unrest, servant risings both real and threatened, plant-cutting riots, and even a full-scale civil war had plagued the colony. But by the end of the century Virginia had achieved internal peace. Several elements contributed to the growth of social tranquility. First, by 1700 the ruling gentry were united as they had never been before. The great planters of the seventeenth century had been for the most part aggressive English immigrants. They fought among themselves for political and social dominance, and during Bacon's Rebellion in 1676 various factions within the gentry attempted to settle their differences on the battlefield. By the end of the century, however, a sizable percentage of the Virginia gentry, perhaps a majority, had been born in the colony. The members of this native-born elite—one historian calls them a "creole elite"—cooperated more frequently in political affairs than had their immigrant fathers. They found it necessary to unite in resistance against a series of interfering royal governors such as Thomas Lord Culpeper, Francis Nicholson, and Alexander Spotswood. After Bacon's Rebellion the leading planters—the kind of men whom Durand watched gamble the night away—successfully consolidated their control over Virginia's civil, military, and ecclesiastical institutions. They monopolized the most important offices; they patented the best lands.

A second and even more far-reaching element in the creation of this remarkable solidarity among the gentry was the shifting racial composition of the plantation labor force. Before the

1680s the planters had relied on large numbers of white indentured servants to cultivate Virginia's sole export crop, tobacco. These impoverished, often desperate servants disputed their masters' authority and on several occasions resisted colonial rulers with force of arms. In part because of their dissatisfaction with the indenture system, and in part because changes in the international slave trade made it easier and cheaper for Virginians to purchase black laborers, the major planters increasingly turned to Africans. The blacks' cultural disorientation made them less difficult to control than the white servants. Large-scale collective violence such as Bacon's Rebellion and the 1682 plant-cutting riots consequently declined markedly. By the beginning of the eighteenth century Virginia had been transformed into a relatively peaceful, biracial society in which a few planters exercised almost unchallenged hegemony over both their slaves and their poorer white neighbors.

The growth of gambling among the great planters during a period of significant social change raises important questions not only about gentry values but also about the social structure of late seventeenth-century Virginia. Why did gambling, involving high stakes, become so popular among the gentlemen at precisely this time? Did it reflect gentry values or have symbolic connotations for the people living in this society? Did this activity serve a social function, contributing in some manner to the maintenance of group cohesion? Why did quarter-horse racing, in particular, become a gentry sport? And finally, did public displays such as this somehow reinforce the great planters' social and political dominance?

In part, of course, gentlemen laid wagers on women and horses simply because they enjoyed the excitement of competition. Gambling was a recreation, like a good meal among friends or a leisurely hunt in the woods—a pleasant pastime when hard-working planters got together. Another equally acceptable explanation for the gentry's fondness for gambling might be the transplanting of English social mores. Certainly, the upper classes in the mother country loved betting for high stakes, and it is possible that the all-night card games and the frequent horse races were staged attempts by a provincial gentry to transform itself into a genuine landed aristocracy. While both views possess merit, neither is entirely satisfactory. The great planters of Virginia presumably could have favored less risky forms of competition. Moreover, even though several planters deliberately emulated English social styles, the widespread popularity of gambling among the gentry indicates that this type of behavior may have had deeper, more complex cultural roots than either of these explanations would suggest.

In many societies competitive gaming is a device by which the participants transform abstract cultural values into observable social behavior. In his now-classic analysis of the Balinese cockfight Clifford Geertz describes contests for extremely high stakes as intense social dramas. These battles not only involve the honor of important villagers and their kin groups but also reflect in symbolic form the entire Balinese social structure. Far from being a simple pastime, betting on cocks turns out to be an expression of the way Balinese perceive social reality. The rules of the fight, the patterns of wagering, the reactions of winners and losers—all these elements help us to understand more profoundly the totality of Balinese culture.

The Virginia case is analogous to the Balinese. When the great planter staked his money and tobacco on a favorite horse or spurred a sprinter to victory, he displayed some of the central elements of gentry culture—its competitiveness, individualism, and materialism. In fact, competitive gaming was for many gentlemen a means of translating a particular set of values into action, a mechanism for expressing a loose but deeply felt bundle of ideas and assumptions about the nature of society. The quarter-horse races of Virginia were intense contests involving personal honor, elaborate rules, heavy betting, and wide community interest; and just as the cockfight opens up hidden dimensions of Balinese culture, gentry gambling offers an opportunity to improve our understanding of the complex interplay between cultural values and social behavior in Virginia.

A notice of a horse race in Anne Arundel County, Maryland, as seen in the *Maryland Gazette,* May 17, 1745.

Gambling reflected core elements of late seventeenth- and early eighteenth-century gentry values. From diaries, letters, and travel accounts we discover that despite their occasional cooperation in political affairs, Virginia gentlemen placed extreme emphasis upon personal independence. This concern may in part have been the product of the colony's peculiar settlement patterns. The great planters required immense tracts of fresh land for their tobacco. Often thousands of acres in size, their plantations were scattered over a broad area from the Potomac River to the James. The dispersed planters lived in their "Great Houses" with their families and slaves, and though they saw friends from time to time, they led for the most part isolated, routine lives. An English visitor in 1686 noted with obvious disapproval that "their Plantations run over vast Tracts of Ground. . . whereby the Country is thinly inhabited; the Living solitary and unsociable." Some planters were uncomfortably aware of the problems created by physical isolation. William Fitzhugh, for example, admitted to a correspondent in the mother country, "Society that is good and ingenious is very scarce, and seldom to be come at except in books."

Yet despite such apparent cultural privation, Fitzhugh and his contemporaries refused to alter their life styles in any way that might compromise their freedom of action. They assumed it their right to give commands, and in the ordering of daily plantation affairs they rarely tolerated outside interference. Some of these planters even saw themselves as law-givers out of the Old Testament. In 1726 William Byrd II explained that "like one of the Patriarchs, I have my Flocks and my Herds, my Bondmen and Bondwomen, and every Soart of Trade amongst my own Servants, so that I live in a kind of Independence every one but Providence." Perhaps Byrd exaggerated for literary effect, but forty years earlier Durand had observed, "There are no lords [in Virginia], but each is sovereign on his own plantation." Whatever the origins of this independent spirit, it bred excessive individualism in a wide range of social activities. While these powerful gentlemen sometimes worked together to achieve specific political and economic ends, they bristled at the least hint of constraint. Andrew Burnaby later noted that "the public or political character of the Virginians corresponds with their private one: they are haughty and jealous of their liberties, impatient of restraint, and can scarcely bear the thought of being controuled by any superior power."

The gentry expressed this uncompromising individualism in aggressive competitiveness, engaging in a constant struggle against real and imagined rivals to obtain more lands, additional patronage, and high tobacco prices. Indeed, competition was a major factor shaping the character of face-to-face relationships among the colony's gentlemen, and when the stakes were high the planters were not particular about the methods they employed to gain victory. In large part, the goal of the competition within the gentry group was to improve social position by increasing wealth.

Some gentlemen believed that personal honor was at stake as well. Robert "King" Carter, by all accounts the most successful planter of his generation, expressed his anxiety about losing out to another Virginian in a competitive market situation. "In discourse with Colonel Byrd, Mr. Armistead, and a great many others," he explained, "I understand you [an English merchant] had sold their tobaccos in round parcels and at good rates.

I cannot allow myself to come behind any of these gentlemen in the planter's trade." Carter's pain arose not so much from the lower price he had received as from the public knowledge that he had been bested by respected peers. He believed he had lost face. This kind of intense competition was sparked, especially among the less affluent members of the gentry, by a dread of slipping into the ranks of what one eighteenth-century Virginia historian called the "common Planters." Gov. Francis Nicholson, an acerbic English placeman, declared that the ordinary sort of planters knew full well "from whence these mighty dons derive their originals." The governor touched a nerve; the efforts of "these mighty dons" to outdo one another were almost certainly motivated by a desire to disguise their "originals," to demonstrate anew through competitive encounters that they could legitimately claim gentility.

Another fact of Virginia gentry culture was materialism. This certainly does not mean that the great planters lacked spiritual concerns. Religion played a vital role in the lives of men like Robert Carter and William Byrd II. Nevertheless, piety was largely a private matter. In public these men determined social standing not by a man's religiosity or philosophic knowledge but by his visible estate—his lands, slaves, buildings, even by the quality of his garments. When John Bartram, one of America's first botanists, set off in 1737 to visit two of Virginia's most influential planters, a London friend advised him to purchase a new set of clothes, "for though I should not esteem thee less, to come to me in what dress thou will—yet these Virginians are a very gentle, well-dressed people—and look, perhaps, more at a man's outside than his inside." This perception of gentry values was accurate. Fitzhugh's desire to maintain outward appearances drove him to collect a stock of monogrammed silver plates and to import at great expense a well-crafted, though not very practical, English carriage. One even finds hints that the difficulty of preserving the image of material success weighed heavily upon some planters. When he described local Indian customs

in 1705, Robert Beverley noted that native Americans lived an easy, happy existence "without toiling and perplexing their mind for Riches, which other people often trouble themselves to provide for uncertain and ungrateful Heirs."

The gentry were acutely sensitive to the element of chance in human affairs, and this sensitivity influenced their attitudes toward other men and society. Virginians knew from bitter experience that despite the best-laid plans, nothing in their lives was certain. Slaves suddenly sickened and died. English patrons forgot to help their American friends. Tobacco prices fell without warning. Cargo ships sank. Storms and droughts ruined the crops. The list was endless. Fitzhugh warned an English correspondent to think twice before allowing a son to become a Virginia planter, for even "if the best husbandry and the greatest forecast and skill were used, yet ill luck at Sea, a fall of a Market, or twenty other accidents may ruin and overthrow the best Industry." Other planters, even those who had risen to the top of colonial society, longed for greater security. "I could wish," declared William Byrd I in 1685, "wee had Some more certain Commodity [than tobacco] to rely on but see no hopes of itt." However desirable such certainty may have appeared, the planters always put their labor and money into tobacco, hoping for a run of luck. One simply learned to live with chance. In 1710 William Byrd II confided in his secret diary, "I dreamed last night . . . that I won a tunfull of money and might win more if I had ventured."

Gaming relationships reflected these strands of gentry culture. In fact, gambling in Virginia was a ritual activity. It was a form of repetitive, patterned behavior that not only corresponded closely to the gentry's values and assumptions but also symbolized the realities of everyday planter life. This congruence between actions and belief, between form and experience, helps to account for the popularity of betting contests. The wager, whether over cards or horses, brought together in a single, focused act the great planter's competitiveness, independence, and materialism, as well as the element of chance. It represented a social agreement in which each individual was free to determine how he would play, and the gentleman who accepted a challenge risked losing his material possessions as well as his personal honor.

The favorite household or tavern contests during this period included cards, backgammon, billiards, nine-pins, and dice. The great planters preferred card games that demanded skill as well as luck. Put, piquet, and whist provided the necessary challenge, and Virginia gentlemen—Durand's hosts, for example—regularly played these games for small sums of money and tobacco. These activities brought men together, stimulated conversation, and furnished a harmless outlet for aggressive drives. They did not, however, become for the gentry a form of intense, symbolic play such as the cockfight in Bali. William Byrd II once cheated his wife in a game of piquet, something he would never have dared to do among his peers at Williamsburg. By and large, he showed little emotional involvement in these types of household gambling. The exception here proves the rule. After an unusually large loss at the gaming tables of Williamsburg, Byrd drew a pointed finger in the margin of his secret diary and swore a "solemn resolution never at once to lose more than 50 shillings and to spend less time in gaming, and I beg the God Almighty to give me grace to keep so good a resolution . . ." Byrd's reformation was short-lived, for within a few days he dispassionately noted losing another four pounds at piquet.

Horse racing generated far greater interest among the gentry than did the household games. Indeed for the great planters and the many others who came to watch, these contests were preeminently a social drama. To appreciate the importance of racing in seventeenth-century Virginia, we must understand the cultural significance of horses. By the turn of the century possession of one of these animals had become a social necessity. Without a horse, a planter felt despised, an object of ridicule. Owning even a slow-footed saddle horse made the common planter more of

a man in his own eyes as well as in those of his neighbors; he was reluctant to venture forth on foot for fear of making an adverse impression. As the Rev. Hugh Jones explained in 1724, "Almost every ordinary Person keeps a Horse; and I have known some spend the Morning in ranging several Miles in the Woods to find and catch their Horses only to ride two or three Miles to Church, to the Court-House, or to a Horse-Race, where they generally appoint to meet upon Business." Such behavior seems a waste of time and energy only to one who does not comprehend the symbolic importance which the Virginians attached to their horses. A horse was an extension of its owner; indeed, a man was only as good as his horse. Because of the horse's cultural significance, the gentry attempted to set its horsemanship apart from that of the common planters. Gentlemen took better care of their animals, and, according to John Clayton, who visited Virginia in 1688, they developed a distinctive riding style. "They ride pretty sharply," Clayton reported; "a Planter's Pace is a Proverb, which is a good sharp hand-Gallop." A fast-rising cloud of dust far down a Virginia road probably alerted the common planter that he was about to encounter a social superior.

The contest that generated the greatest interest among the gentry was the quarter-horse race, an all-out sprint by two horses over a quarter-mile dirt track. The great planters dominated these events. In the records of the country courts—our most important source of information about specific races—we find the names of some of the colony's most prominent planter families—Randolph, Eppes, Jefferson, Swan, Kenner, Hardiman, Parker, Cocke, Batte, Harwick (Hardidge), Youle (Yowell), and Washington. Members of the House of Burgesses, including its powerful speaker, William Randolph, were frequently mentioned in the contests that came before the courts. On at least one occasion the Rev. James Blair, Virginia's most eminent clergyman and a founder of the College of William and Mary, gave testimony in a suit arising from a race run between Capt. William Soane and Robert Napier. The tenacity with which the gentry pursued these cases, almost continuations of the race itself, suggests that victory was no less sweet when it was gained in court.

Many elements contributed to the exclusion of lower social groups from these contests. Because of the sheer size of wagers, poor freemen and common planters could not have participated regularly. Certainly, the members of the Accomack County Court were embarrassed to discover that one Thomas Davis, "a very poore Man," had lost 500 pounds of tobacco or a cow and calf in a horse race with an adolescent named Mr. John Andrews. Recognizing that Davis bore "a great charge of wife and Children," the justices withheld final judgment until the governor had an opportunity to rule on the legality of the wager. The Accomack court noted somewhat gratuitously that if the governor declared the action unlawful, it would fine Davis five days' work on a public bridge. In such cases country justices ordinarily made no comment upon a plaintiff's or defendant's financial condition, assuming, no doubt, that most people involved in racing were capable of meeting their gaming obligations.

The gentry actively enforced its exclusive control over quarter-horse racing. When James Bullocke, a York County tailor, challenged Mr. Mathew Slader to a race in 1674, the county court informed Bullocke that it was "contrary to Law for a Labourer to make a race being a Sport for Gentlemen" and fined the presumptuous tailor two hundred pounds of tobacco and cask. Additional evidence of exclusiveness is found in early eighteenth-century Hanover County. In one of the earliest issues of the colony's first newspaper, the *Virginia Gazette,* an advertisement appeared announcing that "some merry-dispos'd gentlemen" in Hanover planned to celebrate St. Andrew's Day with a race for quarter-milers. The Hanover gentlemen explained in a later, fuller description that "all Persons resorting there are desir'd to behave themselves with Decency and Sobriety, the Subscribers being resolv'd to discountenance all Im-

morality with the utmost Rigour." The purpose of these contests was to furnish the county's "considerable Number of Gentlemen, Merchants, and credible Planters" an opportunity for "cultivating Friendship." Less affluent persons apparently were welcome to watch the proceedings provided they acted like gentlemen.

In most match races the planter rode his own horse, and the exclusiveness of these contests meant that racing created intensely competitive confrontations. There were two ways to set up a challenge. The first was a regularly scheduled affair usually held on Saturday afternoon. By 1700 there were at least a dozen tracks, important enough to be known by name, scattered through the counties of the Northern Neck and the James River valley. The records are filled with references to contests held at such places as Smith's Field, Coan Race Course, Devil's Field, Yeocomico, and Varina. No doubt, many races also occurred on nameless country roads or convenient pastures. On the appointed day the planter simply appeared at the race track and waited for a likely challenge. We know from a dispute heard before the Westmoreland County Court in 1693 that John Gardner boldly "Challeng'd all the horses then upon the ground to run with any of them for a thousand pounds of Tobo and twenty shillings in money." A second type of contest was a more spontaneous challenge. When gentlemen congregated over a jug of hard cider or peach brandy, the talk frequently turned to horses. The owners presumably bragged about the superior speed of their animals, and if one planter called another's bluff, the men cried out "done, and done," marched to the nearest field, and there discovered whose horse was in fact the swifter.

Regardless of the outcome, quarter-horse races in Virginia were exciting spectacles. The crowds of onlookers seem often to have been fairly large, as common planters, even servants, flocked to the tracks to watch the gentry challenge one another for what must have seemed immense amounts of money and tobacco. One witness before a Westmoreland County Court reported in 1674 that Mr.

Stone and Mr. Youle had run a challenge for £10 sterling "in sight of many people." Attendance at race days was sizable enough to support a brisk trade in cider and brandy. In 1714 the Richmond County Court fined several men for peddling liquors "by Retaile in the Race Ground." Judging from the popularity of horses throughout planter society, it seems probable that the people who attended these events dreamed of one day riding a local champion such as Prince or Smoaker.

The magnitude of gentry betting indicates that racing must have deeply involved the planter's self-esteem. Wagering took place on two levels. The contestants themselves made a wager on the outcome, a main bet usually described in a written statement. In addition, side wagers were sometimes negotiated between spectators or between a contestant and spectator. Of the two, the main bet was far the more significant. From accounts of disputed races reaching the county courts we know that gentlemen frequently risked very large sums. The most extravagant contest of the period was a race run between John Baker and John Haynie in Northumberland County in 1693, in which the two men wagered 4,000 pounds of tobacco and 40 shillings sterling on the speed of their sprinters, Prince and Smoaker. Some races involved only twenty or thirty shillings, but a substantial number were run for several pounds sterling and hundreds of pounds of tobacco. While few, if any, of the seventeenth-century gentlemen were what we would call gambling addicts, their betting habits seem irrational even by the more prudential standards of their own day: in conducting normal business transactions, for example, they would never have placed so much money in such jeopardy.

To appreciate the large size of these bets we must interpret them within the context of Virginia's economy. Between 1660 and 1720 a planter could anticipate receiving about ten shillings per hundredweight of tobacco. Since the average grower seldom harvested more than 1,500 pounds of tobacco a year per man, he probably never enjoyed an annual income from tobacco in excess of eight pounds sterling. For most Virginians the conversion of tobacco into sterling occurred only in the neat columns of account books. They themselves seldom had coins in their pockets. Specie was extremely scarce, and planters ordinarily paid their taxes and conducted business transactions with tobacco notes—written promises to deliver to the bearer a designated amount of tobacco. The great preponderance of seventeenth-century planters were quite poor, and even the great planters estimated their income in hundreds, not thousands, of pounds sterling. Fitzhugh, one of the wealthier men of his generation, described his financial situation in detail. "Thus I have given you some particulars," he wrote in 1686, "which I thus deduce, the yearly Crops of corn and Tobo, together with the surplusage of meat more than will serve the family's use, will amount annually to 60,000lb. Tobo wch. at 10 shilling per Ct. is 300 £ annum." These facts reveal that the Baker-Haynie bet—to take a notable example—amounted to approximately £22 sterling, more than 7 percent of Fitzhugh's annual cash return. It is therefore not surprising that the common planters seldom took part in quarter-horse racing: this wager alone amounted to approximately three times the income they could expect to receive in a good year. Even a modest wager of a pound or two sterling represented a substantial risk.

Gentlemen sealed these gaming relationships with a formal agreement, either a written statement laying out the terms of the contest or a declaration before a disinterested third party of the nature of the wager. In either case the participants carefully stipulated what rules would be in effect. Sometimes the written agreements were quite elaborate. In 1698, for example, Richard Ward and John Steward, Jr., "Covenanted and agreed" to race at a quarter-mile track in Henrico County known as Ware. Ward's mount was to enjoy a ten-yard handicap, and if it crossed the finish line within five lengths of Steward's horse, Ward would win five pounds sterling; if Steward's obviously superior animal won by a greater distance, Ward promised to pay six pounds sterling.

In another contest William Eppes and Stephen Cocke asked William Randolph to witness an agreement for a ten-shilling race: "Each horse was to keep his path, they not being to crosse unless Stephen Cocke could gett the other Riders Path at the start at two or three Jumps."

Virginia's county courts treated race covenants as binding legal contracts. If a gentleman failed to fulfill the agreement, the other party had legitimate grounds to sue; and the county justices' first consideration during a trial was whether the planters had properly recorded their agreement. The Henrico court summarily dismissed one gambling suit because "noe Money was stacked down nor Contract in writing made [,] one of wch in such cases is by the law required." Because any race might generate legal proceedings, it was necessary to have a number of people present at the track not only to assist in the running of the contest but also to act as witnessess if anything went wrong. The two riders normally appointed an official starter, several judges, and someone to hold the stakes.

Almost all of the agreements included a promise to ride a fair race. Thus two men in 1698 insisted upon "fair Rideing"; another pair pledged "they would run fair horseman's play." By such agreements the planters waived their customary right to jostle, whip, or knee an opponent, or to attempt to unseat him. During the last decades of the seventeenth century the gentry apparently attempted to substitute riding skill and strategy for physical violence. The demand for "fair Rideing" also suggests that the earliest races in Virginia were wild, no-holds-barred affairs that afforded contestants ample opportunity to vent their aggressions.

The intense desire to win sometimes undermined a gentleman's written promise to run a fair race. When the stakes were large, emotions ran high. One man complained in a York County court that an opponent had interfered with his horse in the middle of the race, "by meanes whereof the s[ai]d Plaintiff lost the said Race." Joseph Humphrey told a Northumberland County

court that he would surely have come in first in a challenge for 1,500 pounds of tobacco had not Capt. Rodham Kenner (a future member of the House of Burgesses) "held the defendt horses bridle in running his race." Other riders testified that they had been "Josselled" while the race was in progress. An unusual case of interference grew out of a 1694 race which Rodham Kenner rode against John Hartly for one pound sterling and 575 pounds of tobacco. In a Westmoreland County court Hartly explained that after a fair start and without using "whipp or Spurr" he found himself "a great distance" in front of Kenner. But as Hartly neared the finish line, Kenner's brother, Richard, suddenly jumped onto the track and "did hollow and shout and wave his hat over his head in the plts [plaintiff's] horse's face." The animal panicked, ran outside the posts marking the finish line, and lost the race. After a lengthy trial a Westmoreland jury decided that Richard Kenner "did no foule play in his hollowing and waveing his hatt." What exactly occurred during this race remains a mystery, but since no one denied that Richard acted very strangely, it seems likely that the Kenner brothers were persuasive as well as powerful.

Planters who lost large wagers because an opponent jostled or "hollowed" them off the track were understandably angry. Yet instead of challenging the other party to a duel or allowing gaming relationships to degenerate into blood feuds, the disappointed horsemen invariably took their complaints to the courts. Such behavior indicated not only that the gentlemen trusted the colony's formal legal system—after all, members of their group controlled it—but also that they were willing to place institutional limitations on their own competitiveness. Gentlemen who felt they had been cheated or abused at the track immediately collected witnessess and brought suit before the nearest county court. The legal machinery available to the aggrieved gambler was complex; and no matter how unhappy he may have been with the final verdict, he could rarely claim that the system had denied due process.

The plaintiff brought charges before a group of justices of the peace sitting as a county court; if these men found sufficient grounds for a suit, the parties—in the language of seventeenth-century Virginia—could "put themselves upon the country." In other words, they could ask that a jury of twelve substantial freeholders hear the evidence and decide whether the race had in fact been fairly run. If the sums involved were high enough, either party could appeal a local decision to the colony's general court, a body consisting of the governor and his council. Several men who hotly insisted that they had been wronged followed this path. For example, Joseph Humphrey, loser in a race for 1,500 pounds of tobacco, stamped out of a Northumberland County court, demanding a stop to "farther proceedings in the Common Law till a hearing in Chancery." Since most of the General Court records for the seventeenth century were destroyed during the Civil War, it is impossible to follow these cases beyond the county level. It is apparent from the existing documents, however, that all the men involved in these race controversies took their responsibilities seriously, and there is no indication that the gentry regarded the resolution of a gambling dispute as less important than proving a will or punishing a criminal. It seems unlikely that the colony's courts would have adopted such an indulgent attitude toward racing had these contests not in some way served a significant social function for the gentry.

Competitive activities such as quarter-horse racing served social as well as symbolic functions. As we have seen, gambling reflected core elements of the culture of late seventeenth-century Virginia. Indeed, if it had not done so, horse racing would not have become so popular among the colony's gentlemen. These contests also helped the gentry to maintain group cohesion during a period of rapid social change. After 1680 the great planters do not appear to have become significantly less competitive, less individualistic, or less materialistic than their predecessors had been. But while the values persisted, the forms in which they were expressed changed. During the last decades of the century unprecedented external pressures, both political and economic, coupled with a major shift in the composition of the colony's labor force, caused the Virginia gentry to communicate these values in ways that would not lead to deadly physical violence or spark an eruption of blood feuding. The members of the native-born elite, anxious to preserve their autonomy over local affairs, sought to avoid the kinds of divisions within their ranks that had contributed to the outbreak of Bacon's Rebellion. They found it increasingly necessary to cooperate against meddling royal governors. Moreover, such earlier unrest among the colony's plantation workers as Bacon's Rebellion and the plant-cutting riots had impressed upon the great planters the need to present a common face to their dependent laborers, especially to the growing number of black slaves who seemed more and more menacing as the years passed.

Gaming relationships were one of several ways by which the planters, no doubt unconsciously, preserved class cohesion. By wagering on cards and horses they openly expressed their extreme competitiveness, winning temporary emblematic victories over their rivals without thereby threatening the social tranquility of Virginia. These nonlethal competitive devices, similar in form to what social anthropologists have termed "joking relationships," were a kind of functional alliance developed by the participants themselves to reduce dangerous, but often inevitable, social tensions.

Without rigid social stratification racing would have lost much of its significance for the gentry. Participation in these contests publicly identified a person as a member of an elite group. Great planters raced against their social peers. They certainly had no interest in competing with social inferiors, for in this kind of relationship victory carried no positive meaning: the winner gained neither honor nor respect. By the same token, defeat by someone like James Bullocke, the tailor from York, was painful, and to avoid such incidents gentlemen rarely allowed poorer whites to enter their gaming relationships—particularly the heavy betting on quarter horses. The common planters certainly gambled among themselves. Even the slaves may have laid wagers. But when the gentry competed for high stakes, they kept their inferiors at a distance, as spectators but never players.

The exclusiveness of horse racing strengthened the gentry's cultural dominance. By promoting these public displays the great planters legitimized the cultural values which racing symbolized—materialism, individualism, and competitiveness. These colorful, exclusive contests helped persuade subordinate white groups that gentry culture was desirable, something worth emulating; and it is not surprising that people who conceded the superiority of this culture readily accepted the gentry's right to rule. The wild sprint down a dirt tract served the interests of Virginia's gentlemen better than they imagined.

STUDY QUESTIONS

1. Breen notes that the "great planter's passion for gaming . . . coincided with a period of far-reaching social change in Virginia." How was Virginia changing?

2. Why did the Virginia gentry feel the need to display solidarity in the face of their social and economic inferiors? Why were members of the gentry reluctant to compete against social inferiors?

3. How important was excitement in work and play for the Virginia gentry?

4. What were the "core values" of Virginia society, and how did gambling illustrate those values?

5. What does Breen mean by the "role of chance" in colonial Virginia?

6. How did a member of the Virginia gentry view his best horse as an extension of himself? What were the symbolic aspects of horse racing in colonial Virginia?

7. How do sports and games illustrate the "core values" of American society?

BIBLIOGRAPHY

Clifford Geertz's masterful essay "Deep Play: Notes on the Balinese Cockfight," *Daedalus,* 101 (1972) demonstrates the relationship between how people play and how they live. Recently sports historians have continued Geertz's line of investigation. They have shown that sports and games play important roles in society. Benjamin G. Rader, *American Sports: From the Age of Folk Games to the Age of Spectators* (1983) presents a balanced and insightful overview of the subject.

Several historians have studied English sports and pastimes of the seventeenth and eighteenth centuries. Among the better studies are Roger Longrigg, *The English Squire and His Sport* (1977); Patricia Ann Lee, "Play and the English Gentleman in the Early Seventeenth Century," *Historian,* 31 (1969); Dennis Brailsford, *Sport and Society: Elizabeth to the Anne* (1969); Robert W. Malcolmson, *Popular Recreations in English Society, 1700-1850* (1980); and E. P. Thompson, "Patrician Society, Plebian Culture," *Journal of Social History,* 7 (1974). For American attitudes toward sports and games see Winton V. Salberg, *Redeem the Times: The Puritan Sabbath in Early America* (1977); Nancy L. Struna, "Sport and Societal Values: Massachusetts Bay," *Quest,* 27 (1977); and C. Robert Barnett, "Recreational Patterns of the Colonial Virginia Aristocrat," *Journal of the West Virginia Historical Association,* 2 (1978).

SWILLING THE PLANTERS WITH BUMBO

Charles S. Sydnor

During the eighteenth century, colonial American assemblies gained strength and expanded their jurisdiction. Aggressively independent, the popularly elected colonial legislatures jealously guarded their rights and frequently opposed the governors appointed by the Crown. Although in theory the governors enjoyed broad privileges, in practice the local leaders in the assemblies wielded considerable power. According to Jack P. Greene, the leading authority on the subject, by the middle of the century the royal governors were on the defensive.

Many historians have held up the assemblies as examples of the early success of democracy in America. If these historians are correct, however, it was a form of democracy that few contemporary Americans would recognize. In the South, the men elected to the assemblies were from the rich and powerful colonial families. Poorer landowners deferred to their economic superiors in politics as naturally as they did in literature or science.

Charles Sydnor takes a hard look at the election process in colonial Virginia. He demonstrates that a candidate's position on an important issue and even his character were often less important than the quality and quantity of rum he passed out on election day. As James Madison learned when he ran for office without distributing free liquor, the "voter preferred free rum to the high ideals of a young reformer."

It would be pleasant to think that voters were good and wise in the bright, beginning days of the American nation; that in Jefferson's Arcadia, to use a popular euphemism, the sturdy, incorruptible freeholders assembled when occasion demanded and, with an eye only to the public good and their own safety, chose the best and ablest of their number to represent them in the Assembly. It is true that the voters of early Virginia chose their representatives and that often they chose remarkably well; but it is an error to think that the voters were the only positive active force at work in elections. For good or ill, the candidates and their friends also played an important part by using many forms of persuasion and pressure upon the voters.

A play called *The Candidates; or, the Humours of a Virginia Election,* written about 1770 by Colonel Robert Munford of Mecklenburg County, Virginia, provides valuable insight into the part played by candidates in the elections of eighteenth-century Virginia. In this play one of the former delegates to the Assembly, Worthy by name, has decided not to stand for re-election. The other, Wou'dbe, offers himself once more "to the humours of a fickle croud," though with reluctance, asking himself: "Must I again resign my reason, and be nought but what each voter pleases? Must I cajole, fawn, and wheedle, for a place that brings so little profit?" The second candidate, Sir John Toddy, "an honest blockhead," with no ability except in consuming liquor and no political strength except his readiness to drink with the poor man as freely as with the rich, looks for support among the plain people who like him because he "wont turn his back upon a poor man, but will take a chearful cup with one as well as another." Scorned by the leading men of the county, the other two candidates, Smallhopes and Strutabout, a vain, showy

fellow, are adept in the low arts of winning the support of ignorant men.

Each of these candidates had some influence, following, or support which, in the language of that day, was known as his interest. It was common practice at this time for two candidates to join interests, as the phrase went, in hopes that each could get the support of the friends of the other. When Sir John suggests to Wou'dbe a joining of interests by asking him "to speak a good word for me among the people," Wou'dbe refuses and tells him plainly "I'll speak a good word to you, and advise you to decline" to run. Because Wou'dbe could not, from principle, join interests with any one of the three other candidates, he loses votes by affronting first one and then another of them. Just in the nick of time, Wou'dbe's colleague Worthy descends from the upper reaches of respectability and greatness to save Wou'dbe from defeat and political virtue from ruin. With stilted phrase Worthy denounces "the scoundrels who opposed us last election" and directs Wou'dbe to "speak this to the people, and let them know I intend to stand a poll." The good men of the county rally to the side of righteousness; Sir John (between alcoholic hiccoughs) announces "I'm not so fitten" as "Mr. Worthy and Mr. Wou'dbe"; Strutabout and Smallhopes, looking as doleful as thieves upon the gallows, are ignominiously defeated; and Worthy and Wou'dbe are triumphantly reelected.

Among the more important of the unwritten rules of eighteenth-century Virginia politics, a rule which the candidates and their advisers often mentioned was the necessity for candidates to be present at elections. Judge Joseph Jones, out of his ripe experience, wrote in 1785 to his young nephew James Monroe, "respecting your offering your service for the County the coming year, . . . it would be indispensibily necessary you should be in the County before the election and attend it when made." In 1758 several of Washington's friends wrote him to "come down" from Fort Cumberland, where he was on duty with his troops, "and show your face" in Frederick County where he was a candidate for burgess.

One of his supporters warned him that "you being elected absolutely depends on your presence." Thanks to the hard work of his friends and the patriotic circumstances of his absence, Washington was elected; but it is evident that the absence of a candidate from the county before and during the taking of the poll was regarded as a distinct handicap.

Fifty years later Henry St. George Tucker, who planned to stand for election at Winchester, was delayed by bad weather and other circumstances at Staunton. He wrote to his father: "I shall not be able to reach Winchester time enough for the election and I presume I shall be withdrawn in consequence of what I have written to my friends in Winchester." But by hard driving he made it, arriving "a few moments before the polls were opened;" and he was elected. As late as 1815 Tucker continued to place himself personally before the people while the voting was in process. Even though he was "still very weak" from illness, he played his part in an election of that year while the enormous number of 737 votes was polled until, as he wrote his father, "fatigue well nigh overcame me."

A sharp distinction must be made between election-day and pre-election behavior of the candidate toward the voter. The code of the times required that in the days before the election the candidate maintain a dignified aloofness from the voters; however, this rule was broken perhaps as often as it was observed. The tipsy Sir John Toddy, in *The Candidates,* assisted by his henchman Guzzle, tries unabashedly to work himself into the good graces of three freeholders named Prize, Twist, and Stern. As they and their wives are sitting on a rail fence, with other freeholders standing about, Sir John comes up to a group. At his shoulder stands Guzzle to whisper the names of the prospective voters to him.

SIR JOHN: *Gentlemen and ladies, your servant, hah! my old friend Prize, how goes it? how does your wife and children do?*

SARAH: *At your service, sir.* (making a low courtsey.)

PRIZE: *How the devil come he to know me so well, and never spoke to me before in his life?* (aside)

GUZZLE: (whispering to Sir John) *Dick Stern.*

SIR JOHN: *Hah! Mr. Stern, I'm proud to see you; I hope your family are well; how many children? does the good woman keep to the told stroke?*

CATHARINE: *Yes, an't please your honour, I hope my ladys' well, with your honour.*

SIR JOHN: *At your service, madam.*

GUZZLE: (whispering [to] Sir John) *Roger Twist.*

SIR JOHN: *Hah! Mr. Roger Twist! your servant, sir. I hope your wife and children are well.*

TWIST: *There's my wife. I have no children, at your service.*

James Littlepage, a candidate for burgess in Hanover County in 1763, practiced nearly every art known to his generation for getting his candidacy before the people and winning their support. The gathering of worshippers at church services afforded him an opportunity to meet people; but unfortunately, he could not be at two churches at the same time. Deciding that it was more important to go to a dissenting congregation, he prepared the way by letters to two freeholders in which he announced that he would "be at your Church To-morrow Se'nnight," and asked their support, setting forth the platform on which he was campaigning and circulating the false rumor that his opponent had "declined serving this Country."

To take care of matters at the other church which he was unable to attend personally, he sent a letter to three freeholders for them to read and pass about among those in attendance. As one of those who saw the letter recalled its substance, Littlepage wrote that he "was that Day gone to the lower Meeting House of the Dissenters, to know their Sentiments whether they would submit to the damned Tobacco Law, and desired to know whether they also would submit to it; that if they would send him Burgess he would be hanged, or burnt (or Words to that Effect) if he did not get

Spirits were often responsible for bringing men together for the sake of politics. Depicted above is an eighteenth century political club, where we get the impression that men met not for the sake of philosophy, but for their love of revelry.

that Part of it, directing a Review of Tobacco, repealed, as being an Infringement on the Liberty of the Subjects, the Inspectors being so intimidated by it that they refused the greater Part of their Tobacco; and that he would endeavor to have the Inspectors chosen by the People."

To meet the voters who could not be found in assemblies, Littlepage went on a house-to-house canvass. After discussing his chances in one part of the country with his friend John Boswell, and being assured that "he might have a good Chance, if he would go up amongst them," Littlepage "accordingly went up, and the said *Boswell* rode about with him among the People." He was the soul of hospitality, inviting those who lived at some distance from the courthouse to spend the night with him on their way to the poll. Littlepage was elected.

James Madison in his old age recalled that when he entered politics it was "the usage for the candidates to recommend themselves to the voters . . . by personal solicitation." Madison thoroughly disliked this practice. Shortly before the election of representatives to the first Congress of the United States he wrote from Philadelphia to George Washington: "I am pressed much in several quarters to try the effect of presence on the district into which I fall, for electing a Representative; and am apprehensive that an omission of that expedient, may eventually expose me to blame. At the same time I have an extreme distaste to steps having an electioneering appearance, altho' they should lead to an appointment in which I am disposed to serve the public; and am very dubious moreover whether any step which might seem to denote a solicitude on my part would not be as likely to operate against as in favor of my pretensions."

Colonel Landon Carter, writing in 1776, said that he had once been "turned out of the H. of B." because "I did not familiarize myself among the People," whereas he well remembered his "son's going amongst them and carrying his Election." The contrasting experiences of father and son suggest that going among the people was important to get a man elected. However, the son, Robert Wormeley Carter, lost his seat in an election in Richmond County in 1776 even though, according to his father, he had "kissed the——of the people, and very seriously accommodated himself to others." With mounting anger the Colonel wrote: "I do suppose such a Circumstance cannot be paralleled, but it is the nature of Popularity. She, I long discovered to be an adultress of the first order." The son was likewise displeased with the decision of the voters, but he naturally thought that his campaign methods were above reproach. He wrote in his diary "as for myself I never ask'd but one man to vote for me since the last Election; by which means I polled but 45 votes an honorable number."

Father and son were miles apart in describing what the son had done; but they were in complete agreement as to what he ought to have done. Both thought that candidates should not solicit votes, and there were other men who thought exactly as they did. Henry St. George Tucker wrote to his father before an election to be held on April 6, 1807, "Please to take notice also, that I am no *electionerer.*" "I have studiously avoided anything like canvassing. . . . My opponents are sufficiently active I learn." Of his victory he wrote: "it has been entirely without solicitation on my part." Eight years later he was again elected though he declared that he had "never attended a public meeting or been at the home of a single individual, and though my adversary and his friends had ransacked the county in the old Electioneering Style."

The contrast between ideal and reality was well illustrated by statements made during an election quarrel in Accomac County. The following advice was given to the freeholders: "If a man solicits you earnestly for your vote, avoid him; self-interest and sordid avarice lurk under his forced smiles, hearty shakes by the hand, and deceitfully enquires after your wife and family." However, it was said, referring to the candidates, that "every person who observes the two gentlemen, allows that the smiles of Mr. S——h are more forced than Mr. H——ry's, and of this Mr. S——h himself is so conscious that he has declared, he would give an Hundred Pounds could he shake hands with the freeholders, and smile in their faces with as good a grace as Col. Pa——e, that he might be more equally match'd."

Some candidates sought to injure a rival by starting the rumor that he was withdrawing from the race, that he had joined interests with an unpopular man, that he was a common drunkard, that he despised poor folks, or that "It's his doings our levies are so high." If the rumor was false, it was better for the candidate to keep silent and let one of his supporters circulate it. More often, the candidate, with the help of his friends, undertook to set himself and his views on current issues in a favorable light.

Sir John Toddy, whose supporters were great lovers of rum, promised to get the price of that article reduced, and it is said of Strutabout that "he'll promise to move mountains. He'll make the rivers navigable, and bring the tide over the tops of hills, for a vote." The noble Worthy promised no more than to "endeavour faithfully to discharge the trust you have reposed in me." And Wou'dbe answered the questions of the voters with carefully measured words. When asked if he would reduce the price of rum and remove an unpopular tax, he answered, "I could not," explaining that it would be beyond his power to accomplish these things. His position on other matters is set forth in the following dialogue.

STERN: *Suppose, Mr. Wou'dbe, we that live over the river, should want to come to church on this side, is it not very hard we should pay ferryage; when we pay as much to the church as you do?*

WOU'DBE: *Very hard.*

STERN: *Suppose we were to petition the assembly could you get us clear of that expense?*

WOU'DBE: *I believe it to be just; and make no doubt but it would pass into a law.*

STERN: *Will you do it?*

WOU'DBE: *I will endeavour to do it.*

STERN: *Huzza for Mr. Wou'dbe! Wou'dbe forever!*

PRIZE: *Why don't you burgesses, do something with the damn'd pickers? If we have a hogshead of tobacco refused, away it goes to them; and after they have twisted up the best of it for their own use, and taken as much as will pay them for their trouble, the poor planter has little for his share.*

WOU'DBE: *There are great complaints against them; and I believe the assembly will take them under consideration.*

PRIZE: *Wil you vote against them?*

WOU'DBE: *I will, if they deserve it.*

Littlepage, it will be recalled, promised to fight the existing system of tobacco inspection, and thereby was said to have gained much favor with the people. He also proposed to have the inspectors chosen yearly by the freeholders of the county, an extension of democracy which must have seemed radical to some men of the time. Friends of George Wythe, appealing to those who felt burdened by taxes, declared that "he would serve as Burgess for the said County for nothing," and they offered to "give Bond to repay any Thing that should be levied on the county for him." A rival candidate, William Wager, realizing that he must follow suit, immediately upon "hearing this Declaration, came up and said, he would serve on the same terms."

There is some evidence that the House of Burgesses frowned upon commitments by candidates, especially upon those which reflected upon the prerogative of the House by promising that it would act according to the will of a single member. The powerful Committee of Privileges and Elections investigated the making of campaign promises by some of the candidates, and the committee gave detailed reports to the House of its findings. Perhaps it was to protect himself against the disapproval of the House that Littlepage, who had promised much during his campaign, "Just before the Poll was opened . . . publickly and openly declared, in the Court House, before a great Number of People, that he did not look upon any of the Promises he had made to the People as binding on him but that they were all void."

There is no way of knowing how many of the candidates followed the rule approved by the Carters, Tucker, and Munford's character Wou'dbe: "never to ask a vote for myself," and how many of them followed the example of Littlepage in unashamedly and energetically courting the voters wherever they could find them, even going on house-to-house canvasses. Most of the candidates seem to have operated between these extremes. While they did not insulate themselves from the voters before elections, they avoided unseemly and ostentatious activity in their mingling with the people. The distinction between approved and disapproved conduct was close, and it is easier to be sure that a line was drawn than to be sure just where it was drawn. A man was likely to shift it a bit, depending on whether he was judging his own actions or those of his rival. John Clopton once gave his candidate son shrewd ad-

vice about cultivating the people and tricking a rival at the very time that he was fulminating against the tricks, deceptions, and intimidations practiced by the son's opponents!

Whether the candidates actively campaigned or not, a good many votes were committed before the election. The Quakers or the Presbyterians, the men along the south side of a river or in the northern corner of a county—these and other groups might discuss the candidates and decide which of them to support. Similarly, powerful men would let their friends, relatives, and dependents know how they stood toward the candidates. Thus, elections were often settled before they were held. A curious attempt to hold back this natural operation of democracy was made in a brief notice published in the *Virginia Gazette*. It was addressed "To the free and independent ELECTORS of the borough of NORFOLK," and it desired them "not to engage your votes or interest until the day of election, as a Gentleman of undoubted ability intends to declare himself as a candidate on that day, and hopes to succeed."

From these cases it is evident that although many candidates entered the race several weeks before election day, a few of them, like the unnamed gentleman of Norfolk or like Worthy in Munford's play, waited until the last minute before announcing their decision to stand a poll. John Marshall recalled in his old age that he had had the unusual experience of being made a candidate contrary to his wishes. He described the event, which occurred at Richmond during an election to the Virginia legislature in the spring of 1795, in the following words.

"I attended at the polls to give my vote early & return to the court which was then in session at the other end of the town. As soon as the election commenced a gentleman came forward and demanded that a poll should be taken for me. I was a good deal surprized at this entirely unexpected proposition & declared my decided dissent. I said that if my fellow citizens wished it I would become a candidate at the next succeeding election, but that I could not consent to serve this year because my wishes & my honour were engaged for one of the candidates. I then voted for my friend & left the polls for the court which was open and waiting for me. The gentleman said that he had a right to demand a poll for whom he pleased, & persisted in his demand that one should be opened for me—I might if elected refuse to obey the voice of my constituents if I chose to do so. He then gave his vote for me.

"As this was entirely unexpected—not even known to my brother who though of the same political opinions with myself was the active & leading partisan of the candidate against whom I voted, the election was almost suspended for ten or twelve minutes, and a consultation took place among the principal freeholders. They then came in and in the evening information was brought me that I was elected. I regretted this for the sake of my friend. In other respects I was well satisfied at being again in the assembly."

Many of the candidates may have been perfectly circumspect in their pre-election behavior, but all of them, with hardly an exception, relied on the persuasive powers of food and drink dispensed to the voters with open-handed liberality. Theoderick Bland, Jr., once wrote with apparent scorn that "Our friend, Mr. Banister, has been very much ingaged ever since the dissolution of the assembly, in swilling the planters with bumbo." When he supplied the voters with liquor Banister was in good company; it included Washington, Jefferson, and John Marshall.

The favorite beverage was rum punch. Cookies and ginger cakes were often provided, and occasionally there was a barbecued bullock and several hogs. The most munificent as well as democratic kind of treat was a public occasion, a sort of picnic, to which the freeholders in general were invited. George Washington paid the bills for another kind of treat in connection with his Fairfax County campaigns for a seat in the House of Burgesses. It consisted of a supper and ball on the night of the election, replete with fiddler, "Sundries &ca." On at least one occasion he shared the cost of the ball with one or more persons, perhaps with the other successful candidate, for his memorandum of expenses closes with the words: "By Cash paid Captn. Dalton for my part of ye Expense at the Election Ball. £ 8.5.6."

A supper and ball of this kind was probably more exclusive than a picnic-type of treat. Hospitality was often shown also to small groups, usually composed of important and influential men. Munford describes a breakfast given the morning of the election by Wou'dbe for the principal freeholders. Worthy was the guest of honor; fine salt shad, warm toast and butter, coffee, tea, or chocolate, with spirits for lacing the chocolate, were set before the guests; and although it was said that "we shall have no polling now," it was understood that all were for Worthy and Wou'dbe.

It was a common practice for candidates to keep open house for the freeholders on their way to the election, and it is a marvel where space was found for all to sleep. When Littlepage heard that some of the voters who lived more than twenty-five miles from the courthouse were unwilling to ride so far in cold weather, he invited them to call at his house which was about five miles from the courthouse. Some ten of them came and were hospitably entertained, "though their Entertainment was not more than was usual with him." Some of the company "were pretty merry with Liquor when they came" to his home. That evening "they chiefly drank Cider." "Some of them drank Drams in the Morning, and went merry to the Court House."

Candidates frequently arranged for treats to be given in their names by someone else. Lieutenant Charles Smith managed this business for George Washington during a campaign in Frederick County in 1758. Two days after the election, which Washington had not been able to attend, Smith sent him receipts for itemized accounts that he had paid to five persons who had supplied refreshments for the voters. A year or two earlier in Elizabeth City County Thomas Craghead sought to repay William Wager, a candidate for burgess, for help he had once received in time of distress. He invited several people to Wager's house and out of his own purse entertained them with "Victuals and Drink." He also had a share in treating all who were present at a muster of Captain Wager's militia company, after which they drank Wager's health.

Samuel Overton, a candidate in Hanover County, directed Jacob Hundley "to prepare a Treat for some of the Freeholders of the said County at his House." Later, Overton withdrew from the race, but a group of freeholders, perhaps ignorant of Overton's withdrawal, came to Hundley's house. He thereupon sent a messenger, desiring Overton's "Directions whether they were to be treated at his Expense," and Overton ordered him "to let them have four gallons of Rum made into punch, and he would pay for it."

At this juncture some of the finer points of campaigning begin to appear. Littlepage, an active candidate, was among those present at Hundley's house; and Littlepage had agreed in return for Overton's withdrawal to reimburse Overton the sum of £75, which was the expense he had incurred in this and a previous election. As a codicil it was agreed that Littlepage would pay only £50 in case "Mr. Henry," presumably Patrick Henry, should enter the race and be elected. While the treat was in progress Hundley told Littlepage "that the Liquor was all drank." He immediately ordered two gallons more, telling Hundley that he supposed Overton would pay for it. Whether any of the company heard this conversation is in doubt; but this much is clear, that Littlepage paid Overton to withdraw, that Littlepage attended a treat for Overton's friends, and that Littlepage succeeded, according to the testimony of one of the guests, in winning "the interest" of most of them.

On election day the flow of liquor reached high tide. Douglas S. Freeman calculated that during a July election day in Frederick County in the year 1758, George Washington's agent supplied 160 gallons to 391 voters and "unnumbered hangers-on." This amounted to more than a quart and a half a voter. An itemized list of the refreshments included 28 gallons of rum, 50 gallons of rum punch, 34 gallons of wine, 46 gallons of beer, and 2 gallons of cider royal. During the close and bitter struggle between John Marshall and John Clopton for a seat in Congress in 1799,

a "barrel of whiskey . . . with the head knocked in" was on the courthouse green.

Defeated candidates often complained of the wrongdoing of their successful opponents. George Douglas of Accomac County alleged before the Committee of Privileges and Elections that Edmund Scarburgh, shortly before the issuance of the writ of election, had twice given "strong Liquors to the People of the said County; once at a Race, and the other Time at a Muster; and did, on the Day of Election cause strong Liquor to be brought in a Cart, near the Courthouse Door, where many People drank thereof, whilst the Polls of the Election were taking; and one Man in particular, said, *Give me a Drink, and I will go and vote for Col. Scarburgh,* . . . and drink was accordingly given him out of the said Cart, where several People were merry with Drink: But it doth not appear, whether that Person voted for the said *Scarburgh,* or not; or was a Freeholder." Contrary to the recommendation of the Committee, Scarburgh was seated.

Captain Robert Bernard was charged with intimidation as well as improper treating in his efforts to help Beverley Whiting win an election in Gloucester County. He attended a private muster of Captain Hayes' men and solicited the freeholders among them to vote for Whiting. "And the next Day, at a Muster of his own Company, the said *Bernard* brought 40 Gallons of Cyder, and 20 Gallons of Punch into the Field, and treated his Men, solliciting them to vote for Mr. *Whiting,* as they came into the Field; and promised one *James Conquest,* to give him Liquor, if he would vote for Mr. *Whiting,* which *Conquest* refused; and then *Bernard* said he should be welcome to drink, tho' he would not vote for him: That the said *Bernard* promised one *Gale,* a Freeholder to pay his Fine, if he would stay from the Election; which *Gale* accordingly did: That the Day of Election, the said *Bernard* treated several Freeholders, who said they would vote for Mr. *Whiting,* at one *Sewell's* Ordinary: And that, at the Election, one of the Freeholders said, he was going to vote for Mr. *Whiting,* because he had promised Capt. *Bernard* so to do; but that he had rather give Half a Pistole than do it: And other Freeholders, who were indebted to Col. *Whiting,* said, that Capt. *Bernard* told them, that Col. *Whiting* would be angry with them if they voted against Mr. *Whiting;* which the said *Bernard* denied, upon his Oath, before the Committee."

The House of Burgesses compelled Bernard to acknowledge his offense, to ask the pardon of the House, and to pay certain fees; and it requested the Governor to issue a writ for a new election in Gloucester County.

The law strictly prohibited any person "directly or indirectly" from giving "money, meat, drink, pre- sent, gift, reward, or entertainment . . . in order to be elected, or for being elected to serve in the General Assembly;" but in one way or another nearly all the candidates gave treats, and seldom was a voice raised in protest. One of the rare protests was adopted at a general meeting of the citizens of Williamsburg two years before the Declaration of Independence. In an address to Peyton Randolph, who was a candidate for re-election to the House of Burgesses, the townsmen declared themselves to be "greatly scandalized at the Practice which has too much prevailed throughout the Country of entertaining the Electors, a Practice which even its Antiquity cannot sanctify; and being desirous of setting a worthy Example to our Fellow Subjects, in general, for abolishing every Appearance of Venality (that only Poison which can infect our happy Constitution) and to give the fullest Proof that it is to your singular Merit alone you are indebted for the unbought Suffrages of a free People; moved, Sir, by these important Considerations, we earnestly request that you will not think of incurring any Expense or Trouble at the approaching Election of a Citizen, but that you will do us the Honour to partake of an Entertainment which we shall direct to be provided for the Occasion."

Three years later young James Madison, feeling that "the corrupting influence of spiritous liquors, and other treats," was "inconsistent with the purity of moral and republican principles," and wishing to see the adoption of "a more chaste mode of conducting elections in Virginia," determined "by

an example, to introduce it." He found, however, that voters preferred free rum to the high ideals of a young reformer; "that the old habits were too deeply rooted to be suddenly reformed." He was defeated by rivals who did not scruple to use "all the means of influence familiar to the people." For many years to come liquor had a large part in Virginia elections. In 1795 Jefferson wrote that he was in despair because "the low practices" of a candidate in Albermarle County were "but too successful with the unthinking who merchandize their votes for grog." In 1807 Nathaniel Beverley Tucker, writing from Charlotte Court House, informed his father, St. George Tucker, that "In this part of the state . . . every decent man is striving to get a seat in the legislature. There are violent contests every where that I have been, to the great anoyance of old John Barleycorn, who suffers greatly in the fray."

Although the custom of treating was deeply ingrained, the law was not entirely disregarded. It did not prohibit a man's offering refreshment to a friend; it only prohibited treating "in order to be elected." Through various interpretations of these words most of the candidates found ways of dispensing largess to the freeholders without incurring the censure of the House of Burgess and perhaps without suffering from an uneasy conscience. Everyone would agree that it was wrong to give liquor to "one *Grubbs,* a Freeholder," who announced at an election that "he was ready to vote for any one who would give him a Dram." Neither should a candidate ask votes of those whom he was entertaining though it was perhaps all right for him to make the general remark "that if his Friends would stand by him he should carry his Election." Some men thought that there should be no treating after the election writ was issued until the poll had been taken. James Littlepage "expressly ordered" Paul Tilman, whom he had employed "to prepare his Entertainment at the Election . . . not to give the Freeholders any Liquor until after the closing of the Poll," and Littlepage produced evidence to show that "none of them had any Liquor, except some few who insisted on it, and paid for it themselves."

To avoid the appearance of corruption, it was well for the candidate to have the reputation of being hospitable at all times. When William Wager's campaign was under investigation, especially in the matter of the treat given in his home by one of his friends and another treat given in his honor to his militia company, Wager introduced evidence to show that he customarily entertained all who came to his house, strangers as well as freeholders, and that he usually treated the members of his militia company with punch after the exercises were over. "They would after that come before his Door and fire Guns in Token of their Gratitude, and then he would given them Punch 'til they dispersed, and that this had been a frequent Practice for several Years."

To avoid the reality as well as the appearance of corruption, the candidates usually made a point of having it understood that the refreshments were equally free to men of every political opinion. If a candidate's campaign was under investigation, it was much in his favor if he could show that among his guests were some who had clearly said that they did not intend to vote for him. Washington reflected an acceptable attitude when he wrote while arranging for the payment of large bills for liquor consumed during a Fred- erick County election: "I hope no Exception were taken to any that voted against me but that all were alike treated and all had enough; it is what I much desir'd." Washington seems to have followed this policy in subsequent elections. A young Englishman, who witnessed an election at Alexandria in 1774 when Washington was one of the two successful candidates, wrote: "The Candidates gave the populace a Hogshead of Toddy (what we call Punch in England). In the evening the returned Member gave a Ball to the Freeholders and Gentlemen of the town. This was conducted with great harmony. Coffee and Chocolate, but no Tea. This Herb is in disgrace among them at present."

Bountiful supplies of free liquor were responsible for much rowdiness, fighting, and drunkenness, but the fun and excitement of an election and the prospect of plentiful refreshments of the kind customarily consumed in that day helped to bring the voters to the polls. Thus in a perverse kind of way treating made something of a contribution to eighteenth-century democracy. Although one sometimes found a man who lived by the rule, "never to taste of a man's liquor unless I'm his friend," most of the voters accepted such refreshments as were offered. As they drank, they were less likely to feel that they were incurring obligations than that the candidate was fulfilling his obligation. According to the thinking of that day, the candidate ought to provide refreshments for the freeholders. His failure to fulfill this obligation would be interpreted as a sign of "pride or parsimony," as a "want of respect" for the voters, as James Madison found to his sorrow.

The Virginia voter expected the candidate to be manly and forthright, but he wanted the candidate to treat him with due respect. He had the power to approve and reject, and the sum total of this consciousness of power among the voters was a strong and significant aspect of the democratic spirit in eighteenth-century Virginia.

STUDY QUESTIONS

1. How were candidates for office supposed to behave during the preelection weeks and on election day? How did they actually behave?

2. What was the fate of candidates who tried to reform election practices?

3. Did "treating" the voters promote or retard the development of a democratic election process?

4. How did the normal election practices affect the deferential pattern of relations in colonial Virginia?

5. How did eighteenth-century elections differ from modern elections? What brought the eighteenth-century voter to the polls? What brings the twentieth-century voter to the election booth?

BIBLIOGRAPHY

The above essay is from Charles Sydnor, *Gentlemen Freeholders: Political Practices in Washington's Virginia* (1952). The classic work on the growth of American assemblies in the Southern colonies is Jack P. Greene, *The Quest for Power: The Lower Houses of Assembly in the Southern Royal Colonies, 1689–1776* (1963). The question of who could vote is ably discussed in Chilton Williamson, *American Suffrage from Property to Democracy, 1760–1860* (1960). The kinds of men who filled the colonial assemblies is treated in Carl Bridenbaugh, *Seat of Empire: The Political Role of Eighteenth-Century Williamsburg* (1950); Jack P. Greene, "Foundations of Political Power in the Virginia House of Burgesses, 1720–1776," *William and Mary Quarterly,* 3rd Ser., 16 (1959); and R. M. Zemsky, *Merchants, Farmers, and River Gods: An Essay on Eighteenth-Century American Politics* (1971). All three works trace the upper-class character of colonial Virginia leadership.

Part Three

THE REVOLUTIONARY GENERATION

When Thomas Jefferson proclaimed in the Declaration of Independence that people had the right to dissolve their government when it ceased to protect their "unalienable rights," he helped set in motion a crusade against European imperialism that lasted well into the twentieth century. Beginning with the "shot heard 'round the world" at Lexington, Massachusetts on April 19, 1775, colonial rebellions swept through Latin America early in the nineteenth century and through Africa and Asia in the twentieth century. By 1776, after nearly 170 years in the New World, the American colonists were ready for independence. With an English heritage and experience from trial and error, they had developed a political culture that emphasized localism, representative government, popular sovereignty, and individual rights. They had also acquired an American identity clearly distinguishing them from their English cousins. When the French and Indian War initiated changes in British imperial policy, colonists rebelled in a desperate and ultimately successful attempt to preserve a moral order.

But the destruction of one set of political relationships did not automatically create new ones. In the summer of 1776, the Second Continental Congress was a government without constitutional authority. The colonies were at best a loose alliance of competing states with limited resources, trying to make war against a major world power. The war also revealed strains between the rich and poor. The Continental army, for example, was periodically weakened by the struggles for power between well-to-do officers and enlisted men, as well as by the lack of support from civilians and politicians. The colonists triumphed by winning the war in the court of world opinion and by draining England of its financial and emotional resources. Their first attempt at constitution making, the Articles of Confederation, ended in failure. Although that government managed to bring the Revolution to a successful conclusion, Americans realized that a

central government had to be able to support itself economically and maintain public order. When Shays's Rebellion in 1786 raised doubts about the latter, the Founding Fathers gathered in Philadelphia in the summer of 1787 to try again.

They were eminently successful. The Constitution was a model political document, even though it represented the vested interests of a conservative minority. After its ratification in 1788, the Constitution became the symbol of the new republic. Americans considered themselves a free people blessed with a fundamental consensus about politics and power. They took their place among independent nations of the world confident that God had destined them for greatness.

Life was not easy. Older rivalries between the lower and upper classes, as well as between the seaboard region and the frontier, still manifested themselves. In 1794, a rebellion of poor farmers in western Pennsylvania challenged the authority of the new government. There were also political tensions within the ruling elite. During the 1790s a two-party system gradually emerged in the United States. George Washington, Alexander Hamilton, and John Adams led the Federalist Party, and Thomas Jefferson and James Madison headed the Democratic-Republicans. Both parties struggled for power throughout the 1790s and early 1800s. Despite the challenges, the new nation survived.

A "MOST UNDISCIPLINED, PROFLIGATE CREW"

James Kirby Martin

Few events in United States history have generated as much mythical rhetoric as the American Revolution. The struggle to separate from the British empire spawned an intense debate about freedom, equality, opportunity, and patriotic loyalty. Historians, usually servants of the status quo, then transformed the American Revolution into a crusade for liberty, creating an image of unity and commitment that never really existed. History has a way of telescoping reality, sometimes to distortion. The American Revolution was a complicated phenomenon of diverse groups competing for influence and power; it was hardly a unified crusade. Most people were not directly engaged in the conflict, and those who were had a variety of motivations. Many slaves, for example, saw the Revolution as an opportunity to secure freedom. Some poor people hoped to acquire land of their own and to enjoy full civil rights. Western land developers and eastern merchants believed the Revolution would eliminate British commercial restrictions. Some Virginia planters hoped to avoid repaying debts to London tobacco brokers. And many colonists, but certainly not a majority, genuinely wanted the Revolution to restore their civil liberties—to return the divinely guaranteed rights so recently taken from them by an autocratic king and an arbitrary Parliament. Amidst such contrary goals, as well as concerted opposition to the Revolution from many other colonists, the 1770s and 1780s constituted an era of conflict and competition in American history.

In "Protest and Defiance in the Ranks," James Kirby Martin surveys the public mood during the American Revolution by looking at the morale problems of the Continental army. Traditionally, historians studying the American Revolution have focused their attention on elites—wealthy businessmen, educated philosophers, prosperous planters, and Continental congressmen—to determine public attitudes. By looking at different groups, such as army officers and enlisted personnel, Martin sees different forces at work during the Revolution. Instead of finding a unified country engaged in a righteous crusade against evil, Martin describes dissension and mutiny in the army, with enlisted men alienated from officers and the entire army alienated from the society at large. Plagued by shortages of food, clothing, and pay, the soldiers felt abandoned by an apathetic public. Their protests became a minor rebellion against social customs in the larger struggle against the British Empire.

A sequence of events inconceivable to Americans raised on patriotic myths about the Revolution occurred in New Jersey during the spring of 1779. For months the officers of the Jersey brigade had been complaining loudly about everything from lack of decent food and clothing to pay arrearages and late payments in rapidly depreciating currency. They had petitioned their assembly earlier, but nothing had happened. They petitioned again in mid-April 1779, acting on the belief that the legislature should "be informed that our pay is now only *minimal,* not *real,* that four months' pay of a private will not procure his wretched wife and children a single bushel of wheat." Using "the most plain and unambiguous terms," they stressed that "unless a speedy and ample remedy be provided, the total dissolution of your troops is inevitable." The Jersey assembly responded to this plea in its usual fashion—it forwarded the petition to the Continental Congress without comment. After all, the officers, although from New Jersey, were a part of the Continental military establishment.

The assembly's behavior only further angered the officers, and some of them decided to demonstrate their resolve. On May 6 the brigade received orders to join John Sullivan's expedition against the Six Nations. That same day, officers in the First Regiment sent forth yet another petition. They again admonished the assembly about pay and supply issues. While they stated that they would prepare the regiment for the upcoming campaign, they themselves would resign as a group unless the legislators addressed their demands. Complaints had now turned into something more than gentlemanly protest. Protest was on the verge of becoming nothing less than open defiance of civil authority, and the Jersey officers were deadly serious. They had resorted to their threatened resignations to insure that the assembly would give serious attention to their demands—for a change.

When George Washington learned about the situation, he was appalled. "Nothing, which has happened in the course of the war, . . . has given me so much pain," the commander in chief stated anxiously. It upset him that the officers seemingly had lost sight of the "principles" that governed the cause. What would happen, he asked rhetorically, "if their example should be followed and become general?" The result would be the "ruin" and "disgrace" of the rebel cause, all because these officers had "*reasoned wrong about the means of obtaining a good end.*"

So developed a little known but highly revealing confrontation. Washington told Congress that he would have acted very aggressively toward the recalcitrant officers, except that "the causes of discontent are too great and too general and the ties that bind the officers to the service too feeble" to force the issue. What he did promise was that he would not countenance any aid that came "in [such] a manner extorted." On the other hand, the officers had been asking the assembly for relief since January 1778, but to no avail. They, too, were not about to be moved.

The New Jersey legislature was the political institution with the ability to break the deadlock. Some of the legislators preferred disbanding the brigade. The majority argued that other officers and common soldiers might follow the First Regiment's lead and warned that the war effort could hardly succeed without a Continental military establishment. The moment was now ripe for compromise. The assemblymen agreed to provide the officers with whatever immediate relief could be mustered in return for the latter calling back their petitions. That way civil authorities would not be succumbing to intimidation by representatives of the military establishment, and the principle of subordination of military to civil authority would remain inviolate. The assembly thus provided an immediate payment of £200 to each officer and

"A 'Most Undisciplined, Profligate Crew': Protest and Defiance in the Continental Ranks, 1776–1783" by James Kirby Martin in *Arms and Independence: The Military Character of the American Revolution,* edited by Ronald Hoffman and Peter J. Albert, 1984. Reprinted by permission of the publisher, The University Press of Virginia.

$40 to each soldier. Accepting the compromise settlement as better than nothing, the brigade moved out of its Jersey encampment on May 11 and marched toward Sullivan's bivouac at Easton, Pennsylvania. Seemingly, all now had returned to normal.

The confrontation between the New Jersey officers and the state assembly serves to illuminate some keys points about protest and defiance in the Continental ranks during the years 1776–83. Most important here, it underscores the mounting anger felt by Washington's regulars as a result of their perceived (and no doubt very real) lack of material and psychological support from the society that had spawned the Continental army. It is common knowledge that Washington's regulars suffered from serious supply and pay shortages throughout the war. Increasingly, historians are coming to realize that officers and common soldiers alike received very little moral support from the general populace. As yet, however, scholars have not taken a systematic look at one product of this paradigm of neglect, specifically, protest and defiance. The purpose of this essay is to present preliminary findings that will facilitate that task.

Given that there was a noticeable relationship between lack of material and psychological support from the civilian sector and mounting protest and defiance in the ranks, it is also important to make clear that patterns of protest were very complex. A second purpose of this essay is to outline those basic patterns and to indicate why protest and defiance did not result in serious internal upheaval between army and society in the midst of the War for American Independence. To begin this assessment, we must bring Washington's Continentals to the center of the historical arena.

During the past twenty years, historians have learned that there were at least two Continental armies. The army of 1775–76 might be characterized as a republican constabulary, consisting of citizens who had respectable amounts of property and who were defending hearth and home. They came out for what they believed would be a rather short contest in which their assumed virtue and moral commitment would easily carry the day over seasoned British regulars not necessarily wedded to anything of greater concern than filling their own pocketbooks as mercenaries.

The first army had a militialike appearance. Even though phrases of commitment were high sounding, there was not much discipline or rigorous training. These early soldiers had responded to appeals from leaders who warned about "our wives and children, with everything that is dear to us, [being] subjected to the merciless rage of uncontrolled despotism." They were convinced that they were "engaged . . . in the cause of virtue, of liberty, of *God*." Unfortunately, the crushing blows endured in the massive British offensive of 1776 against New York undercut such high-sounding phrases about self-sacrifice. The message at the end of 1775 had been "Persevere, ye guardians of liberty." They did not.

The second Continental establishment took form out of the remains of the first. Even before Washington executed his magnificent turnabout at Trenton and Princeton, he had called for a "respectable army," one built on long-term enlistments, thorough training, and high standards of discipline. The army's command, as well as many delegates in Congress, now wanted soldiers who could stand up against the enemy with more than notions of exalted virtue and moral superiority to upgird them. They called for able-bodied men who could and would endure for the long-term fight in a contest that all leaders now knew could not be sustained by feelings of moral superiority and righteousness alone.

To assist in overcoming manpower shortages, Congress and the states enhanced financial promises made to potential enlistees. Besides guarantees about decent food and clothing, recruiters handed out bounty moneys and promises of free land at war's end (normally only for long-term service). Despite these financial incentives, there was no great rush to the Continental banner. For the remainder of the war, the army's command, Congress, and the states struggled to maintain minimal numbers of Continental soldiers in the ranks.

In fact, all began to search diligently for new recruits. Instead of relying on propertied freeholders and tradesmen of the ideal citizen-soldier type, they broadened the definition of what constituted an "able-bodied and effective" recruit. For example, New Jersey in early 1777 started granting exemptions to all those who hired substitutes for long-term Continental service—and to masters who would enroll indentured servants and slaves. The following year Maryland permitted the virtual impressment of vagrants for nine months of regular service. Massachusetts set another kind of precedent in 1777 by declaring blacks (both slave and free) eligible for the state draft. Shortly thereafter, Rhode Islanders set about the business of raising two black battalions. Ultimately, Maryland and Virginia permitted slaves to substitute for whites. The lower South, however, refused to do so, even in the face of a successful British invasion later in the war.

The vast majority of Continentals who fought with Washington after 1776 were representative of the very poorest and most repressed persons in Revolutionary society. A number of recent studies have verified that a large proportion of the Continentals in the second establishment represented ne'er-do-wells, drifters, unemployed laborers, captured British soldiers and Hessians, indentured servants, and slaves. Some of these new regulars were in such desperate economic straits that states had to pass laws prohibiting creditors from pulling them from the ranks and having them thrown in jail for petty debts. (Obviously, this was not a problem with the unfree.)

The most important point to be derived from this dramatic shift in the social composition of the Continental army is that few of these new common soldiers had enjoyed anything close to economic prosperity or full political (or legal) liberty before the war. As a group, they had something to gain from service. If they could survive the rigors of camp life, the killing diseases that so often ravaged the armies of their times, and the carnage of skirmishes and full-scale battles, they could look forward to a better life for themselves at the end of the war. Not only were they to have decent food and clothing and regular pay until the British had been irrevocably beaten, they had also been promised free land (and personal freedom in the cases of indentured servants, black slaves, and criminals). Recruiters thus conveyed a message of personal upward mobility through service. In exchange for personal sacrifice in the short run, there was the prospect of something far better in the long run, paralleling and epitomizing the collective rebel quest for a freer political life in the New World.

To debate whether these new Continentals were motivated to enlist because of crass materialism or benevolent patriotism is to sidetrack the issue. A combination of factors was no doubt at work in the mind of each recruit or conscript. Far more important, especially if we are to comprehend the ramifications of protest and defiance among soldiers and officers, we must understand that respectably established citizens after 1775 and 1776 preferred to let others perform the dirty work of regular, long-term service on their behalf, essentially on a contractual basis. Their legislators gave bounties and *promised* many other incentives. Increasingly, as the war lengthened, the civilian population and its leaders did a less effective job in keeping their part of the agreement. One significant outcome of this obvious civilian ingratitude, if not utter disregard for contractual promises, was protest and defiance coming from Washington's beleaguered soldiers and officers.

That relations between Washington's post-1776 army and Revolutionary society deteriorated dramatically hardly comes as a surprise to those historians who have investigated surviving records. Widespread anger among the rank and file became most demonstrable in 1779 and 1780, at the very nadir of the war effort. Pvt. Joseph Plumb Martin captured the feelings of his comrades when he reflected back on support for the army in 1780. He wrote: "We therefore still kept upon our parade in groups, venting our spleen at our country and government, then at our officers, and then at ourselves for our imbecility in staying there and starving in detail for an ungrateful people who did not care what became of us, so they could enjoy themselves while we were keeping a cruel enemy from them." Gen. John Paterson, who spoke out in

Protest among the ranks stemmed from the poor conditions of camp life, bad food, irregular pay, and a lack of clothing.

March 1780, summarized feelings among many officers when he said, "It really gives me great pain to think of our public affairs; where is the public spirit of the year 1775? Where are those flaming *patriots* who were ready to sacrifice their lives, their fortunes, their all, for the public?"Such thoughts were not dissimilar from those of "A Jersey Soldier" who poured his sentiments into an editorial during May 1779 in support of those regimental officers who were trying to exact some form of financial justice from their state legislature. The army, he pointed out, had put up with "a load. . . grown almost intolerable." "It must be truly mortifying to the virtuous soldier to observe many, at this day, displaying their cash, and sauntering in idleness and luxury," he went on, including "the gentry . . . [who] are among the foremost

to despise our poverty and laugh at our distress." He certainly approved the actions of his comrades because he resented "the cruel and ungrateful disposition of the people in general, in withholding from the army even the praise and glory justly due to their merit and services," just as he resented society's failure to live up to its contract with the soldiers. These statements, which are only a representative sampling, indicate that the army had come to believe that Revolutionary civilians had taken advantage of them—and had broken their part of the contract for military services.

There were real dangers hidden behind these words. With each passing month beginning in 1777, Washington's regulars, especially that small cadre that was signing on for the long-term fight, became more professional in military demeanor.

Among other things, including their enhanced potential effectiveness in combat, this meant that soldiers felt the enveloping (and reassuring) bonds of "unit cohesion." The immediate thoughts of individual soldiers, whether recruited, dragooned, or pressed into service, became attached to their respective primary units in the army, such as the particular companies or regiments in which they served. The phenomenon was nothing more than a developing comradeship in arms. Any threat or insult thus became an assault on the group, especially if that threat or insult were directed at all members of the group. The bonding effect of unit cohesion suggests that collective protest and defiance would become more of a danger to a generally unsupportive society with each passing month, unless civilians who had made grand promises started to meet their contractual obligations more effectively.

Indeed, the most readily observable pattern in Continental army protest and defiance was that it took on more and more of a collective (and menacing) character through time. At the outset, especially beginning in 1776, most protest had an individual character. Frequently it was the raw recruit, quite often anxious for martial glory but quickly disillusioned with the realities of military service once in camp, who struck back against undesirable circumstances. Protest could come through such diverse expressions as swearing, excessive drinking, assaulting officers, deserting, or bounty jumping. One source of such behavior was the dehumanizing, even brutal nature of camp life. Another had to do with broken promises about pay, food, and clothing. A third was a dawning sense that too many civilians held the soldiery in disregard, if not utter contempt.

It must be remembered that middle- and upper-class civilians considered Washington's new regulars to be representative of the "vulgar herd" in a society that still clung to deferential values. The assumption was that the most fit in terms of wealth and community social standing were to lead while the least fit were to follow, even when that meant becoming little more than human cannon fodder. Perhaps James Warren of Massachu-

setts summarized the social perceptions of "respectable" citizens as well as any of the "better sort" when he described Washington's troops in 1776 as "the most undisciplined, profligate Crew that were ever collected" to fight a war.

While civilians often ridiculed the new regulars as riffraff, troublemakers, or mere hirelings (while conveniently ignoring the precept that military service was an assumed obligation of all citizens in a liberty-loving commonwealth), individual soldiers did not hold back in protesting their circumstances. In many cases, they had already acknowledged the personal reality of downtrodden status before entering the ranks. Acceptance of these circumstances and the conditions of camp life did not mean, however, that these new soldiers would be passive. Thus it may be an error to dismiss heavy swearing around civilians or repeated drunkenness in camp as nothing more than manifestations of "time-honored military vices," to borrow the words of one recent student of the war period.

At least in some instances, individual soldiers could have been making statements about their sense of personal entrapment. Furthermore, protest through such methods as drunkenness (this was a drinking society but not one that condoned inebriety) was a defensive weapon. One of Washington's generals, for instance, bitterly complained in 1777 that too many soldiers consistently made it "a practice of getting drunk . . . once a Day and thereby render themselves unfit for duty." To render themselves unfit for duty was to give what they had received—broken promises. Defiance that came in the form of "barrel fever" for some soldiers thus translated into statements about how society looked upon and treated them.

Only over time did individual acts of protest take on a more collective character. That transition may be better comprehended by considering the phenomenon of desertion. While it is true that a great many soldiers did not think of desertion as a specific form of protest, they fled the ranks with greater frequency when food and clothing were in very short supply or nonexistent, as at Valley Forge. However, primary unit cohesion worked to militate against unusually high desertion levels. Sustained involvement with a company or regiment reduced the likelihood of desertion. Hence as soldiers came to know, trust, and depend upon one another, and as they gained confidence in comrades and felt personally vital to the long-term welfare of their primary group, they were much less likely to lodge a statement of individual protest through such individualized forms as desertion.

So it appears to have been with Washington's new regulars. Thad W. Tate discovered that, in the regiments of New York, Maryland, and North Carolina, about 50 percent of all desertions occurred within six months of enlistments. Mark Edward Lender, in studying New Jersey's Continentals, also found that the rate of desertion dropped off dramatically for those soldiers who lasted through just a few months of service. The first few days and weeks in the ranks were those in which these poor and desperate new regulars asked themselves whether vague promises of a better lot in life for everyone, including themselves, in a postwar republican polity was worth the sacrifice now being demanded. Many enlistees and conscripts concluded that it was not, and they fled. Since they had little proof that they could trust the civilian population and its leaders, they chose to express their defiance through desertion. Unit cohesion, in turn, helped sustain those who read the equation differently, and it eased the pain of enduring a long war in return for the remote prospect of greater personal freedom, opportunity, and prosperity.

Then there were those individuals who neither deserted nor became hard-core regulars. By and large, this group defied civil and military authority through the practice of bounty jumping. The procedure, which Washington once referred to as "a kind of business" among some soldiers, was straightforward. It involved enlisting, getting a bounty, and deserting, then repeating the same process with another recruiting agent in another location. Some of the most resourceful bounty jumpers got away with this maneuver seven, eight, or even nine times, if not more. Most jumpers appear to have been very poor young men without family roots. The most careful of them went through the war unscathed. Bounties thus provided a form of economic aggrandizement (and survival) in a society that generally treated its struggling classes with studied neglect. To accept a bounty payment, perhaps even to serve for a short period, and then to run off, was a strongly worded statement of personal defiance.

Bounty jumping was invariably the act of protesting individuals; looting and plundering (like desertion) combined individual with collective protest. Certainly there were numerous occasions when hungry soldiers looted by themselves. Just as often, groups of starving men "borrowed" goods from civilians. Even before the second establishment took form, looting had become a serious problem. Indeed, it probably abetted unit cohesion. One sergeant, for example, described how he and his comrades, searching desperately for food, "liberated" some geese belonging to a local farmer in 1776 and devoured them "Hearty in the Cause of Liberty of taking what Came to their Hand." Next "a sheep and two fat turkeys" approached this band of hungry soldiers, but "not being able to give the countersign," they were taken prisoner, "tried by fire and executed" for sustenance "by the whole Division of the freebooters."

When army looting of civilian property continued its unabated course in 1777, General Washington threatened severe penalties. He emphasized that the army's "business" was "to give protection, and support, to the poor, distressed Inhabitants; not to multiply and increase their calamities." These pleas had little impact. Incident after incident kept the commander in chief and his staff buried in a landslide of civilian complaints. Threats of courts martial, actual trials, and severe punishments did not deter angry, starving, protesting soldiers. In 1780 and 1781 Washington was still issuing pleas and threats, but to little avail. Not even occasional hangings contained an increasingly defiant and cohesive soldiery that wondered who the truly poor and distressed inhabitants were—themselves or civilians ostensibly prospering because of the army's travail. To strike back at hoarding, unsupportive citizens, as they had come to perceive the populace whom they were defending, seemed only logical, especially when emboldened by the camaraderie of closely knit fellow soldiers.

Above all else, two patterns stand out with respect to common soldier protest. First, as the war effort lengthened, defiance became more of a collective phenomenon. Second, such protest had a controlled quality. While there was unremitting resentment toward civilians who were invariably perceived as insensitive and unsupportive, protest rarely metamorphosed into wanton violence and mindless destruction. Soldiers may have looted and pillaged, they may have grabbed up bounties, and they may have deserted. But they rarely maimed, raped, or murdered civilians. Pvt. Joseph Plumb Martin attempted to explain why. Even though "the monster Hunger, . . . attended us," he wrote, and the new regulars "had borne as long as human nature could endure, and to bear longer we considered folly," he insisted that his comrades had become, in the end, "truly patriotic." They were persons who "loved their country, and they had already suffered everything short of death in its cause." The question by 1779 and 1780 was whether these hardened, cohesive veterans would be willing to endure even more privation.

In reflecting positively on the loyalty of his comrades, Martin was commenting on a near mutiny of the Connecticut Line in 1780. Indeed, the specter of collective defiance in the form of line mutinies had come close to reality with the near insubordination of the New Jersey officers in 1779. They had not demonstrated in the field, but they had made it clear that conditions in the army were all but intolerable—and that civil society, when desperate to maintain a regular force in arms, could be persuaded to concede on basic demands. Washington had used the phrase "extorted"; he had also pointed out that, "notwithstanding the expedient adopted for a saving appearances," this confrontation "cannot fail to operate as a bad precedent." The commander in chief was certainly right about the setting of precedents.

Among long-term veterans, anger was beginning to overwhelm discipline. There had been small-scale mutinies before, such as the rising of newly recruited Continentals at Halifax, North Carolina, in February 1776. In 1779 Rhode Island and Connecticut regiments threatened mutinies, but nothing came of these incidents. Then in 1780 another near uprising of the Connecticut Line occurred. Invariably, the issues had the same familiar ring: lack of adequate civilian support as demonstrated by rotten food, inadequate clothing and worthless pay (when pay was available). On occasion, too, the heavy hand of company- and field-grade officers played its part. The near mutiny of the Connecticut Line in 1780 had been avoided by a fortuitous shipment of cattle and by promises from trusted officers of better treatment. In the end, the Connecticut Line calmed itself down, according to Martin, because the soldiery was "unwilling to desert the cause of our country, when in distress." Nevertheless, he explained that "we knew her cause involved our own, but what signified our perishing in the act of saving her, when that very act would inevitably destroy us, and she must finally perish with us."

By the end of 1780, there were some veterans who would have disputed Martin's reasoning. They had all but given up, let come what might for the glorious cause. On January 1, 1781, the Pennsylvania Line proved that point. Suffering through yet another harsh winter near Morristown, New Jersey, the Pennsylvanians mutinied. Some one thousand determined comrades in arms (about 15 percent of the manpower available to Washington) ostensibly wanted nothing more to do with fighting the war. On a prearranged signal, the Pennsylvanians paraded under arms, seized their artillery, and marched south toward Princeton, their ultimate target being Philadelphia. These veterans had had their fill of broken promises, of the unfulfilled contract. They maintained that they had signed on for three years, not for the duration. If they were to stay in the ranks, then they wanted the same benefits (additional bounty payments, more free land, and some pay in specie) that newer enlistees had obtained.

Formal military discipline collapsed as the officers trying to contain the mutineers were brushed aside. The soldiers killed one and wounded two other officers, yet their popular commander, Anthony Wayne, trailed along, attempting to appeal to their sense of patriotism. Speaking through a committee of sergeants, the soldiers assured Wayne and the other officers that they were still loyal to the cause, and they proved it by handing over two spies that Sir Henry Clinton had sent out from New York to monitor the situation. Moreover, the mutineers, despite their anger and bitterness, behaved themselves along their route and did not unnecessarily intimidate civilians who got in their way.

Later checking demonstrated that many of the mutineers were duration enlistees, yet that was a moot point. When the soldiers reached Trenton, representatives of Congress and the Pennsylvania government negotiated with them and agreed to discharge any veteran claiming three years in rank. Also, they offered back pay and new clothing along with immunity from prosecution for having defied their officers in leaving their posts. Once formally discharged, the bulk of the mutineers reenlisted for a new bounty. By late January 1781 the Pennsylvania Line was once more a functioning part of the Continental army.

These mutineers won because Washington was in desperate need of manpower and because they had resorted to collective defiance, not because their society wanted to address what had been grievances based on the contract for service. Unlike their officers, who had just won a major victory in driving for half-pay pensions, they were not in a position to lobby before Congress. Hence they employed one of the most threatening weapons in their arsenal, collective protest against civil authority, but only after less extreme measures had failed to satisfy their claims for financial justice. They were certainly not planning to overthrow any government or to foment an internal social revolution against better-placed members of their society. They had staked their hopes on a better life in the postwar period and had already risked their lives many times for the proposed republican polity. All told, the extreme nature of this mutiny demonstrated,

paradoxically, both that Washington's long-term Continentals were the most loyal and dedicated republican citizens in the new nation, and that they were dangerously close to repudiating a dream that far too often had been a personal nightmare because of the realities of societal support and of service in the Continental army.

More worrisome in January 1781 than the matter of appropriate appreciation of the soldiers' action was whether this mutiny, and its stillborn predecessors, would trigger further turbulence in the ranks. Also camped near Morristown during the winter of 1780–81 were veteran soldiers of the New Jersey Line. Their officers were aware that the Jersey regulars sympathized with the Pennsylvanians and had been in constant communication with them. Then, on January 20, 1781, the New Jersey Line, having witnessed the success of its comrades, also mutinied. The soldiers had each recently received $5 in specie as a token toward long overdue pay, but they were bothered by the better bounties and terms of enlistment offered newer recruits. Their leaders urged them on by shouting: "Let us go to Congress who have money and rum enough but won't give it to us!"

Within a few days, the Jersey Line had won acceptable concessions and was back under control. Washington, however, had decided that enough was enough. "Unless this dangerous spirit can be suppressed by force," he wrote to Congress, "there is an end to all subordination in the Army, and indeed to the Army itself." To back up his strong words, the commander ordered Gen. Robert Howe and about five hundred New England troops near West Point to march to the Jersey camp at Pompton to make sure that the mutineers were back in line and summarily to execute the most notorious leaders. Howe did as instructed. He reached Pompton on January 27, three days after grievances had been redressed. Deploying his men around the campsite just before dawn, Howe caught the Jersey soldiers off guard. He ordered them to fail in without arms, then singled out three ringleaders and ordered their summary execution, to be shot to death by nine of their comrades. A Jersey officer intervened in one case, but the other two were put to death by firing squad.

It was a brutal ending for men who had dreamed of a better future despite all of society's violations of the contract. Perhaps because of the calculated coldheartedness of Washington's orders, or perhaps because the war picture began to brighten in 1781, there were no major uprisings among Washington's regulars after the mutiny of the New Jersey Line. Then again, the soldiery may have been too worn down physically and mentally to continue their protest and defiance in the name of financial justice, humane treatment, and psychological support. They may have passed beyond the point of despair to that of quiet acceptance of whatever came their way, whether just or unjust.

An important question that must be raised in conclusion has to do with political perceptions and fears: given real concerns in Revolutionary society that a regular army could obtain too much power, could corrupt the political system, and could threaten the civilian sector with some form of tyranny, such as a military dictatorship, why did officers and soldiers never unite effectively and put maximum pressure on the frail Revolutionary political structure by protesting in unison? They could have easily played on fears of a coup. But about the closest such union was the Jersey officers' defiance of 1779. Thus, while common soldiers got drunk, deserted, looted, or mutinied, officers pursued their own (and largely separate) avenues of protest. This is curious, especially since the officers too worried about the personal financial cost of service; they too came to resent civilian indifference, ineptitude, and greed; and they too were dismayed over society's inability to treat them with respect. They feared that their virtuous behavior and self-sacrifice would go unappreciated if not completely unrecognized and unrewarded. Having so much in common with their brethren in the rank and file, then, it is worth considering why the officers almost never aligned with them. For if they had, the alliance might have been powerful enough to have fomented something truly menacing to the vitals of Revolutionary society.

The officer corps developed its own forms of protest, and the pattern paralleled that of the common soldiers. The movement was from a dominant expression of individual defiance (resignations in 1776 and 1777) to collective protest (the drive for half-pay pensions which began in earnest during the fall of 1777 and climaxed with the Newburgh Conspiracy of 1782–83). Like common soldiers, the officers had collectivized their protest. In that sense, unit cohesion among comrades had come into play, but such cohesion never broke through the vertical hierarchy of military rank.

Part of the reason lay in the social gulf separating the two groups. As befit the deferential nature of their times as well as their concern for maintaining sharp distinctions in rank as a key to a disciplined fighting force, officers, many of whom were drawn from the "better sort" in society, expected nothing less than steady, if not blind obedience to their will from the rank and file. In their commitment to pursuing the goals of the Revolution, the officers were anything but social levelers. Indeed, many of them feared that the Revolution might get out of hand and lead to actual internal social upheaval, particularly if the "vulgar herd" gained too much influence and authority, whether in or out of the army. They hesitated to turn their troops against society because these same soldiers could always turn against them as well and, through brute force, undermine all assumed claims to economic and social preeminence in Revolutionary America.

Washington's veteran officers, even though they complained and protested with vehemence, also willingly accepted their responsibilities as the army's leadership cadre. The officers administered harsh discipline to deserters, looters, bounty jumpers, and mutineers whenever it seemed necessary—and sometimes when it was not. They generally supported Washington's desire to set the legal limit for lashes at 500 strokes, and many of them often sanctioned whippings of more than 100 lashes, despite the Articles of War of 1776. For example, officers took relish to Washington's general orders at Morristown in

1780 to inflict 100 to 500 lashes on duty tried plunderers and to administer up to 50 lashes on the spot, even before formal hearings, when soldiers were caught breaking military laws.

Many officers thus used their authority with impunity and rarely expressed sympathy for the plight of common soldiers in the ranks. They were much more concerned with societal stability and the protection of property, as well as with military decorum and hierarchy, all of which precluded the officer corps from working in harmony with the soldiery when protesting common grievances against the civilian sector.

Washington's officers, in reality, were caught between the rank and file, for which they had little sympathy, and the larger society, which had little sympathy for them. They pursued their half-pay pension demands, resorting to such defiant acts as threatening to resign en masse during the late summer of 1780. Later they became even more extreme as some toyed with the idea of a full mutiny, if not the possibility of a coup, during the Newburgh crisis. In the end, they failed in their short-term quest for pensions or commutation, as the soldiery fell short in its drive for minimal levels of respectable support. Perhaps those quests would have been more successful had officers and regulars been able to unite in a common bond transcending social class and military rank. If they had, the story of the Revolution might have been quite different. Recalling the common well of bitterness, the ending might well have had more of a Napoleonic cast to it.

That it did not is more than a mere testament to class, hierarchy, and rank. It is also a statement about the evolving feelings among both hard-core officers and regulars, regardless of the multifold reasons that brought them to the service in the first place, that they were fighting for something worthwhile, something of consequence for their particular lives. If they protested, they still maintained residual faith in their personal dreams. They also came to comprehend that, for all of the pain and suffering that was their lot, they could make a lasting contribution. Henry Knox stated the proposition aptly in 1783 when he noted that there was "a favorite toast in the army," that of " 'A hoop to the barrel,' or 'Cement to the Union.'" That is the way that these protesting, defying, long-term Continentals should be remembered, not as a "most undisciplined, profligate Crew," but as individuals who, for all of their defiance, made the necessary personal sacrifice to insure that the Revolution and its ideals would succeed when so many about them in their society did not.

STUDY QUESTIONS

1. Despite the desire of many colonists to separate from Great Britain, there was not much unanimity among Americans. Why? How would you explain the dissension?

2. Historians have frequently looked back on American society in the colonial period as the least aristocratic in the world. Do you agree? Were there any aristocratic values in colonial America? Describe them. How does class conflict in the Continental army expose those aristocratic values?

3. In the 1770s, soldiers complained that the public really did not care much about what was happening to them. Do you agree that the public was apathetic toward the soldiers in the 1770s? Why or why not?

BIBLIOGRAPHY

For a standard treatment of the military dimension of the American Revolution, see J. R. Alden, *A History of the American Revolution* (1969). More analytical treatments can be found in Don Higginbotham, *The War of American Independence: Military Attitudes, Policies and Practice, 1763–1789* (1971) and John Shy's *A People Numerous and Armed: Reflections on the Military Struggle for American Independence* (1976). For the classic study of social change during the Revolution, see J. Franklin Jameson, *The American Revolution Considered as a Social Movement* (1926). A more recent, though still supportive, interpretation of the social dimension of the revolutionary era is Jackson T. Main's *The Social Structure of Revolutionary America* (1969). Jesse Lemisch's article "Listening to the 'Inarticulate': William Widger's Dream and the Loyalties of American Revolutionary Seamen in British Prisons," *Journal of Southern History,* 35 (1969) offers an additional look at the feelings of lower-class Americans at the time. Finally, for an excellent description of American attitudes toward the Revolution over the past two hundred years, see Michael Kammen, *A Season of Youth: The American Revolution and the Historical Imagination* (1978). Also see Gordon Wood, The *Radicalism of the American Revolution* (1992).

ESTABLISHING A GOVERNMENT, 1789

Forrest McDonald

Thoughts of George Washington often lead to images preserved in stone. The marble of the Washington Monument, the rocky peak of Mount Washington, the sculptured side of Mount Rushmore—the first president of the United States has been immortalized in stone. In the American imagination he stands alone, above the other Founding Fathers, as the symbol of the country and the republic. Even during his life, Americans regarded him as different, destined to be remembered in the permanent marble of statues.

Like the statue he became, the man struck many people who met him as cold and distant. His biographers claim that he had a passionate nature, but that he kept rigid control over his emotions. Perhaps so. Perhaps his outward equanimity and courtly manners masked an inward fire that burned to be released. Washington did have two deep passions—the country and the nation that played such an important part in his life. America may have won its independence from England and the United States may have become a reality without George Washington, but it is difficult to imagine either outcome. Rare for his time, he was a man who could accept great powers and then relinquish them. He moved gracefully from soldier to citizen and from head of state back to citizen again. He sought the counsel of people with whom he agreed and disagreed, and he listened to both.

In the following essay, Forrest McDonald discusses the crucial role that Washington and his group of supports played in the establishment of the government of the United States. Amid the swirl of confusion and odd personalities, Washington provided the indispensable center. Success was by no means guaranteed with him—and certainly less so without him.

The new government got off to a slow and erratic start, one suitably gauche for a band of yokels who had arrogantly declared themselves able to get along without the guidance of kings, nobles, or bishops. On March 4, 1789, the day appointed for the meeting of the First Congress, only a quarter of the members showed up. A week passed, and the Senate was still four members short of a constitutional quorum (half the membership), and the House of Representatives was twelve short of a quorum. Another week passed, and another, and another, until, at last, the House obtained a bare quorum by April 1, the Senate on April 6.

Then there was the matter of the presidency. Presidential electors had been chosen the previous fall, had met in the several states as the Constitution required, had cast their unanimous ballot for George Washington, and had made John Adams vice president by giving him the second most votes. Everyone knew before the balloting began that Washington would be president, and the newspapers announced the results early in 1789. Any other man than Washington would have been in the temporary capital, New York, in time for the opening of Congress. But the Father of His Country was ever concerned with propriety, and since he would not be officially elected until a joint session of Congress tallied the votes of the electors, he stayed at home in Mount Vernon. When Congress obtained a quorum, counted the votes, and notified him accordingly, he still tarried, lest unseemly haste suggest that he was improperly eager for the office. He took a leisurely trip northward, incidentally wallowing in the popular adulation shown him in every hamlet along the way, and finally arrived in New York in time to be inaugurated on April 30.

Compelling practical considerations dictated more promptness from all quarters. Anti-Federalists

had by no means given up in their efforts to defeat the Constitution, and every delay worked in their favor. More tangibly, there was the matter of revenues for the new government. Everyone knew that the old Congress of the Confederation was bankrupt, and everyone knew that the financial health of the new system would depend upon the funds derived from import duties. Everyone also knew that Americans normally did most of their importing in the spring and that part of the duties were paid when goods arrived from abroad, the remainder six months later. Thus if the new Congress failed to enact a schedule of tariffs before the spring importing season of 1789 was over, it could count on no appreciable revenues for twelve to eighteen months. In fine, unless someone acted quickly, the babe Constitution could die stillborn.

In these circumstances only one man appeared with the energy and awareness that the occasion demanded. Washington himself could not take the lead, for he had but a limited understanding of what was happening; and besides, he knew, if only instinctively, that he could contribute best by serving as a symbol. Nor could John Adams, he who had been so bold in seizing the initiative on the eve of independence, repeat his earlier performance; this pompous man was as devoid of understanding of present circumstances as he was lacking in followers. The Senate over which Adams presided, regarded by many as potentially the fount of enlightened leadership that the nation needed, quickly proved to be as inept as the vice president. Most members of the House were scarcely better.

Fortunately for the infant States, James Madison was on hand, and Madison both understood and knew how to translate understanding into action. He had been instrumental in having the Constitutional Convention of 1787 called, had been instrumental in the work of that convention, and had been instrumental in bringing about the ratification of the Constitution. After 1789 he would lose control over, and sometimes lose contact with, the tide of events; but in 1789 he was the man of the hour.

Acceptance of the presidency was one of the most painful decisions of Washington's life. For years his abiding, overriding concern, amounting

From *The Presidency of George Washington* by Forrest McDonald, copyright © 1974 by the University Press of Kansas. Used by permission of the publisher.

almost to an obsession, had been his reputation—or, as he put it, his desire for the "approval of his fellow-citizens" and for a favorable judgment from "posterity." Liberty and republicanism mattered to him, to be sure, but less for their own sake than because of their connection with his reputation: if they did not survive, neither would his reputation as the First Character of the Age, the Father of His Country. He had hoped that problems of government would solve themselves, for he had had little experience in dealing with them and had even less talent; but things had not worked out that way, and the call had come. He could not afford to refuse, and he could not afford to fail; for if he should fail now, his entire life's work would retroactively have been a failure.

Thus, despite his preferences and protestations, there had never been any likelihood that he would spurn the office. He was indispensable, and he knew it. As a man idolized by the people—almost all the people, whatever their station in life—he could make it possible for them to indulge their habitual adulation of a monarch without reneging on their commitment to republicanism. As a symbol of the Union, he could stimulate, at least for a time, the emotional attachment to the Nation that normally requires centuries in the building. As a man with a thoroughly justified reputation for integrity, dignity, candor, and republican virtue, he could inspire the trust that was crucial to the radical experiment in federal government. He could do these things, and no other man could. The circumstance stretches the imagination—possibly it was unprecedented in history, and it would certainly never recur in the history of the American presidency—but the fact is that Washington was the only man who measured up to the job.

Yet Washington was mean as well as grand, and it was the pettiness that showed most during his first few months in office. No sooner had he taken the oath of office than he found himself in a dilemma or, perhaps more appropriately, a tizzy. His large rented house in New York was overrun with visitors, a few there on serious business, most total strangers come to solicit jobs with the new government or simply to gawk at the Great

Man. All acted as if they had every right to be there. Between invasions he found it impossible, from breakfast to bedtime, to be "relieved from the ceremony of one visit before I had to attend to another." He inquired as to the practice of his partial predecessors, the presidents of the old Confederation Congress, and learned that they had been "considered in no better light than as a maître d'hôtel . . . for their table was considered as a public one." Thoroughly peeved, Washington published an advertisement in the newspapers, announcing that he would thenceforth receive "visits of compliment" only between two and three on Tuesday and Friday afternoons, would return no visits, and would accept no invitations.

The more austere republicans howled that the president was thereby proposing to shut himself off from the public "like an eastern Lama," forgetting that he was merely an official chosen by the people. Almost desperately, Washington now sent inquiries to several people—Madison, Adams, Alexander Hamilton, John Jay—asking advice on rules of behavior that would strike a balance between "too free an intercourse and too much familiarity" (which would reduce the responsibility of the office) and "an ostentatious show" of monarchical aloofness (which would be improper in a republic). It was a matter of the gravest moment, Washington said, for precedents set now would affect the course of government for many years to come.

Rules were worked out. Dinners were to be held every Thursday at four, the guests being only government officials and their families, invited in an orderly system of rotation to avoid charges of favoritism. As to the general public, Washington established two occasions a week for greeting them: a "levee" for men only on Tuesdays from three to four, and tea parties for men and women, held on Friday evenings. Anyone respectably dressed could attend either public function without invitation or prior notice, but at least the traffic was reduced. Habitually, Washington found the levees insufferable, for people came, saluted him, and otherwise ignored him while freeloading on the refreshments he provided. The tea parties, presided over by his wife Martha after she

George Washington achieved great status and reputation for his devotion to the new nation and, perhaps equally as important, for his modesty.

arrived at the end of May, were much more to his liking, for he loved to circulate among and charm the ladies. (Charming the ladies was not difficult for him. Abigail Adams, wife of the vice president and a veteran of receptions at the Court of St. James, fully expected to dislike the president, but was almost moon-struck upon meeting him. He moved, she gushed, "with a grace, dignity, and ease that leaves Royal George far behind him.")

The program of entertainment was not unrelated to another delicate matter considered in the first few months. Washington magnanimously—or so it seemed—offered to serve without salary, asking Congress only to pay his expenses. Remembering that he had fared rather handsomely under such an arrangement during the Revolutionary War, the General was almost insistent, but Congress instead voted him a $25,000 salary and no expense account. Washington's concern is understandable when it is realized that his liquor bill alone ran to almost $2,000 in 1789.

Two other aspects of the presidency during the early months proved even more vexing. The first was that at first there was precious little for the president to do except entertain. Until the Congress should take some action, there were no national laws to enforce, no officers to appoint, not even any criminals to pardon. The one area in which the Constitution empowered the executive to act without legislation was the conduct of foreign relations, and even there the extent of his discretionary authority was not clear, for his powers were hampered by the requirement that they be exercised with the "advice and consent" of the Senate. Therein lay a second vexing aspect of the office. Washington was an experienced and skillful administrator, but he could function only with an expert corps of advisers—from whom opinions could be solicited and to whom authority could be delegated, but who had to be devoted to and obey the commands of the leader. The Constitution provided for no such body of advisers, and many persons, including Washington's neighbor and old friend George Mason, had opposed it at least partly for that reason. Instead, the document (which Washington interpreted literally, almost as if it were a manual of instructions) authorized the president to require "the Opinion, in writing," of department heads, whenever Congress got around to establishing the departments; otherwise, there was officially nothing but the advice and consent of the Senate.

For a time Washington made do with administrative relics of the defunct Confederation: John Jay, superintendent of foreign affairs, and his one-man diplomatic corps, Minister to France Thomas Jefferson; and Superintendent of War Henry Knox, who oversaw Indian affairs with the assistance of an authorized army of 840 men, of whom no more than two-thirds were actually in service and almost all were in arrears of pay. Through Jay and Knox, meetings were arranged between the president and foreign envoys already on the premises; and negotiations with various Indian tribes, already underway, proceeded for a time. Then it became necessary to issue further instructions in regard to the Indian negotiations, and a minor constitutional impasse ensued.

The president and the secretary of war conferred and decided that they were constitutionally bound to seek the advice and consent of the Senate. One Saturday morning, just as the Senate was beginning its deliberations, Washington and Knox sauntered in, told the doorkeeper to announce their presence, and informed the senators that they were there seeking advice and consent. Knox handed a paper to Washington, who handed it to Adams, who read it just as several carriages were rolling by. Some could make out the word "Indians," but few heard anything else. When the reading was finished, Washington said something about seven points in regard to which advice and consent was requested, but outside noises again prevented anyone from hearing. An embarrassed silence followed. Senator Robert Morris of Pennsylvania, erstwhile Financier of the Revolution and one of the few intimates of the president, deferentially asked that everything be read again. Everything was read again, whereupon Vice President Adams put the question: "Do you advise and consent?" on each of Washington's seven proposals, one by one. On point after point the senators, conceiving of themselves as a deliberative body, were disposed to debate and ended up postponing the question. Washington, accustomed to dealing with advisers as subordinates, grew visibly irritated, his face flaming red as his hair. Finally he rose and declared that "this defeats every purpose of my coming here," and general embarrassment pervaded the room. He gradually cooled down, and so did the senators; but after another confrontation the following Monday, it was mutually if tacitly agreed that advice, like consent, should come after and not before the president acted.

Trivial as the circumstances of that decision were, the decision itself was of considerable importance. For one thing, it ruled out the possibility that the presidency might evolve into something resembling the prime ministership in Great Britain. For another, it set a pattern in the conduct of foreign relations. Thenceforth, Washington initiated foreign policy on his own, seeking no counsel from the Senate at all. Furthermore, ever after, only "weak" presidents, those who entrusted foreign affairs to the secretary of state, worked through the Senate as a matter of course; every "strong" president, like Washington, had as little to do with the Senate as possible.

For all its fumbling, the executive branch had a saving grace that the Senate lacked. Washington and his minions escaped laughability for much the same reason that Napoleon and his marshals later did: people who defeat the best armies of Europe are somehow not very funny. The upper house of the new government, lacking any such basis for pretensions, was a pretty sorry spectacle.

The comedy started almost with the first rap of John Adams's gavel. Unlike those who followed him in the office, Adams participated in as well as presided over the doings of the Senate. From the outset, he was disposed to interrupt the debates with pedantic little lectures or even speeches, alternately attempting to impress the senators with his learning and with his experience, both of which were in fact vast. Most of the senators, in their turn, seemed scarcely able to speak without citing a dozen ancient authorities, so as to display their erudition and prove the timeless rectitude of their views. It was as if a dialogue—or debate—were being held between Polonious and a Greek Chorus.

The comedy began in earnest when a hassle developed over the proper way to address the president. Adams, once a radical republican, had acquired a taste for pomp and ceremony during his many years as a minister in the courts of Europe, and he ardently desired that regal "dignity and splendor" be made a part of the American system. Characteristically, he rationalized the matter. Society, he maintained, was held together by customs, prejudices, and superstitions—a reasonable enough assumption, but from it he concluded that only an elaborate system of titles would instill in the people the awe and veneration that would give permanency to the government. A large number of the senators, conceiving of themselves as a virtual American House of Lords, agreed with the vice president and proposed, for openers, a series of exalted titles for the president. After lengthy discussion "his elective majesty," "his excellency," and others were rejected in favor of "His Highness the President of the United States and Protector of the Rights of the Same." Only three senators opposed such nonsense, and two of them, curiously, were among the nation's richest men: Charles Carroll of Maryland and Ralph Izard of South Carolina, who owned thousands of acres of rich plantation lands and more than a thousand slaves between them. The third was William Maclay, a militant republican and back-country Scotch-Irishman from Pennsylvania.

The House of Representatives refused to concur in the Senate's resolution respecting a presidential title, and the Senate peevishly wrangled about whether to compromise on this grave matter. At one point Richard Henry Lee of Virginia, who strongly supported Adams, stood up and read off "the titles of all the princes and potentates of the earth," to show that the term "highness" was in almost universal use. At another point Adams interrupted the debate by declaring that the president could communicate to the Senate in three ways—in person, through a "minister of state," or through a personal aide. As everyone looked blank, wondering what this had to do with anything, Adams solemnly declared that "it may become a great constitutional question." The subject of titles, which had consumed almost all the Senate's time since April 23, was finally closed on May 14 with a general Senate endorsement of the principle of a title for the president.

The comic climax came four days later. Habitually and in keeping with British practice, colonial and state legislatures had, upon being convened, heard a speech by the executive and subsequently responded by calling on him and presenting an answering address of their own. The Senate called upon the president for that purpose on May 18. Adams, followed by the eighteen senators, filed into the president's levee room, where Washington stood with two aides. "His Rotundity," as Izard dubbed the fat vice president, was trembling so badly that he was able to read only by placing the senatorial address in his hat and holding on to the hat with both hands. That made for some difficulty in turning the pages, but Adams finally managed to get through.

Washington had prepared a brief reply, which he now removed from his coat pocket, only to create a minor dilemma. He had the paper in his right hand and his hat in his left, and no hand left over to remove his spectacles from his vest pocket. After some Chaplinesque shifting of objects he got his hat under his left arm and the paper in his left hand, somehow extracted the glasses from their case and got them on his nose, but was left with the case occupying the right hand. He overcame this "small distress" by placing the case on the chimney piece. Then, "having adjusted his spectacles, which was not very easy, considering the engagements of his hands, he read the reply with tolerable exactness and without much emotion." The president then invited everyone to sit, but Adams, perhaps because he found it difficult to sit gracefully while wearing his sword, declined, and the Senate bowed and left.

Beneath all this nonsensical ostentation and formality, however, lay some deadly serious jockeying for power, collective and individual. On one level, the Senate was looking out for its interests as a body. The exaggerated deference toward the president was designed, at least in part, to ensure that if court politics developed, the senators would have first rank as courtiers. The exaggerated insistence on formality, on the other hand, was part of a design by the senators to protect their prerogatives against executive encroachment. Their jealousy in this regard was revealed in June, when a move was made to require the president to have senatorial approval in removing as well as appointing executive officers. The senators were borne down on that occasion by doubts among their own members and by overpowering constitutional arguments emanating from the House of Representatives, led by James Madison; but the very effort was symptomatic of a trait that would endure.

On another level, the frippery in the Senate was the surface manifestation of a struggle for power inside the body. In broad terms, senators from Virginia and New England were seeking to reestablish the alliance that had triumphed in the old Congress and brought independence in 1776, and those from the Middle States and the lower South were groping toward reestablishing their own coalition, which had prevailed in 1774–1775. On this more personal level, Richard Henry Lee, mistakenly figuring that Adams controlled the New England senators, kowtowed to Adams to aggrandize his own influence. The New Englanders, overestimating Adams's influence with the president and misreading the doings of Lee and his southern supporters, sought to strengthen their own hands by backing Adams and Lee on matters that they regarded as trivial. And so on.

The proceedings of the Senate (unlike those of the House) were closed to the public, but had there been any careful and seasoned Senate-watchers, the man they would have watched was Senator Oliver Ellsworth of Connecticut. His fellow senators, in fact, began to watch him more and more as the summer progressed. And well they might, for he was a shrewder political operator than all the others combined. Moreover, Ellsworth had some grand schemes afoot, and when he executed them—so skillfully that his colleagues never knew quite how it happened—the Senate could claim a large share of the credit for the achievements of 1789.

James Madison, however, was the person most nearly in command of national affairs. Madison was and is perhaps the most difficult of all the Founding Fathers to understand. His contemporaries were almost unanimous in regarding him as remarkably learned, candid, open, and of a sweet and amiable disposition. On all counts but the first they were entirely mistaken: he was, in actuality, so carefully contrived and controlled that in comparison to him Hamilton, Jefferson, and even Burr were open books. Possibly the key to his character is that he was either an epileptic or a victim of epileptiform hysteria and that he devoutly guarded the secret of his infirmity, lest he be regarded (in keeping with the superstitious science of his time) as being insane. Almost certainly he had not yet worked out what various psychiatrists and historians have described as the "identity crisis"—that is, making one's peace with one's own finiteness.

In keeping with the psyche that in many cases stems from such internal stresses, Madison had fervently embraced a cause, that of enlarging national power as a means of creating a balanced system of government; and in keeping with the dictates of a finely honed mind and a highly developed skill in manipulating other men, he had been engaged for some time and with considerable success in support of his cause. Without him, Virginia might never have ratified the Constitution; and without Virginia the Union was entirely unworkable. Patrick Henry prevented Madison's election to the Senate and gerrymandered his representative district to make it unlikely that he could win a seat in the House; but Madison conducted a veritable door-to-door campaign and won a seat in the House anyway. Now, almost awesomely versed in the immediate problems facing the new government, he was better prepared than anyone to take the lead in making it workable.

One large problem quickly proved itself to be temporarily insoluble, and Madison shrewdly perceived that it should therefore be treated as a means by which other problems might be solved. This was the question of the location of the permanent capital of the United States. Every town of any pretensions to consequence between New Haven and Norfolk vied for the honor and the expected wealth that would arise from the choice. More importantly, every politician of consequence sought to have the location fixed as close as possible to his own constituency, on the theory that proximity would influence attendance and therefore influence the locus of power. As a practical matter, the outside limits seemed to lie between New York City and Annapolis. As a practical matter also, James Madison doubtless foresaw that in the rivalry lay the ingredients of a deal, whenever there arose a controversy in which the stakes were large enough to justify some trading.

Meanwhile, there was another large problem, which was almost as thorny but had to be resolved quickly: the matter of a tariff law to raise revenue. Madison's thinking on the subject had been worked out in consultations with Washington but was much more sharply refined than was the president's. The two Virginians agreed that revenue measures should be so devised as to implement a second consideration of national policy—to discriminate somewhat against the nation's late enemy, Great Britain, and to give a favored position to its ally, France, and to those few European powers with which the United States had been able to negotiate commercial treaties.

Madison introduced a bill toward this end on April 8, the very first day on which the House settled down to serious legislative business. He proposed a schedule of specific duties (taxes of so much a gallon or pound) on imported rum, liquor, wine, molasses, sugar, tea, cocoa, and coffee, and duties ad valorem (taxes based on a fixed percentage of value) on all other imported commodities. He also proposed a graded system of tonnage duties—taxes on the carrying capacity of vessels—on ships and smaller cargo craft arriving from foreign ports. Vessels owned by Americans would pay the smallest duties, those owned by subjects of nations "in treaty" with the United States would pay somewhat more, and those of Great Britain and other "untreatied" powers, considerably more.

A conflict of interests immediately arose, to foreshadow every debate on every proposed tariff for more than a century. Thomas Fitzsimons of Pennsylvania suggested that the list of specific duties be expanded to "protect our infant industries," which is to say the handcrafted goods that were produced mainly in his state and surrounding states. Fitzsimons also had an ulterior motive, however, or at least so supposed William Maclay, his fellow Pennsylvanian in the Senate. Fitzsimons was an affluent importing merchant, and together with others of that description, including the erstwhile anti-Federalist Elbridge Gerry of Massachusetts, he apparently set out to delay the enactment of tariff legislation until the spring importing season was past. Meanwhile, merchants could raise their prices on the pretense that the duties were forthcoming, and thereby take in a million or two from their customers on their own account.

Besides such shenanigans, there were more substantial interests at stake, but few understood quite what their interests were. Madison's proposed discrimination was a bonanza to New England shippers, or so it seemed, at the expense of tobacco planters in Maryland, Virginia, and North Carolina. Because freight rates were such a large part of the cost of marketing American tobacco in Europe, southerners objected to discriminatory tonnage duties, on the theory that Europeans would thereby be taxed out of the trade and New Englanders, thus endowed with a virtual monopoly, could raise freight rates at will. In point of fact, precious few Yankees were in the freighting business, preferring instead to buy cargoes and sell them for their own accounts; and so their congressmen counted this proposal as no boon at all, even as the southerners wailed against it as an unfair advantage to New England. Simultaneously the New Englanders objected to Madison's proposed duties on molasses, as being destructive of their rum industry.

In this maze of interests, real and imagined, Madison and reason prevailed. Few were entirely satisfied with the measure as it finally passed both houses of Congress, which was to be the way of things with tariff legislation nearly ever after. The average duty was around 7 or 8 percent. The secondary considerations of policy that motivated Washington and Madison did not lead to law, for full discrimination against Britain was not carried, nor was the protective principle espoused by Fitzsimons. Moreover, the bill did not pass until the spring importing season was almost over. Even so, by mid-summer the government had a regular and potentially large source of revenue, which meant that it might be able to survive. That, in itself, was a monumental fact, for the Confederation Congress and the British Empire itself had, within living memory, foundered on proposals to create just such a system of taxation.

As the tariff was being debated, Madison was already engaged on another front, that concerning a bill of rights to the Constitution. In 1787 the Constitutional Convention, with the wholehearted support of Madison, had rejected proposals for a bill of rights, on the logically impeccable ground that it made no sense to create a federal government by listing the powers it could exercise and then to cloud the issue by listing powers it could not exercise. But opponents of the Constitution had created a considerable stir by demanding a bill of rights and had used that commotion as an excuse for demanding the calling of a second constitutional convention, ostensibly to rectify the oversights of the first but actually to subvert the Constitution entirely.

Understanding the perils of what was involved, Madison announced on May 4 that three weeks hence he would propose certain amendments to the Constitution. The reaction was gradual and complex. Some of the staunchest Federalists in the House, including Roger Sherman of Connecticut and Fisher Ames of Massachusetts, adhered blindly to the original Federalist position and strongly denounced the very idea of a bill of rights. Anti-Federalists, the erstwhile champions of amendments, caught on one by one: Aedanus Burke and Thomas Sumter of South Carolina, Elbridge Gerry of Massachusetts, and James Jackson of Georgia, who less than a year earlier had tried to prevent the adoption of the Constitution on the pretended ground that it had no bill of rights, now joined the likes of Sherman and Ames to oppose the introduction of amendments.

But Madison understood that a bill of rights was not primarily a substantive issue, and fortunately for the Nation, a majority of his colleagues went along with him. He had meticulously studied the proposals that had emanated from the various state ratifying conventions. Not counting North Carolina and Rhode Island, which so far had refused to ratify, formal requests for restrictive amendments had come in from five states, and informal requests had come from two others. Because he recognized that the motivation underlying the demand was more political than ideological, Madison disregarded the fact that only three of these states had bills of rights of their own. Instead, he gathered and organized the proposed amendments.

Eliminating duplicates, Madison found eighty proposals. From all nine states he catalogued requests for a prohibition against interference by Congress with the time and place of holding elections, for restrictions on the taxing power, and for a declaration that all powers not delegated to the general government should be reserved to the states. Seven states spoke for jury trials; six called for an increase in the number of members of Congress, protection of religious freedom, and a prohibition of standing armies in times of peace. Five wanted prohibitions against quartering troops and against unreasonable searches and seizures and demanded protection of the right of the states to control the militias, the right of the people to bear arms, and the rights of freedom of speech and of the press. Four states requested guarantees of due process of law, speedy and public trials, the rights of assembly and petition, limits on the power of the federal judiciary, and bans on monopolies, excessive bail, unconstitutional treaties, and the holding of appointive federal offices by members of Congress.

Madison dismissed the least popular and most impractical of these suggestions and reduced the remainder to nineteen substantive amendments. (He introduced one impractical proposal of his own: that the amendments be woven into the text of the Constitution, rather than tacked on at the end.) On June 8 the House resolved itself into a committee of the whole house to debate the proposals, and by August 24, after intermittent debates, it had approved the amendments. They differed little from Madison's original proposals, save for being consolidated into seventeen amendments and being so worded as to be added onto the end of the Constitution. As they emerged from the House, the amendments were designed to apply to state governments as well as to the national government. (Hence, for example, states as well as the national government would have been required to have trials by jury and prohibited from restricting freedom of speech.)

On September 2 the Senate took up the proposals. Right away, that body removed the applicability of the bill of rights to the states (hence, for example, states remained free to tax all citizens for the support of established churches, as Connecticut did until 1818 and Massachusetts did until 1833). Otherwise, however, the Senate largely concurred, though it and a joint committee that met on September 25 further consolidated the amendments so that only twelve were left. The first two, concerning the number and salaries of congressmen, were never ratified; the other ten, known as the Bill of Rights, became part of the Constitution on December 15, 1791.

The next great legislative task—taken up after but completed before the drafting of the Bill of Rights—was also constitutional in nature, namely the creation of the executive departments. On May 19 Congressman Elias Boudinot of New Jersey opened the subject, but Madison soon took charge of the debate. It was readily agreed that three departments were necessary and that they should comprehend the same activities as the earlier administrative arms of the Confederation: Foreign Affairs, War, and Finance.

Only three serious issues arose during the debate. One surfaced when John Vining of Delaware proposed that a Home Department be created, to exercise general supervision over the records of the government, relations with the states, establishment of post roads, the census, western territories, patents, geographical surveys, and similar matters. Vining received little support and was barraged by some who argued that the functions should not be exercised and by others who held that they should be assigned to the three great departments. By and large, the latter group prevailed; not for many years would the various domestic departments begin to materialize.

A second and much more delicate matter concerned the Treasury Department. First a group of arch-republicans, led by Elbridge Gerry, expressed great concern at the enormous power that would be lodged in the department and proposed to render the power safe by vesting it in a three-man board (as the arrangement had been since 1784) rather than in a single secretary. Tempers flashed hot; it was really a renewal of an old controversy, that between those who had supported Robert Morris as superintendent of finance in 1781–1783 and those who had almost hysterically opposed Morris's administration. That controversy, in turn, had arisen from conflicts of personalities and interests as well as of principles and had pitted the Lee-Adams "junto" of Virginia and Massachusetts against Philadelphia and New York.

The advocates of a single secretary prevailed by a handful of votes, but the uneasiness aroused by the debate led to another decision that was of great consequence in both the short range and the long. Bit by bit, as the subject arose intermittently in the early summer, the House began to add restrictions on the powers of the secretary of the treasury—not to reduce his powers, but to tie them to the House instead of to the independent executive authority. The design was to curtail the executive and aggrandize the House. The effect, as things worked out, was to plunge the Treasury Department into the most important activities of Congress. Indeed, the way was unwittingly paved for a brilliant and energetic secretary of the treasury to become, for practical purposes, an American "prime minister," even as the chancellor of the exchequer served that function in Britain.

The third subject of dispute, the removal power of the president, has already been mentioned. Fear of executive power was widespread and strong. Repeatedly, the more cautious congressmen warned that some powers which might be safely entrusted to Washington were dangerous in principle, for Washington could not live forever, and that it was best to err now on the side of checking presidential authority by making it subject to senatorial approval. Madison and others in what might have been styled the "court party" argued persuasively that if the president could not remove appointees without the permission of the Senate, appointees would serve for "good behaviour" or even life, since the only other way of removing them was the cumbersome impeachment process. Doubtless a few congressmen supported Madison out of jealousy of the Senate's powers. In any event, the principle of unilateral executive removal of executive appointees passed the House by a margin of six or seven votes in each of the bills creating executive offices. When the Senate approved the House measures in July (apparently, more than once by a tie vote broken by the vice president), the principle became a part of established constitutional custom. Along the way, it was also established that clerical and other "inferior" personnel could even be appointed without the Senate's approval, by the president or by the heads of departments.

The bills establishing the departments were enacted in the late summer. The Department of Foreign Affairs (redesignated the State Department on September 15) was created by law on July 27, the War Department on August 7, the Treasury Department on September 2. In addition, Congress also provided for two federal agencies that had less than departmental status. It established the office of attorney general, wherein a lawyer was to be placed on retainer to advise the president on matters of constitutionality and law, and the office of postmaster general, which was to oversee the execution of the Constitution's mandate that Congress establish post offices and post roads.

As the summer of 1789 progressed and as these various enactments became law, President Washington found himself with almost a thousand offices to fill. Several times that number of applicants for jobs besieged him, directly or through intermediaries, but Washington scrupulously declined to exploit the opportunity to develop a system of patronage. Only in one special sense were his appointments partisan: he appointed only persons "of known attachment to the Government we have chosen"—that is, he refused to appoint anyone who was a known enemy of the Constitution.

In screening applicants for the minor jobs, he generally followed one of three rules of thumb. The first was a reflection of the aristocratic lifestyle: if Washington did not know the candidate personally, he made inquiries until he found a trusted acquaintance who did; and no appointment was forthcoming unless someone Washington trusted attested to the applicant's good character. The second was that Washington allowed his upper-level appointees to choose their own immediate inferiors. The third rule was one imposed upon Washington against his will, the practice that came to be called "senatorial courtesy." The president nominated Benjamin Fishbourne to be naval officer of the port of Savannah, but when Georgia Senators James Gunn and William Few objected, the Senate, on the strength of their preferences alone, refused to confirm the appointment. Washington was miffed, but he withdrew the nomination, and subsequently it became regular practice to appoint no one to whom the appointee's senators personally objected.

In making the major appointments, Washington consulted with several intimates, notably Madison, and considered the matter carefully. For secretary of state, the position generally regarded as the most prestigious, he preferred John Jay; but Jay indicated that he wanted to be chief justice, and Washington granted his wish. Instead, to head the State Department, Washington chose Thomas Jefferson, who was on his way to Virginia on leave from his post as minister to France. Henry Knox was continued in the War Department, and at Madison's urging, Washington named his former aide-de-camp, Alexander Hamilton, to be secretary of the treasury. Rounding out the major appointments, Edmund Randolph of Virginia became attorney general, and Samuel Osgood of Massachusetts became postmaster general.

As to setting the executive departments into operation, three general philosophies of public administration—indeed three different philosophies regarding the proper nature of the presidency—were advanced. One was that held by a number of senators and others who believed the Senate should be the repository of power for a strong aristocracy, namely, that the Senate should serve as the president's executive council and, as had been the tradition with the upper houses of several colonial governments, exercise a full share of the executive authority. Washington was temperamentally opposed to such an arrangement, and any doubts he may have held were dispelled by the fiasco of seeking advise and consent from the Senate in person. Moreover, Madison's efforts in working out the laws establishing the departments were carefully designed to minimize the Senate's influence in the executive branch—in matters of administrative detail as well as such broader questions as the power of removal.

A second view, more subtle and more complex, is most closely identifiable with Alexander Hamilton. Hamilton preferred an executive branch modeled after that of Great Britain, where the ministers (including heads of departments), acting in the name of the Crown, in fact constituted "the Government." Such a ministry would not only implement policy, as defined by Congress, but would initiate policy as well, both by exercising an independent administrative power and by drafting legislation and guiding it through Congress. Hamilton's position ran counter to the ideas of both Washington and Madison, and decisions

Washington "very "hands on"

made before Hamilton took office prevented him from fully implementing his ideas. Nonetheless, the nature of Hamilton's responsibilities, carried out in the context of the administrative system that Washington chose to put into force, partially permitted Hamilton to have his way.

The view that prevailed was Washington's own, that executive authority was solely the president's, that the Senate had no share in it beyond that of approving or rejecting his appointments and treaties, and that department heads were responsible directly to him. Not even Hamilton settled any matter of consequence without consulting Washington and obtaining his approval, and all department heads submitted matters of both detail and administrative policy to him. In turn, Washington expected departmental subordinates to be responsible to their heads in just the way the heads were responsible to the president.

Administration was therefore highly personal, after the fashion of the pre-bureaucratic eighteenth-century world. That is to say, subordinate officials normally did not act in accordance with rules or objectively defined codes of procedure, but in accordance with the direct instructions of their immediate superiors. To be sure, it became necessary in carrying out many of the routine activities of the Treasury Department, such as the acceptance of merchants' bonds for the payment of customs duties, to work out strict and uniform procedures, and Hamilton labored effectively to systematize all such activities. But in general, administration was ad hoc and personal; and thus, for example, Congress normally voted money in lump appropriations to the several departments, leaving the administrators a wide latitude of discretion in the actual spending. Washington personally decided how much to pay American ministers abroad, and department heads and even their subordinates often spent money for one purpose when Congress clearly had intended that it be spent for another.

In day-to-day practice, Washington supervised the activities of his department heads closely. In keeping with the Constitution's stricture that the president could seek their opinions *in writing,* he kept them all busy penning reports on matters he had referred to their attention, opinions of proposed plans of action, judgments of the constitutionality of legislation, drafts of his public papers, and compendiums of information. Commonly, moreover, after an exchange of letters Washington would invite the subordinate to breakfast, where discussion would go on until the president was perfectly satisfied.

Jefferson's description of the way the system worked is an excellent one:

Letters of business came addressed sometimes to the President, but most frequently to the heads of departments. If addressed to himself, he referred them to the proper department to be acted on; if to one of the secretaries, the letter, if it required no answer, was communicated to the President, simply for his information. If an answer was requisite, the secretary of the department communicated the letter & his proposed answer to the President. Generally they were simply sent back after perusal, which signified his approbation. Sometimes he returned them with an informal note, suggesting an alteration or a query. If a doubt of any importance arose, he reserved it for conference. By this means, he was always in accurate possession of all facts and proceedings in every part of the Union, and to whatsoever department they related; he formed a central point for the different branches; preserved an unity of object and action among them; exercised that participation in the suggestion of affairs made incumbent on him; and met himself the due responsibility for whatever was done. . . . [Washington's system] gave, indeed, to the heads of departments the trouble of making up, once a day, a packet of all their communications for the perusal of the President; it commonly also retarded one day their despatches by mail. But in pressing cases, this injury was prevented by presenting that case singly for immediate attention; and it produced us in return the benefit of his sanction for every act we did.

Some variations in the routine arose from differences in the talents and temperaments of the administrators. In affairs of the State Department, Washington believed himself an expert; and in the affairs of the War Department he unquestionably was an expert; and thus he was in practice his own foreign secretary and war secretary, Jefferson and Knox often being reduced virtually to clerical roles. Jefferson, who was not at all fond of clerical work, was not always as diligent an administrator as he might have been. Given a free hand on a subject that interested him, he worked promptly and thoroughly; but if he was given only a passive role or (as increasingly happened as time went by) Washington adopted policies that he disagreed with, Jefferson tended to obstruct things through studied lackadaisicalness. Knox was a diligent administrator who loved his work and loved his boss, never initiated or questioned anything, and executed orders with promptness and dispatch. Hamilton, on the other hand, was an expert on finance and commerce, matters clearly beyond Washington's ken and outside his area of interest. Necessarily, Hamilton had a freer rein than did his colleagues. But what was more, Hamilton was hyperenergetic, impatient, and a compulsive meddler; and he often took the liberty, when policies in the province of the War or State departments were of interest to him, of attempting to initiate policy by preparing unsolicited position papers for the president's attention and even by making private commitments that Washington was unaware of.

In regard to the Post Office Department, Congress kept the power of laying out post roads for itself, despite Federalist efforts to vest it in the president; and since Washington was not especially interested in the department anyway, its affairs drifted without presidential direction. Timothy Pickering, who succeeded Osgood as postmaster general, went so far in the discretionary exercise of authority as to drop the customary practice of advertising for bids for mail contractors, until Congress made the practice mandatory in 1792. Postmasters were appointed by the postmaster general, not the president, and were almost never removed from office.

The last grand constitutional task of the First Congress, that of creating the federal judiciary, was the only one carried out by the Senate. It was also the most complex, for it involved the settlement of knotty problems on three essentially unrelated levels: legal, ideological, and economic. In all three areas Senator Oliver Ellsworth took the lead and, with assistance from Senator William Paterson of New Jersey, was largely responsible for the outcome of the debate.

The legal problems were awesome. Anglo-Saxon jurisprudence, from which American law and legal procedures were derived, was itself a maze, involving as it did common law, equity, chancery, and statutory law as well as a myriad of both local and special variations. American law was Anglo-Saxon law compounded by a factor of thirteen. To cite but one relatively simple example, in regard to the manner of directing new trials when an appellate court found something wrong with the way a lower court had conducted a trial, New York, New Jersey, and Virginia followed the procedures of British common law; Massachusetts had long since worked out a different system and had recently confirmed that system by statute; Connecticut was in process of devising a new and especially fuzzy system.

Ellsworth, a man of limited formal training but great common sense and a most diligent and energetic student, had briefed himself as thoroughly on legal procedures as Madison had on bills of rights. He also drew from Paterson, tough minded and thoroughly trained, and Caleb Strong of Massachusetts, fairly short on intellect but long on training and experience. When their combined knowledge was not enough, Ellsworth simply incorporated Connecticut practice into the bill for the national judiciary or invented a commonsense procedure of his own. In the doing, he had the advantage of minimal political opposition to this aspect of the work. Senator Maclay and a few others grumbled, in accordance with an attitude that was widespread in New England and in the back country elsewhere, that the lawyers were making things unnecessarily complicated so as to preserve a secure and comfortable living for themselves; but such prejudice occasioned little opposition in Congress.

Ideological differences, on the other hand, were much less easily resolved. The basic issue in question was fairly simple: how far the power of federal courts should overshadow that of state courts. Extreme nationalists wanted to create a full network of federal courts, to endow them with as much power as the Constitution allowed, and to minimize the powers of the state courts. Extreme states' righters wanted to confine the Supreme Court to the narrow original jurisdiction prescribed by the Constitution, to vest it with as little appellate jurisdiction as possible, and to deposit most of the judicial power in the existing state courts.

Neither view was likely to prevail, but compromise would be difficult. Archfederalists feared state legislatures as the most dangerous enemies of union, but those who were trained in the law viewed the state courts with scarcely less anxiety. As for the anti-Federalists, the great republican orator Patrick Henry had predicted that the national government would swallow up the states and that the main agent of the devouring would be the federal judiciary; and his personal representatives in the Senate, Richard Henry Lee and William Grayson, echoed that sentiment.

Faced with such opposition, Ellsworth produced some creative innovations. He proposed that there be, in addition to a six-member Supreme Court, one district court for each state. The district courts would be federal, but the judges had to be residents of the state from which they were appointed. That insured the following of traditional local procedures except when different procedures were carefully specified by national law, and thus imposed little that was alien upon local lawyers. Moreover, Ellsworth and his associates proposed the creation of circuit courts, to consist of two traveling members of the Supreme Court and the district-court judge in the state in which trials were held, the main function of the district judge being to make sure that trials were conducted according to local rules. Finally, Ellsworth proposed to arrange jurisdictions so that in many cases state courts would have concurrent jurisdiction with federal courts, the sanctity of the Constitution being preserved by provision for direct appeal to the United States Supreme Court when the constitutionality of state law was in question. Such a mixture of jurisdic-

tions confounded the enemy, and Ellsworth's court structure passed the Senate by a 14 to 6 vote and the House by 29 to 22.

The complexities underlying the judicial act in its third aspect, the conflict of economic-interest groups, were so tangled as to make the legal and ideological problems seem simple by comparison. Those involving maritime law, admiralty courts, and similar commercial matters—which anyone learned in British law might have expected to occasion difficulties—were solved with surprisingly little friction. What was less simple was the matter of conflicting claims to land titles.

These conflicts were long in developing. Before the end of the seventeenth century, Americans had begun to realize that the great wealth to be reaped in their continent lay neither in farming for market nor in trade and shipping, but in acquiring large tracts of vacant land and selling it at a profit to newcomers from Europe. That land could be bought and sold like any other commodity was itself a departure from the European norm, and it was bound to have legal and political repercussions. By the 1730s political factions had begun to form in Massachusetts, Pennsylvania, Maryland, and Virginia, with rivalry over land grants and the means of paying for them as their base. By the 1750s and 1760s such rivalries were setting off conflicts that would (in conjunction with other forces) lead to revolution. During the Revolution and under the Confederation, conflicts over land claims were among the few genuinely vital determinants of political positions. In sum, for nearly a century the questions of "home rule, and who should rule at home," to employ Carl Becker's celebrated phrase, had had meaning largely in terms of the unspoken question, "Who shall have control over land grants?"

That was the larger background. The more immediate background had to do with the recent formation of large companies and groups of powerful individual speculators to obtain huge tracts of the public domain—lands acquired by the United States or by individual states as a result of the Revolution. In 1787 the Ohio Company (originally consisting of investors from Connecticut, Massachusetts, and Rhode Island, but ultimately consisting almost exclusively of Connecticutters) had arranged for the purchase from Congress of a million acres of land on the Ohio River at less than a dollar an acre and payable in public securities at their par value, though these bonds could be acquired from individual owners at less than twenty cents on the dollar. In 1788 a group of New Jersey investors, calling themselves the Miami Company, arranged a similar purchase. In 1789 the legislature of Georgia succumbed to large-scale bribery and made its first sales of "Yazoo Lands" (in what became Alabama and Mississippi) to outsiders for a nominal price. In the "western reserve" of Pennsylvania, claimed by Connecticut, dubious sales were also made. In the "triangle" of western New York, northwestern Pennsylvania, and the northeastern portion of the Ohio country, Oliver Phelps and Nathaniel Gorham purchased a huge tract, and it was rumored that every influential New England politician was in on the deal. New York and Pennsylvania speculator-politicians—including William Bingham, William Constable, Secretary of War Henry Knox, and Senator Robert Morris—negotiated and concluded a number of large-scale deals for acquisition of lands owned or claimed by individual states.

The Constitution potentially gave the federal courts jurisdiction over all the litigation that would arise from these various grants. Oliver Ellsworth and William Paterson, as investors in two of the companies that were sure to become involved in litigation, had an interest in seeing to it that jurisdiction was in fact lodged in the federal courts, for they, like other Connecticut and New Jersey investors, purchased directly from the federal government. After the Ohio Company and the Miami Company purchases, most speculators bought from state governments with rival claims and figured to fare better in the courts of the states from which they made their purchases. In short, it was as important to land buyers before 1789 that claims be adjudicated in federal courts as it was important to subsequent buyers that claims be decided in state courts. The judiciary act of 1789, as devised by Ellsworth and Paterson in the Senate and as defended by Roger Sherman

of Connecticut in the House, loaded the deck in favor of federal adjudication.

Despite the narrow considerations upon which the judiciary bill turned, however, it was passed into law and became, for practical purposes, a part of the Constitution itself. As things worked out, the Supreme Court did not become especially important either during Washington's presidency or during that of his successor. Washington's appointments to the bench were distinguished enough: Jay as Chief Justice and, as associate justices, John Rutledge of South Carolina, James Iredell of North Carolina, John Blair of Virginia, James Wilson of Pennsylvania, and William Cushing of Massachusetts. But with few exceptions, the court was not called upon to adjudicate the pressing issues that faced the nation in the 1790s, and much of the time of the justices was taken up with the tedious, onerous, and largely fruitless business of "riding circuit." Moreover, when the court did begin to become important, it came under political attack, and demagogues ever after would exploit popular prejudice to attack the system on one pretense or another. And yet, despite revisions in 1801, 1802, and occasionally thereafter, the system created by Oliver Ellsworth and his associates and allies in 1789 would endure.

Congress adjourned on September 29, and then everyone—or almost everyone—took a breather. Congressmen went home to rest, congratulate themselves, tend to private business, and scheme for the second session, convening on January 4. Washington set off on a triumphal tour of the New England states.

The one man for whom there could be no rest was Hamilton. In keeping with Madison's plan to make the Treasury Department subordinate to the House of Representatives, the House instructed Hamilton to make a survey of the public debts and come up, by the time Congress reconvened, with a plan for servicing them.

The assignment was herculean, but Hamilton did it. In the doing, something quite unexpected took place: Madison's scheme backfired, for Hamilton himself emerged as the most powerful man in the government.

STUDY QUESTIONS

1. What role did George Washington play in launching the new national government? What problems did this new entity encounter in 1789?

2. What immediate financial problems did the new government face, and what were some of the solutions policymakers arrived at to solve these problems?

3. What current practices or institutional arrangements in the federal government can you find precedents for in the events of 1789?

4. What did James Madison do in 1789 that made him the "man of the hour"? What political issues rising from the American Revolution surfaced in Madison's proposed "bill of rights"?

5. How were the executive departments organized, and how were employees chosen and paid in these new positions? Whose view of executive department organization prevailed, and what was that view?

6. Who was most responsible for organizing the federal judiciary? How was it organized, and why is it important? Why did contemporaries think it was important?

BIBLIOGRAPHY

Forrest McDonald is a noted historian of America's early national period; a good place to start reading about this era would be the study from which this chapter was drawn, Forrest McDonald, *The Presidency of George Washington* (1974). For a larger view of the period, the best single-volume survey of American politics in the late 1780s and the 1790s is probably Stanley Elkins and Eric McKitrick, *The Age of Federalism: The Early American Republic, 1788–1800* (1993). A somewhat different reading of the political philosophies employed by men like Jefferson, Madison, Adams, and Hamilton comes from Drew R. McCoy, *The Elusive Republic: Political Economy in Jeffersonian America* (1980). And finally, crucial to understanding the social context of these political debates is the Pulitzer-Prize winning study by Gordon S. Wood, *The Radicalism of the American Revolution* (1991). Besides historical monographs such as those above, one of the best ways to truly understand an historical era—and especially its politics—is to read biographies of the major players. Excellent one-volume biographies of the most prominent personalities in this reading include Forrest McDonald, *Alexander Hamilton: A Biography* (1979); Merrill Peterson, *Thomas Jefferson and the New Nation: A Biography* (1970); Peter Shaw, *The Character of John Adams* (1976); and Drew R. McCoy, *The Last of the Fathers: James Madison and the Republican Legacy* (1989).

"BUT A COMMON MAN" : DANIEL BOONE

John Mack Faragher

For generations historians portrayed Anglo-Americans' drive westward as the spread of civilization. These historians perceived a neat frontier line. On one side of the line were the fruits of European society—Christianity, refined behavior, written records, and rule by law. On the other side lurked danger and savagery—untamed lands, wild animals, and blood-thirsty Indians. Today no serious historian would ascribe to such glib and misleading stereotypes. The neat frontier line never existed; complex Native American and European civilizations flourished throughout America, mixing with each other in an area best described as a "middle ground" to create new hybrid cultures. In the late-eighteenth and early-nineteenth centuries the middle ground was the huge territory between the Appalachian Mountains and the Mississippi River. There Native Americans and European Americans negotiated and traded, formed alliances, and fought battles. Each took and gave, influencing and being influenced by the other. Hunters from both cultures dressed in composite European and Indian styles—moccasins, linen or deerskin hunting shirts, often even breechcloths. Like the Native Americans, European-American hunters wore their hair long and swept it back with bear grease; like the English and French Americans, Native Americans prized European rifles and iron goods. Both groups valued freedom and independence and were loyal to their families and clans.

The most famous European American of the middle ground was Daniel Boone, a Quaker born in Pennsylvania who drifted steadily westward. A man full of contradictions, whose fame grew even after he died, Boone's life demonstrated the dangers and joys of the middle ground. A man who had a deep respect for Native Americans, he nevertheless epitomized the movement of people that ultimately destroyed a way of life.

During the years preceding Daniel Boone's death in 1820 at age nearly eighty-six, a stream of visitors beat a path to the door of the woodsman's Missouri home—"induced by curiosity to visit this extraordinary person."

"Seeing strangers approaching," the aged frontiersman would, as his son Nathan re-called, "take his cane and walk off to avoid them," but if cornered, he usually agreed to talk. "Though at first reserved and barely answering questions," remembered one such visitor, Boone "soon became communicative, warmed up, and became animated in narrating his early adventures in the West."

"Many heroic actions and chivalrous adventures are related of me," the modest living legend would declare, "yet I have been but a common man."

Both extraordinary and common—this is but one of many paradoxes that distinguish the life and character of Daniel Boone, the prototype in American lore of the wilderness-ranging frontiersman. Contradictions—both within Boone himself and between the man and the legend that grew to overshadow him—abound:

Within his own lifetime Boone was elevated to near-mythic stature as a renowned hunter and Indian fighter. Yet he had been raised to honor a code of Quaker tolerance, and he objected to his notoriety for Indian-killing.

Boone was a devoted son, husband, and father, and throughout his life he treasured a close-knit community of kith and kin. Yet he often left home and family for months (even years) at a stretch to hunt and trap in the solitude of the western forests—in the process acquiring a reputation as a "natural man" of the woods or misanthrope who longed for "elbow room."

"But A Common Man" by John Mack Faragher. This article is reprinted from the November/December 1992 issue, Volume XXVII/No. 5, pp. 28-37, 66-70, 73 of *American History Illustrated* with the permission of Cowles History Group, Inc. Copyright *American History Illustrated* magazine.

Boone was a courageous frontier leader of the American Revolution; yet many fellow officers and soldiers suspected him of harboring loyalty to the crown and treasonous sympathy for England's Native American allies.

And, though Boone described himself as a simple woodsman, in midlife he strove mightily to transform himself into a man of property and standing.

These contradictions may be explained in part both by the scanty documentary record of the frontiersman's life and by the extent to which the real Boone quickly became obscured by folklore and legend. Fundamentally, however, the complexity the Boone's character itself was what allowed Americans to imagine him in so many guises.

The quintessential frontier hero was born on October 22, 1734 in a log house in the upper Schuylkill River valley of Pennsylvania. The son of English Quaker emigrants—Squire and Sarah Morgan Boone—he grew up surrounded by family. The farm of his father was bounded by the land of Daniel's aunts and uncles, and nearby was the stone house and gristmill of his grandfather, the patriarch of the clan and local justice of the peace. The Boones were prominent members of the Society of Friends in the township of Exeter, and Squire was an overseer of the brown-stone meeting house, situated on land donated by the family. Here Daniel was, in the words of his son Nathan, "reared under the peaceful influence of the Quaker faith."

Family stories depict a happy household that included eleven rambunctious children. Sixth-born Daniel was responsible for his share of pranks—including dismantling meddlesome neighbors' wagons and hanging the wheels from barn roofs or treetops.

When Squire Boone felt compelled to discipline his boys for such misdeeds, his policy was to beat them only until their first cry, then put down his rod to reason with them, Quaker fashion. But the technique never worked with Daniel, who always endured his punishment in silence. One old tale has Squire "wishing to gain his point in government," appealing to Daniel: "'Canst thou not beg?' But he could not beg, leaving his anxious parent to close the matter at his pleasure."

Thus the stubborn youth missed the opportunity for his father's embrace—an estrangement that in later years would haunt him. After Squire's death in 1765, Daniel frequently dreamed of his father. On several occasions he imagined an angry confrontation with no reconciliation; disaster, he told his children later, invariably followed these visions.

Daniel came by his independent streak quite naturally; his father was equally stubborn and headstrong. In 1747 the Exeter Quaker meeting reprimanded Squire for allowing his eldest son to marry a "worldling"—the second instance in which one of his children had wed outside the circle of Friends. Previously the senior Boone had promised "to be more careful for the future," but this time he was defiant. After repeated attempts to bring squire "to a Sense of his Error," the meeting finally expelled him.

Squire Boone's withdrawal from the central institution of community life surely wrought considerable conflict for Daniel, who continued to attend Quaker meetings with his mother. But Squire's defiance encouraged Daniel's own quest for independence. Boone once professed that he had "always loved God ever since I recollect," but after his youth he never again joined a church.

In addition to raising a large brood of children, Daniel's Welsh mother Sarah Morgan Boone managed the family garden, hen house, and dairy. One of Boone's fondest memories of his childhood was of spending each "grass season" with her at a distant pasture, tending the cows while she milked and churned, then listening to her sing before the open fire. He fashioned a wooden shaft that he called his "herdsman's club," and with it killed small game for their supper.

Those memorable sojourns molded Boone's life course. His "love for the wilderness and hunter's life," Daniel later stated, began with "being a herdsman and thus being so much in the woods." Growing increasingly found of solitude he took to remaining at the meadow after his

mother returned home with her season's bounty of butter and cheese.

When Boone was twelve or thirteen, his father gave him a "short rifle gun." Roaming pasture and wood, the youth developed into an excellent marksman. It was common for him to be gone for several days, then to appear at the cabin door with meat enough to supply the family for a week. Thus did the strapping boy find resolution for his adolescent tensions, spending less time at home where the strong wills of father and son collided, and more time in the woods, a domain he identified with his beloved mother.

In those years, the Pennsylvania backcountry was the most peaceful of North American frontiers. Quaker authorities organized no militia or army, negotiated with indigenous peoples over the titles to land, and promised natives "the full and free privileges and Immunities of all the Said Laws as any other Inhabitants." Attracted by these policies, a number of Native American groups, whose homelands had been disrupted by the reverberating effects of colonization, relocated to Penn's Woods. Numerous communities of Delawares, Shawnees, and other native peoples settled within twenty or thirty miles of the Boone farm. Grandfather Boone often befriended native hunters who passed through the neighborhood, and Daniel had ample opportunity to see and meet the peoples of many tribes.

In this mixed cultural world young Boone found his teachers in woodcraft—both Europeans and Native Americans—who instructed him in the hunting way of life. On the frontier, males of both native and European cultures sought meat, hides, and furs for subsistence and trade, while the women raised corn and tended hogs and cattle. The American long rifle, developed by the German gunsmiths of southeastern Pennsylvania, served both cultures as well, as did native calls, disguises, decoys, surrounds, and fire hunts. Hunters adopted a composite of frontier clothing: deerskin moccasins, breechclouts, and leggings in combination with linen hunting shirts and beaver hats. Although some Americans wore fur caps, Boone despised their un-

Portrait of Daniel Boone.

and grandchildren. Daniel acted as hunter and guide as the family followed the Virginia Road down the Shenandoah Valley, the first of many highways that would lead Americans to the beckoning western country.

Daniel by now had nearly attained his adult stature and physique—five-feet-eight-inches in height, with broad shoulders and chest, muscular arms, and thick legs. A friend later described him as "a sort of pony-built man," a bit undersized but as strong as a horse. He bore pronounced facial features: a high forehead and heavy brow, prominent cheekbones, a tight wide mouth, and long, slender nose. He inherited his father's penetrating blue-gray eyes and ruddy complexion, but had his mother's dark hair, which he always kept "plaited and clubbed" in Native American fashion.

Within a year or two, the Boones were plowing the red clay at the Forks of the Yadkin River in North Carolina. But this agrarian life held few attractions for Daniel. "He never took any delight in farming," recalled a nephew, and Boone himself admitted to his children that while working his father's fields he would pray for rain, and if the storms came, he grabbed his rifle and headed for the woods—"and though the rain would cease in an hour, yet he was so fond of gunning, he would be sure to remain out till evening."

By age eighteen Boone had become a professional hunter, and during the next several years he established a reputation as a marksman. Legend claims that Bear Creek on the Yadkin took its name from the season Daniel shot ninety-nine bears along its waters; he and a companion also are credited with once downing thirty dear between sunup and sundown. The young woodsman competed eagerly at shooting matches, always scoring and sometimes employing his favorite trick shot in which he used only one of his powerful arms to support and fire his long rifle. Then, as one woman recalled, he would strut before the other competitors, "pat them on the shoulders, and tell them they couldn't shoot up to Boone."

When war threatened between England and France, twenty-year-old Boone signed on as a

couth look and always stuck with his Quaker-style beaver.

Boone made this way of life his own during his youth in Pennsylvania, growing in his understanding of the ways of the woods and native culture. But he retained a Quaker approach: "Always meet [Indians] frankly and fearlessly," he advised, and "by kind acts and just treatment, keep on the friendly side of them." This simple code of conduct, he declared, insured that when forced to "seek refuge with my deadliest foes and trust to their magniminity," his native hosts would be "kind and generous in their intercourse with me."

In 1750, soon after his expulsion from the meeting, Squire Boone moved his family south, seeking good land on which to settle his children

teamster with a military company headed north to join British General Edward Braddock. On July 9, 1755, near present Pittsburgh, French and Native American forces ambushed Braddock's column, killing or wounding more than nine hundred of the nearly fourteen hundred British and American troops. Steadying his team at the rear, Boone heard the cry of battle and saw men falling; with the panicked retreat of the survivors he jumped onto his lead horse, slashed its harness free, and galloped away in terror.

An equally perilous encounter took place only a day or two later, when Boone made his way back alone to his Quaker relations in Exeter. As the woodsman crossed the bridge over the gorge of the Juniata River, a big, inebriated Native American suddenly confronted him. "He drew his knife on me," Boone remembered years later, "flourishing it over his head, boasting that he had killed many a Long Knife, and would kill some more on his way home." Unable to avoid a fight as the man lurched toward him, Boone drove his shoulder under his assailant's ribs, catapulting him off his feet and over the side of the bridge to the jagged rocks forty feet below.

Boone related this tale to an admiring group of visitors shortly before his death. In truth, he complained of his reputation as an Indian fighter, "I never killed but three," of which the man lying dead on the rocks was the first. "I am very sorry to say that I ever killed any," he said, "for they have always been kinder to me than the whites."

In the summer of 1756, the year following his return from the war, Boone began to court his future bride. Although no likeness of Rebecca Bryan Boone exists, contemporary descriptions endow her with jet-black hair and dark, penetrating eyes. Rebecca made her first appearance in Boone folklore as "a buxom daughter," and one of her nephews called her "a rather over common sized woman." In fact, in midlife Rebecca stood nearly as tall and broad as her husband, and she could handle a gun or an axe as well as many men. Yet Boone always called her "my little girl," reflecting back, perhaps, on his first sight of her when she was scarcely fifteen.

Boone likely won his future bride's devotion in part through his wit. In one family tale, Daniel, in order to demonstrate his skills as a provider, brings a deer to Rebecca's house. He dresses the carcass outdoors while she cooks him a first meal at the hearth. Without thought, the young hunter then joins the family at the table, his shirt still bloody from his task. The daughters of the relatively well-to-do Bryans ridicule the suitor for this social blunder, but according to the story Boone quickly evens the score by examining his cup and declaring, "You, like me hunting shirt, have missed many a good washing."

Daniel was twenty-one and Rebecca seventeen when the couple married in August 1756. When they took up residence in a cabin owned by Daniel's father, Rebecca found herself mistress of a household that included two of Boone's orphaned nephews. The couple's firstborn, a son, arrived nine months later.[*]

For the first seventeen years of their lives together, the Boones lived in obscurity in the Yadkin valley of North Carolina. To support his growing family, Boone intensified his hunting and trapping, each winter going on a "long hunt" for deerskins and beaver pelts, and gradually shifting his range westward to the Blue Ridge mountains and the valleys beyond. Frequently he was joined by other men from the Yadkin country, but Boone preferred hunting by himself. He would construct a little "half-faced camp"—a three-sided shanty covered with brush, with the open end facing the campfire—and there take his evening meals. He usually carried a Bible, or a book of history (which he loved), or *Gulliver's Travels* (his favorite), to read by the firelight. Then he bedded down on a cushion of hemlock or dried leaves, his feet toward the fire to prevent the rheumatism that con-

---

[*]During the first quarter-century of the couple's marriage, Rebecca delivered ten children—six sons and four daughters. When the oldest children married, they often lived in Rebecca's household, adding grandchildren to the brood already in her care. And, following the death of Rebecca's widowed brother, the Boones also adopted and raised six more nephews and nieces.

stantly plagued old hunters, leaving his moccasins tied to his gun, which stood primed and ready.

Boone's love of solitude later was criticized as evidence of an antisocial nature. The woodsman's family responded defensively. "His wanderings were from duty," declared a niece after his death; "no man loved society better, nor was more ardently attached to his family." Rebecca, eulogized a granddaughter, was "the Companion of his toils, Pleasures, Sorrows for more than a half century," and Daniel "hardly Could live without her."

But outside the family others wondered why, if Boone could not live without Rebecca, he insisted on roaming away from her and the children for such long periods. After Daniel completed the spring plowing, it was Rebecca and the children who cropped the farm while he hunted. His neighbors whispered that Boone "wouldn't live at home" because he "didn't live happily with his family, [and] didn't like to work."

This gossip found a focus in an oft-repeated story that during one of Boone's long absences Rebecca bore an illegitimate child. When the woodsman returns home, so goes the tale, Rebecca meets him at the cabin door, weeping. "What's the matter," asks Boone. "You were gone so long," she replies, "[that] we had supposed you dead." In her sorrow Rebecca has found company with another man, and now there is a new baby in the house. "Oh well," Boone is said to have responded after a pause, "the race will be continued."

But that is only part of the confession: Rebecca admits that the baby's father is Boone's own brother—he "looked so much like Daniel," she confesses, that she "couldn't help it." This revelation, too, Boone is said to have taken in stride: "So much the better. It's all in the family."

The story cannot be taken as gospel, but combined with other circumstantial evidence it lends credence to the speculation that the Boones' daughter Jemima was conceived in 1762, when Daniel was absent on a two-year hunting and exploring expedition. This and other versions of the tale charitably conclude not by slandering the character of either Rebecca or Daniel, but instead by sympathizing with the plight of frontier women and by portraying Boone as a man of deliberation, slow to anger and ready to forgive.

In 1769, when Boone was in his mid-thirties, he led five other hunters across the Appalachian Mountains and into present-day Kentucky. In the Yadkin valley, as one of Boone's nephews put it, "game [had begun] to be scarce and harder to take." Like other hunter/farmers of his time and place, Boone required a freehold of fertile land large enough to settle his children and near enough to rich hunting territory to enable him to make his living. This long hunt, then, was also a land hunt.

After crossing the mountain barrier, Boone climbed a hill and "saw with pleasure the beautiful level of Kentucke," a fertile land of cane and clover, with forests where "we found everywhere abundance of wild beasts of every sort." It was exactly the kind of place for which he had been searching.

From their very first movement into Kentucky, however, the hunters were opposed by the Shawnees, who after their sojourn in Pennsylvania had returned West to farming communities north of the Ohio River. A Shawnee party discovered Boone and his companions with a six-months' accumulation of deerskins and confiscated the entire cache, as well as their horses and supplies. Probably because of Boone's straightforward manner, the Shawnees released the intruders unharmed, but left them with a warning: "Now brothers, go home and stay there. Don't come here any more, for this is the Indians' hunting ground, and all the animals, skins, and furs are ours. And if you are so foolish as to venture here again, you may be sure the wasps and yellow-jackets will sting you severely."

Boone ignored the admonition. Instead, he and his brother-in-law pursued the natives and stole back their horses—only to be recaptured. Finally they succeeded in escaping, but several weeks later Boone's companion disappeared, presumably the victim of native retribution.

Still Boone refused to leave Kentucky. Joined by his younger brother Squire Boone, Jr., the woodsman hunted and explored the region until the spring of 1771. But during their return east the brothers were overwhelmed by yet another party of Native Americans, who again relieved the hapless hunters of their catch.

Despite these setbacks, Boone returned to Kentucky during the winter of 1772–73. This time he found that he was not the only white visitor. Virginia land speculators had dispatched agents to survey large parcels along the Ohio River, and at least two parties found their way to the Kentucky River country where Boone had established his base camp. No white American, however, knew the region as well as Boone. When he recrossed the mountains in the spring, he knew that a western land rush was imminent, and he resolved that his family would be among the first settlers.

The following fall of 1773, Boone led the first attempt to plant an American settlement in Kentucky. The party of forty or fifty immigrants, including Rebecca and the children, brother Squire's family, and several members of the Bryan clan, traveled by pack train over the roughest of mountain trails. They got only as far as the white-cliffed eastern entrance to the Cumberland Gap, where natives ambushed the men herding cattle at the rear of the march, killing six, including the Boones' oldest son James, only sixteen.

Boone "felt worse than ever in his life," and the attack "discouraged the whole company." Concluding that it was too dangerous to proceed, the pioneers retreated back to the settlements of southwest Virginia. The encounter was the opening shot of what became known as Lord Dunmore's War, during which Boone distinguished himself as a popular leader of the Virginia defense against Mingo and Shawnee attacks.

A published report of the incident at the Cumberland Gap marked the first time Boone's name appeared in print. Soon it would be linked indelibly with the American struggle to wrest Kentucky from the Shawnees, a war that would continue for more than twenty years and claim the lives of thousands on both sides—including Boone's second-born son Israel, another of his brothers, and many kinfolk, neighbors, and comrades. It was the single bloodiest phase in the

three-century campaign for the conquest of North America.

Despite his deep personal losses, Boone never demonized his Native American opponents. He later characterized the origins of the conflict with candor: "We Virginians had for some time been waging a war of intrusion upon them. I, amongst the rest, rambled through the woods in pursuit of their race, as I now would follow the tracks of a ravenous animal." For their part, according to Boone, the natives "saw the approaching hour when the Long Knife would dispossess them of their desirable habitations," and they "determined utterly to extirpate the whites out of Kentucke." In Boone's view, war came not because Americans and Indians were so alien, but because the two races were competing for the same resources.

By the end of Lord Dunmore's War, Boone's name was well known all along the southern Appalachian frontier. Thus, when Richard Henderson, a North Carolina land speculator, organized a company to purchase from the Cherokees their rights to Kentucky, it was natural that he would ask Boone to direct the marking of a road over the mountains and the fortification of a town site. In exchange, Boone was to have his choice of two thousand acres of Kentucky land.

At Sycamore Shoals in March 1775, Henderson's "Transylvania Company" and a contingent of Cherokees negotiated the purchase of twenty million acres. Before Boone left the treaty grounds to begin marking the path later known as the wilderness Road, the old Cherokee chief Oconostota took him aside. "Brother," he said, grasping Boone's hand, "we have given you a fine land, but I believe you will have much trouble in settling it." The chief's words proved prophetic.

Trouble began soon after the roadmakers hacked a trace over the mountains. As they slept in their camp south of the Kentucky River, Native Americans fired on them, killing two men and wounding another.

Boone dashed off a message to Henderson, still east of the mountains with the main party. "The people are very uneasy, but are willing to stay and venture their lives with you," he wrote. "Now is the time to flusterate [the Indians'] intentions . . . and keep the country, whilst we are in it. If we give way to them now, it will ever be the case."

The dauntless frontiersman then led his men the final fifteen miles to a broad floodplain along the south side of the Kentucky River, where they established the settlement of Boonesborough. "It was owing to Boone's confidence in us, and the people's in him," Henderson later wrote, "that a stand was ever attempted."

Boone remained through the summer to begin construction of a fort, then returned east to bring his family over the mountains. "My wife and daughter," he declared with pride, were "the first white women that ever stood on the banks of Kentucke river."

With his family settled at Boonesborough, the woodsman had invested his all in the founding of an American community in Kentucky. By the end of 1775, a stream of settlers filed more than nine hundred claims to the land of the bluegrass, and Boonesborough was one of several expanding population centers. Henderson's Transylvania Company, however, soon disappeared, its title to the land (along with Boone's promised two thousand acres) ruled invalid by the government of Virginia, which assumed jurisdiction.

The Shawnees and Mingos continued to harass the settlement during the next year. The culmination of these raids came in July 1776 when five natives kidnapped Boone's thirteen-year-old daughter Jemima and two other girls. Boone, after two days of trailing the kidnappers, led an ambush of their camp that brilliantly succeeded in rescuing the girls unharmed. This dramatic episode, which James Fenimore Cooper later immortalized in *The Last of the Mohicans,* marked the *summum bonum* of Boone's reputation among his contemporaries.

With the American Revolution now under way in the east, the British engaged the western Indians in a strategy designed to demoralize the border settlements. Hard-hit by war parties, Kentucky settlers abandoned their outlying farms and sought refuge within Boonesborough's rough fortifications, swelling the population.

Forced to remain within the log walls, Boonesborough's inhabitants ran dangerously low on food by late 1777. The gravest problem was that they were "almost destitute of the necessary article of salt" required for preserving game. The supply was so exhausted by January 1778 that Boone was forced to risk leaving Boonesborough dangerously undermanned while he led a party of men to the springs on the Licking River to make salt.

Thus began the most controversial episode of Boone's life. While hunting to supply the saltmakers, he was captured by a large Shawnee war party, and to divert the natives' attention from the weakened settlement, agreed to surrender his twenty-nine men. They were taken to the Shawnee town of Chillicothe, north of the Ohio River.

About half of the Americans ended up as prisoners of the British, where they endured great suffering—some toiling at forced labor, others rotting in damp dungeons until the end of the Revolution. The rest, including Boone, were adopted into Shawnee families. Boone became *Sheltowee,* "Big Turtle," the son of Blackfish, a chief of the Chillicothe Shawnees.

Because of his familiarity with native ways, Boone, unlike most of his men, took well to life at Chillicothe. His apparent pleasure with his lot baffled many of the other white captives; but it was all part of his plan, he later explained: "always appearing as chearful and satisfied as possible," watching all the while for an opportunity to escape.

The stories that Boone later told his family about his captivity, however, suggest there was more to it than that. He became very attached to Blackfish and his family, who were "friendly and sociable and kind to him." Blackfish addressed Boone as "my son," and Boone described his native father as "one of Nature's noblemen."

Boone "completely deceived Blackfish and his simple-hearted people," doing everything he could to win their confidence. Gradually their trust increased to the point where Boone was allowed to hunt, and he was able to secrete a small cache of ammunition in the fold of his hunting shirt.

But Boone also deceived his own men, who suspected him of treason. Boone had consulted with the British commander, hunted with the Shawnee warriors, even lived in the lodge of Blackfish himself. When one of the saltmakers escaped and reached an American settlement, he claimed that "Boone was a Tory, and had surrendered them all up to the British, and taken the oath of allegiance to the British at Detroit."

In fact, some of Rebecca's people were Loyalists; this only aggravated Boone's cause. Tormented by gossip and fearing that her husband had been killed, in May she took the children back to North Carolina. When Boone finally made a heroic escape from the Shawnees in June 1778, he arrived at Boonesborough to find his family gone and the settlers sullen and suspicious.

He brought news that the Shawnees were planning a massive attack against the outpost. Whatever the settlers' feelings about him, he declared, they "must make what preperration they could" for "the Indeans would certainly be their in a few Days." When Blackfish's army of four hundred arrived, all Boonesborough watched suspiciously from the walls as Boone went out to parley with his Shawnee "father." Their apparently warm reunion panicked the settlers, who feared that Boone "intended to surrender the fort." Instead, he reported that Blackfish had proposed negotiations to avoid bloodshed. Stalling for time while awaiting reinforcements, the Kentuckians agreed to the proposal. Adopting a ruse similar to that employed by Boone at Chillicothe, they agreed to recognize the Ohio as a boundary, and both sides promised "allegiance to the King of Great Britain." Although "we could not avoid suspicions of the savages," as Boone put it, "the articles were formally agreed to and signed" with a good deal of ceremony. But neither the whites nor the Shawnees trusted their opponents, and both had instructed their marksmen to fire at the first sign of trouble. As the ceremony concluded, a scuffle broke out; in the ensuing confusion riflemen opened fire. The Kentucky negotiators succeeded in reaching the cover of the fort, and the siege of Boonesborough began.

Lasting eleven days, this battle has taken its place in American history as a classic confrontation between Indians and Americans. The Shawnees made several attempts to storm the walls, and failing this began to dig a tunnel to undermine the fort. On what became the final night of the siege, the Shawnees set up an intense barrage of covering fire as warriors ran forward with torches in an attempt to burn the walls. But this tactic cost them enormous casualties, and a heavy rain late in the evening put out the fires and collapsed their tunnel. Accepting failure, the Shawnees slipped away under night's cover; the siege had cost them thirty-seven men to two Kentuckians killed.

Boone was then charged with treason, and a formal court-martial produced testimony that the frontiersman "was in favour of the British government; all his conduct proved it." Boone repeated his explanation that he had surrendered his men to protect Boonesborough, where "the fort was in bad order and the Indeans would take it easy." The panel quickly rendered its verdict: "The court Marshall Deseded in Boon's favour," wrote an observer, "and they at that time advanced Boon to a Major."

Boone clearly not only had been acquitted but vindicated. Nevertheless, a whispered debate, of which he was painfully aware, continued for years. One Boonesborough woman, who admitted that she could "never bear an Indian's presence," gossiped that the Shawnees surrounding the fort had called often for Boone, and he "would rise up, and go out freely to and among the Indians; did so repeatedly." For her, it was Boone's obvious ease with the Shawnees that made him suspect. "Boone was willing and wished to surrender," she believed, and she taught her children that "Boone never deserved any thing of the country."

Boone, always hypersensitive to criticism, felt crushed by the mere fact of the accusations. After the siege, he never lived at Boonesborough again. "I am a Woodsman," Boone once wrote. When it came to money, he professed to be "ignorant [of] how to acquire it, except from the chase or by the regular fruits of honest industry." But after the Revolution, when all of Kentucky came down with the fever of land speculation, he put all his effort into becoming a successful businessman.

In 1783 Boone moved his family to the port of Limestone on the Ohio, where he kept a tavern, a store, and a warehouse, and engaged in river commerce. Putting to good use his knowledge of geography, he became one of the busiest of Kentucky surveyors. Without proper training or tools, men like Boone "shingled" tracts of land one atop the other in a confusing maze that kept generations of attorneys well fed. But he brought to his business dealings the same frank and open manner that made him a popular leader. "Sorry to here of the Dath of your brother," he wrote one of his clients, "however We must submit to providence, and provide for the Living, and talk of our Lands."

All the wealth he could accumulate he invested in land. It was an enterprise not a little like gambling, and for Boone and other small investors this was a game in which the house enjoyed an extraordinary advantage. A man risked his capital not at the close of the round, when title was granted, but at the opening bid, when he procured land certificates or warrants. Boone's total investment in warrants, certificates, and rights purchased from individuals during the 1780s was in the range of seven to ten thousand pounds. These entitled him to make entries on thousands of acres of land. An entry, however, was merely a claim on a particular tract and had to be defended through a torturous process of official survey and grant of patent. Were other claimants to demonstrate prior rights, or superior surveys shingling his tract, the entry was lost and with it the investment.

During the mid-1780s, according to Nathan Boone, his father "thought himself worth a fortune in the wild lands of the country." Public records indicate that Boone filed claims to at least thirty-nine thousand acres, which qualified him as one of the largest resident land speculators in Kentucky. His strategy was to enter all the claims he could afford, reasoning that this would offer him the best insurance against caveats, challenges, and failures. In fact, though many of the claims failed to prove up, his entries resulted in the eventual granting to him of more than twelve

thousand acres. This certainly was not the record of a man ignorant of the means of acquiring property. Boone knew what he was doing, though things did not turn out the way he planned.

"Little by little," said Nathan of his father, "his wealth melted away," the result of a number of factors. One of Boone's first priorities was to provide for his children, and while this cost him land, it certainly cannot be counted a loss. But Boone was as trusting as he was generous, and he often suffered as a result. "So confiding" was Boone, said Nathan, that he once stood as security for the five-hundred-pound debt of a man with whom he did business, then thought nothing of loaning him a horse, saddle, and bridle, and his only male slave, never considering that the man would use them to abscond. But he did, and Boone not only lost his property but had to pay off the obligation.

Boone lacked the ruthless instincts that speculation demanded. For him business obligations were personal matters, and doing the right thing frequently meant taking a financial loss. When he sold land, he usually bonded it against challenge, pledging to "forever Defend the land and premises hereby bargained." Unfortunately, many of his claims were faulty, and as a nephew put it. "Boone's honour compel'd him to pay up his bond while he owned one acre of land."

But these factors were really incidental to the failure of Boone's investment strategy itself. In the heavily speculative environment of Kentucky, Virginia decided to assess not merely lands held under title but land claims as well, and thus Boone's property taxes reflected a valuation of tens of thousands of acres. In order to hold onto his most valuable entries, he began to sell perfected titles to other tracts, often "for a trifle." In this manner Boone disposed of most of the land granted to him. Eventually he even began to sell his entries. In some cases, where his entries were threatened by shingled claims, he sold his interest at deep discount to speculators endeavoring to buy up all the competing claims. The failure of many of these claims meant the Boone frequently had to make good the losses, further increasing his need for cash. The speculative structure Boone had built soon collapsed of its own weight.

His entrance into the speculative world of business, Boone later said, "plunged him into difficulty" with the law, and legal matters soon began to consume most of his time and drive him to distraction. "I am to pay a Large sum of money at Cort on tusday Next," Boone wrote one of his clients, "I hope you will Come Down and satel on Monday Next at my house as I am very on well myself." From 1786 to 1789 he was a party to at least ten lawsuits. Men sued him for faulty surveys, for failed claims, for breech of contract, for the debts of his own and for the debts of others for whom he had posted bond. He lost most of these cases.

Authorities also called on Boone to testify in numerous other suits, usually asking him, as the surveyor, to identify corner trees or landmarks. The record books of Kentucky counties are filled with Boone depositions, and when one reviews the numerous cases it is easy to understand why his patience was tried. At the end of his testimony, the lawyer for the opposing side usually asked whether or not Boone stood to benefit by the outcome of the case. It was one of those pro-forma legal questions, but he always took it as an insinuation about his character. Was it not the case that the defendant had paid him a certain sum of money for his testimony, one lawyer inquired. He had "not received one shilling," Boone replied angrily, "nor was never offered any sum." Will you gain if the land claimed in this entry is saved, asked another lawyer. "Not a farthing!" Boone shot back. His testimony inevitably enraged those who lost their claims as a result, and Boone again began to fear the resentments of his neighbors. He told his children that his life had been threatened a number of times, and fearing assassination he hesitated to travel alone through the country. "Even in time of peace," he said sadly, "his own Kentucky was as dangerous to him as in time of Indian dangers."

In 1799 Boone and most of his clan left the United States to settle in Missouri, where the Spanish governor had promised him a large estate.** There Boone served as "syndic" of the Femme Osage district, and played a mediating role in the transition to American power after the purchase of Louisiana.

But as had been his misfortune in Kentucky, 1809 the federal commission appointed to consider the validity of the Spanish grants rejected his title. At seventy-five, "Unable to call a single acre his own," he wrote, Boone was once again "a wanderer in the world."

Boone first had achieved fame as the result of a narrative written by John Filson in 1784, in which the Kentucky promoter portrayed the woodsman as a triumphant hero. Later folklore dwelt on the resulting paradoxes in the woodsman's situation. As Boone prepares for his final departure from Kentucky, relates one such story, he goes to a young neighbor to say goodbye. "Where in the world are you going and what for?" asks his shocked friend. "To some point beyond the bounds of civilization and spend the remnant of my days in the woods," answers Boone. "For all my privations and toils I thought I was entitled to a home for my family," but "another bought the land over my head." He offers these parting words of wisdom: "I have lived to learn that your boasted civilization is nothing more than improved ways to overreach your neighbor." Boone throws his arms about his friend's neck and weeps like a child, then departs, leading Rebecca and their youngest son Nathan on horseback, in a scene reminiscent of the flight of Joseph and Mary into the wilderness.

Congress in fact later confirmed Boone's Missouri title; his children possessed fine farms of their own; and he spent his declining years in reasonable comfort. But the folklore struck at an essential truth. While the image of the poor pioneer "unable to call a single acre his own" may not have

---

**As they departed, the sheriff of Fayette County was attempting to serve Boone with an arrest warrant for his failure to appear in a suit against him for six thousand pounds; at the same moment, the Kentucky assembly named a new county in Boone's honor.

fit Boone's case precisely, it applied full well to many of his contemporaries. Many of the Kentucky settlers failed to prove their land claims, and by the 1790s fewer than half of the households in the Bluegrass owned land. Boone's troubles were taken to stand for the experience of his fellow pioneers. He had attempted to make the transition from frontier to plantation, moving away from his past as a woodsman and hunter, but he did not have the temperament. And so in his last quarter-century, he returned to hunting and trapping.

Many tales were told about Boone's final move back to the life of the woods. In one, as he moves down the Ohio toward Missouri, someone asks what had induced him to leave "so rich and flourishing a country as his dear Kentucky, which he discovered and had helped to win from the Indians," "Too crowded," Boone exclaims, "too crowded—I want more elbow room!" In another, set in Missouri, Boone tells a traveler that "I wanted to go where I would not be around so much by neabors," but that in Missouri "I am too much crowded." Well, how close are your neighbors, the man inquires, and he is incredulous at Boone's reply. Only twenty miles away!

Such stories angered Boone. "Nothing embitters my old age," he told a visitor, like "the circulation of absurd stories that I retire as civilization advances, that I shun the white men and seek the Indians, and that now even when old, I wish to retire beyond the second Alleganies." Indeed, there is frequently a double edge to the folklore of Boone's wanderlust, for while it celebrates migration, the very essence of American pioneering, it also raises questions about his social commitments. Boone "did not stay one plase long [enough] to get acquainted," declared one of his Kentucky neighbors; he "always lived in a world of his own." The settlers depended upon mutual assistance for survival and mistrusted men who refused to be neighborly.

A few years after Boone's death, Kentucky frontiersman Simon Kenton was asked for his reaction to debunking views of his old friend. Kenton was a quick-tempered man, but resigned to the inevitability of revisionist opinions, he summed up his feelings with a rhetorical shrug of his shoulders: "They may say what they please of Daniel Boone."

By considering Boone's life and legend, Americans have always sought to learn something of themselves. Boone was a woodsman, a man who loved the wilderness and sought a place to hunt and live at ease—but he also was a trailblazer who opened the way for thousands to follow. He was a husband and father devoted to his family—but also a man who craved solitude. He was a man who loved and respected Native Americans and hated violence—but also one who rose to fame as the leader of a war of dispossession. He was a man of contradictions—extraordinary, "but a common man."

STUDY QUESTIONS

1. What paradoxes and contradictions are contained in the life of Daniel Boone and the legend of Daniel Boone? How are the life and legend similar and different?

2. How did European American and Native American cultures mix on the frontier? How would you characterize Boone's relationships with the Native Americans of Pennsylvania, Virginia, North Carolina, and Kentucky? What did Boone believe was the origin of the hostility between Native Americans and Anglo-American settlers?

3. What was life on the frontier like for Rebecca Bryan Boone? How did men and women divide work on the frontier?

4. What characterized the Revolutionary warfare on the frontier? How did the war strain relations between the new settlers and Native Americans? How did the war alter Boone's reputation?

5. How did Boone make and lose a paper fortune in land?

BIBLIOGRAPHY

The best study of Daniel Boone's life and times is John Mack Faragher, *Daniel Boone: The Life and Legend of an American Pioneer* (1992). Much of what we know of Boone comes from John Filson, *The Discovery, Settlement, and Present State of Kentucke* (1784), which has been reprinted in numerous versions. Boone was essentially a man of the "middle ground" where Native American and European peoples and cultures mixed and created original forms. A fine study of this "middle ground" is Richard White, *The Middle Ground: Indians, Empire, and Republics in the Great Lakes Region, 1650–1815* (1991). Also see Terry G. Jordan and Matti Kaups, *The American Backwoods Frontier: An Ethnic and Ecological Interpretation* (1989) and Francis Jennings, *Empire of Fortune: Crowns, Colonies, & Tribes in the Seven Years War in America* (1988). For information on the backwoods during the Revolutionary War see Jack M. Sosin, *The Revolutionary Frontier, 1763–1783* (1967). For the development of the West in the American imagination, a fine starting point is Henry Nash Smith, *Virgin Land: The American West as Symbol and Myth* (1950).

WOUNDED AND PRESUMED DEAD: DYING OF BREAST CANCER IN EARLY AMERICA

James S. Olson

The half-century between the end of the French and Indian War in 1763 and the outbreak of the War of 1812 was an extraordinary period in American history. The Founding Fathers unleashed the American Revolution, declaring their independence from Great Britain, and then won a military victory in the War for American Independence. They wrote the Constitution and the Bill of Rights, launched a new government, and developed a two-party system that has governed the United States ever since. Few people in the history of the world have lived through such dangerous and propitious times and accomplished so much. But while they were dealing with revolution, war, and nation building, they also had private lives and all of the personal challenges that go along with raising a family and making a living. John Adams—the first vice president and the second president of the United States—and his wife Abigail established what remains today one of the most distinguished families in American history. Their children brought them great joy. But as in all families, joy is often mixed with tragedy. In the essay below, historian James S. Olson describes how breast cancer ultimately killed their only daughter Nabby and how the family dealt with her illness.

It was just a tiny dimple. On a man's chin it would have looked rugged and distinguished. On a woman's cheek it might have been called a "beauty mark." But this was a different dimple, a killer dimple. It was on her left breast and "Nabby" Smith wondered what it was. She had never noticed it before, nor had her husband William. Perhaps it was just another physical sign of age, they thought, an indicator that she was not a young woman anymore. It was a sign, to be sure, but not of old age. The dimple was as much a symbol of premature death as a skull and crossbones, and within a few years, it would turn Nabby into a virtual skeleton before killing her in pain-wracked stupor. Actually, the dimple itself was not really the problem. Beneath the dimple, buried an inch below the skin, a small malignant tumor was attaching itself to surface tissues and drawing them in, like a sinking ship pulling water down in its own whirlpool. It was 1808 and Nabby was forty-four years old. She had a husband and three children, but she did not have much of a life left.

At first Nabby did not give it much thought, only noticing it now and then when she bathed or dressed in the morning. Nor did she talk about it. Nabby Smith was a shy and somewhat withdrawn woman, quiet and cautious in the expression of ideas, more comfortable with people who guarded their feelings than with those who exposed them. She blushed easily and rarely laughed out loud, allowing only a demure, half-smile to crease her face when she was amused. She had a pleasant disposition and a mellow temperament, both of which endeared her to family and friends. Nabby was a beautiful woman, blessed with long, red hair, a round face, deep-blue eyes, and a creamy, porcelain complexion. She commanded respect, not because of an aggressive personality but simply because of the quality of her mind and a powerful sense of personal dignity.

"Wounded and Presumed Dead: Dying of Breast Cancer in Early America," by James S. Olson. Copyright © 1992 by James S. Olson. Reprinted by permission.

At least some of that dignity came from her background. Nabby Smith was a member of one of the most distinguished families in the United States. She was born in Quincy, Massachusetts, in 1766. Her parents named her Abigail Adams. They began calling her "Nabby" when she was little. Nabby had an extraordinary childhood. Her father was John Adams, the future president of the United States, and her mother was Abigail Adams, the most prominent woman in early American society. Her little brother John Quincy was destined to become president of the United States. From the time of her birth, Nabby's parents were busily engaged in colonial politics, eventually played leading roles in the American Revolution and the War for American Independence. They raised her on a steady diet of dinner table and parlor political talk—animated discussions of freedom, liberty, rights, despotism, war, and foreign policy. Nabby absorbed it all; political philosophy in her family was not a mere abstraction. Her position in the family was secure.

She was the apple of their eyes. As an only daughter, Nabby enjoyed the special attentions of her father, who felt the need to protect her and pamper her. Abigail had always doted upon her, dressing her up in the latest fashions when she was little and counseling her when she was an adolescent. When Nabby grew up their relationship quickly evolved into a deep friendship. In spite of the devoted attentions of her parents, Nabby took it all in stride, never becoming spoiled or self-indulgent. She was even-handed, thick-skinned, and not afraid of responsibility—the daughter every parent dreamed of having.

When the War for Independence ended in 1783, Nabby was just seventeen years old, but she was in for an adventure. Congress appointed her father to serve as the first United States minister to England, and in 1785 the family crossed the Atlantic and took up residence in a house on Grosvener Square in London. They were immediately caught up in the social and political life of the world's greatest city, meeting King George III at court and other prominent politicians and attending the whirlwind of parties, meetings, banquets, and festivals common to the life of an ambassador.

For the first few months in London, Nabby was somewhat depressed, mostly because of homesickness because she had left behind a boyfriend who soon quit writing letters. Her mood caught her parents off guard—it was uncharacteristic of her—and they tried to reassure her that soon she would be feeling better. They were right. Soon Nabby had noticed a young man who was part of the American diplomatic staff in London. Colonel William Smith, a young veteran of the Continental Army and secretary to the American legation in London, had also noticed Nabby.

Smith was a dashing and handsome figure, racing around London in a two-seated carriage, something equivalent to a sports car today. He dressed well—a weakness for silk coats and shirts—and kept company with a variety of people in London's ex-patriot community, especially with Latin American liberals and radicals interested in securing independence from Spain. He was bold and impetuous, inspired by courage and limited by poor judgment. Because of his work with the American legation in London, and his role as secretary to Minister John Adams, Smith saw a great deal of the Adams family, and Nabby fell secretly in love with him. It was not long before he felt the same way, drawn to Nabby's beauty, grace, and intelligence. He proposed late in 1785 and they were married in June 1786, after a courtship which John and Abigail Adams felt was too short. They excused it because "a soldier is always more expeditious in his courtships than other men."

But Colonel William Smith was a soldier without a war, a dinosaur at the age of twenty-eight, and Nabby was in for a difficult life, an innocent victim of what her brother John Quincy called "fortune's treacherous game." Colonel Smith was not cruel. In fact, he always loved and cared for Nabby, and they had three children. With a stoicism that would have made the most devout Puritan proud, Nabby was more than willing to accept her financial fate and make a life for her family wherever Smith settled. The problem was

that Smith never really settled down. He wasted his life away, always searching but never finding a place for himself, winning and losing political appointments, dabbling in Latin American *coup d'etats* and revolutions, dragging Nabby and the kids back and forth between New York and London trying to influence a new power broker or close another deal. He spent far more money than he ever earned, and Nabby was forever worrying about the bills and their reputation. By the early 1800s, Smith was trying to make his fortune in shady real estate schemes, hoping to profit from the desire of so many Americans to move west and get their own land, but he lost everything he had. He was bold but not shrewd enough for the life of an entrepreneur. In 1808, when Nabby first noticed the dimple, they were living on the edge of the frontier, in a small farmhouse along the Chenago River in western New York, where he spent the days behind an iron plow and a mule working a small plot of land. The Smiths were a long way, economically and geographically, from the heady world of Boston and London politics.

During the next year the dimple became more pronounced and more worrisome to Nabby, but it was not until late in 1809 that she felt a hard lump beneath the skin. Nabby Adams was an intelligent, well-informed woman, and throughout her adult life the Adams family had been close friends with Dr. Benjamin Rush, the country's most prominent physician. Breast cancer was as much the dreaded disease in the early 1800s as it is today, something educated women knew about and feared. Well-informed people had been aware of breast cancer for two thousand years, since Greek physicians first called it *karkinos* (carcinoma), or crab, because of its tenacious ability to hold on, to defy all attempts to cure it or cut it out. In fact, breast cancer in women was really the first cancer human beings ever identified, probably because it was more visible than other deadly tumors. And they knew breast cancer started with a hard lump. No records exist describing Nabby Smith's initial reaction to the lump in her breast, but it is safe to say that the intermittent, low-key concern about the dimple was instantly transformed into a chronic, persistent worry that would never quite go away.

Like so many women then and today, Nabby tried to ignore the lump, hoping that in the daily, busy routines of running a small farm and household she would not have time to think about it. But cancer has a way of asserting itself, finally obliterating even the most elaborate attempts at procrastination and denial. Nabby's cancer was no exception. The lump underwent an ominous growth, in spite of the efforts of local healers who prescribed a dizzying variety of external salves and potions. She wrote home to John and Abigail Adams in February 1811 that her doctor had discovered "a cancer in my breast." As soon as they received the letter, her parents began urging their daughter to come to Boston for medical advice. Some things do not change. Even today, people suffering from cancer often head to the major cities where comprehensive cancer centers can treat them.

In June 1811, with the lump now visible to the naked eye, a desperate Nabby returned to Massachusetts. As soon as she arrived in Quincy, Massachusetts, Nabby wrote to Benjamin Rush in Philadelphia, describing her condition and seeking his advice. When Abigail Adams first looked at her daughter's breast, she found the condition "alarming." The tumor was large enough to distend the breast into a misshapen mass. John and Abigail took Nabby to see several physicians in Boston—Drs. Holbrook and Welsh and Tufts and Johnson—and they were cautiously reassuring, telling her that the situation and her general health were "so good as not to threaten any present danger." They prescribed hemlock pills to "poison the disease."

Soon after that round of reassuring examinations, however, the Adams family received a more ominous reply from Dr. Benjamin Rush. In her initial letter, Nabby told the famous physician that the tumor was large and growing, but that it was "movable"—not attached to the chest wall. Rush found the news encouraging, as do most cancer specialists today. Malignant tumors which are "movable" are better candidates for surgery, since it is more likely that the surgeon can get what is termed a "clean margin"—a border of non-cancerous tissue surrounding the tumor—reducing the chances that the cancer will recur or spread.

Knowing that Nabby had already traveled from western New York to Boston to seek more medical advice and to be cared for by her parents, Rush wrote a letter to John and Abigail Adams, telling them to gently break his news to Nabby. Dr. Rush wrote:

I shall begin my letter by replying to your daughter's. I prefer giving my opinion and advice in her case in this way. You and Mrs. Adams may communicate it gradually and in such a manner as will be least apt to distress and alarm her.

After the experience of more than 50 years in cases similar to hers, I must protest against all local applications and internal medicines for relief. They now and then cure, but in 19 cases out of 20 in tumors in the breast they do harm or suspend the disease until it passes beyond that time in which the only radical remedy is ineffectual. This remedy is the knife. From her account of the moving state of the tumor, it is now in a proper situation for the operation. Should she wait till it suppurates or even inflames much, it may be too late. . . . I repeat again, let there be no delay in flying to the knife. Her time of life calls for expedition in this business. . . . I sincerely sympathize with her and with you and your dear Mrs. Adams in this family affliction, but it will be but for a few minutes if she submit to have it extirpated, and if not, it will probably be a source of distress and pain to you all for years to come. It shocks me to think of the consequences of procrastination in her case.

Benjamin Rush knew that there were no home remedies or folk cures for breast cancer; Nabby Adams needed surgery—a mastectomy—and she needed it immediately.

Rush wrote to John and Abigail Adams, rather than replying directly to Nabby's inquiry, because he wanted them to break the news to her gently, to help her in overcoming the initial terror she was going to feel about going "under the knife." Surgery in the early nineteenth century was a brutal affair. Cutting instruments were crude and there was no such thing as anesthesia. Patients were wide awake during the operation, and they had to be belted down and restrained from moving or screaming. It was not at all uncommon for sick people to choose death rather than "the knife." And if they survived the surgery, they then faced the threat of massive infections. Nobody understood the principle of microscopic life, of germs which cause disease, or how careful, antiseptic procedures could prevent infections. Patients ran the risk of dying of massive infections within days of the operation. Surgery was always a last resort. But Benjamin Rush was convinced that Nabby's condition had reached the desperate point, and he wanted John and Abigail to talk her into it, to let her know that "the pain of the operation is much less than her fears represent it to be." Amputation of the diseased breast was her only chance.

They first had to convince their son-in-law. Fear of the "dread disease" had pushed William Smith into an advanced state of denial. When he learned of Rush's recommendation, he reacted indignantly, heading for libraries to learn whatever he could about the disease and its prognosis, hoping against hope to spare Nabby the operation. He talked and talked, trying to convince himself that maybe the tumor would just go away, that Nabby could probably live with it, that it was not so bad. Abigail Adams's mother had more faith in Rush and wrote to Smith: "If the operation is necessary as the Dr. states it to be, and as I fear it is, the sooner it is done the better provided Mrs. Smith can bring herself along, as I hope she will consent to it." She even asked her son-in-law, if Nabby agreed to the surgery, to be with "Nabby through the painful tryal." Smith finally acquiesced to Rush's opinion and Abigail's persistence. Nabby was also convinced that surgery was her only chance. They scheduled the operation for October 8, 1811.

There was nothing new about amputating a cancerous breast. Some surgeons in Europe had

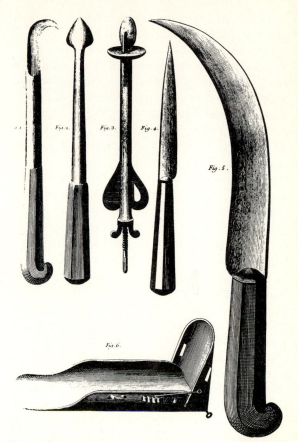

"State of the art" surgical instruments in the late eighteenth century.

been performing the operation for more than a century, and the surgery was well known among Boston physicians. In 1728 Dr. Zabdiel Boylston amputated the breast of Sarah Winslow to remove a malignant tumor. The patient survived the surgery and lived another thirty-nine years, dying in 1767 of old age, and local physicians were convinced that the operation had brought about the cure. Amputation was not however, the treatment of choice for breast cancer in the late 1700s and early 1800s because the surgery itself was so harrowingly painful and the outcomes so problematic. Most patients undergoing surgery in the nineteenth century had to deal with the problem of massive, post-operative infections. Surgery was always a last resort.

Nabby and William Smith, along with their daughter Caroline, and Abigail Adams travelled from Quincy to Boston the day before the operation. Late in the afternoon, they met with John Warren, widely considered to be the city's most skilled surgeon. Warren gave Nabby a brief physical examination and told her what to expect. It was hardly reassuring. In fact, his description of the surgery, of what Nabby was about to go through, was nightmarishly terrifying, enough to make Nabby, William, Abigail, and Caroline rethink the decision. But Rush's warning—"It shocks me to think of the consequences of procrastination in her case"—reverberated through all of their minds. Nabby had no choice if she ever hoped to live to see her grandchildren.

The operation was as bad as they had feared. John Warren was assisted by his son Joseph, who was destined to become a leading physician in his own right, and several other doctors who had examined Nabby back in July. Warren's surgical instruments, laying in a wooden box on a table, were quite simple. One was a large fork with two six-inch prongs sharpened to a needle point. He also had a wooden-handled razor. A pile of compress bandages was in the box as well. In the corner of the room there was a small oven, full of red-hot coals, into which a flat, thick, heavy iron spatula had been inserted.

Nabby came into the room dressed for a Sunday service. She was a proper woman from the best family, and she felt obligated to act the part. The doctors were in professional attire—frock coats, with shirts and ties. Modesty demanded that Nabby unbutton only the top of her dress and slip it off her left shoulder, exposing the diseased breast but little else. She remained fully clothed. Since they knew nothing of bacteria in the early 1800s, there were no gloves or surgical masks, no need for Warren to scrub his hands or wash Nabby's chest before the operation or cover his own hair and beard. Warren had her sit down and lean back in a reclining chair. He belted her waist, legs, feet, and right arm to the chair and had her raise her left arm above her head so that the pectoralis major muscle would push the breast up.

One of the physicians took Nabby's raised arm by the elbow and held it, while another stood behind her, pressing her shoulders and neck to the chair. Warren told Nabby to shut her eyes, grit her teeth, and get ready. Abigail, Caroline, and William stood off to the side to witness the ordeal.

Warren then straddled Nabby's knees, leaned over her semi-reclined body, and began his work. Like a father carving a Thanksgiving turkey, he took the two-pronged fork and thrust it deep into Nabby's breast. With his left hand, he held onto the fork and raised up on it, lifting the breast from the chest wall. He reached over for the large razor and started slicing into the base of the breast, moving from the middle of her chest toward her left side. When the breast was completely severed, Warren lifted it away from Nabby's chest with the fork. But the tumor was larger and more widespread than he had anticipated. Breast cancer often spreads to regional lymph nodes, and Warren discovered that Nabby already had visible tumor tissue in the nodes of her axilla—under her left armpit. He took the razor in there as well and with his fingers pulled out nodes and tumor.

There was a real premium on speed in early nineteenth-century surgery. No wonder. Nabby was grimacing and groaning, flinching and twisting in the chair, with blood staining her dress and Warren's shirt and pants. Her hair was soon matted in sweat. Abigail, William, and Caroline had to turn their faces and eyes away from the gruesome struggle. With the patient writhing in pain and her family eyewitnessing the spectacle, Warren wanted to get the job done as quickly as possible. To stop the bleeding, he pulled the red-hot spatula from the oven and applied it several times directly to the wound, cauterizing the worst bleeding points. With each touch, steamy wisps of smoke hissed into the air and filled the room with the distinct smell of burning flesh. Warren then sutured the wounds together, bandaged them, stepped back from Nabby, and mercifully told her that it was over. The whole procedure had taken less than twenty-five minutes. Abigail and Caroline quickly went to the surgical chair and helped Nabby pull her dress back over her left shoulder. Modesty demanded it. William helped her out of the chair and they all walked outside to the carriage. The two-hour ride to Quincy proved to be agony of its own for Nabby, with each bump in the road sending spasms of pain throughout her body.

Nabby had a long recovery from the surgery. Miraculously, she did not suffer from any serious post-surgical infections, but for months after the operation she was weak and feeble, barely able to get around. She could not use her left arm at all, and left it in a sling. Going back to the wilds of western New York was out of the question, so she stayed in Quincy with her mother, hoping to regain the strength she needed to return home. What sustained all of them during the ordeal of Nabby's recovery was the faith that the operation had cured the cancer. Within two weeks of the surgery, Dr. Benjamin Rush wrote John Adams congratulating him "in the happy issue of the operation performed upon Mrs. Smith's breast . . . her cure will be radical and durable. I consider her as rescued from a premature grave." Abigail wrote to a friend that although the operation had been a "furnace of affliction. . . what a blessing it was to have extirpated so terrible an enemy." In May 1812, seven months after the surgery, Nabby Adams felt well again. She returned home to the small farm along the Chenago River in western New York.

But Nabby Adams was not cured. Even today, breast cancer victims whose tumors have already spread to the lymph nodes do not have very good survival rates, even with modern surgery, radiation treatments, and chemotherapy. In Nabby's case, long before Dr. Warren performed the mastectomy, the cancer had already spread throughout her body. She was going to die, no matter what, and the horrific surgery in 1811 had served no purpose. Nabby suspected something was wrong within a few weeks of arriving home in New York. She began to complain of headaches and severe pain in her spine and abdomen. A local physician attributed the discomfort to rheumatism. The diagnosis relieved some of Nabby's anxiety, since she was already worried that the pain had something to do with cancer. Cancer patients grasp at straws,

hoping against hope that there is an alternative explanation for their distress, something simple and common, like a cold or the flu or rheumatism, anything but a recurrence of the dread disease.

For Nabby Adams, however, it was not the flu or "the rheumatism." The cancer was back. That became quite clear in 1813 when she suffered a local recurrence of the tumors. When Warren amputated her breast and excised tissues from her axilla, he thought he had "gotten it all," removing the visible tumor tissue. But cancer is a cellular disease and millions of invisible, microscopically tiny malignant cancers were left behind. Some of them had grown into tumors of their own by the spring of 1813—visible tumors below the scar where Nabby's breast had once been and on the skin as well. Nabby's doctor in New York then changed his diagnosis: her headaches and now excruciating body pains were not rheumatism. The cancer was back and had spread throughout her body. Nabby Adams was terminal. She was going to die in a matter of months.

Nabby declined steadily in the late spring, finally telling her husband that she "wanted to die in her father's house." William Smith wrote John and Abigail Adams in May that the cancer had returned and that Nabby wanted "to spend her state of convalescence within the vortex of your kindness and assiduities than elsewhere." The colonel was back into denial, refusing to voice the certainty that his wife was going to die. Since the country was in the midst of the War of 1812, Smith told his in-laws, he had to go to Washington D.C., to obtain a military appointment, and that he would return to Quincy, Massachusetts, as soon as the congressional session was over. John and Abigail prepared Nabby's room and waited for her arrival.

The trip was unimaginably painful—more than 300 miles in a carriage, over bumpy roads where each jolt meant stabbing pain. Her son John drove the carriage. When Nabby finally reached Quincy on July 26, she was suffering from grinding, constant, multiple-site pain. John and Abigail were shocked when they saw her. She was gaunt and thin, wracked by a deep cough, and her eyes had a moist, rheumy look to them. She groaned and sometimes screamed every time she moved. Huge, dark circles shadowed her cheeks, and a few minutes after she settled into bed, the smell of death was in the air. Cancer cells not only divide rapidly, they also die rapidly, and when a patient has a body full of tumors, the body is also full of an increasing volume of dead, necrotic tissue. Those tissues are rancid and rotten, full of bacteria, and they give off a foul odor. Scientists today call the condition "cachexia"—the body seems to be feeding on itself—but in the early 1800s it was known as "the odor of death."

Nabby's pain was so unbearable, and her misery so unmitigated, that Abigail went into a depression of her own, a depression so deep she could not stand even to visit her daughter's room. It was her husband John Adams, the second president of the United States, who ministered to his dying daughter, feeding her, cleaning her and seeing to her personal needs, combing her hair and holding her hand. He tried to administer several recommended pain killers, but nothing seemed to help, not until she lapsed into a pain-numbing coma. Her husband returned from Washington, D.C., and the deathwatch began. On the morning of August 9, Nabby's breathing became more shallow and the passage of time between breaths more extended. The family gathered around her bedside. She took her last breath early in the afternoon. A few days later, in a letter to Thomas Jefferson, John Adams wrote: "Your Friend, my only Daughter, expired, Yesterday Morning in the Arms of Her Husband, her Son, her Daughter, her Father and Mother, her Husbands two Sisters and two of her Nieces, in the 49th. Year of Age, 46 of which She was the healthiest and firmest of Us all: Since which, She has been a monument to Suffering and to Patience."

Except for a chosen few victims, breast cancer was a death sentence in the early nineteenth century, and the surgical treatment for it was almost as bad as the disease. From the moment she first noticed the lump, Nabby was doomed. During the rest of the century, physicians learned about anesthesia, which dramatically eased the trauma of surgery. They also learned about bacteria and started washing their hands before putting the scalpel to a patient's breast. They discovered that all tissue was composed of tiny cells, and that cancer was a disease process involving those cells. Around 1900, when surgeons developed the radical mastectomy—a new surgical procedure for removing a cancerous breast—patient survival rates increased. Seventy-five years after Nabby Adams died of breast cancer, women with the disease had a better chance of survival.

But even today, nearly 170 years after Nabby's death, breast cancer remains a frighteningly unpredictable disease. More limited surgical procedures, radiation therapy, and chemotherapy provide new treatments, but nearly 50,000 American women die of breast cancer every year. According to statistics released in 1992, one out of nine American women—a total of nearly 15 million people—will develop breast cancer during their lifetime. And according to existing survival rates, approximately forty percent of them will die from it. The only real answer is early detection, hopefully from a mammogram examination when the cancer is tiny and curable. Nabby Adams did not have that option. We do.

STUDY QUESTIONS

1. What did Nabby Adams do when she first noticed the lump? What kind of medical attention did she get from her physicians in New York and Boston?

2. What did Dr. Benjamin Rush recommend and why did he give his advice to Nabby's parents rather than directly to her?

3. How did Nabby's husband, William Smith, react to the news of her illness and Dr. Rush's recommendation?

4. Why was Nabby Adams probably doomed to death from breast cancer no matter what she would have done after learning she had the disease?

5. How can a woman today greatly improve her chances of surviving breast cancer?

BIBLIOGRAPHY

For an excellent description of Abigail "Nabby" Adams's marriage to William Smith, see Lida Mayo, "Miss Adams in Love," *American Heritage*, 16 (February 1965), 36–49, 80–89. Carl Binger's *Revolutionary Doctor, Benjamin Rush (1746–1813)* (1966) is a good introduction to the life of early America's most prominent physician. For the correspondence of Benjamin Rush with John and Abigail Adams, see L. H. Butterfield, *Letters of Benjamin Rush,* Vol. II: 1793–1813 (1951). The best biography of Abigail Adams is Phyllis Lee Levin's *Abigail Adams: A Biography* (1987). Also see Lynne Withay, *Dearest Friend: A Life of Abigail Adams* (1981). For a biography of John Adams, see John Ferling, *John Adams: A Life* (1992). A brief history of the mastectomy can be found in Bernard Fisher and Mark C. Gebhardt, "The Evolution of Breast Cancer Surgery: Past, Present, and Future," *Seminars in Oncology,* 5 (December 1978), 385–394.

Part Four

ADJUSTING TO AMERICA

The nineteenth century was a time of extraordinary social and economic upheaval in the Western World, even though the historic forces were subtle and evolutionary in their impact. For a number of reasons—the absence of war in Europe after the Napoleonic era, improved sanitation and public health, the smallpox vaccine, and the dissemination of the potato and mass-produced grains—population growth was extraordinary. The European population exploded from 140 million people in 1750, to 260 million in 1850, to 400 million in 1914. Farm sizes dwindled, and younger sons and laborers began moving to cities to look for work. The industrial economy was also changing, destroying home production in favor of mass-produced factory goods. Traditional village lifestyles were altered forever. The Atlantic economy was slowly integrating America and Western Europe.

In the United States, a tremendous demand for labor attracted millions of the European peasants. Rapid industrialization, unprecedented economic growth, tremendous population increases, and steady expansion into the western territories created a dynamic society. At the same time, more and more workers were moving into the great American cities to work on the assembly lines. Never before in human history had the way people made their livings undergone more dramatic change.

Within that larger economy, there were many distinct cultures of people trying to cope with the changes around them. Minority groups were especially vulnerable to social and economic change because they usually had little political power to control the forces affecting their lives. In the South, millions of black slaves were managing to develop a unique African-American culture that sustained them emotionally amidst gross discrimination and exploitation. They substituted cultural vitality for political power and succeeded in surviving psychologically and in ordering their lives. In the

(a) Baron Biesele, upon his arrival in America (in German): "Hey, fellow countryman, where can we find a German tavern?" Countryman (in German): "Damme. Do you think I'm a no-good like you? I am an American."

(b) Baron Biesele, first week after arrival (in German): "Well, Marianel, how do you like it in America?" Marianel (in German): "Oh, Baron, the language, the language. I'll never learn it in all my life."

(c) Baron Biesele, two weeks after arrival (in German): "Can you tell us—Hey, beautiful Marianel, isn't that you?" Marianel (in English): "You are mistaken. I don't talk Dutch."

Southwest, acquired from Mexico in 1848, perhaps 80,000 Hispanics were engaged in a similar struggle, frustrated about being under Anglo power and struggling to retain their land and culture. Throughout the United States, women too were trying to cope with changing circumstances. People, confused by the social changes accompanying the Industrial Revolution, tried to preserve a sense of the mythical past by creating a "cult of domesticity" for women. In addition, hundreds of thousands of Native Americans were finding their way of life incompatible with the growth-oriented, materialistic economy of industrial America. For all these people, the changing nature of American society was an extraordinary challenge, one that required adjustment and accommodation.

THE CULT OF TRUE WOMANHOOD: 1820–1860

Barbara Welter

In an interview with the Public Broadcasting System, American feminist Gloria Steinem was asked if her opinions about the women's movement had changed at all in the last twenty years. After reflecting for a moment, she remarked that over the years she had become increasingly aware that the problem of sexism was rooted more deeply than she had first assumed. One look at public policy debated in the United States during the 1990s confirms her belief. Most of the major domestic public policy questions in the United States today directly involve the place of women in society: wage discrimination, affirmative action and promotion, abortion and freedom of choice, Social Security and retirement benefits, child care, the Equal Rights Amendment, pornography and censorship, rape and sexual abuse, insurance and annuity rate differentials, divorce and child support, poverty and welfare, and gay rights. Virtually all of these problems have their roots in the gender stereotyping so common in American culture. Gender stereotyping is a residue from before the industrial and even modern eras when divisions of labor in society were directly tied to pregnancy, birthing, nursing, and child rearing. Although the economic institutions dictating such divisions of labor are now disappearing, the gender stereotypes have lives of their own, continuing to shape public expectations of men and women.

In "The Cult of True Womanhood: 1820–1860," historian Barbara Welter looks at the antebellum decades of the nineteenth century and describes an important stage in public expression of gender stereotypes. By making virtues of domesticity, submissiveness, passivity, and chastity for women, and leaving men free to exhibit a much wider range of behaviors, American culture hoped to promote industrialization while preserving some semblance of premodern values. The irony, of course, was that the relevance of the "cult of womanhood" declined in direct proportion to the pace of industrialization. Women gradually became confined to an increasingly unreal world of impossible expectations; the underside of domesticity and submissiveness, for many women, was anger, guilt, and extraordinary frustration. Even after the Nineteenth Amendment was ratified in 1920, the "cult of womanhood" still influenced American attitudes, and the modern feminist movement had to turn its attention to changing those attitudes as a prerequisite to realizing freedom and equality for both genders.

The nineteenth-century American man was a busy builder of bridges and railroads, at work long hours in a materialistic society. The religious values of his forebears were neglected in practice if not in intent, and he occasionally felt some guilt that he had turned this new land, this temple of the chosen people, into one vast countinghouse. But he could salve his conscience by reflecting that he had left behind a hostage, not only to fortune, but to all the values which he held so dear and treated so lightly. Woman, in the cult of True Womanhood presented by the women's magazines, gift annuals and religious literature of the nineteenth century, was the hostage in the home. In a society where values changed frequently, where fortunes rose and fell with frightening rapidity, where social and economic mobility provided instability as well as hope, one thing at least remained the same—a true woman was a true woman, wherever she was found. If anyone, male or female, dared to tamper with the complex virtues which made up True Womanhood, he was damned immediately as an enemy of God, of civilization and of the Republic. It was a fearful obligation, a solemn responsibility, which the nineteenth-century American woman had—to uphold the pillars of the temple with her frail white hand.

The attributes of True Womanhood, by which a woman judged herself and was judged by her husband, her neighbors, and society could be divided into four cardinal virtues—piety, purity, submissiveness, and domesticity. Put them all together and they spell mother, daughter, sister, wife—woman. Without them, no matter whether there was fame, achievement, or wealth, all was ashes. With them she was promised happiness and power.

Barbara Welter, "The Cult of True Womanhood: 1820–1860" in *American Quarterly,* Vol. 18 (Summer 1966): 151–174. Copyright © The Johns Hopkins University Press. Reprinted by permission.

Religion or piety was the core of woman's virtue, the source of her strength. Young men looking for a mate were cautioned to search first for piety, for if that were there, all else would follow. Religion belonged to woman by divine right, a gift of God and nature. This "peculiar susceptibility" to religion was given her for a reason: "the vestal flame of piety, lighted up by Heaven in the breast of woman" would throw its beams into the naughty world of men. So far would its candle power reach that the "Universe might be Enlightened, Improved, and Harmonized by WOMAN!!" She would be another, better, Eve, working in cooperation with the Redeemer, bringing the world back "from its revolt and sin." The world would be reclaimed for God through her suffering, for "God increased the cares and sorrows of woman, that she might be sooner constrained to accept the terms of salvation." A popular poem by Mrs. Frances Osgood, "The Triumph of the Spiritual Over the Sensual" expressed just this sentiment, woman's purifying passionless love bringing an erring man back to Christ.

Dr. Charles Meigs, explaining to a graduating class of medical students why women were naturally religious, said that "hers is a pious mind. Her confiding nature leads her more readily than men to accept the proffered grace of the Gospel." Caleb Atwater, Esq., writing in *The Ladies' Repository,* saw the hand of the Lord in female piety: "Religion is exactly what a woman needs, for it gives her that dignity that best suits her dependence." And Mrs. John Sandford, who had no very high opinion of her sex, agreed thoroughly: "Religion is just what a woman needs. Without it she is ever restless or unhappy. . . ." Mrs. Sandford and the others did not speak only of that restlessness of the human heart, which St. Augustine notes, that can only find its peace in God. They spoke rather of religion as a kind of tranquilizer for the many undefined longings which swept even the most pious young girl, and about which it was better to pray than to think.

One reason religion was valued was that it did not take a woman away from her "proper sphere," her home. Unlike participation in other societies or movements, church work would not make her less domestic or submissive, less a True Woman. In religious vineyards, said the *Young Ladies' Literary and Missionary Report,* "you may labor without the apprehension of detracting from the charms of feminine delicacy." Mrs. S. L. Dagg, writing from her chapter of the Society in Tuscaloosa, Alabama, was equally reassuring: "As no sensible woman will suffer her intellectual pursuits to clash with her domestic duties" she should concentrate on religious work "which promotes these very duties."

The women's seminaries aimed at aiding women to be religious, as well as accomplished. Mt. Holyoke's catalogue promised to make female education "a handmaid to the Gospel and an efficient auxiliary in the great task of renovating the world." The Young Ladies' Seminary at Bordentown, New Jersey, declared its most important function to be "the forming of a sound and virtuous character." In Keene, New Hampshire, the Seminary tried to instill a "consistent and useful character" in its students, to enable them in this life to be "a good friend, wife and mother" but more important, to qualify them for "the enjoyment of Celestial Happiness in the life to come." And Joseph M. D. Matthews, Principal of Oakland Female Seminary in Hillsborough, Ohio, believed that "female education should be preeminently religious."

If religion was so vital to a woman, irreligion was almost too awful to contemplate. Women were warned not to let their literacy or intellectual pursuits take them away from God. Sarah Josepha Hale spoke darkly of those who, like Margaret Fuller, threw away the "One True Book" for others, open to error. Mrs. Hale used the unfortunate Miss Fuller as fateful proof that "the greater the intellectual force, the greater and more fatal the errors into which women fall who wander from the Rock of Salvation, Christ the Saviour. . . ."

One gentleman, writing on "Female Irreligion" reminded his readers that "Man may make himself a brute, and does so very often, but can woman brutify herself to his level—the lowest level of human nature—without exerting special wonder?" Fanny Wright, because she was godless,

"was no woman, mother though she be." A few years ago, he recalls, such women would have been whipped. In any case, "woman never looks lovelier than in her reverence for religion" and, conversely, "female irreligion is the most revolting feature in human character."

Purity was as essential as piety to a young woman, its absence as unnatural and unfeminine. Without it she was, in fact, no woman at all, but a member of some lower order. A "fallen woman" was a "fallen angle," unworthy of the celestial company of her sex. To contemplate the loss of purity brought tears; to be guilty of such a crime, in the women's magazines at least, brought madness or death. Even the language of the flowers had bitter words for it: a dried white rose symbolized "Death Preferable to Loss of Innocence." The marriage night was the single great event of a woman's life, when she bestowed her greatest treasure upon her husband, and from that time on was completely dependent upon him, an empty vessel, without legal or emotional existence of her own.

Therefore all True Women were urged, in the strongest possible terms, to maintain their virtue, although men, being by nature more sensual than they, would try to assault it. Thomas Branagan admitted in *The Excellency of the Female Character Vindicated* that his sex would sin and sin again, they could not help it, but woman, stronger and purer, must not give in and let man "take liberties incompatible with her delicacy." "If you do," Branagan addressed his gentle reader, "You will be left in silent sadness to bewail your credulity, imbecility, duplicity, and premature prostitution."

Mrs. Eliza Farrar, in *The Young Ladies' Friend,* gave practical logistics to avoid trouble: "Sit not with another in a place that is too narrow; read not out of the same book; let not your eagerness to see anything induce you to place your head close to another person's."

If such good advice was ignored the consequences were terrible and inexorable. In *Girlhood and Womanhood: Or Sketches of My Schoolmates,* by Mrs. A. J. Graves (a kind of mid-nineteenth-century *The Group*), the bad ends of a boarding school class of girls are scrupulously recorded. The worse end of all is reserved for "Amelia Dorrington: The Lost One." Amelia died in the almshouse "the wretched victim of depravity and intemperance" all because her mother had let her be "high-spirited not prudent." These girlish high spirits had been misinterpreted by a young man, with disastrous results. Amelia's "thoughtless levity" was "followed by a total loss of virtuous principle" and Mrs. Graves editorializes that "the coldest reserve is more admirable in a woman a man wishes to make his wife, than the least approach to undue familiarity."

A popular and often-reprinted story by Fanny Forester told the sad tale of "Lucy Dutton." Lucy "with the seal of innocence upon her heart, and a rose-leaf on her cheek" came out of her vine-covered cottage and ran into a city slicker. "And Lucy was beautiful and trusting, and thoughtless: and he was gay, selfish, and profligate. Needs the story be told? . . . Nay, censor, Lucy was a child—consider how young, how very un-taught—oh! her innocence was no match for the sophistry of a gay, city youth! Spring came and shame was stamped upon the cottage at the foot of the hill." The baby died; Lucy went mad at the funeral and finally died herself. "Poor, poor Lucy Dutton! The grave is a blessed couch and pillow to the wretched. Rest thee there, poor Lucy!" The frequency with which derangement follows loss of virtue suggests the exquisite sensibility of woman, and the possibility that, in the women's magazines at least, her intellect was geared to her hymen, not her brain.

If, however, a woman managed to withstand man's assaults on her virtue, she demonstrated her superiority and her power over him. Eliza Farnham, trying to prove this female superiority, concluded smugly that "the purity of women is the everlasting barrier against which the tides of man's sensual nature surge."

A story in *The Lady's Amaranth* illustrates this dominance. It is set, improbably, in Sicily, where two lovers, Bianca and Tebaldo, have been separated because her family insisted that she marry a rich old man. By some strange circumstance the two are in a shipwreck and cast on a desert is-

land, the only survivors. Even here, however, the rigid standards of True Womanhood prevail. Tebaldo unfortunately forgets himself slightly, so that Bianca must warn him: "We may not indeed gratify our fondness by caresses, but it is still something to bestow our kindest language, and looks and prayers, and all lawful and honest attentions on each other." Something, perhaps, but not enough, and Bianca must further remonstrate: "It is true that another man is my husband, but you are my guardian angel." When even that does not work she says in a voice of sweet reason, passive and proper to the end, that she wishes he wouldn't but "still, if you insist, I will become what you wish; but I beseech you to consider, ere that decision, that debasement which I must suffer in your esteem." This appeal to his own double standards holds the beast in him at bay. They are rescued, discover that the old husband is dead, and after "mourning a decent season" Bianca finally gives in, legally.

Men could be counted on to be grateful when women thus saved them from themselves. William Alcott, guiding young men in their relations with the opposite sex, told them that "Nothing is better calculated to preserve a young man from contamination of low pleasures and pursuits than frequent intercourse with the more refined and virtuous of the other sex." And he added, one assumes in equal innocence, that youths should "observe and learn to admire, that purity and ignorance of evil which is the characteristic of well-educated young ladies, and which, when we are near them, raises us above those sordid and sensual considerations which hold such sway over men in their intercourse with each other."

The Rev. Jonathan F. Stearns was also impressed by female chastity in the face of male passion, and warned woman never to compromise the source of her power: "Let her lay aside delicacy, and her influence over our sex is gone."

Women themselves accepted, with pride but suitable modesty, this priceless virtue. *The Ladies' Wreath,* in "Woman the Creature of God and the Manufacturer of Society," saw purity as her greatest gift and chief means of discharging her duty to save the world: "Purity is the highest beauty—the true pole-star which is to guide humanity aright in its long, varied, and perilous voyage."

Sometimes, however, a woman did not see the dangers to her treasure. In that case, they must be pointed out to her, usually by a male. In the nineteenth century any form of social change was tantamount to an attack on woman's virtue, if only it was correctly understood. For example, dress reform seemed innocuous enough and the bloomers worn by the lady of that name and her followers were certainly modest attire. Such was the reasoning only of the ignorant. In another issue of *The Ladies' Wreath* a young lady is represented in dialogue with her "Professor." The girl expresses admiration for the bloomer costume— it gives freedom of motion, is healthful and attractive. The "Professor" sets her straight. Trousers, he explains, are "only one of the many manifestations of that wild spirit of socialism and agrarian radicalism which is at present so rife in our land." The young lady recants immediately: "If this dress has any connection with Fourierism or Socialism, or fanaticism in any shape whatever, I have no disposition to wear it at all . . . no true woman would so far compromise her delicacy as to espouse, however unwittingly, such a cause."

America could boast that her daughters were particularly innocent. In a poem on "The American Girl" the author wrote proudly:

> Her eye of light is the diamond bright,
> Her innocence the pearl,
> And these are ever the bridal gems
> That are worn by the American girl.

Lydia Maria Child, giving advice to mothers, aimed at preserving that spirit of innocence. She regretted that "want of confidence between mothers and daughters on delicate subjects" and suggested a woman tell her daughter a few facts when she reached the age of twelve to "set her mind at rest." Then Mrs. Child confidently hoped that a young lady's "instinctive modesty" would "prevent her from dwelling on the information until she was called upon to use it." In the same vein, a book of advice to the newly married was titled *Whisper to a Bride*. As far as intimate infor-

mation was concerned, there was no need to whisper, since the book contained none at all.

A masculine summary of this virtue was expressed in a poem "Female Charms":

> *I would have her as pure as the snow*
> *   on the mount—As true as the smile*
> *   that to infamy's given—As pure as*
> *   the wave of the crystalline fount,*
> *Yet as warm in the heart as the*
> *   sunlight of heaven.*
> *With a mind cultivated, not boastingly*
> *   wise,*
> *I could gaze on such beauty, with*
> *   exquisite bliss;*
> *With her heart on her lips and her soul*
> *   in her eyes—What more could I*
> *   wish in dear woman than this.*

Man might, in fact, ask no more than this in woman, but she was beginning to ask more of herself, and in the asking was threatening the third powerful and necessary value, submission. Purity, considered as a moral imperative, set up a dilemma which was hard to resolve. Woman must preserve her virtue until marriage and marriage was necessary for her happiness. Yet marriage was, literally, an end to innocence. She was told not to question this dilemma, but simply to accept it.

Submission was perhaps the most feminine virtue expected of women. Men were supposed to be religious, although they rarely had time for it, and supposed to be pure, although it came awfully hard to them, but men were the movers, the doers, the actors. Women were the passive, submissive responders. The order of dialogue was, of course, fixed in Heaven. Man was "woman's superior by God's appointment, if not in intellectual dowry, at least by official decree." Therefore, as Charles Elliott argued in *The Ladies' Repository*, she should submit to him "for the sake of good order at least." In *The Ladies' Companion* a young wife was quoted approvingly as saying that she did not think woman should "feel and act for herself" because "When, next to God, her husband is not the tribunal to which her heart and intellect

Domesticity was considered a great virtue. The "true woman" was expected to stay at home and serve her family.

appeals—the golden bowl of affection is broken." Women were warned that if they tampered with this quality they tampered with the order of the Universe.

The Young Lady's Book summarized the necessity of the passive virtues in its readers' lives: "It is, however, certain that in whatever situation of life a woman is placed from her cradle to her grave, a spirit of obedience and submission, pliability of temper, and humility of mind, are required from her."

Woman understood her position if she was the right kind of woman, a true woman. "She feels herself weak and timid. She needs a protector," declared George Burnap, in his lectures on *The Sphere and Duties of Woman*. "She is in a measure dependent. She asks for wisdom, constancy, firmness, perseverance, and she is willing to repay it all by the surrender of the full treasure of her affections. Woman despises in man every thing like herself except a tender heart. It is enough that she is effeminate and weak; she does not want another like herself." Or put even more strongly by Mrs. Sandford: "A really sensible woman feels her dependence. She does what she can, but she is conscious of inferiority, and therefore grateful for support."

Mrs. Sigourney, however, assured young ladies that although they were separate, they were equal. This difference of the sexes did not imply inferiority, for it was part of that same order of Nature established by Him "who bids the oak brave the fury of the tempest, and the alpine flower lean its cheek on the bosom of eternal snows." Dr. Meigs had a different analogy to make the same point; contrasting the anatomy of the Apollo of the Belevedere (illustrating the male principle) with the Venus de Medici (illustrating the female principle). "Woman," said the physician, with a kind of clinical gallantry, "has a head almost too small for intellect but just big enough for love."

This love itself was to be passive and responsive "Love, in the heart of a woman," wrote Mrs. Farrar, "should partake largely of the nature of gratitude. She should love, because she is already loved by one deserving her regard."

Woman was to work in silence, unseen, like Wordsworth's Lucy. Yet, "working like nature, in secret" her love goes forth to the world "to regulate its pulsation, and send forth from its heart, in pure and temperate flow, the life-giving current." She was to work only for pure affection, without thought of money or ambition. A poem, "Woman and Fame," by Felicia Hemans, widely quoted in many of the gift books, concludes with a spirited renunciation of the gift of fame:

> *Away! to me, a woman, bring*
> *Sweet flowers from affection's spring.*

"True feminine genius," said Grace Greenwood (Sara Jane Clarke) "is ever timid, doubtful, and clingingly dependent; a perpetual childhood." And she advised literary ladies in an essay on "The Intellectual Woman"—"Don't trample on the flowers while longing for the stars." A wife who submerged her own talents to work for her husband was extolled as an example of a true woman. In *Women of Worth: A Book for Girls,* Mrs. Ann Flaxman, an artist of promise herself, was praised because she "devoted herself to sustain her husband's genius and aid him in his arduous career."

Caroline Gilman's advice to the bride aimed at establishing this proper order from the beginning of a marriage: "Oh, young and lovely bride, watch well the first moments when your will conflicts with his to whom God and society have given control. Reverence his *wishes* even when you do not his *opinions.*"

Mrs. Gilman's perfect wife in *Recollections of a Southern Matron* realizes that "the three golden threads with which domestic happiness is woven" are "to repress a harsh answer, to confess a fault, and to stop (right or wrong) in the midst of self-defense, in gentle submission." Woman could do this, hard though it was, because in her heart she knew she was right and so could afford to be forgiving, even a trifle condescending. "Men are not unreasonable," averred Mrs. Gilman. "Their difficulties lie in not understanding the moral and physical nature of our sex. They often wound through ignorance, and are surprised at having offended." Wives were advised to do their best to reform men, but if they couldn't, to give up gracefully. "If any habit of his annoyed me, I spoke of it once or twice calmly, then bore it quietly."

A wife should occupy herself "only with domestic affairs—wait till your husband confides to you those of a high importance—and do not give your advice until he asks for it," advised the *Lady's Token.* At all times she should behave in a manner becoming a woman, who had "no arms other than gentleness." Thus "if he is abusive, never retort." *A Young Lady's Guide to the Harmonious Development of a Christian Character* suggested that females should "become as little children" and "avoid a controversial spirit." *The Mother's Assistant and Young Lady's Friend* listed "Always Conciliate" as its first commandment in "Rules for Conjugal and Domestic Happiness." Small wonder that these same rules ended with the succinct maxim: "Do not expect too much."

As mother, as well as wife, woman was required to submit to fortune. In *Letters to Mothers* Mrs. Sigourney sighed: "To bear the evils and sorrows which may be appointed us, with a patient mind, should be the continual effort of our sex. . . .It seems, indeed, to be expected of us; since the passive and enduring virtues are more immediately within our province." Of these trials "the hardest was to bear the loss of children with submission" but the indomitable Mrs. Sigourney found strength to murmur to the bereaved mother: "The Lord loveth a cheerful giver." *The Ladies' Parlor Companion* agreed thoroughly in "A Submissive Mother," in which a mother had already buried two of her children and was nursing a dying baby and saw her sole remaining child "probably scalded to death. Handing over the infant to die in the arms of a friend, she bowed in sweet submission to the double stroke." But the child "through the goodness of God survived, and the mother learned to say 'Thy will be done.'"

Woman then, in all her roles, accepted submission as her lot. It was a lot she had not chosen or deserved. As *Godey's* said, "the lesson of submission is forced upon woman." Without comment or criticism the writer affirms that "To suffer and to be silent under suffering seems the great command she has to obey." George Burnap referred to a woman's life as "a series of suppressed emotions." She was, as Emerson said, "more vulnerable, more infirm, more mortal than man." The death of a beautiful woman, cherished in fiction, represented woman as the innocent victim, suffering without sin, too pure and good for this world but too weak and passive to resist its evil forces. The best refuge for such a delicate creature was the warmth and safety of her home.

The true woman's place was unquestionably by her own fireside—as daughter, sister, but most of all as wife and mother. Therefore domesticity was among the virtues most prized by the women's magazines. "As society is constituted," wrote Mrs. S. E. Farley, on the "Domestic and Social Claims on Woman," "the true dignity and beauty of the female character seemed to consist in a right understanding and faithful and cheerful performance of social and family duties. Sacred Scripture re-enforced social pressure: "St. Paul knew what was best for women when he advised them to be domestic," said Mrs. Sandford. "There is composure at home; there is something sedative in the duties which home involves. It affords security not only from the world, but from delusions and errors of every kind."

From her home woman performed her great task of bringing men back to God. *The Young Ladies' Class Book* was sure that "the domestic fireside is the great guardian of society against the excesses of human passions." *The Lady at Home* expressed its convictions in its very title and concluded that "even if we cannot reform the world in a moment, we can begin the work by reforming ourselves and our households—It is woman's mission. Let her not look away from her own little

family circle for the means of producing moral and social reforms, but begin at home."

Home was supposed to be a cheerful place, so that brothers, husbands, and sons would not go elsewhere in search of a good time. Woman was expected to dispense comfort and cheer. In writing the biography of Margaret Mercer (every inch a true woman) her biographer (male) notes: "She never forgot that it is the peculiar province of women to minister to the comfort, and promote the happiness, first, of those most nearly allied to her, and then of those, who by the Providence of God are placed in a state of dependence upon her." Many other essays in the women's journals showed woman as comforter: "Woman, Man's Best Friend," "Woman, the Greatest Social Benefit," "Woman, A Being to Come Home To," "The Wife: Source of Comfort and the Spring of Joy."

One of the most important functions of woman as comforter was her role as nurse. Her own health was probably, although regrettably, delicate. Many homes had "little sufferers," those pale children who wasted away to saintly deaths. And there were enough other illnesses of youth and age, major and minor, to give the nineteenth-century American woman nursing experience. The sickroom called for the exercise of her higher qualities of patience, mercy, and gentleness as well as for her housewifely arts. She could thus fulfill her dual feminine function—beauty and usefulness.

The cookbooks of the period offer formulas for gout cordials, ointment for sore nipples, hiccough and cough remedies, opening pills and refreshing drinks for fever, along with recipes for pound cake, jumbles, stewed calves head and currant wine. *The Ladies' New Book of Cookery* believed that "food prepared by the kind hand of a wife, mother, sister, friend" tasted better and had a "restorative power which money cannot purchase."

A chapter of *The Young Lady's Friend* was devoted to woman's privilege as "ministering spirit at the couch of the sick." Mrs. Farrar advised a soft voice, gentle and clean hands, and a cheerful smile. She cautioned against an excess of female delicacy. That was all right for a young lady in the parlor, but not for bedside manners. Leeches, for example, were to be regarded as "a curious piece of mechanism. . . their ornamental stripes should recommend them even to the eye, and their valuable services to our feelings." And she went on calmly to discuss their use. Nor were women to shrink from medical terminology, since "If you cultivate right views of the wonderful structure of the body, you will be as willing to speak to a physician of the bowels as the brains of your patient."

Nursing the sick, particularly sick males, not only made a woman feel useful and accomplished, but increased her influence. In a piece of heavy-handed humor in *Godey's* a man confessed that some women were only happy when their husbands were ailing that they might have the joy of nursing him to recovery "thus gratifying their medical vanity and their love of power by making him more dependent upon them." In a similar vein a husband sometimes suspected his wife "almost wishes me dead—for the pleasure of being utterly inconsolable."

In the home women were not only the highest adornment of civilization, but they were supposed to keep busy at morally uplifting tasks. Fortunately most of the housework, if looked at in true womanly fashion, could be regarded as uplifting. Mrs. Sigourney extolled its virtues: "The science of housekeeping affords exercise for the judgment and energy, ready recollection, and patient self-possession, that are the characteristics of a superior mind." According to Mrs. Farrar, making beds was good exercise, the repetitiveness of routine tasks inculcated patience and perseverance, and proper management of the home was a surprisingly complex art: "There is more to be learned about pouring out tea and coffee than most young ladies are willing to believe." *Godey's* went so far as to suggest coyly, in "Learning vs. Housewifery" that the two were complimentary, not opposed: chemistry could be utilized in cooking, geometry in dividing cloth, and phrenology in discovering talent in children.

Women were to master every variety of needlework, for, as Mrs. Sigourney pointed out, "Needlework, in all its forms of use, elegance, and ornament, has ever been the appropriate occupation of woman." Embroidery improved taste; knit-

ting promoted serenity and economy. Other forms of artsy-craftsy activity for her leisure moments included painting on glass or velvet, Poonah work, tussy-mussy frames for her own needlepoint or water colors, stands for hyacinths, hair bracelets, or baskets of feathers.

She was expected to have a special affinity for flowers. To the editors of *The Lady's Token* "A woman never appears more truly in her sphere, than when she divides her time between her domestic avocations and the culture of flowers." She could write letters, an activity particularly feminine since it had to do with the outpourings of the heart, or practice her drawingroom skills of singing and playing an instrument. She might even read.

Here she faced a bewildering array of advice. The female was dangerously addicted to novels, according to the literature of the period. She should avoid them, since they interfered with "serious piety." If she simply couldn't help herself and read them anyway, she should choose edifying ones from lists of morally acceptable authors. She should study history since it "showed the depravity of the human heart and the evil nature of sin." On the whole, "religious biography was the best."

The women's magazines themselves could be read without any loss of concern for the home. *Godey's* promised the husband that he would find his wife "no less assiduous for his reception, or less sincere in welcoming his return" as a result of reading their magazine. *The Lily of the Valley* won its rights to be admitted to the boudoir by confessing that it was "like its namesake humble and unostentatious, but it is yet pure, and, we trust, free from moral imperfections."

No matter what later authorities claimed, the nineteenth century knew that girls *could* be ruined by book. The seduction stories regard "exciting and dangerous books" as contributory causes of disaster. The man without honorable intentions always provides the innocent maiden with such books as a prelude to his assault on her virtue. Books which attacked or seemed to attack woman's accepted place in society were regarded as equally dangerous. A reviewer of Harriet Martineau's *Society in America* wanted it kept out of the hands of American women. They were so susceptible to persuasion, with their "gentle yielding natures" that they might listen to "the bold ravings of the hard-featured of their own sex." The frightening result: "Such reading will unsettle them for their true station and pursuits, and they will throw the world back again into confusion."

The debate over women's education posed the question of whether a "finished" education detracted from the practice of housewifely arts. Again it proved to be a case of semantics, for a true woman's education was never "finished" until she was instructed in the gentle science of homemaking. Helen Irving, writing on "Literary Women," made it very clear that if women invoked the muse, it was as a genie of the household lamp. "If the necessities of her position require these duties at her hands, she will perform them nonetheless cheerfully, that she knows herself capable of higher things." The literary woman must conform to the same standards as any other woman: "That her home shall be made a loving place of rest and joy and comfort to those who are dear to her, will be the first wish of every true woman's heart." Mrs. Ann Stephens told women who wrote to make sure they did not sacrifice one domestic duty. "As for genius, make it a domestic plant. Let its roots strike deep in your house. . . ."

The fear of "blue stockings" (the eighteenth-century male's term of derision for educated or literary women) need not persist for nineteenth-century American men. The magazines presented spurious dialogues in which bachelors were convinced of their fallacy in fearing educated wives. One such dialogue took place between a young man and his female cousin. Ernest deprecates learned ladies ("A *Woman* is far more lovable than a *philosopher*") but Alice refutes him with the beautiful example of their Aunt Barbara who, "although she *has* perpetrated the heinous crime of writing some half dozen folios" is still "a model of the spirit of feminine gentleness." His memory prodded, Ernest concedes that, by George, there was a woman: "When I last had a cold she not only made me a bottle of cough syrup, but when I complained of nothing new to read, she set to work and wrote some twenty stanzas on consumption."

The magazines were filled with domestic tragedies in which spoiled young girls learned that when there was a hungry man to feed French and china painting were not helpful. According to these stories many a marriage is jeopardized because the wife has not learned to keep house. Harriet Beecher Stowe wrote a sprightly piece of personal experience for *Godey's,* ridiculing her own bad housekeeping as a bride. She used the same theme in a story "The Only Daughter," in which the pampered beauty learns the facts of domestic life from a rather difficult source, her mother-in-law. Mrs. Hamilton tells Caroline in the sweetest way possible to shape up in the kitchen, reserving her rebuke for her son: "You are her husband—her guide—her protector—now see what you can do," she admonishes him. "Give her credit for every effort: treat her faults with tenderness; encourage and praise whenever you can, and depend upon it, you will see another woman in her." He is properly masterful, she properly domestic and in a few months Caroline is making lumpless gravy and keeping up with the darning. Domestic tranquillity has been restored and the young wife moralizes: "Bring up a girl to feel that she has a responsible part to bear in promoting the happiness of the family, and you make a reflecting being of her at once, and remove that lightness and frivolity of character which makes her shrink from graver studies." These stories end with the heroine drying her hands on her apron and vowing that *her* daughter will be properly educated, in piecrust as well as Poonah work.

The female seminaries were quick to defend themselves against any suspicion of interfering with the role which nature's God had assigned to women. They hoped to enlarge and deepen that role, but not to change its setting. At the Young Ladies' Seminary and Collegiate Institute in Monroe City, Michigan, the catalogue admitted few of its graduates would be likely "to fill the learned professions." Still, they were called to "other scenes of usefulness and honor." The average woman is to be "the presiding genius of love" in the home, where she is to "give a correct and elevated literary taste to her children, and to assume that influential station that she ought to possess as the companion of an educated man."

At Miss Pierce's famous school in Litchfield, the students were taught that they had "attained the perfection of their characters when they could combine their elegant accomplishments with a turn for solid domestic virtues." Mt. Holyoke paid pious tribute to domestic skills: "Let a young lady despise this branch of the duties of woman, and she despises the appointments of her existence." God, nature and the Bible "enjoin these duties on the sex, and she cannot violate them with impunity." Thus warned, the young lady would have to seek knowledge of these duties elsewhere, since it was not in the curriculum at Mt. Holyoke. "We would not take this privilege from the mother."

One reason for knowing her way around a kitchen was that America was "a land of precarious fortunes," as Lydia Maria Child pointed out in her book *The Frugal Housewife: Dedicated to Those Who Are Not Ashamed of Economy*. Mrs. Child's chapter "How to Endure Poverty" prescribed a combination of piety and knowledge— the kind of knowledge found in a true woman's education, "a thorough religious *useful* education." The woman who had servants today, might tomorrow, because of a depression or panic, be forced to do her own work. If that happened she knew how to act, for she was to be the same cheerful consoler of her husband in their cottage as in their mansion.

An essay by Washington Irving, much quoted in the gift annuals, discussed the value of a wife in case of business reverses: "I have observed that a married man falling into misfortune is more apt to achieve his situation in the world than a single one . . . it is beautifully ordained by Providence that woman, who is the ornament of man in his happier hours, should be his stay and solace when smitten with sudden calamity."

A story titled simply but eloquently "The Wife" dealt with the quiet heroism of Ellen Graham during her husband's plunge from fortune to poverty. Ned Graham said of her: "Words are too poor to tell you what I owe to that noble woman. In our darkest seasons of adversity, she has been the angel of consolation—utterly forgetful of self and anxious only to comfort and sustain me." Of course she had a little help from "faithful Dinah who absolutely refused to leave her beloved mistress," but even so Ellen did no more than would be expected of any true woman.

Most of this advice was directed to woman as wife. Marriage was the proper state for the exercise of the domestic virtues. "True Love and a Happy Home," an essay in *The Young Ladies' Oasis,* might have been carved on every girl's hope chest. But although marriage was best, it was not absolutely necessary. The women's magazines tried to remove the stigma from being an "Old Maid." They advised no marriage at all rather than an unhappy one contracted out of selfish motives. Their stories showed maiden ladies as unselfish ministers to the sick, teachers of the young, or moral preceptors with their pens, beloved of the entire village. Usually the life of single blessedness resulted from the premature death of a fiancé, or was chosen through fidelity to some high mission. For example, in "Two Sisters," Mary devotes herself to Ellen and her abandoned children, giving up her own chance for marriage. "Her devotion to her sister's happiness has met its reward in the consciousness of having fulfilled a sacred duty." Very rarely, a "woman of genius" was absolved from the necessity of marriage, being so extraordinary that she did not need the security or status of being a wife. Most often, however, if girls proved "difficult," marriage and a family were regarded as a cure. The "sedative quality" of a home could be counted on to subdue even the most restless spirits.

George Burnap saw marriage as "that sphere for which woman was originally intended, and to which she is so exactly fitted to adorn and bless, as the wife, the mistress of a home, the solace, the aid, and the counsellor of that ONE, for whose sake alone the world is of any consequence to her." Samuel Miller preached a sermon on women: "How interesting and important are the duties devolved on females as WIVES . . . the counsellor and friend of the husband; who makes it her daily study to lighten his cares, to soothe his sorrows, and to augment his joys; who, like a guardian angel, watches over his interests, warns him against dangers, comforts him under trials; and by her pious, assiduous, and attractive deportment, constantly endeavors to render him more virtuous, more useful, more honourable, and more happy." A woman's whole interest should be focused on her husband, paying him "those numberless attentions to which the French give the title of *petits soins* and which the woman who loves knows so well how to pay. . . she should consider nothing as trivial which could win a smile of approbation from him."

Marriage was seen not only in terms of service but as an increase in authority for women. Burnap concluded that marriage improves the female character "not only because it puts her under the best possible tuition, that of the affections, and affords scope to her active energies, but because it gives her higher aims, and a more dignified position." *The Lady's Amaranth* saw it as a balance of power: "The man bears rule over his wife's person and conduct. She bears rule over his inclinations: he governs by law; she by persuasion. . . . The empire of the woman is an empire of softness . . . her commands are caresses, her menaces are tears."

Woman should marry, but not for money. She should choose only the high road of true love and not truckle to the values of a materialistic society. A story "Marrying for Money" (subtlety was not the strong point of the ladies' magazines) depicts Gertrude, the heroine, rueing the day she made her crass choice: "It is a terrible thing to live without love. . . . A woman who dares to marry for aught but the purest affection, calls down the just judgments of heaven upon her head."

The corollary to marriage, with or without true love, was motherhood, which added another dimension to her usefulness and her prestige. It also anchored her even more firmly to the home. "My Friend," wrote Mrs. Sigourney, "If in becoming a mother, you have reached the climax of your happiness, you have also taken a higher place in the scale of being . . . you have gained an increase of power." The Rev. J. N. Danforth pleaded in *The Ladies' Casket,* "Oh, mother, acquit thyself well in thy humble sphere, for thou mayest affect the

world." A true woman naturally loved her children; to suggest otherwise was monstrous.

America depended upon her mothers to raise up a whole generation of Christian statesmen who could say "all that I am I owe to my angel mother." The mothers must do the inculcating of virtue since the fathers, alas, were too busy chasing the dollar. Or as *The Ladies' Companion* put it more effusively, the father "weary with the heat and burden of life's summer day, or trampling with unwilling foot the decaying leaves of life's autumn, has forgotten the sympathies of life's joyous springtime. . . . The acquisition of wealth, the advancement of his children in worldly honor—these are his self-imposed tasks." It was his wife who formed "the infant mind as yet untainted by contact with evil . . . like wax beneath the plastic hand of the mother."

The Ladies' Wreath offered a fifty-dollar prize to the woman who submitted the most convincing essay on "How May An American Woman Best Show Her Patriotism." The winner was Miss Elizabeth Wetherell who provided herself with a husband in her answer. The wife in the essay of course asked her husband's opinion. He tried a few jokes first—"Call her eldest son George Washington," "Don't speak French, speak American"—but then got down to telling her in sober prize-winning truth what women could do for their country. Voting was no asset, since that would result only in "a vast increase of confusion and expense without in the smallest degree affecting the result." Besides, continued this oracle, "looking down at their child," if "we were to go a step further and let the children vote, their first act would be to vote their mothers at home." There is no comment on this devastating male logic and he continues: "Most women would follow the lead of their fathers and husbands," and the few who would "fly off on a tangent from the circle of home influence would cancel each other out."

The wife responds dutifully: "I see all that. I never understood so well before." Encouraged by her quick womanly perception, the master of the house resolves the question—an American woman best shows her patriotism by staying at home, where she brings her influence to bear "upon the right side for the country's weal." That woman will instinctively choose the side of right he has no doubt. Besides her "natural refinement and closeness to God" she has the "blessed advantage of a quiet life" while man is exposed to conflict and evil. She stays home with "her Bible and a well-balanced mind" and raises her sons to be good Americans. The judges rejoiced in this conclusion and paid the prize money cheerfully, remarking "they deemed it cheap at the price."

If any woman asked for greater scope for her gifts the magazines were sharply critical. Such women were tampering with society, undermining civilization. Mary Wollstonecraft, Frances Weight, and Harriet Martineau were condemned in the strongest possible language—they were read out of the sex. "They are only semi-women, mental hermaphrodites." The Rev. Harrington knew the women of America could not possibly approve of such perversions and went to some wives and mothers to ask if they did not want a "wider sphere of interest" as these nonwomen claimed. The answer was reassuring. "'NO!' they cried simultaneously, 'Let the men take care of politics, *we will take care of the children!*'" Again female discontent resulted only from a lack of understanding: women were not subservient, they were rather "chosen vessels." Looked at in this light the conclusion was inescapable: "Noble, sublime is the task of the American mother."

"Women's Rights" meant one thing to reformers, but quite another to the True Woman. She knew her rights,

The right to love whom others scorn,
The right to comfort and to mourn,
The right to shed new joy on earth,
The right to feel the soul's high worth. . .
Such women's rights, and God will bless
And crown their champions with
    success.

The American woman had her choice—she could define her rights in the way of the women's magazines and insure them by the practice of the requisite virtues, or she could go outside the home, seeking other rewards than love. It was a decision on which, she was told, everything in her world depended. "Yours it is to determine," the Rev. Mr. Stearns solemnly warned from the pulpit, "whether the beautiful order of society. . . shall continue as it has been" or whether "society shall break up and become a chaos of disjointed and unsightly elements." If she chose to listen to other voices than those of her proper mentors, sought other rooms than those of her home, she lost both her happiness and her power—"that almost magic power, which, in her proper sphere, she now wields over the destinies of the world."

But even while the women's magazines and related literature encouraged this ideal of the perfect woman, forces were at work in the nineteenth century which impelled woman herself to change, to play a more creative role in society. The movements for social reform, westward migration, missionary activity, utopian communities, industrialism, the Civil War—all called forth responses from woman which differed from those she was trained to believe were hers by nature and divine decree. The very perfection of True Womanhood, moreover, carried within itself the seeds of its own destruction. For if woman was so very little less than the angels, she should surely take a more active part in running the world, especially since men were making such a hash of things.

Real women often felt they did not live up to the ideal of True Womanhood: some of them blamed themselves, some challenged the standard, some tried to keep the virtues and enlarge the scope of womanhood. Somehow through this mixture of challenge and acceptance, of change and continuity, the True Woman evolved into the New Woman—a transformation as startling in its way as the abolition of slavery or the coming of the machine age. And yet the stereotype, the "mystique" if you will, of what woman was and ought to be persisted, bringing guilt and confusion in the midst of opportunity.

The women's magazines and related literature had feared this very dislocation of values and blurring of roles. By careful manipulation and interpretation they sought to convince woman that she had the best of both worlds—power and virtue—and that a stable order of society depended upon her maintaining her traditional place in it. To that end she was identified with everything that was beautiful and holy.

"Who Can Find a Valiant Woman?" was asked frequently from the pulpit and the editorial pages. There was only one place to look for her—at home. Clearly and confidently these authorities proclaimed the True Woman of the nineteenth century to be the Valiant Woman of the Bible, in whom the heart of her husband rejoiced and whose price was above rubies.

STUDY QUESTIONS

1. Summarize the "cult of true womanhood" and the behavioral expectations it imposed on American women.

2. Welter argues that the "cult of true womanhood" was an attempt to preserve premodern values in the industrial age. What does she mean? In what sense was industrialization incompatible with the "cult of true womanhood"? Why did the "cult of true womanhood" often leave nineteenth-century women feeling guilty?

3. To what extent was the "cult of true womanhood" an attempt by men in literary circles to prevent women from taking advantage of new opportunities provided by the rise of an industrial society? Was this a conspiracy or an unconscious cultural attempt to prevent change?

4. If the "cult of true womanhood" was indeed an attempt to retard modernization, what were people worried about? If they demanded domesticity, submissiveness, and chastity of women, why did they so fear professionalism, assertiveness, and sexual freedom?

BIBLIOGRAPHY

For general histories of the women's movement in the United States, see Andrew Sinclair, *The Better Half* (1965) and Page Smith, *Daughters of the Promised Land* (1970). Important scholarly work has been done on the origins of the feminist movement in early American history. See Barbara J. Berg, *The Remembered Gate: Origins of American Feminism—The Woman and the City, 1800–1860* (1977); Ann Douglas, *The Feminization of American Culture* (1977); and Nancy F. Cott, *The Bonds of Womanhood: "Women's Sphere" in New England, 1780–1835* (1977). Ellen DuBois's *Feminism and Suffrage: The Emergence of an Independent Woman's Movement in America, 1848–1869* (1978) deals with the early years of the crusade for the right to vote and how this crusade led to a much broader demand for equality. Philip Greven's *The Protestant Temperament* (1977) analyzes family roles and religious training in early America. Also see Barbara Leslie Epstein, *The Politics of Domesticity* (1981); M. P. Ryan, *Womanhood in America* (1983); and Nancy Woloch, *Women and the American Experience* (1984).

Reading 14

"MAKING NIGHT HIDEOUS": CHRISTMAS REVELRY AND PUBLIC ORDER IN NINETEENTH-CENTURY PHILADELPHIA

Susan G. Davis

Most Americans associate Christmas with a bundle of images and emotions—perhaps a blanket of snow, or presents under an evergreen tree. For the month between Thanksgiving and Christmas, malls and shopping centers play non-stop Christmas music, DJ's observe a countdown to Christmas, and families plan holiday get-togethers. Some try, usually unsuccessfully, to ignore the commercialism of the season, while others revel in an orgy of spending, giving, and getting. It seems the only controversies caused by Christmas involve credit card debt and rap versions of traditional Christmas songs.

There was a time, however, when many Americans viewed Christmas with feelings of fear and loathing. In the mid-seventeenth century, the Massachusetts Bay colony passed a law making the celebration of Christmas a criminal offense. What upset the authorities was not the private devotion but the "disorders" that accompanied Christmas celebrations. This concern for excessive, loud, and at times violent Christmas activities became more pronounced in the mid-nineteenth century. In cities like New York and Philadelphia—cities with sharp economic, ethnic, and racial divisions—Christmas was often a time of threatening mob actions, when gangs of young working-class males, often unemployed due to seasonal swings in the economy, dressed up as women or blacks, fortified themselves with liquor, and took to the streets. Often they ranged into wealthier neighborhoods—talking and singing loudly, beating on drums and ringing bells, firing guns and mouthing discontents, and generally "making night hideous." These mobs reminded the wealthier classes that violence and class conflict seethed under the surface of Jacksonian America.

In the following essay Susan G. Davis discusses the form and meaning of Christmas in nineteenth-century America. She demonstrates that society's core values are present in its celebrations and leisure moments.

For most of the nineteenth century respectable Philadelphians condemned Christmas as a disgrace. Philadelphia's Christmas was then an essentially public celebration, unfolding in taverns, alleys, and squares, and although it grew out of European festive patterns and rural customs, the festival took its shape and meaning from the city's working class and the changing conditions of urban life. Riot and revelry, disguise and debauch gave police and property owners reason to fear the approach of the holiday.

The history of Christmas in Philadelphia exemplifies the conflict within and between classes over behavior in public; confrontation over the form and enactment of the street festival was sharp and recurring. Middle-class disapproval and hostility were recorded in reportage, editorials, ordinances, and municipal policies, while celebrants' resistance found expression in the streets and the evolving forms of revelry. Press accounts of holiday activities provide a unique year-by-year record, not only of this conflict, but of working peoples' festive behavior. Moreover, the evolution of the street Christmas into an organized, sanctioned New Year's pageant—the Philadelphia Mummers Parade—provides an example of the transformation of urban public culture in the nineteenth century. The history of Christmas and its transformation can be examined along several dimensions: its origins in older customs and urban social life, its enactment in relation to the identities of its creators, and the attempts to suppress it by its opponents. Critical to its history are ethnic and class relations in the city and the special position of urban youth.

This street festival emerged in the early nineteenth century, with urban working-class culture

in general, from the convergence of older ways of life with unprecedented conditions. Cultural diversity distinguished Philadelphia's working people: the mingling of Germans, former slaves, Carribbeans, "native" Americans, Catholic and Protestant Irish, and migrants from the countryside was punctuated by their often violent clashes. Working-class heterogeneity found expression in patterns of residence, for the city's poorer districts were ethnic and racial patchworks, and ghettoes remained few and small until late in the century. Urban life was shaped by a more decisive segregation, however, as the new working-class suburbs spread out around the concentration of shops, businesses, and middle-class residences in the city center. Social life in the working-class districts grew out of the experience of labor, and although Philadelphians toiled in large workshops and mechanized factories, the lives of the majority were defined by hand labor, seasonal industry, and irregular employment. Working people blended intense labor with bouts of hard play, rejecting the rationalism and piety of their respectable neighbors and middle-class reformers. Their social life and recreation similarly combined the familiar and the new as they found leisure in commercial and customary entertainments. The most vibrant novelty, the musical theatre, spoke to an unprecedented male working-class audience, but entertainments could also be found in the tavern, dance hall, groggery, and street. The edges of town, still rural, provided livelihood and sport, both legal and illegal, complementing the free and easy, open atmosphere of the markets, amusement halls, and fairs. Thus city life in the early decades of the century was marked by the interpenetration of work and leisure, an incomplete spatial segregation of peoples and activities, and a blending of the informal and the emergent commercial.

Sacred and secular holidays were important expressions of this mixed culture, at once old- and new-fashioned. Christmas was the major punctuation of the European traditional year, and Philadelphians kept this emphasis, marking the season with relaxation and drinking, visiting and

Susan G. Davis, "Making Night Hideous": Christmas Revelry and Public Order in Nineteenth-Century Philadelphia in *American Quarterly*, Vol. 34.2 (Summer 1982): 185–199. © The Johns Hopkins University Press. Reprinted by permission.

Christmas revelry in 19th century Philadelphia.

ceremony. In the first half of the nineteenth century Christmas comprised a week of amusements and celebrations such as horse races, pig chases, pigeon shoots, ox roasts, and hunting and skating parties. The thriving theatre district counted on heavy attendance at harlequinades and minstrel shows. Militia troops and clubs held balls and concerts, church women gave fairs, fire companies paraded new equipment, set fires, and brawled. Hundreds of pubs, groggeries, and cookshops treated patrons to the specialities of the season with extra liberality.

Such intense socializing was possible, in part, because the holiday fell at a time of sharp contrast between work and leisure. As December's cold deepened, the creeks and rivers froze, and the workshops, factories, and docks stood still. In this time of hardship and unemployment for working people, the line between seasonal relaxation and distress was a fine one. Desperation often combined with customary license to turn suburban lanes and central streets into scenes of beggary, drunkenness, and riot. From early in the century observers found this face of Christmas

both alarming and disgraceful, a threat to public order.

Against this pattern of stepped-up socializing, disorder, and violence, two special activities took place that became the focus of outrage and suppression. "Masking" and "shooting" stood out in the street Christmas, associated with disturbances in the city's working-class suburbs. "Shooting"—a pan-European custom—celebrated the death of the old year and "fired in" the new, although explosive noisemaking occurred on Christmas Eve as well. "Masking"—assuming a new, often inverted or paradoxical identity through disguise— reflected the varied folk-cultural backgrounds of Philadelphians. Until about 1830, "belsnickling," a type of masking that involved disguised adults visiting houses to query children about their conduct, was popular in the city, an importation from the German-speaking countryside. Another form of disguised house-visit, masking (sometimes called mumming) became common after the 1820s. Costumed processions from door to door, with or without the performance of a folk play, were familiar to immigrants from the British Isles and the coastal South.

The record of a new kind of masking and shooting began in the 1830s, when descriptions of Christmas Eve processions of young men started to appear in newspapers. Though they were often in costume, these processions were different from rural German and British Isles traditions. Unlike the single, inquisitorial belsnickle, who was known to the families who let him in, these young men roved in bands, stopping at taverns and brawling on street corners. And although they paraded in their own neighborhoods, probably visiting the houses of friends and relatives, they also marched from the suburbs to sport in the city's crowded thoroughfares.

Observers found new names for these urban maskers: "fantasticals" and "callithumpians" designated their distinct but overlapping themes of disguise. Callithumpians made charivari-like rough music, taking the conventions of marching bands and fife and drum corps and turning them inside out. Dressed in burlesque, they mocked real music with cracked pots, cowbells, kitchen utensils, bent horns, cow horns, fake trumpets, and the whole folk repetoire of homemade and pretend instruments.

The fantasticals flew even further into anti-sense. In extravagant parody of the militia, they marched in drill form, bearing mock weapons and pseudo-military names. Appearing in both city and outlying towns, fantasticals drew their identities from real events and from the minstrel stage, mingling "Santa Ana's Cavalry" with the "Strut-Some Guards." Accounts of a mock-militia parade held in Easton, in early January, 1834, give the fullest description of fantastical dress and behavior. Led by a "Colonel" mounted on a jackass, one hundred men dressed as soldiers, with huge hats and weapons, wearing paintbrushes, hogs' ears, and tobacco plugs for epaulettes and strings of bones and fish around their necks, conducted elaborate sham manoeuvres. They were accompanied by a callithumpian band made up of "Indians, hunters, Falstaffs, Jim Crows, and nondescripts," wearing tent-sized hats and ballooning trousers. The exaggeration and inversion of military ceremony at play in this parody, as well as the theatrical borrowings, served as common devices of city maskers.

Though remarkable, such fantastical and callithumpian processions were not highly framed or specialized performances. On the contrary, noise and disguise, the two enduring and basic motifs of the festival, found endless repetition and myriad forms in the crowd's "rude revelry" of gun firing, drum beating, bell ringing, and simpler disguises.

Costumes were spare and dramatic, varying within a narrow range of imagery. Occasionally a lone belsnickle—half-demon, half-man—turned out. But in contrast to older, rural themes of semi-human disguise, Philadelphians commonly impersonated kinds of people, in conventionalized but differing interpretations of racial and national types. "Red Indians," "Chinamen," "Dutchmen" (standing both for German-speaking farmers and later, German immigrants), and rural New Englanders—"Brother Jonathans"—all appeared. But the most familiar disguises treated very familiar people: women and blacks. Wearing women's clothing was an easy transformation and popular, although arrests for transvestism brought stiff fines. Dressing as a woman could be as simple as filching a sister's dress or as elaborate as an impersonation of Jenny Lind or "Mrs. Langtry."

Blackface was a popular theme in the street Christmas from the 1830s. Here, as with the stereotyped images mentioned above, there was an intimate connection to performances in city theatres and their most successful form, the Negro minstrel show. "Jim Crow" began to march in parades and processions almost immediately after his debut in 1832. Like transvestism, blacking-up was quick and cheap, but could sustain elaboration into a stage character or a marching minstrel troupe. Female clothing often combined with blackface to make an "Aunt Sally," a double inversion of race and sex.

Though masks and disguises varied, the real identities of the holiday revelers stood clear: the Christmas and New Year's crowds were always described as young and male. Year after year the newspapers railed against the "drunken men and boys in the streets," the "half-grown boys," the "young rioters," "the inebriated young men," the "groups of hobbledehoys," and "black sheep" "who made night hideous with Galathumpian doings." Similarly, those arrested for masking and shooting and worse were uniformly young and male. The facts of youth and maleness illuminate the specific meanings of the festival for participants and observers, for the noisy, often violent crowds were not anomalous or extraordinary. Revelry crystalized the city's year-round youth problem. In a period of rapidly increasing industrialization, and before universal public education, the breakdown of the apprenticeship system and the decline of craft skills meant that young men were a severely underemployed group. Youthful criminals caused anxiety in all parts of the city, but the notorious gangs were only the most visible aspect of male street life. Most boys and young men diverted themselves less violently than the "Killers" and "Stingers"; still, their ever-present "destructionism," petty gambling, and hanging out annoyed gentle citizens, reminding them that the city seemed to corrupt youth.

In the street Christmas, rowdy youth culture reached its apotheosis; concern over riotous holiday nights was constant from the 1830s on. The editor of the *Chronicle* complained that on Christmas Eve, 1833, ". . . riot, noise, and uproar prevailed, uncontrolled and uninterrupted in many of our central and most orderly streets. Gangs of boys howled as if possessed by the demon of disorder." In 1844 the *Ledger's* New Year's editorial deplored the "riotous spirit raging" in the streets and declared that "our city has almost daily been the theatre of disorders which practically nullify civil government." The mid-1840s were especially uproarious, but tumult and commotion seemed ominous for decades.

Anxieties over youth and holiday crowds came together in outrage over the volunteer fire companies, who contributed heavily to the ceremonial and rowdy aspects of Christmas week and set the tone of the wild night. Key institutions of working-class peer culture, these all-male fraternities reflected ethnic and ideological splits among workers, as well as local rivalries over gang territory and fire-fighting prerogatives. The volunteers' love of parades, costumes, and machinery was surpassed only by their enthusiasm for fighting; by the 1840s firemen ranked as leading incendiaries and rioters in a city well known for violent upheavals. During Christmas week, firemen filled the theatre of the streets with their horse races, promenade dances, fantastical troupes, and less benign celebrations.

Many firemen and other "rowdies" lived in the new suburbs, where on holiday nights they created masquerades and uproars. In 1845 the *Public Ledger* remarked of Southwark's brawls, "the people who live in this region are demons." But as fantasticals and callithumpians, young men sought their largest audiences in the main business and theatre district, Chestnut between Fourth and Broad, where playgoers and promenaders thronged to view shop-window illuminations. The sense of threat, then, turned in part on the influx of carousers into the city's respectable heart; many of those arrested downtown for masking began their sport in Spring Garden, the Liberties, Passyunk, or Moyamensing.

Observers understood from suburban residence and demeanor the revellers' membership in the growing, heavily foreign-born, and poor stratum of the working class. There is, however, little information about the nativity of the crowds, and as noted above, masking customs would have been familiar to many of the city's natives and immigrants. Just as they came from all areas of the city, so the maskers likely sprang from different national backgrounds. Neither were the crowds all white, despite the mocking convention of blackface, for blacks made fantastical parades and played music in the streets as well. One of the first clear descriptions of a Christmas procession reports the attack on a black fife and drum corps by a white gang. Given the size of the city's black population, its concentration near the center, and the steady influx of blacks from the coastal South where slaves developed distinct mumming traditions, it is likely that Afro Americans contributed much to the shape of Christmas revelry.

These, then, were the revellers: young men from the city's poorer districts, ethnically and racially diverse, invading the respectable and propertied downtown. Fantasticals and callithumpians, highly visible because of their costumes and antics, became the focus of uneasiness and the objects of attempts to suppress the wearing of disguise. Maskers' own customs also led to notoriety and outrage. For instance, a favored callithumpian sport was collecting free drinks in neighborhood taverns. But if treats were ungenerous or refused, rough musicians were likely to retaliate. Crossing neighborhood boundaries probably provoked more fights than did stingy proprietors, and tavern owners seem to have preferred the noise of maskers to interference by authorities. In 1854 watchmen who tried to stop a callithumpian performance at William Myers's tavern found themselves mobbed by the band, the clientele, and the owner.

A New Year's Eve murder in 1857 illustrates the involvement of gangs and the night's use for the expression of ethnic antipathy. Witnesses to the stabbing death of Andrew Beiche, a young German, described his attack by a group of fantasticals. Calling themselves the "Ruggers" and sporting blackened faces, white robes, and plumes, the fantasticals followed Beiche's serenading party, beating them with wooden swords, fence stakes, and brickbats. References at the inquest to the Ruggers' code words, headquarters, and activities make it clear that they were one of the city's numerous gangs. Maskers and undisguised gangs fought each other, or joined up to attack "outsiders" and immigrants. White assaults on blacks, mobbings of black churches, battles between white and black gangs, and attacks on the watch were venerable holiday traditions.

Nighttime violence could be still more capricious: shootings and knifings errupted from disputes between maskers, and accidents were common, as when firing out the old year resulted in chance shootings of bystanders. The holidays seemed to offer endless possibilities for crime, violence, arson, riot, and misadventure.

The street Christmas held different and antagonistic meanings for those who created it and those who opposed it, meanings and interpretations located in the social identities of the maskers, in their disguises, and in their violent, disorderly behavior. For the boys and young men, "making night hideous" was a condensed statement made to and about three groups of people: themselves, their social superiors, and those they saw as outsiders or inferiors. For the young of the working class, the custom of masquerading forged and perpetuated group identity in particular neighborhoods or for particular gangs. Dressing up together, carousing and collecting free drinks, and finding and thrashing common enemies all created sensations of solidarity. At the same time, those denied power, recognition, and adult status because of their class and in particular because of their weak position in the city's economy could for once take over the respectable central district. In streets lined with the shops and residences of businessmen, the world turned upside down as maskers forced the most decried features of their peer culture on the entire city. The young men created a giant exemplary display of noise, intemperance, and riot, and they seem to have delighted in the outrage they caused.

Disguise expressed the point of view of working-class youth: in the patterned and selective transformation of identity, they discussed local social relations, outlining and emphasizing differences between kinds of people. The street Christmas shared this central motif—the delineation of the traits of inferiors—with much of nineteenth-century popular culture. But the racial and ethnic stereotypes that preoccupied maskers did not spring from an abstract repertoire; they reflected immediate conflicts and complexities in local and national life. Germans, whether rural or urban newcomers, were an important group in Philadelphia and the objects of joking and hostility in daily life, on stage, and in broadsheets. Chinese people were only a little removed, presented as subhuman idiots in newspapers and on the minstrel stage from San Francisco to Philadelphia. News of Indian removals and wars circulated constantly; Indian plays and later Wild West shows served as staple Christmas entertainments. The rural hick or "Brother Jonathan" strode the stage for most of the century, and Philadelphians witnessed his idiosyncracies in comic publications, the press, and at first hand.

But the group closest to home was the Negro, whose inferiority was delineated, celebrated, and reproduced in print and in the popular theatre. Young white men who dressed as blacks did not merely borrow imagery from commercial culture, they created a kind of localized commentary on central tensions in Philadelphia neighborhoods. From the early nineteenth century blacks competed with working-class whites for jobs and resources, achieving before the Civil War a position of relative strength in a few unskilled occupations and all-black guilds. Blacks were barely tolerable to whites when they acted like slaves: since the eighteenth century they had been permitted to hold festive dances in Potter's Field. But as the black population in the central city and South-wark grew in the 1830s and 1840s, black attempts at full social and political participation drew mockery, abuse, and violence from the majority of their white neighbors.

Christmas impersonations, like minstrel shows, mocked urban blacks' attempts to "act white"; that is, to participate equally in city life. But the homemade masquerades were unique in that they were not performed for commercial consumption, but as part of an informal means of creating group unity. In derogatory repetition of familiar images, popular ideas moved easily between stage and street and were enacted by neighbors for neighbors. On the other hand, masking made an ambiguous statement about race despite its violent mocking tone, for black-face found use as a way to play with racial identity, important in a city where black inferiority was taken for granted yet segregation was incomplete. John Szwed has described processes of moving back and forth across racial and cultural boundaries, involving the use of gesture, specific behaviors, voice, dialect, and other linguistic features. Such play, often the preserve of youth, paradoxically accomplishes learning and absorption of "alien" culture. Theatricals are only heightened examples of this play with socially constructed boundaries between kinds of people. Part of Christmas's delight was the liberty to "act black," all the more enjoyable because maskers could count on a safe return to their real identities.

The popularity of transvestism at Christmas is more difficult to explain, if only because we know so little about the lives of Philadelphia's working women. But the festival, like carnivals elsewhere, expressed vivid male/female, home/street oppositions. The heavily male tavern life and fighting mystique of peer culture opposed a respectable world of home, marriage, and family, so that in an era of absolute male supremacy in public life, sexual inversion made a strikingly complete identity transformation. Perhaps sexual boundary-crossing voiced anxiety about the definition of sex roles, for women's new activities as industrial workers

and their involvement in evangelical religion, temperance, trade unions, abolitionism, and feminism all seemed worthy of derision and violence from men.

Mockery and parody could also aim upward: the fantastical takeoffs of militia drills appeared in Philadelphia at the same time that the city's artisans organized against the unequal and oppressive compulsory militia system. This antiauthority strain continued in later impersonations of policemen, dog-catchers, and even mounted policemen, all municipal innovations resented in working-class neighborhoods.

Inferiority, then, was the street Christmas's subject, and masking, inequality's spare but complete enactment. Revelry took for its text acceptance of the fundamental divisions on which the republic of equals rested and asserted the right of the white male to take what was his—jobs, education, a limited measure of political power—by force, if necessary. This margin of privilege was reconstructed daily in laws, informal practices, and by riot, so that it is not surprising to find masquerades shaded into violence against blacks and immigrants, and rioters disguised as blacks and women at times other than Christmas. Playful and serious assertions of power, maskings, and mobbings marked proximate points along a continuum of antagonistic expression.

The racial and ethnic antagonisms within the working class served middle-class interests, fragmenting the potential for class-wide labor and political organization. Not one of the public complaints against masking objected to the strands of mocking supremacism it contained, but as the century progressed fear of the festival's form and tone increased. Arrests, stiff fines for masking and shooting, denunciations in the press, and attempts to keep crowds from forming expressed the mingled annoyance and anxiety with which middle-class Philadelphians viewed "the Christmas disgrace."

Gentle citizens felt rankled by more than noise. The "young black sheep of the community" were the group the authorities could least control, and imprecations hurled by the press—"rag-tag," "loafers," "vagrants"—reveal recognition of and uneasiness about youths' unemployment and the distress of winter. Precisely because of the year-round boisterousness of working-class youth, the street Christmas made the worst fears of the respectable seem about to come true. When the street Christmas was called a threat to property, authorities proved especially sensitive to complaints from downtown storekeepers. So the watch made forays into the suburbs to quell masking and shooting, but from early on concentrated their efforts on Eighth and Chestnut Streets.

The deepest threat loomed for moral and symbolic order, as defined by center city residents. Christmas focussed uneasiness through the lens of concern over youth, but at the same time that outrage over rowdyism swelled, the middle class was attaching its own new meanings to the festival. By the 1840s Christmas was becoming the apotheosis of middle-class ideals of childhood and family. Though still a holy day for the pious, affluent people now sought the day's meaning in the cozy, innocent delights of gift-giving, stocking-filling, and a family dinner celebrated at the altar of the hearth. The new icon of the holiday press—jolly, doting Santa Claus—barely resembled his country cousin, the whip-cracking belsnickle. This is not to argue that working-class families enjoyed no domestic Christmas; however, the elaboration and commercialization of this domestic holiday were accomplished largely by popular magazines, especially women's magazines, speaking to a newly prosperous and growing urban middle class.

The street Christmas collided with this celebration of private sentiment, throwing the disparity between middle-class expectations for behavior in public and anxieties about working-class youth into sharp relief. Hopes that the lower orders would raise themselves through temperance, piety, and self-denial (hopes held by some among the working class as well) found contradiction in the defiant rudeness of the festival. Most ironically, the exposition of irrationality unfolded on the holiest night of the pious year, openly, freely, and in public. Despite its critics' denunciations, it annually grew more disreputable.

In the 1860s, with the exception of the war years, the crowds of revelers swelled and their music grew rougher. Chestnut Street from Eighth to Independence Hall was "completely blockaded," and the firing of guns and blowing of trumpets incessant. Now the street Christmas reached a turning point: in the past masking and shooting had been tolerated when they could not be prevented, but the consolidation of the city's watches into a central police force in 1854 meant that all neighborhoods now experienced a more consistent presence of authority. Disorder could be met, at least in theory, in a concerted and forceful way. Thus, as the Christmas disgrace reached a new peak, the city government could begin a campaign to establish control over the holiday streets. Christmas Eve now saw the theatre district lined with hundreds of armed, uniformed men stationed in front of the shops. Proclamations forbidding masking, guns, and horns were issued from year to year, and "reasonable restraints" resulted in hundreds of arrests annually, mostly for drunkeness. These attempts at supression continued into the 1870s, but none worked. Instead of withering away, processions of fantasticals and callithumpians became more numerous, and the themes of noise-making and disguise persisted with resilience. In years when the city issued bans on "the horn nuisance," crowds of boys turned out ringing bells. When the little tin horns sold by hawkers were prohibited, men and boys blew brass trumpets, fog horns, rams horns—anything not made of tin.

Pressure from above did shift the locations, forms, and interpretations of the festival. Massed police kept celebrants out of the business district and closer to home in the suburbs, until masqueraders, long active in all parts of town and even in Camden, began to be thought of as "belonging" to the southern wards. But the most important and symbolic effect of organized crowd control was to shift the theatre of disorder from holy Christmas Eve to secular New Year's Eve and eventually to New Year's Day. New Year's had always been a nonreligious if less well-loved holiday, and seemed less susceptible to defilement than the night of Christ's birth.

At the same time, attitudes toward a more restricted range of festive activities softened. In 1880, describing a scene on Chestnut Street, the *Inquirer* commented that although fantasticals created pandemonium with their mock weapons and voices, ". . . it is the prerogative of New Year's that as long as the people do not violently break the peace, they can be as noisy and jolly as they will." Why was condescending tolerance possible after decades of complaint, contempt, and suppression? It was the growing tendency of the maskers to organize themselves into clubs and to give coordinated performances that proved decisive in forcing the city's acceptance of modified mummery. While early fantasticals and callithumpians had gathered spontaneously among age cohorts, by the mid-1880s Philadelphia maskers participated in New Year's social clubs. A few "Socials" were active year after year under the same names, prefiguring the famous twentieth-century string bands and comic clubs. Socials with money to spend paraded in "fancy dress," yet themes of racial and sexual parody persisted. These more elaborate marches earned approval from commentators who distinguished between the "tasteful" and the "crude," and between mock musicians and troupes with hired brass bands.

The beginnings of the organized clubs and the stepped-up efforts at crowd control coincided with the city's victory in 1871 in its long battle to bring the volunteer fire departments under municipal authority. There is some evidence that the social functions of the fire companies flowed into the activities of the New Year's clubs, a shift from one heavily invested all-male institution to another. The socials retained the volunteers' names and ties to firemen in other cities, and behaved much as the hose and engine crews had done, parading, giving dances, and brawling. Women participated in auxiliaries, sewing banners and costumes. The cycle of ceremony and social exchange remained dense and busy.

Masking gradually became a very different kind of activity. In the eighties, participation shifted toward family involvement, often across generations, and families identified with particular clubs. In club life, maskers adapted and modified the older forms of revelry, following the general tendency toward more organized urban recreations. As a result, revelry shifted away from the domain of rowdy youth. Though working-class youth and gangs still prompted anxiety, the noisy strains of youth culture receded from the festival's core. Mummery now tended to become—and could become—more "creditable." Costumes became flashy and elaborate; "furs, feathers, bullion and embroidery" appeared in the crowds. Formally making a masquerade more of a performance and less a wild revel provided one way of being in control of being out of control. With increasing elaboration, structure, and conciousness of form the wild night was becoming a parade, and the disgrace could be recast into an appropriate and rational part of the city's self-image.

Most important, the clubs gave the city authorities a flexible means of control over maskers' performances. In 1884 the mayor issued permits, making the leader of each troupe responsible for the actions of all its members. By requiring maskers to carry permits and present them like licenses, the city assured that mummery took place not in the face of authority but under its sponsorship. This authority maskers accepted to a degree, by desisting from impersonating local politicians and policemen, and by further organizing and differentiating themselves from the crowd. When merchants offered prizes for the best troupes and costumes, the shift in public meaning was assured—the disgrace transformed into an entertaining custom. All that remained was to shift the theatre of disorders from the night to the day.

Still, the transformation of the wild night into an official tradition did not take place in one year or even over one decade. In 1883–1884 several large clubs and fife and drum corps applied for the first permits. Yet of 190 applications more than 140 were filed by individuals and unnamed persons, and many of these, the *Inquirer* remarked, were boys. Requests were "respectfully submitted" for "a few friends [to have] a sociable time," for "six private citizens to maskerade [sic]," and "for blakin up as colored men to serenade a few friends." Though tortuous callithumpian notes still prevailed over brass bands, large associations did the main streets decked out in spangles and satins, their clowns in blackface at the rear. But as the *Inquirer* commented, the majority of masquerades took place on a "cheap and shabby scale": that is, they were homemade and neighborhood oriented.

As a result of pressures and counter pressures, the rude street festival had been changed and contained, yet it expanded into a formal parade. In 1900 the Mummers Parade, as observers now called it, received the city's official sanction and sponsorship. Although arbiters of culture occasionally offered suggestions for making the parade more "artistic," the clubs retained control of their performances' content and good relations prevailed between Mummers and officials until the 1960s. Except for regulations prohibiting the impersonation of local politicians, content was self-regulated, or rather, Mummers' and official notions of parade-worthy topics did not diverge significantly.

In the parade, a selective and distilled statement of working-class culture and point of view found institutionalized, public expression. One segment of the city's working class, a mostly white, self-organizing portion, wrested for itself and was allowed to gain an important medium of communication. Enmeshed in a complex binding of kin, neighborhood, and ethnic ties, the new parade linked working-class recreation and social life to commerce, advertising, and more recently, to tourism. But in the process of transformation, the possibility of the wild night as a means to explore alternate interpretations and orderings of society—a possibility that flickered and threatened in the nineteenth century—was foreclosed. Thus it is no surprise to find that while the parade has remained a stoutly working-class activity, black participation in the festival withered away after 1900. Official sanction alone did not diffuse revelry's rowdy threat and redirect its social commentary. The ideology celebrated in the street Christmas—Jacksonian masculinity, white supremacy—saturated the challenge to order implied in the explosion of youth culture. Along with other new features of popular culture, the street Christmas delineated inferiors, foreigners, and social "others," and this aspect of revelry, never challenged by authorities, persists most vibrantly today. It was not inevitable that the Mummers Parade become a joyful elaboration of the primacy of racial and sexual divisions and loyalties over other social values and larger class interests, but this was the result of the process of organization, incorporation, and control. Decisively changed was the social definition of what might be enacted in public.

STUDY QUESTIONS

1. How would you characterize the relationships between the various racial and ethnic groups which comprised Philadelphia's working class in the first half of the nineteenth century? How might we consider the processions of "fantasticals" and "callithumpians" as an expression of these relationships?

2. What were "masking" and "shooting," and why did the working classes want to make a "mockery" and "parody" of middle-class respectability and governmental authority? If Christmas revelry was a way for the white male working classes to assert their "rights" and create a "sensation of solidarity," why was the middle class so upset at these activities?

3. What were some of the activities of the volunteer fire companies which particularly offended middle-class reformers? How were the fire companies eventually brought under control?

4. How did Philadelphia's middle classes begin to celebrate Christmas starting in the 1840s? How did this new mode of celebration reflect social and economic changes in this class?

5. How did "respectable" Philadelphians finally manage to tame the tradition of riotous Christmas revelry in the city?

BIBLIOGRAPHY

An extended treatment of the material in this article can be found in Susan G. Davis, *Parades and Power: Street Theater in Nineteenth-Century Philadelphia* (1986). Another good exploration of antebellum urban "disorder" is Paul A. Gilje, *The Road to Mobocracy: Popular Disorder in New York City, 1763–1834* (1987). Further changes and controversies associated with the celebration of Christmas in America are explored in Stephen Nissenbaum, *The Battles for Christmas* (1996) and Clement A. Miles, *Christmas in Ritual and Tradition, Christian and Pagan* (1912, reissued in 1976). Excellent studies of urban working-class life in antebellum America include Bruce Laurie, *Working People of Philadelphia, 1800–1850* (1980) and Sean Wilentz, *Chants Democratic: New York City and the Rise of the American Working Class, 1788–1850* (1984). Both Laurie and Wilentz—and a whole generation of labor historians—were inspired by the classic study by E. P. Thompson, *The Making of the English Working Class* (1966).

THE ANIMAL TRICKSTER

Lawrence W. Levine

For more than 350 years, Americans have debated the questions of slavery, arguing continually over the nature of slavery and the black personality, but always agreeing that the unique relationship between black and white people has had an enormous impact on United States history. An early generation of historians looked upon the slaves as genetically inferior people—lazy, childlike, obsequious, and quite incapable of dealing independently with civilized society. By the 1950s, historians were rejecting the idea of genetic inferiority, but they were still looking back on slavery with a white perspective. While one group argued that the viciousness of slavery had transformed black people into a frightened, weak mass, another group tried to undermine plantation slavery by claiming that blacks were rebellious and bitterly unhappy. Recently, historians have taken a more complex approach to the history of black slavery, arguing that a delicate and symbiotic relationship existed between whites and blacks in the antebellum South, and that the slaves developed a rich African-American culture, despite the pains of bondage, which provided them fulfillment, power, and a sense of self-worth. Lawrence W. Levine's book *Black Culture and Black Consciousness: Afro-American Folk Thought from Slavery to Freedom* (1977) is a major contribution to the contemporary interpretation of slavery. The following selection, "The Animal Trickster," clearly illustrates how slaves developed a folk culture enabling them to interpret their environment, vent frustration, and provide forms of symbolic association necessary to group survival.

Although the range of slave tales was narrow in neither content nor focus, it is not surprising or accidental that the tales most easily and abundantly collected in Africa and among Afro-Americans in the New World were animal trickster tales. Because of their overwhelmingly paradigmatic character, animal tales were, of all the narratives of social protest or psychological release, among the easiest to relate both within and especially outside the group.

The propensity of Africans to utilize their folklore quite consciously to gain psychological release from the inhibitions of their society and their situation. . . needs to be reiterated here if the popularity and function of animal trickster tales is to be understood. After listening to a series of Ashanti stories that included rather elaborate imitations of afflicted people—an old woman dressed in rags and covered with sores, a leper, an old man suffering from the skin disease yaws—which called forth roars of laughter from the audience, the English anthropologist R. S. Rattray suggested that it was unkind to ridicule such subjects. "The person addressed replied that in everyday life no one might do so, however great the inclination to laugh might be. He went on to explain that it was so with many other things: the cheating and tricks of priests, the rascality of a chief—things about which everyone knew, but concerning which one might not ordinarily speak in public. These occasions gave every one an opportunity of talking about and laughing at such things; it was 'good' for every one concerned," he said. Customs such as these led Rattray to conclude "beyond a doubt, that West Africans had discovered for themselves the truth of the psychoanalysts' theory of 'repressions,' and that in these ways they sought an outlet for what might otherwise become a dangerous complex."

From *Black Culture and Black Consciousness: Afro-American Folk Thought from Slavery to Freedom* by Lawrence W. Levine. Copyright © 1977 by Oxford University Press, Inc. Reprinted by permission of the author.

Certainly this was at the heart of the popularity of animal trickster tales. Whether it is accurate to assert, as Rattray has done, that the majority of "beast fables" were derived from the practice of substituting the names of animals for the names of real individuals whom it would have been impolitic or dangerous to mention, there can be no question that the animals in these tales were easily recognizable representations of both specific actions and generalized patterns of human behavior. "In the fable," Léopold Senghor has written, "the animal is seldom a totem; it is this or that one whom every one in the village knows well; the stupid or tyrannical or wise and good chief, the young man who makes reparation for injustice. Tales and fables are woven out of everyday occurrences. Yet it is not a question of anecdotes or of 'material from life.' The facts are images and have paradigmatic value." The popularity of these tales in Africa is attested to by the fact that the Akan-speaking people of the West Coast gave their folk tales the generic title *Anansesem* (spider stories), after the spider trickster Anansi, whether he appeared in the story or not, and this practice was perpetuated by such New World Afro-American groups as the South American Negroes of Surinam who referred to all their stories, whatever their nature, as *Anansitori,* or the West Indian blacks of Curaçao who called theirs *Cuenta de Nansi.*

For all their importance, animals did not monopolize the trickster role in African tales; tricksters could, and did, assume divine and human form as well. Such divine tricksters as the Dahomean Legba or the Yoruban Eshu and Orunmila did not survive the transplantation of Africans to the United States and the slaves' adaptation to Christian religious forms. Human tricksters, on the other hand, played an important role in the tales of American slaves. By the nineteenth century, however, these human tricksters were so rooted in and reflective of their new cultural and social setting that outside of function they bore increasingly little resemblance to their African counterparts. It was in the animal trickster that the most easily perceivable correspondence in form and usage between African and Afro-American tales can be found. In both cases the primary trickster figures of animal tales were weak, relatively powerless creatures who attain their ends through the application of native wit and guile rather than power or authority: the Hare or Rabbit in East Africa, Angola, and parts of Nigeria; the Tortoise among the Yoruba, Ibo, and Edo peoples of Nigeria; the Spider throughout much of West Africa including Ghana, Liberia, and Sierra Leone; Brer Rabbit in the United States.

In their transmutation from their natural state to the world of African and Afro-American tales, the animals inhabiting these tales, though retaining enough of their natural characteristics to be recognizable, were almost thoroughly humanized. The world they lived in, the rules they lived by, the emotions that governed them, the status they craved, the taboos they feared, the prizes they struggled to attain were those of the men and women who lived in this world. The beings that came to life in these stories were so created as to be human enough to be identified with but at the same time exotic enough to allow both storytellers and listeners a latitude and freedom that came only with much more difficulty and daring in tales explicitly concerning human beings.

This latitude was crucial, for the one central feature of almost all trickster tales is their assault upon deeply ingrained and culturally sanctioned values. This of course accounts for the almost universal occurence of trickster tales, but it has not rendered them universally identical. The values people find constraining and the mechanisms they choose to utilize in their attempts at transcending or negating them are determined by their culture and their situation. "It is very well to speak of 'the trickster,'" Melville and Frances Herskovits have noted, "yet one need but compare the Winnebago trickster [of the North American Indians] . . . with Legba and Yo in Dahomey to find that the specifications for the first by no means fit the second." The same may be said of the slave trickster in relation to the trickster figures of the whites around them. Although animal trickster tales do not seem to have caught a strong hold among American

whites during the eighteenth and the first half of the nineteenth century, there were indigenous American tricksters from the tall, spare New Englander Jonathan, whose desire for pecuniary gain knew few moral boundaries, to the rough roguish confidence men of southwestern tales. But the American process that seems to have been most analogous in function to the African trickster tale was not these stories so much as the omnipresent tales of exaggeration. In these tall tales Americans were able to deal with the insecurities produced by forces greater than themselves not by manipulating them, as Africans tended to do, but by overwhelming them through the magnification of the self epitomized in the unrestrained exploits of a Mike Fink or Davy Crockett. "I'm . . . half-horse, half-alligator, a little touched with the snapping turtle; can wade the Mississippi, leap the Ohio, ride upon a streak of lightning, and slip without a scratch down a honey locust; can whip my weight in wildcats, . . . hug a bear too close for comfort, and eat any man opposed to Jackson," the latter would boast.

It is significant that, with the exception of the stories of flying Africans, mythic strategies such as these played almost no role in the lore of nineteenth-century slaves; not until well after emancipation do tales of exaggeration, with their magnification of the individual, begin to assume importance in the folklore of Afro-Americans. Nor did the model of white trickster figures seem to have seriously affected the slaves, whose own tricksters remained in a quite different mold—one much closer to the cultures from which they had come. In large part, African trickster tales revolved around the strong patterns of authority so central to African cultures. As interested as they might be in material gains, African trickster figures were more obsessed with manipulating the strong and reversing the normal structure of power and prestige. Afro-American slaves, cast into a far more rigidly fixed and certainly a more alien authority system, could hardly have been expected to neglect a cycle of tales so ideally suited to their needs.

This is not to argue that slaves in the United States continued with little or no alteration in the trickster lore of their ancestral home. The divergences were numerous: divine trickster figures disappeared; such important figures as Anansi the spider were at best relegated to the dim background; sizable numbers of European tales and themes found their way into the slave repertory. But we must take care not to make too much of these differences. For instance, the fact that the spider trickster retained its importance and its Twi name, Anansi, among the Afro-Americans of Jamaica, Surinam, and Curaçao, while in the United States Anansi lived only a peripheral existence in such tales as the Aunt Nancy stories of South Carolina and Georgia, has been magnified out of proportion by some students. "The sharp break between African and American tradition," Richard Dorson has written, "occurs at the West Indies, where Anansi the spider dominates hundreds of cantefables, the tales that inclose songs. But no Anansi stories are found in the United States." The decline of the spider trickster in the United States can be explained by many factors from the ecology of the United States, where spiders were less ubiquitous and important than in either Africa or those parts of the New World in which the spider remained a central figure, to the particular admixture of African peoples in the various parts of the Western Hemisphere. Anansi, after all, was but one of many African tricksters and in Africa itself had a limited influence. Indeed, in many parts of South America where aspects of African culture endured overtly with much less alteration than occurred in the United States, Anansi was either nonexistent or marginal.

What is more revealing than the life or death of any given trickster figure is the retention of the trickster tale itself. Despite all of the changes that took place, there persisted the mechanism, so well developed throughout most of Africa, by means of which psychic relief from arbitrary authority could be secured, symbolic assaults upon the powerful could be waged, and important lessons about authority relationships could be imparted. Afro-Americans in the United States were to make extended use of this mechanism throughout their years of servitude.

In its simplest form the slaves' animal trickster tale was a cleanly delineated story free of ambiguity. The strong assault the weak, who fight back with any weapons they have. The animals in these tales have an almost instinctive understanding of each other's habits and foibles. Knowing Rabbit's curiosity and vanity, Wolf constructs a tar-baby and leaves it by the side of the road. At first fascinated by this stranger and then progressively infuriated at its refusal to respond to his friendly salutations, Rabbit strikes at it with his hands, kicks it with his feet, butts it with his head, and becomes thoroughly enmeshed. In the end, however, it is Rabbit whose understanding of his adversary proves to be more profound. Realizing that Wolf will do exactly what he thinks his victim least desires, Rabbit convinces him that of all the ways to die the one he is most afraid of is being thrown into the briar patch, which of course is exactly what Wolf promptly does, allowing Rabbit to escape.

This situation is repeated in tale after tale: the strong attempt to trap the weak but are tricked by them instead. Fox entreats Rooster to come down from his perch, since all the animals have signed a peace treaty and there is no longer any danger: "I don't eat you, you don' boder wid me. Come down! Le's make peace!" Almost convinced by this good news, Rooster is about to descend when he thinks better of it and tests Fox by pretending to see a man and a dog coming down the road. "Don' min' fo' comin' down den," Fox calls out as he runs away. "Dawg ain't got no sense, yer know, an' de man got er gun." Spotting a goat lying on a rock, Lion is about to surprise and kill him when he notices that Goat keeps chewing and chewing although there is nothing there but bare stone. Lion reveals himself and asks Goat what he is eating. Overcoming the momentary paralysis which afflicts most of the weak animals in these tales when they realize thay are trapped, Goat saves himself by saying in his most terrifying voice: "Me duh chaw dis rock, an ef you dont leff, wen me done . . . me guine eat you."

At its most elemental, then, the trickster tale consists of a confrontation in which the weak use their wits to evade the strong. Mere escape, however, does not prove to be victory enough, and in a significant number of these tales the weak learn the brutal ways of the more powerful. Fox, taking advantage of Pig's sympathetic nature, gains entrance to his house during a storm by pleading that he is freezing to death. After warming himself by the fire, he acts exactly as Pig's instincts warned him he would. Spotting a pot of peas cooking on the stove, he begins to sing:

Fox and peas are very good,
But Pig and peas are better.

Recovering from his initial terror, Pig pretends to hear a pack of hounds, helps Fox hide in a meal barrel, and pours the peas in, scalding Fox to death.

In one tale after another the trickster proves to be as merciless as his stronger opponent. Wolf traps Rabbit in a hollow tree and sets it on fire, but Rabbit escapes through a hole in the back and reappears, thanking Wolf for an excellent meal, explaining that the tree was filled with honey which melted from the heat. Wolf, in his eagerness to enjoy a similar feast, allows himself to be sealed into a tree which has no other opening, and is burned to death. "While eh duh bun, Buh Wolf bague an pray Buh Rabbit fuh leh um come out, but Buh Rabbit wouldnt yeddy [hear] um." The brutality of the trickster in these tales was sometimes troubling ("Buh Rabbit. . . hab er bad heart," the narrator of the last story concluded), but more often it was mitigated by the fact that the strong were the initial aggressors and the weak really had no choice. The characteristic spirit of these tales was one not of moral judgment but of vicarious triumph. Storytellers allowed their audience to share the heartening spectacle of a lion running in terror from a goat or a fox fleeing a rooster; to experience the mocking joy of Brer Rabbit as he scampers away through the briar patch calling back to Wolf, "Dis de place me mammy fotch me up,—dis de place me mammy fotch me up"; to feel the joyful relief of Pig as he turns Fox's song upside down and chants:

Pig and peas are very good,
But Fox and peas are better.

Had self-preservation been the only motive driving the animals in these stories, the trickster tale need never have varied from the forms just considered. But Brer Rabbit and his fellow creatures were too humanized to be content with mere survival. Their needs included all the prizes human beings crave and strive for: wealth, success, prestige, honor, sexual prowess. Brer Rabbit himself summed it up best in the following

De rabbit is de slickest o' all de animals de Lawd ever made. He ain't de biggest, an' he ain't de loudest but he sho' am de slickest. If he gits in trouble he gits out by gittin' somebody else in. Once he felt down a deep well an' did he holler and cry? No siree. He set up a mighty mighty whistling and a singin', an' when de wolf passes by he heard him an' he stuck his head over an' de rabbit say, "Git 'long 'way f'om here. Dere ain't room fur two. Hit's mighty hot up dere and nice an' cool down here. Don' you git in dat bucket an' come down here." Dat made de wolf all de mo' onrestless and he jumped into the bucket an' as he went down de rabbit come up, an' as dey passed de rabbit he laughed an' he say, "Dis am life; some go up and some go down."

There could be no mistaking the direction in which Rabbit was determined to head. It was in his inexorable drive upward that Rabbit emerged not only as an incomparable defender but also as a supreme manipulator, a role that complicated the simple contours of the tales already referred to.

In the ubiquitous tales of amoral manipulation, the trickster could still be pictured as much on the defensive as he was in the stories which had him battling for his very life against stronger creatures. The significant difference is that now the panoply of his victims included the weak as well as the powerful. Trapped by Mr. Man and hung from a sweet gum tree until he can be cooked, Rabbit is buffeted to and fro by the wind and left to contemplate his bleak future until Brer

Although the animals in the trickster tales were physically recognized as animals, they were thoroughly human in their actions.

Squirrel happens along. "This yer my cool air swing," Rabbit informs him. "I taking a fine swing this morning." Squirrel begs a turn and finds his friend surprisingly gracious: "Certainly, Brer Squirrel, you do me proud. Come up here, Brer Squirrel, and give me a hand with this knot." Tying the grateful squirrel securely in the tree, Rabbit leaves him to his pleasure—and his fate. When Mr. Man returns, "he take Brer Squirrel home and cook him for dinner."

It was primarily advancement not preservation that led to the trickster's manipulations, however. Among a slave population whose daily rations were at best rather stark fare and quite often a barely minimal diet, it is not surprising that food proved to be the most common symbol of enhanced status and power. In his never-ending quest for food the trickster was not content with mere acquisition, which he was perfectly capable of on his own; he needed to procure the food through guile from some stronger animal. Easily the most popular tale of this type pictures Rabbit and Wolf as partners in farming a field. They have laid aside a tub of butter for winter provisions, but Rabbit proves unable to wait or to share. Pretend-

ing to hear a voice calling him, he leaves his chores and begins to eat the butter. When he returns to the field he informs his partner that his sister just had a baby and wanted him to name it. "Well, w'at you name um?" Wolf asks innocently. "Oh, I name um Buh Start-um," Rabbit replies. Subsequent calls provide the chance for additional assaults on the butter and additional names for the nonexistent babies: "Buh Half-um," "Buh Done-um," After work, Wolf discovers the empty tub and accuses Rabbit, who indignantly denies the theft. Wolf proposes that they both lie in the sun, which will cause the butter to run out of the guilty party. Rabbit agrees readily, and when grease begins to appear on his own face he rubs it onto that of the sleeping wolf. "Look, Buh Wolf," he cries, waking his partner , "de buttah melt out on you. Dat prove you eat um." "I guess you been right," Wolf agrees docilely, "I eat um fo' trute." In some versions the animals propose a more hazardous ordeal by fire to discover the guilty party. Rabbit successfully jumps over the flames but some innocent animal—Possum, Terrapin, Bear—falls in and perishes for Rabbit's crime.

In most of these tales the aggrieved animal, realizing he has been tricked, desperately tries to avenge himself by setting careful plans to trap Rabbit, but to no avail. Unable to outwit Rabbit, his adversaries attempt to learn from him, but here too they fail. Seeing Rabbit carrying a string of fish, Fox asks him where they came from. Rabbit confesses that he stole them from Man by pretending to be ill and begging Man to take him home in his cart which was filled with fish. While riding along, Rabbit explains, he threw the load of fish into the woods and then jumped off to retrieve them. He encourages Fox to try the same tactic, and Fox is beaten to death, as Rabbit knew he would be, since Man is too shrewd to be taken in the same way twice.

And so it goes in story after story. Rabbit cheats Brer Wolf out of his rightful portion of a cow and a hog they kill together. He tricks Brer Fox out of his part of their joint crop year after year "until he starved the fox to death. Then he had all the crop, and all the land too." He leisurely watches all the other animals build a house in which they store their winter provisions and then sneaks in, eats the food, and scares the others, including Lion, away by pretending to be a spirit and calling through a horn in a ghostly voice that he is a "better man den ebber bin yuh befo." He convinces Wolf that they ought to sell their own grandparents for a tub of butter, arranges for his grandparents to escape so that only Wolf's remain to be sold, and once they are bartered for the butter he steals that as well.

The many tales of which these are typical make it clear that what Rabbit craves is not possession but power, and this he acquires not simply by obtaining food but by obtaining it through the manipulation and deprivation of others. It is not often that he meets his match, and then generally at the hands of an animal as weak as himself. Refusing to allow Rabbit to cheat him out of his share of the meat they have just purchased, Partridge samples a small piece of liver and cries out, "Br'er Rabbit, de meat bitter! Oh, 'e bitter, bitter! bitter, bitter! You better not eat de meat," and tricks Rabbit into revealing where he had hidden the rest of the meat. "You is a damn sha'p feller," Partridge tells him. "But I get even wid you." Angry at Frog for inviting all the animals in the forest but him to a fish dinner, Rabbit frightens the guests away and eats all the fish himself. Frog gives another dinner, but this time he is prepared and tricks Rabbit into the water. "You is my master many a day on land, Brer Rabbit," Frog tells him just before killing and eating him, "but I is you master in the water."

It is significant that when these defeats do come, most often it is not brute force but even greater trickery that triumphs. Normally, however, the trickster has more than his share of the food. And of the women as well, for sexual prowess is the other basic sign of prestige in the slaves' tales. Although the primary trickster was occasionally depicted as a female—Ol' Molly Hare in Virginia, Aunt Nancy or Ann Nancy in the few surviving spider stories—in general women played a small role in slave tales. They were not actors in their own right so much as attractive possessions to be fought over. That the women for whom the animals compete are frequently the daughters of the most powerful creatures in the forest makes it evident that the contests are for status as well as pleasure. When Brer Bear promises his daughter to the best whistler in the forest, Rabbit offers to help his only serious competitor, Brer Dog, whistle more sweetly by slitting the corner of his mouth, which in reality makes him incapable of whistling at all. If Rabbit renders his adversaries figuratively impotent in their quest for women, they often retaliate in kind. In the story just related, Dog chases Rabbit, bites off his tail, and nothing more is said about who wins the woman.

More often than not, though, Rabbit is successful. In a Georgia tale illustrating the futility of mere hard work, Brer Wolf offers his attractive daughter to the animal that shucks the most corn. Rabbit has his heart set on winning Miss Wolf but realizes he has no chance of beating Brer Coon at shucking corn. Instead, he spends all of his time during the contest singing, dancing, and charming Miss Wolf. At the end he sits down next to Coon and claims that he has shucked the great pile of corn. Confused, Wolf leaves the decision up to his daughter:

Now Miss Wolf she been favoring Brer Rabbit all the evening. Brer Rabbit dancing and singing plum turned Miss Wolf's head, so Miss Wolf she say, "It most surely are Brer Rabbit's pile." Miss Wolf she say she "plum 'stonished how Brer Coon can story so." Brer Rabbit he take the gal and go off home clipity, lipity. Poor old Brer Coon he take hisself off home, he so tired he can scarcely hold hisself together.

In another Georgia tale the contest for the woman seems to be symbolically equated with freedom. Fox promises his daughter to any animal who can pound dust out of a rock.

Then Brer Rabbit, he feel might set down on, 'cause he know all the chaps can swing the stone hammer to beat hisself, and he go off sorrowful like and set on the sand bank. He sat a while and look east, and then he turn and set a while and look west, but may be you don't know, sah, Brer Rabbit sense never come to hisself 'cepting when he look north.

Thus inspired, Rabbit conceives of a strategy allowing him to defeat his more powerful opponents and carry off the woman.

In the best known and most symbolically interesting courting tale, Rabbit and Wolf vie for the favors of a woman who is pictured as either equally torn between her two suitors or leaning toward Wolf. Rabbit alters the contest by professing surprise that she could be interested in Wolf, since he is merely Rabbit's riding horse. Hearing of this, Wolf confronts Rabbit, who denies ever saying it and promises to go to the woman and personally refute the libel as soon as he is well enough. Wolf insists he go at once, and the characteristic combination of Rabbit's deceit and Wolf's seemingly endless trust and gullibility allows Rabbit to convince his adversary that he is too sick to go with him unless he can ride on Wolf's back with a saddle and bridle for support. The rest of the story is inevitable. Approaching the woman's house Rabbit tightens the reins, digs a pair of spurs into Wolf, and trots him around crying, "Look here, girl! what I told you? Didn't I say I had Brother Wolf for my riding horse?" It was in many ways the ultimate secular triumph in slave tales. The weak doesn't merely kill his enemy: he mounts him, humiliates him, reduces him to servility, steals his woman, and, in effect, takes his place.

Mastery through possessing the two paramount symbols of power—food and women—did not prove to be sufficient for Rabbit. He craved something more. Going to God himself, Rabbit begs for enhanced potency in the form of a larger tail, greater wisdom, bigger eyes. In each case God imposes a number of tasks upon Rabbit before his wishes are fulfilled. Rabbit must bring God a bag full of blackbirds, the teeth of a rattlesnake or alligator, a swarm of yellowjackets, the "eyewater" (tears) of a deer. Rabbit accomplishes each task by exploiting the animals' vanity. He tells the blackbirds that they cannot fill the bag

and when they immediately prove they can, he traps them. He taunts the snake, "dis pole *swear* say you ain't long as him." When Rattlesnake insists he is, Rabbit ties him to the stick, ostensibly to measure him, kills him, and takes his teeth. Invariably Rabbit does what is asked of him but finds God less than pleased. In some tales he is chased out of Heaven. In others God counsels him, "Why Rabbit, ef I was to gi' you long tail aint you see you'd 'stroyed up de whol worl'? Nobawdy couldn' do nuttin wid you!" Most commonly God seemingly complies with Rabbit's request and gives him a bag which he is to open when he returns home. But Rabbit cannot wait, and when he opens the bag prematurely "thirty bull-dawg run out de box, an' bit off Brer Rabbit tail again. An' dis give him a short tail again."

The rabbit, like the slaves who wove tales about him, was forced to make do with what he had. His small tail, his natural portion of intellect—these would have to suffice, and to make them do he resorted to any means at his disposal—means which may have made him morally tainted but which allowed him to survive and even to conquer. In this respect there was a direct relationship between Rabbit and the slaves, a relationship which the earliest collectors and interpreters of these stories understood well. Joel Chandler Harris, as blind as he could be to some of the deeper implications of the tales he heard and retold, was always aware of their utter seriousness. "Well, I tell you dis," Harris had Uncle Remus say, "ef deze yer tales wuz des fun, fun, fun, en giggle, giggle, giggle, I let you know I'd a-done drapt um long ago." From the beginning Harris insisted that the animal fables he was collecting were "thoroughly characteristic of the negro," and commented that "it needs no scientific investigation to show why he selects as his hero the weakest and most harmless of all animals, and brings him out victorious in contests with the bear, the wolf, and the fox."

Harris's interpretations were typical. Abigail Christensen noted in the preface to her important 1892 collection of black tales: "It must be remembered that the Rabbit represents the colored man.

He is not as large nor as strong, as swift, as wise, nor as handsome as the elephant, the alligator, the bear, the deer, the serpent, the fox, but he is 'de mos' cunnin' man dat go on fo' leg' and by this cunning he gains success. So the negro, without education or wealth, could only hope to succeed by stratagem." That she was aware of the implications of these strategies was made evident when she remarked of her own collection: "If we believe that the tales of our nurseries are as important factors in forming the characters of our children as the theological dogmas of maturer years, we of the New South cannot wish our children to pore long over these pages, which certainly could not have been approved by Froebel." In that same year Octave Thanet, in an article on Arkansas folklore, concluded, "Br'er Rabbit, indeed, personifies the obscure ideals of the negro race. . . . Ever since the world began, the weak have been trying to outwit the strong; Br'er Rabbit typifies the revolt of his race. His successes are just the kind of successes that his race have craved."

These analyses of the animal trickster tales have remained standard down to our own day. They have been advanced not merely by interpreters of the tales but by their narrators as well. Prince Baskin, one of Mrs. Christensen's informants, was quite explicit in describing the model for many of his actions:

You see, Missus, I is small man myself; but I aint nebber 'low no one for to git head o' me. I allers use my sense for help me 'long jes' like Brer Rabbit. 'For de wah ol' Marse Heywood mek me he driber on he place, an' so I aint hab for work so hard as de res'; same time I git mo' ration ebery mont' an' mo' shoe when dey share out de cloes at Chris'mus time. Well, dat come from usin' my sense. An' den, when I ben a-courtin' I nebber 'lowed no man to git de benefit ob me in dat. I allers carry off de purties' gal, 'cause, you see, Missus, I know how to play de fiddle an' allers had to go to every dance to play the fiddle for dem.

More than half a century later, William Willis Greenleaf of Texas echoed Baskin's admiration:

De kinda tales dat allus suits mah fancy de mo'es' am de tales de ole folks used to tell 'bout de ca'iens on of Brothuh Rabbit. In de early days Ah heerd many an' many a tale 'bout ole Brothuh Rabbit what woke me to de fac' dat hit tecks dis, dat an't'othuh to figguh life out—dat you hafto use yo' haid fo om'n a hat rack lack ole Brothuh Rabbit do. Ole Brothuh Rabbit de smaa'tes' thing Ah done evuh run 'crost in mah whole bawn life.

This testimony—and there is a great deal of it—documents the enduring identifications between black storytellers and the central trickster figure of their tales. Brer Rabbit's victories became the victories of the slave. This symbolism in slave tales allowed them to outlive slavery itself. So long as the perilous situation and psychic needs of the slave continued to characterize large numbers of freedmen as well, the imagery of the old slave tales remained both aesthetically and functionally satisfying. By ascribing actions to semi-mythical actors, Negroes were able to overcome the external and internal censorship that their hostile surroundings imposed upon them. The white master could believe that the rabbit stories his slaves told were mere figments of a childish imagination, that they were primarily humorous anecdotes depicting the "roaring comedy of animal life." Blacks knew better. The trickster's exploits, which overturned the neat hierarchy of the world in which he was forced to live, became their exploits; the justice he achieved, their justice; the strategies he employed, their strategies. From his adventures they obtained relief; from his triumphs they learned hope.

To deny this interpretation of slave tales would be to ignore much of their central essence. The problem with the notion that slaves completely identified with their animal trickster hero whose exploits were really protest tales in disguise is that it ignores much of the complexity and ambiguity inherent in these tales. This in turn flows from the propensity of scholars to view slavery as basically a relatively simple phenomenon which produced human products conforming to some unitary behavioral pattern. Too frequently slaves emerge from the pages of historians' studies either as docile, accepting beings or as alienated prisoners on the edge of rebellion. But if historians have managed to escape much of the anarchic confusion so endemic in the Peculiar Institution, slaves did not. Slaveholders who considered Afro-Americans to be little more than subhuman chattels converted them to a religion which stressed their humanity and even their divinity. Masters who desired and expected their slaves to act like dependent children also enjoined them to behave like mature, responsible adults, since a work force consisting only of servile infantiles who can make no decisions on their own and can produce only under the impetus of a significant other is a dubious economic resource, and on one level or another both masters and slaves understood this. Whites who considered their black servants to be little more than barbarians, bereft of any culture worth the name, paid a fascinated and flattering attention to their song, their dance, their tales, and their forms of religious exercise. The life of every slave could be altered by the most arbitrary and amoral acts. They could be whipped, sexually assaulted, ripped out of societies in which they had deep roots, and bartered away for pecuniary profit by men and women who were also capable of treating them with kindness and consideration and who professed belief in a moral code which they held up for emulation not only by their children but often by their slaves as well.

It would be surprising if these dualities which marked the slaves' world were not reflected in both the forms and the content of their folk culture. In their religious songs and sermons slaves sought certainty in a world filled with confusion and anarchy; in their supernatural folk beliefs they sought power and control in a world filled with arbitrary forces greater than themselves; and in their tales they sought understanding of a world in which, for better or worse, they were forced to live. All the forms of slave folk culture afforded their creators physical relief and a sense of mastery. Tales differed from the other forms in that they were more directly didactic in intent and therefore more compellingly and realistically reflective of the irrational

and amoral side of the slaves' universe. It is precisely this aspect of the animal trickster tales that has been most grossly neglected.

Although the vicarious nature of slave tales was undeniably one of their salient features, too much stress has been laid on it. These were not merely clever tales of wish-fulfillment through which slaves could escape from the imperatives of their world. They could also be painfully realistic stories which taught the art of surviving and even triumphing in the face of a hostile environment. They underlined the dangers of acting rashly and striking out blindly, as Brer Rabbit did when he assaulted the tar-baby. They pointed out the futility of believing in the sincerity of the strong, as Brer Pig did when he allowed Fox to enter his house. They emphasized the necessity of comprehending the ways of the powerful, for only through such understanding could the weak endure. This lesson especially was repeated endlessly. In the popular tales featuring a race between a slow animal and a swifter opponent, the former triumphs not through persistence, as does his counterpart in the Aesopian fable of the Tortoise and the Hare, but by outwitting his opponent and capitalizing on his weaknesses and short-sightedness. Terrapin defeats Deer by placing relatives along the route with Terrapin himself stationed by the finish line. The deception is never discovered, since to the arrogant Deer all terrapins "am so much like anurrer you cant tell one from turrer." "I still t'ink Ise de fas'est runner in de worl'," the bewildered Deer complains after the race. "Maybe you air," Terrapin responds, "but I kin head you off wid sense." Rabbit too understands the myopia of the powerful and benefits from Mr. Man's inability to distinguish between the animals by manipulating Fox into taking the punishment for a crime that Rabbit himself commits. "De Ole Man yent bin know de diffunce tween Buh Rabbit an Buh Fox," the storyteller pointed out. "Eh tink all two bin de same animal." For black slaves, whose individuality was so frequently denied by the whites above them, this was a particularly appropriate and valuable message.

In many respects the lessons embodied in the animal trickster tales ran directly counter to those of the moralistic tales considered earlier. Friendship, held up as a positive model in the moralistic tales, was pictured as a fragile reed in the trickster tales. In the ubiquitous stories in which a trapped Rabbit tricks another animal into taking his place, it never occurs to him simply to ask for help. Nor when he is being pursued by Wolf does Hog even dream of asking Lion for aid. Rather he tricks the Lion into killing Wolf by convincing him that the only way to cure his ailing son is to feed him a piece of half-roasted wolf liver. The animals in these stories seldom ask each other for disinterested help. Even more rarely are they caught performing acts of altruism—and with good reason. Carrying a string of fish he has just caught, Fox comes upon the prostrate form of Rabbit lying in the middle of the road moaning and asking for a doctor. Fox lays down his fish and hurries off to get help—with predictable results: "Ber Fox los' de fish. An' Ber Rabbit got de fish an' got better. Dat's da las' of it." Brer Rooster learns the same lesson when he unselfishly tries to help a starving Hawk and is rewarded by having Hawk devour all of his children.

Throughout these tales the emphasis on the state of perpetual war between the world's creatures revealed the hypocrisy and meaninglessness of their manners and rules. Animals who called each other brother and sister one moment were at each other's throats the next. On his way to church one Sunday morning, Rabbit meets Fox and the usual unctuous dialogue begins. "Good-mornin', Ber Rabbit!" Fox sings out. "Good-mornin', Ber Fox!" Rabbit sings back. After a few more pleasantries, the brotherliness ends as quickly as it had begun and Fox threatens: "Dis is my time, I'm hungry dis mornin'. I'm goin' to ketch you." Assuming the tone of the weak suppliant, Rabbit pleads: "O Ber Fox! leave me off dis mornin'. I will sen' you to a man house where he got penful of pretty little pig, an' you will get ye brakefus' fill." Fox agrees and is sent to a pen filled not with pigs but hound dogs who pursue and kill him. Reverting to his former Sabbath piety, Rabbit

calls after the dogs: "Gawd bless yer soul! dat what enemy get for meddlin' Gawd's people when dey goin' to church." "I was goin' to school all my life," Rabbit mutters to himself as he walks away from the carnage, "an learn every letter in de book but *d*, an' D was death an' death was de en' of Ber Fox."

Such stories leave no doubt that slaves were aware of the need for role playing. But animal tales reveal more than this; they emphasize in brutal detail the irrationality and anarchy that rules Man's universe. In tale after tale violence and duplicity are pictured as existing for their own sake. Rabbit is capable of acts of senseless cruelty performed for no discernible motive. Whenever he comes across an alligator's nest "didn' he jes scratch the aigs out for pure meaness, an' leave 'em layin' around to spile." In an extremely popular tale Alligator confesses to Rabbit that he doesn't know what trouble is. Rabbit offers to teach him and instructs him to lie down on the broom grass. While Alligator is sleeping in the dry grass, Rabbit sets it on fire all around him and calls out: "Dat's trouble Brer 'Gator, dat's trouble youse in." Acts like this are an everyday occurance for Rabbit. He sets Tiger, Elephant, and Panther on fire, provokes Man into burning Wolf to death, participates in the decapitation of Raccoon, causes Fox to chop off his own finger, drowns Wolf and leaves his body for Shark and Alligator to eat, boils Wolf's grandmother to death and tricks Wolf into eating her. These actions often occur for no apparent reason. When a motive is present there is no limit to Rabbit's malice. Nagged by his wife to build a spring house, Rabbit tricks the other animals into digging it by telling them that if they make a dam to hold the water back they will surely find buried gold under the spring bed. They dig eagerly and to Rabbit's surprise actually do find gold. "But Ole Brer Rabbit never lose he head, that he don't, and he just push the rocks out the dam, and let the water on and drown the lastest one of them critters, and then he picks up the gold, and of course Ole Miss Rabbit done get her spring house." It is doubtful, though, that she was able to enjoy it for very long, since in another tale Rabbit coolly sacrifices his wife and little children in order to save himself from Wolf's vengeance.

Other trickster figures manifest the identical amorality. Rabbit himself is taken in by one of them in the popular tale of the Rooster who tucked his head under his wing and explained that he had his wife cut his head off so he could sun it. "An' de rabbit he thought he could play de same trick, so he went home an' tol' his ol' lady to chop his head off. So dat was de las' of his head." All tricksters share an incapacity for forgetting or forgiving. In a North Carolina spider tale, Ann Nancy is caught stealing Buzzard's food and saves herself only by obsequiously comparing her humble lot to Buzzard's magnificence, stressing "how he sail in the clouds while she 'bliged to crawl in the dirt," until he takes pity and sets her free. "But Ann Nancy ain't got no gratitude in her mind; she feel she looked down on by all the creeters, and it sour her mind and temper. She ain't gwine forget anybody what cross her path, no, that she don't, and while she spin her house she just study constant how she gwine get the best of every creeter." In the end she invites Buzzard to dinner and pours a pot of boiling water over his head, "and the poor old man go baldheaded from that day." At that he was lucky. When Rabbit's friend Elephant accidentally steps on Rabbit's nest, killing his children, Rabbit bides his time until he catches Elephant sleeping, stuffs leaves and grass in his eyes, and sets them on fire. Hare, unable to forgive Miss Fox for marrying Terrapin instead of himself, sneaks into her house, kills her, skins her, hangs her body to the ceiling, and smokes her over hickory chips.

The unrelieved violence and brutality of these tales can be accounted for easily enough within the slave-as-trickster, trickster-as-slave thesis. D. H. Lawrence's insight that "one sheds one's sickness in books" is particularly applicable here. Slave tales which functioned as the bondsmen's books were a perfect vehicle for the channelization of the slaves' "sicknesses": their otherwise inexpressible angers, their gnawing hatreds, their pent-up frustrations. On one level, then, the animal trickster tales were expressions of the slaves' unrestrained

fantasies: the impotent become potent, the brutalized are transformed into brutalizers, the undermen inherit the earth. But so many of these tales picture the trickster in such profoundly ambivalent or negative terms, so many of them are cast in the African mold of not depicting phenomena in hard-and-fast, either-or, good-evil categories, that it is difficult to fully accept Bernard Wolfe's argument that it is invariably "the venomous American slave crouching behind the Rabbit." Once we relax the orthodoxy that the trickster and the slave are necessarily one, other crucial levels of meaning and understanding are revealed.

"You nebber kin trus Buh Rabbit," a black storyteller concluded after explaining how Rabbit cheated Partridge. "Eh all fuh ehself; an ef you listne ter him tale, eh gwine cheat you ebry time, an tell de bigges lie dout wink eh yeye." Precisely what many slaves might have said of their white masters. Viewed in this light, trickster tales were a prolonged and telling parody of white society. The animals were frequently almost perfect replicas of whites as slaves saw them. They occasionally worked but more often lived a life filled with leisure-time activities: they fished, hunted, had numerous parties and balls, courted demure women who sat on verandas dressed in white. They mouthed lofty platitudes and professed belief in noble ideals but spent much of their time manipulating, oppressing, enslaving one another. They surrounded themselves with meaningless etiquette, encased themselves in rigid hierarchies, dispensed rewards not to the most deserving but to the most crafty and least scrupulous. Their world was filled with violence, injustice, cruelty. Though they might possess great power, they did not always wield it openly and directly but often with guile and indirection. This last point especially has been neglected; the strong and not merely the weak could function as trickster. Jenny Proctor remembered her Alabama master who was exceedingly stingy and fed his slaves badly. "When he go to sell a slave, he feed that one good for a few days, then when he goes to put 'em pu on the auction block he takes a meat skin and greases all around that nigger's mouth and makes 'em look like they been eating plenty meat and such like and was good and strong and able to work." Former slaves recalled numerous examples of the master as trickster:

There was one old man on the plantation that everybody feared. He was a good worker but he didn't allow anybody to whip him. Once he was up for a whipping and this is the way he got it. Our young master got a whole gang of paddy-rollers and hid them in a thicket. Then he told old man Jack that he had to be whipped. "I won't hit you but a few licks," he told him, "Papa is going away and he sent me to give you that whipping he told you about." Old man Jack said, "Now, I won't take nairy a lick." Young master took out a bottle of whiskey, took a drink and gave the bottle to old man Jack and told him to drink as much as he wanted. Old man Jack loved whiskey and he drank it all. Soon he was so drunk he couldn't hardly stand up. Young Mars called to the men in hiding, "Come on down, I got the wild boar." They whipped the old man almost to death. This was the first and last time he ever got whipped.

Slave tales are filled with instances of the strong acting as tricksters: Fox asks Jaybird to pick a bone out of his teeth, and once he is in his mouth, Fox devours him; Buzzard invites eager animals to go for a ride on his back, then drops them to their deaths and eats them; Wolf constructs a tar-baby in which Rabbit almost comes to his end; Elephant, Fox, and Wolf all pretend to be dead in order to throw Rabbit off guard and catch him at their "funerals"; Fox tells Squirrel that he had a brother who could jump from the top of a tall tree right into his arms, and when Squirrel proves he can do the same, Fox eats him. Tales like these, which formed an important part of the slaves' repertory, indicate that the slave could empathize with the tricked as well as the trickster. Again the didactic function of these stories becomes apparent. The slaves' interest was not always in being like the trickster but often in avoiding being like his victims from whose fate

they could learn valuable lessons. Although the trickster tales could make a mockery of the values preached by the moralistic tales—friendship, hard work, sincerity—there were also important lines of continuity between the moralistic tales and the trickster stories. Animals were taken in by the trickster most easily when they violated many of the lessons of the moralistic tales: when they were too curious, as Alligator was concerning trouble; too malicious, as Wolf was when he tried to kill Rabbit by the most horrible means possible; too greedy, as Fox and Buzzard were when their hunger for honey led to their deaths; overly proud and arrogant, as Deer was in his race with Terrapin; unable to keep their own counsel, as Fox was when he prematurely blurted out his plans to catch Rabbit; obsessed with a desire to be something other than what they are, as the Buzzard's victims were when they allowed their desire to soar in the air to overcome their caution.

The didacticism of the trickster tales was not confined to tactics and personal attributes. They also had important lessons to teach concerning the nature of the world and of the beings who inhabited it. For Afro-American slaves, as for their African ancestors, the world and those who lived in it were pictured in naturalistic and unsentimental terms. The vanity of human beings, their selfishness, their propensity to do anything and betray anyone for self-preservation, their drive for status and power, their basic insecurity, were all pictured in grim detail. The world was not a rational place in which order and justice prevailed and good was dispensed. The trickster, as Louise Dauner has perceived, often functioned as the eternal "thwarter," the symbol of "the irrational twists of circumstance." His remarkably gullible dupes seldom learned from their experience at his hands any more than human beings learn from experience. There was no more escape from him than there is escape from the irrational in human life. The trickster served as agent of the world's irrationality and as a reminder of man's fundamental helplessness. Whenever animals became too bloated with their power or importance or sense of control, the trickster was on hand to remind them of how things really were. No animal escaped these lessons; not Wolf, not Lion, not Elephant, indeed, not the trickster himself. Throughout there is a latent yearning for structure, for justice, for reason, but they are not to be had, in this world at least. If the strong are not to prevail over the weak, neither shall the weak dominate the strong. Their eternal and inconclusive battle served as proof that man is part of a larger order which he scarcely understands and certainly does not control.

If the animal trickster functioned on several different symbolic levels—as black slave, as white master, as irrational force—his adventures were give coherence and continuity by the crucial release they provided and the indispensable lessons they taught. In the exploits of the animal trickster, slaves mirrored in exaggerated terms the experiences of their own lives.

STUDY QUESTIONS

1. Animal trickster tales were common features of European and African folk culture. What is a "trickster," and how did the African-American trickster stories differ from their European and African counterparts?

2. When southern whites living in the antebellum plantation society heard the slave trickster tales, how did they interpret them? How did the slaves interpret them?

3. To what extent did the trickster tales offer slaves a form of power as well as a means of releasing the frustrations of bondage? What did the trickster tales reveal about African-American slave culture?

4. How might a contemporary feminist interpret the slave trickster tales of the eighteenth and nineteenth centuries?

BIBLIOGRAPHY

For the most traditional, and now classic, interpretation of slavery and the slave personality, see Ulrich B. Phillips's *American Negro Slavery* (1918). The major revision of Phillips's work came in Herbert Aptheker's *American Negro Slave Revolts* (1943) and especially Kenneth Stampp's *The Peculiar Institution* (1956). Both books emphasize the constant rebelliousness of black slaves in the United States. In 1959, Stanley B. Elkins wrote *Slavery: A Problem in American Intellectual and Institutional Life,* where he argued that the brutality of slavery had transformed black people into an infantile generation, plagued by laziness, confusion, and ineptitude. For more recent works that emphasize the strength and complexity of African-American slave culture, see John H. Blassingame, *The Slave Community* (1972); Gerald W. Mullin, *Fight and Rebellion* (1972); Leslie Howard Owen, *This Species of Property* (1976); George P. Rawick, *From Sundown to Sunup* (1972); Eugene D. Genovese, *Roll, Jordan, Roll: The World the Slaves Made* (1974); and Herbert Gutman, *The Black Family in Slavery and Freedom, 1750–1925* (1976). Also see John B. Boles, *Black Southerners, 1619–1869* (1983); Jacqueline Jones, *Labor of Love, Labor of Sorrow* (1985); and Sterling Stuckey, *Slave Culture* (1987).

Reading 16

FOLKLORE AND LIFE EXPERIENCE

Arnoldo De Leon and Saul Sanchez

Although Hispanic values are deeply rooted in American culture, more than three centuries of contact in the Southwest have produced little understanding between Anglos and their Spanish-speaking neighbors. A tenuous accommodation has replaced the violence of the nineteenth century, but an enormous gulf of suspicion, ignorance, and confusion still divides Anglos and Mexican Americans. Until recently, historians and anthropologists have reinforced the misunderstandings by giving ethnocentrism an intellectual legitimacy. Writing always from an Anglo perspective, albeit a liberal one, they have described Mexicans as a pleasant but inscrutable people, blessed with a love of life but cursed with a cultural malaise, a fatalism enabling them to survive tragedy but crippling any hope for triumph. Passive and childlike, ready to accept the course of history and quietly absorb stress, Mexicans were, according to the scholarly stereotype, unwilling and incapable of influencing their environment. Success, vertical mobility, and entrepreneurial opportunity were hopelessly beyond them.

But just as a new generation of historians have rewritten the African-American past, so too have young scholars taken another look at Mexican-American ethnicity. The foremost revisionary work is Arnoldo De Leon's *The Tejano Community, 1836–1900,* a study of Spanish-speaking people in nineteenth-century Texas. Combining the research techniques of history and anthropology with a Hispanic perspective, De Leon rejects the long-held notion of Mexican passivity and fatalism. Instead, he portrays a people who confidently exercised great control over their cultural and physical world through hard work, a vibrant folk culture and ethnoreligion, and strong extended families. These were hardly the hapless and helpless people of so many scholarly discourses. This selection from De Leon's work clearly illustrates the richness and vitality of Tejano culture.

Historians searching for the role of folklore in the lives of Tejanos confront serious difficulties. Generally speaking, Mexicanos, like other poor and illiterate classes, did not record their lore; historians who seek access to this oral tradition have to rely upon what Mexicanos related to inquisitive whites. Although these compilations are reliable, what Mexicans relayed to these collectors must be scrutinized rigorously. It is possible, for instance, that Mexicanos did not trust the interviewers and told them only what they wanted them to hear. In addition, Tejanos may have been reluctant to relate tales that verged on the pornographic or those that revealed intimate feelings about race and other features of Mexican-American culture that they believed whites could not comprehend. The tales, moreover, surely lost something in the cultural and linguistic translation. Anglo folklorists could not have captured the teller's intonation, stress, chants, and mimicking, all of which are common to Mexican-American storytelling traditions.

Equally disturbing for the historian and folklorist is that these legends, myths, and other tales, collected in the twentieth century, forfeited the flavor of their nineteenth-century milieu. Yet, grouped together from different sources and different times, they give a clearer indication of the part folklore played in the belief system and world view that characterized nineteenth-century Mexican-Americans.

In Texas, itinerants, historians, journalists, and other observers recorded the folklore of the state's Spanish-speaking community. But all historians owe a debt to the Texas Folklore Society for its indefatigable efforts in collecting Mexican-American materials. Organized in 1909, issuing its first volume in 1916, and continuing until the pre-

sent, the Society regularly published scores of items relating to Tejano life. Long uninterpreted or simply ignored, these and other collections reveal the views of a preindustrial folk as they came into contact with the predominantly agrarian society. They reveal not the behavior of a people living in the culture of poverty, but rather the culture of Tejanos who just happened to be poor. They identify the autonomous spirit of a community socialized, partly by choice, partly by force, as Mexican American.

Folklore provided an intrinsic survival tool for Tejanos; it identified them with the past and thus with an experience at once contiguous and familiar. It gave them a sense of history and thus the psychological affirmation necessary to endure in a setting that constantly reminded them that they came from practically nothing.

Because Tejano folklore was firmly planted in the Texas pre-Revolutionary War experience, it lent a profound sense of cultural continuity traceable to Mexico's colonial period. Legends about buried treasures, the naming of places, the origin of certain plants, miracles, and events involving the presence of Spaniards all related to Spanish themes, settings, characters, and the like.

No other aspects of folklore revealed the legacy of the Spanish experience as much as the legends about buried treasures. Spanish *entradas* into Texas and searches by Spanish Mexicans in later decades engendered a rich lore about mythical wealth and tales of hidden treasures. According to legends told by nineteenth-century Tejanos, Spaniards had hidden fortunes in moments of crises (usually Indian attacks) only to be prevented by some happenstance from returning at a later date to retrieve them. Thus, precious treasures lay hidden in diverse areas of the state from El Paso to East Texas. This folklore, passed on to Anglo Americans who migrated to the state in later generations, became part of the fantasy of the new arrivals.

The Spanish past manifested itself in many other ways. Such folktales as that of "Pedro de Urdemalas" for example, revealed the presence of Spanish characters. Border *corridos* (ballads) that appeared around the 1860s were a link to Spanish *romances,* although their subject matter and structure belonged to the New World, while the *tragedia* (a ballad of tragedy) tended to resemble the epics of Medieval France and Spain (*La Chanson de Roland* and *El Cantar de Mío Cid*) in origin and theme.

When Spanish domination ended for Tejanos in 1821, the post-Spanish experience threaded its way into folklore as had the colonial historical past. Thus an evolving and unfolding experience embraced tales of buried treasures left in Texas by Antonio López de Santa Anna or by *bandidos* and *rancheros.* For varied reasons associated with accidents, the law, or Indian attacks, Mexicans had left their goods at various points in McMullen County in hopes of returning some day. Tejanos related these legends to whites who themselves continued the search for the elusive treasure in following generations.

Also, folklore exposed Tejanos as the bicultural people they became after the Texas Revolution. On the one hand, it displayed the interest that Mexican Americans still retained in affairs that occurred in the mother country. Through songs, for example, they eulogized Mexican heroes: with the *coplas* of *los franceses,* Tejanos of the lower border hailed the exploits of Mexican president Benito Juárez in his struggle against the French imperialists of the 1860s. Corridos praised the victory of Texas-born Ignacio Zaragoza over the French at Puebla on May 5, 1862, and immortalized Catarino Garza for his revolution of 1891–1892 against Mexican President Porfirio Díaz. Social types, settings, traditions, and other elements similarly pointed to the Mexican cultural presence. On the other hand, as a folklore in flux, it displayed the Tejano's familiarity with the people who controlled Texas politics, economics, and society. Old legends about buried treasures, for one, showed a modification that included the presence of the *americanos.* In legends surrounding the battles of Palo Alto and Resaca de la Palma (May 8 and 9, 1846), the Mexican Army, pressed by Zachary Taylor's troops, lightened the retreat by burying its pay money and other valuables in the battlefield. Other tales had Anglos, rather than Spaniards or Mexicans, burying treasure and then, because of unforeseen contingencies, never returning to retrieve it. Still others had the ghosts of white men guarding buried treasures, instead of the ghosts of Mexicans or Spaniards who had protected them before white men became part of the life experience of Tejanos.

Similarly, corridos reflected the Tejano adaptation to the American setting and their evolving nature as a bicultural people. While the corridos about Ignacio Zaragoza celebrated the exploits of a Mexican national hero, it also celebrated the fame of a native Tejano (*General de la frontera*). And surely, Mexicanos would not have eulogized the exploits of Ulysses S. Grant in song (or even have been aware of him) had they retained immutable ties to Mexico and repudiated all interest in the United States. Because those two corridos were sung during the same period, they indicated the familiarity of the border people with the significance of the two men and the fact that the Tejano mind naturally identified with both. Additionally, the corridos about the Catarino Garza revolution of 1891–1892 displayed a Tejano familiarity with both Texan and Mexican events. *El Corrido de los Pronunciados* eulogized the attack of Garza upon Mexican territory, while the *Corrido de Capitán Jol* depicted Texas Ranger Captain Lee Hall as a coward and an ineffective fighter compared to the *pronunciados* that defeated him. This type of ethnocentrism attested to a way of life on the border colored by the interaction between Mexican Americans and white Texans.

More aspects of folklore pointed to an experience of Tejanos well acquainted both with their past and their present. Folkloric themes indicated familiarity with time, featured settings, characters, and stylistic arrangements intimate to the narrator. Place names like Presidio, San Elizario, and San Antonio, ranchos belonging to well-to-do families, the Big Bend, and the *Chaparral* country of South Texas, local flora like *el cenizo* and the *guadalupana* vine, all permeated the folklore and thus revealed the Tejano's closeness to his environment. Allusions to personalities like the widow Doña Fidencia Ortega of San Elizario, Bartolo Mendoza of El Paso County, the Cantú family of South Texas, to the peasant José Días and to the rich Don Pedro Carrasco, similarly reflected the reality of their daily experience. Descriptive detail, symbolism, and other stylistic forms added specificity and a localized frame of reference, more plausible characters, strength of purpose, and a more meaningful and convincing portrait to that folklore.

The benevolence of a Christian God, common to folklore universally, was also shown in the religious dimension of their folk stories. In their case, He was an altruistic God, seemingly an integral part of a world of disadvantaged people. A beneficent God took care of His people, intervened on their behalf in desperate moments, and fought off evil forces. He was a concerned God who intervened directly in order to give Tejanos relief from natural calamities. *Kineños* (residents of the King Ranch of South Texas), for example, related the story of a compassionate God bursting into tears that became the rain which brought relief to the drought-stricken countryside and His suffering people.

Also, folklore revealed a protective God who intervened in times of great desperation. Time after time, He had come to the assistance of the legendary Father Antonio Margil de Jesús, the ubiquitous folkloric figure. Nineteenth-century folklore credited Margil, accompanying the Domingo Ramón expedition in 1716, with working a miracle through the agency of prayer by turning an attacking "swarm of savages" near San Antonio into inoffensive deer. Then, as the expedition approached the city, Margil again rescued the thirsty party through another miracle that begot the San Antonio River. That same year, he delivered another thirsty missionary party from its plight near Nacogdoches by a miracle that produced a living stream of cool water from a site that came to be called the Holy Springs of Father Margil.

Folktales such as "El Cenizo" (which explained the creation of the cenizo shrub) and "La Guadalupana Vine" (which related how the *guadalupana*

vine acquired its medicinal value) and the song "Nuestra Señora de los Dolores" (which recounted the powers of such a statue in Webb County) likewise revealed a faith, a moral uprightness, and a humility that testified to the privileged status and special relationship that Tejano vaqueros understood themselves to have with their Creator. In each, the miraculous intervention of the Divine warded off imminent catastrophe. In "El Cenizo," vaqueros arose on Ash (cenizo) Wednesday to rejoice over the desperately needed rain sent to them in response to their prayers. Likewise, the Virgen de Guadalupe had intervened directly to teach vaqueros that the guadalupana vine dipped in *mescal* had extraordinary medicinal values. And "Nuestra Señora de los Dolores," an old statue of the Virgin Mary kept at La Becerra Ranch in Webb County, invariably responded to the pleas of drought-stricken *rancheros* in the latter half of the century. During dry spells they carried the unprepossessing image in solemn procession while mothers marched praying the rosary and chanting "Nuestra Señora de los Dolores" (the song relating in ten assonantal *cuartetas* the affliction of the Virgin upon learning of the imminent crucifixion of the Lord). Legend had it that rain fell within days after marchers arrived at the drought-stricken ranch.

In each case, the Divine had intervened to bestow His blessings, not in behalf of one individual, but characteristically for the benefit of an entire community or group. In the legend of "La Guadalupana Vine" the Virgin intended the gift, in the form of the medicinal vine, for Mexicanos in general and the vaquero specifically. The wooden statue of the Virgin Mary ("of a dark color" and its paint "a kind of sticky-looking clay") to which Tejanos sang the verses of "Nuestra Señora de los Dolores," ostensibly represented God's people, the Mexicanos. In the legend of "El Cenizo," a considerate God delivered His blessings to *la gente* in the form of the rain.

A guardian God similarly defended His people from evil forces. In the legend of "The Devil's Grotto," a priest used the holy cross to overcome Satan and deliver the pagan people of Presidio, Texas, from the havoc wreaked upon them by the

A strong sense of filial responsibility permeated nineteenth-century Mexican American life.

Devil. Converted to the Christian faith, the people thenceforth enjoyed good health, their crops grew abundantly, and they no longer feared Satan's evil designs. Similarly, a legend concerning the old Mission de Nuestra Señora de la Purísima Concepción de Acuña supposed that the Virgin, responding to the prayers of a supplicating *padre* seeing his neophytes retreating into the safety of the Mission with Comanches close on their heels, had interceded at the gates and somehow held back the "wild tribes" at the very lintel as the neophytes rushed into the safety of the Mission just as the gates closed behind them. In another legend, San Miguel, the patron saint of Socorro (in the El Paso Valley) came to the aid of the community when, during the Civil War, wild marauders from Major T. T. Teel's command commenced bombarding the old church at Socorro. San Miguel appeared in the tower waving a flaming sword and thus held them in check until the Major arrived from Ysleta to end the indiscriminate attack.

Likewise, Tejanos carried on their traditional world view that explained the mysteries of nature and the universe. *Kineños,* for example, employed folk yarns to explain astronomical phenomena. They borrowed freely from Catholic theology and their experiences as vaqueros at the King Ranch in giving subjective renditions of the arrangements of the heavenly bodies. For others, a similar world perception begot explanations of such things as the origin of the Earth's inhabitants, their place in the world order, their functions, and so on. Explanatory stories about birds especially followed such a scheme. Through folktales, Tejanos explained the mysteries in the *aves* (birds): the *paisano* (roadrunner) ran among the chaparral in order to hide his shame and disgrace after being punished for his vanity and arrogance; the owl called "Cú, Cú, Cú, Cú, Cú," as he searched for the Pájaro Cú who had become arrogant after receiving a coat of feathers from other birds that had clothed his naked body (the owl had posted bond that the Pájaro Cú would remain humble after receiving the coat); the male cardinal was beautiful while the female was a wonderful singer because the spirit of the plains could give only one gift to each; and the song of the dove was a sob because she never saw the Christ Child when all the other creatures of the world came to worship Him (the dove was so humble and unassuming that no one thought of telling her the wonderful news). Similarly, *la cigarra* (locust or *cicada*) achieved its ugly form when his wife called upon the eagle, the monarch of all birds, to check the *cigarra's* roaming ways. The *cigarra's* eyes thus became popped and round and his colored wings turned an ashy gray (his wife, then wanting to be happy with the ugly creature, asked the eagle to make her like her husband).

Hence, by borrowing from their theology and everyday experiences and then combining that with their worldly wisdom, Tejanos rendered seemingly rational explanations of phenomena with which they had daily contact. Structured around such a prosaic framework, the explanations achieved credibility. Folklore provided a vehicle through which rational explanations untangled the supernatural, be it prairie lights, ghosts and spirits, mysterious lakes, physical ailments, or psychological states of mind. Thus, in explaining *la luz del llano,* that mysterious red light that appears at night on the prairie, which scientists believe is caused by peculiar atmospheric conditions, Kineño folklore held that it originated out of a covenant between an old woman and an old wizard. In exchange for food for her starving girls, the woman had agreed to surrender them to the wizard four years later. When the wizard took them the mother was so disconsolate that she set out searching for them, risking the wizard's warning that she not hunt for them on the penalty of immolation. Finally caught and burned alive, the old woman nevertheless kept up the search. Hence, *la luz del llano* was a bundle of fire held together by the spirit of the old woman who still traversed the llanos seeking her lost daughters. Unexplainable lights at night often were believed to indicate precious metals underground. Thus, legend held that the lights about Fort Ramírez (on Ramireño Creek in Nueces County) pointed to the money Ramírez had buried before Indians killed him in the early part of the century. Strange and unexplainable events such as those occurring at Rancho El Blanco, an old Spanish ranch in what is now Jim Hogg County, could be explained similarly—for ghosts and spirits in different forms haunted buried treasures. The appearance of a wraith at San Pedro's sparkling springs in San Antonio also signified the spirit of the tragic Francisco Rodríguez family that guarded the family's hidden treasure. Anyone daring to search for it confronted the specter of Don Francisco or his son or daughter, or the daughter's lover, who had, during Texas' colonial period, been part of a tragic scenario that had led to the treasure's burial. Likewise the feared presence at Espantosa (part of a multiplicity of pools—*tinajas*—and small lakes situated for many miles up and down the west side of the Nueces River and fifteen to twenty miles back) of huge alligators with a horn on their noses, was a result of God's wrath upon Mexican robbers who had once upon a time enticed the most beautiful señoritas to the lake's banks and kidnapped them. In his terrible vengeance, God created reptiles to prey on the children, the women, and the bandits. But after exterminating the band, the monsters still craved for human flesh and, hence, Tejanos in the 1870s still dreaded the Espantosa.

Tejanos also used folk tales as a means of explaining physical or psychological ailments. Such was the case concerning the robust young Eutiquio Holguín of nineteenth-century San Elizario who suffered from a strange malady that rendered him paralytic. After all remedies failed, it became obvious he was the victim of the local witch of Cenecú. Traumatized nightly by the *bruja* (witch), Eutiquio finally managed to grab her hand and struggle with her one night. He gradually recovered after that and, when fully recuperated, paid a visit to the *bruja*. Finding all her *monos* (figurines), he threw them into the fire, and with that the witch of Cenecú lost her powers.

And not illogically, a particularly distressing psychological state of mind caused by shock or tragedy found convenient explanation through folklore, as in the case of Elisa Valdez of San Antonio in 1888. A widow, she reluctantly consented to marry a second time. Still harboring feelings of guilt about infidelity to her dead husband, she had wandered away from the wedding festivity to be alone. Then she heard the musicians sing:

*Toma el arpa con que canto Las haza-
   ñas de los
reyes y de amor las dulces leyes De tu
   imperio
seductor*

At that moment she felt something pulling on her dress and, turning around, she saw a turkey. Frightened, the conviction forced itself upon her that the turkey was her dead husband coming to upbraid her for her forgetfulness and faithlessness to his memory. She knew then that her marriage could not be consummated, and, indeed, all Eliza did after that was wander around Mission Espada tending to her goat and her pet, the large turkey over which she sang Mexican love songs.

The strength, the durability, and the phenomenal endurance of the mortar of which the Mission de Nuestra Señora de la Purísima Concepción de Acuña in San Antonio consisted, also found its explanation in folklore. It was as strong as brass and had resisted the effects of time because, according to legend, the priest had explained to the Indian workers that as the mission and church were to be erected in honor of the Virgin who was without sin, the mortar was to be mixed each day with fresh pure milk as a tribute to her purity. So also could the beneficent properties of particular plants that rendered Tejanos so much curative services be explained.

Stylized romantic tales and legends, ballads and *canciones* (songs), fables, and other folkloric stories focused on the notions Tejanos held about disenchantment with the opposite sex, filial responsibility, friendships, and other special relationships. The theme of love—especially be-

tween sweethearts—persisted in such tragic romances as the one involving María Morales and Alfonso Salinas. Legend held that María had defied her betrothal to a man of her father's choice by marrying Alfonso secretly. But as the newly wedded pair rowed along the San Antonio River, a deep whirlpool caught and swallowed them. So profound was their love that, when their lifeless bodies were found, they were clasped inseparably in each other's arms and had to be buried in the same casket. Similarly, nineteenth-century vaqueros and *campesinos* (farm workers) expressed their feelings of endearment toward special ladies in such canciones as "Adelita" and "La Trigueña."

Folklore also employed elements of the supernatural to show the power of love over evil. In the tale of "Blanca Flor," the gambler Juan had given his soul to the Devil in exchange for five years of good luck. At the end of the period, Juan went to the Devil's retreat at the Hacienda of Qui-quiri-qui to fulfill his commands. While there he fell in love with the Devil's beautiful daughter, Blanca Flor, and through her help escaped his commitment to the Devil. Upon marrying Blanca Flor, the legend held, he renounced his former evil ways and both lived happily ever after. Love had redeemed the former gambler.

Tejanos expressed the intimacy of filial relationships through folklore as well. In the tale of "La Luz del Llano," the mother's love for her daughters had been so eternal that the spirit of the old woman in the form of "la luz del llano" still searched for her lost daughters. In contrast, the wrath of God visited the childbeater or unprincipled parent who abused little *inocentes* (innocents). In the "Devil on the Border," Tejanos related the story of a childbeating father who took his new born baby from his wife to starve it. She cursed the brute: "May the Devil get you." About midnight a terrific whirlwind enveloped the rancho; the smell of sulfur became suffocating, and a dust of ashes choked the people. At daylight, the people hurried toward the place where the father had taken the baby. There they found the dead child, a white dove hovering over its corpse. All that remained of the father was a heap of greenish yellow sulfur.

Filial responsibility necessarily included socializing the young, and nineteenth-century Tejano folklore contained abundant tales on morals, lessons, and good examples to be imitated by the young. Advice, counsel, and admonitions played prominent roles in these stories. Among the many tales told to impatient children was the story of King Solomon, the wise man who had discovered the secret of returning from death. Telling his most faithful servant that he would die on a certain day, he instructed him further on how to wrap his body, how to dig it up after three weeks, and how to unwrap it so that it would be resurrected. The servant was to tell no one. But people soon started wondering about Solomon's disappearance and threatened the servant with death. Realizing that if he talked, Solomon would never return but that, if he did not, both he and Solomon would be dead forever, the servant revealed the story. "They had not been patient with time, and just for that the secret of returning alive from death was lost forever."

Another didactic story concerned a little boy with three bad habits: aimlessness, asking about people's affairs, and not controlling his temper. One day while running away from home he encountered an old man who gave him three pieces of advice for his last three *pesos:* don't leave a highway for a trail; don't ask about things that don't concern you; and don't lose your temper. Leaving empty handed and feeling swindled, the boy soon encountered three crises to which the *viejito's* (old man) advice applied. By following it, he came into a thriving business and a lovely wife as rewards.

Other tales, such as "Baldheads," were intended to warn the young of certain deceptive types. A country boy had entrusted his money to a bald-headed man who owned a *Casa de Encargos,* which the boy thought to be a bank. Returning a few hours later, he was told that he had deposited nothing. To recover the money, his father designed a plan. He took a bag full of buttons and washers to the *Casa de Encargos* and as

he arranged for its deposit, the son entered asking for his money. The clerk, fearing to lose the larger sum the old man possessed, returned the boy's cash. The father then revealed the plot and, turning to his son, advised him: "Keep an eye on baldheads."

And a tale of the Alamo sought to inculcate children with the value of courtesy by alerting them that someday they might meet the *"padre."* According to this legend, the *padre* rewarded courtesy with gifts.

As a cultural form, folklore defined the Tejano sense of values, ideals, and collective behavior. Those folktales that articulated the theme of retributive justice, for example, contained a repugnant, sometimes grotesque manifestation of supernatural evil that dramatized the consequences of unacceptable behavior. In the legend of "The Devil's Grotto," Satan arrived to bring all manners of distress to the unconverted people of the Presidio, Texas, area and left them in peace only after they were converted. In the legend of "La Casa de la Labor," Doña Fidencia Ortega of San Elizario refused the parish priest Father Pedro a little wine to celebrate the feast of San Isidro and saw her beautiful ranch burn down the next day; the smouldering remains gave "testimony of the wrath of God." Shortly afterward she was seen "riding to the *laguna* on a bull that snorted fire" and plunged into the water never to be seen again. (More terrestrial though no less gruesome as symbols of punishment for bad behavior were "two slender hands" that drove Don Miguel mad for killing his lover's fiancé in the tale of "The Little White Dog." Similarly, in the tale "A Boom in Guarache Leather," a set of mean-looking bandits met their punishment at the hands of the destitute José Días, who, sharing their camp overnight, innocently placed an ugly devil's mask over his face as protection from the bitter night's cold.) Waking to find what they thought to be the very devil, the malefactors fled the campsite, scrambling over a cliff to their deaths.

Stories that dramatized the favorable outcome or retributive justice, as adduced by the rewards granted the obedient in recompense for their desirable behavioral traits, were as common. In "A Hanged Man Sends Rain," Bartolo Mendoza, a convict destined for execution on a day that "seemed to grow hotter with each moment that passed," repented of his crime before God and thus summoned Providence to send relief to drought-stricken San Elizario. Upon expiring on the gallows, he sent rain from Heaven. In a legend of the Big Bend country told by Natividad Luján in the early 1880s, his uncle Santiago had been killed by Indians sometime around mid-century and became "among the blessed who died for the Faith among the heathens" and his soul had journeyed to purgatory, there to be rescued by prayers said by his faithful descendants.

Folktales featuring the compensation of those who lived acceptably and the punishment of those who lived unacceptably were as frequent. Juan Verdadero was one person whose exemplary behavior resulted in his being handsomely rewarded. According to the story, Juan never lied. But he became an innocent pawn between his *patrón* (boss) and a neighboring landowner who bet his farm that "any man under the urge of necessity will lie." Certain that Juan could be induced into a falsehood, the neighbor sent his daughter to Juan with an offer to exchange her valuable ring for the heart of the prize bull Juan herded. After an excruciatingly difficult decision, Juan killed the bull for the ring. As he approached the ranch house, his *patrón* queried:

"Juan Verdadero, how is the herd?" "Some fat, some poor, upon my word." "And the white and greenish-colored bull?" "Dead, señor, dead," replied Juan.

Juan had not lied, so his *patrón* made him the administrator of the new estate that the neighbor surrendered. But the case of Doña Carolina who lived in mid-century El Paso Valley was different. She was haughty and arrogant until she suffered a harrowing experience while searching for her absent husband. After the ordeal, she was no longer the supercilious woman of former days, and everyone noticed her new behavior. *Disobedi-*

entes (disobedients), *malcridos* (ill-bred persons), *sin-vergüenzas* (no 'counts) and other nonconformists received the severest castigations. Tejanos had little tolerance for culprits who abused their children or their spouses. One wife-beater was Don Paniqua, a magically powerful person everyone feared. One day his wife gave birth to a devil-baby who prophesied various horrors, both for the world and Don Paniqua. The raging Don Paniqua took the baby into the thicket and returned without it. No one knew what happened, but, when Don Paniqua died, the Kineños said, he became the foreman of the *infierno's* (hell) *corrida*. Other evil men, the Kineños maintained, went to work in Don Paniqua's outfit.

Brief and pithy animal tales that took the form of fables focused on deviant and unacceptable behavior. For being too proud, the mockingbird had suffered the loss of part of his beautiful feathers; for being audacious in addressing his superiors as cousins, the *paisano* had been condemned to forget to fly and to feed on unclean things; for growing overbearing and cruel toward his ugly and less gifted wife, the male cardinal suffered the loss of his wife's respect; and for being a spirited adventurer who ignored his mate, the *cicada* incurred its repugnant appearance.

Like fables, corridos pointed to the Tejano value system. Lyrics often extolled the deeds of such great men as Ignacio Zaragoza, Ulysses Grant, and Catarino Garza, heroes who Tejanos looked upon as the personification of courage, liberty, and justice. The corridos not only exalted the adventures of those who challenged the powerful through defiance or confrontation, but they expressed delight in seeing the antagonist demeaned or denigrated—especially if he represented injustice and oppression.

Folktales also expressed a reality in which Tejanos could poke fun at the world, at its inhabitants, and at themselves. They ridiculed the Devil in a tale involving Pedro de Urdemañas (or Urdemalas), a well-traveled and much-experienced *cabellero* who arrived in hell to regale the Devil with the wonders of Texas. Hastening to see the marvels of Texas firsthand, the Devil arrived in the state only to face a series of calamities with chili peppers, prickly pears, and an unruly cow. Returning swiftly to hell, he expelled Urdemañas who happily returned to Texas to pursue the lifestyle of his former days.

Also popular was the tale of Chano Calanche, who, for a bottle of wine, agreed to help some bandits rid themselves of a priest's body. Tricked by the killers into thinking that he had not buried the corpse—each time he returned to claim the bottle, he found the body of the *padrecito,* not knowing that the bandits had actually killed three priests—the drunken Chano finally decided to dispose of it once and for all. Lighting fire to the corpse, he stayed with it until he fell asleep. He awoke, however to find the padrecito at his campfire; it was actually a traveling priest that happened to stop to warm his morning meal. After the incident, the story held, Chano never claimed the wine and it was said that the prize occupied a place of esteem in the *cantina* (bar) for years after that and was never put up for sale.

In a tale with a more universal theme, Tejano common folks mocked female curiosity. "My wife is not inquisitive," retorted a husband to his friend's suggestion that "all women are curious." But, when his partner took a box to the first man's wife with instructions to keep it sealed, the wife could not resist her curiosity. Upon opening the box, she unwittingly allowed the bird inside to fly away, thereby ridiculing the husband and her own ineptness at keeping secrets.

And they could demean themselves, as in the song of "Coplas del payo," which portrayed in a jesting manner the general misfortune of their lives. In this story, an overseer encouraged a forlorn lover—an ordinary worker like the narrator—to jump over a cliff.

As poor and disadvantaged people, Tejanos employed folklore as a means of expressing wish fulfillment, wishful fantasizing, and ambitiousness. Such tales generally expressed expectations of winning against misfortune. One of those tales involved a poor, elderly couple who owned a miraculous dog capable of acting as a beast of burden, a hunter, and a racer. One day, a stranger arrived in a nearby town with a very swift horse that made short work of the local opposition. With a chance to make $10,000, the poor man matched his dog against the visiting steed. The dog won easily—in fact did not stop at the finish line but ran all the way to the moon—and the poor, elderly couple gained their ambition to be wealthy. Another tale involved a *conducta* (convoy) of weary, hungry men preparing to cook their meager meal at the end of the day. At that point Agapito Cercas spoke up: "Don't bother to cook anything. This very day a hog was slaughtered at my home. Just wait and I will bring you *carne adobada, chile con asadura,* and *tortillas calientes.*" He withdrew from the group, and, according to a witness, took off his clothes and disappeared. In a while, he called for his clothes and reappeared with the food he had promised. Some of the men started eating the appetizing meal they wished for, but others refused it suspecting the work of the supernatural.

As an ambitious people not fatalistically resigned to their lot, Tejanos used folklore to constantly question their social condition. They displayed confidence in themselves and showed that they regarded themselves to be as good as the next man and that, if granted more favorable circumstances, they could overcome their problems. Further revealed was the high regard Tejanos had of themselves: that they were good enough to outwit more formidable antagonists, whether it be a wily coyote, a rich *compadre* or a more fortunate neighbor.

This displayed itself conspicuously in several of the trickster tales. As a genre, these tales include the antagonistic forces of the weak (the underdog) and the strong (the opposer) with a scenario in which the weak used their wit to overcome the powerful. Such was the case of the innocent man outsmarted by a wily coyote who had rescued him from a snake; the man had originally rescued the snake from a trap whereupon the snake had turned on him because "to repay good with evil" was *la costumbre*—the custom. Beholden to the coyote, the man compensated the animal "with good" (contrary to custom). The man soon learned that he had been too generous, for the coyote kept increasing the payment. Tricking the coyote, he finally unleashed his dog upon the opportunist. "It isn't right to repay good with evil," called the outwitted coyote. "Perhaps," answered the man, "*pero es la costumbre.*"

Commonly, the antagonist was a compadre, for Tejanos spoke in terms of their own culture and social conditions as ordinary people. One tale involved two compadres—one rich and the other poor, and the former arrogant and snobbish toward the latter. One day the poor man was so desperate for survival that he schemed to extract money from his more affluent compadre. But his rich compadre grew so angry at his tricks that he finally sought to drown his nemesis by putting him in a bag and dumping him in the sea. But the poor compadre slyly escaped the bag and surfaced to report that he had recovered the rich man's lost pearls at the bottom of the water. Eager to retrieve more jewels, the rich compadre persuaded the poor man to tie him in a sack and dump him in the ocean—all his worldly goods would be put in trust to the poor man for the favor. The poor man did as his compadre wished and became wealthy and was held in great esteem by the people of the town for his innocent little pranks.

In a similar tale, a poor man sought to get even with a rich compadre who looked condescendingly upon him because of his poverty. He succeeded in convincing the rich man of the powers of a newly purchased cap. All that was necessary to obtain items at the store was to say "*Debo de gorra*" (put it on the cap, cuff). "What a marvelous cap," said the rich man, "Sell it to me for $30,000." Feigning reluctance, the poor man surrendered it. But when the rich man attempted to buy an expensive diamond necklace with it, he found himself in jail for failing to pay. The poor man went on to live a life of luxury, while the rich fellow wound up in the mad house.

A tale indicating the awareness Tejanos felt concerning social distance involved Don Pedro Carrasco, the owner of many cattle, and José Días, the owner of a single but fat and very productive cow. Jealous of José, Don Pedro tricked José into killing his only cow, telling him of the high price *guarache* leather was bringing in the neighboring town of Aldama. Disappointed at being tricked into killing his only cow (the price of leather at Aldama was rock bottom), José was making his way slowly homeward when he came upon some money left by bandits. Taking his newfound wealth, he arrived home to show the people the money which, he said, he had made off his cow. Don Pedro, thinking that the price of *guarache* leather was indeed high, killed his herd, only to find himself tricked by his sly compadre. Now José and his family became wealthy and gave money to the *santitos* (saints) and the poor. Such trickster tales allowed Tejanos to engage the enemy and triumph over him. It also permitted the psychic relief from oppressive conditions.

Nineteenth-century Texas folklore revealed an aspiring, scheming, dreaming, and changing people concerned with a multiplicity of things affecting them both as human beings and as an oppressed people. Like dependent classes elsewhere, Tejanos employed folklore to question their existence, to explain it, and to satisfy the mind as to the universe about them; but folklore was not limited to that. It also functioned as entertainment, as a way of eulogizing heroes and expressing discontent with "no 'counts", a means of expressing kinship, a vehicle for inculcating values and behavior patterns, a mode of teaching the lessons of acceptable ideals both to adults and the young, an art of poking fun at themselves, a manner of engaging in wishful fantasizing, and, much more importantly, a technique for passing on survival skills through fictionalized accounts where the weak could indeed triumph over powerful forces. Folklore, encompassing all these functions, acted not only to give identity and solidarity to a community that shared a similar experience, but it also provided them with a covert and subconscious form of resistance to oppression.

Folklore, of course, is a universal cultural feature among all classes, and it was present long before Tejanos met Anglos in the 1820s. It persisted as a vital force of the Tejano nineteenth-century experience, and it continued long after 1900. Indeed, it was in the first four or five decades of the twentieth century that the aforementioned Texas Folklore Society collected most of its materials. Primarily the tales and legends of Tejanos from the rural areas, that folklore, while manifesting the changes of the twentieth century, reflected themes, settings, and stylistic forms similar to the folklore of nineteenth-century agrarian Texas. It continued being a part of the intimate side of the Texas Mexican experience—like that of raising families, worshipping in particular ways, and maintaining a language. That folklore thrived meant it was part of an expressive culture defined from within but that also took and rejected from outside standards, observances, and patterns as it saw fit.

STUDY QUESTIONS

1. De Leon argues that Tejano culture was a fusion of Mexican and Anglo experiences. Do you agree? Why or why not?

2. Evaluate the traditional Anglo argument that Tejano culture was passive and fatalistic, with Tejanos taking a negative view of themselves and assuming they had little power over their own lives.

3. How did the Anglo view of Tejanos reinforce the existing social and economic institutions of nineteenth-century Anglo society?

4. Modern societies have increasingly distinguished between magic and formal religion. Can such distinctions be made for Tejano culture? Why or why not?

BIBLIOGRAPHY

For portraits of Mexican Americans perceived as passive and fatalistic people, see William Madsen, *Mexican-Americans of South Texas* (1964) or Norman D. Humphrey, "The Cultural Background of the Mexican Immigrant," *Rural Sociology*, 13 (1948). More recent treatments of Mexican American history that employ liberal outrage over past discrimination as their major focus include Rodolfo Acuña, *Occupied America: The Chicano's Struggle for Liberation* (1972) and Carey McWilliams, *North from Mexico* (1968). For the best treatments of Mexican American ethnicity, which transcend the Anglo perspective, see Arnoldo De Leon, *The Tejano Community, 1836–1900* (1982); Leonard Pitt, *The Decline of the Californios: A Social History of Spanish-Speaking Californians, 1848–1890* (1966); and Louise Ano Nuevo Kerr, "Mexican Chicago: Chicago Assimilation Aborted, 1939–1952," in Melvin G. Holli and Peter d'A. Jones, *The Ethnic Frontier: Group Survival in Chicago and the Midwest* (1977). Also see James Officer, *Hispanic Arizona* (1987); David Montejano, *Anglos and Mexicans in the Making of Texas* (1987); and Douglas Monroy, *Thrown Among Strangers* (1990).

FORGOTTEN FORTY-NINERS

JoAnn Levy

Throughout the twentieth century, American popular culture and scholarly histories have maintained a keen interest in the frontier. Stories about explorers, mountain men, cowboys, buffalo hunters, gunslingers, Indians, and cavalry soldiers have captured the American imagination, and literally tens of thousands of books and movies have created nearly as many myths and stereotypes. No stereotypes have been more rigid, or more long-lived, than those involving women in the frontier West. They were either the stoic heroine mothers and wives of the John Wayne films or the heart-of-gold "dance hall girls" who populated the ubiquitous saloons of dusty frontier towns. But the social structure of the American West was far more complicated than that. Millions of women settled the frontier, engaging in virtually every conceivable occupation and occupying every level of society. In the following essay, JoAnn Levy looks at the women who headed for California during the gold-rush days of the late 1840s and early 1850s.

If Concord, Massachusetts, is remembered for the "shot heard 'round the world," Sutter's Mill, in the foothills of California's Sierra Nevada, is remembered for the "shout heard 'round the world"—"Eureka!" As that cry reverberated across the globe in 1848 (and echoed into the 1850s), a flood of humanity converged on the land of golden opportunity. This human tide irrevocably changed the West, opening up the frontier as no other force in the nation's history has, before or since.

One of the most common assumptions about gold-rush-era California is that it was almost exclusively a male domain—and that such women as could be found there were prostitutes. As recently as 1983, a California historian asserted that "it was, literally, mankind which participated in the gold rush, for woman kind, at least of the 'proper' variety, was almost totally absent."

A careful study of surviving diaries, memoirs, newspapers, and census records from the period refutes this longstanding misperception, revealing that the vast wave of migration to California included thousands of "respectable" women—and numerous children, too.

Many of these adventurous women accompanied or followed their husbands, fathers, or brothers to the golden land; others arrived entirely on their own. Once in California, enterprising women engaged in almost every occupation and inhabited every level of society. They mined for gold, raised families, earned substantial sums by their domestic and entrepreneurial labors, and stayed on to help settle the land—contributing a facet of gold-rush history that until now has been largely overlooked or forgotten.

In actually, so-called respectable women outnumbered prostitutes in California, even in 1850, by four to one. While 25 percent represents a

"Forgotten Forty-Niners" by JoAnn Levy. This article is reprinted from the January/February 1992 issue of *American History Illustrated* 26, pp. 38–49, with the permission of Cowles History Group, Inc. Copyright *American History Illustrated* magazine.

large number, even if not in this instance a "respectable" one, it is far from a majority.

Before they could avail themselves of the opportunities afforded by the gold rush, women argonauts, like their male counterparts, had to undertake and survive the arduous journey to California. Many travelers chose the Cape Horn route, braving gale, storm, and shipwreck on a voyage that consumed from five to seven months; others shortened the ocean journey by making the difficult crossing of the Isthmus of Panama via small boat and mule. In 1849, more than twenty thousand gold-seekers arrived at San Francisco by sea, and nearly twenty-five thousand more followed in 1850. Many journals and letters mention the presence of women on these routes, which travelers generally regarded as being safer for families than the even more daunting overland crossings.

Despite the hardships and dangers involved, thousands of other wealth-seekers trekked overland by wagon or on foot, crossing plains, deserts, and forbidding mountain ranges while carrying with them—and then often abandoning for survival's sake—their worldly possessions. Trail-journal entries suggest that of the twenty-five thousand people traveling overland in 1849, at least three thousand were women and fifteen hundred children. Forty-four thousand people crossed the plains the following year, and, given California's census of 1850, about ten percent of these may be assumed to have been female. News of hardship, starvation, and cholera stemmed the tide of overland emigrants in 1851 to little more than a thousand, but in 1852 an estimated fifty thousand again surged across the continent. By July 13, 1852 the Fort Kearny register had tallied for that year alone the passage of more than seven thousand women and eight thousand children.

"The country was so level that we could see long trains of white-topped wagons for many miles," recorded one woman of her experiences on the eastern segment of the overland trail. "And, when we drew nearer to the vast multitude, and saw them in all manner of vehicles and conveyances, on horseback and on foot, all eagerly driving and hurrying forward, I thought, in my excitement, that if one-tenth of these teams and these people got [there] ahead of us, there would be nothing left for us in California worth picking up."

On June 28, 1849, the "Buckeye Rovers," a company of young men heading from Ohio to California's gold fields, camped near Independence Rock on the overland trail. One of the group, John Banks, wrote in his diary that night of seeing "an Irish woman and daughter without any relatives on the way for gold. It is said she owns a fine farm in Missouri." Two weeks later, on the banks of the Green River, their paths converged again: "Last night the Irish woman and daughter were selling liquor near us . . . . Fifty cents a pint, quite moderate."

Some distance beyond the Green River, near the Humbolt River, a woman named Margaret Frink recorded in her journal for August 12, 1850: "Among the crowds on foot, a negro woman came tramping along through the heat and dust, carrying a cast-iron bake oven on her head, with her provisions and blanket piled on top—all she possessed in the world—bravely pushing on for California."

Frink and her husband had begun their westward trek in Indiana. Along the way they stopped at the home of a Mr. and Mrs. McKinney near St. Joseph, Missouri. "Mrs. McKinney," wrote Margaret in hear diary, "told me of the wonderful tales of abundance of gold that she had heard; 'that they kept flour-scoops to scoop the gold out of the barrels that they kept it in, and that you could soon get all that you needed for the rest of your life. And as for a woman, if she could cook at all, she could get $16.00 per week for each man that she cooked for, and the only cooking required to be done was just to boil meat and potatoes and serve them on a big chip of wood, instead of a plate, and the boarder furnished the provisions.' I began at once to figure in my mind how many men I could cook for, if there should be no better way of making money."

These vivid images of independent and determined women are strikingly at odds with the stereotypical picture of the long-suffering and sad-eyed pioneer wife peering wearily westward while a creaking covered wagon carries her even farther from the comforts of home. Perhaps more startling is the departure from the perception of the gold rush as an exclusively male adventure.

All travelers endured hardships en route to California, but the lure of gold enticed and beckoned like a rainbow's promise. Upon reaching the golden ground, numbers of women, as eager as any male red-shirted miner, grubbed in the dirt and creekbeds for the glittering ore. Gold fever raged in epidemic proportions, and women were not immune.

The journal of schoolteacher Lucena Parsons, married but a year, reveals her infection's daily progress. On May 30, 1851, Parsons confessed to "a great desire to see the gold diggings"; she accompanied the men and watched them mine for gold. On May 31, she wrote: "This morning the gold fever raged so high that I went again with the rest but got very little gold. . . ." On June 2, "again went to the canion [*sic*] to find that bewitching ore"; and June 3, "a general turn out to the mines . . . we made 10 dollars to day." On June 4, she went again "and did very well."

Elizabeth Gunn, who had sailed around the Horn with four young children to join her prospecting husband in Sonora, observed to her family back East that "a Frenchman and his wife live in the nearest tent, and they dig gold together. She dresses exactly like her husband—red shirt and pants and hat."

The editor of the *Alta California* reported a similar sighting: "We saw last April, a French woman, standing in Angel's Creek, dipping and pouring water into the washer, which her husband was rocking. She wore short boots, white duck pantaloons, a red flannel shirt, with a black leather belt and a Panama hat. Day after day she could be seen working quietly and steadily, performing her share of the gold digging labor. . . . "

Many of the women who tried mining, however, found the prize unworthy of the effort it required. Eliza Farnham, famed for attempting to deliver one hundred marriageable women to California, wrote that she "washed one panful of earth, under a burning noon-day sun. . . and must frankly confess, that the small particle of gold, which lies this day safely folded in a bit of tissue paper . . . did not in the least excite the desire to continue the search."

Louisa Clapp, wife of a doctor at Rich Bar, concurred, writing to her sister in the East: "I have become a *mineress;* that is, if the having washed a pan of dirt with my own hands, and procured therefrom three dollars and twenty-five cents in gold dust . . . will entitle me to the name. I can truly say, with the blacksmith's apprentice at the close of his first day's work at the anvil, that 'I am sorry I learned the trade'; for I wet my feet, tore my dress, spoilt a pair of new gloves, nearly froze my fingers, got an awful headache, took cold and lost a valuable breastpin, in this my labor of love."

Mary Ballou, at the mining camp of Negro Bar, wrote her son Selden, left behind in New Hampshire, that she "washed out about a Dollars worth of gold dust . . . so you see that I am doing a little mining in this gold region but I think it harder to rock the cradle to wash out gold than it is to rock the cradle for Babies in the States."

The labor was indeed discouraging, and most gold-rushing women found it easier—and more profitable—to market their domestic skills in exchange for the glittering metal. As Margaret Frink had heard, if "a woman could cook at all," she could earn her living. Boasted one fiercely independent woman: "I have made about $18,000 worth of pies—about one third of this has been clear profit. One year I dragged my own wood off the mountain and chopped it, and I have never had so much as a child to take a step for me in this country. $11,000 I baked in one little iron skillet, a considerable portion by a campfire, without the shelter of a tree from the broiling sun. . . . "

Forty-niner Sarah Royce, who journeyed overland to California with her husband and three-year-old daughter, met a woman at Weaverville who "evidently felt that her prospect of making money was very enviable." The woman received one hundred dollars a month to cook three meals a day, was provided an assistant, and did no dishwashing.

In San Francisco, Chastina Rix supplemented the family income by ironing. In one week she noted that she had ironed sixty shirts, thirty-five starched and twenty-five plain, plus "hosts of other clothes & I have made twelve dollars by my labor." Her husband Alfred wrote to friends in the East that Chastina "is making money faster than half the good farmers in Peacham. She has just bought her another silk dress & lots of toggery & cravats & gloves for me and all the nice things & has quite a fund at interest at 3 percent a month."

Laundresses were in especially high demand in the gold fields: during the early days of the rush some desperate miners shipped their laundry to the Sandwich [Hawaiian] Islands and even to China, waiting for as long as six months for its return. Abby Mansur, at the Horseshoe Bar camp, wrote to her sister in New England about a neighbor who earned from fifteen to twenty dollars a month washing, "so you can see that women stand as good a chance as men[;] if it was not for my heart I could make a great deal but I am not stout enough to do it."

Whether washing or cooking, mining or ironing, women at work in frontier California toiled arduously. No labor, however, seemed more intimidating than keeping a boarding house. In 1850, about one out of every hundred persons gainfully employed in California ran some sort of hotel. Many were women, and none attested more eloquently to the labor involved than forty-niner Mary Jane Megquier, who had crossed the Isthmus from Winthrop, Maine to run a San Francisco boarding house.

"I should like to give you an account of my work if I could do it justice," Megquier wrote. "I get up and make the coffee, then I make the biscuit, then I fry the potatoes then broil three pounds of steak, and as much liver, while the [hired] woman is sweeping, and setting the table, at eight the bell rings and they are eating until nine. I do not sit until they are nearly all done . . . after breakfast I bake six loaves of bread (not very big) then four pies, or a pudding then we have lamb, for which we have paid nine dollars a quarter, beef, pork, baked, turnips, beets, potatoes, radishes, sallad [*sic*], and that everlasting soup, every day, dine at

Life in the California gold fields in the late 1840s and early 1850s was one of hard work and drudgery.

two, for tea we have hash, cold meat bread and butter sauce and some kind of cake and I have cooked every mouthful that has been eaten excepting one day and a half that we were on a steamboat excursion. I make six beds every day and do the washing and ironing[.] you must think that I am very busy and when I dance all night I am obliged to trot all day and if I had not the constitution of six horses I should [have] been dead long ago but I am going to give up in the fall whether or no, as I am sick and tired of work. . . . ”

Although Megquier fails to mention how much she earned from these herculean exertions, another female forty-niner formerly of Portland, Maine earned $189 a week from her ten boarders, clearing $75 after expenses. The accommodations she shared with them were minimal, if not spartan:

“[We] have one small room about 14 feet square, and a little back room we use for a store room about as large as a piece of chalk. Then we have an open chamber over the whole, divided off by a cloth. The gentlemen occupy the one end, Mrs. H—and a daughter, your father and myself, the other. We have a curtain hung between our beds, but we do not take pains to draw it, as it is of no use to be particular here. . . . We sleep on a cot without any bedding or pillow except our extra clothing under our heads.”

California’s inflated economy required that everyone work who could, as forty-niner Luenza Wilson, an overlander with her husband Mason and two young sons, vigorously affirmed: “Yes, we worked; we did things that our high-toned servants would now look at aghast, and say it was impossible for a woman to do. But the one who did not work in ’49 went to the wall. It was a hand to hand fight with starvation at the first. . . . ”

William Tecumseh Sherman, a gold-rush banker before history called him to greater fame as a Union general in the Civil War, confessed to a friend that keeping his wife Ellen in California ruined him financially: "No man should have a wife in California. . . . Unless she be a working woman, no man can by his own labor support her."

Many women like Ellen Sherman, accustomed to servants and unaccustomed to labor, gave up and returned east. Those willing to work, however, received substantial rewards in an economy where a washerwoman earned more than a United States congressman. Writing from San Francisco in 1850, one woman declared: "A smart woman can do very well in this country—true there are not many comforts and one must work all the time and work hard but [there] is plenty to do and good pay[.] If I was in Boston now and know what I now know of California I could come out here[.] If I had to hire the money to bring me out. It is the only country I ever was in where a woman received anything like a just compensation for work."

Many other gold-rushing women both affirmed the necessity to work and observed that there were "not many comforts." Those who had arrived via the overland trail, for example, often continued to make their beds in tents and wagons, like Mrs. John Berry, who protested: "Oh! you who lounge on your divans & sofas, sleep on your fine, luxurious beds and partake of your rich viands at every meal know nothing of the life of a California emigrant. Here are we sitting, on a pine block, a log or a bunk; sleeping in beds with either a quilt or a blanket as substitute for sheets, (I can tell you it is very aristocratic to have a bed at all), & calico pillow-cases for our pillows."

Harriet Ward, already a fifty-year-old grandmother when she journeyed overland, wrote happy descriptions of her roomy cabin and pine-stump furniture in remote Sierra Country. But of the beds she penned only, "Oh, such beds! I will say nothing of them!"

One report of a comfortable California bed does survive in the reminiscence of a guest at a celebrated gold-rush hostelry. The St. Francis boasted that it was the first San Francisco hotel to offer sheets on its beds. The lady confirmed that her bed there was "delightful." Two "soft

hair mattresses" and "a pile of snowy blankets" hastened her slumbers. On this occasion, however, the California deficiency was not the bed, but the *walls:*

"I was suddenly awakened by voices, as I thought, in my room; but which I soon discovered came from two gentlemen, one on each side of me, who were talking to each other from their own rooms *through* mine; which, as the walls were only of canvas and paper, they could easily do. This was rather a starting discovery, and I at once began to cough, to give them notice of my *interposition,* lest I should become an unwilling auditor of matters not intended for my ear. The conversation ceased, but before I was able to compose myself to sleep again . . . a nasal serenade commenced, which, sometimes a duet and sometimes a solo, frightened sleep from my eyes. . . . "

The walls of most early California habitations consisted of bleached cotton cloth stretched tightly and fastened to the dwelling's frame, then papered over. "These partitions look as firm and solid as they do made the usual way," noted Mrs. D. B. Bates, wife of a ship's captain, "but they afford but a slight hindrance to the passage of sounds."

California construction astonished Sarah Walsworth, a missionary's wife, who watched a house being built in Oakland: "Only a slight underpinning is laid on the ground, upon which rest the joists of the floor which is carefully laid down the *first thing.* This looked so odd to me at first, that I could but laugh[.] Give a carpenter a few feet of *lumber,* a few doors, & windows, a few pounds of nails & screws a few hinges; to a paper-hanger, a few yards of cloth & a few rolls of paper—to them *both a good deal of gold* & you may have a house in 6 days—perhaps in less time. You will have no trouble with 'digging cellars,' laying wall, 'having a *raising'* nor with dirty 'masons'—but after it is all done it is but an improved speaking-trumpet[.]"

At Santa Cruz, forty-niner Eliza Farnham built her own house. "Let not ladies lift their hands in horror," she wrote, "[but] I designed supplying the place of journeyman carpenter with my own hands." She succeeded so well, she confessed, "that during its progress I laughed . . . at the idea of promising to pay a man $14 or $16 per day for doing what I found my hands so dexterous in."

While most women made do with tents, cabins, and flimsily constructed clapboard houses, a very few enjoyed luxurious surroundings. "See yonder house," wrote a San Francisco chronicler. "Its curtains are of the purest white lace embroidered, and crimson damask. . . . All the fixtures are of a keeping, most expensive, most voluptuous, most gorgeous. . . . " Upon the Brussels carpet "whirls the politician with some sparkling beauty," he added, "as fair as frail. . . . "

The house described is thought to have been that of Belle Cora, a beauty from Baltimore by way of New Orleans, who crossed the Isthmus in 1849 with gambler Charles Cora. Belle and a handful of other successful parlorhouse madams lived extravagantly, but such magnificence was the exception—even among California's demimonde population.

The first prostitutes to gold-rush California sailed from Valparaiso, Chile, where news of the gold discovery arrived in August 1848 via the Chilean brig *J.R.S.* Many of these women not only married argonauts, but enjoyed the luxury of choosing among their suitors.

Other Latin women, however, fared poorly. Hundreds, through indenture arrangements, were destined for fandango houses, the poor man's brothels. José Fernández, the first alcalde at San Jose under American rule, wrote: "They did not pay passage on the ships, but when they reached San Francisco the captains sold them to the highest bidder. There were men who, as soon as any ship arrived from Mexican ports with a load of women, took two or three small boats, or a launch, went on board the ship, paid to the captain the passage of ten to twelve unfortunates and took them immediately to their cantinas, where the newcomers were forced to prostitute themselves for half a year, during which the proprietors took the bulk of their earnings."

China, like Chile, received news of California's gold discovery in 1848. By 1854, San Francisco's burgeoning Chinatown included hundreds of Chinese girls imported for prostitution. Typically, agents took arriving Chinese girls to a basement in Chinatown where they were stripped for examination and purchase. Depending on age, beauty, and the prevailing market, they sold from $300 to $3,000.

American women were not exempt from similar exploitation, albeit more subtly executed. In late 1849 and early 1850, several prostitutes in the East received passage to California by signing contracts as domestics. Some unethical agencies subsequently adopted the ploy of advertising that "servants" were wanted in California and receiving exceptional wages. A number of girls innocently responded to these procurement fronts that masqueraded as employment offices.

France similarly pounced on the fortuitous discovery at Sutter's Mill. Recruiting agents, as well as the French government, assisted the emigration of French women, who arrived in California literally by the boatload. Testified one eyewitness: "They have done the wildest kinds of business you can imagine in San Francisco, such as auctioning off women in the public square. I got there when matters had settled down somewhat: a ship arrived with sixty French women, none of them had paid her passage, so they offered a girl to anyone who would pay what she owed. Next day they did not have a single one left."

A knowledgeable Frenchman noted that his countrywomen profitably hired themselves out to stand at gambling tables: "All in all, the women of easy virtue here earn a tremendous amount of money. This is approximately the tariff."

"To sit with you near the bar or at a card table, a girl charges one ounce ($16) an evening. She had to do nothing save honor the table with her presence. This holds true for the girls selling cigars, when they sit with you. Remember they only work in the gambling halls in the evening. They have their days to themselves and can then receive all the clients who had no chance during the night. . . ."

"Nearly all these women at home were streetwalkers of the cheapest sort. But out here, for only a few minutes, they ask a hundred times as much as they were used to getting in Paris. A whole night costs from $200 to $400."

Providing theatrical entertainment for lonesome miners offered a less notorious but equally profitable means of amassing California gold. Everywhere forty-niners could be found, from San Francisco's gilt-decorated theaters to the rough boards of a mining camp stage lit by candles stuck in whiskey bottles, actresses, dancers, singers, and musicians performed before appreciative audiences.

The pay varied as much as the venue. In Grass Valley, a black woman presented public piano concerts, charging fifty cents admission. The miners of Downieville bestowed $500 in gold on a young female vocalist who made them homesick by sweetly singing old familiar ballads. A Swiss organ-girl, by playing in gambling halls, accumulated $4,000 in about six months. A Frenchwoman who played the violin at San Francisco's Alhambra gambling hall earned two ounces of gold daily, about $32.

In 1850, three French actresses opened at San Francisco's Adelphi Theatre. A critic observed that two of them "have been on the stage for a long time (I was about to write too long a time), and . . . have never definitely arrived." The women succeeded despite the quality of the performances, for the critic noted that they "have not done badly from a financial point of view, as they now own the building, the lot, and the scenery."

Renowned female performers willing to try their fortunes in far-off California achieved enormous success. Soprano Catherine Hayes, a tall blonde woman of imposing appearance, introduced costumed operatic presentations to the San Francisco stage and was rumored to have departed from the golden state with an estimated quarter-

million dollars. Lola Montez cleared $16,000 a week for performing her titillating spider dance.

California's free and open society also permitted women to pursue a variety of other employments normally deemed unacceptable for their gender. The editor of the *Alta California* welcomed a female doctor with a cheerfully delivered jibe: "So few ladies in San Francisco the New M.D. may attend them all. . . . No circumlocutions necessary. . . . Simply, as woman to woman: 'Saw my leg off!'"

The same newspaper advised "those wishing to have a good likeness are informed that they can have them taken in a very superior manner, by a real live lady, in Clay street, opposite the St. Francis Hotel, at a very moderate charge. Give her a call, gents."

The editor also boosted the business of a female barber with a shop on Commercial street by admitting that it was "not an unpleasant operation . . . to take a clean shave at the hands of a lady fair."

Advertising her own skills in the San Francisco paper was "Madame St. Dennis—Late of Pennsylvania," who could be "consulted on matters of love, law and business, from 8 a.m. to 8 p.m. Office second brown cottage from Union street, between Stockton and Dupont." Similarly self-promoting was the linguistically talented Madame de Cassins: "The celebrated diviner, explains the past and predicts the future. Can be consulted in English, French, Italian, Greek, Arabic, and Russian . . . No. 69 Dupont st." And, at the site of the future state capital, "Miss Chick begs to inform the inhabitants of Sacramento, that she has taken a suite of rooms . . . for the purpose of teaching all the new and fashionable dances."

California's early newspapers are a mother lode of rich and often surprising information about female gold-rushers; tidbits are as diverse as the experiences of these women.

Three women, for example, made one newspaper's December 14, 1850 listing of San Francisco's millionaires: Mrs. Elizabeth Davis, Mrs.

Fuller, and Mrs. Wm. M. Smith. And in September 1850, noted another article, a fire destroyed the capacious dwelling house of Mrs. Jane Smith, "erected a few months since at an expense of $10,000."

At the opposite end of the spectrum, on March 10, 1852, the *Alta* reported the particulars of a washerwomen's meeting at which laundry fees were discussed and jointly agreed.

Newspapers also reported what we would term gossip-column material today, such as an item appearing in the September 14, 1852 *Alta:* "Forlorn: This was the charge written against Eliza Hardscrabble's name on the Recorder's docket. Unacquainted with the peculiar character of this offense, we referred to Webster, and found perhaps the proper definition, 'a lost forsaken, solitary person.' Yes, Eliza is one of 'em. Whether blighted affection, harrowing care, or an erring be the cause, she is now an incurable rum-drinker, and is no longer fit to take care of herself."

Quite able to take care of herself was Dorothy Scraggs. Nonetheless, she advertised in a Marysville newspaper that she wanted a husband. She advised that she could "wash, cook, scour, sew, milk, spin, weave, hoe, (can't plow), cut wood, make fires, feed the pigs, raise chicks . . . saw a plank, drive nails, etc." She added that she was "neither handsome nor a fright, yet an *old* man need *not* apply, nor any who have not a little more education than she has, and a great deal more gold, for there must be $20,000 settled on her before she will bind herself to perform all of the above."

Court records, too, provide intriguing glimpses into the lives of gold-rushing women. In July 1850 Mrs. Mary King testified in the Sacramento justice court that persons unknown had stolen from her two leather bags containing gold dust and California coin worth about $3,500.

According to the record of *People v. Seymour alias Smith,* Fanny Seymour was indicted on a charge of assault with intent to commit murder when she shot stage-driver Albert Putnam for refusing to pay for a bottle of wine.

In *People v. Potter,* Sarah Carroll's case against William Potter, whom she claimed stole $700 in gold coin from her trunk, was dismissed because she was black and Potter was white.

Equally interesting are the surviving letters, diaries, and reminiscences of men who encountered women during their California adventures. For instance, Enos Christman, a young miner, witnessed a bullfight in Sonora at which a "magnificently dressed" *matadora* entered the arena: "She plunged the sword to the hilt into the breast of the animal. She was sprinkled with crimson dye. . . and greeted with a shower of silver dollars."

In Weaverville, Franklin Buck, a trader, was smitten by a young woman who owned a train of mules by which she delivered flour to the distant mining community: "I had a strong idea of offering myself . . . but Angelita told me she had a husband somewhere in the mines . . . so I didn't ask."

Lawyer John McCrackan met a woman who, while en route to California, brought fresh produce from a Pacific island as a speculative venture: "She sold some pieces of jewelry . . . which cost her about twenty dollars at home [and] purchased onions which she sold on arriving here for eighteen hundred dollars, quite a handsome sum, is it not? . . . She also brought some quinces & made quite a nice little profit on them."

Most fascinating, however, are the women's own observations on life in the gold regions. Wrote Abby Mansur from Horseshoe Bar: "I tell you the women are in great demand in this country no matter whether they are married or not[.] You need not think [it] strange if you see coming home with some good looking man some of these times with a pocket full of rocks . . . it is all the go here for Ladys to leave there [*sic*] Husbands[.] two out of three do it."

In fact, the divorce rate in gold-rush California was startlingly high. One judge, growing impatient with incessant requests for divorces under California's permissive divorce law, sought to deter further applications to his court by publishing his negative decision in *Avery v. Avery* in the *Sacramento Daily Union.*

By the end of 1853, a contemporary historian estimated California's female population at more than sixty thousand, plus about half that many children. In San Francisco alone, women numbered about eight thousand.

By that time, energy and gold had transformed San Francisco from a city of tents into a booming metropolis. No longer a hamlet, the city reflected the changes taking place throughout the newly admitted state. Its people were no longer simply transient miners. Men were bankers and businessmen, lawyers and doctors, farmers and manufacturers. They intended to stay.

So did the women, as California pioneer Mallie Stafford later recalled. "Very few, if any, in those [first] days contemplated permanently settling in the country. . . . But as time wore on . . . they came to love the strange new country . . . and found that they were wedded to the new home, its very customs, the freedom of its lovely hills and valleys."

Thus tens of thousands of women, through choice, chance, or circumstance, found themselves in California during the "great adventure." And, after the gold fever eventually subsided, many of them remained to help settle the land. Although they are today a neglected part of gold-rush history, the "forgotten forty-niners" were there when history was being made—and they helped to make it.

STUDY QUESTIONS

1. What does the author say about the argument that the California gold rush was exclusively a "man's domain"?

2. In 1850, what percentage of women in California were prostitutes? Does this number surprise you? Why or why not?

3. Did women engage in mining? What does the author mean by the statement that women "found it easier—and more profitable—to market their domestic skills in exchange for the glittering metal"?

4. What were the "domestic skills" many women used to make a living?

5. What was life like for women in early California?

6. How did Hispanic and Chinese women immigrants fare in early California?

7. Were there more economic opportunities in frontier California for women than in other parts of the country? Why or why not?

BIBLIOGRAPHY

An increasing volume of scholarly literature addresses the experiences of women in the West. Two books by Patricia Limerick are especially useful: *Desert Passages* (1985) and *The Legacy of Conquest* (1990). Also see Annette Kolodny, *The Land Be-*

fore Her (1984) and Joanna L. Stratton, *Pioneer Women* (1981). For works dealing with women in early California, see JoAnn Levy, *They Saw the Elephant: Women in the California Gold Rush* (1990); Louisa Clapp's *Shirley Letters from the California Mines, 1851–1852* (1983); and Sarah Royce, *A Frontier Lady: Recollections of the Gold Rush and Early California* (1977).

Part Five

THE AGE OF IMAGINATION

For more than a century, historians have described the era of the 1830s and 1840s as "The Age of Jackson" or "The Age of Democracy." It was a propitious time for the young nation. A vast hinterland of apparently limitless resources beckoned to a generation of land-hungry settlers from both the Old World and the New. Two oceans protected them from the threats of foreign powers. With traditions vastly overwhelmed by expectations, it was the "age of imagination"—a time when Americans saw themselves as the hope of the world, and their country as the place where human potential would ultimately be fulfilled. Such vision translated into "Manifest Destiny," a slogan capturing the national imagination in the 1840s and justifying the march across the continent. A generation of Americans believed that God intended that they assume sovereignty over North America. It was also their intention to obliterate any vestige of aristocratic privilege, governmental oppression, or corporate hegemony. "Young America" glorified individual rights, common people, and popular sovereignty.

The origins of democratic individualism were buried deep in the European past and the American environment. From their English ancestors, the American colonists had inherited Lockean values—the belief that government was designed to protect individual rights, primarily life, liberty, and property. The settlers themselves were young, adventurous, ambitious, and unwilling to tolerate the status quo. Had they been otherwise, they would have stayed forever in the Old World. In America, they encountered the harsh frontier wilderness where individualism, self-reliance, and hard work were taken for granted. Unencumbered by aristocratic privilege and free to establish their own political institutions, the settlers of the United States accepted democratic individualism as the natural order of things.

Andrew Jackson personified the age of democracy. His humble roots in the Tennessee frontier gave poverty a certain social status, at least among politicians. In his assault on the Second Bank of the United States, Jackson stood as an enemy of economic privilege and as a friend of competition and laissez-faire. Impatient with those who prized wealth and social standing, Jackson inspired an unprecedented national infatuation with the democratic ideal. He was a politician of extraordinary charisma.

The national preoccupation with democracy also inspired a wide variety of reform movements during the 1830s and 1840s. Led by Horace Mann of Massachusetts, educational reformers campaigned for a public school system in which the future of democracy could be guaranteed by a literate electorate. Dorothea Dix led a crusade for mental health reform, primarily in the treatment of emotional illnesses. During the age of Andrew Jackson, the last property requirements for holding public office disappeared. William Ladd spearheaded a drive for international peace. Bible tract and temperance societies campaigned across the nation to purify society through the abolition of alcohol. And the great crusade of the antebellum period, led by people like William Lloyd Garrison and Theodore Dwight Weld, was the assault on slavery, a bitter issue that eventually tore the nation apart in a civil war. But that was only a distant threat in the 1830s and 1840s. Confidence and hope were the symbols of Jacksonian America.

THE CHOICE:
THE JACKSON–DICKINSON DUEL

William A. DeGregorio

For generations philosophers have debated the role of the individual in history—whether the force of historical events automatically produces "the great man or woman" or whether great individuals actually shape the course of history. Because they have traditionally worshipped at the altar of individualism and created a political culture to match, Americans have always preferred the latter interpretation, allowing great people to affect destiny. At best, historical greatness is an ephemeral blessing, frequently bestowed too quickly and always subject to the capricious mood of public opinion. Those who achieve it are usually lucky to have their personal skills tested by some great national crisis. Any list of the "great presidents" will include George Washington, Abraham Lincoln, and Franklin D. Roosevelt, primarily because they had to confront the founding of a new nation, a civil war, and a great depression and global war, respectively. Others who aspire to greatness may link their careers to some great event, such as Theodore Roosevelt and the charge up San Juan Hill in 1898 or John F. Kennedy and the exploits of PT-109. Carved out of an enormous, forbidding wilderness by restless immigrants assuming tremendous risks, American society has placed a great premium on individual determination, courage, and perseverance.

Andrew Jackson has also been considered a "great man," one whose character and resolve were tested in battle and crisis. In the 1820s and 1830s Jackson seemed the perfect person to lead a young nation. In his exploits against the British at the Battle of New Orleans, the Creek Indians in the frontier wars, and the National Bank during his presidency, Andrew Jackson had demonstrated an unrivaled determination to achieve whatever he wanted, regardless of the opposition. For a new youthful country preoccupied with its own destiny, Jackson seemed a "symbol for an age"—a man whose skills were complemented by the forces of history.

In the following essay, William A. DeGregorio closely examines Jackson's famous duel with Charles Dickinson. For his contemporaries, this event, as much as any other, attested to Jackson's courage and determination, and also his brutality and violent nature. And the glorification of the duel says much about the qualities that were admired in the mid-nineteenth century.

Gentlemen, are you ready?"

Andrew Jackson and Charles Dickinson squared off, facing each other eight paces (about twenty-four feet) apart. Each held a single-shot pistol at his side.

Dickinson, a handsome figure nattily dressed in a short blue coat and gray trousers, calmly replied, "Yes." Jackson, his spare, lanky frame concealed beneath a carelessly buttoned, full-length frock coat, fixed his icy blue eyes on his opponent and awaited the signal.

"Fire!"

Even before that Friday morning, May 30, 1806, news of the duel had swept Nashville. Residents placed bets furiously, with the smart money on Dickinson. At age twenty-seven, he was widely regarded as the best marksman in Tennessee. He was a rising attorney of some repute in the western part of the state, and had prospered by speculating in commodities, land, livestock, and slaves. Dickinson's arrogance and incessant bragging annoyed some, but his wit and charm allowed him to remain quite popular in Nashville.

Jackson, the man who nonetheless challenged this sharpshooter to a duel, had at age thirty-nine already served in both houses of Congress and as a judge in Tennessee's highest court, and held the rank of major general in the Tennessee militia. He had demonstrated many important leadership qualities—courage, vision, and an ability to motivate others. But there was a darker side to Jackson's character—a side he exposed during the events surrounding his duel with Dickinson.

Of course, those who knew Jackson well were aware that he had a visceral, forceful personality. He was combative, often stubborn, and had an explosive temper. His closest confidant and eventual

"The Choice" by William A. DeGregorio. This article is reprinted from the January/February 1990 issue, Volume XXIV/No. 7, pp. 33–36, 72 of *American History Illustrated* with the permission of Cowles History Group, Inc. Copyright *American History Illustrated* magazine.

presidential successor Martin Van Buren marveled at the way Jackson turned his anger on and off like a switch.

Some speculated that Jackson simply showed his temper for effect. Perhaps, but genuine rage often boiled within this rawboned veteran who, having been orphaned by age fourteen, had needed to grow up in a hurry, and who still bore the physical and emotional scars from his boyhood internment in a prisoner of war camp during the Revolution.

Thomas Jefferson observed Jackson regularly during the latter's brief Congressional career and was appalled at his inability to control his temper. "His passions are terrible," Jefferson said of Jackson. "When I was President of the Senate, he was senator, and he could never speak on account of the rashness of his feelings. I have seen him attempt it repeatedly, and as often choke with rage. His passions are, no doubt, cooler now; he has been much tried since I knew him, but he is a dangerous man."

"When Andrew Jackson hated," writes Robert V. Remini, Jackson's principal modern biographer, "It often became grand passion. He could hate with a Biblical fury and would resort to petty and vindictive acts to nurture his hatred and keep it bright and strong and ferocious. He needed revenge. He always struck back."

Especially in defense of his wife's honor.

When Jackson "married" Rachel Donelson Robards in 1791, neither realized that she was still legally wed to another man. Rachel thought she had been divorced, but because of a technicality that Jackson, though a lawyer, had somehow overlooked, the divorce was not yet finalized when she and Andrew exchanged vows. A few years later they discovered the error and were married in a second ceremony, this time legally. But whenever Jackson ran for office or was otherwise in the public spotlight, his adversaries and the opposition press hurled charges of adultery.

In October 1803, for example, Jackson was the target of a harsh verbal attack by former Tennessee governor John Sevier in a public confrontation on Knoxville's town square. "I know of

This grand statue of Jackson stands in Jackson Park in New Orleans; it is indicative of Jackson's reputation, and plays upon a romanticized view of militance, strength, and honor.

no great service you have rendered the country," taunted Sevier, "except taking a trip to Natchez with another man's wife." A scuffle punctuated by gunshots ensued between the enraged Jackson and his bitter political rival; during the weeks that followed Jackson repeatedly challenged Sevier to duel and published charges that he was "a base coward and poltroon" who "will basely insult, but has not the courage to repair the wound." The satisfaction with arms that Jackson sought was barely averted at the last minute through the efforts of the two men's seconds.

Tradition credits the Jackson-Dickinson duel to similar circumstances: learning that Dickinson had made irreverent remarks about Rachel, the story goes, Jackson confronted the young lawyer. Dickinson apologized and blamed his loose tongue on too many drinks. Soon thereafter, however, Dick-

inson repeated the slanders, and escalating tempers eventually led to the dueling ground.

Although no authentic document survives to confirm that Dickinson besmirched the honor of Jackson's wife as legend and some historical accounts maintain, the degree of enmity Jackson felt toward Dickinson suggests this could well have been the case. But the sequence of events leading to the ultimate confrontation between the two men was far more complex than that, and it was set in motion by a wager over a horse race.

An avid horseman, Jackson owned a superb stallion named Truxton. In November 1805 Jackson and two partners arranged a $2,000 match race between Truxton and Ploughboy, a horse owned by Dickinson's uncle and partner, Captain Joseph Ervin. Ploughboy went lame before the appointed day, however, and Ervin and Dickinson canceled the race, paying Jackson the $800 forfeit in the form of promissory notes they held. A brief disagreement arose regarding whether the notes paid were the same as those presented when the race had been arranged, but the matter was settled amicably.

That would have been the end of the affair had not a third party—a young lawyer and newcomer to Nashville named Thomas Swann—meddled. Apparently seeking attention and notoriety, Swann incited both Dickinson and Jackson by repeating to each man inflammatory statements supposedly made by the other about the promissory notes. Misunderstandings compounded and tempers flared. Finally, in a letter published in the Nashville newspaper *Impartial Review and Cumberland Repository,* Jackson charged Swann with being a "puppet and lying valet for a worthless, drunken, blackguard scounderal [*sic*]." Dickinson, replying publicly in the same newspaper, declared Jackson to be "a worthless scoundrel" and "a paltroon [*sic*] and a coward."

Jackson not unexpectedly responded by challenging Dickinson to duel. Although dueling was illegal in Tennessee, Jackson was prepared to defy the law to satisfy his passion. Nevertheless, for propriety's sake he and Dickinson agreed to meet outside of Tennessee—just across the state border in a popular forest clearing at Harrison's Mills, Kentucky, about thirty-five miles north of Nashville.

The day before the scheduled showdown, Jackson arose at 5 A.M., ate breakfast, and told his wife that he was leaving for a couple of days, adding parenthetically that he might have a bit of trouble to settle with Charles Dickinson. Rachel typically did not press him for details but easily could have surmised his mission. At 6:30 A.M. Jackson met his second in the duel, John Overton, and three other companions in Nashville; together they turned north toward Kentucky.

En route, Jackson was in a serious but talkative mood. Never hesitant to speak his mind on national affairs, Jackson criticized President Thomas Jefferson for not standing up to the British over the issue of impressment on the high seas, calling him "the best Republican in theory and the worst in practice." He criticized Aaron Burr, ironically in light of events about to unfold, for killing Alexander Hamilton in a duel two years earlier.

Jackson spoke little of his pending duel except to reveal his strategy of letting Dickinson shoot first. Jackson, only a fair shot himself, was aware of Dickinson's reputation as one of Tennessee's best marksmen. Some said Dickinson was capable of shooting apart a piece of string from eight yards away. Jackson reasoned that he had no chance to beat Dickinson to the draw, and that if he were to fire hastily, his aim was sure to be spoiled by the impact of Dickinson's bullet. Jackson was almost certain that he would be hit and believed that his only chance was to survive Dickinson's shot, then take careful aim.

Dickinson, his second, Dr. Hanson Catlett, and a half-dozen friends traveled ahead of the Jackson party in a carnival mood. Before setting off, Dickinson cheerily kissed his wife farewell and reassured her that he would return home safely the following evening. Boasting to all within earshot that he would shoot Jackson handily, he placed hundreds of dollars in wagers on himself in Nashville. Dickinson paused at times during the journey to demonstrate his marksmanship, delighting onlookers, and he repeated his vow to drop Jackson with one shot.

Before noon the Jackson party stopped for refreshments and a few hours' rest. Jackson had not had his usual morning ration of whiskey, wanting to keep a clear head for the business at hand, but did allow himself a single mint julep at the rest stop.

Later, at about 8 P.M., Jackson settled into David Miller's tavern near the site of the duel, displaying none of the jitters one would expect in a man about to put his life on the line. The prospect of the next morning's potentially fatal encounter disturbed neither his appetite nor his sleep. He enjoyed a full-course supper of fried chicken, sweet potatoes, waffles, and coffee. He then went out on the tavern porch to smoke his pipe for a bit and, at 10 P.M., went to bed. He was asleep in ten minutes. Throughout his life, Jackson was supremely confident of his ability to face any challenge—even a crack shot like Dickinson. Jackson slept so soundly that night that Overton had trouble rousing him at dawn.

Just after sunrise that morning the duelists stood ready in their positions with the seconds, Overton and Catlett, alert to gun down the opposing principal if either should fire prematurely.

Dickinson had won the toss for position, but because it was too early for the sun to break the horizon, this made little difference. Jackson had chosen the weapons—a pair of his own pistols with nine-inch barrels firing 70-caliber balls. Dickinson, therefore, had his pick of the two. Jackson won the right to have his second give the signal to fire.

Upon Overton's signal to "Fire!," Dickinson instantly raised his pistol and, as expected, got off the first shot. Kicking up dust from Jackson's coat as it entered, the bullet struck him full in the chest. Everyone watching knew that Jackson had been hit. Astonishingly, Jackson did not fall but remained standing, ramrod straight, though the ball had chipped off his breastbone, broken two ribs, plowed through chest muscle, and lodged so close to his heart that it could never be removed.

Jackson raised his left hand to the wound. Blood drained down his left leg and began to fill his boot, but except for a slight wince Jackson gave no outward appearance of how badly he had been hurt. His lips concealed how tightly he clenched his teeth.

Dickinson, dumfounded to see his gaunt target still erect, stumbled back off his mark and cried out, "Great God, have I missed him?" But he knew his aim had been sure; he had seen the bullet hit. Everyone there had seen it.

"Back to the mark, sir!" ordered Jackson's second, brandishing a gun. Dickinson had no honorable alternative but to return to the mark and await his fate. He was now at Jackson's mercy.

A man in Jackson's situation, if he did not believe himself to be mortally wounded, customarily raised his pistol, aimed it at his disarmed opponent, then pointed it at the sky and fired. Many present, especially Dickinson, no doubt anticipated this magnanimous, though not mandatory, gesture.

While Dickinson stood frozen at the mark, his arms folded across his chest, his eyes fixed on the ground, Jackson raised his pistol, took level aim—and pulled the trigger.

A harmless "click" followed. The hammer had mercifully failed to strike.

Jackson now had a second chance to consider his actions, to remind himself that Dickinson's wife was pregnant. Jackson had been born after his own father's death and so knew from experience the hardship of growing up fatherless on the frontier.

As Dickinson waited helplessly in place, Jackson carefully recocked his pistol and again took deliberate aim at his opponent. And for the second time he pulled the trigger. This time the weapon did not misfire.

The heavy bullet struck Dickinson in the abdomen, penetrating his intestines and leaving a gaping wound. Overton, satisfied that the figure writhing in agony on the ground would not survive the day, hurried over to Jackson and said, "He won't want anything more of you, General."

As the winning team strode off the field, Overton noted Jackson's left boot sloshing with blood and finally realized that his friend had been seriously wounded. "Oh, I believe that he pinked me," Jackson observed in typical understatement. "I don't want those people to know. Let's move on."

On examining the wound, the duelist's companions concluded that what had apparently saved Jackson was the set of his ill-fitting coat. With the frock hung askew, Dickinson had probably misjudged the location of his opponent's heart. But he had missed it by only an inch.

To those who wondered how Jackson had found the strength to remain standing and shoot Dickinson after having been so severely wounded, Jackson responded, "I should have hit him if he had shot me through the brain!"

Jackson showed no repentance for having shot Dickinson in cold blood. His notion of magnanimity was sending a bottle of wine to his victim and offering his surgeon's services. Dickinson's only comfort in his last hours was the lie friends told him: that Jackson was also on his deathbed, mortally wounded. At about 9 P.M. Dickinson asked, "Why did you put out the candles?" and died.

Throughout his career, Jackson never felt restrained to use the minimum force necessary to repel a threat. And in his encounter with Dickinson he felt fully justified in killing a man who had tried, albeit unsuccessfully, to kill *him.* No further excuse, he believed, was necessary; nor was any forthcoming. Jackson's apologists over the years have maintained that when he shot Dickinson he believed his own wound was fatal. If that is so, Jackson left no record of it.

The episode and the bullet Dickinson fired would haunt Jackson the rest of his life. The full ounce of lead was lodged so close to his heart that doctors never dared to attempt removing it. The bullet immobilized him for weeks. He recovered slowly and thereafter experienced sporadic chest pain that increased in frequency with old age.

Dickinson's funeral was one of the largest ever held in Nashville. A group of more than seventy angry mourners met after the services to petition the *Impartial Review* to run a memorial edition dedicated to Dickinson as an expression of regret for his death. When Jackson heard about this, he sent an angry letter to the editor demanding that the petitioners' names also be printed so that he would know who his enemies were. Confronted with such publicity, twenty-six people withdrew their names from the document, but the remainder, including some community leaders, agreed to take a public stand.

Erwin, the father of Dickinson's pregnant widow, publicly charged that Jackson, by pulling the trigger a second time after the pistol had jammed at half-cock, had violated the agreement governing the duel and therefore killed his opponent dishonorably. This accusation came to nothing, however; Catlett, Dickinson's second, joined Overton in a public statement attesting that the duel had been fought within the terms of the agreement.

Until he subsequently gained fame as "Old Hickory" during the War of 1812, Jackson remained something of a pariah in western Tennessee. Even after he became a national figure, the duel was occasionally dredged up and cited by political opponents as a good reason why Jackson should be denied public office.

Some saw the episode as part of a pattern of ruthless and belligerent behavior. Jackson's critics pointed out that the Dickinson shooting was not an isolated incident:

- In the 1803 fight previously noted, Jackson used his heavy walking stick to attack former Tennessee governor John Sevier on the steps of the Knoxville courthouse. The two men later met for a duel that was only narrowly averted before shots were exchanged.
- While preparing to defend New Orleans against imminent British attack during the War of 1812, Jackson executed deserters, imposed martial law on the city, dissolved the Louisiana legislature, suppressed free expression, and ignored a federal judge's writ of habeas corpus.
- In 1814 Jackson went gunning for Thomas Hart Benton in Nashville's City Hotel, but was shot in the back by Benton's brother, Jesse. The bullet tore Jackson's left shoulder and greatly reduced the mobility in that arm until the lead was removed nearly twenty years later.
- During the First Seminole War (1816–1818), Jackson occupied Spanish Florida without authorization from the administration in Washing-

ton, D.C. He also captured, court-martialed, and executed British citizens Alexander Arbuthnot and Robert Ambrister for having incited the Seminoles against the United States. The killings drew a sharp diplomatic rebuke from Britain.

During Jackson's first successful presidential campaign in 1828 the opposition compiled a résumé of brutality, the so-called Coffin Handbill, from such incidents. Under the bold, grim headline "Account of some of the Bloody Deeds of GENERAL JACKSON," it depicted clusters of caskets, eighteen in all, each with the name of an individual killed by Jackson's order and a brief narrative of how that person died.

Despite Jackson's vulnerability on what today is called the character issue, Americans twice elected him president and he went on to become perhaps the greatest chief executive in the half-century between Jefferson and Abraham Lincoln. Jackson was a founder of the modern activist presidency. He was the first to harness the latent powers of the office to implement his programs and thwart the will of the opposition. In so doing he vetoed more bills than all of his predecessors combined.

In the strictest sense, Jackson was the first common man to become president; his predecessors were either Virginia aristocrats or Boston lawyers. He was the first president to represent the interests of the burgeoning West. He destroyed the Bank of the United States, symbol to many of the moneyed interests' exploitation of the working class. And, in a showdown with South Carolina over its claimed right to nullify federal laws within its borders (1832–1833), Jackson stood firm and stamped out, at least temporarily, budding secessionist sentiment in the South.

The Dickinson episode, then, revealed some significant character flaws in Jackson, but these did not prove fatal to his presidency. Had voters focused on Jackson's temper and ruthless, unforgiving nature to the exclusion of his courage, integrity, tenacity, and unquestionable leadership ability, the nation would have been denied an outstanding president.

STUDY QUESTIONS

1. Why did Jackson and Dickinson get involved in a duel? Had these men been involved in other duels, and what circumstances prompted those confrontations?

2. Do the activities of the Southern "gentlemen" in this piece—especially the gambling, horse racing, and fighting—remind you of events described in an earlier reading in this text? What conclusions might you draw from the comparison?

3. What was a "second," and what role did he play in the elaborate protocol of duels?

4. Despite killing Dickinson in the duel described here, Andrew Jackson went on to become President of the United States and the most famous American of his era. In fact, some historians refer to the 1820–1840 period as the "Age of Jackson." Considering the importance we currently place on the "character issue" in choosing our president, why do you think the majority of American voters not only elected a man with such a violent past to the White House, but considered him the living embodiment of the "American character" as well? Did Jackson display positive character traits which might have balanced out his violent temper?

BIBLIOGRAPHY

The first place to go for superlative Jackson biography is Robert V. Remini, *Andrew Jackson and the Course of American Freedom, 1822–1833* (1981); and also by Remini, *Andrew Jackson and the Course of American Democracy, 1833–1845* (1984). For an introduction to the Age of Jackson, see Glyndon G. Van Deusen, *The Jacksonian Era, 1828–1848* (1959). Also see Edward Pessen, *Jacksonian America: Society, Personality, and Politics* (1978). A dated but still important interpretation of the phenomenon of Jacksonianism is Arther M. Schlesinger, Jr., *The Age of Jackson* (1945). Additionally, see John William Ward, *Andrew Jackson: Symbol for an Age* (1955) and Marvin Meyers, *The Jacksonian Persuasion* (1957) for analyses of the culture of Jacksonian democracy. Finally, for the role of duels and the code of Southern "honor" see Bertram Wyatt-Brown, *Southern Honor: Ethics and Behavior in the Old South* (1982) and Edward L. Ayers, *Vengeance and Justice: Crime and Punishment in the Nineteenth-Century American South* (1984).

THE ALAMO: AN AMERICAN EPIC

Paul Andrew Hutton

All that remains today of the original Alamo complex is the chapel. A maze of hotels, businesses, fast-food restaurants, and crowded streets has replaced the infamous mission where men once struggled for—and ultimately lost—their lives. But inside the chapel, even on the busiest days, is an eerie silence, a quiet reverence shared between the living and the dead. In the United States the Alamo has become a symbol of ultimate sacrifice. The men who fought and died there could have escaped, but chose instead to make a stand for independence. As Col. William Barret Travis, commander of the Alamo, wrote the man who was taking care of his young son, "if . . . I should perish, he [his son] will have nothing but the proud recollection that he is the son of a man who died for his country."

This display of sacrifice is one of the reasons for the enduring fascination of the battle of the Alamo. Another contributor to the battle's mystique are the larger-than-life personalities involved in the event. Although much is known of David Crockett and James Bowie—and a bit less about William Travis—all three men remain something of a mystery. Was Crockett a bumbling politician or a shrewd, backwoods philosopher? Was Bowie a get-rich-quick slave trader or a man wholly committed to Texas independence? And Travis, who was this man with a shadowy past who arrived on the scene so late and died so early? One final reason for the continued interest in the Alamo is the many mysteries that swirl around the event. How many independence fighters died inside the Alamo? We know that the traditional number of 183 is too low. How did Crockett die—making a last stand or by execution? Because no defenders survived, many questions will never be fully answered.

In the following essay, historian Paul Andrew Hutton masterfully recounts what is known of the battle.

Williiam Barret Travis was an unhappy young man as he led a band of thirty dusty, bedraggled soldiers into San Antonio de Bexar on February 3, 1836. His bright dreams of martial glory were fading fast. Events seemed to be conspiring against him—even the splendid dress uniform he had ordered had failed to arrive before his departure from San Felipe de Austin. He was clad in homemade Texas jeans, hardly the proper attire for a twenty-seven-year-old cavalry officer of soaring ambition and Byronic temperament.

Travis had worked hard to win a commission as a lieutenant colonel of the Texas cavalry, a martial arm in keeping with his chivalric sensibilities and aristocratic pretensions. He had been enraged when ordered to San Antonio with only thirty men, and had threatened to resign unless reassigned to another command. "I am unwilling to risk my reputation (which is ever dear to a volunteer)," he wrote to Provisional Texas Governor Henry Smith, "by going off into the enemy's country with so little means, so few men, and these so badly equipped—the fact is there is no necessity for my services to command these few men. The company officers will be sufficient."

Governor Smith ignored Travis's tirade. He was used to them by now, for this was the young officer's third letter of resignation. Smith was busy with more pressing matters, for the Texas army was splintering into factions, and the shaky provisional government was collapsing from within from incessant bickering. The commander of the virtually nonexistent army, Sam Houston, had gone off in disgust under the pretext of negotiating with the northern Indians to ensure their neutrality, while rumors abounded that the president of Mexico, Antonio López de Santa Anna, was

marching against Texas with a strong army to suppress the rebellion. Smith needed men he could count on to guard the borders of Texas, and William Barret Travis was such a man.

Born in 1809 near Red Bank, South Carolina, William was the first of ten children of Mark and Jemima Travis. In 1818 the family moved west to Sparta, Alabama, where William grew to be a bright, ambitious six-footer with a fiery disposition to match his red hair. In his late teens he taught school and, in October 1828, married one of his students. Rosanna Cato and William Barret Travis seemed destined to happiness. Travis studied law with James Delett, a leading Alabama lawyer, and soon had a promising legal practice. Rosanna bore him a son, Charles, and was soon pregnant again.

Then, in 1831, everything suddenly fell apart. Travis discovered that his wife had been unfaithful, even doubted that the child she carried was his. He sought out her lover and killed him. With his reputation sullied and his legal career destroyed—despite the tolerance extended by the community concerning the killing—Travis mounted his horse and headed west toward Texas to begin life anew.

Despite vague assurances to Rosanna that he would send for her and the children, Travis listed himself as "single" and even as "widower" on legal documents in Texas. He settled in the port town of Anáhuac in May 1831, but soon moved inland to bustling San Felipe and opened a law practice. Travis began a cryptic but meticulous diary that recorded his passionate pursuit of the good life. He dressed stylishly, gambled incessantly, and enjoyed a rather staggering number of liaisons with various ladies—these latter adventures recorded in Spanish in his diary, with everything else in English.

When Rosanna suddenly appeared in 1834 to demand either a reconciliation or a divorce, she promptly got the divorce. Travis, however, retained custody of Charles.

Soon after arriving in Texas, Travis identified himself with radicals opposed to Mexican rule. His sentiments were similar to those of many recent emigrants to the northern Mexican province.

"The Alamo: An American Epic" by Paul Andrew Hutton. This article is reprinted from the March 1986 issue, Volume XX/No. 11, pp. 12–26, 35–37 of *American History Illustrated* with the permission of Cowles History Group, Inc. Copyright *American History Illustrated* magazine.

Shortly after winning independence from Spain in 1821, the new Mexican government had offered generous land grants and exemption from taxes and trade duties to induce colonists to settle in Texas. The only requirements had been to swear allegiance to the Mexican government and to become a nominal Catholic. Men such as Stephen F. Austin had received enormous grants of land in exchange for bringing bands of colonists to develop Texas under this *empresario* system. The first settlers were sober, orderly, and law-abiding, but by the 1830s adventurers of every sort were flocking to Texas in search of new fortune. Some, like Sam Houston—the Tennessee governor whose marriage had collapsed in scandal, leading him to resign and seek a new life elsewhere— were already famous. Others, like William Barret Travis, were not. But their stories were similar and their goals the same—to make a fresh start in this rich, exotic, and vast land.

By 1830 Americans made up over 75 percent of the population of Texas and were growing increasingly restless under inefficient, if benign, Mexican rule. Smuggling had become a way of life in Texas, illegal slavery was practiced flagrantly, and taxes were ignored. Cultural arrogance and racial antipathy further exacerbated the deteriorating situation.

In response, the Mexican government passed a new law in April 1830 that outlawed American migration into Texas, banned slavery, restricted trade, and imposed new taxes. The Texans, already angry over the refusal of the central government to consider separating them from the state of Coahuila, were incensed. To make matters worse, the Mexicans actually intended to enforce their new law. General Manuel y Terán established a string of garrisons across Texas to enforce compliance.

In June 1832, when tensions were running high, Travis decided to play a practical joke on Colonel John Bradburn, a former Kentuckian now serving Mexico as garrison commander at Anáhuac. He and a friend, Patrick Jack, warned Bradburn that a mob of armed Texans was about to descend on Anáhuac because of the colonel's

rigorous enforcement of the antismuggling laws. After a tense night awaiting the onslaught, the colonel failed to share Travis's sense of humor when informed that it was all a ruse. He threw both Travis and Jack into jail.

Now the Americans really did rise—just as Travis had hoped they would—and marched on Anáhuac. The armed rebels found the prisoners tied to the ground, with muskets pointed at their heads. Travis, an avid reader of the novels of Sir Walter Scott, seized on the moment to become the Ivanhoe of Texas. He called on his rescuers to fire, for he would rather die in martyr to freedom than live under tyranny. But cooler heads prevailed, and the Americans withdrew to lay siege to Anáhuac.

All over east Texas men answered the call to arms. War seemed inevitable until events in Mexico thwarted young Travis's scheme. General Santa Anna, a supposed liberal, had overthrown the anti-American regime of President Anastacio Bustamente. Customs duties were temporarily suspended, Bradburn was fired, and Travis and Jack were released. Stephen F. Austin and other advocates of accommodation were elated, and their opinion now prevailed.

Seeking a peaceful solution to their grievances, the so-called "peace party" drafted petitions requesting the separation of Coahuila and Texas, repeal of the anti-immigration clause of the 1830 law, and tariff exemption. Texans at San Felipe in April 1833 also drafted a proposed state constitution, based on the Massachusetts charter of 1780. Austin was chosen to carry the petitions and constitution to Mexico City and present the views of Texans to Santa Anna.

At first Austin was successful, for Santa Anna rescinded the immigration restrictions as of May 1834. The Mexican leader also prodded the Coahuila legislature to placate the Texans by increasing the number of Texas delegates to the joint legislature, establishing trial by jury and an appellate court system for Texas, and instituting other administrative reforms.

These impressive Mexican concessions were all forgotten, however, when news reached Texas that Austin had been imprisoned. An inflammatory letter he had written to the *ayuntamiento* [governing council] of San Antonio de Bexar, urging that Texas form a state even if the central government would not consent, had fallen into the hands of government agents.

Austin remained in prison for a year before winning release on bond early in 1835. But he was still detained in Mexico City, effectively silencing the most influential voice for moderation in Texas.

With Austin out of the way, Travis and the "war party" saw their chance. The Customs House at Anáhuac had been reopened, and its commander, Captain Antonio Tenorio, was vigorously pursuing smugglers. Tensions ran high along the coast, and Travis was confident that the moment for action had come. With twenty-five men, he marched on Anáhuac and seized the Customs House on June 27, 1835.

Captain Tenorio fled to San Felipe, where the colonists were horrified by Travis's audacity. Throughout Texas, communities passed resolutions condemning Travis in the strongest terms. Humiliated, the impetuous agitator retreated into seclusion to brood over his folly. "The peace party are the strongest," he grumbled in a letter to James Bowie, "unless we could be united, had we not better be quiet, and settle down for a while?"

But just when Travis and the "war party" were in total disgrace and the moderates were gaining the upper hand, Santa Anna decided to tighten his control over Texas—and in doing so played right into the hands of the radicals. Naturally enraged over the seizure of Anáhuac, and perplexed as to why Texas civil authorities had not arrested Travis and his men, Santa Anna ordered his brother-in-law, General Martín Perfecto de Cós, to march north with four hundred troops and establish martial law.

The news swept across Texas, and "Committees of Public Safety" were quickly organized. Travis was in the thick of the organizing, feeling jubilant and vindicated. "Although the Mexican or Tory party made a tremendous effort to put us

down," Travis wrote a friend on August 31, "principle has triumphed over prejudice, passion, cowardice and knavery. All their measures have recoiled upon them and they are routed horse and foot . . . The people call now loudly for a convention in which their voices shall be heard. They have become almost completely united. And now let Tories, submission men and Spanish invaders look out."

Stephen F. Austin now suddenly returned from Mexico, landing at Velasco on September 1. When a thousand Texans honored him at a banquet in Brazoria, they found his voice turned against moderation. Texans, he declared, must unite against any invading force and must organize a government.

When news reached Austin on September 19 that Cós's troops were poised to occupy San Antonio de Bexar, he issued a clarion call to all patriots: "War is our only resource. There is no other remedy but to defend our rights, ourselves, and our country by force of arms."

War was not long in coming. Government troops from San Antonio de Bexar marched seventy miles east to Gonzales to confiscate a rusty six-pounder that the colonists had been given for protection against the Indians. The Gonzales militia, under its thirty-year-old captain, Albert Martin, and a young Tennessee blacksmith, Almeron Dickinson, gathered to block the Mexicans. Numbering but eighteen, they taunted the troops with a little banner on which was emblazoned, "Come and Take It." The Mexicans hesitated and then went into camp.

While the troops dallied, volunteers swelled the ranks of the Gonzales militia to 167 men by October 1. At dawn the next day, the two bands of soldiers faced each other. Somebody fired a shot, and then the little cannon that had caused the confrontation sputtered forth. The Mexicans broke, retreating to Bexar, and the Texas rebellion was underway.

Austin arrived at Gonzales on October 11, and was immediately elected commander of the ragtag Volunteer Army of Texas. The presidio at Goliad soon fell on to the rebels, giving them valuable military supplies. Austin led some four hundred men to Bexar and laid siege to that strongly fortified town. Although General Cós had twice as many troops, they were short on food and tormented by low morale. The town was finally assaulted, and after five days of bitter street fighting Cós surrendered on December 11, 1835. He and his men were paroled and allowed to peacefully withdraw from Texas.

Travis had distinguished himself in several scouting expeditions and hit-and-run raids against the Mexicans, but was absent when Bexar was finally assaulted. Austin was also gone, having been sent to the United States to seek aid. By this time a convention had finally gathered in San Felipe and organized a state government for Texas under the Mexican Federalist constitution of 1824—a liberal charter that Santa Anna had overthrown. Henry Smith was elected as provisional governor with a twelve-member council appointed to assist and advise him. Smith and the council immediately set to quarreling, much to the consternation of the newly appointed commander of the Texas army, Maj. General Sam Houston.

After the victory over Cós, the army quickly disintegrated. Military stores left at Bexar by the defeated Mexicans were looted by followers of Dr. James Grant and Colonel Francis Johnson, who proposed a bold strike south into Mexico against Matamoros. Houston bitterly opposed the scheme, but was helpless to stop it. Colonel James Neill, in command at Bexar, gloomily reported that most of his men had joined the Matamoros venture. "We have 104 men and two distinct fortresses to garrison, and about 24 pieces of artillery," he wrote Governor Smith on January 6, 1836. "You doubtless have learned that we have no provisions nor clothing in this garrison since Johnson and Grant left."

Governor Smith, in response, ordered Lieutenant Colonel Travis, then on recruiting duty in San Felipe, to reinforce Neill. Travis departed San Felipe on January 23, dragging his feet every step of the way in hope he might be recalled as requested. No recall came, and on February 3 he reported to Colonel Neill in San Antonio de Bexar.

Travis was surprised to find Colonel James Bowie with Neill.

There was hardly a man in Texas better known than the forty-year-old Bowie. The big-boned, sandy-haired giant had a personality as forceful and oversized as his physical presence. All across the Old Southwest men recounted his legendary deeds of daring—roping wild mustangs, riding alligators, smuggling slaves with the pirate Lafitte, battling Indians, and searching for the San Saba silver mine. But mostly they spoke of his knife, a monstrous, double-edged blade—and of the men he had slain with it. As his fame spread, men began to ask blacksmiths to make them knives "just like Bowie's" and the most peculiarly American of weapons was baptised.

Born in Kentucky in 1796, Bowie had been reared in the Louisiana bayou country. As he grew to strapping manhood he made a local name for himself as a hunter and mustanger. He made a living cutting lumber and barging it down to New Orleans. Soon he felt as comfortable among the courtly citizens of the Crescent City as with the rough folk of the backwoods.

Bowie had first visited Texas in 1819 in company with his brother Rezin. They fell in with Jean Lafitte at his Galveston Island outpost. The old pirate had fallen on hard times since his glory days operating off Barataria Island, but he still turned a tidy profit smuggling slaves into the United States. The Bowies paid Lafitte a dollar a pound for the blacks, and then made the dangerous journey into Louisiana with their human cargo. Slaves were worth between five hundred and a thousand dollars at auction in those days, and the Bowie brothers did quite well, making over sixty-five thousand dollars before they parted company with Lafitte.

They invested these ill-gotten funds in land speculation. These land deals, many of them rather shady, led Bowie into conflict with Major Norris Wright, a neighbor in Rapides Parish, Louisiana, and set in motion a chain of events culminating in the bloodiest duel in the history of the Old Southwest. On September 19, 1827, the antagonists met at Vidalia Sandbar, a little island on the Mississippi River near Natchez. Neither Bowie nor Wright were principals in the duel to be fought that morning, but when the duelists exchanged ineffectual shots and shook hands, their seconds pulled weapons and a general melee resulted. Two men were killed and three others badly wounded. Bowie, wounded several times, managed to plunge his terrible knife into Major Wright before collapsing from loss of blood.

The sandbar fray made Bowie the most celebrated mankiller on the frontier. There were other fights, always with the knife, and for every real killing there were a dozen fanciful ones. Always Bowie was the victor, and always someone else started the fracas.

Although he possessed a violent temper, Bowie was generally regarded as courtly and courteous. His deference to women became a trademark. An equally famous American, Henry Clay, shared a stagecoach ride with Bowie in 1832. Clay reported that when a fellow passenger refused to put out his pipe upon a lady's request, Bowie instantly sprang into action. The ill-mannered traveler suddenly felt the cold steel of Bowie's knife against his throat and quickly extinguished his smoke amidst profuse apologies to the lady.

In 1828 Bowie again headed for Texas, leaving the states before some fraudulent land speculations he had engaged in in Arkansas with his brother John began to unravel. He passed as a man of wealth and position, and although his notoriety as a knife-fighter had preceded him, he was accepted into the upper circles of Texas society.

Prim and proper Stephen F. Austin immediately disliked Bowie, sizing him up as an extravagant adventurer, but he nevertheless introduced him to Don Juan Martin de Veramendi, vice governor of Texas-Coahuila and the most important Hispanic figure in Texas. His wife, Doña María Josefa Navarro de Veramendi, was from the other major Hispanic family in Texas, and they were proud parents of a seventeen-year-old girl of uncommon beauty, keen intelligence, and a warm disposition. Maria Ursula de Veramendi quickly

won Jim Bowie's heart, and within a few months he was baptized into the Roman Catholic Church and took up Mexican citizenship. Bowie and Ursula were married in the San Fernando Church in San Antonio de Bexar on April 25, 1831, and it seemed as if an adventurous life had reached a quiet, domestic conclusion.

But Bowie, although devoted to his wife, could never be still for long. In November he set out across central Texas with his brother Rezin and nine others in search of the legendary lost San Saba silver mine. They never found the mine, but they did encounter over 150 Indians, and there followed one of the most desperate Indian-white clashes in Southwest history. When it was over, one of Bowie's men was dead, and three wounded, while the defeated Indians lost forty dead and another thirty wounded.

Bowie led other parties out against the Indians, eventually ranking as colonel in an early formation of Texas Rangers, and he kept up his search for the silver mines as well. Rumors persisted that he actually found the San Saba mine, which came to be called the Lost Bowie Mine, and that only he knew its true location.

Bowie traveled across Texas, and often back to the United States, making business deals and engaging in wild land speculations, all financed by his father-in-law. Soon he owned over a million acres of prime Texas land.

Then, while on a business trip to Mississippi in 1832, Bowie received the shattering news that cholera had swept Monclova, where the Veramendis kept a summer home. His wife, his two children, and his in-laws were all dead. Bowie's grief was unbearable, and for solace he took more and more to the bottle. He lived alone in the big Veramendi house in Bexar, surrounded by ghosts; a tormented, lonely man. For years he had been wracked by a terrible cough, but now it grew more vicious, exacerbated by his alcoholic binges.

As tensions increased between Mexico and Texas, Bowie threw in with the "war party." Here was a cause a man could lose himself in, a cause that could help him forget the past. Stephen Austin despised Bowie, but Sam Houston was his warm friend and trusted in him completely. "There is no man on whose forecast, prudence, and valor I place a higher estimate," wrote Houston of Bowie. It was Houston who ordered his friend to go to Bexar in January 1836. Houston wanted Bowie to destroy the fortifications at the old Spanish mission called the Alamo, and retreat with Neill's men to Gonzales.

Bowie rode into Bexar on January 19, 1836, with thirty volunteers, and immediately began to reconsider Houston's orders. He liked the fiber of the men with Neill, for they had withstood the blandishments of the Matamoros adventurers; and in the Alamo he saw a fortress worth holding. Mexican friends informed him that Santa Anna was on the march. To Bowie, Bexar now became the key to the defense of Texas. Of course, it was also his home, where his family had lived, and where his many Mexican friends still lived, and he was not about to abandon it to an invading army.

By February 2, Bowie had made a firm commitment to make his stand. "The salvation of Texas depends in great measure on keeping Bexar out of the hands of the enemy," he wrote to Governor Smith. "It serves as the frontier picquet [picket] guard, and if it were in the possession of Santa Anna, there is no stronghold from which to repel him in his march toward the Sabine. Colonel Neill and myself have come to the solemn resolution that we will rather die in these ditches than give it up to the enemy."

The ditches that Bowie was determined to defend were hardly imposing. The mission San Antonio de Valero had been founded by Franciscans in 1718 to Christianize the Indians. Construction had finally been completed during the 1750s. After 1801 the compound was converted into a fort by Spanish troops. Some of the soldiers were from the Company of the Alamo of Parras, Coahuila, and their name stuck to the old mission. San Antonio de Valero was similar in construction to other Spanish missions in Texas and the Southwest. There was a large rectangular plaza of about three acres, lined by stone walls that were from nine to twelve feet high and up to three thick. The main entrance lay on the south side

and ran through a single-story building called the low barracks.

A series of adobe dwellings lined the west wall and faced toward Bexar, some four hundred yards distant. The north wall was similar, while the east wall was composed of the two-story "long barracks." This imposing structure was further fortified by a corral to its rear.

Just south of the long barracks was a ruined Alamo church with four-foot-thick walls, some twenty-two feet high. Its roof had collapsed in the 1760s, but several small rooms along its side wall were still covered.

There was a fifty-yard gap between the church and the low barracks, and Bowie promptly set his engineering officer, Green Jameson, to constructing a low log-and-earthen wall to cover the gap. It would take hundreds of men to hold this sprawling compound, but numbers did not worry Jim Bowie. He had twenty pieces of artillery and a hundred determined men with which to defend the Alamo, and he was confident that others would rally to the defense of Bexar.

The defenders, cheered by the arrival of Travis and his thirty men on February 3, had their spirits further bolstered five days later when Colonel David Crockett and a dozen companions—dubbed the Tennessee Mounted Volunteers—rode into Bexar.

World of Crockett's arrival spread quickly, and before long most of the Alamo garrison and many of the citizens of Bexar had gathered around him in the Main Plaza, demanding a speech. Giving speeches was what the fifty-year-old politician did best, and he gave them all a roaring one that day. He had told his Tennessee constituents that if they did not reelect him to Congress they could all go to hell, and he would go to Texas—and here he was at Bexar.

"I have come to aid you all that I can in your noble cause," he informed the assembled crowd. "I shall identify myself with your interests, and all the honor I desire is that of defending as a high private, in common with my fellow citizens, the liberties of our common country." Old Davy Crockett had not become one of the most celebrated men in America for nothing. It was a fine speech, and it established him immediately as a natural, democratic leader of the Bexar garrison.

Crockett, like Houston, Travis, and Bowie, had come to Texas to start over. Born in northeastern Tennessee on August 17, 1786, Davy had grown up on the frontier as his father, John Crockett, a veteran of the American Revolution, moved ever westward in search of elusive fortune. Davy ran away from home at age twelve to avoid a thrashing and worked for several years as a wagoneer. He eventually returned home and even went to school for six months before taking a wife, lovely Polly Finley, in August 1806.

The Crocketts settled in central Tennessee, near the Alabama border, but their efforts at farming were interrupted by the outbreak of the Creek Indian War in 1813. Davy promptly volunteered to fight, and served in Andrew Jackson's successful campaign against the Indians.

Soon after Crockett returned from the war, his wife died, leaving him with three children. He soon married Elizabeth Patton, a widow with two small children, and they combined their families, eventually adding three more children of their own to the brood.

Crockett did not prosper as a farmer. In search of better land he moved his growing family west of the Tennessee River, to lands recently wrested from the Creeks. It was there that Crockett began his political career, first as a magistrate, then as a colonel of militia, and finally, in 1821, as a delegate to the state legislature. He was a forceful stump speaker, winning over the voters with tall tales and humorous anecdotes. Although of independent mind, he was strongly identified with the Jackson forces, and as a result was elected to Congress in 1827. He championed Jacksonian democracy and squatters' rights, and became a picturesque and celebrated figure in Washington.

Crockett eventually broke with Jackson over land and Indian policy, and briefly aligned himself with the Whigs. They exploited his backwoods credentials and attempted to build him up into a Whig frontier symbol to counter Jackson, but the

effort failed. He lost his bid for reelection in 1835 by 230 votes. His Whig friends promptly abandoned him, and his political career lay in shambles. So Davy Crockett, as he had done countless times before, packed up and headed westward to regain his fortunes. This time he headed for Texas, giving speeches all along the way.

On February 10 a grand fandango was thrown in Crockett's honor by the Alamo garrison. The drinking and dancing was still going strong after midnight when a scout hurried in with the news that Santa Anna had reached the Rio Grande, only one hundred and fifty miles to the southwest. A hurried officer's call followed, but after a quick meeting everyone returned to the party convinced that the Mexicans were still far away. Colonel Neill, however, was having second thoughts about holding Bexar, and the next morning he departed on "twenty-days' leave." Before leaving, Neill appointed Travis, the senior regular army officer in Bexar, to take over command of the Alamo.

This did not please the volunteers. They demanded an election to decide who their commander would be, to which Travis reluctantly agreed. Jim Bowie was overwhelmingly elected to command the volunteers, and the humiliated Travis, who still commanded the few regulars, retreated to his rooms to brood. He took up his pen and bitterly complained to Governor Smith that his situation was "truly awkward and delicate." Since Bowie's election, Travis priggishly noted, "He has been roaring drunk all the time; has assumed all command—is proceeding in a most disorderly and irregular manner—interfering with private property, releasing prisoners sentenced by court martial and by Civil Court and turning everything topsy-turvey. If I did not feel my honor and that of my country compromised I would leave here instantly for some other point with the troops under my immediate command as I am unwilling to be responsible for the drunken irregularities of any man."

By February 14, however, Bowie had sobered up, and he and Travis reached agreement to share the command, making all decisions jointly.

While Travis and Bowie bickered, and their soldiers occasionally labored at fortifying the Alamo, the Mexican army struggled on toward Bexar. Santa Anna commanded the army, reinforced at Saltillo by Cós's retreating soldiers and on the Rio Grande by 1,541 men under General Ramirez y Sesma. This force, some 5,500 strong with twenty cannons, crossed the Great River on February 16, 1836.

The march from Saltillo to Bexar, some 365 miles, was a hard one, marked both by a ghastly blizzard and long, dusty miles of dry desert. Many of the soldiers, including both the polished, professional *Zapadores* (fighting engineers) and the illiterate Mayan Indians of the Yucatan battalion, were felled along the trail by exposure or disease. The general had not bothered to bring along a single doctor for his men, nor even a priest to administer last rites. Nevertheless, the Mexican advance guard was within striking distance of Bexar by February 21, and only a rain-swollen river prevented them from launching a surprise attack on the town.

When Lieutenant Colonel Travis awoke on February 23, he found Bexar a scene of wild commotion. The citizens of the town were in motion, with every wagon and cart pressed into service to take them out of town. Travis had been receiving warnings for days that the enemy host was near, but he had not believed the reports. Now, however, he was finally becoming a believer; he hurried to place a sentinel high in the tower of the imposing San Fernando Church.

Hours of fretful worry passed, and then suddenly the bell of the church rang out over and over. The enemy was in view, claimed the agitated sentry, but no one else could see anything. Two volunteers, Dr. John Sutherland and John W. Smith, rode out of town to have a closer look. They had not gone far before they came upon the Mexican cavalry. Back toward Bexar they galloped. In the church tower the vindicated sentry saw them coming and once again jerked on the bell rope.

The defenders of the Alamo gathered together their possessions and hurried toward the old mission. Some had families to look after. Jim Bowie rushed to the Veramendi house to gather in his two young sisters-in-law, while Almeron Dickinson, the Gonzales blacksmith who now commanded the Alamo's artillery, galloped to his quarters to get his eighteen-year-old wife, Susannah, and infant daughter. "Give me the baby," he cried. "Jump on behind and ask me no questions!" Soon they were within the protective walls of the Alamo.

Travis, in his headquarters in the mission, scratched out messages requesting reinforcements. As he sent Dr. Sutherland off to Gonzales with one appeal, Davy Crockett reported to him. "Colonel, here am I," declared the old frontiersman. "Assign me to a position, and I and my twelve boys will try to defend it." Travis assigned him to the rough palisade between the church and low barracks, the weakest point in the fort.

Within two hours Santa Anna arrived in nearly abandoned Bexar with a strong force, although much of his army was still strung out all the way back to the Rio Grande. As the Mexican band played, a blood-red flag fluttered in the breeze over the San Fernando church, a symbol of no quarter to the enemy.

Emissaries now ushered out of the Alamo under flags of truce. Green Jameson went first at the instigation of Bowie, to be followed a few minutes later by Captain Albert Martin, the hero of Gonzales, sent out by Travis.

Both men received the same response from the Mexicans—a demand for unconditional surrender. Travis sent a simple and unmistakably clear answer with a blast from the Alamo's eighteen-pounder.

It was dawn on the twenty-fourth before the Mexican artillery responded. From the partial cover of the riverbank, some four hundred yards from the Alamo, two nine-pounders and a small howitzer bombarded the fort the rest of the day. But the shells caused little damage, and none of the defenders were injured. There was, however, great loss to the garrison that day. Bowie's strange and terrible illness had been growing worse for weeks, and now he completely collapsed. Unable to even stand, he relinquished his share of the command to Travis.

They placed Bowie in a room in the low barracks. He waited in the cool, dimly lit room, often in and out of delirium, wracked by coughing fits, for the inevitable arrival of death. Bowie had faced death many times before and it held no fear for him now. It had already claimed those most dear to him, and he must have welcomed this final confrontation. But Jim Bowie would not go quietly. The great blade lay on a table beside his bed: he was ready for his final duel.

As darkness approached, Travis was also alone with his thoughts in the Alamo's headquarters, just a few yards from Bowie's room. His eloquent pen dashed out another appeal for assistance, this one addressed "To the People of Texas & All Americans in the World":

Fellow citizens & compatriots—I am besieged, by a thousand or more of the Mexicans under Santa Anna—I have sustained a continual bombardment & cannonade for 24 hours & have not lost a man—The enemy has demanded a surrender at discretion, otherwise, the garrison are to be put to the sword, if the fort is taken—I have answered the demand with a cannon shot, & our flag still waves proudly from the walls—I shall never surrender or retreat. Then, I call on you in the name of Liberty, of patriotism & everything dear to the American character, to come to our aid, with all dispatch—The enemy is receiving reinforcements daily & will no doubt increase to three or four thousand in four or five days. If this call is neglected, I am determined to sustain myself as long as possible & die like a soldier who never forgets what is due to his honor & that of his country—Victory or Death.

Travis underlined those last three words three times. Then he handed the message to Captain Albert Martin, with instructions to carry it the sixty-five miles to Gonzales. After dark Martin raced out of the south gate and then turned east. "Hurry on all the men you can," the captain scribbled on the back of Travis's letter when he reached Gonzales late on the twenty-fifth. Another messenger galloped on to San Felipe, another eighty-five miles to the northeast, with the letter. From there other men carried Travis's words to the various American settlements in Texas, and then across the Sabine and Red rivers into the United States.

February 25 was a day of a sharp combat at the Alamo. Santa Anna sent elements of the Matamoros and Jiménez battalions against the fort, at midmorning, only to have them stopped short by Captain Dickinson's artillery. A small band of Texans then sallied forth and burned some nearby huts that had provided cover to the attackers. Again the Texans suffered no casualties, while the Mexicans did not fare nearly so well. Still, Santa Anna pulled his ring of soldiers even tighter around the Alamo, placing new batteries south and southeast of the fort.

That evening Travis dashed off a report of the day's fighting—lavishly praising Dickinson, Crockett, and others for gallantry in repelling the Mexican attack—and again appealing for assistance. He reluctantly agreed that Juan Seguín should make the dangerous ride through the encircling Mexicans to carry the letter to Sam Houston. Travis hated to lose Seguín, who commanded a company of Tejanos, or Mexican-Texans, for he could prove invaluable in any future negotiations with Santa Anna.

Seguín hurried to Jim Bowie's room to ask for the use of his fine horse. Bowie, so wracked by fever that he barely recognized his old friend, muttered his assent. Then Seguín, accompanied by his orderly, dashed out of the Alamo, past a squad of surprised Mexican dragoons, and vanished into the darkness.

Scion of a wealthy and influential Hispanic family, Seguín had long been a friend to the American settlers in Texas. His liberal sensibilities bridled at the centralist dictatorship of Santa Anna. His father, Erasmo, was a warm friend of both Austin and Bowie, and had been elected as a delegate to the convention that ultimately declared Texas independence on March 2, 1836. In the early days of the war, Seguín's company of Tejano cavalry had proven invaluable as scouts. Seguín, who held the rank of captain in the Texas army, had

Robert Onderdonk's "Fall of the Alamo" depicts the vicious battle at what was once a Spanish mission.

scouted with Travis to insure that General Cós's defeated army withdrew from Texas late in 1835 and then had accompanied Travis to the Alamo.

After delivering his message, Seguín raised another company of Tejanos, some twenty-five in number, and hurried back toward the Alamo. Word reached him that Colonel James Fannin was now marching toward the Alamo with three hundred men, so he halted at Cibola to await this larger force. Day after day passed as the impatient Tejano captain looked in vain for Fannin's men, well knowing that time was running out.

Fannin, timid and unsure of his own ability to command, had lost his nerve. He had started for the Alamo on February 26, with over three hundred men and four cannons. But while still in sight of the fort at Goliad, ninety miles southeast of Bexar, several of the wagons had broken down. The expedition soon became a tragic comedy of errors, with oxen wandering off while the wagons were being repaired. Fannin held a council of war, and decided to return to Goliad. He had abandoned the Alamo. A month later, on March 27, 1836, he would surrender his own force to the Mexicans and be murdered along with over three hundred of his men, on orders of Santa Anna.

The men of Gonzales, however, were made of sterner stuff. There George Kimball, a former New York hatter, was organizing a company of militia to march to the relief of the Alamo. By February 27 Kimball had assembled his men, and they set out for Bexar, guided by two of Travis's messengers, Albert Martin and John W. Smith. Skirting Mexican patrols in the darkness, they dashed safely into the fort at 3:00 A.M. on March 1. These thirty-two gallant men would prove to be the only reinforcements the Alamo would receive.

But Travis was still optimistic that relief would be sent, and the arrival of the men from Gonzales further buoyed his spirits. Fannin would surely come to his aid, and to insure that, he had sent out his most trusted and influential officer, James Butler Bonham.

Like Travis, Bonham was a South Carolina lawyer of soaring ambition and romantic sensibilities. Ironically, he had been born just a few miles from the Travis homestead, in 1807. But Bonham's family was aristocratic, and it is unlikely that the two boys knew each other. Bonham, always looking for a fight, had been expelled from South Carolina College before manning an artillery battery as a young colonel during the state's Nullification Crisis of 1832. A failed romance had brought him west. When he learned of the Texas war he helped to raise a company of Alabama volunteers—the Mobile Greys—reaching Bexar on December 12, 1835. Bonham was commissioned a lieutenant in the cavalry, and quickly won the admiration of Houston, Bowie, Travis, and almost everyone who came in contact with him. "His influence in the army is great," Houston noted, "more so than some who would be generals."

Bonham reached Goliad on February 29, but all his powers of influence were wasted on Fannin. The colonel would not budge, and he urged Bonham to remain with him. But Bonham quickly rode on to Gonzales in search of volunteers. He found the town empty, for Kimball's men had already left for the Alamo.

Bonham learned that Seguín's company was still at Cibola, now reinforced by a dozen men under Dr. John Sutherland, and he presumed that they would soon leave for Bexar as well. At Gonzales Bonham met another of Travis's messengers, young Ben Highsmith, who had just returned from a futile attempt to get back through Santa Anna's lines. Weary and nervous after having been chased several miles by the Mexican cavalry, Highsmith warned Bonham that no one could get into the Alamo. "I will report the result of my mission to Travis or die in the attempt," responded Bonham. On March 3 he galloped past startled Mexicans and into the Alamo to report to his commander that Fannin was not coming.

Bonham's gloomy report was punctuated by the arrival of more of Santa Anna's army and the movement of Mexican artillery batteries to within 250 yards of the Alamo. The continual bombardment was beginning to wear down the walls. That night Travis again busied himself writing appeals for assistance. The ever-reliable John W. Smith

was to venture forth once more to rally men to reinforce the fort.

Others hurriedly scribbled notes to their families for Smith to carry out. Isaac Millsaps's poignant letter to his blind wife and seven children in Gonzales is probably typical of those final messages:

We are in the fortress of the Alamo a ruined church that has most fell down. The Mexicans are here in large numbers they have kept up a constant fire since we got here. All of our boys [the Gonzales militia] are well and Capt. Martin is in good spirits . . . Col. Bowie is down sick and had to be to bed. I saw him yesterday and he is still ready to fight. He didn't know me from last spring but did remember Wash. He tells all that help will be here soon and it makes us feel good . . . I have not seen Travis but 2 times since here. He told us all this morning that Fanning was going to be here early with many men and there would be a good fight. He stays on the wall some but mostly to his room. I hope help comes soon cause we can't fight them all . . . If we fail here get to the river with the children. All Texas will be before the enemy. We get so little news here we know nothing. There is no discontent in our boys—some are tired from loss of sleep and rest. The Mexicans are shooting every few minutes, but most of the shots fall inside and do no harm. I don't know what else to say they is calling for all letters, kiss the dear children for me and believe as I do that all will be well and God protects us all. . . .

Even the duty-bound Travis took a minute to write a personal note to his friend who was boarding his son, Charles. "Take care of my little boy," Travis wrote on a sheet of yellow wrapping paper. "If the country should be saved, I may make him a splendid fortune; but if the country should be lost and I should perish, he will have nothing but the proud recollection that he is the son of a man who died for his country."

Smith gathered together his precious cargo— the last messages of the doomed garrison—and mounted his horse. It was near midnight when a party of Texan skirmishers made their way out of the Alamo and fired into the sleeping Mexicans. In the confusion that followed, Smith galloped out of the fort and into the safety of the darkness beyond.

What optimism remained among the garrison rapidly faded over the next two days as the intensity of the bombardment increased, and as the Mexican cannon moved ever closer to the crumbling walls of the old mission. Even the normally ebullient Crockett grew weary, confessing to Susannah Dickinson that he preferred to "march out and die in the open air. I don't like to be hemmed up." From his post Crockett could see the Mexicans building scaling ladders. He would not have long to wait.

On Saturday afternoon, March 5, there was a lull in the bombardment, and Travis took advantage of the respite to call his men together in the Alamo plaza. Calmly facing them, he broke the news that Fannin was not coming. The Alamo was doomed. Although there was no longer any hope of victory, he was determined to stay in the fort and sell his life as dearly as possible to buy more time for Texas. Travis asked the men to join him, but left to each that ultimate decision. Anyone who wished to leave was free to go.

It was a moment of sublime democratic choice as, one by one, each man made his decision to die for liberty rather than submit to tyranny. Only one member of the garrison was not prepared to die: after dark Frenchman Louis "Moses" Rose, a friend of Bowie's, climbed over the wall and vanished into the oblivion beyond.

Later during that same night, after eleven days of almost continual bombardment, the Mexican artillery stopped firing. The unaccustomed silence soon lulled the weary defenders of the Alamo into sleep. Not so in the Mexican camp. All night officers and men busied themselves in preparation for assaulting the fort. Santa Anna, as usual, had carefully planned every detail of the attack. For the assault he relied on his veteran troops, with some 1,100 actually to be engaged. General Cós was to attack from the northwest with 350 men. Colonel Francisco Duque would lead 350 more in from the

northeast. From the east, Colonel José María Romero was to advance with 300 soldiers, while Colonel Juan Morales would assault Crockett's position at the southern stockade wall with 100 men.

General Sesma's cavalry would be strung out east of the Alamo to prevent any escape, as well as to keep an eye out for Texan reinforcements. In reserve, under his personal command, Santa Anna kept the crack *Zapadores* and the infantry grenadiers.

By four in the morning on Sunday, March 6, the Mexican troops were in position. They shivered on the cold ground, denied even the comfort of moonlight, for the clouds were thick. Santa Anna seemed caught in indecision, failing to give the order to attack. For an hour the soldiers fidgeted in cruel anticipation, their cold hands grasped tight around old surplus British muskets. Finally a soldier could contain himself no longer. "Viva Santa Anna!" went up the cry, which quickly grew into a chorus of hundreds of voices. The decision made for him, Santa Anna signaled his bugler to sound the call for attack. As one, the columns rushed toward the Alamo.

Travis, instantly awake, grabbed his sword and a shotgun, and rushed from his room followed by his slave, Joe. The Alamo was alive with running men as the shouts of the Mexicans and blaring bugles rent the air. "Come on boys," Travis shouted. "The Mexicans are upon us and we'll give them hell!"

Waving his men to the walls, Travis saw several of Captain Seguín's Tejanos and called out to them in Spanish, "¡No rendirse, muchachos!" ["Don't surrender, comrades!"] Hurrying to his post at the twelve-pounder on the northwest wall, he could see in the dim light that the enemy was already dangerously close. Now the field was sporadically illuminated by fiery blasts from the Texan cannon and spits of flame from American long rifles and Mexican muskets.

The Texan artillery did terrible work as grapeshot raked the advancing ranks. Forty men fell around one soldier in an instant. Colonel Duque was wounded, and then trampled to death by his own advancing troops. The columns wavered, broke, and retreated, only to be reformed and sent in again. Once more the carnage was terrible as long rifles and cannons extracted their heavy price from the attackers. Again the Mexicans fell back.

Incredibly, the decimated Mexican columns regrouped and plunged once again into the storm of fire. High courage was the rule on both sides that bloody morning. Romero's column was again stopped at the east wall, but instead of retreating, veered off to the north, mingling with Duque's column, now commanded by General Manuel fernandez Castrillión. Cós's column, mauled by Travis's twelve-pounder on the northwest wall, drifted to the east, joining the mass of soldiers surging against the center of the north wall.

Santa Anna was infuriated. Everything was going wrong. He angrily ordered in the four hundred reserves. Cheering and firing their *escopetas* [muskets], the hardened *Zapadores* and the tough grenadiers rushed into the fray. Now, above the cacophony of explosions, gunfire, and screaming men rose a new and terrible sound. Santa Anna had ordered the massed bands of all the battalions to play the "Degüello"—the ancient Spanish cutthroat song of no quarter.

Milling soldiers bunched up against the north wall, pressed by those behind who sought the relative shelter the wall provided from the Texan cannon. The scaling ladders had long since been lost, and now men climbed onto each other's backs and grasped chinks in the rough wall—hard climbing, but not impossible for desperate men. As they clambered over the top of the wall they were met with Bowie knives and clubbed rifles—but the Texans were stretched too thin, and soon Mexicans began spilling into the compound.

Travis, his cannon now useless against the Mexicans bunched directly below him, fired his shotgun into the swirling mass of soldiers. Then, as Joe watched in horror, his master suddenly spun around and tumbled down the parapet, a single bullet wound in his head. Stunned and dying, he sat up against the sloping ramp. Mexicans were quickly upon him, but as an officer approached, the wounded man summoned a last reserve of defiant strength and drove his sword into him. They died together.

The Texans began to fall back from the wall, firing as they retreated toward the long barracks. Mexicans now poured over the north wall, unchecked by defenders. On the west wall Texans turned their cannons around to fire into the plaza at the advancing enemy. The attackers were mowed down, but for every man who fell ten others took his place.

Morales's column, cut to pieces by Crockett's gunners at the stockade, veered to the left and stormed the southwest corner, while defenders there were busy firing into ranks advancing across the plaza from the north. Within minutes the eighteen-pounder was captured and turned against the Texans.

Crockett's men were caught in the open in front of the church. Some managed to reach momentary sanctuary in the church or long barracks, but most were trapped by advancing Mexicans from the north or west. Bowie knife, tomahawk, and clubbed rifle met Mexican bayonet in fierce hand-to-hand combat. It lasted but a few moments, but they made a fine end.

Inside the church sacristy, Susannah Dickinson clutched her daughter to her breast as the sounds of combat grew louder. Suddenly Almeron Dickinson, powder-stained and wild-eyed, burst into the room. "Great God, Sue, the Mexicans are inside our walls!" he cried, embracing her for a final time. "If they spare you, save my child!" Moments later he was gone, climbing back to his battery atop the church. It was not long, however, before Dickinson's guns fell silent, their crews cut down by the powerful eighteen-pounder now in Mexican hands.

Jim Bowie waited in his room in the low barracks, a brace of pistols across his lap and the knife at his side. Pale and emaciated, he was not far from death anyway. The door crashed open and angry, determined faces peered in at the bedridden man. As they rushed upon him, Bowie's pistols snapped in defiance, and the acrid smell of powder filled the tiny room. In their rage the Mexicans tossed him on their bayonets like so much hay.

In the long barracks the Texans fought bitterly from room to room, contesting every inch. The darkness of the chambers was compounded by the swirl of black powder so that men grappled, died, or conquered without ever seeing the faces of their enemy. Finally Mexican gunners pulled the captured cannons into the doorways and fired point-blank into the rooms. Overhead, on the roof of the long barracks, a brave young lieutenant gave his life to raise the Mexican tricolor over the Alamo.

Next the Mexicans battered down the doors of the church and quickly overwhelmed the last defenders. To the distant wail of the "Degüello," the wounded were murdered in a frenzied orgy of slaughter. General Castrillón, sickened by this carnage, halted the advance of his men on a knot of seven bloodied, defiant defenders.

Bowie knives and clubbed rifles in hand, this pitiful remnant was all that was left on the garrison of the Alamo. Castrillón begged them to surrender, offering them clemency and asserting that further resistance served no purpose. Their situation clearly hopeless, the cornered men agreed to this gallant offer. Among this handful of survivors was Davy Crockett.

It was now 6:30 A.M., and a cold, hazy dawn illuminated the ghastly scene as Santa Anna inspected the work of his troops. His elation over victory was tempered by early casualty figures. The attacking columns had lost over six hundred men, a full one-third of the troops involved in the battle. Santa Anna and his staff were between the church and the long barracks when Castrillón approached with his seven prisoners.

Lieutenant Colonel José Enrique de la Peña of the *Zapadores* battalion, standing near Santa Anna, was particularly impressed by the bearing and courage of one of the prisoners, a man "of great stature, well-proportioned, with regular features, in whose face there was the imprint of adversity, but in whom one also noticed a degree of resignation and nobility that did him honor."

Castrillón presented this captive to Santa Anna as "the naturalist David Crockett, well known in North America for his unusual adventures," and implored his commander to spare him and the other prisoners. Santa Anna angrily cut Castrillón off short, and turning to a group of nearby sappers, ordered the immediate execution of the Americans. Horrified by this base order, both offi-

cers and men hesitated to comply, but several of Santa Anna's staff officers drew their previously unbloodied sabers and fell upon the helpless prisoners. Lieutenant Colonel de la Peña turned his face from the carnage, sickened and disgusted, while the enraged Castrillóon stormed off to his tent. The battle of the Alamo was over.

Minutes later soldiers escorted the noncombatant survivors out of the ruined church. There were ten Mexican women and children, including Bowie's two sisters-in-law and the widow of Alamo defender Gregorio Esparza and her four children, along with Susannah Dickinson and her daughter, Angelina.

Two members of the garrison survived as well. Brigido Guerrero, of Seguín's company, somehow managed to convince his captors that he had been a prisoner of the Texans, and talked his way out of the Alamo. Travis's slave, Joe, had hidden himself in one of the barracks rooms after his master's death and, although slightly wounded, was saved by a Mexican officer. Santa Anna did not make war on slaves, Joe was informed. He was taken before the general and ordered to point out the bodies of Travis and Bowie. The bodies of the 183 slain defenders of the Alamo were then stacked in three pyres and burned.

The following day Mrs. Dickinson was set at liberty. Santa Anna instructed her to carry the story of the Alamo to the rest of Texas, with the admonition that further resistance to the central government was hopeless. She was joined on the road to Gonzales by Joe, and they reached Sam Houston's camp on March 13.

Houston, who had already received news of the fall of the Alamo, now ordered a general retreat. The retreat of his tiny army soon turned into a mass exodus, as the American settlers packed up and scurried eastward in what came to be called the "Runaway Scrape."

At first Houston's army grew fat with volunteers, but as the retreat continued, morale plummeted, compounded by the news of the massacre of Fannin and his men at Goliad on March 27. There were many desertions, but by mid-April the army had stabilized at eight hundred untrained men. Santa Anna, in hot pursuit, unwisely divided his command, sending General Antonio Gaona off to the north with seven hundred men. When finally he faced Houston far to the east on the plain of San Jacinto he had but 1,250 men.

The Mexican troops, exhausted from forced marches, were settling into a drowsy siesta at 4:30 P.M. on April 21, 1836, when Houston led his army forward to the attack. Houston's fifers played a popular ballad of the day, "Will You Come to the Bower?" as the troops silently advanced across the open plain. The musical strain was suddenly lost amidst the spontaneous cries of "Remember the Alamo!" Captain Juan Seguín and his Tejano scouts took it up in Spanish as well—"¡Recuerden el Alamo!"—and the fierce cry echoed down the line.

The surprised Mexicans barely had time to unstack their muskets before the enraged Texans were upon them. Most fled in panic only to be shot down. General Castrillón attempted to rally his stricken troops, but it was hopeless. Atop an ammunition box he calmly folded his arms and faced the Texans, proudly calling out in Spanish: "I've been in forty battles and never showed my back. I'm too old to do it now." Despite the efforts of Texan officers to save him, the gallant Castrillón was soon riddled with bullets. Santa Anna, awakened from an opium-induced slumber by the assault, mounted his horse and escaped, only to be captured the next day.

Houston, his ankle shattered by a musket ball, was lying on a blanket, propped up against a tree when Santa Anna was brought before him. "That man may consider himself born to no common destiny who has conquered the Napoleon of the West," Santa Anna haughtily announced. "And now it remains for him to be generous to the vanquished."

"You should have remembered that at the Alamo," Houston snapped back.

It was a stunning victory. The Texans lost but nine dead and thirty-four wounded, while the Mexican army suffered six hundred killed and six hundred and fifty captured. Santa Anna obligingly ordered his remaining four thousand troops out of Texas and was held hostage until November to insure their compliance. The independence of Texas was won, and for a decade it remained a republic before joining the Union as the twenty-eighth state on December 29, 1845.

It was February 1837 before Juan Seguín, promoted to lieutenant colonel and appointed military governor of Bexar, returned to bury the remains of the defenders of the Alamo. Seguín gathered up what ashes and bones remained from the three funeral pyres and placed them in a coffin engraved with the names of Travis, Bowie, and Crockett. On February 25, 1837, he conducted a somber funeral ceremony for his compatriots in arms.

"These remains which we have had the honor of carrying on our shoulders are the ones of the brave heroes who died in the Alamo," Seguín declared in his funeral oration. "Yes, my friends, they preferred a thousand deaths rather than surrender to serve the yoke of the tyrant. What a brilliant example. Worthy indeed of being recorded in the pages of history. . . The worthy remains of our venerable companions bearing witness, I ask you to tell the world: Texas shall be free and independent or we shall perish with glory in battle."

It was a fitting epitaph.

STUDY QUESTIONS

1. What sort of person was William Barret Travis? Why did he venture to Texas, and why did he join the revolution? What did he hope to gain?

2. What were the sources of tension between the central government in Mexico City and the largely Anglo region of Texas? Was revolution inevitable?

3. How did the Texans embody the ideals of the American Revolution?

4. Why did James Bowie move to Texas, and why did he enlist in the revolutionary cause?

5. Why did Davy Crockett travel to Texas, and why did he join the revolution?

6. What was the fighting like inside and outside the Alamo on the morning of March 6, 1836?

BIBLIOGRAPHY

Although it is a bit dated in parts, Walter Lord, *A Time to Stand: The Epic of the Alamo* (1961) remains the best book on the siege and battle of the Alamo. Stephen L. Hardin, *Texian Iliad: A Military History of the Texas Revolution* (1994) expertly puts the battle into the proper military context, and Paul D. Lack, *The Texas Revolutionary Experience: A Political and Social History, 1835–1836* (1992) does an outstanding job of discussing the political aspects of the Texas revolution. Susan Prendergast Schoelwer with Tom W. Glaser, *Alamo Images: Changing Perceptions of the Texas Experience* (1985) is a unique blend of picture and prose, showing how the Alamo—the place and the battle—has changed and been reinterpreted over the years. Five other books deserve special mention: Archie P. McDonald, *William Barret Travis: A Biography* (1976); James Atkins Shackford, *David Crockett: The Man and the Legend* (1956); Michael A. Lofaro, ed., *Davy Crockett: The Man, the Legend, the Legacy, 1786–1986* (1985); Holly Beachley Brear, *Inherit the Alamo: Myth and Ritual at an American Shrine* (1995); and Timothy M. Matovina, *The Alamo Remembered: Tejano Accounts and Perspectives* (1995).

FROM UTOPIA TO MILL TOWN

Maury Klein

In Massachusetts in the nineteenth century descendants of the early Puritans built a new city upon the hill and called it Lowell. In an age of brimming optimism, humanitarian reform, and exuberant capitalism, Lowell stood for the proposition that making money and improving the lot of the poor were not mutually exclusive. The builders of the city also believed that capitalism need not degrade its struggling masses, that it had the capability to morally and spiritually uplift workers. Few stories tell more about the age of imagination than the attempt at Lowell to put a human face on capitalism. The impulses that led to the construction of the factories and the reasons that the experiment failed tell much about American capitalism and social thought during the generation before the Civil War.

But the history of Lowell's mills is more than a tale of capitalism; as much if not more than its builders, its workers fascinated visitors in the nineteenth century and historians in the twentieth century. They were young farm women mostly, women in search of a way to contribute to their parents and siblings back on the farm and at the same time support themselves. When Lowell was as young and fresh as its workers it seemed to sparkle; clean dormitories, green open spaces, libraries, and educational facilities adorned the town, causing European visitors to make invidious comparisons to their own blackened and inhumane industrial cities. The women who labored at Lowell seemed something more than industrial laborers; they seemed as if they were partners in some noble communal enterprise. But appearances can be deceiving, and the "mill girls" were laborers, not owners, managers, or investors. During hard times, when the mills struggled to make a profit, the mill girls discovered how vulnerable their positions were.

In the following essay Maury Klein looks both at the myth and reality of Lowell. From its capitalist entrepreneurs to its female workers, he illustrates the high hopes and sometimes sad realities of life in a mill town.

They flocked to the village of Lowell, these visitors from abroad, as if it were a compulsory stop on the grand tour, eager to verify rumors of a utopian system of manufacturers. Their skepticism was natural, based as it was on the European experience where industry had degraded workers and blighted the landscape. In English manufacturing centers such as Manchester, observers had stared into the pits of hell and shrank in horror from the sight. Charles Dickens used this gloomy, putrid cesspool of misery as a model in *Hard Times,* while Alexis de Tocqueville wrinkled his nose at the "heaps of dung, rubble from buildings, putrid, stagnant pools" amid the "huge palaces of industry" that kept "air and light out of the human habitations which they dominate. . . . A sort of black smoke covers the city. . . . Under this half daylight 300,000 human beings are ceaselessly at work. A thousand noises disturb this damp, dark labyrinth, but they are not at all the ordinary sounds one hears in great cities."

Was it possible that America could produce an alternative to this hideous scene? It seemed so to the visitors who gaped in wonderment at the village above the confluence of the Concord and Merrimack rivers. What they saw was a planned community with mills five to seven stories high flanked by dormitories for the workers, not jammed together but surrounded by open space filled with trees and flower gardens set against a backdrop of the river and hills beyond. Dwelling houses, shops, hotels, churches, banks, even a library lined the streets in orderly, uncrowded rows. Taken whole, the scene bore a flavor of meticulous composition, as if a painting had sprung to life.

The contrast between so pristine a vision and the nightmare of Manchester startled the most

jaded of foreigners. "It was new and fresh, like a setting at the opera," proclaimed Michel Chevalier, a Frenchman who visited Lowell in 1834. The Reverend William Scoresby, an Englishman, marveled at how the buildings seemed "as fresh-looking as if built within a year." The indefatigable Harriet Martineau agreed, as did J.S. Buckingham, who pronounced Lowell to be "one of the most remarkable places under the sun." Even Dickens, whose tour of America rendered him immune to most of its charms, was moved to lavish praise on the town. "One would swear," he added "that every 'Bakery,' 'Grocery' and 'Bookbindery' and every other kind of store, took its shutters down for the first time, and started in business yesterday."

If Lowell and its social engineering impressed visitors, the mill workers dazzled them. Here was nothing resembling Europe's *Untermenschen,* that doomed proletariat whose brief, wretched lives were squeezed between child labor and a pauper's grave. These were not men or children or even families as found in the Rhode Island mills. Instead Lowell employed young women, most of them fresh off New England farms, paid them higher wages than females earned anywhere else (but still only half of what men earned), and installed them in dormitories under strict supervision. They were young and industrious, intelligent, and entirely respectable. Like model citizens of a burgeoning republic they saved their money, went to church, and spent their leisure hours in self-improvement.

More than one visitor hurried home to announce the arrival of a new industrial order, one capable of producing goods in abundance without breaking its working class on the rack of poverty. Time proved them wrong, or at best premature. The Lowell experiment lasted barely a generation before sliding back into the grinding bleakness of a conventional mill town. It had survived long enough to tantalize admirers with its unfulfilled promise and to reveal some harsh truths about the incompatibility of certain democratic ideals and the profit motive.

The founding fathers of Lowell were a group known as the Boston Associates, all of whom belonged to that tight knit elite whose dominance of

"Utopia to Mill Town" Part I, by Maury Klein. This article is reprinted from the October 1981 issue of *American History Illustrated* 6, Volume XVI, pp. 35-40, with the permission of Cowles History Group, Inc. Copyright *American History Illustrated* magazine.

The Lowell Mills time table reflects strict organization, long work hours, and seasonal variations in the schedule.

Boston society was exceeded only by their stranglehold on its financial institutions. The seed had been planted by Francis Cabot Lowell, a shrewd, far-sighted merchant who took up the manufacture of cotton cloth late in life. A trip abroad in 1810 introduced him to the cotton mills of Lancashire and to a fellow Boston merchant named Nathan Appleton. Blessed with a superb memory and trained in mathematics, Lowell packed his mind with details about the machinery shown him by unsuspecting mill owners. The Manchester owners jealously hoarded their secrets and patents, but none regarded the wealthy American living abroad for his health as a rival.

Once back in America, Lowell recruited a mechanical genius named Paul Moody to help replicate the machines he had seen in Manchester.

After much tinkering they designed a power loom, cottonspinning frame, and some other machines that in fact improved upon the English versions. As a hedge against inexperience Lowell decided to produce only cheap, unbleached cotton sheeting. The choice also enabled him to use unskilled labor, but where was he to find even that? Manchester drew its workers from the poorhouses, a source lacking in America. Both the family system and use of apprentices had been tried in Rhode Island with little success. Most men preferred farming their own land to working in a factory for someone else.

But what about women? They were familiar with spinning and weaving, and would make obedient workers. Rural New England had a surplus of daughters who were considered little more than drains on the family larder. To obtain their services Lowell need only pay decent wages and overcome parental reservations about permitting girls to live away from home. This could be done by providing boarding houses where the girls would be subject to the strict supervision of older women acting as chaperones. There would be religious and moral instruction enough to satisfy the most scrupulous of parents. It was an ingenious concept, one that cloaked economic necessity in the appealing garb of republican ideals.

Lowell added yet another wrinkle. Instead of forming a partnership like most larger businesses, he obtained a charter for a corporation named the Boston Manufacturing Company. Capitalized at $300,000, the firm started with $100,000 subscribed by Lowell and a circle of his caste and kin: Patrick Tracy Jackson and his two brothers, Nathan Appleton, Israel Thorndike and his son, two brothers-in-law, and two other merchants. Jackson agreed to manage the new company, which chose a site at the falls on the Charles River at Waltham. By late 1814 the first large integrated cotton factory in America stood complete, along with its machine shop where Lowell and Moody reinvented the power loom and spinner.

Production began in 1815, just as the war with England drew to a close. The mill not only survived the return of British competition but prospered in spectacular fashion: during the years 1817–1824 dividends averaged more than nineteen percent. Moody's fertile mind devised one new invention after another, including a warp-yarn dresser and double speeder. His innovations made the firm's production methods so unique that they soon became known as the "Waltham system." As Gilman Ostrander observed, "The Waltham method was characterized by an overriding emphasis upon standardization, integration, and mechanization." The shop began to build machinery for sale to other mills. Even more, the company's management techniques became the prototype on which virtually the entire textile industry of New England would later model itself.

Lowell did not live to witness this triumph. He died in 1817 at the age of forty-two, having provided his associates with the ingredients of success. During the next three years they showed their gratitude by constructing two more mills and a bleachery, which exhausted the available water power at Waltham. Eager to expand, the Associates scoured the rivers of New England for new sites. In 1821 Moody found a spot on the Merrimack River at East Chelmsford that seemed ideal. The river fell thirty-two feet in a series of rapids and there were two canals, one belonging to the Pawtucket Canal Company and another connecting to Boston. For about $70,000 the Associates purchased control of the Canal Company and much of the farmland along the banks.

From that transaction arose the largest and most unique mill town in the nation. In this novel enterprise the Associates seemed to depart from all precedent, but in reality they borrowed much from Waltham. A new corporation, the Merrimack Manufacturing Company, was formed with Nathan Appleton and Jackson as its largest stockholders. The circle of investors was widened to include other members of the Boston elite such as Daniel Webster and the Boott brothers, Kirk and John. Moody took some shares but his ambitions went no further; he was content to remain a mechanic for the rest of his life. The memory of Francis Cabot Lowell was honored by giving the new village his name.

The task of planning and overseeing construction was entrusted to Kirk Boott. The son of a wealthy Boston Anglophile, Boott's disposition and education straddled the Atlantic. He obtained a commission in the British army and fought under Wellington until the War of 1812 forced his resignation. For several years he studied engineering before returning home in 1817 to take up his father's business. A brilliant, energetic, imperious martinet, Boott leaped at the opportunity to take charge of the new enterprise. As Hannah Josephson observed, he became "its town planner, its architect, its engineer, its agent in charge of production, and the leading citizen of the new community."

The immensity of the challenge appealed to Boott's ordered mind. He recruited an army of 500 Irish laborers, installed them in a tent city, and began transforming a pastoral landscape into a mill town. A dam was put across the river, the old canal was widened, new locks were added, and two more canals were started. The mills bordered the river but not with the monotony of a wall. Three buildings stood parallel to the water and three at right angles in a grouping that reminded some of Harvard College. Trees and shrubs filled the space between them. The boarding houses, semi-detached dwellings two-and-a-half stories high separated by strips of lawn, were set on nearby streets along with the superintendents' houses and long brick tenements for male mechanics and their families. It was a standard of housing unknown to working people anywhere in the country or in Europe. For himself Boott designed a Georgian mansion ornamented with a formidable Ionic portico.

Lowell emerged as the nation's first planned industrial community largely because of Boott's care in realizing the overall concept. At Waltham the boarding houses had evolved piecemeal rather than as an integral part of the design. The Associates took care to avoid competition between the sites by confining Lowell's production to printed calicoes for the higher priced market. While Waltham remained profitable, it quickly took a back seat to the new works. The machine shop provided a true barometer of change. It not only produced machinery and water wheels for Lowell but also oversaw the construction of mills and housing. Shortly before Lowell began production in 1823, the Associates, in Nathan Appleton's words, "arranged to equalize the interest of all the stockholders in both companies" by formally purchasing Waltham's patterns and patent rights and securing Moody's transfer to Lowell. A year later the entire machine shop was moved to Lowell, leaving Waltham with only a maintenance facility.

The success of the Lowell plant prompted the Associates to unfold ambitious new plans. East Chelmsford offered abundant water power for an expanding industry; the sites were themselves a priceless asset. To use them profitably the Associates revived the old Canal Company under a new name, the Locks and Canals Company, and transferred to it all the land and water rights owned by the Merrimack Company. The latter then bought back its own mill sites and leased the water power it required. Thereafter the Locks and Canals Company sold land to other mill companies, leased water power to them at fixed rates per spindle, and built machinery, mills, and housing for them.

This organizational arrangement was as far advanced for the times as the rest of the Lowell concept. It brought the Associates handsome returns from the mills and enormous profits from the Locks and Canals Company, which averaged twenty-four percent in dividends between 1825 and 1845. As new companies like the Hamilton, Appleton, and Lowell corporations were formed, the Associates dispersed part of their stock among a widening network of fellow Brahmins. New partners entered their exclusive circle, including the Lawrence brothers, Abbott and Amos. Directories of the companies were so interlocked as to avoid any competition between them. In effect the Associates had created industrial harmony of the sort J.P. Morgan would later promote under the rubric "community of interest."

By 1836 the Associates had invested $6.2 million in eight major firms controlling twenty five-story mills with more than 6,000 employees. Lowell had grown into a town of 18,000 and ac-

quired a city charter. It boasted ten churches, several banks to accommodate the virtue of thrift on the part of the workers, long rows of shops, a brewery, taverns, schools, and other appurtenances of progress. Worldwide attention had transformed it into a showcase. Apart from the influx of foreigners and other dignitaries, it had already been visited by a president the Associates despised (Andrew Jackson), and by a man who would try three times to becomes president (Henry Clay).

The Associates basked in this attention because they viewed themselves as benevolent, far-seeing men whose sense of duty extended far beyond wealth. To be sure the life blood of the New England economy flowed through their counting houses from their domination of banks, insurance companies, railroads, shipping, and mills elsewhere in New England. Yet such were the rigors of their stern Puritan consciences that for them acquisition was all consuming without being all fulfilling. Duty taught that no fortune was so ample that more was not required. Economist Thorstein Veblen later marveled at the "steadfast cupidity" that drove these men "under pain of moral turpitude, to acquire a 'competence,' and then unremittingly to augment any competence acquired."

Not content with being an economic and social aristocracy, the Associates extended their influence to politics, religion, education, and morality. Lowell fit their *raison d'etre* so ideally because it filled their coffers while at the same time reflecting their notion of an orderly, paternal community imbued with the proper values. The operatives knew their place, deferred to the leadership of the Associates, shared their values.

Or so they thought. In reality the homogeneity of Lowell had always been, like a painting, somewhere between an illusion and a contrivance. The planned community stopped just beyond the border of the mills and boarding houses. No provision had been made for the Irish who built the mills; they huddled together in a squalid settlement, the pioneer settlers of what became the town. Shopkeepers overwhelmed the space provided by the Associates until their stores and homes sprawled in the same indiscriminate manner of other towns. Gradually the growth of Lowell threw the Associates into the familiar role of dominant taxpayer demanding economy and reluctant to approve services that cost money.

In promoting their mills as an industrial utopia [the Associates] were quick to realize that the girls were the prime attraction, the trump card in their game of benevolent paternalism. As early as 1827 Captain Basil Hall, an Englishman, marveled at the girls on their way to work at six in the morning, "nicely dressed, and glittering with bright shawls and showy-colored gowns and gay bonnets . . . with an air of lightness, and an elasticity of step, implying an obvious desire to get to their work."

Observers who went home to rhapsodize about Lowell and its operatives as a model for what the factory system should become, trapped themselves in an unwitting irony. While there was much about the Lowell corporations that served later firms as model, the same did not hold true for their labor force. The young women who filled the mills, regarded by many as the heart of the Lowell system, were in fact its most unique element and ultimately its most transient feature. They were of the same stock and shared much the same culture as the men who employed them. This relative homogeneity gave them a kinship of values absent in later generations of workers. Benita Eisler has called them "the last WASP labor force in America."

The women who flocked to Lowell's mills came mostly from New England farms. Some came to augment the incomes of poor families, others to earn money for gowns and finery, to escape the bleak monotony of rural life, or sample the adventure of a fresh start in a new village. Although their motives were mixed, they chose

"Utopia to Mill Town" Part II, by Maury Klein. This article is reprinted from the November 1981 issue of *American History Illustrated* 7, Volume XVI, pp. 36–43, with the permission of Cowles History Group, Inc. Copyright *American History Illustrated* magazine.

the mills over such alternatives as teaching or domestic service because the pay was better and the work gave them a sense of independence. Lucy Larcom, one of the most talented and articulate of the mill girls, observed that:

Country girls were naturally independent, and the feeling that at this new work the few hours they had of everyday leisure were entirely their own was a satisfaction to them. They preferred it to going out as "hired help." It was like a young man's pleasure in entering upon business for himself.

Leisure hours were a scarce commodity. The mill tower bells tolled the girls to work before the light of day and released them at dusk six days a week, with the Sabbath reserved for solemn observance. The work day averaged twelve-and-a-half hours, depending on the season, and there were only three holidays a year, all unpaid: Fast Day, the Fourth of July, and Thanksgiving. Wages ranged between $2 and $4 a week, about half what men earned. Of this amount $1.25 was deducted for board, to which the company contributed another twenty-five cents. Meager as these sums appear, they exceeded the pay offered by most other mills.

The work rooms were clean and bright for a factory, the walls whitewashed and windows often garnished with potted flowers. But the air was clogged with lint and fumes from the whale-oil lamps hung above every loom. Since threads would snap unless the humidity was kept high, windows were nailed shut even in the summer's heat, and the air was sprayed with water. Delicate lungs were vulnerable to the ravages of tuberculosis and other respiratory ailments. More than one critic attributed the high turnover rate to the number of girls "going home to die."

The machines terrified newcomers with their thunderous clatter than shook the floor. Belts and wheels, pulleys and rollers, spindles and flyers, twisted and whirled, hissing and buzzing, always in motion, a cacophonous jungle alien to rural ears. At first the machines looked too formidable to master. One girl, in a story recalling her first days at Lowell, noted that:

> she felt afraid to touch the loom, and she was almost sure she could never learn to weave; the harness puzzled and the reed perplexed her; the shuttle flew out and made a new bump on her head; and the first time she tried to spring the lathe she broke a quarter of the threads. It seemed as if the girls all stared at her, and the overseers watched every motion, and the day appeared as long as a month had at home. . . . At last it was night. . . . There was a dull pain in her head, and a sharp pain in her ankles; every bone was aching, and there was in her ears a strange noise, as of crickets, frogs and jew-sharps, all mingling together.

Once the novelty wore off, the strangeness of it all gave way to a more serious menace: monotony.

The boarding houses provided welcome havens from such trials. These were dwellings of different sizes, leased to respectable high-toned widows who served as housemothers for fifteen to thirty girls. They kept the place clean and enforced the company rules, which were as strict as any parent might want. Among other things they regulated conduct, imposed a ten o'clock curfew, and required church attendance. The girls were packed six to a bedroom, with three beds. One visitor described the small rooms as "absolutely choked with beds, trunks, bandboxes, clothes, umbrellas and people," with little space for other furniture. The dining room doubled as sitting room, but in early evening it was often besieged by peddlers of all sorts.

This cramped arrangement suited the Associates nicely because it was economical and reinforced a sense of group standards and conformity. Lack of privacy was old hat to most rural girls, though a few complained. Most housemothers set a good table and did not cater to dainty appetites. One girl reported dinner as consisting of "meat and potatoes, with vegetables, tomatoes and pickles, pudding or pie, with bread, butter, coffee or tea." English novelist Anthony Trollope

was both impressed and repulsed by the discovery that meat was served twice a day, declaring that for Americans "to live a day without meat would be as great a privation as to pass a night without a bed."

The corporations usually painted each house once a year, an act attributed by some to benevolence and others to a shrewd eye for public relations and property values. Their zeal for cleanliness did not extend to bathing facilities, which were minimal at best. More than one visitor spread tales of dirt and vermin in the boarding houses, but these too were no strangers to rural homes. Like the mills, later boarding houses were built as long dormitory rows unleavened by strips of lawn or shrubbery, but the earlier versions retained a quaint charm for visitors and inhabitants.

Above all the boarding houses were, as Hannah Josephson stressed, "a woman's world." In these cluttered cloisters the operatives chatted, read, sewed, wrote letters, or dreamed about the day when marriage or some better opportunity would take them from the mills. They stayed in Lowell about four years on the average, and most married after leaving. The mill experience was, in Thomas Dublin's phrase, simply "a stage in a woman's life cycle before marriage." For many girls the strangeness of it all was mitigated by the presence of sisters, cousins, or friends who had undertaken the same adventure.

Outside the boarding house the girls strolled and picnicked in the nearby countryside, attended church socials, paid calls, and shopped for the things they had never had. Dozens of shops vied with the savings banks for their hard-earned dollars and won more than their share of them. Those eager to improve their minds, and there were many, patronized the library and the Lyceum, which for fifty cents offered a season ticket for twenty-five lectures by such luminaries as Ralph Waldo Emerson, Horace Mann, John Quincy Adams, Horace Greeley, Robert Owen, and Edward Everett. Some were ambitious enough to attend evening classes or form study groups of their own in everything from art to German.

Above all the girls read. Their appetite for literature was voracious and often indiscriminate. So strong was this ardor that many slipped their books into the mills, where such distractions were strictly forbidden. It must have pained overseers to confiscate even Bibles from transgressors, but the large number that filled their drawers revealed clearly the Associates' determination to preserve the sharp distinction between the Lord's business and their own.

No one knows how many of the girls were avid readers, but the number probably exceeded the norm for any comparable group. Where so many read, it was inevitable that some would try their hand at writing. By the early 1840s Lowell boasted seven Mutual self-improvement Clubs. These were the first women's literary clubs in America, and the members consisted entirely of operatives. From two of these groups emerged a monthly magazine known as the *Lowell Offering* which in its brief life span (1841–1845) achieved a notoriety and reputation far in excess of its literary merits. The banner on its cover described the contents as *A Repository of Original Articles, Written Exclusively by Females Actively Employed in the Mills.*

No other aspect of Lowell rivaled the *Offering* as a symbol for the heights to which an industrial utopia might aspire. Observers at home and abroad were astounded at the spectacle of factory workers—women no less—capable of producing a literary magazine. Even Charles Dickens, that harsh critic of both English industrialism and American foibles, hurried this revelation to his readers:

I am now going to state three facts, which will startle a large class of readers on this side of the Atlantic very much. First, there is a joint-stock piano in a great many of the boarding-houses. Secondly, nearly all these young ladies subscribe to circulating libraries. Thirdly, they have got up among themselves a periodical . . . which is duly printed, published, and sold; and whereof I brought away from Lowell four hundred good solid pages, which I have read from beginning to end.

As the *Offering*'s fame grew, the Associates were not slow to appreciate its value. Nothing did more to elevate their esteem on both sides of the Atlantic. Contrary to the belief of some, the magazine never became a house organ. Both editors, Harriet Farley and Harriott Curtis, were veterans of the mills who opened their columns to critics and reformers while keeping their own editorial views within more discreet and refined bounds. For their part the Associates were too shrewd not to recognize that the *Offering*'s appeal, its effectiveness as a symbol of republican virtues, lay in its independence. To serve them best it must not smack of self-serving, and it did not.

Although the magazine's prose and poetry seldom rose above mediocre, the material offered revealing insights into every aspect of factory life. Inevitably it attracted authors eager to voice grievances or promote remedies. The editors trod a difficult path between the genteel pretensions of a literary organ and a growing militancy among operatives concerned with gut issues. Few of the girls subscribed to the *Offering* anyway; most of the copies went to patrons in other states or overseas. Small wonder that critics charged the magazine had lost touch with actual conditions in the mills or the real concerns of their operatives.

The *Offering* folded in part because it reflected a system hurrying toward extinction. By the 1840s, when Lowell's reputation as an industrial utopia was still at its peak, significant changes had already taken place. Hard times and swollen ranks of stockholders clamoring for dividends had dulled the Associates' interest in benevolent paternalism. It had always been less a goal than a by-product and not likely to survive a direct conflict with the profit motive. The result was a period of several years during which Lowell coasted on its earlier image while the Associates dismantled utopia in favor of a more cost-efficient system.

The self-esteem of the Associates did not permit them to view their actions in this light, but the operatives felt the change in obvious ways. Their work week increased to seventy-five hours with four annual holidays compared to sixty-nine hours and six holidays for the much maligned British textile workers. To reduce unit costs, girls tended faster machines and were paid lower wages for piecework. That was called speedup; in another practice known as stretch-out, girls were given three or four looms where earlier they had tended one or two. Overseers and second hands were offered bonuses for wringing more productivity out of the workers.

At heart the utopian image of Lowell, indeed the system itself, rested on the assumption that grateful, obedient workers would not bite the hands of their masters. When operatives declined to accept this role, factory agents countered with dismissals and blacklists. The result was a growing sense of militancy among the girls and the first stirrings of a labor movement. In 1834 and 1836 there occurred spontaneous "turnouts" or strikes in Lowell, the first protesting wage cuts and the second an increase in the board charge. Neither achieved much, although a large number of girls (800 and 2,500) took part. The Associates showed their mettle in one instance by turning a widow with four children out of her boarding house because her eleven-year-old daughter, a bobbin girl, had followed the others out. "Mrs. Hanson, you could not prevent the older girls from turning out," the corporate agent explained sternly, "but your daughter is a child, and *her* you could control."

Between 1837 and 1842 a national depression drove wages down and quieted labor unrest at Lowell. When conditions improved and wages still fell, the disturbances began anew. In December 1844 five mill girls met to form the Lowell Female Labor Reform Association; within a year the organization had grown to 600 members in Lowell and had branches elsewhere in New England. Since unions had no legal status or power to bargain directly, LFLRA could only appeal to public opinion and petition the General Court (state legislature) for redress.

For three years the organization dispatched petitions and testified before legislative commissions on behalf of one issue in particular: the ten hour workday. Led by Sarah Bagley and other women of remarkable energy and intelligence,

LFLRA joined hands with workingmen's groups in the push for shorter hours. Their efforts were dogged, impressive, and ultimately futile. As their ranks swelled, they suffered the usual problems of divided aims and disagreement over tactics. More than that, the LFLRA failed in the end simply because it had determination but no leverage. Legislators and other officials did not take them seriously because they were women who had no business being involved in such matters and could not vote anyway. By 1847 LFLRA was little more than a memory. The ten-hour movement lived on, but did not succeed until 1874.

During its brief life LFLRA did much to shatter the image of Lowell as an industrial utopia. The Associates held aloof from controversy and allowed editors, ministers, and distinguished visitors to make their case. There were those who preserved Lowell as a symbol because they wanted to believe, needed to believe in what it represented. After several years of constant labor strife, however, few could overlook the problems pointed up by LFLRA: more work for less pay, deteriorating conditions in the mills and boarding houses, blacklists, and more repressive regulations. Lowell had lost much of what had made it special and was on the verge of becoming another bleak and stifling mill town.

Gradually the river and countryside disappeared behind unbroken walls of factory or dormitory. Nature approached extinction in Lowell, and so did the girls who had always been the core of its system. In 1845 about ninety percent of the operatives were native Americans, mostly farm girls; by 1850 half the mill workers were Irish, part of the flood that migrated after the famine years of 1845–1846. The Irish girls were illiterate, docile, and desperate enough to work for low wages. They preferred tenements with their friends and family to boarding houses, which relieved the Associates of that burden. It did not take the Associates long to appreciate the virtues of so helpless and undemanding a work force. In these immigrants they saw great promise for cheap labor comparable to that found in English mill towns like Manchester.

So it was that Lowell's utopian vision ended where industrialism began. In time the Irish would rise up in protest as their predecessors had done, but behind them came waves of Dutch, Greek, and French Canadian immigrants to take their places in the mills. The native New England girls continued to flee the mills or shy away from them in droves, until by 1860 they were but a small minority. Their departure marked the emergence of Lowell as a mill town no different than any other mill town. One of the girls, peering from her boarding house window, watched the growing stories of a new mill snuff out her view of the scenery beyond and caught the significance of her loss. In her lament could be found an epitaph for Lowell itself:

Then I began to measure . . . and to calculate how long I would retain this or that beauty. I hoped that the brow of the hill would remain when the structure was complete. But no! I had not calculated wisely. It began to recede from me . . . for the building rose still higher and higher. One hope after another is gone. . . one image after another, that has been beautiful to our eye, and dear to our heart has forever disappeared. How has the scene changed! How is our window darkened!

STUDY QUESTIONS

1. What "harsh truths about the incompatibility of certain democratic ideals and profit motive" does the story of the Lowell mills demonstrate? Why, ultimately, does Klein believe the "Lowell experiment" failed?

2. How did the founders of the Lowell mills cloak "economic necessity in the appealing garb of republican ideals"? Was profit motive or humane industrialism the founders' most important motive?

3. What values of the owners did the mills reflect?

4. What type of females found work in the Lowell mills? What did the owners and managers expect of them, and what did they hope to gain from the work?

5. How did their living and working conditions change over the years? How did the workers respond to the changes?

BIBLIOGRAPHY

Two outstanding general treatments of the reform impulse in the first half of the nineteenth century are Steven Mintz, *Moralists and Modernizers: America's Pre-Civil War Reformers* (1995) and Ronald G. Walters, *American Reformers, 1815–1860* (1978). The concerns over the impact that industrialism and the machine would have on American life are explored in John F. Kasson, *Civilizing the Machine: Technology and Republican Values in America, 1776–1900* (1976). Women, labor, and the textile industry are examined in Barbara M. Tucker, *Samuel Slater and the Origins of the American Textile Industry, 1790–1860* (1984); Steve Dunwell, *The Run of the Mill* (1978); and Hannah Josephson, *The Golden Threads: New England's Mill Girls and Magnates* (1949).

THE GREAT ONEIDA LOVE-IN

Morris Bishop

By the early nineteenth century, the Puritan impulse to change the world was still alive, but its energies were now dissipated in a multitude of crusades. One such crusade was the utopian movement. Blessed with few class distinctions or entrenched traditions, as well as with abundant land and space, America became a laboratory for dramatic social exchange. Periodically, utopian idealists consciously tried to start society anew—creating social institutions from scratch instead of dealing with normal conventions. Most of these proved to be feeble attempts destined for historical oblivion, but a few succeeded, not so much because they changed individual perceptions but because they managed to stimulate debate about fundamental American values. The most unique of the utopian experiments took place at Oneida Lake, New York, and it also provoked bitter controversy in American society.

Morris Bishop's "The Great Oneida Love-in" describes the dream and the reality of John Humphrey Noyes's utopian community. While American culture placed a premium on private property and individual progress, Noyes preached a socialistic gospel of group property and community progress. In a society worshipping monogamy and sexual propriety, Noyes called for "complex marriage" in which all men and women were united together sexually. In a country where religious sectarianism was the norm, Noyes worked for a "community of believers" without churches and denominational competition. Despite his dreams, Noyes failed to reform American society; indeed, American culture eventually transformed the Oneida community.

Sin, the conviction of sin, the assurance of punishment for sin, pervaded pioneer America like the fever and ague, and took nearly as many victims. Taught that in Adam's fall we had sinned all, threatened with hell-fire by revivalist preachers, tortured by the guilt of intimate offenses, earnest youths whipped themselves into madness and suicide, and died crying that they had committed the sin against the Holy Ghost, which is unforgivable, though no one knows quite what it is.

The year 1831 was known as the Great Revival, when itinerant evangelists powerfully shook the bush and gathered in a great harvest of sinners. In September of that year John Humphrey Noyes, a twenty-year-old Dartmouth graduate and a law student in Putney, Vermont, attended such a revival. He was in a mood of metaphysical despair, aggravated by a severe cold. During the exhortings the conviction of salvation came to him. Light gleamed upon his soul. "Ere the day was done," he wrote later, "I had concluded to devote myself to the service and ministry of God."

Noyes was a young man of good family. His father was a Dartmouth graduate, a successful merchant in Putney, and a congressman. John was a bookish youth, delighting in history, romance, and poetry of a martial character, such as lives of Napoleon or of the Crusaders or Sir Walter Scott's *Marmion*. He was red-haired and freckled, and thought himself too homely ever to consider marriage. But when he began preaching his face shone like an angel's: one of his sons later averred that "there was about him an unmistakable and somewhat unexpected air of spiritual assurance."

According to his phrenological analysis, his bumps of amativeness, combativeness, and self-esteem were large, his benevolence and philoprogenitiveness very large. His life confirmed these findings.

"The Great Oneida Love-In" by Morris Bishop in *American Heritage,* February 1969. Reprinted by permission of *American Heritage* Magazine, a division of Forbes, Inc.,© Forbes Inc., 1969.

After his mystical experience in Putney, Noyes spent a year in the Andover Theological Seminary (Congregational). He found his teachers and companions lukewarm in piety, and devoted himself to an intensive study of the New Testament, most of which he could recite by heart. A divine direction—"I know that ye seek Jesus which was crucified. He is not here"—sent him from Andover to the Yale theological Seminary in New Haven. There he came in contact with the doctrine of perfectionism and was allured by it.

Perfectionism asserted that men may be freed from sin and attain in this life the perfect holiness necessary to salvation. It rejected therefore the consequences of original sin and went counter to the Calvinistic dogma of total depravity. Perfectionism took shape early in the nineteenth century and found lodgment among adventurous groups in New Haven, Newark, Albany, and in villages of central New York, "the burned-over district," where religion smote with a searing flame. Perfectionism was likely to develop into antinomianism, the contention that the faithful are "directly infused with the holy spirit" and thus free from the claims and obligations of Old Testament moral law. And antinomianism led readily to scandal, as when three perfectionist missionaries, two men and a sister of one of them, were tarred and feathered for sleeping together in one bed.

Though suspected of perfectionist heresy, Noyes was licensed to preach in August, 1833. At about the same time, he made a sensational discovery: Jesus Christ had announced that He would return during the lifetime of some of His disciples. Jesus could not have been mistaken; therefore the Second Coming of Christ had taken place in A.D. 70. The "Jewish cycle" of religious history then ended and a "Gentile cycle" began, in which the Church has improperly usurped the authority of the apostles. We live no longer in an age of prophecy and promise, but in an age of fulfillment. Perfect holiness is attainable in this life, as well as guaranteed deliverance from sin.

Noyes found this revelation by fasting, prayer, and diligent search of the Scriptures. At divine command he announced it in a sermon to the

Free Church of New Haven on February 20, 1834. "I went home with a feeling that I had committed myself irreversibly, and on my bed that night I received the baptism which I desired and expected. Three times in quick succession a stream of eternal love gushed through my heart, and rolled back again to its source. 'Joy unspeakable and full of glory' filled my soul. All fear and doubt and condemnation passed away. I knew that my heart was clean, and that the Father and the Son had come and made it their abode."

This was all very well, but next day the word ran through New Haven, "Noyes says he is perfect!" with the inevitable corollary, "Noyes is crazy!" The authorities promptly expelled him from the seminary and revoked his license to preach. But the perfect are proof against imperfect human detractors. "I have taken away their license to sin, and they keep on sinning," said Noyes. "So, though they have taken away my license to preach, I shall keep on preaching." This he did, with some success. His first convert was Miss Abigail Merwin of Orange, Connecticut, with whom he felt himself sealed in the faith.

Nevertheless his way was far from smooth. He had yet to pass through what he called "the dark valley of conviction." He went to New York and wandered the streets in a kind of frenzy, catching a little sleep by lying down in a doorway, or on the steps of City Hall, or on a bench at the Battery. He sought the most ill-famed regions of the city. "I descended into cellars where abandoned men and women were gathered, and talked familiarly with them about their ways of life, beseeching them to believe in Christ, that they might be saved from their sins. They listened to me without abuse." Tempted by the Evil One, he doubted all, even the Bible, even Christ, even Abigail Merwin, whom he suspected to be Satan in angelic disguise. But after drinking the dregs of the cup of trembling he emerged purified and secure. He retreated to Putney for peace and shelter. His friends, even his sister, thought him deranged. But such was the power of his spirit that he gathered a little group of adepts, relatives, and friends to accept his revelation.

Miss Abigail Merwin, however, took fright, married a schoolteacher, and removed to Ithaca, New York. Noyes followed her there—a rather ungentlemanly procedure. After a few months she left her husband, but not for Noyes's arms—only to return to her father in Connecticut.

Noyes was delighted with the pretty village of Ithaca, with his lodging in the Clinton House, and especially with the broad-minded printers, unafraid of publishing heresies and liberal with credit. On August 20, 1837, he established a periodical, the *Witness,* for a subscription rate of one dollar; or, if a dollar should be inconvenient, for nothing. The issue of September 23 reverberated far beyond the subscription list of faithful perfectionists. Noyes had written a private letter expressing his radical views on marriage among the perfect. By a violation of confidence, this had reached the free-thinking editor of a paper called the *Battle-Axe.* Noyes, disdaining evasion, acknowledged in the *Witness* his authorship of the letter and reiterated his startling conclusions. The essential of "the *Battle-Axe* letter" lies in the concluding words: "When the will of God is done on earth as it is in heaven, *there will be no marriage.* The marriage supper of the Lamb is a feast at which *every dish is free to every guest.* Exclusiveness, jealousy, quarreling, have no place there, for the same reason as that which forbids the guests at a thanksgiving dinner to claim each his separate dish, and quarrel with the rest for his rights. In a holy community, there is no more reason why sexual intercourse should be restrained by law, than why eating and drinking should be—and there is as little occasion for shame in the one as in the other. . . . The guests of the marriage supper may each have his favorite dish, each a dish of his own procuring, and that without the jealousy of exclusiveness."

Ungallant as this statement is in its characterization of women as dishes to pass, it states a reasonable protest against the egotisms of marriage. One may readily perceive in it also a secret resentment against the unfaithful Abigail Merwin. One may even interpret it as the erotic outburst of repressed impulse. Noyes, an impassioned, amorous type, was still a virgin.

Noyes was soon vouchsafed a sign, almost a miracle. When he was eighty dollars in debt to an Ithaca printer, he received from a disciple in Vermont, Miss Harriet A. Holton of Westminster, a letter enclosing a gift of exactly eighty dollars. He paid his bill, returned to Putney, and after a decent interval, forgetting the perfectionist views of the *Battle-Axe* letter, proposed exclusive marriage to Miss Holton. The two were formally united in Chesterfield, New Hampshire, on June 28, 1838. For a honeymoon they drove to Albany to buy a second-hand printing press, with more of Harriet's money.

Thus began the Putney Community, which at first consisted only of Noyes and his wife, several of his brothers and sisters, and a small cluster of converts from the neighborhood. They lived in a group, sharing possessions and duties. Their chief occupations were spiritual exercises in pursuit of holiness and the printing of the *Witness* on their own press. Noyes had no great liking for sheer honest toil for its own sake; he wished to secure for all the freedom for spiritual development. The women prepared one hot meal a day—breakfast. Thereafter the hungry had to help themselves in the kitchen.

Noyes was restless in the monotonous peace of Putney. His wife inherited $9,000 in 1844; Noyes was provoked to fantastic visions. He wrote his wife: "In order to subdue the world to Christ we must carry religion into money-making." He proposed first a theological seminary for perfectionism, then agencies in Boston and New York to distribute their spiritual goods. "Then we must advance into foreign commerce, and as our means enlarge we must cover the ocean with our ships and the whole world with the knowledge of God. This is a great scheme, but not too great for God. . . . Within ten years we will plant the standard of Christ on the highest battlements of the world."

Though allured by such shimmering visions, he had to deal with present problems. An urgent personal problem was that of sex. His wife was pregnant five times in six years. She endured long agonies ending in four stillbirths. The only surviving child was Theodore, born in 1841. John Noyes suffered with his wife, and he protested against cruel nature, perhaps against God. Surely women were not made to suffer so. Surely there was a better way. A perfectionist could not brook flagrant imperfection. Noyes's habit was to seek and find a better way, and then sanctify it. The better way turned out to be male continence.

Noyes had been trained in the Puritan ethic, which did not regard marital sex as unholy. Nevertheless the consequences of male egoism horrified him. "It is as foolish and cruel to expend one's seed on a wife merely for the sake of getting rid of it," he wrote, "as it would be to fire a gun at one's best friend merely for the sake of unloading it." After his wife's disasters he lived for a time chaste by her side. But chastity proving to be no solution at all, he embraced male continence, of which the definition embarrasses the chaste pen. When embarrassed, the chaste pen may decently quote. One of the community disciples, H. J. Seymour, thus defined the practice: "checking the flow of amative passion before it reaches the point of exposing the man to the loss of virile energy, or the woman to the danger of undesired childbearing." Or, with Latin decorum, *coitus reservatus;* or, more colloquially, everything but. This was not actually the beginning of birth-control advocacy. In 1832 a Boston physician, Charles Knowlton, published *The Fruits of Philosophy; or the Private Companion of Young Married People,* pointing to the menace of excessive childbearing and eventual overpopulation, and recommending contraception. Dr. Knowlton and his publisher were accused of blasphemy. Their case was carried to the Supreme Court, and they were condemned to several months in jail. Robert Dale Owen, the reformer of New Harmony, Indiana, supported by Miss Frances Wright, "the Priestess of Beelzebub," carried on the work. In his *Moral Physiology* (1836), Owen recommended *coitus interruptus,* which Noyes scored as substituting self-indulgence for self-control.

"Amativeness is to life as sunshine is to vegetation," wrote Noyes twelve years later in his *Bible Argument Defining the Relation of the Sexes in the Kingdom of Heaven.* "Ordinary sexual intercourse (in which the amative and propagative functions are confounded) is a momentary affair, terminating in exhaustion and disgust. . . . Adam and Eve . . . sunk the spiritual in the sensual in their intercourse with each other, by pushing prematurely beyond the amative to the propagative, and so became ashamed." In the future society, "as propagation will become a science, so amative intercourse will become one of the 'fine arts.' Indeed it will rank above music, painting, sculpture, &c.; for it combines the charms and the benefits of them all."

All this is very noble and high-minded; but we are trained to look for—and we usually find—a casuistical serpent in the gardens, who is able to transform impulse into ideals, even into new theologies. The serpent in this case was Mary Cragin, who with her husband, George, had joined Putney Community. Mary was a charmer, and, to put it baldly, sexy. (Do not condemn her; some are, some aren't. This is a well-known fact.) Noyes feared that she might "become a Magdalene" if he did not save her. One evening in the woods, Noyes and Mary discovered that they were united by a deep spiritual bond. "We took some liberty of embracing, and Mrs. George distinctively gave me to understand that she was ready for the full consummation." But Noyes insisted on a committee meeting with the respective spouses. "We gave each other full liberty, and so entered into marriage in quartette form. The last part of the interview was as amiable and happy as a wedding, and a full consummation . . . followed."

This was Noyes's first infidelity, according to the world's idiom. He found a more grandiloquent term for it—complex marriage, to contrast with the restrictiveness of simple marriage. Heaven beamed upon the participants. "Our love is of God; it is destitute of exclusiveness, each one rejoicing in the happiness of the others," said Mary. The Putney Community, in general, applauded; some, under direction, adopted the new cure for marital selfishness. It appears that some puritan wives, as well as husbands, were secretly weary of the "scanty and monotonous fare" provided by monogamy.

But righteous Putney soon had hints of goings-on and uprose in anger. On October 26, 1847, Noyes was arrested, charged with adultery, and released, pending trial, on $2,000 bail. Noyes declared himself guiltless, insisting that in common law no tort has been committed if no one is injured. "The head and front and whole of our offense is communism of love. . . . If this is the unpardonable sin in the world, we are sure it is the beauty and glory of heaven." But in fear of mob violence from "the barbarians of Putney" he thought it well to jump bail, following the counsel of the highest authority: "When they persecute you in this city, flee ye into another."

A refuge awaited the persecuted saints in the burned-over district of central New York, a region familiar to Noyes. A group of perfectionists offered the Putneyans a sawmill and forty acres of woodland on Oneida Creek, halfway between Syracuse and Utica. It was a bland, fertile, welcoming country, suitable for an Eden. By good omen, the spot was the exact geographical center of New York, if one over-looked Long Island.

In mid-February of 1848, "the year of the great change," the pilgrims began to arrive. Defying the upstate winter, lodging in abandoned cabins, they set to with a will to build a community dwelling and workshops. Some of the neighbors looked at them askance; most welcomed these honest, pious, industrious newcomers, and some even were converted to perfectionism and threw in their lot with the colony.

The early years were the heroic age of Oneida. All worked together, cutting and sawing timber, digging clay for bricks, building simple houses, clearing land for vegetable gardens. Everyone took his or her turn at the household tasks. All work was held in equal honor, without prestige connotations. Noyes recognized that most American experiments in communal life had foundered because they were established on the narrow base of agriculture; his communism would live on industry. Thus Oneida marketed canned fruits and vegetables, sewing silk, straw hats, mop sticks, travelling bags, and finally, silver tableware. Its traps for animals, from rodents to bears, became fa-

Members of the Oneida community standing outside of the Mansion House. This community home, with its towers, mansard roofs, and tall French windows, carried a message of security, peace, and material comfort.

mous as far as Alaska and Siberia. The cruelty of traps seldom occurred to the makers, who were frontiersmen as well as perfectionists. Sympathy with suffering beasts and the conservation of wildlife were concepts still underdeveloped. To a critic, Noyes replied that since God had covered the earth with vermin, Oneida simply had to cleanse it. Salesmen, known only as peddlers, were sent out to market the wares. On their return, they were given a Turkish bath and a sharp examination on faith and practice, a spiritual rubdown to expunge the stains of the unregenerate world.

The Oneida Community prospered. The numbers of the faithful rose. The great Mansion House, the community home, was begun in 1860 and completed a dozen years later. It is a far-wandering red-brick building or group of buildings, standing on a knoll amid magnificent fat trees. Harmoniously proportioned, with its towers, mansard roofs, and tall French windows, it is a superb example of mid-nineteenth-century architecture. Its message is security, peace, and material comfort.

The interior is graced with fine woodwork and decorations. The parlors, the excellent library, the lovely assembly hall, are redolent with memories, jealously preserved and proudly recounted. Here live a number of descendants of the original Oneidans, together with some lodgers, still regarded with kindly pity as "foreign bodies."

The memories, second-hand though they are, are all of a happy time, of a golden age long lost. John Humphrey Noyes, affectionately referred to by his grandchildren as "the Honorable John," was a cheerful person, and imposed happiness on his great family. The story is told of a visitor who asked her guide: "What is the fragrance I smell here in this house?" The guide answered: "It may be the odor of crushed selfishness." There was no money within the Oneida economy, no private possession, no competition for food and shelter, and hence little rivalry.

All worked and played together. Whenever possible, work was done on the "bee" system; thus a party of men and women would make handbags on the lawn, while a dramatic voice read a novel aloud. Classes were conducted in such recondite subjects as Greek and Hebrew. Dances and respectable card games, like euchre and whist, were in favor. Amateur theatricals were a constant diversion. The productions of the *The Merchant of Venice, The Merry Wives of Windsor,* and especially of *H. M. S. Pinafore,* were famous as far as Utica and Syracuse. Music was encouraged, with an orchestra and much vocalization. Music, Noyes mused, was closely related to sexual love; it was an echo of the passions. However, music contained a menace; it gave rise to rivalries, jealousies, and vanities, to what Noyes reproved as "prima donna fever."

Noyes had strong views on dress. He called the contrast of men's and women's costumes immodest, in that it proclaimed the distinction of sex. "In a state of nature, the difference between a man and a woman could hardly be distinguished at a distance of five hundred yards, but as men and women dress, their sex is telegraphed as far as they can be seen. Woman's dress is a standing lie. It proclaims that she is not a two-legged animal, but some-thing like a churn, standing on castors. . . . Gowns operate as shackles, and they are put on that sex which has most talent in the legs."

From the beginning at Oneida, a new dress for women was devised, loose skirts to the knee with pantalets below, thus approximating a gentleman's frock coat and trousers. Some visitors were shocked, some were amused; few were allured. Indeed the specimens remaining in the community's collections and the representations in photographs hardly seem beautiful. But the wearers rejoiced in their new freedom of movement. They cut their hair, in despite of Saint Paul. It was asserted they looked and felt younger.

For thirty years the community, a placid island amid the stormy seas of society, lived its insulated life. It numbered, at its peak, three hundred members. It was undisturbed, except by invasions of visitors brought on bargain excursions by the railroads. As many as a thousand appeared on a single day, picnicking on the grounds, invading the workshops and private quarters. They were welcomed;

but on their departure all the Oneidans turned out in order to collect the scatterings, to scrub out the tobacco stains on the parquet floors.

The structure, the doctrine, the persistence of Oneida made a unique social phenomenon. It was consciously a family, with Noyes as father. As Constance Noyes Robertson says, it substituted "for the small unit of home and family and individual possessions the larger unit of group-family and group-family life." Its faith was "Bible Communism." Though it held aloof from all churches and deconsecrated the Sabbath, it was pietistic in demanding the regeneration of society by rejecting competition, a money economy, and private ownership, whether of goods or persons. But it was not Marxian, for it made no mention of class warfare, of a revolution to come, of proletarian dictatorship.

The internal organization of the community was loose and vague, depending largely on the will of Noyes. Justice and discipline were administered informally, if at all. To provide correction, Noyes trusted chiefly to a procedure known as mutual criticism. Saint Paul had said: "Speak every man truth with his neighbor; for we are members of one another"; and the Apostle James: "Confess your faults to one another." When an individual offered himself for criticism, or was designated from above, a committee prepared his "trial," but any member might join in the proceedings. The trial was a game, though a serious one. The subject was informed of his secret faults, of shortcomings he had not suspected. He learned that his very virtues, on which he had flattered himself, were only disguised vices. The critics would pounce on an unpopular fellow-member with glee, seizing the opportunity to reveal to him some home truths, at the same time revealing their hidden rancors. A transcript of the proceedings was posted and often printed. The subject of this primitive psychoanalysis was likely to suffer dreadfully from his new self-knowledge. "I was shaken from center to circumference," said one. "I was metaphorically stood upon my head and allowed to drain until all the self-righteousness had dripped out of me." Afterward the subject felt enlightened, purified, happy. "Mutual criticism," said Noyes, "subordinates the I-spirit to the We-spirit." It also made the subjects, mostly brooding introspectives, for a time the center of interest and concern for the whole community. Mutual criticism, under the name "krinopathy," was even used as a therapeutic device to cure children's colds, with, it was said, remarkable success.

Of the various Oneida institutions, the most fascinating to the prudent observer is the organization of sex behavior. Since the community was a single great family, there could be within it no marrying and giving in marriage. Each was married to all, Noyes insisted; every man was husband and brother to every woman. Love, far from being a sin, was holy, a sacrament; in the sexual experience one escaped from egotism and self-hood into the ecstasy of communion. Every effort must be to "abound"—one of Noyes's favorite words. One must spend, not hoard. The human heart seldom realized its possibilities; it "is capable of loving any number of times and any number of persons; the more it loves the more it can love." One had only to look at surrounding society to recognize the evils of exclusive marriage, the chains binding unmatched natures, the secret adulteries, actual or of the heart, the hate-filled divorces, women's diseases, prostitution, masturbation, licentiousness in general.

Noyes maintained that sexual love was not naturally restricted to pairs, that second marriages were often the happiest. "Men and women find universally (however the fact may be concealed) that their susceptibility to love is not burned out by one honeymoon, or satisfied by one lover." The body should assert its rights; religion should make use of the senses as helpers of devotion. Sexual shame, the consequence of the fall of man, was fictitious and irrational. "Shame ought to be banished from the company of virtue, though in the world it has stolen the very name virtue. . . . Shame gives rise to the theory that sexual offices have no place in heaven. Anyone who has true modesty would sooner banish singing from heaven than sexual music." Beware, said Noyes, of

one who proclaims that he is free from sexual desire, beware of religious teachers with fondling hands. Beware especially of Dr. Josiah Gridley of Southampton, Massachusetts, who boasts that he could carry a virgin in each hand without the least stir of passion. In short, "you must not serve the lusts of the flesh; if you do you will be damned. You must not make monks of yourself; if you do you will be damned."

One might suspect that these doctrines would have led to oughtright antinomianism and to general orgies. Nothing of the sort occurred, thanks to the watchful care of Noyes and thanks to the character of the Oneidans, devout and rather humorless seekers for perfection. The system of complex marriage, or pantagamy, begun in Putney, was instituted. A man might request the privilege of a private visit with a lady, or a lady might take the initiative, for "in all nature the female element invites and the male responds." The request was submitted to a committee of elders, headed by Noyes, who gave the final approval or disapproval. The mate besought had the right of refusal. It was recommended that older women initiate young men, and vice versa. Thus the young men were expertly guided in the practice of male continence, while the maturer men undertook without complaint the education of the maidens. The committee was also concerned to break up "exclusive and idolatrous attachments" of two persons of the same age, for these bred selfishness. We are assured that complex marriage worked admirably, and that for many life became a continuous courtship. "Amativeness, the lion of the tribe of human passions, is conquered and civilized among us." But the records are unwontedly reticent on the details of the system's operation. Only one scandal is remembered, when an unworthy recruit tried to force his attentions on the women, and was expelled through a window into a snowdrift. One suspects that in spite of all the spiritual training, there were heartaches and hidden anger, and much whispering and giggling at the sound of midnight footsteps on the stairs.

The flaw in the system of continence was the threatening sterilization of the movement—the fate of the Shakers. Noyes recognized the danger, and in his *Bible Argument* of 1848 had proposed scientific propagation to replace random or involuntary propagation. But the time was not yet ripe. In the difficult early years of Oneida, Noyes discouraged childbearing, and his docile followers produced only forty-four offspring in twenty years. Then increasing prosperity permitted him to take steps for the perpetuation of his community. Early in 1869, he proposed the inauguration of stirpiculture, or the scientific improvement of the human stock by breeding. "Every race-horse, every straight-backed bull, every premium pig tells us what we can do and what we must do for men." Oneida should be a laboratory for the preparation of the great race of the future.

The Oneidans, especially the younger ones, greeted the proposal with enthusiasm. Fifty-three young women signed these resolutions:

1. *That we do not belong to ourselves in any respect, but that we do belong to God, and second to Mr. Noyes as God's true representative.*
2. *That we have no rights or personal feelings in regard to childbearing which shall in the least degree oppose or embarrass him in his choice of scientific combinations.*
3. *That we will put aside all envy, childishness and selfseeking, and rejoice with those who are chosen candidates; that we will, if necessary, become martyrs to science, and cheerfully resign all desire to become mothers, if for any reason Mr. Noyes deem us unfit material for propagation. Above all, we offer ourselves "living sacrifices" to God and true Communism.*

At the same time thirty-eight young men made a corresponding declaration to Noyes:

The undersigned desire you may feel that we most heartily sympathize with your purpose in regard to scientific propagation, and offer ourselves to be used in forming any combinations that may seem to you desirable. We claim no rights. We ask no privileges. We desire to be servants of the truth. With a prayer that the grace of God will help us in this resolution, we are your true soldiers.

Thus began the first organized experiment in human eugenics. For several years Noyes directed all the matings, on the basis of physical, spiritual, moral, and intellectual suitability. In 1875 a committee of six men and six women was formed to issue licenses to propagate. The selective process bore some bitter fruit. The eliminated males particularly were unhappy, unconsoled by the reflection that in animal breeding one superior stud may serve many females. Noyes relented in his scientific purpose so far as to permit one child to each male applicant. There was also some covert grumbling that Noyes, then in his sixties, elected himself to father nine children, by several mates. Eugenically, to be sure, he was entirely justified; there could be no doubt of his superiority.

The results of the stirpicultural experiment have not been scientifically studied, though an article by Hilda Herrick Noyes, prepared in 1921, offered some valuable statistical information. About one hundred men and women took part; eighty-one became parents, producing fifty-eight living children and four stillborn. No mothers were lost during the experiment; no defective children were produced. The health of the offspring was exceptionally good; their longevity has far surpassed the average expectations of life. The children, and the children's children, constitute a very superior group, handsome, and intelligent. Many have brilliantly conducted the affairs of their great manufacturing corporation; others have distinguished themselves in public service, the arts, and literature.

The integration of the children into the community caused some difficulties. The mother kept her child until he was weaned and could walk; then he was transferred to the Children's House, though he might return to his mother for night care. Noyes, with this ideal of the community family, disapproved of egotistic, divisive "special love"; the mothers were permitted to see their children only once or twice a week. The children were excellently educated in the nursery school, the kindergarten, and the grammar school, by teachers chosen for their competence and natural liking for the young. If the children cried for their mothers, they were severely reproved for "partiality" or "stickiness." One graduate of the Children's House remembered that when he was forbidden to visit his mother he went berserk. Another recalled her agony when she caught sight of her mother after a fortnight's enforced separation. The child begged her mother not to leave her—and her mother fled for fear of a penalty of an additional week's separation from her child.

The atmosphere of the Children's House was, in short, that of a friendly orphanage. If the disruption of the family units had any bad psychic effects on the children, they have not been recorded. Children accept their world as it is; they know no other. The memories of the Oneida boys and girls are mostly of happy schooldays under kind teachers, days of laughter, play, and delightful learning. The judgment of one eminent product, Pierrepont B. Noyes, is surely correct, that the community system was harder on the mothers than on the children.

The fathers were more remote from their children than were the mothers. Pierrepont Noyes admitted "Father never seemed a father to me in the ordinary sense." The system reflected indeed the character of John Humphrey Noyes. He was the Father of his people, the semidivine begetter of a community, and he loved the community communally. He saw no reason to encourage family bonds, "partiality," among the faithful, at cost to the community spirit. He seems to have shown little personal affection for his sons after the flesh. No doubt a phrenologist would have noted that his bump of parental love was small. One is tempted to go further, to see in his disregard for his children a certain horror of paternity, a deep-implanted remembrance of his four stillborn babies, of his wife's sufferings and his own.

The rumors of strange sex practices roused the righteous and the orthodox, already angered by Oneida's nonobservance of the Sabbath and rejection of church affiliations. A professor at Hamilton College, John W. Mears, still the bogeyman of Oneida after a hundred years, began in 1873 a long campaign to destroy the community and its band of sinners. Though most of the inhabitants and newspaper editors of the region defended Noyes and his followers, though local justice could find no grounds for prosecution, the churches demanded action against "the ethics of the barnyard," and sought enabling legislation from the state. The menace mounted until, in June, 1879, Noyes fled to Canada, as, thirty-one years before, he had fled from Vermont. From a new home in Niagara Falls, Ontario, he continued to advise and inspire his old companions until his death, on April 13, 1886.

With the Father's departure the community system collapsed. In August, 1879, complex marriage was abandoned. Most of the Oneidans paired off and married, to legitimize their children. There were distressing cases of mothers whose mates were already taken, of the children of Noyes himself, left high and dry. In the reorganization into conventional families, it was necessary to establish rights of private property. As Noyes had foreseen, the demons of greed, self-seeking, jealousy, anger, and uncharitableness invaded the serene halls of the Mansion House.

The Oneida industries were converted into a joint-stock company, the shares distributed to the members of the community. After a period of drifting and fumbling, the widely varied enterprises came under the inspired management of Pierrepont Noyes and became models of welfare capitalism, or the partnership of owners and workers. To the present day, high wages are paid, profits are shared, schools, country clubs, aids for home-building are provided. Oneida is the leading producer of stainless-steel flatware, the second largest producer of silver-plated ware in the United states. It has over three thousand employees in the Oneida plants, and many more in the factories in Canada, Mexico, and the United Kingdom. Its net sales in 1967 amounted to fifty-four million dollars, with net profits of two and a half million.

This outcome is not the least surprising feature of the Oneida story. Nearly all other communistic experiments in this country have long since disappeared leaving nothing more than a tumble-down barracks or a roadside marker. Oneida found a transformation into the capitalist world. It did so at the cost of losing its religious and social doctrines; but it has never lost the idealism, the humanitarianism, and the communitarian love of John Humphrey Noyes.

STUDY QUESTIONS

1. Some psychohistorians have argued that the early life of John Humphrey Noyes explains better than anything else the eccentric radicalism of his social philosophy. What is the basis for this argument? Do you agree? Why or why not?

2. Most Americans found Noyes's ideas to be outrageous at best and satanic at worst. Why? Is there any realistic hope that Noyes could have succeeded had he lived in our era? Why or why not?

3. Although Noyes set out to change America, his vision and community were eventually transformed by the environment. What went wrong with the Oneida experiment? What significance do you see in the change in Oneida from a socialist commune to a modern corporation?

BIBLIOGRAPHY

The classic study of reform movements during the Jacksonian period is Alice Felt Tyler, *Freedom's Ferment* (1944). Also see Ronald G. Walter, *American Reformers, 1815–1860* (1978) and William G. McLoughlin, *Revivals, Awakenings, and Reform* (1978). Arthur Bestor's *Backwoods Utopias: The Sectarian and Owenite Phases of Communitarian Socialism in America, 1663–1829* (1950) remains an excellent survey. For sexual radicalism in early America, see Raymond Muncy, *Sex and Marriage in Utopian Communities* (1950). The best studies of John Humphrey Noyes and Oneida are M. L. Carden, *Oneida: Utopian Community to Modern Corporation* (1971) and R. D. Thomas, *The Man Who Would Be Perfect: John Humphrey Noyes and the Utopian Impulse* (1977). Also see Louis J. Kern, *An Ordered Love: Sex Roles and Sexuality in Victorian Utopias* (1981).

GOUGE AND BITE, PULL HAIR AND SCRATCH

Elliott J. Gorn

The tidewater aristocracy of Virginia enjoyed horse racing, "the sport of kings." If no kings could be found among the gentry, there was not lack of royal pretensions. Gentlemen raced their horses against other gentlemen, and at stake was more than just money or glory. Riding on the outcome was a gentleman's sense of self-worth. Robert "King" Carter, the most successful planter of his time, believed that if he lost a race, he lost face in the eyes of his peers. As T. H. Breen demonstrated in an earlier selection, gambling and horse racing provide the keys for unlocking the planters' attitudes toward themselves and life in general.

In the following essay, historian Elliott Gorn examines the brutal pastimes of the working-class men of the South and West. In particular, he focuses on gouging matches, in which the object was to pry the opponent's eye out of its socket using a thumb as the fulcrum. Like Breen, Gorn uses this activity as a means for understanding the world of working-class men in the southern and western backcountry. He uncovers a world in which violence was common, and "Indians, wild animals, lawless criminals, and natural forces threatened life." It was also a world in which work was physically hard and dangerous, and in which men spent more time in the company of other men than with women. In this environment, Gorn notes, "a man's role in the all-male society was defined less by his ability as a breadwinner than by his ferocity. . . . Violent sports, heavy drinking, and impulsive pleasure seeking were appropriate for men whose lives were hard, whose futures were unpredictable, and whose opportunities were limited."

"I would advise you when You do fight Not to act like Tygers and Bears as these Virginians do—Biting one anothers Lips and Noses off, and *gowging* one another—that is, thrusting out one anothers Eyes, and kicking one another on the Cods, to the Great damage of many a Poor Woman." Thus, Charles Woodmason, an itinerant Anglican minister born of English gentry stock, described the brutal form of combat he found in the Virginia backcountry shortly before the American Revolution. Although historians are more likely to study people thinking, governing, worshiping, or working, how men fight—who participates, who observes, which rules are followed, what is at stake, what tactics are allowed—reveals much about past cultures and societies.

The evolution of southern backwoods brawling from the late eighteenth century through the antebellum era can be reconstructed from oral traditions and travelers' accounts. As in most cultural history, broad patterns and uneven trends rather than specific dates mark the way. The sources are often problematic and must be used with care; some speculation is required. But the lives of common people cannot be ignored merely because they leave few records. "To feel for a feller's eyestrings and make him tell the news" was not just mayhem but an act freighted with significance for both social and cultural history.

As early as 1735, boxing was "much in fashion" in parts of Chesapeake Bay, and forty years later a visitor from the North declared that, along with dancing, fiddling, small swords, and card playing, it was an essential skill for all young Virginia gentlemen. The term "boxing," however, did not necessarily refer to the comparatively

tame style of bare-knuckle fighting familiar to eighteenth-century Englishmen. In 1746, four deaths prompted the governor of North Carolina to ask for legislation against "the barbarous and inhuman manner of boxing which so much prevails among the lower sort of people." The colonial assembly responded by making it a felony "to cut out the Tongue or pull out the eyes of the King's Liege People." Five years later the assembly added slitting, biting, and cutting off noses to the list of offenses. Virginia passed similar legislation in 1748 and revised these statutes in 1772 explicitly to discourage men from "gouging, plucking, or putting out an eye, biting or kicking or stomping upon" quiet peaceable citizens. By 1786 South Carolina had made premediated mayhem a capital offense, defining the crime as severing another's bodily parts.

Laws notwithstanding, the carnage continued. Philip Vickers Fithian, a New Jerseyite serving as tutor for an aristocratic Virginia family, confided to his journal on September 3, 1774:

By appointment is to be fought this Day near Mr. Lanes two fist Battles between four young Fellows. The Cause of the battles I have not yet known; I suppose either that they are lovers, and one has in Jest or reality some way supplanted the other; or has in a merry hour called him a Lubber or a thick-Skull, or a Buckskin, or a Scotsman, or perhaps one has mislaid the other's hat, or knocked a peach out of his Hand, or offered him a dram without wiping the mouth of the Bottle; all these, and ten thousand more quite as trifling and ridiculous are thought and accepted as just Causes of immediate Quarrels, in which every diabolical Strategem for Mastery is allowed and practiced.

The "trifling and ridiculous" reasons for these fights had an unreal quality for the matter-of-fact Yankee. Not assaults on persons or property but slights, insults, and thoughtless gestures set young southerners against each other. To call a man a "buckskin," for example, was to accuse him of the

"Gouge and Bite, Pull Hair and Scratch: The Social Significance of Fighting in the Southern Backcountry" by Elliott J. Gorn in *American Historical Review*, Vol. 90, No. 1, pp.18–43, February 1985. Reprinted by permission of the author.

poverty associated with leather clothing, while the epithet "Scotsman" tied him to the low-caste Scots-Irish who settled the southern highlands. Fithian could not understand how such trivial offenses caused the bloody battles. But his incomprehension turned to rage when he realized that spectators attended these "odious and filthy amusements" and that the fighters allayed their spontaneous passions in order to fix convenient dates and places, which allowed time for rumors to spread and crowds to gather. The Yankee concluded that only devils, prostitutes, or monkeys could sire creatures so unfit for human society.

Descriptions of these "fist battles," as Fithian called them, indicate that they generally began like English prize fights. Two men, surrounded by onlookers, parried blows until one was knocked or thrown down. But there the similarity ceased. Where as "Broughton's Rules" of the English ring specified that a round ended when either antagonist fell, southern bruisers only began fighting at this point. Enclosed not inside a formal ring—the "magic circle" defining a special place with its own norms of conduct—but within whatever space the spectators left vacant, fighters battled each other until one called enough or was unable to continue. Combatants boasted, howled, and cursed. As words gave way to action, they tripped and threw, gouged and butted, scratched and choked each other. "But what is worse than all," Isaac Weld observed, "these wretches in their combat endeavor to their utmost to tear out each other's testicles."

Around the beginning of the nineteenth century, men sought original labels for their brutal style of fighting. "Rough-and-tumble" or simply "gouging" gradually replaced "boxing" as the name for these contests. Before two bruisers attacked each other, spectators might demand whether they proposed to fight fair—according to Broughton's Rules—or rough-and-tumble. Honor dictated that all techniques be permitted. Except for a ban on weapons, most men chose to fight "no holts barred," doing what they wished to each other without interference, until one gave up or was incapacitated.

The emphasis on maximum disfigurement, on severing bodily parts, made this fighting style unique. Amid the general mayhem, however, gouging out an opponent's eye became the sine qua non of rough-and-tumble fighting, much like the knockout punch in modern boxing. The best gougers, of course, were adept at other fighting skills. Some allegedly filed their teeth to bite off an enemy's appendages more efficiently. Still, liberating an eyeball quickly became a fighter's surest route to victory and his most prestigious accomplishment. To this end, celebrated heroes fired their fingernails hard, honed them sharp, and oiled them slick. "You have come off badly this time, I doubt?" declared an alarmed passerby on seeing the piteous condition of a renowned fighter. "'Have I,' says he triumphantly, shewing from his pocket at the same time an eye, which he had extracted during the combat, and preserved for a trophy."

As the new style of fighting evolved, its geographical distribution changed. Leadership quickly passed from the southern seaboard to upcountry counties and the western frontier. Although examples could be found throughout the South, rough-and-tumbling was best suited to the backwoods, where hunting, herding, and semisubsistence agriculture predominated over market-oriented, stable crop production. Thus, the settlers of western Carolina, Kentucky, and Tennessee, as well as upland Mississippi, Alabama, and Georgia, became especially known for their pugnacity.

The social base of rough-and-tumbling also shifted with the passage of time. Although brawling was always considered a vice of the "lower sort," eighteenth-century Tidewater gentlemen sometimes found themselves in brutal fights. These combats grew out of challenges to men's honor—to their status in patriarchal, kin-based, small-scale communities—and were woven into the very fabric of daily life. Rhys Isaac has observed that the Virginia gentry set the tone for a fiercely competitive style of living. Although they valued hierarchy, individual status was never permanently fixed, so men frantically sought to assert their prowess—by grand boasts over tavern gaming tables laden with money, by whipping and tripping each other's horses in violent quarter-races, by wagering one-half year's earnings on the flash of a fighting cock's gaff. Great planters and small shared an ethos that extolled courage bordering on foolhardiness and cherished magnificent, if irrational, displays of largess.

Piety, hard work, and steady habits had their adherents, but in this society aggressive self-assertion and manly pride were the real marks of status. Even the gentry's vaunted hospitality demonstrated a family's community standing, so conviviality itself became a vehicle for rivalry and emulation. Rich and poor might revel together during "public times," but gentry patronage of sports and festivities kept the focus of power clear. Above all, brutal recreations toughened men for a violent social life in which the exploitation of labor, the specter of poverty, and a fierce struggle for status were daily realities.

During the final decades of the eighteenth century, however, individuals like Fithian's young gentlemen became less inclined to engage in rough-and-tumbling. Many in the planter class now wanted to distinguish themselves from social inferiors more by genteel manners, gracious living, and paternal prestige than by patriarchal prowess. They sought alternatives to brawling and found them by imitating the English aristocracy. A few gentlemen took boxing lessons from professors of pugilism or attended sparring exhibitions given by touring exponents of the manly art. More important, dueling gradually replaced hand-to-hand combat. The code of honor offered a genteel, though deadly, way to settle personal disputes while demonstrating one's elevated status. Ceremony distinguished antiseptic duels from lower-class brawls. Cool restraint and customary decorum proved a man's ability to shed blood while remaining emotionally detached, to act as mercilessly as the poor whites but to do so with chilling gentility.

Slowly, then, rough-and-tumble fighting found specific locus in both human and geographical landscapes. We can watch men grapple with the transition. When an attempt at a formal duel aborted, Savannah politician Robert Watkins and United States Senator James Jackson resorted to gouging. Jackson bit Watson's finger to save his eye. Similarly, when "a low fellow who pretends to gentility" insulted a distinguished doctor, the gentleman responded with a proper challenge. "He had scarcely uttered these words, before the other flew at him, and in an instant turned his eye out of the socket, and while it hung upon his cheek, the fellow was barbarous enough to endeavor to pluck it entirely out." By the new century, such ambiguity had lessened, as rough-and-tumble fighting was relegated to individuals in backwoods settlements. For the next several decades, eye-gouging matches were focal events in the culture of lower-class males who still relished the wild ways of old.

"I saw more than one man who wanted an eye, and ascertained that I was now in the region of 'gouging,'" reported young Timothy Flint, a Harvard educated, Presbyterian minister bound for Louisiana missionary work in 1816. His spirits buckled as his party turned down the Mississippi from the Ohio Valley. Enterprising farmers gave way to slothful and vulgar folk whom Flint considered barely civilized. Only vicious fighting and disgusting accounts of battles past disturbed their inertia. Residents assured him that the "blackguards" excluded gentlemen from gouging matches. Flint was therefore perplexed when told that a barbarous-looking man was the "best" in one settlement, until he learned that best in this context meant not the most moral, prosperous, or pious but the local champion who had whipped all the rest, the man most dexterous at extracting eyes.

Because rough-and-tumble fighting declined in settled areas, some of the most valuable accounts were written by visitors who penetrated the backcountry. Travel literature was quite popular during America's infancy, and many profit-minded authors undoubtedly wrote with their audience's expectations in mind. Images of heroic frontiersmen, of crude but unencumbered natural men, enthralled both writers and readers. Some who toured the new republic in the decades following the Revolution had strong prejudices against America's democratic pretensions. English travelers in particular doubted that the upstart nation—in which the lower class shouted its equality and the upper class was unable or unwilling to exercise proper authority—could survive. Ironically, backcountry fighting became a symbol for both those who inflated and those who punctured America's expansive national ego.

Frontier braggarts enjoyed fulfilling visitors' expectations of backwoods depravity, pumping listeners full of gruesome legends. Their narratives projected a satisfying, if grotesque, image of the American rustic as a fearless, barbaric, larger-than-life democrat. But they also gave Englishmen the satisfaction of seeing their former countrymen run wild in the wilderness. Gouging matches offered a perfect metaphor for the Hobbesian war of all against all, of men tearing each other apart once institutional restraints evaporated, of a heart of darkness beating in the New World. As they made their way from the northern port towns to the southern countryside, or down the Ohio to southwestern waterways, observers concluded that geographical and moral descent went hand in hand. Brutal fights dramatically confirmed their belief that evil lurked in the deep shadows of America's sunny democratic landscape.

And yet, it would be a mistake to dismiss all travelers' accounts of backwoods fighting as fictions born of prejudice. Many sojourners who were sober and careful observers of America left detailed reports of rough-and-tumbles. Aware of the tradition of frontier boasting, they distinguished apocryphal stories from personal observation, wild tales from eye-witness accounts. Although gouging matches became a sort of literary convention, many travelers compiled credible descriptions of backwoods violence.

"The indolence and dissipation of the middling and lower classes of Virginia are such as to give pain to every reflecting mind," one anonymous visitor declared. "Horse-racing, cock-fighting, and boxing-matches are standing amusements, for which they neglect all business; and in the latter of which they conduct themselves with a barbarity worthy of their savage neighbors." Thomas Anburey agreed. He believed that the Revolution's leveling of class distinctions left the "lower people" dangerously independent. Although Anburey found poor whites usually hospitable and generous, he was disturbed by their sudden outbursts of impudence, their aversion to labor and love of drink, their vengefulness and savagery. They shared with their betters a taste for gaming, horse racing, and cockfighting, but "boxing matches, in which they display such barbarity, as fully marks their innate ferocious disposition," were all their own. Anburey concluded that an English prize fight was humanity itself compared to Virginia combat.

Another visitor, Charles William Janson, decried the loss of social subordination, which caused the rabble to reinterpret liberty and equality as licentiousness. Paternal authority—the font of social and political order—had broken down in America, as parents gratified their children's whims, including youthful tastes for alcohol and tobacco. A national mistrust of authority had brought civilization to its nadir among the poor whites of the South. "The lower classes are the most abject that, perhaps, ever peopled a Christian land. They live in the woods and deserts and many of them cultivate no more land than will raise them corn and cabbages, which, with fish, and occasionally a piece of pickled pork or bacon, are their constant food. . . . Their habitations are more wretched than can be conceived; the huts of the poor of Ireland, or even the meanest Indian wig-wam, displaying more ingenuity and greater industry." Despite their degradation—perhaps because of it—Janson found the poor whites extremely jealous of their republican rights and liberties. They considered themselves the equals of their best-educated neighbors and intruded on whomever they chose. The gouging match this fastidious Englishman witnessed in Georgia was the epitome of lower-class depravity:

We found the combatants . . . fast clinched by the hair, and their thumbs endeavoring to force a passage into each other's eyes; while several of the bystanders were betting upon the first eye to be turned out of its socket. For some time the combatants avoided the thumb stroke *with dexterity. At length they fell to the ground, and in an instant the uppermost sprung up with his antagonist's eye in his hand!!! The savage crowd applauded, while, sick with horror, we galloped away from the infernal scene. The name of the sufferer was John Butler, a Carolinian, who, it seems, had been dared to the combat by a Georgian; and the first eye was for the honor of the state to which they respectively belonged.*

Janson concluded that even Indian "savages" and London's rabble would be outraged by the beastly Americans.

While Janson toured the lower South, his countryman Thomas Ashe explored the territory around Wheeling, Virginia. A passage, dated April 1806, from his *Travels in America* gives us a detailed picture of gouging's social context. Ashe expounded on Wheeling's potential to become a center of trade for the Ohio and upper Mississippi valleys, noting that geography made the town a natural rival of Pittsburgh. Yet Wheeling lagged in "worthy commercial pursuits, and industrious and moral dealings." Ashe attributed this backwardness to the town's frontier ways, which attracted men who specialized in drinking, plundering Indian property, racing horses, and watching cockfights. A Wheeling Quaker assured Ashe that mores were changing, that the underworld element was about to be driven out. Soon, the godly would gain control of the local government, enforce strict observance of the Sabbath, and outlaw vice. Ashe was sympathetic but doubtful. In Wheeling, only heightened violence and debauchery distinguished Sunday from the rest of the week. The citizens' willingness to close up shop and neglect business on the slightest pretext made it a questionable residence for

any respectable group of men, let alone a society of Quakers.

To convey the rough texture of Wheeling life, Ashe described a gouging match. Two men drinking at a public house argued over the merits of their respective horses. Wagers made, they galloped off to the race course. "Two thirds of the population followed:—blacksmiths, shipwrights, all left work: the town appeared a desert. The stores were shut. I asked a proprietor, why the warehouses did not remain open? He told me all good was done for the day: that the people would remain on the ground till night, and many stay till the following morning." Determined to witness an event deemed so important that the entire town went on holiday, Ashe headed for the track. He missed the initial heat but arrived in time to watch the crowd raise the stakes to induce a rematch. Six horses competed, and spectators bet a small fortune, but the results were inconclusive. Umpires' opinions were given and rejected. Heated words, then fists flew. Soon, the melee narrowed to two individuals, a Virginian and a Kentuckian. Because fights were common in such situations, everyone knew the proper procedures, and the combatants quickly decided to "tear and rend" one another—to rough-and-tumble—rather than "fight fair." Ashe elaborated: "You startle at the words tear and rend, and again do not understand me. You have heard these terms, I allow, applied to beasts of prey and to carnivorous animals; and your humanity cannot conceive them applicable to man: It nevertheless is so, and the fact will not permit me the use of any less expressive term."

The battle began—size and power on the Kentuckian's side, science and craft on the Virginian's. They exchanged cautious throws and blows, when suddenly the Virginian lunged at his opponent with a panther's ferocity. The crowd roared its approval as the fight reached its violent denouement:

The shock received by the Kentuckyan, and the want of breath, brought him instantly to the

A REGULAR ROW IN THE BACKWOODS.

Men in the primitive southern backcountry used violence in sports, jokes, and talk as a means of release from life's hardships.

ground. The Virginian never lost his hold; like those bats of the South who never quit the subject on which they fasten till they taste blood, he kept his knees in his enemy's body; fixing his claws in his hair, and his thumbs on his eyes, gave them an instantaneous start from their sockets. The sufferer roared aloud, but uttered no complaint. The citizens again shouted with joy. Doubts were no longer entertained and bets of three to one were offered on the Virginian.

But the fight continued. The Kentuckian grabbed his smaller opponent and held him in a tight bear hug, forcing the Virginian to relinquish his facial grip. Over and over the two rolled, until, getting the Virginian under him, the big man "snapt off his nose so close to his face that no manner of projection remained." The Virginian quickly recovered, seized the Kentuckian's lower lip in his teeth, and ripped it down over his enemy's chin.

This was enough: "The Kentuckyan at length *gave out,* on which the people carried off the victor, and he preferring triumph to a doctor, who came to cicatrize his face, suffered himself to be chaired round the ground as the champion of the times, and the first *rougher-and-tumbler.* The poor wretch, whose eyes were started from their spheres, and whose lip refused its office, returned to the town, to hide his impotence, and get his countenance repaired." The citizens refreshed themselves with whiskey and biscuits, and then resumed their races.

Ashe's Quaker friend reported that such spontaneous races occurred two or three times a week and that the annual fall and spring meets lasted fourteen uninterrupted days, "aided by the licentious and profligate of all the neighboring states." As for rough-and-tumbles, the Quaker saw no hope of suppressing them. Few nights passed without such fights; few mornings failed to reveal a new citizen with mutilated features. It was a regional taste, unrestrained by law or authority, an inevitable part of life on the left bank of the Ohio.

By the early nineteenth century, rough-and-tumble fighting had generated its own folklore. Horror mingled with awe when residents of the Ohio Valley pointed out one-eyed individuals to visitors, when New Englanders referred to an empty eye socket as a "Virginia Brand," when North Carolinians related stories of mass rough-and-tumbles ending with eyeballs covering the ground, and when Kentuckians told of battle-royals so intense that severed eyes, ears, and noses filled bushel baskets. Place names like "Fighting Creek" and "Gouge Eye" perpetuated the memory of heroic encounters, and rustic bombast reached new extremes with estimates from some counties that every third man wanted an eye. As much as the style of combat, the rich oral folklore of the backcountry—the legends, tales, ritual boasts, and verbal duels, all of them in regional vernacular—made rough-and-tumble fighting unique.

It would be difficult to overemphasize the importance of the spoken word in southern life. Traditional tales, songs, and beliefs—transmitted orally by blacks as well as whites—formed the cornerstone of culture. Folklore socialized children, inculcated values, and helped forge a distinct regional sensibility. Even wealthy and well-educated planters, raised at the knees of black mammies, imbibed both Afro-American and white traditions, and charismatic politicians secured loyal followers by speaking the people's language. Southern society was based more on personalistic, face-to-face, kin-and-community relationships than on legalistic or bureaucratic ones. Interactions between southerners were guided by elaborate rituals of hospitality, demonstrative conviviality, and kinship ties—all of which emphasized personal dependencies and reliance on the spoken word. Through the antebellum period and beyond, the South had an oral as much as a written culture.

Boundaries between talk and action, ideas and behavior, are less clear in spoken than in written contexts. Psychologically, print seems more distant and abstract than speech, which is inextricably bound to specific individuals, times, and places. In becoming part of the realm of sight rather than sound, words leave behind their personal, living qualities, gaining in fixity what they lose in dynamism. Literate peoples separate thought from action, pigeon-holing ideas and behavior. Nonliterate ones draw this distinction less sharply, viewing words and the events to which they refer as a single reality. In oral cultures generally, and the Old South in particular, the spoken word was a powerful force in daily life, because ideation and behavior remained closely linked.

The oral traditions of hunters, drifters, herdsmen, gamblers, roustabouts, and rural poor who rough-and-tumbled provided a strong social cement. Tall talk around a campfire, in a tavern, in front of a crossroads store, or at countless other meeting places on the southwestern frontier helped establish communal bonds between disparate persons. Because backwoods humorists possessed an unusual ability to draw people together and give expression to shared feelings, they often became the most effective leaders and preachers. But words could also divide. Fithian's observation in the eighteenth century—that seemingly innocuous remarks led to sickening violence—remained true for several generations. Men were so touchy about their personal reputations that any slight required an apology. This failing, only retribution restored public stature and self-esteem. "Saving face" was not just a metaphor.

The lore of backwoods combat, however, both inflated and deflated egos. By the early nineteenth century, simple epithets evolved into verbal duels—rituals well known to folklorists. Backcountry men took turns bragging about their prowess, possessions, and accomplishments, spurring each other on to new heights of self-magnification. Such exchanges heightened tension and engendered a sense of theatricality and display. But boasting, unlike insults, did not always lead to combat, for, in a culture that valued oral skills, the verbal battle itself—the contest over who best controlled the power of words—was a real quest for domination:

"I am a man; I am a horse; I am a team. I can whip any man in all Kentucky, *by G—d!" The other replied, "I am an alligator, half man, half horse; can whip any man on the* Mississippi, *by G—d!" The first one again, "I am a man; have the best horse, best dog, best gun and handsomest wife in all Kentucky, by G—d." The other, "I am a Mississippi snapping turtle: have bear's claws, alligator's teeth, and the devil's tail; can whip* any man, *by G—d."*

Such elaborate boasts were not composed on the spot. Folklorists point out that free-phrase verbal forms from Homeric epics to contemporary blues, are created through an oral formulaic process. The singer of epics, for example, does not memorize thousands of lines but knows the underlying skeleton of his narrative and, as he sings, fleshes it out with old commonplaces and new turns of phrase. In this way, oral formulaic composition merges cultural continuity with individual creativity. A similar but simplified version of the same process was at work in backwoods bragging.

A quarter-century after the above exchange made its way into print, several of the same phrases still circulated orally and were worked into new patterns. "'By Gaud, stranger,' said he, 'do you know me?—do you know what stuff I'm made of? Clear steamboat, sea horse, alligator—run agin me, run agin a snag—jam up—whoop! Got the prettiest sister, and biggest whiskers of any man hereabouts—I can lick my weight in wild cats, or any man in all Kentuck!'" Style and details changed, but the themes remained the same: comparing oneself to wild animals, boasting of possessions and accomplishments, asserting domination over others. Mike Fink, legendary keelboatman, champion gouger, and fearless hunter, put his own mark on the old form and elevated it to an art:

"I'm a salt River roarer! I'm a ring tailed squealer! I'm a regular screamer from the old Massassip! Whoop! I'm the very infant that refused his milk before its eyes were open and called out for a bottle of old Rye? I love the women and I'm chockful o' fight! I'm half wild horse and half cock-eyed alligator and the rest o' me is crooked snags an' red-hot snappin' turtle.... I can out-run, out-jump, out-shoot, out-brag, out-drink, an' out-fight, rough-an'-tumble, no holts barred, any man on both sides the river from Pittsburgh to New Orleans an' back ag'in to St. Louiee. Come on, you flatters, you barger, you milk white mechanics, an' see how tough I am to chaw! I ain't had a fight for two days an' I'm spilein' for exercise. Cock-a-doodle-doo!"

Tall talk and ritual boasts were not uniquely American. Folklore indexes are filled with international legends and tales of exaggeration. But inflated language did find a secure home in America in the first half of the nineteenth century. Spread-eagle rhetoric was tailor-made for a young nation seeking a secure identity. Bombastic speech helped justify the development of unfamiliar social institutions, flowery oratory salved painful economic changes, and lofty words masked aggressive territorial expansion. In a circular pattern of reinforcement, heroic talk spurred heroic deeds, so that great acts found heightened meaning in great words. Alexis de Tocqueville observed during his travels in the 1830s that clearing land, draining swamps, and planting crops were hardly the stuff of literature. But the collective vision of democratic multitudes building a great nation formed a grand poetic ideal that haunted men's imaginations.

The gaudy poetry of the strapping young nation had its equivalent in the exaggeration of individual powers. Folklore placing man at the center of the universe buttressed the emergent ideology of equality. Tocqueville underestimated Americans' ability to celebrate the mundane, for ego magnification was essential in a nation that extolled self-creation. While America prided itself on shattering old boundaries, on liberating individuals from social, geographic, and cultural encumbrances, such freedom left each citizen frighteningly alone to succeed or fail in forging his own identity. To hyperbolize one's achievements was a source of power and control, a means of amplifying the self while bringing human, natural, and social obstacles down to size. The folklore of exaggeration could transform even the most prosaic commercial dealings into great contests. Early in the nineteenth century, legends of crafty Yankee peddlers and unscrupulous livestock traders abounded. A horse dealer described an animal to a buyer in the 1840s: "'Sir, he can jump a house or go through a pantry, as it suits him; no hounds are too fast for him, no day too long for him. He has the courage of a lion, and the docility of a lamb, and you may ride him with a thread. Weight did you say? Why, he would carry the national debt and not bate a penny.'" The most insipid marketplace transactions were transfigured by inflated language, legends of heroic salesmanship, and an ethos of contest and battle.

The oral narratives of the southern backcountry drew strength from these national traditions yet possessed unique characteristics. Above all, fight legends portrayed backwoods men reveling in blood. Violence existed for its own sake, unencumbered by romantic conventions and claiming no redeeming social or psychic value. Gouging narratives may have masked grimness with black humor, but they offered little pretense that violence was a creative or civilizing force. Thus, one Kentuckian defeated a bear by chewing off its nose and scratching out its eyes. "They can't stand Kentucky play," the settler proclaimed, "biting and gouging are too hard for them." Humor quickly slipped toward horror, when Davy Crockett, for example, coolly boasted, "I kept my thumb in his eye, and was just going to give it a twist and bring the peeper out, like taking up a gooseberry in a spoon." To Crockett's eternal chagrin, someone interrupted the battle just at this crucial juncture.

Sadistic violence gave many frontier legends a surreal quality. Two Mississippi raftsmen engaged in ritual boasts and insults after one accidentally nudged the other toward the water, wetting his shoes. Cheered on by their respective gangs, they stripped off their shirts, then pummeled, knocked out teeth, and wore skin from each other's faces. The older combatant asked if his opponent had had enough. "Yes," he was told, "when I drink your heart's blood, I'll cry enough, and not till then." The younger man gouged out an eye. Just as quickly, his opponent was on top, strangling his adversary. But in a final reversal of fortunes, the would-be victor cried out, then rolled over dead, a stab wound in his side. Protected by his clique, the winner jumped in the water, swam to a river island, and crowed: "Ruoo-ruoo-o! I can lick a steamboat. My fingernails is related to a sawmill on my mother's side and my daddy was a double breasted catamount! I wear a hoop snake for a neck-handkerchief, and the brass buttons on my coat have all been boiled in poison."

The danger and violence of daily life in the backwoods contributed mightily to sanguinary oral traditions that exalted the strong and deprecated the weak. Early in the nineteenth century, the Southwest contained more than its share of terrifying wild animals, powerful and well-organized Indian tribes, and marauding white outlaws. Equally important were high infant mortality rates and short life expectancies, agricultural blights, class inequities, and the centuries-old belief that betrayal and cruelty were man's fate. Emmeline Grangerford's graveyard poetry—set against a backdrop of rural isolation shattered by sadistic clan feuds—is but the best-known expression of the deep loneliness, death longings, and melancholy that permeated backcountry life.

At first glance, boisterous tall talk and violent legends seem far removed from sadness and alienation. Yet, as Kenneth Lynn has argued, they grew from common origins, and the former allowed men to resist succumbing to the latter. Not passive acceptance but identification with brutes and brawlers characterized frontier legendry. Rather than be overwhelmed by violence, acquiesce in an oppressive environment, or submit to death as an escape from tragedy, why not make a virtue of necessity and flaunt one's unconcern? To revel in the lore of deformity, mutilation, and death was to beat the wilderness at its own game. The storyteller's art dramatized life and converted nameless anxieties into high adventure; bravado helped men face down a threatening world and transform terror into power. To claim that one was sired by wild animals, kin to natural disasters, and tougher than steam engines—which were displacing rivermen in the antebellum era—was to gain a momentary respite from fear, a cathartic, if temporary, sense of being in control. Symbolically, wild boasts overwhelmed the very forces that threatened the backwoodsmen.

But there is another level of meaning here. Sometimes fight legends invited an ambiguous response, mingling the celebration of beastly acts with the rejection of barbarism. By their very nature, tall tales elicit skepticism. Even while men identified with the violence that challenged them, the folklore of eye gouging constantly tested the limits of credibility. "Pretty soon I got the squatter down, and just then he fixed his teeth into my throte, and I felt my windpipe begin to loosen." The calculated coolness and understatement of this description highlights the outrageousness of the act. The storyteller has artfully maneuvered his audience to the edge of credulity.

Backwoodsmen mocked their animality by exaggerating it, thereby affirming their own humanity. A Kentuckian battled inconclusively from ten in the morning until sundown, when his wife showed up to cheer him on:

"So I gathered all the little strength I had, and I socked my thumb in his eye, and with my fingers took a twist on his snot box, and with the other hand, I grabbed him by the back of the head; I then caught his ear in my mouth, gin his head a flirt, and out come his ear by the roots! I then flopped his head over, and caught his other ear in my mouth, and jerked that out

in the same way, and it made a hole in his head that I could have rammed my fist through, and I was just goin' to when he hollered: 'Nuff!' "

More than realism or fantasy alone, fight legends stretched the imagination by blending both. As metaphoric statements, they reconciled contradictory impulses, at once glorifying and parodying barbarity. In this sense, gouging narratives were commentaries on backwoods life. The legends were texts that allowed plain folk to dramatize the tensions and ambiguities of their lives: they hauled society's goods yet lived on its fringe; they destroyed forests and game while clearing the land for settlement; they killed Indians to make way for the white man's culture; they struggled for self-sufficiency only to become ensnared in economic dependency. Fight narratives articulated the fundamental contradiction of frontier life—the abandonment of "civilized" ways that led to the ultimate expansion of civilized society.

Foreign travelers might exaggerate and backwoods storytellers embellish, but the most neglected fact about eye-gouging matches is their actuality. Circuit Court Judge Aedamus Burke barely contained his astonishment while presiding in South Carolina's upcountry: "Before God, gentlemen of the jury, I never saw such a thing before in the world. There is a plaintiff with an eye out! A juror with an eye out! And two witnesses with an eye out!" If the "ring-tailed roarers" did not actually breakfast on stewed Yankee, washed down with spike nails and epsom salts, court records from Sumner County, Arkansas, did describe assault victims with the words "nose was bit." The gamest "gamecock of the wilderness" never really moved steamboat engines by grinning at them, but Reuben Cheek did receive a three-year sentence to the Tennessee penitentiary for gouging out William Maxey's eye. Most backcountrymen went to the grave with their faces intact, just as most of the southern gentry never fought a duel. But as an extreme version of the common tendency toward brawling, street fighting, and seeking personal vengeance, rough-and-tumbling gives us insight into the deep values and assumptions—the *mentalité*—of backwoods life.

Observers often accused rough-and-tumblers of fighting like animals. But eye gouging was not instinctive behavior, the human equivalent of two rams vying for dominance. Animals fight to attain specific objectives, such as food, sexual priority, or territory. Precisely where to draw the line between human aggression as a genetically programmed response or as a product of social and cultural learning remains a hotly debated issue. Nevertheless, it would be difficult to make a case for eye gouging as a genetic imperative, coded behavior to maximize individual or species survival. Although rough-and-tumble fighting appears primitive and anarchic to modern eyes, there can be little doubt that its origins, rituals, techniques, and goals were emphatically conditioned by environment; gouging was learned behavior. Humanistic social science more than sociobiology holds the keys to understanding this phenomenon.

What can we conclude about the culture and society that nourished rough-and-tumble fighting? The best place to begin is with the material base of life and the nature of daily work. Gamblers, hunters, herders, roustabouts, rivermen, and yeomen farmers were the sorts of persons usually associated with gouging. Such hallmarks of modernity as large-scale production, complex division of labor, and regular work rhythms were alien to their lives. Recent studies have stressed the premodern character of the southern uplands through most of the antebellum period. Even while cotton production boomed and trade expanded, a relatively small number of planters owned the best lands and most slaves, so huge parts of the South remained outside the flow of international markets or staple crop agriculture. Thus, backcountry whites commonly found themselves locked into a semisubsistent pattern of living. Growing crops for home consumption, supplementing food supplies with abundant game, allowing small herds to fatten in the woods,

spending scarce money for essential staples, and bartering goods for the services of parttime or itinerant trades people, the upland folk lived in an intensely local, kin-based society. Rural hamlets, impassable roads, and provincial isolation—not growing towns, internal improvements, or international commerce—characterized the backcountry.

Even men whose livelihoods depended on expanding markets often continued their rough, premodern ways. Characteristic of life on a Mississippi barge, for example, were long periods of idleness shattered by intense anxiety, as deadly snags, shoals, and storms approached. Running aground on a sandbar meant backbreaking labor to maneuver a thirty-ton vessel out of trouble. Boredom weighed as heavily as danger, so tale telling, singing, drinking, and gambling filled the empty hours. Once goods were taken on in New Orleans, the men began the thousand-mile return journey against the current. Before steam power replaced muscle, bad food and whiskey fueled the gangs who day after day, exposed to wind and water, poled the river bottoms or strained at the cordelling ropes until their vessel reached the tributaries of the Missouri or the Ohio. Hunters, trappers, herdsmen, subsistence farmers, and other backwoodsmen faced different but equally taxing hardships, and those who endured prided themselves on their strength and daring, their stamina, cunning, and ferocity.

Such men played as lustily as they worked, counterpointing bouts of intense labor with strenuous leisure. What travelers mistook for laziness was a refusal to work and save with compulsive regularity. "I have seen nothing in human form so profligate as they are," James Flint wrote of the boatmen he met around 1820. "Accomplished in depravity, their habits and education seem to comprehend every vice. They make few pretensions to moral character; and their swearing is excessive and perfectly disgusting. Although earning good wages, they are in the most abject poverty; many of them being without anything like clean or comfortable clothing." A generation later, Mark Twain vividly remembered those who manned the great timber and coal rafts gliding past his boyhood home in Hannibal, Missouri: "Rude, uneducated, brave, suffering terrific hardships with sailor-like stoicism; heavy drinkers, course frolickers in moral sties like the Natchez-under-the-hill of the day, heavy fighters, reckless fellows, every one, elephantinely jolly, foul witted, profane; prodigal of their money, bankrupt at the end of the trip, fond of barbaric finery, prodigious braggarts; yet, in the main, honest, trustworthy, faithful to promises and duty, and often picaresquely magnanimous." Details might change, but penury, loose morality, and lack of steady habits endured.

Boatmen, hunters, and herdsmen were often separated from wives and children for long periods. More important, backcountry couples lacked the emotionally intense experience of the bourgeois family. They spent much of their time apart and found companionship with members of their own sex. The frontier town or crossroads tavern brought males together in surrogate brotherhoods, where rough men paid little deference to the civilizing role of women and moral uplift of the domestic family. On the margins of a booming, modernizing society, they shared an intensely communal yet fiercely competitive way of life. Thus, where work was least rationalized and specialized, domesticity weakest, legal institutions primitive, and the market economy feeble, rough-and-tumble fighting found fertile soil.

Just as the economy of the southern back country remained locally oriented, the rough-and-tumblers were local heroes, renowned in their communities. There was no professionalization here. Men fought for informal village and county titles; the red feather in the champion's cap was pay enough because it marked him as first among his peers. Paralleling the primitive division of labor in backwoods society, boundaries between entertainment and daily life, between spectators and participants, were not sharply drawn. "Bully of the Hill" Ab Gaines from the Big Hatchie Country, Neil Brown of Totty's Bend, Vernon's William Holt, and Smithfield's Jim Willis—all of them were renowned Tennessee fighters, local heroes in their day. Legendary champions were real individuals, tested gang leaders who attained their status by being the meanest, toughest, and most ruthless fighters, who faced disfigurement and never backed down. Challenges were ever present; yesterday's spectator was today's champion, today's champion tomorrow's invalid.

Given the lives these men led, a world view that embraced fearlessness made sense. Hunters, trappers, Indian fighters, and herdsmen who knew the smell of warm blood on their hands refused to sentimentalize an environment filled with threatening forces. It was not that backwoodsmen lived in constant danger but that violence was unpredictable. Recreations like cockfighting deadened men to cruelty, and the gratuitous savagery of gouging matches reinforced the daily truth that life was brutal, guided only by the logic of superior nerve, power, and cunning. With families emotionally or physically distant and civil institutions weak, a man's role in the all-male society was defined less by his ability as a breadwinner than by his ferocity. The touchstone of masculinity was unflinching toughness, not chivalry, duty, or piety. Violent sports, heavy drinking, and impulsive pleasure seeking were appropriate for men whose lives were hard, whose futures were unpredictable, and whose opportunities were limited. Gouging champions were group leaders because they embodied the basic values of their peers. The successful rough-and-tumbler proved his manhood by asserting his dominance and rendering his opponent "impotent," as Thomas Ashe put it. And the loser, though literally or symbolically castrated, demonstrated his mettle and maintained his honor.

Here we begin to understand the travelers' refrain about plain folk degradation. Setting out from northern ports, whose inhabitants were increasingly possessed by visions of godly perfection and material progress, they found southern upcountry people slothful and backward. Ashe's Quaker friend in Wheeling, Virginia, made the point. For Quakers and northern evangelicals, labor was a means of moral self-testing, and earthly success was a sign of God's grace, so hard work and steady habits became acts of piety. But not only Yankees endorsed sober restraint. A growing number of southern evangelicals also embraced a life of decorous self-control, rejecting the hedonistic and self-assertive values of old. During the late eighteenth century, as Rhys Isaac has observed, many plain folk disavowed the hegemonic gentry culture of conspicuous display and found individual worth, group pride, and transcendent meaning in religious revivals. By the antebellum era, new evangelical waves washed over class lines as rich and poor alike forswore such sins as drinking, gambling, cursing, fornication, horse racing, and dancing. But conversion was far from universal, and, for many in backcountry settlements like Wheeling, the evangelical idiom remained a foreign tongue. Men worked hard to feed themselves and their kin, to acquire goods and status, but they lacked the calling to prove their godliness through rigid morality. Salvation and self-denial were culturally less compelling values, and the barriers against leisure and self-gratification were lower here than among the converted.

Moreover, primitive markets and the semi-subsistence basis of upcountry life limited men's dependence on goods produced by others and allowed them to maintain the irregular work rhythms of a precapitalist economy. The material base of backwoods life was ill suited to social transformation, and the cultural traditions of the past offered alternatives to rigid new ideals. Closing up shop in mid-week for a fight or horse race had always been perfectly acceptable, because men labored so that they might indulge the joys of the flesh. Neither a compulsive need to save time and money nor an obsession with progress haunted people's imaginations. The backcountry folk who lacked a bourgeois or Protestant sense of duty were little disturbed by exhibitions of human passions and were resigned to violence as part of daily life. Thus, the relative dearth of capitalistic values (such as delayed gratification and accumulation), the absence of a strict work ethic, and a cultural tradition that winked at lapses in moral rigor limited society's demands for sober self-control.

Not just unconverted poor whites but also large numbers of the slave-holding gentry still lent their prestige to a regional style that favored conspicuous displays of leisure. As C. Vann Woodward has pointed out, early observers, such as Robert Beverley and William Byrd, as well as modern-day commentators, have described a distinctly "southern ethic" in American history. Whether judged positively as leisure or negatively as laziness, the southern sensibility valued free time and rejected work as the consuming goal of life. Slavery reinforced this tendency, for how could labor be an unmitigated virtue if so much of it was performed by despised black bondsmen? When southerners did esteem commerce and enterprise, it was less because piling up wealth contained religious or moral value than because productivity facilitated the leisure ethos. Southerners could therefore work hard without placing labor at the center of their ethical universe. In important ways, then, the upland folk culture reflected a larger regional style.

Thus, the values, ideas, and institutions that rapidly transformed the North into a modern capitalist society came late to the South. Indeed, conspicuous display, heavy drinking, moral casualness, and love of games and sports had deep roots in much of Western culture. As Woodward has cautioned, we must take care not to interpret the southern ethic as unique or aberrant. The compulsions to subordinate leisure to productivity, to divide work and play into separate compartmentalized realms, and to improve each bright and shining hour were the novel ideas. The southern ethic anticipated human evil, tolerated ethical lapses, and accepted the finitude of man in contrast to the new style that demanded unprecedented moral rectitude and internalized self-restraint.

The American South also shared with large parts of the Old World a taste for violence and personal vengeance. Long after the settling of the southern colonies, powerful patriarchal clans in Celtic and Mediterranean lands still avenged affronts to family honor with deadly feuds. Norbert Elias has pointed out that postmedieval Europeans routinely spilled blood to settle their private quarrels. Across classes, the story was the same:

Two associates fall out over business; they quarrel, the conflict grows violent; one day they meet in a public place and one of them strikes the other dead. An innkeeper accuses another of stealing his clients; they become mortal enemies. Someone says a few malicious words about another; a family war develops. . . . Not only among the nobility were there family vengeance, private feuds, vendettas. . . . The little people too—the hatters, the tailors, the shepherds—were all quick to draw their knives.

Emotions were freely expressed: jollity and laughter suddenly gave way to belligerence; guilt and penitence coexisted with hate; cruelty always lurked nearby. The modern middle-class individual, with his subdued, rational, calculating ways, finds it hard to understand the joy sixteenth-century Frenchmen took in ceremonially burning alive one or two dozen cats every Midsummer Day or the pleasure eighteenth-century Englishmen found in watching trained dogs slaughter each other.

Despite enormous cultural differences, inhabitants of the southern uplands exhibited characteristics of their forebears in the Old World. The Scots-Irish brought their reputation for ferocity to the backcountry, but English migrants, too, had a thirst for violence. Central authority was weak, and men reserved the right to settle differences for themselves. Vengeance was part of daily life. Drunken hilarity, good fellowship, and high spirits, especially at crossroads taverns, suddenly turned to violence. Traveler after traveler remarked on how forthright and friendly but quick to anger the backcountry people were. Like their European ancestors, they had not yet internalized the modern world's demand for tight emotional self-control.

Above all, the ancient concept of honor helps explain this shared proclivity for violence. According to the sociologist Peter Berger, modern men have difficulty taking seriously the idea of honor. American jurisprudence, for example, offers legal recourse for slander and libel because they involve material damages. But insult—publicly smearing a man's good name and besmirching his honor—implies no palpable injury and so does not exist in the eyes of the law. Honor is an intensely social concept, resting on reputation, community standing, and the esteem of kin and compatriots. To possess honor requires acknowledgement from others; it cannot exist in solitary conscience. Modern man, Berger has argued, is more responsive to dignity—the belief that personal worth inheres equally in each individual, regardless of his status in society. Dignity frees the evangelical to confront God alone, the capitalist to make contracts without customary encumbrances, and the reformer to uplift the lowly. Naked and alone man has dignity; extolled by peers and covered with ribbons, he has honor.

Anthropologists have also discovered the centrality of honor in several cultures. According to J. G. Peristiany, honor and shame often preoccupy individuals in small-scale settings, where face-to-face relationships predominate over anonymous or bureaucratic ones. Social standing in such communities is never completely secure, because it must be validated by public opinion whose fickleness compels men constantly to assert and prove their worth. Julian Pitt-Rivers has added that, if society rejects a man's evaluation of himself and treats his claim to honor with ridicule or contempt, his very identity suffers because it is based on the judgment of peers. Shaming refers to that process by which an insult or any public humiliation impugns an individual's honor and thereby threatens his sense of self. By risking injury in a violent encounter, an affronted man—whether victorious or not—restores his sense of status and thus validates anew his claim to honor. Only valorous action, not words, can redeem his place in the ranks of his peer group.

Bertram Wyatt-Brown has argued that this Old World ideal is the key to understanding southern history. Across boundaries of time, geography, and social class, the South was knit together by a primal concept of male valor, part of the ancient heritage of Indo-European folk cultures. Honor demanded clan loyalty, hospitality, protection of women, and defense of patriarchal prerogatives. Honorable men guarded their reputations, bristled at insults, and, where necessary, sought personal vindication through bloodshed. The culture of honor thrived in hierarchical rural communities like the American South and grew out of a fatalistic world view, which assumed that pain and suffering were man's fate. It accounts for the pervasive violence that marked relationships between southerners and explains their insistence on vengeance and their rejection of legal redress in settling quarrels. Honor tied personal identity to public fulfillment of social roles. Neither bourgeois self-control nor internalized conscience determined status; judgment by one's fellows was the wellspring of community standing.

In this light, the seemingly trivial causes for brawls enumerated as early as Fithian's time—name calling, subtle ridicule, breaches of decorum, displays of poor manners—make sense. If a man's good name was his most important possession, then any slight cut him deeply. "Having words" precipitated fights because words brought shame and undermined a man's sense of self. Symbolic acts, such as buying a round of drinks, conferred honor on all, while refusing to share a bottle implied some inequality in social status. Honor inhered not only in individuals but also in kin and peers; when members of two cliques had words, their tested leaders or several men from each side fought to uphold group prestige. Inheritors of primal honor, the southern plain folk were quick to take offense, and any perceived affront forced a man either to devalue himself or strike back violently and avenge the wrong.

The concept of male honor takes us a long way toward understanding the meaning of eye-gouging matches. But backwoods people did not simply acquire some primordial notion without modifying it. Definitions of honorable behavior have always varied enormously across cultures. The southern upcountry fostered a particular style of honor, which grew out of the contradiction between equality and hierarchy. Honorific societies tend to be sharply stratified. Honor is apportioned according to rank, and men fight to maintain personal standing within their social categories. Because black chattel slavery was the basis for the southern hierarchy, slave owners had the most wealth and honor, while other whites scrambled for a bit of each, and bondsmen were permanently impoverished and dishonored. Here was a source of tension for the plain folk. Men of honor shared freedom and equality; those denied honor were implicitly less than equal—perilously close to a slave-like condition. But in the eyes of the gentry, poor whites as well as blacks were outside the circle of honor, so both groups were subordinate. Thus a herdsman's insult failed to shame a planter since the two men were not on the same social level. Without a threat to the gentleman's honor, there was no need for a duel; horsewhipping the insolent fellow sufficed.

Southern plain folk, then, were caught in a social contradiction. Society taught all white men to consider themselves equals, encouraged them to compete for power and status, yet threatened them from below with the specter of servitude and from above with insistence on obedience to rank and authority. Cut off from upper-class tests of honor, backcountry people adopted their own. A rough-and-tumble was more than a poor man's duel, a botched version of genteel combat. Plain folk chose not to ape the dispassionate, antiseptic, gentry style but to invert it. While the gentleman's code of honor insisted on cool restraint, eye gougers gloried in unvarnished brutality. In contrast to duelists' aloof silence, backwoods fighters screamed defiance to the world. As their own unique rites of honor, rough-and-tumble matches allowed backcountry men to shout their equality at each other. And eye-gouging fights also dispelled any stigma of servility. Ritual boasts, soaring oaths, outrageous ferocity, unflinching bloodiness—all proved a man's freedom. Where the slave acted obsequiously, the backwoodsman resisted the slightest affront; where human chattels accepted blows and never raised a hand, plain folk celebrated violence; where blacks could not jeopardize their value as property, poor whites proved their autonomy by risking bodily parts. Symbolically reaffirming their claims to honor, gouging matches helped resolve painful uncertainties arising out of the ambiguous place of plain folk in the southern social structure.

Backwoods fighting reminds us of man's capacity for cruelty and is an excellent corrective to romanticizing premodern life. But a close look also keeps us from drawing facile conclusions about innate human aggressiveness. Eye gouging represented neither the "real" human animal emerging on the frontier, nor nature acting through man in a Darwinian struggle for survival, nor anarchic disorder and communal breakdown. Rather, rough-and-tumble fighting was ritualized behavior—a product of specific cultural assumptions. Men drink together, tongues loosen, a simmering of old rivalry begins to boil; insult is given, offense taken, ritual boasts commence; the fight begins, mettle is tested, blood redeems honor, and equilibrium is restored. Eye gouging was the poor and middling whites' own version of a historical southern tendency to consider personal violence socially useful—indeed, ethically essential.

Rough-and-tumble fighting emerged from the confluence of economic conditions, social relationships, and culture in the southern backcountry. Primitive markets and the semisubsistence basis of life threw men back on close ties to kin and community. Violence and poverty were part of daily existence, so endurance, even callousness, became functional values. Loyal to their localities, their occupations, and each other, men came together and found release from life's hardships in strong drink, tall talk, rude practical jokes, and cruel sports. They craved one another's recognition but rejected genteel, pious, or bourgeois values, awarding esteem on the basis of their own traditional standards. The glue that held men together was an intensely competitive status system in which the most prodigious drinker or strongest arm wrestler, the best tale teller, fiddle player, or log roller, the most daring gambler, original liar, skilled hunter, outrageous swearer, or accurate marksman was accorded respect by the others. Reputation was everything, and scars were badges of honor. Rough-and-tumble fighting demonstrated unflinching willingness to inflict pain while risking mutilation—all to defend one's standing among peers—and became a central expression of the all-male subculture.

Eye gouging continued long after the antebellum period. As the market economy absorbed new parts of the backcountry, however, the way of life that supported rough-and-tumbling waned. Certainly by mid-century the number of incidents declined, precisely when expanding international demand brought ever more upcountry acres into staple production. Towns, schools, churches, revivals, and families gradually overtook the backwoods. In a slow and uneven process, keelboats gave way to steamers, then railroads; squatters, to cash crop farmers; hunters and trappers, to preachers. The plain folk code of honor was far from dead, but emergent social institutions engendered a moral ethos that warred against the old ways. For many individuals, the justifications for personal violence grew stricter, and mayhem became unacceptable.

Ironically, progress also had a darker side. New technologies and modes of production could enhance men's fighting abilities.

"Birmingham and Pittsburgh are obliged to complete . . . the equipment of the 'chivalric Kentuckian,'" Charles Agustus Murray observed in the 1840s, as bowie knives ended more and more rough-and-tumbles. Equally important, in 1835 the first modern revolver appeared, and manufacturers marketed cheap, accurate editions in the coming decade. Dueling weapons had been costly, and Kentucky rifles or horse pistols took a full minute to load and prime. The revolver, however, which fitted neatly into a man's pocket, settled more and more personal disputes. Raw and brutal as rough-and-tumbling was, it could not survive the use of arms. Yet precisely because eye gouging was so violent—because combatants cherished maimings, blindings, even castrations—it unleashed death wishes that invited new technologies of destruction.

With improved weaponry, dueling entered its golden age during the antebellum era. Armed combat remained both an expression of gentry sensibility and a mark of social rank. But in a society where status was always shifting and unclear, dueling did not stay confined to the upper class. The habitual carrying of weapons, once considered a sign of unmanly fear, now lost some of its stigma. As the backcountry changed, tests of honor continued, but gunplay rather than fighting tooth-and-nail appealed to new men with social aspirations. Thus, progress and technology slowly circumscribed rough-and-tumble fighting, only to substitute a deadlier option. Violence grew neater and more lethal as men checked their savagery to murder each other.

STUDY QUESTIONS

1. In which areas of the United States did gouging matches take place? Which class of men were most likely to be involved in such matches?

2. Why did the men fight? What distinguished between fighting "for real" and fighting "for fun"?

3. How did foreign travelers regard the fighting?

4. What does the language of the men in the backcountry tell us about their culture and attitude toward life?

5. How do the gouging matches reflect backcountry life? How did the backcountry environment affect the settlers of the region?

6. Which characteristics of "manliness" were greatly valued by the backcountry settlers?

7. Why did the number of gouging matches eventually decline?

BIBLIOGRAPHY

The work of modern social theorists is evident in Gorn's essay. Clifford Gretz, *The Interpretation of Culture* (1973); Norbert Elias, *The Civilizing Process* (1978); Richard G. Sipes, "War, Sports, and Aggression: An Empirical Test of Two Rival Theories," *American Anthropologist,* New Series, 75 (1973); and Peter Berger, et al., *The Homeless Man* (1973) present valuable insights. The nature of southern and western violence and society is discussed in Bertram Wyatt-Brown, *Southern Honor: Ethics and Behavior in the Old South* (1982); Arthur K. Moore, *The Frontier Mind* (1957); Sheldon Hackney, "Southern Violence," *American Historical Review,* 74 (1969); Richard Slotkin, *Regeneration Through Violence* (1973); James I. Robertson, Jr., "Frolics, Fights, and Firewater in Frontier Tennessee," *Tennessee Historical Quarterly,* 17 (1958); and James Leyburn, *The Scotch-Irish: A Social History* (1962).

Part Six

AMERICANS DIVIDED

In the aftermath of General Andrew Jackson's victory over the British in New Orleans in1815, Americans temporarily sounded a harmonious note. Nationalism was the order of the day. Americans sang a new national anthem and joined together in national enterprises. They built roads and dug canals to tie the country together; they protected fledgling northern industries with a tariff; they hailed the end of political strife; and they boldly issued sweeping foreign policy measures. Americans proudly watched as government agents pushed the flag of the Republic north, south, and west.

Nationalism, however, was short-lived. As early as the Panic of 1819, observers of the national scene noticed fundamental divisions within America. A year later, during the Missouri controversy, these lines of division became clearer. In 1820 Thomas Jefferson denounced the Missouri Compromise as an attempt to restrict the area where slavery could spread. It awoke him, he said, like "a fire-bell in the night" and sounded "the knell of the Union." If sectional tranquility was restored after the controversy, it lacked the optimism and giddiness of the earlier period.

Increasingly Northerners and Southerners found less common ground to stand on and more issues that divided them. In the winter of 1832–1833 a pall hung over the aristocratic festivities of Charleston, South Carolina. Led by the brilliant John C. Calhoun, South Carolina had nullified the tariffs of 1828 and 1832 and had forbidden the collection of customs duties within the state. The Union and the effectiveness of the Constitution swayed in balance. Again, however, the crisis passed. Politicians struck a compromise. But national unity was further weakened.

During the 1840s, Americans looked westward toward vast expanses of land. Some saw opportunity and moved toward it. Others, saw a chance to escape persecution, and they too packed up their belongings and headed west. Indians and Mexicans,

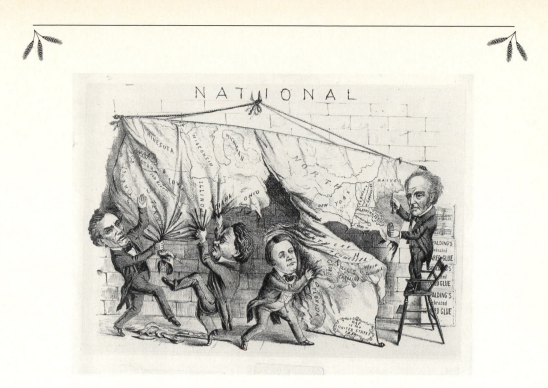

who occupied much of the land, came face to face with a movement of people who were unconcerned with their plight. "Make way, I say, for the young American Buffalo," cried one Democratic orator, "—he has not yet got land enough."

In the spring of 1846, the United States declared war on Mexico. It was a war that unified many Americans—but only for a brief time. The war brought new lands, and the new lands revived old questions. What would be the status of the new lands? Would the new territories and states, once formed, be free or slave? Who would decide the answers to these questions, and how would they decide them?

During the 1850s politicians struggled over these questions. Ultimately they lost the struggle. One solution after another failed. The South, which had contributed greatly to the victory in the Mexican War, demanded the right to move into the newly annexed regions with their "peculiar institution" intact. Northerners were just as determined that the lands would be settled by free labor. By the mid-1850s the subject dominated the national political arena. The issue destroyed one political party, split another, and created yet another. Political rhetoric became increasingly more strident and vitriolic. In 1861 the politicians passed the issue on to the generals.

NOTES ON MORMON POLYGAMY

Stanley S. Ivins

Upstate New York in the 1820s was a "burned-over district" according to one historian because of all the "hell-fire and damnation" preaching going on by competing Protestant denominations. Religion was a topic dear to most people's hearts as they contemplated the salvation or damnation of souls. Near Palmyra, New York, a confused young man, troubled by religious contention, decided to ask God for direct and complete answers to his questions about religion. After offering such a prayer, fourteen-year-old Joseph Smith, Jr., claimed to have been visited by two angelic beings. Identifying themselves as God the Father and Jesus Christ, they told him to join none of the churches and to wait for further instruction. Three years later Smith said he had been visited by an angel who had left him responsible for translating a historical record, engraved on golden plates, of the ancient inhabitants of the American continent. That translation was published in 1829 as the *Book of Mormon,* and the Church of Jesus Christ of Latter-day Saints was organized in 1830.

Under the charismatic leadership of Joseph Smith, the young church grew rapidly in the 1830s and 1840s, and encountered persecution in direct proportion to its success. Their internal cohesiveness and tendency to vote as a bloc usually embittered their neighbors, and the practice of polygamy, introduced by Joseph Smith in the late 1830s, enraged American society. Driven from Ohio and Missouri, the Mormons settled in southern Illinois in 1839. When Joseph Smith was assassinated in 1844, Brigham Young assumed leadership of the Mormons, and in 1846–1847 he led them on an extraordinary journey across the continent to the valley of the Great Salt Lake in present-day Utah. Free of persecution, the Mormons thrived, accepting tens of thousands of converts and colonizing new regions in southern Utah, Nevada, southern California, Idaho, Arizona, and Wyoming.

But for the next half-century, the practice of polygamy created a national uproar as well as a crusade against the Mormons involving an invasion of Utah by the United States Army in 1857, federal antipolygamy laws, and mass jailings of Mormon leaders. In the process, a series of myths about the Mormon practice of polygamy became firmly entrenched in the public mind. In "Notes on Mormon Polygamy," Stanley Ivins describes polygamous marriages in Utah during the nineteenth century.

Time was when, in the popular mind, Mormonism meant only polygamy. It was assumed that every Mormon man was a practical or theoretical polygamist. This was a misconception, like the widespread belief that Mormons grew horns, for there were always many of these Latter-day Saints who refused to go along with the doctrine of "plurality of wives." It was accepted by only a few of the more than fifty churches or factions which grew out of the revelations of the prophet Joseph Smith. Principal advocate of the doctrine was the Utah church, which far outnumbered all other branches of Mormonism. And strongest opposition from within Mormondom came from the second largest group, the Reorganized Church of Jesus Christ of Latter-day Saints, with headquarters at Independence, Missouri.

This strange experiment in family relations extended over a period of approximately sixty-five years. It was professedly inaugurated on April 5, 1841, in a cornfield outside the city of Nauvoo, Illinois, with the sealing of Louisa Beeman to Joseph Smith. And it was brought to an official end by a resolution adopted at the seventy-fourth Annual Conference of the Utah church, on April 4, 1904. Since that time, those who have persisted in carrying on with it have been excommunicated. But the project was openly and energetically prosecuted during only about forty years. For the first ten years the new doctrine was kept pretty well under wraps, and it was not until the fall of 1852 that it was openly avowed and the Saints were told that only those who embraced it could hope for the highest exaltation in the resurrection. And during the fifteen years prior to 1904, there were only a few privately solemnized plural marriages. So it might be said that the experiment was ten years in embryo, enjoyed a vigorous life of forty years, and took fifteen years to die.

"Notes on Mormon Polygamy" by Stanley S. Ivins in *Western Humanities Review,* X, Summer 1956, pp. 229–239. Reprinted by permission of *Western Humanities Review.*

The extent to which polygamy was practiced in Utah will probably never be known. Plural marriages were not publicly recorded, and there is little chance that any private records which might have been kept will ever be revealed.

Curious visitors to Utah in the days when polygamy was flourishing were usually told that about one-tenth of the people actually practiced it. Since the abandonment of the principle this estimate has been revised downward. A recent official published statement by the Mormon church said: "The practice of plural marriage has never been general in the Church and at no time have more than 3 percent of families in the Church been polygamous." This estimate was apparently based upon testimony given during the investigation into the right of Reed Smoot to retain his seat in the United States Senate. A high church official, testifying there, referred to the 1882 report of the Utah Commission, which said that application of the antipolygamy laws had disfranchised approximately 12,000 persons in Utah. The witness declared that, since at least two-thirds of these must have been women, there remained no more than 4,000 polygamists, which he believed constituted less than 2 percent of the church population. The error of setting heads of families against total church membership is obvious. Using the same report, Senator Dubois concluded that 23 percent of Utah Mormons over eighteen years of age were involved in polygamy. Later on in the Smoot hearing the same church official testified that a careful census, taken in 1890, revealed that there were 2,451 plural families in the United States. This suggests that, at that time, 10 percent or more of the Utah Mormons might have been involved in polygamy.

Of more than 6,000 Mormon families, sketches of which are found in a huge volume published in 1913, between 15 and 20 percent appear to have been polygamous. And a history of Sanpete and Emery counties contains biographical sketches of 722 men, of whom 12.6 percent married more than one woman.

From information obtainable from all available sources, it appears that there may have been a time when 15, or possibly 20, percent of the Mormon families of Utah were polygamous. This leaves the great majority of the Saints delinquent in their obligation to the principle of plurality of wives.

While the small proportion of Mormons who went into polygamy may not necessarily be a true measure of its popularity, there is other evidence that they were not anxious to rush into it, although they were constantly reminded of its importance to their salvation.

A tabulation, by years, of about 2,500 polygamous marriages, covering the whole period of this experiment, reveals some interesting facts. It indicates that, until the death of prophet Joseph Smith in the summer of 1844, the privilege of taking extra wives was pretty well monopolized by him and a few of his trusted disciples. Following his death and the assumption of leadership by the Twelve Apostles under Brigham Young, there was a noticeable increase in plural marriages. This may be accounted for by the fact that, during the winter of 1845–1846, the Nauvoo Temple was finished to a point where it could be used for the performance of sacred rites and ordinances. For a few weeks before their departure in search of a refuge in the Rocky Mountains, the Saints worked feverishly at their sealings and endowments. As part of this religious activity, the rate of polygamous marrying rose to a point it was not again to reach for ten years. It then fell off sharply and remained low until the stimulation given by the public announcement, in the fall of 1852, that polygamy was an essential tenet of the church. This spurt was followed by a sharp decline over the next few years.

Beginning in the fall of 1856 and during a good part of the following year, the Utah Mormons were engaged in the greatest religious revival of their history. To the fiery and sometimes intemperate exhortations of their leaders, they responded with fanatical enthusiasm, which at times led to acts of violence against those who were slow to repent. There was a general confession of sins and renewal of covenants through baptism, people hastened to return articles "borrowed" from their neighbors, and men who had not before given a thought to the matter began looking for new wives. And, as one of the fruits of the Reformation, plural marriages skyrocketed to a height not before approached and never again to be reached. If our tabulation is a true index, there were 65 percent more of such marriages during 1856 and 1857 than in any other two years of this experiment.

With the waning of the spirit of reformation, the rate of polygamous marrying dropped in 1858 to less than a third and in 1859 to less than a fifth of what it was in 1857. This decline continued until 1862, when Congress, responding to the clamor of alarmists, enacted a law prohibiting bigamy in Utah and other territories. The answer of the Mormons to this rebuke was a revival of plural marrying to a point not previously reached except during the gala years of the Reformation.

The next noticeable acceleration in the marriage rate came in 1868 and 1869 and coincided with the inauguration of a boycott against the Gentile merchants and the organization of an anti-Mormon political party. But this increased activity was short-lived and was followed by a slump lasting for a dozen years. By 1881 polygamous marrying had fallen to almost its lowest ebb since the public avowal of the doctrine of plurality.

With the passage of the Edmunds Act of 1882, which greatly strengthened the antipolygamy laws, the government began its first serious effort to suppress the practice of polygamy. The Mormons responded with their last major revival of polygamous activity, which reached its height in 1884 and 1885. But, with hundreds of polygamists imprisoned and most of the church leaders driven into exile to avoid arrest, resistance weakened and there was a sudden decline in marriages, which culminated in formal capitulation in the fall of 1890. This was the end, except for a few undercover marriages during the ensuing fifteen years, while the experiment was in its death throes.

II

If there is any significance in this chronicle of polygamous marrying, it is in the lack of evidence that the steady growth of Utah church was

Fleeing persecution, Mormons traveled west and settled in Utah. By the 1850s Mormons could no longer afford draft animals; nevertheless, they crossed the prairies and the Rockies drawing two-wheeled handcarts.

accompanied by a corresponding increase in the number of such marriages. The story is rather one of sporadic outbursts of enthusiasm, followed by relapses, with the proportion of the Saints living in polygamy steadily falling. And it appears to be more than chance that each outbreak of fervor coincided with some revivalist activity within the church or with some menace from without. It is evident that, far from looking upon plural marriage as a privilege to be made the most of, the rank and file Mormons accepted it as one of the onerous obligations of church membership. Left alone, they were prone to neglect it, and it always took some form of pressure to stir them to renewed zeal.

The number of wives married by the men who practiced polygamy offers further evidence of lack of enthusiasm for the principle. A common mistaken notion was that most polygamists maintained large harems, an idea which can be attributed to the publicity given the few men who went in for marrying on a grand scale. Joseph Smith was probably the most married of these men. The number of his wives can only be guessed at, but it might have gone as high as sixty or more. Brigham Young is usually credited with only twenty-seven wives, but he was sealed to more than twice that many living women, and to at least 150 more who had died. Heber C. Kimball had forty-five living wives, a number of them elderly ladies who never lived with him. No one else came close to these three men in the point of marrying. John D. Lee gave the names of his nineteen wives, but modestly explained that, "as I was married to old Mrs. Woolsey for her soul's sake, and she was near sixty years old when I married her, I never considered her really a wife. . . . That is the reason that I claim only eighteen true wives." And by taking fourteen wives, Jens Hansen earned special mention in the *Latter-day Saint Biographical Encyclopedia,* which said: "Of all the Scandinavian brethren who figured prominently in the Church Bro. Hansen distinguished himself by marrying more wives than any other of his countrymen in modern times." Orson Pratt, who was chosen to deliver the first public discourse on the subject of plural marriage and became its most able defender, had only ten living wives, but on two days, a week apart, he was sealed for eternity to more than two hundred dead women.

But these men with many wives were the few exceptions to the rule. Of 1,784 polygamists, 66.3 percent married only one extra wife. Another 21.2 percent were three-wife men, and 6.7 percent went as far as to take four wives. This left a small group of less than 6 percent who married five or more women. The typical polygamist, far from being the insatiable male of popular fable, was a dispassionate fellow, content to call a halt after marrying the one extra wife required to assure him of his chance at salvation.

Another false conception was that polygamists were bearded patriarchs who continued marrying young girls as long as they were able to hobble about. It is true that Brigham Young took a young wife when he was sixty-seven years old and a few others followed his example, but such marriages were not much more common with Mormons than among other groups. Of 1,229 polygamists, more than 10 percent married their last wives while still in their twenties, and more than one half of them before arriving at the still lusty age of forty years. Not one in five took a wife after reaching his fiftieth year. The average age at which the group ceased marrying was forty years.

There appears to be more basis in fact for the reports that polygamists were likely to choose their wives from among the young girls who might bear them many children. Of 1,348 women selected as plural wives, 38 percent were in their teens, 67 percent were under twenty-five and only 30 percent over thirty years of age. A few had passed forty and about one in a hundred had, like John D. Lee's old Mrs. Woolsey, seen her fiftieth birthday.

There were a few notable instances of high-speed marrying among the polygamists. Whatever the number of Joseph Smith's wives, he must have married them all over a period of thirty-nine months. And Brigham Young took eight wives in a single month, four of them on the same day. But only a few enthusiasts indulged in such rapid marrying. As a rule it proceeded at a much less hurried pace. Not one plural marriage in ten followed a previous marriage by less than a year. The composite polygamist was first married at the age of twenty-three to a girl of twenty. Thirteen years later he took a plural wife, choosing a twenty-two-year-old girl. The chances were two to one that, having demonstrated his acceptance of the principle of plurality, he was finished with marrying. If, however, he took a third wife, he waited four years, then selected another girl of twenty-two. The odds were now three to one against his taking a fourth wife, but if he did so, he waited another four years, and once more chose a twenty-two-year-old girl, although he had now reached the ripe age of forty-four. In case he decided to add a fifth wife, he waited only two years, and this time the lady of his choice was twenty-one years old. This was the end of his marrying, unless he belonged to a 3 percent minority.

Available records offer no corroboration of the accusation that many polygamous marriages were incestuous. They do, however, suggest the source of such reports, in the surprisingly common practice of marrying sisters. The custom was initiated by Joseph Smith, among whose wives were at least three pairs of sisters. His example was followed by Heber C. Kimball, whose forty-five wives included Clarissa and Emily Cutler, Amanda and Anna Gheen, Harriet and Ellen Sanders, Hannah and Dorothy Moon, and Laura and Abigail Pitkin. Brigham Young honored the precedent by marrying the Decker sisters, Lucy and Clara, and the Bigelow girls, Mary and Lucy. And John D. Lee told how he married the three Woolsey sisters, Agatha Ann, Rachel, and Andora, and rounded out the family circle by having their mother sealed to him for her soul's sake. Among his other wives were the Young sisters, Polly and Lovina, sealed to him on the same evening. The popularity of this custom is indicated by the fact that of 1,642 polygamists, 10 percent married one or more pairs of sisters.

While marrying sisters could have been a simple matter of propinquity, there probably was some method in it. Many a man went into polygamy reluctantly, fully aware of its hazards. Knowing that his double family must live in one small home, and realizing that the peace of his household would hinge upon the congeniality between its two mistresses, he might well hope that if they were sisters the chances for domestic tranquility would be more even. And a wife, consenting to share her husband with another, could not be blamed for asking that he choose her sister, instead of bringing home a strange woman.

III

The fruits of this experiment in polygamy are not easy to appraise. In defense of their marriage system, the Mormons talked much about the benefits it would bring. By depriving husbands of an excuse for seeking extramarital pleasure, and by making it possible for every woman to marry, it was to solve the problem of the "social evil" by eliminating professional prostitution and other adulterous activities. It was to furnish healthy tabernacles for the countless spirits, waiting anxiously to assume their earthly bodies. It was build up a "righteous generation" of physically and intellectually superior individuals. It was to enhance the glory of the polygamist through a posterity so numerous that, in the course of eternity, he might become the god of a world peopled by his descendants. And there was another blessing in store for men who lived this principle. Heber C. Kimball, Brigham Young's chief lieutenant, explained it this way:

I would not be afraid to promise a man who is sixty years of age, if he will take the counsel of brother Brigham and his brethren, that he will renew his age. I have noticed that a man who has but one wife, and is inclined to that doctrine, soon begins to wither and dry up, while a man who goes into plurality looks fresh, young and sprightly. Why is this? Because God loves that man, and because he honors His work and word. Some of you may not believe this; but I not only believe it—I also know it. For a man of God to be confined to one woman is small business; for it is as much as we can do now to keep up under the burdens we have to carry; and I do not know what we should do if we had only one wife apiece.

It does appear that Mormon communities of the polygamous era were comparatively free from the evils of professional prostitution. But this can hardly be attributed to the fact that a few men, supposedly selected for their moral superiority, were permitted to marry more than one wife. It might better be credited to the common teaching that adultery was a sin so monstrous that there was no atonement for it short of the spilling of the blood of the offender. It would be strange indeed if such a fearful warning failed to exert a restraining influence upon the potential adulterer.

There is, of course, nothing unsound in the theory that a community of superior people might be propagated by selecting the highest ranking males and having them reproduce themselves in large numbers. The difficulty here would be to find a scientific basis for the selection of the favored males. And there is no information from which an opinion can be arrived at as to the results which were obtained in this respect.

When it came to fathering large families and supplying bodies for waiting spirits, the polygamists did fairly well, but fell far short of some of their dreams. Heber C. Kimball once said of himself and Brigham Young: "In twenty-five or thirty years we will have a larger number in our two families than there now is in this whole Territory, which numbers more than seventy-five thousand. If twenty-five years will produce this amount of people, how much will be the increase in one hundred years?" And the *Millennial Star* reckoned that a hypothetical Mr. Fruitful, with forty wives, might, at the age of seventy-eight, number among his seed 3,508,441 souls, while his monogamous counterpart could boast of only 152.

With such reminders of their potentialities before them, the most married of the polygamists must have been far from satisfied with the results they could show. There is no conclusive evidence that any of Joseph Smith's many plural wives bore children by him. Heber C. Kimball, with his forty-five wives, was the father of sixty-five children. John D. Lee, with only eighteen "true wives," fell one short of Kimball's record, and Brigham Young fathered fifty-six children, approximately one for each wife.

Although the issue of the few men of many wives was disappointing in numbers, the rank and file of polygamists made a fair showing. Of 1,651 families, more than four-fifths numbered ten or more children. Half of them had fifteen or more and one-fourth, twenty or more. There were eighty-eight families of thirty or more, nineteen of forty or more, and seven of fifty or more. The average number of children per family was fifteen. And by the third or fourth generation some families had reached rather impressive proportions. When one six-wife elder had been dead fifty-five years, his descendants numbered 1,900.

While polygamy increased the number of children of the men, it did not do the same for the women involved. A count revealed that 3,335 wives of polygamists bore 19,806 children, for an average of 5.9 per woman. An equal number of wives of monogamists, taken from the same general group, bore 26,780 for an average of eight. This suggests the possibility that the overall production of children in Utah may have been less than it would have been without the benefit of plurality of wives. The claim that plurality was needed because of a surplus of women is not borne out by statistics.

There is little doubt that the plural wife system went a good way toward making it possible for every woman to marry. According to Mormon

teachings a woman could "never obtain a fullness of glory, without being married to a righteous man for time and all eternity." If she never married or was the wife of a Gentile, her chance of attaining a high degree of salvation was indeed slim. And one of the responsibilities of those in official church positions was to try to make sure that no woman went without a husband. When a widow or a maiden lady "gathered" to Utah, it was a community obligation to see to it that she had food and shelter and the privilege of being married to a good man. If she received no offer of marriage, it was not considered inconsistent with feminine modesty for her to "apply" to the man of her choice, but if she set her sights too high she might be disappointed. My grandmother, who did sewing for the family of Brigham Young, was fond of telling how she watched through a partly open doorway while he forcibly ejected a woman who was too persistent in applying to be sealed to him. Her story would always end with the same words: "And I just couldn't help laughing to see brother Brigham get so out of patience with that woman." However, if the lady in search of a husband was not too ambitious, her chances of success were good. It was said of the bishop of one small settlement that he "was a good bishop. He married all the widows in town and took good care of them." And John D. Lee was following accepted precedent when he married old Mrs. Woolsey for her soul's sake.

As for Mr. Kimball's claims concerning the spiritual uplift to be derived from taking a fresh, young wife, what man is going to quarrel with him about that?

IV

The most common reasons given for opposition to the plural wife system were that it was not compatible with the American way of life, that it debased the women who lived under it, and that it caused disharmony and unhappiness in the family. To these charges the Mormons replied that their women enjoyed a higher social position than those of the outside world, and that there was less contention and unhappiness in their families than in those of the Gentiles. There is no statistical information upon which to base a judgment as to who had the better of this argument.

In addition to these general complaints against polygamy, its critics told some fantastic stories about the evils which followed in its wake. It was said that, through some mysterious workings of the laws of heredity, polygamous children were born with such peculiarities as feeblemindedness, abnormal sexual desires, and weak and deformed bodies.

At a meeting of the New Orleans Academy of Sciences in 1861, a remarkable paper was presented by Dr. Samuel A. Cartwright and Prof. C.G. Forshey. It consisted mainly of quotations from a report made by Assistant Surgeon Robert Barthelow of the United States Army on the "Effects and Tendencies of Mormon Polygamy in the Territory of Utah." Barthelow had observed that the Mormon system of marriage was already producing a people with distinct racial characteristics. He said:

The yellow, sunken, cadaverous visage; the greenish-colored eye; the thick, protuberant lips; the low forehead; the light, yellowish hair, and the lank, angular person, constitute an appearance so characteristic of the new race, the production of polygamy, as to distinguish them at a glance. The older men and women present all the physical peculiarities of the nationalities to which they belong; but these peculiarities are not propagated and continued in the new race; they are lost in the prevailing type.

Dr. Cartwright observed that the Barthelow report went far "to prove that polygamy not only blights the physical organism, but the moral nature of the white or Adamic woman to so great a degree as to render her incapable of breeding any other than abortive specimens of humanity—a new race that would die out—utterly perish from the earth, if left to sustain itself."

When one or two of the New Orleans scientists questioned the soundness of parts of this paper, the hecklers were silenced by Dr. Cartwright's retort that the facts presented were not so strong as "those which might be brought in proof of the debasing influence of abolitionism on the moral principles and character of that portion of the Northern people who have enacted personal liberty bills to evade a compliance with their constitutional obligations to the Southern States, and have elevated the Poltroon Sumner into a hero, and made a Saint of the miscreant Brown."

Needless to say there is no evidence that polygamy produced any such physical and mental effects upon the progeny of those who practiced it. A study of the infant mortality rate in a large number of Mormon families showed no difference between the polygamous and monogamous households.

It is difficult to arrive at general conclusions concerning this experiment in polygamy, but a few facts about it are evident. Mormondom was not a society in which all men married many wives, but one in which a few men married two or more wives. Although plurality of wives was taught as a tenet of the church, it was not one of the fundamental principles of the Mormon faith, and its abandonment was accomplished with less disturbance than that caused by its introduction. The Saints accepted plurality in theory, but most of them were loath to put it into practice, despite the continual urging of leaders in whose divine authority they had the utmost faith. Once the initial impetus given the venture had subsided it became increasingly unpopular. In 1857 there were nearly fourteen times as many plural marriages for each one thousand Utah Mormons as there were in 1880. Left to itself, undisturbed by pressure from without, the church would inevitably have given up the practice of polygamy, perhaps even sooner than it did under pressure. The experiment was not a satisfactory test of plurality of wives as a social system. Its results were neither spectacular nor conclusive, and they gave little justification for either the high hopes of its promoters or the dire predictions of its critics.

STUDY QUESTIONS

1. List the basic myths surrounding the Mormon practice of polygamy and then describe the social reality of each idea.

2. Ivins feels that the practice of polygamy was really not that popular among the Mormons. What evidence does he use to support that idea?

3. How important was polygamy as a religious principle among the Mormons? What was the relationship between the "Reformation" and the practice of polygamy?

4. What did Mormons believe about the social and spiritual benefits of polygamy?

5. How did the non-Mormon public in the nineteenth century view polygamy? What did they believe about the consequences of polygamy? Why did they have such attitudes?

BIBLIOGRAPHY

The classic study of Mormon settlement in the Intermountain West is Leonard Arrington, *Great Basin Kingdom: An Economic History of the Latter-day Saints, 1830–1900* (1958). Still the best sociological study of the Mormon faith is Thomas F. O'Dea, *The Mormons* (1957). The best survey history of the Mormon Church is James B. Allen and Glen M. Leonard, *The Story of the Latter-day Saints* (1976). For background material to the founding of the Mormon Church, see Whitney Cross, *The Burned-over District* (1950). For biographies of Joseph Smith, see Fawn Brodie, *No Man Knows My History: The Life of Joseph Smith, the Mormon Prophet* (1946) and Donna Hill, *Joseph Smith, The Mormon Prophet* (1977). The drama of the Mormon trek west is described in Wallace R. Stegner, *The Gathering of Zion: The Story of the Mormon Trail* (1964). Robert Flanders, *Nauvoo: Kingdom on the Mississippi* (1965) and Leonard Arrington, *Brigham Young: American Moses* (1984) are excellent sources. Also see Richard Bushman, *Joseph Smith and the Beginnings of Mormonism* (1984).

THE SLAVE WAREHOUSE
from *UNCLE TOM'S CABIN*

Harriet Beecher Stowe

On meeting Harriet Beecher Stowe during the Civil War, President Abraham Lincoln remarked, "So this is the lady who made this big war!" To be sure, Stowe did not cause the Civil War, but her novel, *Uncle Tom's Cabin,* aroused Northerners and angered Southerners. She portrayed slavery as a great moral evil—not at all the benign institution presented by southern apologists. Unlike the abstract writings of some of her contemporaries, Stowe confirmed the reality of slavery to Northerners who had never seen a slave or ventured below the Mason-Dixon line. The novel gave northern abolitionists a new rhetoric to use in condemning slavery, and it helped convince the South that the North was bent on destroying the southern way of life. State after state in the South banned the sale of the book, and southern postmasters routinely intercepted and destroyed all copies of the book mailed from northern book distributors.

Published in 1852, *Uncle Tom's Cabin* became a runaway bestseller, a literary success on both sides of the Atlantic. Stowe's characters—Uncle Tom, Eliza, Simon Legree, and Little Eva—were hailed as universal types. In the following selection, "The Slave Warehouse," good-hearted Christian slaves are purchased at a slave auction by Simon Legree.

A slave warehouse! Perhaps some of my readers conjure up horrible visions of such a place. They fancy some foul, obscure den, some horrible *Tartarus "informis, ingens, cui lumen ademptum."* But no, innocent friend; in these days men have learned the art of sinning expertly and genteelly, so as not to shock the eyes and senses of respectable society. Human property is high in the market; and is, therefore, well fed, well cleaned, tended, and looked after, that it may come to sale sleek, and strong, and shining. A slave warehouse in New Orleans is a house externally not much unlike many others, kept with neatness; and where every day you may see arranged, under a sort of shed along the outside, rows of men and women, who stand there as a sign of the property sold within.

Then you shall be courteously entreated to call and examine, and shall find an abundance of husbands, wives, brothers, sisters, fathers, mothers, and young children, to be "sold separately, or in lots, to suit the convenience of the purchaser;" and that soul immortal, once bought with blood and anguish by the Son of God, when the earth shook, and the rocks were rent, and the graves were opened, can be sold, leased, mortgaged, exchanged for groceries or dry goods, to suit the phases of trade, or the fancy of the purchaser.

It was a day or two after the conversation between Marie and Miss Ophelia, that Tom, Adolph, and about half a dozen others of the St. Clare estate, were turned over to the loving kindness of Mr. Skeggs, the keeper of a depot on ———street, to await the auction next day.

Tom had with him quite a sizable trunk full of clothing, as had most others of them. They were ushered, for the night, into a long room, where many other men, of all ages, sizes, and shades of complexion, were assembled, and from which

---

"The Slave Warehouse" from *Uncle Tom's Cabin* by Harriet Beecher Stowe. New York, 1852.

roars of laughter and unthinking merriment were proceeding.

"Ah, ha! that's right. Go it, boys—go it!" said Mr. Skeggs, the keeper. "My people are always so merry! Sambo, I see!" he said, speaking approvingly to a burly Negro who was performing tricks of low buffoonery, which occasioned the shouts which Tom had heard.

As might be imagined, Tom was in no humor to join these proceedings; and, therefore, setting his trunk as far as possible from the noisy group, he sat down on it, and leaned his face against the wall.

The dealers in the human article make scrupulous and systematic efforts to promote noisy mirth among them, as a means of drowning reflection, and rendering them insensible to their condition. The whole object of the training to which the Negro is put, from the time he is sold in the northern market till he arrives south, is systematically directed towards making him callous, unthinking, and brutal. The slave-dealer collects his gang in Virginia or Kentucky, and drives them to some convenient, healthy place—often a watering-place,—to be fattened. Here they are fed full daily; and, because some incline to pine, a fiddle is kept commonly going among them, and they are made to dance daily; and he who refuses to be merry— in whose soul thoughts of wife, or child, or home, are too strong for him to be gay—is marked as sullen and dangerous, and subjected to all the evils which the ill-will of an utterly irresponsible and hardened man can inflict upon him. Briskness, alertness, and cheerfulness of appearance, especially before observers, are constantly enforced upon them, both by the hope of thereby getting a good master, and the fear of all that the driver may bring upon them, if they prove unsalable.

"What dat ar nigger doin' here?" said Sambo, coming up to Tom, after Mr. Skeggs had left the room. Sambo was a full black, of great size, very lively, voluble, and full of trick and grimace.

"What you doin' here?" said Sambo, coming up to Tom, and poking him facetiously in the side. "Meditatin', eh?"

"I am to be sold at the auction, to-morrow!" said Tom, quietly.

"Sold at auction—haw! haw! boys, an't this yer fun? I wish't I was gwin that ar way!—tell ye, wouldn't I make 'em laugh? but how is it—dis yer whole lot gwine to-morrow?" said Sambo, laying his hand freely on Adolph's shoulder.

"Please to let me alone!" said Adolph, fiercely, straightening himself up, with extreme disgust.

"Law, now, boys! dis yer's one o' yer white niggers—kind o' cream-color, ye know, scented!" said he, coming up to Adolph and snuffing. "O Lor! he'd do for a tobaccershop; they could keep him to scent snuff! Lor, he'd keep a whole shop agwine—he would!"

'I say, keep off, can't you?" said Adolph, enraged.

"Lor, now, how touchy we is—we white niggers! Look at us, now!" and Sambo gave a ludicrous imitation of Adolph's manner; "here's de airs and graces. We's been in a good family, I specs."

"Yes," said Adolph; "I had a master that could have bought you all for old truck!"

"Laws, now, only think," said Sambo, "the gentlemens that we is!"

"I belonged to the St. Clare family," said Adolph, proudly.

"Lor, you did! Be hanged if they aren't lucky to get shet of ye. Spects they 's gwine to trade ye off with a lot o' cracked teapots and sich like!" said Sambo, with a provoking grin.

Adolph, enraged at this taunt, flew furiously at his adversary, swearing and striking on every side of him. The rest laughed and shouted, and the uproar brought the keeper to the door.

"What now, boys? Order—order!" he said, coming in and flourishing a large whip.

All fled in different directions, except Sambo, who, presuming on the favor which the keeper had to him as a licensed wag, stood his ground, ducking his head with a facetious grin, whenever the master made a dive at him.

"Lor, Mas'r, 't an't us—we 's reg'lar stiddy—it's these yer new hands; they 's real aggravatin'—kinder pickin' at us, all time!"

The keeper, at this, turned upon Tom and Adolph, and distributing a few kicks and cuffs without much inquiry, and leaving general orders for all to be good boys and go to sleep, left the apartment.

While this scene was going on in the men's sleeping-room, the reader may be curious to take a peep at the corresponding apartment allotted to the women. Stretched out in various attitudes over the floor, he may see numberless sleeping forms of every shade of complexion, from the purest ebony to white, and of all years, from childhood to old age, lying now asleep. Here is a fine bright girl, of ten years, whose mother was sold out yesterday, and who tonight cried herself to sleep when nobody was looking at her. Here, a worn old Negress, whose thin arms and callous fingers tell of hard toil, waiting to be sold to-morrow, as a cast-off article, for what can be got for her; and some forty or fifty others, with heads variously enveloped in blankets or articles of clothing, lie stretched around them. But, in a corner, sitting apart from the rest, are two females of a more interesting appearance than common. One of these is a respectably dressed mulatto woman between forty and fifty, with soft eyes and a gentle and pleasing physiognomy. She has on her head a high-raised turban, made of a gay red Madras handkerchief, of the first quality, and her dress is neatly fitted, and of good material, showing that she has been provided for with a careful hand. By her side, and nestling closely to her, is a young girl of fifteen—her daughter. She is a quadroon, as may be seen from her fairer complexion, though her likeness to her mother is quite discernible. She has the same soft, dark eyes, with longer lashes, and her curling hair is of a luxuriant brown. She also is dressed with great neatness, and her white, delicate hands betray very little acquaintance with servile toil. These two are to be sold to-morrow, in the same lot with the St. Clare servants; and the gentleman to whom they belong, and to whom the money for their sale is to be transmitted, is a member of a Christian church in New York, who will receive the money, and go thereafter to the sacrament of his Lord and theirs, and think no more of it.

These two, whom we shall call Susan and Emmeline, had been the personal attendants of an amiable and pious lady of New Orleans, by whom they had been carefully and piously instructed and trained. They had been taught to read and write, diligently instructed in the truths of religion, and their lot had been as happy an one as in their condition it was possible to be. But the only son of their protectress had the management of her property; and, by carelessness and extravagance, involved it to a large amount, and at last failed. One of the largest creditors was the respectable firm of B. & Co., in New York. B. & Co. wrote to their lawyer in New Orleans, who attached the real estate (these two articles and a lot of plantation hands formed the most valuable part of it), and wrote word to that effect to New York. Brother B., being, as we have said, a Christian man, and a resident in a free state, felt some uneasiness on the subject. He didn't like trading in slaves and souls of men—of course, he didn't; but, then, there were thirty thousand dollars in the case, and that was rather too much money to be lost for a principle; and so, after much considering, and asking advice from those that he knew would advise to suit him, Brother B. wrote to his lawyer to dispose of the business in the way that seemed to him the most suitable, and remit the proceeds.

The day after the letter arrival in New Orleans, Susan and Emmeline were attached, and sent to the depot to await a general auction on the following morning; and as they glimmer faintly upon us in the moonlight which steals through the grated window, we may listen to their conversation. Both are weeping, but each quietly, that the other may not hear.

"Mother, just lay your head on my lap, and see if you can't sleep a little," says the girl, trying to appear calm.

"I haven't any heart to sleep, Em; I can't it's the last night we may be together!"

"Oh, mother, don't say so! perhaps we shall get sold together—who knows?"

"If't was anybody's else case, I should say so, too, Em," said the woman; "but I'm so 'feared of losin' you that I don't see anything but the danger."

"Why, mother, the man said we were both likely, and would sell well."

Susan remembered the man's looks and words. With a deadly sickness at her heart, she remembered how he had looked at Emmeline's hands, and lifted up her curly hair, and pronounced her a first-rate article. Susan had been trained as a Christian, brought up in the daily reading of the Bible, and had the same horror of her child's being sold to a life of shame that any other Christian mother might have; but she had no hope—no protection.

"Mother, I think we might do first-rate, if you could get a place as cook, and I as chambermaid or seamstress, in some family. I dare say we shall. Let's both look as bright and lively as we can, and tell all we can do, and perhaps we shall," said Emmeline.

"I want you to brush your hair all back straight, to-morrow," said Susan.

"What for, mother? I don't look near so well, that way."

"Yes, but you'll sell better so."

"I don't see why!" said the child.

"Respectable families would be more apt to buy you, if they saw you looked plain and decent, as if you wasn't trying to look handsome. I know their ways better'n you do," said Susan.

"Well, mother, then I will."

"And, Emmeline, if we shouldn't ever see each other again, after to-morrow—if I'm sold way up on a plantation somewhere, and you somewhere else—always remember how you've been brought up, and all Missis has told you; take your Bible with you, and your hymnbook; and if you're faithful to the Lord, he'll be faithful to you."

So speaks the poor soul, in sore discouragement; for she knows that to-morrow any man, however vile and brutal, however godless and merciless, if he only has money to pay for her, may become owner of her daughter, body and soul; and then, how is the child to be faithful? She thinks of all this, as she holds her daughter in her arms, and wishes that she were not handsome and attractive. It seems almost an aggravation to her to remember how purely and piously, how much above the ordinary lot, she has been brought up. But she has no resort but to *pray;* and many such prayers to God have gone up from those same trim, neatly arranged, respectable slave-prisons—prayers which God has not forgotten, as a coming day shall show; for it is written, "Whoso causeth one of these little ones to offend, it were better for him that a mill-stone were hanged about his neck, and that he were drowned in the depths of the sea."

The soft, earnest, quiet moonbeam looks in fixedly, marking the bars of the grated windows on the prostrate, sleeping forms. The mother and daughter are singing together a wild and melancholy dirge, common as a funeral hymn among the slaves:—

"Oh, where is weeping Mary?
Oh, where is weeping Mary?
  'Rived in the goodly land.
She is dead and gone to heaven;
She is dead and gone to heaven;
  'Rived in the goodly land."

These words, sung by voices of a peculiar and melancholy sweetness, in an air which seemed like the sighing of earthly despair after heavenly hope, floated through the dark prison-rooms with a pathetic cadence, as verse after verse was breathed out—

"Oh, where are Paul and Silas?
Oh, where are Paul and Silas?
  Gone to the goodly land.
They are dead and gone to heaven;
They are dead and gone to heaven;
  'Rived in the goodly land."

Sing on, poor souls! The night is short, and the morning will part you forever!

But now it is morning, and everybody is astir; and the worthy Mr. Skeggs is busy and bright, for a lot of goods is to be fitted out for auction. There is a brisk lookout on the toilet, injunctions passed to every one to put on their best face and be spry; and now all are arranged in a circle for a last review, before they are marched up to the Bourse.

Mr. Skeggs, with his palmetto on and his cigar in his mouth, walks around to put farewell touches on his wares.

"How's this?" he said, stepping in front of Susan and Emmeline. "Where's your curls, gal?"

The girl looked timidly at her mother, who, with the smooth adroitness common among her class, answers—

"I was telling her, last night, to put up her hair smooth and neat, and not havin' it flying about in curls; looks more respectable so."

"Bother!" said the man, peremptorily, turning to the girl; "you go right along, and curl yourself real smart!" He added, giving a crack to a rattan he held in his hand, "And he back in quick time, too!"

"You go and help her," he added, to the mother. "Them curls may make a hundred dollars difference in the sale of her."

Beneath a splendid dome were men of all nations, moving to and fro, over the marble pave. On every side of the circular area were little tribunes, or stations, for the use of speakers and auctioneers. Two of these, on opposite sides of the area, were now occupied by brilliant and talented gentlemen, enthusiastically forcing up, in English and French commingled, the bids of connoisseurs in their various wares. A third one, on the other side, still unoccupied, was surrounded by a group, waiting the moment of sale to begin. And here we may recognize the St. Clare servants—Tom, Adolph, and others; and there, too, Susan and Emmeline, awaiting their turn with anxious and dejected faces. Various spectators, intending to purchase, or not intending, as the case might be, gathered around the group, handling examining, and commenting on their various points and faces with the same freedom that a set of jockeys discuss the merits of a horse.

"Hulloa, Alf! what brings you here?" said a young exquisite, slapping the shoulder of a sprucely dressed young man, who was examining Adolph through an eye-glass.

"Well, I was wanting a valet, and I heard that St. Clare's lot was going. I thought I'd just look at his"—

"Catch me ever buying any of St. Clare's people! Spoilt niggers, every one. Impudent as the devil!" said the other.

"Never fear that!" said the first. "If I get'em, I'll soon have their airs out of them; they'll soon find that they've another kind of master to deal with than Monsieur St. Clare. 'Pon my word, I'll buy that fellow. I like the shape of him."

"You'll find it'll take all you've got to keep him. He's deucedly extravagant!"

"Yes, but my lord will find that he *can't* be extravagant with *me*. Just let him be sent to the calaboose a few times, and thoroughly dressed down! I'll tell you if it don't bring him to a sense of his ways! Oh, I'll reform him, up hill and down—you'll see. I buy him that's flat!"

Tom had been standing wistfully examining the multitude of faces thronging around him, for one whom he would wish to call master. And if you should ever be under the necessity, sir, of selecting, out of two hundred men, one who was to become your absolute owner and disposer, you would, perhaps, realize, just as Tom did, how few there were that you would feel at all comfortable in being made over to. Tom saw abundance of men—great, burly, gruff men; little, chirping, dried men; long-favored, lank, hard men; and every variety of stubbed-looking, commonplace men, who pick up their fellow-men as one picks up chips, putting them into the fire or a basket with equal unconcern according to their convenience; but he saw no St. Clare.

A little before the sale commenced, a short, broad, muscular man, in a checked shirt considerably open at the bosom, and pantaloons much the worse for dirt and wear, elbowed his way through the crowd, like one who is going actively into a business; and, coming up to the group, began to examine them systematically. From the moment that Tom saw him approaching, he felt an immediate and revolting horror at him, that increased as he came near. He was evidently, though short, of gigantic strength. His round, bullet-head, large, light-grey eyes, with their shaggy, sandy eyebrows, and stiff, wiry, sunburned hair, were rather unprepossessing items, it is to be confessed; his large, coarse mouth was distended with tobacco, the juice of which, from time to time, he ejected from him with great decision and explosive force; his hands were immensely large, hairy, sunburned, freckled, and very dirty, and garnished with long nails, in a very foul condition. This man proceeded to a very free personal examination of the lot. He seized Tom by the jaw, and pulled open his mouth to inspect his teeth; made him strip up his sleeve, to show his muscle; turned him round, made him jump and spring, to show his paces.

"Where was you raised?" he added, briefly, to these investigations.

"In Kintuck, Mas'r," said Tom, looking about, as if for deliverance.

"What have you done?"

"Had care of Mas'r's farm," said Tom.

"Likely story!" said the other, shortly, as he passed on. He paused a moment before Dolph; then spitting a discharge of tobacco-juice on his well-blacked boots, and giving a contemptuous umph, he walked on. Again he stopped before Susan and Emmeline. He put out his heavy, dirty hand, and drew the girl towards him; passed it over her neck, and bust, felt her arms, looked at her teeth, and then pushed her back against her mother, whose patient face showed the suffering she had been going through at every motion of the hideous stranger.

The girl was frightened, and began to cry.

"Stop that, you minx!" said the salesman; "no whimpering here—the sale is going to begin." And accordingly the sale began.

Adolph was knocked off, at a good sum, to the young gentleman who had previously stated his intentions of buying him; and the other servants of the St. Clare lot went to various bidders.

"Now, up with you, boy! d'ye hear?" said the auctioneer to Tom.

Tom stepped upon the block, gave a few anxious looks round; all seemed mingled in a common, indistinct noise—the clatter of the salesman crying off his qualifications in French and English, the quick fire of French and English bids; and almost in a moment came the final thump of the hammer, and the clear ring on the last syllable of

Families endured forced separation at slave auctions like the one depicted above; here a mother and child are being sold. Contrary to popular belief, slave markets were ususally well-tended warehouses. Slaves were fattened and groomed before auctions in order to bring better prices.

the word *"dollars,"* as the auctioneer announced his price, and Tom was made over. He had a master.

He was pushed from the block; the short, bullet-headed man, seizing him roughly by the shoulder, pushed him to one side, saying in a harsh voice, "Stand there, *you!*"

Tom hardly realized anything; but still the bidding went on—rattling, clattering, now French, now English. Down goes the hammer again—Susan is sold! She goes down from the block, stops, looks wistfully back—her daughter stretches her hands towards her. She looks with agony in the face of the man who has bought her—a respectable, middle-aged man, of benevolent countenance.

"Oh, Mas'r, please do buy my daughter!"

"I'd like to, but I'm afraid I can't afford it!" said the gentleman, looking, with painful interest, as the young girl mounted the block, and looked around her with a frightened and timid glance.

The blood flushes painfully in her otherwise colorless cheek, her eye has a feverish fire, and her mother groans to see that she looks more beautiful than she ever saw her before. The auctioneer sees his advantage, and expatiates volubly in mingled French and English, and bids rise in rapid succession.

"I'll do anything in reason," said the benevolent-looking gentleman, pressing in and joining with the bids. In a few moments they have run beyond his purse. He is silent; the auctioneer grows warmer; but bids gradually drop off. It lies now between an aristocratic old citizen and our bullet-headed acquaintance. The citizen bids for a few turns, contemptuously measuring his opponent; but the bullet-head has the advantage over him, both in obstinacy and concealed length of purse, and the controversy lasts but a moment; the hammer falls—he has got the girl, body and soul, unless God help her.

Her master is Mr. Legree, who owns a cotton plantation on the Red River. She is pushed along into the same lot with Tom and two other men, and goes off, weeping as she goes.

The benevolent gentleman is sorry; but, then, the thing happens every day! One sees girls and mothers crying, at these sales, *always!* it can't be helped, etc.; and he walks off, with his acquisition, in another direction.

Two days after, the lawyer of the Christian firm of B. & Co., New York, sent on their money to them. On the reverse of that draft, so obtained, let them write these words of the great Paymaster, to whom they shall make up their account in a future day: *"When he maketh inquisition for blood, he forgetteth not the cry of the humble!"*

"Thou art of purer eyes than to behold evil, and canst not look upon iniquity: wherefore lookest thou upon them that deal treacherously, and holdest thy tongue when the wicked devoureth the man that is more righteous than he?"—*Hab.* i. 13.

On the lower part of a small, mean boat, on the Red River, Tom sat—chains on his wrists, chains on his feet, and a weight heavier than chains lay on his heart. All had faded from his sky—moon and star; all had passed by him, as the trees and banks were now passing, to return no more. Kentucky home, with wife and children, and indulgent owners; St. Clare home, with all its refinements and splendors; the golden head of Eva, with its saint-like eyes; the proud, gay, handsome, seemingly careless, yet ever-kind St. Clare; hours of ease and indulgent leisure—all gone! and in place thereof, *what* remains?

It is one of the bitterest apportionments of a lot of slavery, that the Negro, sympathetic and assimilative, after acquiring, in a refined family, the tastes and feelings which form the atmosphere of such a place, is not the less liable to become the bond-slave of the coarsest and most brutal—just as a chair or table, which once decorated the su-

perb saloon, comes, at last, battered and defaced, to the bar-room of some filthy tavern, or some low haunt of vulgar debauchery. The great difference is, that the table and chair cannot feel, and the *man* can; for even a legal enactment that he shall be "taken, reputed, adjudged in law, to be a chattel personal," cannot blot out his soul, with its own private little world of memories, hopes, loves, fears, and desires.

Mr. Simon Legree, Tom's master, had purchased slaves at one place and another, in New Orleans, to the number of eight, and driven them, handcuffed, in couples of two and two, down to the good steamer Pirate, which lay at the levee, ready for a trip up the Red River.

Having got them fairly on board, and the boat being off, he came round, with that air of efficiency which ever characterized him, to take a review of them. Stopping opposite to Tom, who had been attired for sale in his best broadcloth suit, with well-starched linen and shining boots, he briefly expressed himself as follows:

"Stand up."

Tom stood up.

"Take off that stock!" and, as Tom, encumbered by his fetters, proceeded to do it, he assisted him, by pulling it, with no gentle hand, from his neck, and putting it in his pocket.

Legree now turned to Tom's trunk, which, previous to this, he had been ransacking, and taking from it a pair of old pantaloons and a dilapidated coat, which Tom had been wont to put on about his stable-work, he said, liberating Tom's hands from the handcuffs, and pointing to a recess in among the boxes—

"You go there, and put these on."

Tom obeyed, and in a few moments returned.

"Take off your boots," said Mr. Legree.

Tom did so.

"There," said the former, throwing him a pair of course, stout shoes, such as were common among the slaves, "put these on."

In Tom's hurried exchange, he had not forgotten to transfer his cherished Bible to his pocket. It was well he did so; for Mr. Legree, having refitted Tom's handcuffs, proceeded deliberately to investigate the contents of his pockets. He drew out a silk handkerchief, and put it into his own pocket. Several little trifles, which Tom had treasured, chiefly because they amused Eva, he looked upon with a contemptuous grunt, and tossed them over his shoulder into the river.

Tom's Methodist hymn-book, which, in his hurry, he had forgotten, he now held up and turned over.

"Humph! pious, to be sure. So, what's yer name—you belong to the church, eh?"

"Yes, Mas'r," said Tom, firmly.

"Well, I'll soon have *that* out of you. I have none o' yer bawling, praying, singing niggers on my place; so remember. Now, mind yourself," he said, with a stamp and a fierce glance of his gray eye, directed at Tom, "*I'm* your church now! You understand—you've got to be as I say."

Something within the silent black man answered *No!* and, as if repeated by an invisible voice, came the words of an old prophetic scroll, as Eva had often read them to him, "Fear not! For I have redeemed thee. I have called thee by my name. Thou art MINE!"

But Simon Legree heard no voice. That voice is one he never shall hear. He only glared for a moment on the downcast face to Tom, and walked off. He took Tom's trunk, which contained a very neat and abundant wardrobe, to the forecastle, where it was soon surrounded by various hands of the boat. With much laughing, at the expense of niggers who tried to be gentlemen, the articles very readily were sold to one and another, and the empty trunk finally put up at auction. It was a good joke, they all thought, especially to see how Tom looked after his things, as they were going this way and that; and then the auction of the trunk, that was funnier than all, and occasioned abundant witticisms.

This little affair being over, Simon sauntered up again to his property.

"Now, Tom, I've relieved you of any extra baggage, you see. Take mighty good care of them clothes. It'll be long enough 'fore you get more. I go in for making niggers careful; one suit has to do for one year, on my place."

Simon next walked up to the place where Emmeline was sitting chained to another woman.

"Well, my dear," he said, chucking her under the chin, "keep up your spirits."

The involuntary look of horror, fright, and aversion with which the girl regarded him, did not escape his eye. He frowned fiercely.

"None o' your shines, gal! you 's got to keep a pleasant face, when I speak to ye—'d ye hear? And you, you old yellow poco moonshine!" he said, giving a shove to the mulatto woman to whom Emmeline was chained, "don't you carry that sort of face! You 's got to look chipper, I tell ye!"

"I say, all on ye," he said, retreating a pace or two back, "look at me—look at me—look me right in the eye—*straight,* now!" said he, stamping his foot at every pause.

As by a fascination, every eye was now directed to the glaring greenish gray eye of Simon.

"Now," said he, doubling his great, heavy fist into something resembling a blacksmith's hammer, "d' ye see this fist? Heft it!" he said, bringing it down on Tom's hand. "Look at these yer bones! Well, I tell ye this yer fist has got as hard as iron *knocking down niggers.* I never see the nigger, yet, I couldn't bring down with one crack," said he, bringing his fist down so near to the face of Tom that he winked and drew back. "I don't keep none o' yer cussed overseers; I does my own overseeing; and I tell you things *is* seen to. You 's every one of ye get to toe the mark, I tell ye; quick—straight—the moment I speak. That's the way to keep in with me. Ye won't find no soft spot in me, nowhere. So, now, mind yerselves; for I don't show no mercy!"

The women involuntarily drew in their breath, and the whole gang sat with downcast, dejected faces. Meanwhile, Simon turned on his heel, and marched up to the bar of the boat for a dram.

"That's the way I begin with my niggers," he said, to a gentlemanly man, who had stood by him during his speech. "It's my system to begin strong—just let 'em know what to expect."

"Indeed!" said the stranger, looking upon him with the curiosity of a naturalist studying some out-of-the-way specimen.

"Yes, indeed. I'm none o' yer gentlemen planters, with lily fingers, to slop round and be cheated by some old cuss of an overseer! Just feel of my knuckles, now; look at my fist. Tell ye, sir, the flesh on't has come jest like a stone, practising on niggers—feel on it.'

The stranger applied his fingers to the implement in question, and simply said,

"'T is hard enough; and, I suppose," he added, "practice has made your heart just like it."

"Why, yes, I may say so," said Simon, with a hearty laugh. "I reckon there's as little soft in me as in any one going. Tell you, nobody comes it over me! Niggers never gets round me, neither with squalling nor soft soap—that's a fact."

"You have a fine lot there."

"Real," said Simon. "There's that Tom, they told me he was suthin uncommon. I paid a little high for him, 'tendin' him for a driver and a managing chap; only get the notions out that he's larnt by being treated as niggers never ought to be, he'll do prime! The yellow woman I got tookin in. I rayther think she's sickly, but I shall put her through for what she's worth; she may last a year or two. I don't go for savin' niggers. Use up, and buy more, 's my way—makes you less trouble, and I'm quite sure it comes cheaper in the end;" and Simon sipped his glass.

"And how long do they generally last?" said the stranger. "Well, donno; 'cordin' as their constitution is. Stout fellers last six or seven years; trashy ones gets worked up in two or three. I used to, when I fust begun, have considerable trouble fussin' with 'em, and trying to make 'em hold out—doctorin' on 'em up when they 's sick, and given' on 'em clothes and blankets, and what not, tryin' to keep 'em all sort o' decent and comfortable. Law, 't wasn't no sort o' use; I lost money on 'em, and 't was heaps o' trouble. Now, you see, I just put 'em straight through, sick or well. When one nigger's dead, I buy another; and I find it comes cheaper and easier, every way."

The stranger turned away, and seated himself beside a gentleman, who had been listening to the conversation with repressed uneasiness.

"You must not take that fellow to be any specimen of southern planters," said he.

"I should hope not," said the young gentleman, with emphasis.

"He is a mean, low, brutal fellow!" said the other.

"And yet your laws allow him to hold any number of human beings subject to his absolute will without even a shadow of protection; and, low as he is, you cannot say that there are not many such."

"Well," said the other, "there are also many considerate and humane men among planters."

"Granted," said the young man; "but, in my opinion, it is you considerate, humane men, that are responsible for all the brutality and outrage wrought by these wretches; because, if it were not for your sanction and influence, the whole system could not keep foothold for an hour. If there were no planters except such as that one," said he, pointing with his finger to Legree, who stood with his back to them, "the whole thing would go down like a mill-stone. It is your respectability and humanity that licenses and protects his brutality."

"You certainly have a high opinion of my good nature," said the planter, smiling; "but I advise you not to talk quite so loud, as there are people on board the boat who might not be quite so tolerant to opinion as I am. You had better wait till I get up to my plantation, and there you may abuse us all, quite at your leisure."

The young gentleman colored and smiled, and the two were soon busy in a game of backgammon. Meanwhile, another conversation was going on in the lower part of the boat, between Emmeline and the mulatto woman with whom she was confined. As was natural, they were exchanging with each other some particulars of their history.

"Who did you belong to?" said Emmeline.

"Well, my Mas'r was Mr. Ellis—lived on Levee Street. P'r'aps you've seen the house."

"Was he good to you?" said Emmeline.

"Mostly, till he tuk sick. He's lain sick, off and on, more than six months, and been orful oneasy. 'Pears like he warn't willin' to have nobody rest, day nor night; and got so curous, there couldn't nobody suit him. 'Pears like he just grew crosser, every day; kep me up nights till I got farly beat out, and couldn't keep awake no longer; and 'cause I got to sleep, one night, Lors, he talk so orful to me, and he tell me he'd sell me to just the hardest master he could find; and he'd promised me my freedom, too, when he died."

"Had you any friends?" said Emmeline.

"Yes, my husband—he's a blacksmith. Mas'r gen'ly hired him out. They took me off so quick, I didn't even have time to see him; and I's got four children. Oh, dear me!" said the woman, covering her face with her hands.

It is a natural impulse, in every one, when they hear a tale of distress, to think of something to say by way of consolation. Emmeline wanted to say something, but she could not think of anything to say. What was there to be said? As by a common consent, they both avoided, with fear and dread, all mention of the horrible man who was now their master.

True, there is religious trust for even the darkest hour. The mulatto woman was a member of the Methodist Church, and had an unenlightened but very sincere spirit of piety. Emmeline had been educated much more intelligently, taught to read and write, and diligently instructed in the Bible, by the care of a faithful and pious mistress; yet, would it not try the faith of the firmest Christians to find themselves abandoned, apparently, of God, in the grasp of ruthless violence? How much more must it shake the faith of Christ's poor little ones, weak in knowledge and tender in years.

The boat moved on—freighted with its weight of sorrow—up the red, muddy, turbid current, through the abrupt, tortuous windings of the Red River; and sad eyes gazed wearily on the steep red-clay banks, as they glided by in dreary sameness. At last the boat stopped at a small town, and Legree, with his party, disembarked.

STUDY QUESTIONS

1. How does Stowe convey the inhumanity of the slave auction?

2. How does Tom accept his fate?

3. How does Stowe portray the evil of Legree?

4. What reactions do you believe Stowe was trying to arouse in her readers?

BIBLIOGRAPHY

For studies of *Uncle Tom's Cabin* and Harriet Beecher Stowe, see Charles A. Foster, *The Wrungless Ladder* (1954); Chester E. Jorgensen, ed., *Uncle Tom's Cabin as Book and Legend* (1952); Forrest Wilson, *Crusader and Crinoline* (1941); and Edmund Wilson, *Patriotic Gore* (1962). Anne Fields, *Life and Letters of Harriet Beecher Stowe* (1898), contains useful information on *Uncle Tom's Cabin,* and Herbert Ross Brown, *The Sentimental Novel in America 1789-1860* (1940), puts the novel into its literary perspective.

THE SOUTHAMPTON SLAVE REVOLT

Henry F. Tragle

The need for some form of involuntary servitude seemed inevitable in the American South. Land was abundant and cheap, but labor was limited and expensive. Unlike the situation in England, American settlers found it fairly easy to acquire land of their own but practically impossible to find people to work it. If Southerners were going to get the most out of their land, they needed labor; if no volunteers were available, slavery seemed a viable alternative. They found their workers in West Africa, importing the first group of slaves to Virginia in 1619. By the time of the Civil War, that handful of blacks had grown to four million people.

Southern life was full of ambiguities, but none of them was more ironic than the role of those four million slaves. Whites needed slaves to plant their land, harvest their crops, clean their houses, cook their food, and suckle their children. Whites needed slaves in order to thrive and prosper, so they imported more and more Africans, making slaves a permanent, visible fixture in southern life.

But the arrival of more and more slaves made southern whites nervous. Despite the prevailing rationale that slavery benefited all concerned, whites knew instinctively that the Africans resented their bondage and yearned to be free. Rumors of slave rebellions were rampant in the nineteenth century. Whites became paranoid about their slaves; they were always on guard, always searching for conspiracies, always afraid of a slave uprising. Then on the morning of August 22, 1831, their worst nightmares came true in Southampton, Virginia. There Nat Turner led a group of slaves on a bloody rampage through white farms and plantations. When the orgy of violence was over, sixty whites were dead, hacked apart by axes wielded by slaves. The South would never be the same.

The voluminous histories of this country written in the nineteenth century, while admirable in many respects, are of little value to a student today who seeks reliable information on the institution of American slavery. Concerned primarily with slavery as a political question, or with its economic, social, and cultural impact on the white population, the historians rarely made any attempt to understand the black man as a human being.

One of the persistent themes pursued by those who have written recently on the subject of American slavery has been to ask why the slave was willing to tolerate his lot. Why, when in many sections of the South the slave population considerably outnumbered the white, was there no more evidence of unrest?

Actually, there was considerable. But one must look beyond the writings of the most respected of the nineteenth-century historians in order to perceive this. The works of James Schouler, John Fiske, Hermann von Holst, John W. Burgess, James Ford Rhodes, and John Bach McMaster simply did not deal with the available evidence on this question. Satisfied to accept the stereotype of the American black man as docile, ignorant, and inherently inferior, they saw no reason to probe very deeply. Fiske did find that the absence of any insurrectionary spirit was, in itself," one of the remarkable facts of American history," and Schouler, when considering the same question, wrote that American Negroes were "a black servile race, . . . brutish, obedient to the whip."

Yet, in order to see that all was not "sweetness and light" in the Southern states one can find countless instances of individual unrest and resistance, and a few uprisings organized on a sufficient scale to be called insurrections or revolts. The contemporary press and the historical archives of the states that were part of the slave-holding South are the best sources of such information. Despite the tendency of Southern newspapers to play down these stories, the black files of any such paper for the period from 1800 up to the time of the Civil War will reveal numerous accounts of homes or barns burned, of property damaged or destroyed, and instances of white masters beaten, or even murdered by their own slaves. A summary prepared by the state auditor of Virginia in 1831 shows that, between 1820 and 1831, the state paid out a total of $124,785 for 313 slaves who were either executed as criminals or were "transported" out of the state for acts judged to be criminal. Since, under existing law, the state was required to reimburse an owner for slave executed or transported, and since neither of these actions could be taken without benefit of trial in a court of law, it can be assumed that the 313 slaves on the list had been judged guilty of serious crimes.

Three well-authenticated attempts at organized slave revolt took place in the first third of the nineteenth century. In 1800 there was the so-called "Gabriel's Insurrection" in Richmond. While the details of the plot have never been fully known, it is clear that a group of slaves living in and near the Virginia capital developed a plan to burn and sack the city and destroy its white inhabitants. Although discovered before any blow was actually struck, the conspiracy caused great excitement. Those believed to be the ringleaders were executed, the laws governing the conduct of slaves as well as of free black people were applied more severely, and the governor, James Monroe, wrote a special report on the matter for the Virginia Legislature.

In 1822 in Charleston, South Carolina, occurred what has come to be known as the "Denmark Vesey Plot." Vesey, who had been the slave of sea-captain, had traveled abroad with his master and had learned to read and write. After purchasing his freedom, he became a respected black artisan in Charleston. In a plot that was revealed through slave informers, Vesey was accused along with a number of other black men, slave and free, of planning and insurrection and was executed.

"The Southampton Slave Revolt" by Henry F. Tragle. This article is reprinted from the November 1971 issue of *American History Illustrated* 6, pp. 4–11, 44–47, with the permissing of Cowles History Group, Inc. Copyright *American History Illustrated* magazine.

Again, no actual uprising took place, but it seems clear that plans had been laid to organize a black rebellion which would have extended well into the interior of the state.

The most famous instance of this sort, and the only one which actually resulted in the deaths of a sizable number of white people, took place in an obscure backwater of Virginia, Southampton County, in August of 1831. Generally referred to as "The Southampton Insurrection," or "the servile insurrection of 1831," it has been called by one historian the "single instance of sustained revolt of slaves against their masters in American history." Whether this description is justified or not depends on the criteria one uses, but there is no question that the revolt led by the slave Nat Turner had a powerful and lasting effect on the institution of slavery throughout the entire South.

Interest in Turner as an individual has recently been intensified by a highly successful fictionalized version of his exploits, as well as by the growing interest in serious study of the culture and history of the American black man as a hitherto neglected aspect of the American heritage. Nat Turner, as symbol and folk hero, has figured frequently in fiction, poetry, and drama in the 140 years since 1831. Harriet Beecher Stowe, in her novel, *Dred,* which she published in 1856, used what little was known of Turner in shaping her principal character, and included as an appendix to her book a portion of the "Confession" which he is supposed to have made while awaiting trial in the Southampton jail. George Payne Rainsford James, a prolific novelist of the nineteenth century and Historiographer Royal to King William IV of England, published a novel in 1853 which he called *The Old Dominion.* The plot is based on what had taken place in Southampton County some twenty years earlier, and Nat Turner emerges as a kind of black mystic. James had served for a short time as British Consul in Norfolk, Virginia, and it is possible that during this period he heard the actual event discussed.

It is possible to reconstruct from contemporary records and the news stories of the time a reasonably accurate account of what happened during the period August 21 through November 11, 1831, on which date Nat Turner was executed. But we know little about the man himself and even less about his basic motivation. He was born the slave of Benjamin Turner on October 2, 1800. The Turner home, located about fifteen miles southwest of Jerusalem, the county seat of Southampton, was characteristic of the style of life which prevailed in that part of Virginia. Most of Southampton's white male citizens farmed small holdings, and only a handful of its most prosperous citizens owned more than twenty-five slaves. In 1830 its population totaled 16,074 of which 6,573 were white and 9,501 black. Jerusalem, the main town, had but 175 inhabitants. The county was unusual in one particular: a relatively high proportion of its black population, 1,745, were what were then known as "free men (or women) of color." This exception from the prevailing pattern in Southside Virginia was due in large part to the activity of the Quakers and the Emancipating Baptists, both of which sects had flourished in the area in the years following the Revolutionary War. Both had taken strong stands against slavery. Little is known about these free black people and their way of life, but it is safe to assume that their existence was marginal at best. Of the fifty persons eventually tried on suspicion of having taken part in the revolt, five of those arraigned were free black men.

Since blacks lived under a legal system which made it a felony to teach a slave to read or write, it is not surprising that illiteracy among them was almost universal. Yet Nat Turner was not only literate, he was known, by black and white alike, for his profound knowledge of the Bible. As surprising as the possession of these skills is the fact that he avoided attracting the serious attention of white members of the community, whose suspicion and animosity could be readily aroused by any signs of intelligence or ability on the part of a slave. Yet the lawyer who recorded his "Confessions," Thomas R. Gray, wrote this evaluation in the concluding lines of his account:

It has been said that he was ignorant and cowardly, and his object was to murder and rob for

the purpose of obtaining money to make his es-
cape. It is notorious that he was never known
to have a dollar in his life, to swear an oath, or
drink a drop of spirits. As to his ignorance, he
certainly never had the advantages of an edu-
cation, but he can read and write (it was
taught him by his parents) and for natural in-
telligence and quickness of apprehension, is
surpassed by few men I have ever seen.

There is no evidence that Nat Turner was a pampered house servant, or that, except for the austerity of his personal life and his habit of reading the Bible in every free moment, he has outwardly much different from any other able-bodied male slave in the county. After the revolt he was characterized in news stories as a "Black Preacher," but white persons in the neighborhood who knew him denied that he had even attended church regularly. When Benjamin Turner died in 1810, Nat passed into the ownership of a younger brother, Samuel, and at his death in 1822, was sold to a neighbor, one Thomas Moore. In his "Confessions," he speaks of having revelations from Heaven, and is quoted as saying, "these confirmed me in the impression that I was ordained for some great purpose in the hands of the Almighty." Speaking further to Gray of the influence he realized that he had obtained over the minds of his fellows in bondage, he said, "I now began to prepare them for my purpose, by telling them that something was about to happen that would terminate in fulfilling the great promise that had been made to me." But he makes it clear that at this point he himself was not aware of the nature of his mission.

Finally, according to his account, he had a vision on May 12, 1828, in which he "heard a loud noise in the heavens, and the Spirit instantly appeared to me and said . . . the time was fast approaching when the first should be last and the last should be first." In the same vision he was told that "until the first sign appeared, I should conceal it from the knowledge of men."

In the meantime, the ordinary round of life went on in Southampton County. Nat Turner's third owner, Thomas Moore, died in 1828 and his nominal ownership passed to Moore's nine-year-old son, Putnam. Within two years the Widow Moore married a local wheelwright, Joseph Travis, who moved into her house and set up his business on the place.

On February 12, 1831, there occurred an eclipse of the sun, and this came to Nat Turner as the sign he had been awaiting. In his words, "the seal was removed from my lips, and I communicated the great work laid out for me to do, to four in whom I had the greatest confidence, (Henry, Hark, Nelson and Sam)." Slaves, of course, had no patronymic. Because many shared the same given name, they generally used the last name of their owner, and when they changed owners, they usually changed names. Hark (who had also belonged to Thomas Moore) subsequently was spoken of as Hark Travis. Yet Nat Turner seemed always to remain Nat Turner. Also, in the trials that eventually ensued, the arraignment usually read "Hark, or Sam, or Jack, a man slave belonging to" so and so. Nat Turner was arraigned as "Nat, alias Nat Turner." He was even mentioned in one news story in a Richmond paper (and not in a facetious manner) as "Mr. Turner."

The first date chosen for the beginning of his "mission of work" was July 4, 1831, but he tells in his "Confessions" that this date had to be abandoned because "I fell sick." Then on August 13 there occurred a day-long atmospheric phenomenon, during which the sun was seen but faintly and appeared to be of a greenish hue. This occurrence, which caused wide-spread consternation in many places in the eastern United States, was accepted by Nat Turner as a direct communication from God. After alerting those whom he had originally chosen as his primary lieutenants, and recruiting two more, he arranged a meeting for Sunday, August 21, deep in the woods near the Travis homestead at a place called Cabin Pond.

The followers met first and roasted a pig and drank brandy. Later in the day Nat Turner appeared and explained the nature of his mission. It is significant that he is also quoted in the "Confessions" as saying, "we expected . . . to concert a plan, as we had not yet determined on any." This, and the fact that no physical preparations, such as the prior secreting of weapons or supplies had been undertaken, gives the impression that Turner saw himself purely as an instrument acting for a higher power which would provide all that was necessary when the time came.

The gist of the plan which emerged was nothing less than the destruction of every white person within reach; again in the words of the "Confessions," "we should commence at home (Mr. J. Travis') on that night, and until we had armed and equipped ourselves, and gathered sufficient force, neither age nor sex was to be spared. . . . "

Beginning at about two o' clock on the morning of Monday, August 22, the plan became reality. Leaving the site of the meeting, the group made its silent way through the woods to the Travis farm. Nat Turner ascended to a second-story window by means of a ladder, opened the door to the others, and they quickly disposed of Mr. and Mrs. Travis, their young child, Nat Turner's legal master, Putnam Moore, and a young apprentice, Joel Westbrook. Thus began the gory crusade, which was to lead in a long, S-shaped path toward the county seat. Having dispatched their first victims with axes and hatchets, they acquired weapons and horses as they went. By dawn, they had visited half a dozen homes and had killed more than twenty men, women, and children. Mounted now, they moved swiftly from house to house, gaining recruits as they went. But, probably to their surprise, many slaves on neighboring places either had to be forced at gun-point to join them, and subsequently had to be guarded almost as hostages, or escaped and gave the alarm. When shortly after daybreak they began to find homes deserted, they realized that a warning had been spread.

The bloody details of the slayings which took approximately sixty lives were described at length in the Richmond and Norfolk newspapers in the days that followed. The stories appear to agree on several aspects which surprised the surviving white community; insofar as was ever known, no female victim was sexually molested, no wanton torture was inflicted, no buildings were burned, and—except for horses and weapons—relatively little in the way of personal property was taken.

At about nine o' clock they arrived at the home of Captain Thomas Barrow, a veteran of the War of 1812. Disdaining to flee, the Captain held off the entire band long enough to permit his wife to escape. According to a local legend, Captain Barrow's determined resistance so impressed his slayers that, having finally killed him by cutting his throat, they wrapped the body in a quilt and placed a plug of tobacco on his chest.

From the gateway of his farm, Barrow had built a road eastward for about five miles to a junction with the highway that ran south from Jerusalem to the North Carolina line. Still known locally as Barrow Road (and officially as County Highway 658), this was one of the few real roads in the county. Nat Turner and his men now followed it eastward, sowing death as they went. They probably numbered between forty and fifty at their peak, and all were mounted. If there is a monument to the Southampton Revolt, it is the Barrow Road itself.

Apples were a principal product of the county, and almost every homestead had its own still where brandy was made. As the day wore on, this potent spirit took its toll of some, but it seemed not to affect the determination of the eight or ten leaders who are responsible for most of the killing. One of the recruits who had joined while still at the Cabin Pond, Will, appears to have been the principal executioner. Most of his victims were decapitated by a razor-sharp axe. Strangely, according to Nat Turner's subsequent "Confessions," he dealt the death blow only once, and that to the young daughter of a Travis neighbor, Margaret Whitehead.

At Levi Waller's, the master of the house saw the band approaching and was able to conceal himself in a nearby field from which he watched the murder of his wife, his children, and a number of other children who attended a school at his homeplace. In all, eleven died at that one home, and their bodies were heaped in one room together. Levi Waller survived to appear as a witness at Nat Turner's trial. At William Williams' after killing the man of the house and his two children, the band caught Mrs. Williams and forced her to lie beside her dead husband, and then shot her. At Jacob Williams' house one of the original group, Nelson, was cheated of his intent to destroy his master, who was away from home, but Mrs. Williams, their two children, the wife of their overseer, Mrs. Caswell Worrell, and her child, as well as a visitor, Edwin Drewry, were left dead.

The final home visited, just about noontime, was that of Mrs. Rebecca Vaughan. Pleading vainly for her life, she was quickly dispatched, as were her niece, Eliza, her young son, Arthur, and their overseer. Although she did not know it, her older son, George, had fallen victim to the band when they encountered him earlier on the road leading to the Thomas Barrow homestead.

The Vaughan house lay close to the junction of the Barrow Road with the highway leading to the county seat, and again, in the words of Nat Turner's "Confessions," we learn that "here I determined on starting for Jerusalem." Presumably his goal was the local armory where weapons, powder, and shot were stored in abundance. In the aftermath, it was frequently speculated that Nat Turner intended to lead his band into the almost impenetrable fastness of the Dismal Swamp, some thirty miles distant; but this is never stated in his "Confessions."

Turning northeast at the crossroads, they rode toward Jerusalem. About half a mile from the junction lay the entrance to James Parker's farm. Some of the participants had friends here, who they thought would join them, and they probably also thought that weapons, and possibly additional brandy, could be obtained there. Apparently against his better judgment, Nat Turner had the party divide, some going toward the Parker house, from which the family had fled, while a small group including Turner himself stayed at the entrance to the farm.

Suddenly a detachment of militia rode into view. They had been tardily assembled when the alarm reached Jerusalem, and here, in Parker's cornfield, the first armed confrontation took place between the slaves in revolt and their em-battled masters. Apparently there were no fatalities on either side, and after an exchange of shots, and a few wounds being inflicted, they broke off contact. But Nat Turner realized that the road to Jerusalem was effectively barred. His force was thrown into confusion by the encounter, was reduced in numbers, and now was much harder to manage. He resolved to try a crossing of the Nottaway River, which lay between him and the town, at a point to the east, Cypress Bridge, but a quick reconnaissance showed it to be well guarded.

Gathering the remnants of his force he turned south, seeking recruits. Discouraged by the obvious evidence that the countryside was now alarmed, he turned north again, crossed the path he had followed earlier, and holed up for the night, with a force of forty or fewer, near the Ridley plantation. During the night a false alarm scared off more than half of his remaining followers.

At dawn on Tuesday, August 23, the last blow of the revolt was struck. Probably believing that the residents had already fled "Belmont," the home of Dr. Simon Blunt, the band entered the lane leading from the main road. Close to the house they were met with withering fire from the doctor, his son, the overseer, and three white neighbors, who, rather than fleeing, had barricaded themselves in the house. At least one of Turner's men fell dead, and several including his principal lieutenant, Hark, were wounded. Blunt's own slaves, having hidden in an out-building, now rallied to the defense of their master and aided in the capture of the wounded and the unhorsed. Nat Turner escaped with a handful of the faithful.

Deciding to return to the vicinity of their starting point, they were met by militia along the Barrow Road. One or more were killed and by late afternoon, Nat Turner found himself alone, a fugitive pursued not only by the aroused citizenry of the county but by a horde of vigilantes from adjoining Virginia and North Carolina counties and by various military forces which had begun to arrive in response to appeals for help.

On Monday, when word of the trouble in the southwestern part of the county reached Jerusalem, the postmaster, James Trezevant, sent a

Nat Turner's 1831 revolt, be it just or unjust, had a significant impact on slavery throughout the south, and brought the issue of slavery to the attention of the nation.

letter by express rider to the mayor of Petersburg, some fifty miles away. This was relayed to Governor John Floyd in Richmond, who received it in the early morning hours of Tuesday, the 24th. He quickly ordered armed militia units to the scene, and arranged for weapons and supplies to be sent as rapidly as possible. Floyd, a veteran of the War of 1812 and a brigadier general in the militia, immediately considered the possibility that what was happening in Southampton could be the prelude to a general slave uprising. For this reason, together with others related to the prestige of the State, he refrained from asking for help from the Federal forces stationed at Fort Monroe, just across Hampton Roads from Norfolk.

However, word of what was happening had reached Norfolk by means of the regular stagecoach, and the mayor, backed by the city council, decided to call for Federal help. No possibility existed for communication with the state authorities in Richmond, so very soon a request had gone to Colonel House at Fort Monroe, to the commander of the United States Naval yard, and to two ships of war lying in the Roads. Within a matter of hours, a joint force of regular army troops, marines, and sailors was alerted and on their way to Southampton. As it turned out, the revolt was quelled before any of the Federal forces could participate and most were turned around and returned to their stations without reaching the site of the action. Governor Floyd, eventually learning of the precipitate action by Norfolk's mayor, was furious. He felt that the psychological impression which the call-out had created was bad. He also pointed out that, had the uprising been of a general character, drawing off the available Federal force from Fort Monroe would have left the area on the north bank of the James River, including numerous plantations and settlements where the blacks outnumbered the whites, entirely without possibility of reinforcement.

But the lot of the innocent blacks in Southampton County itself might have been better if Federal forces had taken charge. As it was, once the scare was over and the true nature of the threat ascertained, the life of every black person in the country was threatened. The spirit of revenge and retaliation ran wild. The editor of one Richmond newspaper, who went as a member of a militia troop of cavalry to the scene, wrote:

It is with pain we speak of another feature of the Southampton Rebellion; for we have been most unwilling to have our sympathies for the sufferers diminished or affected by their misconduct. We allude to the slaughter of many blacks, without trial, and under circumstances of great barbarity.

The militia commander placed in charge by Governor Floyd, Brigadier General Richard Eppes, finally found it necessary to threaten to invoke the Articles of War to halt the indiscriminate slaughter.

Most of those involved were either killed or rounded up. In the meantime, the fear of an uprising had spread to neighboring counties in Virginia and North Carolina. It is impossible to estimate how many innocent blacks paid with their lives for no more than the merest suspicion. For example, a group of citizens from Sampson County in North Carolina, wrote to the governor to report that they had "ten or fifteen Negroes in Jail," and in passing noted that "the people of Duplin County have examined ten or fifteen Negroes, and found two guilty, and have put them to death." It was not even suggested that any of those jailed or executed were known to have participated in any type of threatening action.

Trials began in the Southampton Court of Oyer and Terminer on August 31 and continued into November. During this period more than twenty slaves, including one woman and three boys of less than fifteen years, were convicted and sentenced to death. Some of the sentences were subsequently reduced by the governor to transportation out of the state. All of those who had been part of Nat Turner's original band were either killed in the aftermath of the revolt, or were subsequently executed. Estimates of the number who were killed without trial run to more than one hundred. In many instances, the only witnesses for the prosecution were fellow-slaves of the accused, some of whom were subsequently to go to the gallows.

Through all this, the question remained, "What had become of Nat Turner?" Despite search by several thousand militiamen, augmented by volunteer vigilantes from all over the area, the leader eluded capture. There were almost daily reports that he had been sighted; by one mail, the governor was informed that he had been taken prisoner in Washington; a few days later he was reported to have drowned while trying to escape capture in the western part of the state. On September 14, Floyd proclaimed a reward of $500 for his capture, and persons in the area increased this by another $600. Yet all this time "General Nat," as the papers

frequently called him, was hiding no more than a mile from the place of original assembly at Cabin Pond. Having secured a small stock of food, he scratched a tiny "cave" under a pile of fence rails where he remained concealed for more than four weeks. Later, after two frightened slaves had stumbled onto this hiding place, he concealed himself in a haystack and then moved to the shelter of a hole beneath the branches of a fallen pine tree.

Finally, on October 30, when most of his companions had already been executed or shipped out of the state, he was discovered by a local white man, Benjamin Phipps. Armed only with a small sword, he surrendered and was turned over to the Southampton County jailor the next day. It was while awaiting trial that he agreed to talk with Thomas. R. Gray. These "Confessions," which Gray is supposed to have taken down verbatim, were recorded on the 1st, 2nd, and 3rd of November. Gray is frequently referred to as Nat Turner's counsel at his trial, which took place on November 5. Actually he had no official connection with the case. It seems more likely that, as a local lawyer who had served as court-appointed counsel for some of those tried earlier, and who was familiar with all that had happened, he saw the considerable commercial possibilities in converting Nat Turner's story into a pamphlet. This is what he did, and very speedily. The twenty-three page document, authenticated by a certificate of the justices of the court, and containing lists of the white people who had been killed and all of the persons tried up to that time, was copyrighted by Gray in Washington on November 10, just one day before Nat Turner was, according to the sentence of the court, "taken by the Sheriff to the usual place of execution, and there . . . hanged by the neck until he be dead."

About ten days later the pamphlet was published in Baltimore, and the accuracy of Gray's estimate of public interest in the matter can be gauged by the fact that several other editions were subsequently printed, and it is said to have sold more than 40,000 copies. Yet today copies of the original pamphlet are very rare. A Norfolk newspaper wrote that a "portrait painter" of that town had made a likeness of Nat Turner while in jail. Pictures purporting to depïct Nat Turner have been published, but it has never been established that any of these were drawn from life.

Governor Floyd was convinced, despite the lack of any real evidence, that the revolt was part of a larger plot which extended to many areas of the South. He also felt that the relative freedom which had been accorded black preachers as well as such abolitionist writings as Garrison's *Liberator* and Walker's *Appeal* had been part of the root cause. A resident of western Virginia, he favored the abolition of slavery, provided it was coupled with a removal of all black people from the state. His sentiments were not so much an expression of humanitarian feelings, as they were a conviction that Virginia could make no real economic progress while burdened with "the peculiar institution."

From letters to the newspapers during the fall of 1831, it can be readily seen that Floyd's views were widely shared. During November he wrote in his diary, "Before I leave this Government, I will have contrived to have a law passed gradually abolishing slavery in the State. . . . " Yet the message which he sent to the newly assembled, legislature on December 6 contained no such proposal. Instead, after a lengthy review of the revolt and an analysis of what he believed to be its causes, he proposed the enactment of extremely stern laws which would apply to all of the state's black people, slave and free alike.

Between December 1831 and February 1832, the whole question of slavery was hotly debated by the legislature, and a resolution supporting emancipation failed by a very narrow margin. This debate, which engaged some of the best minds of the state, and which attracted wide attention, has been called the last free and uninhibited discussion of the question of slavery in any Southern legislative body. But once the vote was taken, those who had favored emancipation

seemed to fade away. Floyd's biographer, Charles Ambler, explains the Governor's attitude in this way:

Absorbed as he was in national affairs, Floyd was perfectly willing to turn the whole subject of the state's proper policy regarding negro slavery over to the solution of a master who was at hand in the person of Thomas R. Dew of William and Mary College. . . . The able defense and justification of the institution of negro slavery which followed was accepted by Floyd and most other Virginians of whatever section as final.

In the end we are left with the question of the net effect of Nat Turner's actions on the institution of slavery itself. Did it hasten or retard the thrust toward emancipation? Herbert Aptheker, one of those who has written much on the subject concludes that "The Turner Revolt may be summed up by the one word accelerator." Probably the best assessment is that of John W. Cromwell, a black historian and lawyer, who saw the final results in this fashion:

Whether Nat Turner hastened or postponed the day of the abolition of slavery . . . is a question that admits of little or much discussion in accordance with opinions concerning the law of necessity and free will in national life. Considered in the light of its immediate effects upon its participants, it was a failure, an egregious failure, a wanton crime. Considered in its relation to slavery and as contributory to making it a national issue by deepening and stirring of the then weak local forces, that finally led to the Emancipation Proclamation and the Thirteenth Amendment, the insurrection was a moral success and Nat Turner deserves to be ranked with the great reformers of his day.

STUDY QUESTIONS

1. Nat Turner was not a "typical" Virginia slave. In what ways was he different?

2. In what ways was the black population of Southampton County unique? How might those unique demographic circumstances have contributed to white and black attitudes about slavery there?

3. In your opinion , was Nat Turner "crazy"? Explain your answer.

4. What was the white reaction to the slave uprising? How did the uprising affect the lives of the rest of the blacks—slave and free—in Southampton County?

5. Why did the slave uprising create an intense debate in Virginia about freeing all of the slaves? Why, in your opinion, did that emancipation movement fail?

BIBLIOGRAPHY

William Styron's *The Confessions of Nat Turner* (1968), a novel based on Turner's confession to Thomas Gray, remains a highly readable, if controversial, account of the 1831 rebellion. Herbert Aptheker's *American Negro Slave Revolts* (1943) provides a list of the antebellum slave revolts, but it is flawed by a highly polemical style. For more sophisticated accounts of slave resistance to bondage, see Gerald Mullin, *Flight and Rebellion: Slave Resistance in Eighteenth-Century Virginia* (1972) and Kenneth M. Stampp, *The Peculiar Institution: Slavery in the Antebellum South* (1956). The best book on free blacks in the antebellum South is Ira Berlin, *Slaves Without Masters: The Free Negro in the Antebellum South* (1975). For outstanding descriptions of slave life and culture, see George Rawick, *From Sundown to Sunup: The Making of the Slave Community* (1972); John Blassingame, *The Slave Community: Plantation Life in the Antebellum South* (1972); and Lawrence W. Levine, *Black Culture and Black Consciousness: Afro-American Folk Thought from Slavery to Freedom* (1977).

JOHN BROWN AND THE PARADOX OF LEADERSHIP AMONG AMERICAN NEGROES

David Potter

John Brown was a man given to excess. He fathered twenty children, and in thirty-five years he engaged in more than twenty different businesses. When he was fifty-five, he radically changed professions. He became, in his mind and the minds of his devoted followers, a visionary and a modern-day prophet. His crusade and reason for living was the abolition of slavery. An utterly fearless man of action, he left talking to others and took matters into his own hands. On the night of May 24, 1856, John Brown, four of his sons, a son-in-law, and two other men left their bloodly imprint on history. At Pottawatomie Creek in Kansas, they murdered and mutilated five proslavery settlers. The action, Brown said, had been "decreed by Almighty God, ordained from Eternity."

In October 1859, Brown and a larger group of followers made a more daring raid. They were determined to capture the federal arsenal at Harpers Ferry, Virginia, and from there, to move South and liberate the slaves. The action failed and Brown was captured, tried, and executed. But his legacy lives on. As historian David Potter demonstrates in the following essay, Brown's raid on Harpers Ferry illustrated how far the North and South had grown apart and how much northern as well as southern whites were alienated from slaves. In the North, the dead Brown became a sainted martyr. In the South he became a symbol of bloodthirsty northern aggression. By the late 1850s, the two regions were speaking different languages as they marched toward civil war.

One of the anomalies in the history of American Negroes is that, as a group, they have had only very limited opportunity to choose their own leadership. Historians agree, more or less, on a selected list of men who have been Negro leaders—Frederick Douglass, Booker T. Washington, W. E. B. Du Bois, Marcus Garvey, Martin Luther King. Of course, there have also been other very distinguished figures—Thurgood Marshall, Ralph Ellison, James Baldwin, Walter White, Roy Wilkins, *et al.*, but they have not commanded large mass followings; and there have been still others like Elijah Muhammad, Malcolm X, and Stokeley Carmichael whose role is or was controversial even within the Negro community. But none of these men was ever chosen to leadership by an election in which the body of American Negroes voted for what might be called "the Negroes' choice." Despite the widespread growth of organized groups of Negro activists in recent years, there has never been an organization which we can designate with assurance as expressing the attitudes of the rank and file of American Negroes, unless it was Marcus Garvey's Universal Negro Improvement Association. Most of the others have appealed either to the middle class, as the NAACP has done, or to ideological radicals, and not to the run-of-the-mill American Negro.

This absence of an organizational basis for the selection of leaders has meant that the positions of leadership were gained in special ways, sometimes in arbitrary or, as it were, fictitious ways. For instance, Frederick Douglass received his license as spokesman for four million slaves from a small coterie of abolitionists who later quarreled with him. True, he was an excellent choice and he proved a very able leader indeed—perhaps as able as any American Negro—but the choice was nevertheless an historical accident, as the choice of

"John Brown and the Paradox of Leadership Among American Negroes" from *The South and the Sectional Crisis* by David Potter. Copyright © 1968 by Louisiana State University Press. Reprinted by permission.

many excellent leaders has been. Booker T. Washington, also an able man, did not owe his eminence to the recognition that Negroes gave him, but was appointed to the political leadership of American Negroes by Theodore Roosevelt, and to the economic leadership by Andrew Carnegie. W. E. B. Du Bois received his investiture in an especially ironical way—the anomaly of which he felt as keenly as anyone else. He was made the key figure in the NAACP by a wealthy, highly respectable, and I think one can say smug, self-appointed committee of upper-class white moderate reformers; later, he owed his more or less posthumous canonization to academic Marxist intellectuals whom most Negroes had never heard of. Today some of the militant types whose names flash like meteors across the headlines—Carmichael, Rap Brown, LeRoi Jones—have been fobbed off on American Negroes partly by social revolutionaries who care nothing for civil rights or Negro welfare within our existing society, and partly by the mass media which need sensational and extravagant material to galvanize the attention of a jaded public. If one looks for Negroes who owed their positions of leadership primarily to the support accorded them by other Negroes, the most authentic names are those of Marcus Garvey and Martin Luther King, and perhaps Roy Wilkins, despite the attacks which he has sustained from the left. At a more limited level, I think one should add Elijah Muhammand and Malcolm X.

These comments may seem extraneous indeed to a consideration of the career of John Brown, but indirectly they may have a certain pertinence because though Brown was not a Negro, he probably went farther in plans for launching a Negro revolution in the United States than anyone in history. He intended to become the commander-in-chief of an army of Negroes. Yet he had no Negro lieutenants; he took almost no advice from Negroes and acted in defiance of such advice as he did take; and most paradoxical of all, he completely concealed his intended insurrection from the Negroes who were expected to support it. His was the classic case of a man who acted in the name of American Negroes and relied upon them to follow him, but never really sought to represent them or to find out what they wanted their leader to do.

Historians of the antislavery movement have already complained, with considerable justice I think, that the Negro was neglected even by the abolitionists. Many abolitionists could not see the Negroes, as it were, for the slaves. Thus even the underground railroad became, historiographically, the first Jim Crow transportation in America. Traditional accounts pictured the railroad as an operation in which heroic white conductors braved dangers unspeakable in transporting fugitives from one hideout to the next, while the helpless and passive Negroes lay inert in the bottom of the wagon bed, concealed under a layer of hay. We now know that a good many respectable Yankee families who had never worked on the railroad later decided that they had intended to, or they would have if there had been a fugitive handy, and gradually translated this sentimental ex post facto intention into the legend of a fearless deed. But that is beside the point. What is relevant to the theme of this paper is that historically there was an anomalous relationship between the Negro slaves and their white sympathizers, and the paradox of this relationship shows up in its most striking form in the story of John Brown and Harpers Ferry. The paradox lay in the fact that the white abolitionists believed that the Negroes were all on the brink of a massive insurrection, yet they seldom consulted any Negro for corroboration and they conducted their own abolitionist activities—even John Brown's insurrectionary activities—as if Negroes could be regarded abstractly, like some sort of chemical element which at a certain heat would fuse into a new compound, and not concretely as a plurality of diverse men and women, each one with a temperament and aspirations of his own.

What were John Brown's specific relations with Negroes? It cannot be said that Negroes were entirely an abstraction to him, as they have been to some civil rights enthusiasts, for he knew Negroes, worked with them, and included them, on terms of seeming familiarity, in the intimacy of his little band of followers. But let us examine the record in more detail.

John Brown was apparently reared from an early age to hate slavery. The details may have been over-dramatized, as they have been in the story of the early life of Lincoln, but the fact appears clear. As early as the 1830's, he assisted in the escape of at least one fugitive; he made plans to rear a Negro child with his own children in his home; and he also thought of conducting a school for Negroes. His systematic activity in behalf of Negroes and his actual association with Negroes, however, began in the late 1840's when he agreed to move to North Elba, New York, where Gerrit Smith proposed to make him responsible for a colony of Negroes for which Smith was prepared to give 120,000 acres. At North Elba, Brown tried to help the Negro settlers, including at least one known fugitive. He gave them advice about farming and took some into his home, where they worked and shared the Spartan life of his family. But the North Elba project failed, primarily because the region never has been good farm country; it was frigid and rigorous in a way that made adaptation by Southern Negroes especially difficult. Moreover, Brown's own financial difficulties in the wool business made it impossible for him to stay at North Elba on a regular basis, and compelled him to spend much of his time at Springfield, Massachusetts, instead. At Springfield in 1847, he invited Frederick Douglass to visit him, and there he revealed to Douglass the first version of the plan which ultimately took him to Harpers Ferry. This was a scheme to organize a band of about twenty-five men, who would operate from hideouts in the Southern Appalachians. These men would induce slaves to run away and would assist them in their escape. Douglass had been a fugitive slave himself, had lived among slaves, had known the South at first hand; but there is no evidence that Brown asked him for his opinion about the practicability of the plan or about any aspect of the operations. Douglass probably knew a great deal that might have been useful to Brown, but Brown took no advantage of this potential information. This was characteristic of him throughout his life.

By the time of the enactment of the Fugitive Slave Act in 1850, Brown was in Springfield most of the time. In response to the act, he organized a

League of Gileadites, as he called it, to offer physical resistance to the enforcement of the act. He drew up an "Agreement" and nine resolutions for the League, with an emphasis upon encouraging Negroes to be brave and not to resort to halfway measures: "When engaged, do not do your work by halves, but make clean work with your enemies and be sure you meddle not with any others. . . . All traitors must die, whenever caught and proven to be guilty." Brown wrote to his wife in November, 1850: "I, of course, keep encouraging my colored friends to 'trust in God and keep their powder dry.' I did so today at a Thanksgiving meeting, publicly." Forty-four black men and women of Springfield signed Brown's agreement, but their commitment was never put to the test, for no efforts were made by Federal officials to arrest fugitives in the Springfield area. Still, the League is of great interest, for it was the only case in which this man—who gave so much of his energy while living and finally his life itself to the Negro cause—relied primarily upon Negroes in his work.

As the focus of the slavery controversy shifted to Kansas, Brown shifted his activities to that arena, and the plans which he had revealed to Douglass fell into abeyance. But ultimately it was the Kansas diversion which led him back to the Virginia project. Kansas fed his impulse toward violence, his appetite for leadership, and his hatred of slavery. It also unfitted him for his former prosaic pursuits in the wool trade. If Kansas had continued as a scene of violence, he might have ended his career as a Jayhawker on the Kansas prairies, but by 1857 Kansas was becoming pacified. Robert J. Walker had replaced Geary as governor and was giving the Free-Soilers fair treatment; the Free-Soilers had won control of the legislature when Walker threw out fraudulent proslavery votes. The antislavery party had nothing whatever to gain by a resumption of the border wars. They remembered, unpleasantly, the murders committed by Brown along Pottawatomie Creek (something which Easterners did not know about), and they regarded Brown as a troublemaker—trigger-happy and too much of a lone wolf. Brown began to perceive that his ca-

reer as a Kansas guerrilla was played out, and though he still talked about organizing a crack military unit for Kansas, his thoughts were turning increasingly toward the old idea of some kind of operation in the Southern Appalachians.

Brown left Kansas twice, first in October, 1856, with a divided mind as to whether he ought to return and continue active in the border wars; and again in November, 1857, knowing that his path would lead to Virginia. It is significant that, on both occasions, he stopped off at Rochester to see Douglass (in December, 1856, and in January, 1858). What meaning the visit in 1856 may have had, no one now can tell; at least it showed, as Douglass testifies, that the relationship formed nine years previously had been kept very much alive. But the visit in 1858 lasted for three weeks, and during this time Brown unfolded in full, perhaps for the first time, his second version of a plan for operation in Virginia. Douglass did not, at that time, disassociate himself from the plan, and indeed he later helped Brown to raise funds among well-to-do Negroes. But having been both a slave and a fugitive, Douglass perceived defects in the realism of Brown's plan, and he warned Brown of the pitfalls which were involved. John Brown did with this advice what he always did with all advice—he ignored it.

An interval of twenty months was to elapse between these conferences with Douglass and the final action at Harpers Ferry. This represented a delay of over a year in Brown's original plans. The delay resulted from two things: first, lack of money; and second, the fact that a soldier of fortune named Hugh Forbes, whom Brown had taken on as a military adviser, became disaffected because he did not receive the pay which he thought he had been promised, broke confidence, and revealed much of the plot to Senators Henry Wilson and William H. Seward. This breakdown in security greatly alarmed Brown's financial supporters, who virtually ordered him to suspend his plans.

Thus, during most of 1858 and 1859, Brown, who wanted only to smite the slaveholders, discovered that he had to be a salesman and a fundraiser first. So long as he was soliciting for funds for aid to Free-Soilers in Kansas, he was able to make public appeals. But as his insurrectionary scheme developed, it required the utmost secrecy, and he could appeal only to trusted sympathizers including principally the Secret Six—Gerrit Smith in Peterboro, New York, and five backers in Boston: George L. Stearns, Franklin B. Sanborn, Thomas Wentworth Higginson, Theodore Parker, and Samuel Gridley Howe. These men had been moderately generous since 1857, but they tended to want more action before they gave additional money, and Brown wanted additional money as a preliminary to the action. Often he was actually reduced to asking for handouts, and he never did obtain anything approaching the financial support which was needed for an operation on the scale which he projected.

Somehow, nevertheless, he weathered all these difficulties. Meanwhile, he had been looking to a means of formalizing his plans and raising recruits; and to this end he had made a curious pilgrimage with twelve of his followers, all of them white men except Richard Richardson, to Chatham, Ontario, in May, 1858. Ontario at that time had a population of upwards of thirty thousand Negroes, a vast proportion of whom were former slaves who might be expected to support a campaign against slavery in the South. Among these people, Brown had determined to make his appeal, to relax secrecy, and to seek the sanction and support of the Negro community for his daring plan. He had invited Gerrit Smith, Wendell Phillips, "and others of like kin" to be on hand.

Accordingly, on May 8, 1858, Brown presented to a secret "convention" at Chatham, consisting of twelve of his own followers and thirty-four resident Negroes, a plan of organization entitled "A Provisional Constitution and Ordinances for the people of the United States." This document condemned slavery, defined slavery as war, thus asserting for the slaves a legal status as belligerents, and provided for a provisional government, with a commander-in-chief of the army, an executive, a legislature, and a judiciary. This government was to act against slavery—indeed, to make war against it—and in explaining it Brown stated

where the army would get its troops. "Upon the first intimation of a plan formed for the liberation of the slaves," he said, "they would immediately rise all over the Southern states." By "flocking to his standard" they would enable him to extend his operations outward and southward from the mountain country in which he would begin, until he could operate upon the plantations of the lower South. They could defeat any militia, or even Federal troops sent against them, and "then organize the freed blacks under this provisional Constitution." What John Brown was planning was not a raid but a revolution.

The convention politely voted for the proposed Constitution, and on the next day it elected John Brown commander-in-chief and members of his party Secretaries of State, of the Treasury, and of War. Two men were elected as members of Congress, and one of these, Osborn P. Anderson, was an Ontario Negro. All the others were whites.

But Gerrit Smith was not there; Frederick Douglass was not there; and Wendell Phillips was not there. And when John Brown left Ontario, only two new Negro recruits went with him, one of whom, fearing arrest, soon returned to Canada. This was the only real effort Brown ever made to organize Negro support, and it had failed completely. It indicated clearly that the most famous project for a Negro insurrection in the history of the United States did not have the full support of even a corporal's guard of Negroes. There must have been hundreds of Negroes in Ontario who heard all about Brown's "secret" plan, but they had learned in a realistic school, and far more shrewdly than Emerson and Thoreau, and the litterateurs of Boston, they recognized that there was something unrealistic about this man. What was wrong was that he was recruiting members of a supporting cast for a theatrical melodrama in which the protagonist and principal actor was to be John Brown.

Only a month after the Chatham "convention" Brown sent one of his very earliest recruits, John E. Cook, to Harpers Ferry, Virginia, to live as a spy and to reconnoiter the environs. Cook found employment as a locktender on the canal and maintained his mission for over a year, but Brown was very apprehensive that he would talk too much, and this apprehension must have increased greatly when Cook married a local Harpers Ferry girl.

Fourteen months after the Chatham convention, Brown and a small band of followers began to converge on a farmhouse in Maryland which was to be their rendezvous. At first there were twenty of them, including sixteen whites and four Negroes—two of whom were born free and two of whom had run away from slavery. After they had gathered, Frederick Douglass came down to Chambersburg, Maryland, with a friend of his, Shields Green, who was, like himself, an escaped slave. Brown and Douglass had a final conference, which must have been a strained affair on both sides. Brown now revealed a new and even more alarming design—his purpose to seize the arsenal at Harpers Ferry. To this Douglass instantly took exception. He warned Brown that the position would be a trap from which escape would be impossible, and also that an attack on Federal property would turn the whole country against Brown's plans. He said that this was such a complete change of purpose that he would no longer participate. Brown urged him not to withdraw, saying, "I want you for a special purpose. When I strike, the bees will begin to swarm, and I shall want you to help me hive them." But Douglass still refused, and turning to his friend he asked what Green intended to do. Green's reply was, "I b'lieve I'll go wid de ole man."

Green was later accused of lack of courage, but there was in fact something supremely heroic about his action. His remark showed little confidence in Brown's plan but much loyalty to Brown personally; and he later died on the gallows because he had subordinated his judgment to his sense of personal devotion.

On the evening of October 16, 1859, after waiting three months for additional men, money, and munitions, most of which never arrived, John Brown marched with nineteen of his band, now grown to twenty-two, down to Harpers Ferry. There he seized the Potomac River bridge, the Shenandoah River bridge, and the Federal armory and rifle works. He also sent out a detail to bring

in two of the slaveholders of the neighborhood with their slaves. This mission was accomplished. Then he settled into the arsenal and waited, while first the local militia and later a small Federal force gathered to besiege him. Within thirty-six hours, his hopes were blasted and his force was destroyed—five men had escaped, but ten were dead or dying, and seven were in prison, all to die at the end of a rope.

Technically, Brown's operation had been such an unmitigated disaster that it has lent color to the belief that he was insane. Certain aspects were indeed incongruous. After making melodramatic gestures in the direction of secrecy, he had left behind him on the Maryland farm a large accumulation of letters which revealed all his plans and exposed all his secret supporters among the elite of Boston. As Hugh Forbes wrote, "the most terrible engine of destruction which he (Brown) would carry with him in his campaign would be a carpet-bag loaded with 400 letters, to be turned against his friends, of whom the journals assert that more than forty-seven are already compromised." After three and a half months of preparation, he marched at last without taking with him food for his soldiers' next meal, so that, the following morning, the Commander-in-Chief of the Provisional Army of the North, in default of commissary, was obliged to order forty-five breakfasts sent over from the Wagner House. For the remaining twenty-five hours, the suffering of Brown's besieged men was accentuated by the fact that they were acutely and needlessly hungry. His liaison with allies in the North was so faulty that they did not know when he would strike, and John Brown, Jr., who was supposed to forward additional recruits, later stated that the raid took him completely by surprise. If this was, as is sometimes suggested, because of the disordered condition of young Brown's mind rather than because of lack of information from his father, is still leaves a question why such a vital duty should have been entrusted to one whose mental instability had been conspicuous ever since Pottawatomie. Finally, there was the seemingly incredible folly of seizing a Federal arsenal and starting a war against the state of Virginia with an army of twenty-two men. This latter folly was probably the strongest factor in the later contention that he was insane. In layman's terms, anybody who tried to conquer a state as large as one of the nations of Western Europe with less than two dozen troops might be regarded as crazy. Was John Brown crazy in these terms?

Without trying to resolve the insanity question, to which C. Vann Woodward, Allan Nevins, and others have given extensive attention, let me just make two brief comments: first, that insanity is a clear-cut legal concept concerning a psychological condition which is seldom clear-cut; second, that the insanity concept has been invoked too much by people whose ulterior purposes were too palpable—first by people who hoped to save Brown's life by proving him irresponsible; then by Republicans who wanted to disclaim his act without condemning him morally; and finally by adverse historians who wanted to discredit his deeds by saying that only a madman would do such things. The evidence shows that Brown was very intense and aloof, that he became exclusively preoccupied with his one grand design, that he sometimes behaved in a very confused way, that he alternated between brief periods of decisive action and long intervals when it is hard to tell what he was doing, that mental instability occurred with significant frequency in his family, and that some who knew him believed he had a vindictive or even a homicidal streak with strong fantasies of superhuman greatness. Also, Pottawatomie should be borne in mind. From all this, one may clearly infer that Brown was not, as we would now term it, a well-adjusted man.

But withal, the heaviest count in the argument against Brown's sanity is the seeming irrationality of the Harpers Ferry operation. Yet Harpers Ferry, it might be argued, was irrational if, and only if, the belief in a vast, self-starting slave insurrection was a delusion. But if this was a fantasy, it was one which Brown shared with Theodore Parker, Samuel Gridley Howe, Thomas Wentworth Higginson, and a great many others who have never been called insane. It was an article of faith among the abolitionists that the slaves of the South were

seething with discontent and awaited only a signal to throw off their chains. It would have been heresy for an orthodox abolitionist to doubt this, quite as disloyal as for him to entertain the idea that any slave owner might be a well-intentioned and conscientious man. Gerrit Smith believed it, and two months before Brown's attempted coup he wrote, "The feeling among the blacks that they must deliver themselves gains strength with fearful rapidity." Samuel Gridley Howe believed it, and even after Brown's failure and when war came, he wrote that twenty to forty thousand volunteers could "plough through the South and be followed by a blaze of servile war that would utterly and forever root out slaveholding and slavery." Theodore Parker believed it, and wrote in 1850, "God forgive us our cowardice, if we let it come to this, that three millions of human beings . . . degraded by us, must wade through slaughter to their inalienable rights." After Harpers Ferry, Parker said, "The Fire of Vengeance may be waked up even in an African's heart, especially when it is fanned by the wickedness of a white man; then it runs from man to man, from town to town. What shall put it out? The white man's blood." William Lloyd Garrison was apparently inhibited from making such statements by his opposition on principle to the use of violence, but his *Liberator* constantly emphasized the unrest and resentment among the slaves; and he had once declared that, but for his scruples, he would place himself "at the head of a black army at the South to scatter devastation and death on every side." As J. C. Furnas has expressed it, there was a widespread "Spartacus complex" among the abolitionists, a fascinated belief that the South stood on the brink of a vast slave uprising and a wholesale slaughter of the whites. "It is not easy, though necessary," says Furnas, "to grasp that Abolitionism could, in the same breath warn the South of arson, rape, and murder and sentimentally admire the implied Negro mob leaders brandishing axes, torches, and human heads." This complex arose from the psychological needs of the abolitionists and not from any evidence which Negroes had given to them. No one really asked the Negroes what they wanted, or just how bloodthirsty they felt. There is much evidence that they wanted freedom to be sure, but again there is not much evidence that anyone even asked them how they thought their freedom could best be gained, and how they would like to go about getting it. Certainly John Brown did not ask, when he had a really good opportunity at Chatham, Ontario. All he did was talk. He did not listen at all. In fact there is no evidence that he ever listened at anytime, and this is perhaps the most convincing proof that he lived in the "private world" of an insane man.

But Brown's idea that the South was a waiting torch, and that twenty-two men without rations were enough to put a match to it, far from being a unique aberration, was actually one of the most conventional, least original notions in his whole stock of beliefs. Thus the Boston *Post* spoke much to the point when it said, "John Brown may be a lunatic but if so, then one-fourth of the people of Massachusetts are madmen."

The *Post* certainly did not intend to shift the question from one concerning Brown's personal sanity to one concerning the mass delusions of the abolitionists. A historian may, however, regard the latter as a legitimate topic of inquiry. But if he should do so, he must recognize at once the further fact that the Spartacus delusion—if delusion it was—was not confined to the abolitionists. The Southerners, too, shared this concept, in the sense that they were ever fearful of slave insurrections and were immensely relieved to learn that the slaves had not flocked to Brown's support. Clearly they had felt no assurance that this would be the outcome.

This is no place for me to go into either the extent or the realism of Southern fears of slave insurrection. The only point to make here is that John Brown, believing in the potentiality of a slave insurrection, only believed what both abolitionist and slaveholders believed. But Brown needed to know the specifics of that potentiality as others did not. He needed to know how strong it was, how it could be cultivated, how it could be triggered. The lives of himself and his men depended upon knowing. Yet there is no evidence

American artist Thomas Hovenden's painting of "The Last Moments of John Brown" (1884) depicts an emotional farewell from the most militant and controversial white champion of black freedom in the pre-Emancipation years.

that he ever even asked the questions. He merely said, "When I strike, the bees will swarm." But Negroes are not bees, and when figures of speech are used in argumentation, they are usually a substitute for realistic thinking.

Brown may have been right, at a certain level and in a certain sense, in believing that the Negroes might revolt. But he was completely wrong in the literal-minded way in which he held the idea, and this indiscriminate notion about Negro reactions probably led him to what was really his supreme folly. He supposed that the Negroes of Jefferson County would instantly spring to the support of an insurrection of which they had not been notified—that they would, of their own volition, join a desperate coup to which they had not even been invited. Brown evidently thought of Negroes, as so many other people have done, as abstractions, and not as men and women.

It was not as if he had not been warned: his English soldier of fortune, Hugh Forbes, told him that even slaves ripe for revolt would not come in on an enterprise like this. "No preparatory notice having been given to the slaves," he said, "the invitation to rise might, unless they were already in a state of agitation, meet with no response, or a feeble one." But Brown brushed this aside: he was sure of a response, and calculated that on the first night of the revolt, between two hundred and five hundred slaves would rally to him at the first news of his raid. Again later, when John E. Cook was keeping his lonely and secret vigil for more than a year as Brown's advance agent at Harpers Ferry, and even after Brown had moved to the farm in Maryland, Cook pleaded to be allowed to give the slaves at least some inkling of what was afoot. But Brown sternly rejected this idea. Thus, when the "Negro insurrection" began, the Negroes were as unprepared for it, as disconcerted, and as mystified as anyone else.

Brown, in his grandiose way, boasted of having studied the slave insurrections of history—of Spartacus, of Toussaint. But one wonders what those two, or even Denmark Vesey, would have had to say about John Brown's mode of conducting an insurrection. Abraham Lincoln, with his usual talent for accuracy of statement, later said, "It was not a slave insurrection. It was an attempt by white men to get up a revolt among slaves, in which the slaves refused to participate." But in a way Lincoln did not understand the case. The slaves were never asked to participate. Brown's remarkable technique for securing their participation was to send out a detail in the middle of the night, kidnap them, thrust a pike into their hands, and inform them that they were soldiers in the army of emancipation. He then expected them to place their necks in a noose without asking for further particulars.

Yet he was so supremely confident of their massive support that all the strange errors of October 16 and 17 sprang from that delusion. This was why he marched without rations; it was why thirteen of his twenty-one followers carried commissions as officers in their knapsacks, though none of his five Negro followers was included in this number—thirteen officers would hardly suffice to command the Negro troops who would swarm like bees to his headquarters; it was why he wanted the weapons at Harpers Ferry although he already had several times as many weapons as were needed for the men at the Maryland farm. Finally it was why he sat down at Harpers Ferry and waited while his adversaries closed the trap on him. He was still waiting for the word to spread and for the Negroes to come trooping in.

John Brown wanted to be a leader for the Negroes of America. He dwelled upon this idea almost to the exclusion of all others. Ultimately he died with singular bravery to vindicate his role. Yet he never thought to ask the Negroes if they would accept him as a leader, and if so, what kind of policy they wanted him to pursue. Of course he could not ask them all, but he never even asked Frederick Douglass or the gathering of Negroes at Chatham. He knew what he wanted them to do and did not really care what they themselves wanted to do. John Brown occupies and deserves a heroic place in the gallery of historic leaders of American Negroes. Yet, like many other prominent and less heroic figures in that gallery, he was a self-appointed savior, who was not chosen by the Negroes, who had no Negro following of any magnitude, and whose policies in the name of the Negro were not necessarily the policies of the Negroes themselves.

STUDY QUESTIONS

1. What is the "paradox of leadership among American Negroes?" What was the problem of the traditional relationship between black slaves and their white sympathizers?

2. During his childhood and early adulthood, what relationship did John Brown have with blacks?

3. What motivated John Brown to violently pursue the abolition of slavery? Was he a madman or a realistic reformer?

4. Before the raid on Harpers Ferry, what antislavery activities did Brown pursue? Would you consider him a "radical"?

5. How did Brown think he was going to lead a black rebellion without even consulting or informing blacks of his plans? What was the reason for such poor planning?

6. The raid on Harpers Ferry was an "unmitigated disaster" in Potter's opinion. Why?

7. In your opinion, was John Brown insane? Why or why not?

8. What was the "Spartacus complex"? Did it have any justification in reality? Why or why not?

BIBLIOGRAPHY

John Brown has not been forgotten—at least not by historians. In the 1970s, for example, he was the subject of four biographies. The most balanced biography of Brown is Stephen B. Oates, *To Purge This Land with Blood: A Biography of John Brown* (1970). Two older works that are also valuable are James C. Malin, *John Brown and the Legacy of Fifty-Six* (1942) and Garrison Villard, *John Brown, 1800–1859: A Biography Fifty Years After* (1910). James W. Davidson and Mark H. Lytle attempt a psychological interpretation of Brown in "The Madness of John Brown: The Uses of Psychohistory," *After the Fact: The Art of Historical Detection* (1982). James A. Rawley, *Race and Politics: "Bleeding Kansas" and the Coming of the Civil War* (1969) presents a fine introduction to the section where Brown acquired his initial fame. Students interested in psychohistory should consult Robert J. Lifton, ed., *Explorations in Psychohistory* (1974) and Bruce Mazlish, *Psychoanalysis and History* (1971).

Part Seven

CIVIL WAR AND RECONSTRUCTION

It seemed impossible. Threats and rumors of civil war, rebellion, and secession had circulated throughout the 1850s, but most Americans had confidently assumed they were just talk, not descriptions of what really could come to pass. But when South Carolina military forces fired on Union vessels trying to resupply Fort Sumter in 1861, the rumors suddenly became reality. War was at hand—a war few people wanted. With an attempt at optimism, many people assumed the rebellion would be a short-run affair, decided quickly in the first major military engagement. The Confederate victory at the first battle of Bull Run dashed those hopes. Four years later, the Civil War would prove to have been the bloodiest, most costly conflict in American history.

The sectionalism that brought on the Civil War was evident from the very beginning of the republic. Southerners were devoted to slavery as a source of cheap labor. Southerners also saw slavery as an institution of social control, a way of managing a large, alien black population. To protect their economy and society, Southerners preached a loyalty to laissez-faire and states' rights.

As long as the nation was confined east of the Appalachian Mountains, the North and South were able to coexist peacefully because the two sections were relatively isolated from each other. But early in the nineteenth century, tens of thousands of Americans began pouring into the western territories each year, forcing new issues on the political system. After the War of 1812, a balance of power existed in the United States Senate between free states and slave states, but each time a new territory applied for statehood, its permanent status as a "slave state" or "free state" had to be decided. Most Northerners came to oppose the expansion of slavery into the territories; Southerners believed the survival of their way of life depended on its expansion. Between 1820 and 1860, the country debated this fundamental issue repeatedly. The debate ultimately splintered the nation. Primarily because of their opposition to the expansion of slavery, the Republicans were anathema to the South, and when Abraham Lincoln won the presidency in 1860, the secession movement began.

Although the Civil War was not started as a crusade against slavery, it ended that way. The Emancipation Proclamation and the Thirteenth Amendment to the Constitution ended legal human bondage in the United States, and during Reconstruction Republicans worked diligently to extend full civil rights to former slaves. The Civil Rights Act of 1866 and the Fourteenth and Fifteenth Amendments to the Constitution were designed to bring the emancipated slaves into the political arena and build a respectable Republican party in the South.

Both goals were stillborn. When Congress removed the troops from the last Southern states in 1877, the old planter elite resumed control of Southern politics. They disenfranchised blacks and relegated them to second-class citizenship. The South became solidly Democratic.

As Reconstruction was coming to an end, another era was beginning. Out west, ambitious farmers were rapidly settling the frontier, while cattlemen were forging their own empire by supplying the eastern demand for beef. Civilization was again replacing a wilderness mentality with familiar political, economic, and social institutions. America was trying to forget about the divisions of the past and get on with the business of building a new society.

JOHNNY REB AND BILLY YANK

Bell I. Wiley

General George S. Patton, famous commander of the United States Third and Seventh Armies in Europe during World War II, once remarked that "compared to war, all other forms of human endeavor pale into insignificance." For him, there was an inherent majesty in mobilizing people and resources, as if humanity resembled divinity only in the organized production of death. He undoubtedly looked at the Civil War in the same way.

By the late spring of 1861, throughout the United States—in the North and in the Confederate South—young men were kissing sweethearts good-bye, marching off to war in a mood of confidence, exhilaration, and moral certitude, embarking on a noble adventure. Usually carrying the family rifle and mustering together in neighborhood armies, these young soldiers were setting out as communities to right wrongs and implement the will of God. Each side underestimated its opponent, expected brief engagements where bravery and morality would prevail, and anticipated early, triumphant returns home. In a matter of months, sometimes only weeks, the smell of death and the sickening realization that war might last indefinitely crushed all naive assumptions of a quick victory.

Altogether, more than 600,000 soldiers died during the Civil War, and that many more were wounded. The soldiers of the United States of America and the Confederate States of America shared the suffering and misery of modern combat, spoke the same language, and worshipped the same ideals, but they were not necessarily the same people. Differences existed between the common soldiers of the two armies, and those differences eventually played a critical role in the outcome of the conflict. In "Johnny Reb and Billy Yank," Bell I. Wiley describes the lives and motivations of ordinary people caught up in extraordinary events.

The common soldiers of North and South during the American Civil War were very much alike. As a general rule they came from similar backgrounds, spoke the same language, cherished the same ideals, and reacted in like manner to the hardships and perils of soldiering. They hated regimentation, found abundant fault with their officers, complained often about army rations, and hoped earnestly for speedy return to civilian life. Even so, men of the opposing sides presented some notable and interesting differences.

In the first place, Billy Yanks were more often of foreign background than were their opposites in gray. During the decades preceding the Civil War several million Europeans migrated to America and because of convenience, economic opportunity, and other influences, most of them settled in the North. In 1861 there were about four million persons of alien birth living in the states adhering to the Union as against only about one fourth of a million residing in the Southern Confederacy. Because the immigrants tended to identify themselves with the section in which they settled, far more of them donned the Union blue than the Confederate gray. Probably one out of every four or five Billy Yanks was of foreign birth and only one out of every twenty or twenty-five Johnny Rebs.

On the Northern side the Germans, aggregating about 200,000, were the most numerous of the foreign groups. Next were the Irish, numbering about 150,000, then Canadians and Englishmen each totalling about 50,000 and, down the line, lesser numbers of Scandinavians, Frenchmen, Italians, and other nationalities.

It has been estimated that 15,000 to 20,000 Irishmen marched in Confederate ranks and they apparently outnumbered any other foreign group

"Johnny Reb and Billy Yank" by Bell I. Wiley. This article is reprinted from the April 1968 issue of *American History Illustrated* 3, pp. 4–11, 44–47, with the permission of Cowles History Group, Inc. Copyright *American History Illustrated* magazine.

on the Southern side. But Canada, England, France, and Italy were well represented among wearers of the gray.

On both sides most of the foreigners were enlisted men, but many served as company and field grade officers and a considerable number attained the rank of general. Forty-five of the North's 583 general officers were of foreign birth, and among them were twelve Germans and twelve Irishmen. Among the Confederacy's 425 generals, there were nine foreigners of whom five were Irish.

In both armies the foreign groups added color and variety to camp life by singing their native songs, celebrating festive days, and observing customs peculiar to their homeland. St. Patrick's Day was always a great occasion among Irish units, featuring horse races, athletic contests, and consumption of large quantities of alcohol. As Pat and Mike lingered at flowing bowls their pugnacious tendencies were accentuated, and before night guardhouses were crowded with men suffering from cuts, bruises, or broken bones. Indeed, St. Patrick's Day sometimes produced more casualties among sons of Erin than did encounters on the battlefield.

In combat the foreigners gave a good account of themselves. Meagher's Irish Brigade was one of the best fighting units in the Civil War. Ezra J. Warner in *Generals in Blue* rates Prussian-born Peter J. Osterhaus as "certainly the most distinguished of the foreign-born officers who served the Union," and few, if any, division commanders of any nationality on either side had a better battle record than the Confederacy's beloved Irishman, Patrick R. Cleburne.

Among native participants two groups deserving special mention were the Indians and Negroes. The Confederacy had three brigades of [Indians], mostly Cherokees, Choctaws, and Seminoles. One of the Cherokees, Stand Watie, became a brigadier general. The Union Army had one brigade of Indians, most of whom were Creeks. Muster rolls of Indian units, filed in the National Archives, contain such names as Private Sweetcaller, Private Hog Shooter, Private Hog Toter, Private Flying Bird, and Lieutenant Jumper

Men and boys of every sort were called upon in the bloody war. Countless families were left at the end of the war with only a hurriedly taken photo to remind them of a loved one lost on the battlefield.

Duck. At the Battle of Honey Springs in 1864, Yankee Indians fought Rebel Indians. In combat Indians acquitted themselves well, but between battles they were poor soldiers, since they had only vague ideas of discipline and regimentation.

On the Confederate side, Negroes served almost exclusively in accessory capacities, as cooks, hostlers, musicians, and body servants. On March 13, 1865, after prolonged and acrimonious discussion the Confederate Congress passed a law authorizing recruitment of 300,000 slaves to serve as soldiers. A few companies were organized but the war ended before any of them could get into combat. It seems unreasonable to think that slaves would have fought with any enthusiasm for the perpetuation of their bondage. More than 188,000 Negroes, most of whom were ex-slaves, wore the Union blue. Despite discriminations in pay, equipment, and association with fellow soldiers, and notwithstanding the fact that they had to do far more than their share of labor and garrison duty, Negro Yanks fought well at Port Hudson, Milliken's Bend, Fort Wagner, the Crater, and other Civil War battles in which they participated.

Billy Yanks were better educated than Johnny Rebs, owning to the North's better schools and greater emphasis on public education. In some companies from the rural South, half of the men could not sign the muster rolls. Such companies were exceptional, but so were those that did not have from one to twenty illiterates. Sergeant Major John A. Cobb of the 16th Georgia Regiment wrote a kinsman on September 8, 1861: "Paying off soldiers is a good deal like paying off negroes their cotton money . . . about one third of the men in the regiment can't write their names, so the Pay Roll has a good many X (his mark) on it, and about one half of those that write them you can't read, nor could they themselves." Among Yanks the rate of illiteracy was highest in Negro units, but the typical Union regiment seems to have had no more than a half-dozen illiterates and many had none at all. On both sides, however, spelling and grammar frequently fell far below schoolroom standards. In soldier letters pneumonia sometimes appeared as *new mornion* or *new mony,* once as *wonst,* uneasy as *oneasy,* fought as *fit,* your as *yore* or *yorn,* and not any as *nary.* Other common usages were *tuck* for took, *purty* for pretty, *laig* for leg, and *shore* for sure. Long words were often divided, sometimes with strange results. One Reb complained about the "rashens" issued by a *comma sary;* another stated that he hoped to get a *fur low* when some more *volen teares* joined the *ridge ment.* A Yank wrote that he had been marching through mud that was *nea deap.* Another reported shortly after Lincoln ordered the organization of McClellan's forces into corps: "They are dividing the army up into corpses." While reading the letter of an Illinois soldier I was puzzled by the statement "I had the camp diary a few days ago," for I had not previously found indication that Civil War organizations kept unit journals. But my confusion was cleared up by the rest of the sentence which stated "but now I am about well of it." This soldier was suffering from a malady commonly known as the "Tennessee Quickstep."

A Yank who served under General Frederick Lander wrote in one of his letters: "Landers has the ganders." I read it just as it appeared, with a hard "g." On reflection I realized that the "g" was soft and that what the general really had was the jaundice. Landers was very unpopular with this particular Yank, so he added "I hope the old so and so dies." The next letter began: "Well old Landers is dead, and I'll bet he's down in hell pumping thunder at three cents a clap."

Soldiers in both armies frequently spelled hospital as "horsepittle," and that was a place which they abhorred almost as much as the devil himself. A Reb wrote that the hospital which served his unit "outstinks a ded horse."

Because of differences in northern and southern economy, Billy Yanks were more often town dwellers and factory workers than were Johnny Rebs. The contrast is vividly demonstrated in company descriptive rolls. The occupation columns on typical Southern rolls consist of a monotonous repetition of "farmer," while Northern rolls, except in the case of units recruited from agricultural communities, listed a wide assortment of occupations, including carpenters, clerks, coopers, shoemakers, bricklayers, printers, tinsmiths, mechanics, miners, plumbers, tailors, and boatmen. This diversity of skills among the rank and file gave the North a considerable advantage in what proved to be the first great modern war. It meant that if a wagon, steamboat, or locomotive broke down, or if a railroad needed rebuilding, or if a gun failed to function, a Northern commander could usually find close at hand soldiers who knew how to do the job.

Both during and after the war many people believed that the Confederate forces contained more boys and old men than did those of the Union. Study of descriptive rolls and other records indicates that this was an erroneous impression. There were many boys and old men on both sides. Charles Carter Hay enlisted in an Alabama regiment when he was 11 years old, and when four years later he surrendered at Appomattox he had not celebrated his 15th birthday. He had a counterpart on the Union side in the case of Johnny Clem, who began service as a drummer boy at age 9 in 1861, and who graduated to the fighting ranks after the Battle of Shiloh. E. Pollard enlisted in the 5th North Carolina Regiment at 73, but the oldest Civil War soldier apparently was 80-year-old Curtis King of the 37th Iowa, a non-combatant regiment known as the "Graybeards" because on its rolls there were 145 men who had passed their 60th birthday. But on both sides, most soldiers were neither very young nor very old. The largest single age group were the 18-year-olds, and three-fourths of the men fell in the age bracket 18–30.

Billy Yanks manifested a livelier interest in politics than did the men whom they opposed. This was due in part to the greater literacy of the

Northern soldiers and their easier access to newspapers. On the national level the nature of politics was a contributing factor. Because the Confederate Constitution provided a single term of six years for the Chief Executive, there was only one presidential campaign in the South during the war. This was a very dull affair because Jefferson Davis had no opposition. But in the North the campaign of 1864 between Lincoln and McClellan was a hard-fought contest, and most Yanks thought that the outcome would have a great impact on the prosecution of the war. Electioneering was lively in many units, and soldiers voted in impressive numbers. When ballots were tabulated it was found that the overwhelming majority had voted for "Uncle Abe" and continuance of war until the Union was restored.

Few, if any, other campaigns generated as much enthusiasm among Billy Yanks as did the Lincoln-McClellan contest, but even in the choice of governors, Congressmen, and lesser officials, the men in blue in their letters and diaries revealed considerably more interest than did wearers of the gray.

Billy Yanks' greater involvement in politics reflected a healthier interest in things intellectual, owing to the North's better schools, the more cosmopolitan character of its population, the more varied pattern of its economy, the presence in its borders of more large cities, the greater prosperity of its citizens, better communication, easier access to books and papers, greater freedom of thought and discussion, and sundry other advantages. Union soldiers manifested greater curiosity about things past and present than their opposites in Confederate service. Common soldiers on either side who showed a deep concern for philosophic aspects of the conflict were rare. But the North appears to have had considerably more than its share of the exceptions.

In their religious attitudes and activities Billy Yanks and Johnny Rebs manifested some notable contrasts. Letters and diaries of Southern soldiers contain more references to religion than do those of the men in blue, and Rebs were more emotional in their worship than were Billy Yanks. During the last two years of the conflict, great revivals swept over both the Eastern and Western armies of the Confederacy and men made open confessions of their sins, sought forgiveness at mourners' benches, and raised shouts of joy when relieved of the burden of guilt. Seasons of revival sometimes extended for several weeks as leading ministers from Richmond, New Orleans, Nashville, and other cities joined the army chaplains in promoting the cause of salvation. Revivals also took place in Northern units, but rarely did they extend beyond brigade or division. Certainly, the Union forces experienced no army-wide outbreaks of emotionalism such as occurred among Confederates.

The greater interest in religion manifested by Confederates and their greater susceptibility to revivalism was due to a combination of circumstances. The fact that Southerners were a more homogeneous people than Northerners and more often members of evangelistic sects made for greater religious zeal and emotionalism in Confederate camps. Another factor working to the same end was the South's greater ruralism. Still another factor was the example of high-ranking leaders. Robert E. Lee, Stonewall Jackson, and Leonidas Polk were deeply religious men and they showed far more interest in the spiritual welfare of their commands than did Grant, Sherman, and Sheridan. Jefferson Davis proclaimed more days of fasting and prayer and was more of a church man than was Abraham Lincoln.

The fortunes of war played a part in revivalism. The flood tides of emotionalism that swept over the Southern armies came after Vicksburg and Gettysburg, and to some extent they represent the tendency of a religiously rooted people in times of severe crises to seek supernatural deliverance from the woes that beset them.

The greater religiosity of the confederates does not seem to have produced a higher level of morality in Southern camps. Comments of soldiers, complaints of chaplains, court-martial proceedings, and monthly health reports indicate that profanity, gambling, drunkenness, fornication, and other "sins" flourished as much among Rebs as among Yanks.

The Northern soldiers generally were of a more practical and prosaic bent of mind than were Johnny Rebs. This difference was reflected in the Northerners' greater concern for the material things of life. Billy Yanks more often engaged in buying and selling and other side activities to supplement their army pay. Their letters contain far more references to lending their earnings at interest, investing for profit, and other financial ventures than do those written by the men in gray. Admittedly, Yanks had more money to write about, but their better remuneration, important though it was, was not enough wholly to account for the difference.

Billy Yanks' letters were not so fanciful or poetic as those of Johnny Rebs, nor were they as rich in humor and banter. The Northerners did not so frequently address wives and sweethearts in endearing terms as did their Southern counterparts. Correspondence of the men in blue contains much delightful humor, but I have yet to find any matching that exemplified by the following selections from Confederate sources: A Georgia Reb wrote his wife after absence of about a year in Virginia: "If I did not write and receive letters from you, I believe that I would forgit that I was married. I don't feel much like a maryed man, but I never forgit it so far as to court enny other lady but if I should you must forgive me as I am so forgitful." Another Georgian while on tour of duty in East Tennessee wrote his spouse: "lis, I must tell you that I have found me a Sweat hart heare. . . . I had our pictures taken with her handen me a bunch of flowers. . . . she lets on like she thinks a heep of me and when I told her I was marred she took a harty cry about it . . . she ses that she entends to live singel the balance of her days." A Tar Heel wrote a male friend at home: "Tommy I want you to be a good boy and tri to take cear of the wemmen and children tell I get home and we'll all have a chance. . . . I want you to go . . . and see my wife and children but I want you to take your wife with you [when you go]."

Billy Yank's reasons for fighting were different from those of Johnny Rebs. Some Yanks went to war to free the slaves. One of these was Chauncey Cooke of the 25th Wisconsin Regiment, who wrote home before he heard of Lincoln's issuance of the Emancipation Proclamation: "I have no heart in this war if the slaves cannot be free." But Cooke represented a minority. The overwhelming majority of those who donned the blue did so primarily to save the imperilled Union. Devotion to the Union found eloquent expression in some of their letters. Private Sam Croft, a youth from Pennsylvania, wrote his homefolk about a hard march in September 1861: "I have never once thought of giving out. . . . I am well, hardy, strong, and doing my country a little service. I did not come for money and good living. My Heart beats high and I am proud of being a soldier. When I look along the line of glistening bayonets with the glorious Stars and Stripes floating over them . . . I am proud and sanguine of success." Croft died at Gettysburg.

Most Rebs who commented on their individual motivation indicated that they were fighting to protect their families and homes against foreign invaders and they envisioned the invaders as a cruel and wicked foe. "Teach my children to hate them with that bitter hatred that will never permit them to meet without seeking to destroy each other," wrote a Georgia Reb to his wife in 1862.

Many Confederates were fighting for slavery, though this was rarely indicated in their letters. Usually they represented themselves as fighting for self-government, state rights, or "the Southern way of life." There is no doubt in my mind that most Southerners, non-slaveholders as well as planters, were earnestly desirous of maintaining slavery, not primarily as an economic system, but rather as an established and effective instrument of social control. A North Carolina private wrote a friend in 1863: "You know I am a poor man having none of the property said to be the cause of the present war. But I have a wife and some children to rase in honor and never to be put on an equality with the African race." Thus did one Reb who owned no Negroes avow that he was fighting for slavery; there were many others like him.

Billy Yanks were better fed and better clothed than Johnny Rebs. In the latter part of the war they frequently were better armed. Each side experienced ups and downs of morale, but generally speaking Confederate morale was higher than that of the Northerners during the first half of the war and lower during the second half. The nadir of Union morale came early in 1863, in the wake of Grant's reverses in Mississippi and Burnside's bloody defeat at Fredericksburg. Confederate morale plummeted after Vicksburg and Gettysburg, rose slightly in the spring and summer of 1864, and began its final unabated plunge after the re-election of Lincoln.

What of the combat performance of Johnny Rebs and Billy Yanks? The Southerners apparently fought with more enthusiasm than their opponents; and, after battle, in letters to the folk at home, they wrote more vividly and in greater detail of their combat experiences. In a fight they demonstrated more of dash, elan, individual aggressiveness, and a devil-may-care quality than Billy Yanks. But the men in blue seemed to have gone about the business of fighting with greater seriousness than Johnny Rebs, and they manifested more of a group consciousness and team spirit. In other words, the Rebs thought a battle was a thrilling adventure in which each man was to a large extent on his own; to Yanks it was a formidable task requiring the earnest and coordinated exertion of all those involved—not a gameshooting experience as some Rebs seemed to regard it, but a grim and inescapable chore that ought to be performed with as much efficiency and expedition as possible.

These differences were reflected in the battle cheers of the opposing forces. Southerners charged with the "Rebel yell" on their lips. This was a wild, highpitched, piercing "holler," inspired by a combination of excitement, fright, anger, and elation. The standard Yankee cheer, on the other hand, was a regularly intoned huzza or hurrah. The contrast between Southern and Northern cheering was the subject of much comment by participants on both sides. A Federal officer observed after the second battle of Manassas: "Our own men give three successive cheers and in concert, but theirs is a cheering without any reference to regularity of form—a continual yelling." A Union surgeon who was in the Wilderness Campaign of 1864 stated: "On our side it was a resounding, continuous hurrah, while the famous dread-inspiring 'Rebel yell' was a succession of yelps staccato and shrill."

Unquestionably Johnny Rebs made a better showing in combat during the first half of the war. This was due mainly to better leadership, particularly on the company and regimental levels. On both sides these officers were elected, and in the South, owing largely to the prevalence of the caste system, the successful candidates were usually planters or their sons—privileged persons, recognized community leaders, habituated to the direction of slaves, products of the military academies on which the region principally relied for education of its boys, and strongly indoctrinated with the spirit of *noblesse oblige.*

In the more democratic North, on the other hand, men were chosen as officers because of their effectiveness in persuading neighbors to sign up for military service. In many instances they were deficient in the essentials of leadership. By the summer of 1863, incompetent officers on both sides generally had been weeded out by resignation, dismissal, or hostile bullets. By that time also the Northerners had overcome the initial handicap of being less familiar with firearms than their opponents. During the last two years of the war, there was no discernible difference in the combat performance of Johnny Rebs and Billy Yanks. There was never any significant difference in their determination, pride, courage, devotion to cause, loyalty to comrades, and other basic qualities that go to make good soldiers. From the beginning to the end of the conflict the common soldiers of both sides acquitted themselves in a manner that merited the pride of their descendants and won for them a high standing among fighting men of all time.

STUDY QUESTIONS

1. What role did foreigners play in both armies? Why were foreigners more prominent in the Union Army? What impact might this have had on morale and organization?

2. To what extent did the South employ slaves as soldiers? Why were slaves not used more extensively as combat soldiers in the Confederate Army?

3. To what extent did northern and southern soldiers come from different demographic and economic backgrounds? What impact did these differences have on the outcome of the war?

4. Wiley claims that southern soldiers were more religious than northern soldiers. What evidence does he use to justify his claim?

5. When asked to describe their reasons for risking death in order to fight as soldiers, what explanations did northern soldiers offer? How did their responses differ from those of southern soldiers?

BIBLIOGRAPHY

For a general background study of American military history, see Walter Millis, *Arms and Men: A Study in American Military History* (1956) and Russell F. Weigley, *The American Way of War: A History of United States Military Strategy and Policy* (1973). A number of excellent works detail the history of the Civil War. One of the best general surveys is James G. Randall and David Donald, *The Civil War and Reconstruction* (1961). Also see Allan Nevins, *The War for the Union,* four volumes (1959–1972). Fred A. Shannon's *The Organization and Administration of the Union Army 1861–1865* (1928) and George W. Adams's *Doctors in Blue: The Medical History of the Union Army in the Civil War* (1952) both deal with the problems of mobilizing and caring for a modern army. Bell I. Wiley's *The Life of Johnny Reb* (1943) and *The Life of Billy Yank* (1952) describe the life of a typical soldier, as does Robert Cruden's *The War That Never Ended: The American Civil War* (1973). Stephen Crane's classic novel *The Red Badge of Courage* (1895) exposes the personal pain and tragedy of war. Also see Michael Barton, *Good Men: The Character of Civil War Soldiers* (1981) and Gerald F. Linderman, *Embattled Courage: Combat in the Civil War* (1987).

JOHN WILKES BOOTH AND THE POLITICS OF ASSASSINATION

James W. Clarke

"Right or wrong, God judge me, not man. For be my motive good or bad, of one thing I am sure, the lasting condemnation of the North." So began a letter John Wilkes Booth wrote shortly before his abortive attempt to abduct President Abraham Lincoln. When he later assassinated Lincoln, he was guaranteed the condemnation of the North and most of the South as well. John Wilkes Booth is America's most famous assassin. Hundreds of books and articles have been written about Booth, the assassination, and his motives. Was he a failed actor looking for theatrical immortality by playing a role of his own twisted invention? Were his motives rooted in some childhood trauma or in the need to compensate for some gnawing sense of inferiority? Or were his motives anchored in the external events of his life—the bloody Civil War, the hatred and opposition of Lincoln, the fear of emancipation?

In his book *American Assassins: The Darker Side of Politics,* James W. Clarke argues that not all assassinations can be dismissed simply as the actions of deranged men and women who had easy access to handguns and rifles. Often assassins are motivated by the political context of their age. In the following essay Clarke examines the political context of the Lincoln assassination.

It is commonly assumed that President Lincoln's assassin, John Wilkes Booth, killed to achieve the fame that had eluded him in a floundering career as an actor. Booth's stage career, it is reasoned, had never achieved the distinction of his famous father, the English-born tragedian Junius Brutus Booth, or his older brother Edwin. Realizing this in 1864, and confronted with a bronchial condition that threatened his ability to perform, Booth, in a classically compensatory manner, supposedly decided to resolve his personal disappointments and failures and achieve lasting fame by striking a dramatic political blow for the Confederate cause. Probably the most widely respected and quoted proponent of this view is Stanley Kimmel in his *The Mad Booths of Maryland.*

Drawing upon Kimmel, Booth has been dismissed elsewhere in even less qualified language as merely a deluded, acrobatic, noisy, and alcoholic actor. Other secondary work has imposed a rather strained psychoanalytic interpretation on this general explanation that goes even further in stressing Booth's neurotic motives. Yet even in Kimmel's carefully researched work, numerous facts appear that raise doubts about his interpretation.

The most important qualification of Kimmel's explanation, however, is that it virtually ignores the political context of the assassination: facts such as Lincoln's unpopularity in the North as well as the South, the vicious opposition within his cabinet and the Congress, and the controversy surrounding his re-election in 1864. To ignore the political circumstances and events of the Civil War era is to miss the most important element in Booth's motives. And virtually every account of the assassination that shares Kimmel's conclusion about Booth does just that.

In most cases, the omission is a result of the erroneous assumption that the nation's esteem and affection for Lincoln preceded his death. The fact is that until Appomattox, a week before his death, Lincoln was one of the most criticized and vilified presidents in American history, commonly referred to as "the baboon, the imbecile, the wet rag, the Kentucky mule." Although winning re-election in 1864 by a convincing margin (55 percent of the popular vote), that victory can be best understood, not in terms of Lincoln's personal popularity, but rather in terms of the ineffectiveness and confusion of the opposition—both within his own party as well as among his Democratic opponents—and a final reluctant resignation of party leaders to the principle that in time of war it is best not to change horses in midstream. When considered in this political context, the facts of Booth's life—both his upbringing and his career—suggest a different view of the man and his motives.

Youth and Career

John Wilkes Booth was born on May 10, 1838 near Baltimore. He was almost twenty-seven years of age when he shot himself in a burning barn surrounded by soldiers on April 26, 1865. Of the ten children born to Junius Brutus Booth and his second wife, Mary Ann Holmes Booth, John Wilkes, or "Johnny" as he was called, was their favorite. A beautiful child with shiny black hair and classically sculpted features, he exuded the brightness and exuberance of a happy childhood. His mother and his older sister Asia adored his kind and gentle ways, while his tempestuous but doting father admired his fiery spirit and athletic ability. As we will see, this positive view of Booth was shared by virtually everyone who ever knew him. He made friends easily and was loyal and generous to a fault. Even after he had achieved fame as an actor, Booth did not forget his childhood friends. Throughout his life his friendships endured, uncontaminated by his success, and they would span a sociological range from stable boys and clerks to debutantes and high-ranking public officials.

As a youth, Booth attended private schools where he studied history and the classics, reading Milton, Byron, and Shakespeare, and committing much of the latter to memory in preparation for a stage career virtually assured by family tradition. He also played the flute. He learned to ride early and well, and his sister later remembered fondly their spirited gallops together chasing imaginary villains through the wooded Maryland countryside. A lover of the outdoors, Booth's respect for living creatures prevented him from becoming the hunter and angler so encouraged by the culture of nineteenth-century America. Rather his interest ran toward botany and geology; he was an observer rather than a conqueror of nature. His sister described him as "very tender of flowers, and of insects and butterflies; lightning bugs he considered as 'bearers of sacred torches' and would go out of his way to avoid injuring them."

An unusually articulate youth, Booth's gaiety and exuberance for life had a contagious quality that partly explains his popularity with those who knew him. Often his activities were punctuated with melodramatic exclamations that delighted his friends. His sister recorded one occasion where he exclaimed:

Heaven and Earth! How glorious it is to live! how divine! to breathe this breath of life with a clear mind and healthy lungs! Don't let us be sad. Life is so short—and the world is so beautiful. Just to breathe is delicious.

Booth was fourteen when his famous father died in 1852. During his lifetime, the elder Booth had become the most famous Shakespearean actor in America. Although his career kept him away from home frequently during his son's formative years, there was no question of his love for the handsome boy who had inherited so much of the old man's spirit and flamboyance. Edwin, Booth's talented but more taciturn older brother, had spent a youthful stage apprenticeship with his father and thus logically assumed many of the roles and much of the acclaim previously enjoyed by the elder Booth. The oldest brother, Junius Brutus, Jr., was also an actor, but being some seventeen years older than John Wilkes, a sibling rivalry, which often placed strains on the relationship between the two younger brothers, never developed between them.

When Booth began his acting career at the age of seventeen, three years after his father's death, there is no question that some rivalry developed with respect to his by-now-famous older brother Edwin. No doubt both were intent on carrying on the proud and highly successful tradition their father had established. What is less clear, however, is the familiar contention that Booth fared less well in the views of audiences and critics than did Edwin—the basic premise of the argument upon which so many have explained the Lincoln assassination.

The evidence appears to support the premise only for the first three years of John's career, when his inexperience was acknowledged in his reviews. The sense of inferiority Kimmel claims Booth experienced during these early years of apprenticeship, performing in the shadow of a late and lamented father and an older brother, was no doubt justified. The fact that Booth had himself billed as "J. Wilkes" rather than invoking the renown of the Booth name attests to that fact. It also suggests Booth's desire to make a reputation on his own merits rather than capitalizing on the fame of his father and brother. Determined in this respect, Booth took his critical knocks, as most young actors do, as an obscure "J. Wilkes" before emerging triumphantly on the Richmond stage in the autumn of 1858 where he delighted audiences and was proclaimed then and until his death as the handsomest actor on the American stage.

The argument that Booth's sympathies for the Confederacy had their origins in the applause of Southern audiences and the critical disdain he received in the North has no basis in fact. After his first three apprenticeship years, Booth was never to receive a bad review—North or South. He was a star, a matinee idol whose talents approximated those of Edwin, while his physical attractiveness and flair on stage exceeded his older brother's and placed him in a position of undeniable ascendancy in the American theater. In fact, the only reservations about his abilities cited by Kimmel are those expressed by Edwin in private correspondence. Contrary to Edwin's assessment, Booth's reviews across the country were sufficiently enthusiastic to trigger professional envy from an older brother. Consider the following representative critical comments taken from Booth's reviews:

An artist of the highest order. [*Richard III,* New York, January 1862]

. . . the most brilliant [*Richard III*] *ever* played in the city. [Chicago, January-February 1862]

In Baltimore, his performances were thought superior to Edwin's. Even in New York where Edwin was a special favorite of theater audiences, complementary comparisons were made. His performances also cut through the typical Bostonian reserve of the *Daily Advertiser,* which allowed that with some reservations about "proper treatment of the voice," it was "greatly pleased" by his Richard III. When he returned to Boston in January 1863 for an appearance in *The Apostate* with brother Edwin in the audience, he was "wildly cheered."

In February of the same year, Booth played Macbeth at the Arch Street Theater in Philadelphia where one of his first appearances as a fledgling actor had been poorly received. Nearby at the Chestnut Street Theater, Edwin Forrest, perhaps America's first matinee idol, was performing in the same role. In a convincing demonstration of his great appeal, audiences ignored Forrest and lined up to see the handsome new star of the American stage—John Wilkes Booth. And reviews indicate that they were not disappointed. Advanced billings for Booth's April appearance as Richard III in Washington described him as "a star of the first magnitude." Reviewers later acknowledged that he had established himself as a reigning favorite in the capital. Attracted by such reviews, President Lincoln saw Booth perform in

John Wilkes Booth is infamous in American history because he assassinated President Abraham Lincoln.

The Marble Heart on November 9, 1863. Later that month, the Washington *Daily National Intelligencer* praised his performance of Romeo in the Shakespearean drama as "the most satisfactory of all renderings of that fine character."

Recognition of Booth's talents were not limited to audiences and critics only. Established professionals in the theater acknowledged his superior talents. John Ellsler, Director of the respected Cleveland Academy of Music, who knew and admired all the Booths, observed that John Wilkes had "more of (his famous father's) power in one performance than Edwin can show in a year." He went on to predict that John Wilkes Booth would become "as great an actor as America can produce."

Such appraisals continued as long and wherever Booth performed. At a March 1864 appearance in New Orleans, he gave an emotional performance before a typically appreciative audience in the same role and on the same stage where his father had given his last performance. Similar praise followed his engagements in Boston later that year, where crowds waited after the performance outside the stage exit hoping for another glimpse of the handsome actor as he left the theater. On November 25, 1864, he appeared for the first and last time with his brothers Edwin and Junius in *Julius Caesar* before an ecstatic audience of over two thousand "Bravo"-shouting New Yorkers who crowded the Winter Garden Theater for a command performance. Again, it should be emphasized that from 1858 through his last performance at Ford's Theater less than a month before the assassination, there is *no* evidence that Booth received other than the most complimentary reviews of his work.

In the context, it is surprising that he remained so well-liked by his peers in the acting profession. Although numerous young women succumbed to Booth's dashing good looks and personal charm, he remained a discrete and invariably kind and sensitive Lothario. Such refinement set him apart from the typical nineteenth-century American male; women found him irresistible. Clara Morris, a contemporary of Booth's on the American stage, described him as "so young, so bright, so gay, so kind." Recalling an incident where Booth, hurrying from the stage door of the theater, inadvertently knocked over a small child, the actress described how Booth picked up the little street urchin and carefully wiped the tears from his grimy face. Then satisfied that the child was not injured, Booth kissed him and pressed a pocketful of change into his hand before dashing off. The significance of the act was that it was so characteristic of Booth:

He knew of no witness to the act. To kiss a pretty clean child under the approving eyes of mamma might mean nothing but politeness, but surely it required the prompting of a warm and tender heart to make a young and thoughtful man feel for and caress such a dirty, forlorn bit of babyhood as that.

Nor was Booth's kindness and generosity confined to star-struck young women and children. He remained a close and loving son and brother to his mother and sister Asia. More interesting, however, is that men from seemingly all walks of life valued the friendship of the engaging young actor. Even male peers within his competitive and egocentric profession genuinely seemed to like and admire Booth. A fellow actor, Sir Charles Wyndham, described him as "a man of flashing wit and magnetic manner. He was one of the best raconteurs to whom I ever listened." Another actor who knew Booth explained that he was liked because of his quick good humor, his love of fun, and his unassuming ease with people regardless of social rank. He never permitted his celebrity status to become a barrier to old friends. He was also generous with his money.

Thus an accurate view of John Wilkes Booth— the view of his contemporaries—represents a stark contrast to the image of a frustrated, highly neurotic actor obsessed with achieving fame. Booth's character emerged out of a childhood of great love and affection—a beautiful, self-confident child who never knew unkindness or hardship. Raised in the cultured, if eccentric, environment of a theatrical aristocracy, the transition to the stage was swift, smooth, and highly successful. The acclaim denied to so many in the acting profession was well within grasp by his twenty-first year. By the time of his death, some six years later, his reputation as a fine actor and matinee idol was established. Booth's popularity and success were reflected in his income: in 1862, he wrote that he was averaging 650 dollars per week for his performances—an extraordinary sum for that period. At the time of his death, even after he had cut his performances drastically because of his war-related activities, he wrote that he was earning "more than twenty-thousand dollars a year."

To bolster the unconvincing explanation that professional jealously and an obsessive "greed for fame" motivated Booth, the argument, as previously observed, has also been made that he was threatened with a loss of his voice due to a recurring bronchial condition. Recognizing that his career was limited, he then supposedly turned to political extremism only as a means of eclipsing a loathesome brother's theatrical ascendancy. While this argument cannot be substantiated or denied in the absence of medical evidence, it is true that Booth's sixth performance in New Orleans in March, 1864 was cancelled because of a "cold." But there is simply no other evidence attesting to the alleged seriousness or chronic nature of this problem as Kimmel suggests. Rather it is *assumed* that Booth had permanently damaged his voice and was thus forced to acknowledge that his acting career was over. It is further *assumed* that this circumstance heightened his "neurotic sense of inferiority." Such is the highly questionable basis of the Kimmel explanation.

The Political Context

Political events in 1864, rather than assumptions about chronic laryngitis and sibling rivalry, provide a more accurate context in which to assess Booth's motives. Nearing the completion of his first term in office, Abraham Lincoln enjoyed none of the esteem accorded to him after his death. Lincoln had been elected president, a minority candidate of an upstart new party, with less than 40 percent of the popular vote. He had won only because the Democratic party had divided ranks with two candidates, J. C. Breckenridge and Stephen A. Douglas, splitting 47.5 percent of the vote while the remaining 12.6 percent went to Constitutional Union party candidate John Bell. Undaunted by his lack of a popular mandate, Lincoln quickly embarked upon a course of action with a single overriding purpose in mind—the restoration of the Union between the North and South.

Needless to say, Lincoln was hated in the rebellious states. Not so obvious in history texts, however, was his unpopularity in the North, where growing opposition to the war required drastic—some would say dictatorial—executive actions to control the festering and volatile dissent. Lincoln quickly, and on his own initiative, suspended the constitutionally guaranteed writ of *habeas corpus* and authorized the arbitrary arrest of any sus-

pected opponents of his war policies. In 1863, for example, some 38,000 persons were arrested in the North and imprisoned without trial for suspected anti-war activities. Soon after the first shots were fired at Fort Sumter, he had—without Congressional approval—called up the militia and expanded the size of the regular army. He arbitrarily, and again without congressional approval, transferred some two million dollars to Union agents in New York for assistance in stifling the anti-war movement. Ignoring Congress, he instituted unpopular conscription in 1862 by executive order. He aggressively appointed and removed a succession of politically ambitious Union generals before finding a satisfactory commander in Grant. He issued the Emancipation Proclamation, freeing the slaves in the rebellious states without consulting Congress. He issued executive orders establishing provisional courts in conquered states and appointed military governors in Arkansas, Louisiana, and Tennessee without Congressional approval or clear constitutional authority. In general, President Lincoln ignored the Congress and the Constitution during his first term in office and dramatically exploited his executive authority.

A nation averse to strong central government, sympathetic to states' rights, and embued with notions of Jacksonian democracy did not respond kindly to this unimpressive-looking, obscure midwesterner who was presiding over the bloodiest war in American history with the iron hand of a despot—a war that would kill and maim over a million American boys, many of them drafted as reluctant participants in what had become an All-American holocaust. Such negative public sentiments were reflected most vigorously in the Congress, where Lincoln was especially reviled by members of his own party. He was also condemned and ridiculed by his own cabinet appointees. Prominent and influential newspaper editors charged him with abuses ranging from incompetence to war profiteering. On one side, Democrats blasted him for waging an unconstitutional war against political self-determination; on the other, radical Republicans condemned his restraint in prosecuting the war. By 1864, it was difficult to identify any important segment of support for the President. Strong criticism had developed in the North in response to costly military defeats at Southern hands, racist opposition to emancipation, and resistance to the draft in an exceedingly bloody war to free Negroes most Northerners considered less than human.

Opposition to Lincoln and the draft was particularly vigorous in New York and Philadelphia, as well as smaller towns on the eastern seaboard and Ohio, Kentucky, and Wisconsin in the Midwest, not to mention the strong Southern sympathy in the marginally loyal Border States. Following on the heels of New York Governor Horatio Seymour's denunciation of Lincoln in a July Fourth speech in 1863, draft resisters rioted in New York City, attacking blacks and abolitionists in a murderous three-day rampage.

By early 1864, many prominent Union supporters considered Lincoln's presidency an unqualified failure; it was certain that his renomination would be challenged. As the peace movement grew in 1864, influential newspapers in New York and Philadelphia attacked the use of black soldiers and condemned the Emancipation Proclamation. Moreover, Lincoln's vilification was not confined to this country: London papers also sneered at his manners and ridiculed his homeliness while condemning his policies.

A discouraged Lincoln anticipated defeat in 1864 and prepared a memorandum on the transition as serious challenges to his re-nomination were mounted by Salmon P. Chase, his Treasury Secretary, and former general and "Great Pathfinder" John C. Fremont, as well as another general, Benjamin Butler. Largely as a result of the fragmented quality of his opposition, rather than his own popularity, Lincoln was finally re-nominated in Baltimore by an unenthusiastic party amid feelings of sullen resentment. Prominent Union supporters such as William Cullen Bryant, Theodore Tilton, and Horace Greeley considered Lincoln a failure as president but saw no acceptable alternative.

Undoubtedly, the curious nomination and party platform of opposition Democrats contributed importantly to the beleaguered Lincoln's subsequent re-election. The Democrats nominated another former general, George McClellan, as a candidate committed, like Lincoln, to an uncompromising military solution to the war. They then saddled the general with an incongruous peace platform written by chief anti-war advocate and vice-presidential nominee Clement L. Vallandigham—a man who had been arrested and deported to the South by a military court for his treasonous Confederate sympathies. Confronted with a choice between such a contradiction or the unpopular Lincoln, the electorate held its nose and voted for the incumbent, giving him an unanticipated impressive victory.

Lincoln's surprising re-election and mandate signaled an ominous message for the South. Given Lincoln's unpopularity in the North and the growing anti-war sentiment in that part of the country, many war-weary Southerners had prayed for his defeat and a negotiated end to the war that would recognize, as many Northern papers advocated, an independent Confederacy. The loss of life on both sides during Grant's Wilderness Campaign in May and June 1864 was staggering—an estimated 90,000 casualties. Lincoln, like another president a hundred years and a different war later, was widely blamed for this carnage that many, anticipating a shorter, less costly war, now considered unnecessary. For the South, his re-election meant that the destructive war of attrition Grant was now conducting would grind on toward its humiliating ultimate objective—unconditional surrender. It was a time of desperation in the South. Lincoln, as Commander in Chief of the Union armies now intent on destroying men, not merely capturing territory, was intensely hated throughout the South. The *Richmond Examiner* asked: "What shall we call him? Coward, assassin, savage, murderer of women and babies? Or shall we consider them all embodied in the word of fiend, and call him Lincoln the Fiend."

Booth's Politics and Plan

Few persons loved the South and hated Abraham Lincoln more than John Wilkes Booth. From the beginning of the war, Booth had made his Southern sympathies clear in the most outspoken and unequivocal manner. His hatred for the President was both personal and political, and it grew more intense as the conflict dragged on. He held Lincoln responsible for a bloody and unnecessary war and, as a man of some refinement, he was contemptuous of what he saw as Lincoln's personal coarseness of style and manner. In Booth's eyes, Lincoln was not qualified by birth or training to be president.

As a performer, Booth was permitted to travel throughout the country—North and South—during the war. He used this privilege to smuggle quinine and other war-related material, as well as information, into the South at every opportunity. As prospects for a Southern victory began to dim after Lee's defeat at Gettysburg in 1863, Booth's activities intensified. By 1864, he was preoccupied with the war effort, severely curtailing his professional commitments—not because of bad reviews or throat problems—but because his priorities were now elsewhere.

It is worth noting that Booth's theatrical tours regularly took him to areas of the most intense opposition to the President. In addition to Southern cities, Booth regularly toured New York, Philadelphia, and Baltimore, not to mention the capital itself where the anti-war movement was very strong. It is little wonder that he correctly viewed himself as participating in a widely popular cause.

In September 1864, the same month that Lincoln was renominated for a second term, Sherman's forces swept through Atlanta burning and pillaging as they went. To the north, Lee's army was being forced into a last stand outside Richmond. The situation for the Confederates was desperate. It was at this time that Booth became part of a plan to abduct the President so that subsequently Lincoln could be ransomed for the release of Confederate prisoners of war who were sorely needed to restore Lee's badly depleted ranks. In October, Booth went to Montreal on the first of many trips he would make across the border over the next few months to meet with Con-

federate agents. While there, he opened a bank account and packed his theatrical wardrobe and paraphernalia in a trunk for future shipment to Richmond. Any doubts about the plan were put aside with Lincoln's November re-election. It was now evident that drastic measures would be required to prevent Southern defeat.

Various alternatives were discussed by Confederate agents: plots to sabotage government ships and buildings; raids from Canada on cities such as Buffalo, Detroit, and New York: attacks on prisoner of war camps to release Confederate soldiers; a plot to burn New York City; and a plan to distribute clothes infested with yellow fever, smallpox, and other contagious diseases in Washington—all desperate measures to stem the tide of a war going very badly.

In this context, the plan to abduct the President seems less bizarre. Earlier in April 1864, General Grant had refused a Confederate proposal for a prisoner exchange; a successful abduction could possibly achieve that end. In any case, it was worth the gamble. In November, Booth initiated actual preparations to carry out the abduction. He began to recruit among old friends and acquaintances for persons willing to assist in the operation. He also made trips into southern Maryland to plan the route by which the handcuffed president would be transported across Southern lines. During the year, Booth had spent large sums of his own money in such espionage activities.

Intent on having his purpose and motives for the abduction clearly understood, Booth drafted a sealed letter of explanation and left it with his sister Asia's husband, John Sleeper Clarke, for safekeeping. The letter, which remained unopened until it was discovered after the assassination, reveals the scope and depth of Booth's feeling and his rationale for his anticipated crime:

My Dear Sir:
You may use this as you think best. But as some may wish to know when, who and why, and as I know not how to direct, I give it (in the words of your master).

To whom it may concern,

Right or wrong, God judge me, not man. For be my motive good or bad, of one thing I am sure, the lasting condemnation of the North.

I love peace more than life. Have loved the Union beyond expression. For four years I have waited, hoped and prayed for the dark clouds to break, and for the restoration of our former sunshine. To wait longer would be a crime. All hope for peace is dead. My prayers have proved as idle as my hopes. God's will be done. I go to see and share the bitter end.

I have ever held the South were right. The very nomination of Abraham Lincoln, four years ago, spoke plainly war—war upon Southern rights and institutions. His election proved it. Await an overt act. Yet, till you are bound and plundered. What folly! The South was wise. Who thinks of argument or patience when the finger of his enemy presses the trigger? In a foreign war, I too, could say, country right or wrong. But in a struggle such as ours where the brother tries to pierce the brother's heart, for God's sake, choose the right. When a country like this spurns justice for her side, she forfeits the allegiance of every honest free man, and should leave him untrammelled by any fealty soever, to act as his own conscience may approve.

People of the North, to hate tyranny, to love liberty and justice, to strike at wrong and oppression, was the teaching of our fathers. The study of our early history will not let me forget it and may it never.

This country was formed for the white man and not for the black. And looking upon African slavery from the same standpoint as held by the noble framers of our Constitution, I, for one, have ever considered it one of the greatest blessings for themselves and for us that God ever bestowed upon a favored nation. Witness heretofore our wealth and power; witness their elevation and enlightenment above their race elsewhere. I have lived among it most of my life, and have seen less harsh treatment from master to man than I have beheld in the North from father to son. Yet heaven knows that no one *would be more willing to do more for the negro race than I, could I but see a way* to *still better their* condition.

But Lincoln's policy is only preparing the way to their total annihilation. The South are not nor have they been fighting for the continuance *of slavery. The first battle of Bull Run did away with that idea. The causes since for war have been as* noble, and greater far than those that urged our fathers on. Even though we should allow that they were wrong at the beginning of this contest, cruelty and injustice *have made the wrong become the right, and they now stand before the wonder and admiration of the world, as a noble band of patriotic heroes. Hereafter reading of* their deeds, *Thermopylae will be forgotten.*

When I aided in the capture and execution of John Brown who was a murderer on our western border, who was fairly tried and convicted *before an impartial judge and jury, of treason, and who by the way, has since been made a god, I was proud of my little share in the transaction, for I deemed it my duty, and that I was helping our common country to perform an act of justice. But what was a crime in poor John Brown is now considered by themselves as the greatest and only virtue of the Republican party. Strange transmigration. Vice is to become a virtue, simply because more* indulge *in it.*

I thought then, as now, that the Abolitionists were the only traitors *in the land, and that the entire party deserved the same fate as poor old Brown, not because they wish to abolish slavery, but on account of the means they have endeavored to use to effect that abolition. If Brown were living, I doubt whether he* himself would set slavery against the Union. Most, or many in the North do, and openly curse the Union, if the South are to return and attain a single right *guaranteed to them by every tie which we once* revered as sacred. *The South can make no choice. It is either extermination or slavery* for themselves *worse than death to draw from. I know* my *choice.*

I have also studied hard to discover upon what grounds the right of a state to secede has been denied, when our name, United States and Declaration of Independence, both provide for secession. But this is no time for words. I write in haste. I know how foolish I shall be deemed for undertaking such a step as this, where on one side I have my friends and every thing to make me happy, where my profession alone has gained me an income of more than *twenty thousand dollars a year, and where my great personal ambition in my profession has such a great field of labor. On the other hand the South have never bestowed upon me one kind word, a place where I have no friends except beneath the sod: a place where I must either become a private soldier or a beggar.*

To give up all the former *for the* latter, *besides my mother and sisters whom I love so dearly, although they differ so widely in opinion, seems insane; but God is my judge. I love* justice *more than a country that disowns it; more than fame and wealth; heaven pardon me, if wrong, more than a happy home. I have never been upon the battle field, but, O my countrymen, could all but see the* reality *or effects of this horrid war, as I have seen them in* every state *save Virginia, I know you would think like me, and would pray the Almighty to create in the Northern mind a sense of* right and justice *even should it possess no seasoning of mercy, and then he would dry up this sea of blood between us, which is daily growing wider. Alas, poor country, is she to meet her threatened doom? Four years ago I would have given a thousand lives to see her as I have always known her, powerful and unbroken. And even now I would hold my life as naught, to see her what she was. O, my friends, if the fearful scenes of the past four years had never been enacted or if what had been done were but a frightful dream from which we could now awake with over-flowing hearts, we could bless*

our God and pray for his continued favor. How I have loved the old flag *can never be known.*

A few years since the world could boast of none so pure and spotless. But of late I have been seeing and hearing of the bloody deeds *of which she has been* made the emblem, *and would shudder to think how changed she has grown. Oh, how I have longed to see her break from the midst of blood and death that circles round her folds, spoiling her beauty and tarnishing her honor! But no: day by day she has been dragged deeper into cruelty and oppression, till now in my eyes her once bright red striped look [like]* bloody gashes *on the face of heaven.*

I look now upon my early admiration of her glories as a dream.

My love as things stand today is for the South alone. Nor do I deem it a dishonor in attempting to make for her a prisoner of this man to whom she owes so much misery. *If success attends me, I go penniless to her side They say she has found that last ditch which the North has so long derided and been endeavoring to force her in, forgetting they are our brothers, and it is impolite to goad an enemy to madness. Should I reach her in safety and find it true, I will proudly beg permission to triumph or die in that same ditch by her side.*

A Confederate doing duty on his own responsibility.

J. Wilkes Booth

Booth coolly and rationally recruited five men (all of whom he had known earlier) to assist him: John Surratt, a Confederate spy and a person well acquainted with the geography of southern Maryland; David Herold, a simpleminded but extremely loyal person who also knew the country; George Atzerodt, an experienced boatman who was familiar with the river crossings that would be required; Lewis Payne[1],

---

[1]Variously known as Lewis Powell or Lewis Paine.

a burly, physically powerful ex-Confederate soldier familiar with firearms; and finally, another ex-Confederate soldier, an old boyhood friend, Samuel Arnold. The qualifications of all but possibly Herold, who had only his loyalty to recommend him, suggest Booth's choices were not as ill-considered as some have made them out to be. A number of other persons were indirectly involved in the conspiracy (and theories abound about those who were not involved but were aware of the plot), but these were the main actors.

The plan was to abduct Lincoln on his way to the play, "Still Waters Run Deep," which was being performed at the Soldier's Home on the outskirts of Washington. On either March 16 or 20[2], 1865, the conspirators prepared for the abduction. They hoped to stop the President's carriage, overpower him and any aides (he was rarely escorted by more than one), then drive the handcuffed chief executive south where fresh horses would carry the group beyond to the protection of the Confederate lines.

The plan failed, however, because Lincoln did not appear. Rather, he had asked Treasury Secretary and political adversary Salmon P. Chase to go in his place. The carriage of a startled Chase was stopped by a group of riders, who, seeing the President was not on board, then galloped off.

Military events soon made it clear that abduction was no longer a viable strategy. Lee's army could not hold its positions at Petersburg much longer without an enormous sacrifice of life; surrender appeared inevitable. But on April 4, Confederate President Jefferson Davis, fearing the terms of surrender, urged a continuation of the war as guerrilla campaign "operating in the interior . . . where supplies are more accessible, and where the foe will be far removed from his own base." He went on to ask the South for a renewed commitment to "render our triumph certain."

Lee, closer to the suffering of his troops than the truculent Davis, saw no reason to continue a senseless slaughter. On April 7, he asked for terms, and

two days later he formally surrendered his army. Desperate, Davis continued to press for a continuation of the war west of the Mississippi. With General Joe Johnston's Confederate army still in the field blocking Sherman's way north, he reasoned, perhaps there was a way out yet. Davis, the Southern zealot, was grasping for straws. So was Booth.

The Assassination

After the abduction plot had failed, Booth began to consider other more drastic measures that could throw the Union war effort into disarray permitting the South to regroup militarily long enough, at least, to enhance the possibility of a negotiated settlement rather than an unconditional surrender dictated by the despised Lincoln. The plan that evolved was to strike down by assassination key government and military leaders, thus producing complete chaos in Washington. The targets: the President, Vice President Andrew Johnson, Secretary of State William H. Seward (who would become President in the event of the death of a succeeding Vice President), and General Ulysses S. Grant, commander of the Union army. In so doing, the conspirators hoped to eliminate in one stroke the government's formal political and military leadership.

On April 14, after learning of the President's theater plans with General Grant, a determined Booth decided that this was the opportunity he had been awaiting. It was time to strike. He again wrote a letter to explain what he was about to do and gave it to a fellow actor, John Matthews, in a sealed envelope instructing him to deliver it personally to the publisher of the *National Intelligencer* the next day. An unnerved Matthews tore open the letter after the assassination, then fearing the consequences of having it in his possession, destroyed it. He recalled the closing paragraph, however:

The moment has at length arrived when my plans [to abduct] must be changed. The world may censure me for what I am about to do, but I am sure posterity will justify me.

---

[2]The exact date remains uncertain.

To this Booth signed his name and those of fellow conspirators Payne, Atzerodt, and Herold. Reserving for himself the President and General Grant, who was expected to accompany the President, Booth assigned Atzerodt to kill Vice President Johnson and Payne to kill Secretary of State Seward with Herold's assistance.

Why did Booth choose a public theater for the act? And why the leap to the stage after the fatal shot, unless it was for recognition? Booth's choice of Ford's Theater was in part fortuitous, but it was also a very rational, calculating decision. As a famous actor, he had unlimited access to Ford's. This meant that he could enter and leave the theater when and where he pleased without questions. Thus, he could enter and climb the stairs to the President's box without suspicion. He leaped to the stage after the shooting because that was the quickest, most direct way out of the crowded theater. To go back down the stairs and through the lobby would have meant almost certain capture. This is not to suggest that Booth was averse to the publicity. As his letters and diaries indicate, he was convinced that what he was doing was right and that public opinion would support the elimination of this "tyrant" who had ruled the country and had conducted the bloodiest war in American history. But the desire for notoriety, in this case, was a distinctly secondary consideration—neither necessary nor sufficient as a motive for his act.

Except for whatever fleeting personal satisfaction Booth may have derived from Lincoln's death, the plan was a failure: Payne's attempt to kill Seward ended bloody but unsuccessful; Atzerodt could not bring himself to execute a man he did not know: he made no attempt on the Vice President's life. Grant had declined the President's theater invitation because of plans to visit a daughter in New Jersey. Thus, only the President died.

The conspirators, except for John Surratt, were quickly arrested, although much controversy surrounded the investigation of the conspiracy and many questions remained about its thoroughness and the possibility of other conspirators.[3] If it hadn't been for Booth's broken leg, which he suffered in his leap to the stage, he and the ever faithful Davy Herold, who accompanied him on his flight toward an anticipated sanctuary in Virginia, might have escaped.

Booth's diary records his despair after the event as he realized that his act was poorly timed and misunderstood. The Nation was tired of killing after four long years of war. North and South, a war-weary nation welcomed Appomattox. A year earlier, the result may have been different, but except for zealots like Jefferson Davis and Booth, Americans were ready to lay down their arms and return to their homes and farms. Now in great pain, making his way through the Maryland swamps, Booth wrote:

> *April, 13, 14, Friday, The Ides*
> *Until today nothing was ever thought of sacrificing to our country's wrongs. For six months we have worked to capture. But our cause being almost lost, something decisive and great must be done. But its failure was owing to others who did not strike for their country with a heart. I struck boldly, and not as the papers say. I walked with a firm step through a thousand of his friends, was stopped but pushed on. A colonel was at his side. I shouted Sic semper before I fired. In jumping I broke my leg. I passed all his pickets. Rode sixty miles that night, with the bone of my leg tearing the flesh at every jump.*
> *I can never repent it, though we hated to kill. Our country owed all our troubles to him, and God simply made me the instrument of his punishment.*[4]

---

[3]David Herold, George Atzerodt, Lewis Payne, and Mary Surratt (the latter in a highly questionable judgement) were hanged on July 7, 1865. Other conspirators not directly involved, Samuel Arnold, Samuel Mudd, Edward Spangler, and Michael O'Laughlin were given prison sentences. John Surratt escaped to Europe. After his capture in Cairo in November 1866, he was returned to the country for trial. He was released in August 1867 after the jury failed to reach a verdict.
[4]The final phrase of this sentence is often cited out of context as evidence of Booth's alleged delusion of divine inspiration.

The country is not what it was. This forced union is not what I have loved. I care not what becomes of me. I have no desire to outlive my country. This night [before the deed] I wrote a long article and left it for one of the editors of the National Intelligencer, *in which I fully set forth our reasons for our proceedings. He or the Gov't. . . . (the entry ends)[5]*

A week later, a depressed Booth laments that his act has been misunderstood:

Friday 21

After being hunted like a dog through swamps, woods, and last night being chased by gunboats till I was forced to return wet, cold, and starving, with every man's hand against me, I am here in despair. And why? For doing what Brutus was honored for—what made Tell a hero. And yet I, for striking down a greater tyrant than they ever knew, am looked upon as a common cut-throat. My action was purer than either of theirs. One hoped to be great.[6] The other had not only his country's, but his own, wrongs to avenge. I hoped for no gain. I knew no private wrong. I struck for my country and that alone. A country that groaned beneath this tyranny, and prayed for this end, and yet now behold the cold hand they extend me. God cannot pardon me if I have done wrong. Yet I cannot see my wrong, except in serving a degenerate people. The little, the very little, I left behind to clear my name, the government will not allow to be printed (the letter he had left with John Matthews). So ends all. For my country I have given up all that makes life sweet and holy, brought misery upon my family, and am sure there is no pardon in the Heaven for me, since man condemns me so. I have only heard of what has been done (except what I did myself), and it fills me with horror. God, try and forgive me, and bless my mother. Tonight I will once more try the river with the intent to cross. Though I have a greater desire and almost a mind to return to Washington, and in a measure clear my name—which I feel I can do. I do not repent the blow I struck. I may before my God, but not to man. I think I have done well. Though I am abandoned, with the curse of Cain upon me, when, if the world knew my heart, that one blow would have made me great, though I did desire no greatness.

Tonight I try to escape these blood-hounds once more. Who, who can read his fate? God's will be done. I have too great a soul to die like a criminal. O, may He, may He spare me that, and let me die bravely.

I bless the entire world. Have never hated or wronged anyone. This last was not a wrong, unless God deems it so, and it's with Him to damn or bless me. And for this brave boy with me, who often prays (yes, before and since) with a true and sincere heart—was it crime in him? If so, why can he pray the same?

I do not wish to shed a drop of blood, but "I must fight the course." 'Tis all that's left me.

Given the tone and intensity of Booth's remarks, it is difficult to take seriously an often-quoted subsequent remark he allegedly made to a farm girl, who, unaware of who he was, said to him that she thought Lincoln's assassin had killed for money. Booth was said to have replied that in his opinion "he wasn't paid a cent, but did it for notoriety's sake."

Had Booth been seeking the fame he already possessed, it is likely that he would have welcomed a well-publicized trial where he could have spoken with the dramatic persuasiveness of the skilled actor he was in his own defense. He could have given expression to the many eloquent political statements he had penned in letters and diary. Rather, he chose to die alone "bravely." With that in mind, as he leaned heavily on a crutch, surrounded by Union troops who

---

[5]In the last incomplete sentence, Booth probably intended to express his frustration that "he [John Matthews] or the Gov't" suppressed his letter of explanation.

[6]The sentence, "One hoped to be great" is also cited out of context as evidence of Booth's alleged desire for fame, despite the fact that the reference is clearly to another earlier assassin.

had encircled his refuge in a barn, he shouted back when asked to surrender:

Captain, I know you to be a brave man, and I believe you to be honorable: I am a cripple. I have got but one leg; if you withdraw your men in "line" one hundred yards from the door, I will come out and fight you.

When the officer-in-charge replied that it was his intention to take him and Herold prisoners. Booth shouted back: "Well, my brave boys, prepare a stretcher for me." He then negotiated with the soldiers to permit his panicked companion to surrender alone. Soon after Herold left the barn, it was set afire by the soldiers. Seeing no other honorable alternative, Booth raised his pistol and fired a shot behind his right ear, smashing instead his spinal column and leaving him paralyzed but conscious to die a slow agonizing death. Throughout an ordeal so painful that he pleaded to be killed, he did not recant on his principles. Shortly before he died, he whispered to a soldier bending over him, "Tell mother I die for my country."

Conclusions

Much of the misunderstanding about Booth and his motives has been the result of the failure to consider the political context of his actions. It has been assumed that Lincoln was the revered leader in life that he became after his death: the fact that his assassination is frequently referred to as a martyrdom attests to this point. Thus, it has been further assumed that only a deranged person could have killed so noble a human being. Consequently, writers have interpreted virtually every aspect of Booth's life from this incorrect perspective. As I have indicated, it is unlikely that a "ham" actor would have received the consistently good reviews that Booth did. It is also unlikely that a person consumed with the egocentric and anxiety-induced needs for acclaim attributed to Booth would have had so very many friends and admirers from all walks of life.

Booth was wrong, obviously, on moral grounds; moreover, he was wrong politically, as subsequent events illustrated. But he was not deranged, nor did he kill for neurotic compensatory or nihilistic reasons. His motives were more akin to those of the German officers who conspired and attempted to kill Hitler to end the madness of World War II than they were to a deranged person. Such a conclusion is difficult to accept because it conflicts so directly with the mythology surrounding a slain national hero. But during most of his presidency, Abraham Lincoln was viewed by many Americans, especially in the South, as a cruel, despotic man. As a more restrained but still bitter Jefferson Davis wrote some years later about Lincoln, "[The South] could not be expected to mourn" an enemy who had presided over such misery.

STUDY QUESTIONS

1. Discuss Booth's background. Was there anything in his early life that would suggest psychological troubles?

2. Was Booth an unsuccessful actor? Did his career play a part in his assassination of Lincoln?

3. Describe the political climate in America in 1864 and early 1865. How do political tensions help to explain Booth's actions?

4. How did Booth support the Confederacy during the Civil War? What do Booth's letter and diary entries indicate about his personality and motives?

5. How rational were Booth's plans to abduct and then to assassinate Lincoln?

6. What was Booth's motive for assassinating Lincoln?

BIBLIOGRAPHY

The literature on Abraham Lincoln and his assassination is enormous. The Library of Congress lists more books on Lincoln than any other individual save Jesus and William Shakespeare. The best place to begin to examine the circumstances surrounding Lincoln's assassination is William Hanchett, *The Lincoln Murder Conspiracies* (1983). Harold M. Hyman, *With Malice Toward Some: Scholarship (or Something Less) on the Lincoln Murder* (1978) is also outstanding. Stanley Kimmel, *The Mad Booths of Maryland* (1969) presents the thesis that Booth's actions were psychologically motivated. Jim Bishop, *The Day Lincoln Was Shot* (1955) presents a popularized account of the assassination. Margaret Leech, *Reveille in Washington, 1861–1865* (1945) describes the feelings toward Lincoln during the Civil War.

THE KNIGHTS OF THE RISING SUN

Allen W. Trelease

The Civil War, which started in 1861 and ended in 1865, was like a nightmare come true for most Americans. More than 600,000 young men were dead, countless others wounded and permanently maimed, and the South a prostrate ruin. For the next twelve years, northern Republicans tried to "reconstruct" the South in a chaotic crusade mixing retribution, corruption, and genuine idealism. Intent on punishing white Southerners for their disloyalty, northern Republicans, especially the Radicals, tried to extend full civil rights—via the Fourteenth and Fifteenth Amendments—to the former slaves. For a variety of reasons, the attempt at giving equality to southern blacks failed, and by 1877 political power in the South reverted to the white elite.

A major factor in the failure of Radical Republicans to "reconstruct" the South was the rise of the Ku Klux Klan. Enraged at the very thought of black political power, the Klan resorted to intimidation and violence, punishing southern blacks even suspected of sympathizing with Radicals' goals for the South. In "The Knights of the Rising Sun," historian Allen W. Trelease describes Klan activities in Texas during the late 1860s. Isolated from the main theaters of the Civil War, much of Texas remained unreconstructed, and the old white elite, along with their Klan allies, succeeded in destroying every vestige of black political activity and in eliminating the Republican party from the political life of the state.

Large parts of Texas remained close to anarchy through 1868. Much of this was politically inspired despite the fact that the state was not yet reconstructed and took no part in the national election. In theory the Army was freer to take a direct hand in maintaining order than was true in the states which had been readmitted, but the shortage of troops available for this duty considerably lessened that advantage. At least twenty counties were involved in the Ku Klux terror, from Houston north to the Red River. In Houston itself Klan activity was limited to the holding of monthly meetings in a gymnasium and posting notices on lampposts, but in other places there was considerable violence.

By mid-September disguised bands had committed several murders in Trinity County, where two lawyers and both justices of the peace in the town of Sumter were well known as Klansmen. Not only did the crimes go unpunished, but Conservatives used them to force a majority of the Negroes to swear allegiance to the Democratic party; in return they received the familiar protection papers supposedly guaranteeing them against further outrage. "Any one in this community opposed to the Grand Cyclops and his imps is in danger of his life," wrote a local Republican in November. In Washington County the Klan sent warning notices to Republicans and committed at least one murder. As late as January 1869 masked parties were active around Palestine, shaving heads, whipping, and shooting among the black population, as well as burning down their houses. The military arrested five or six men for these offenses, but the Klan continued to make the rounds of Negroes' and Union men's houses, confiscating both guns and money. Early in November General J. J. Reynolds, military commander in the state, de-

clared in a widely quoted report that "civil law east of the Trinity river is almost a dead letter" by virtue of the activities of Ku Klux Klans and similar organizations. Republicans had been publicly slated for assassination and forced to flee their homes, while the murder of Negroes was too common to keep track of. These lawless bands, he said, were "evidently countenanced, or at least not discouraged, by a majority of the white people in the countries where [they] are most numerous. They could not otherwise exist." These statements did not endear the general to Conservative Texans, but they were substantially true.

The worst region of all, as to both Klan activity and general banditry, remained northeast Texas. A correspondent of the Cincinnati *Commercial* wrote from Sulphur Springs early in January 1869:

Armed bands of banditti, thieves, cut-throats and assassins infest the country; they prowl around houses, they call men out and shoot or hang them, they attack travellers upon the road, they seem almost everywhere present, and are ever intent upon mischief. You cannot pick up a paper without reading of murders, assassinations and robbery. . . . And yet not the fourth part of the truth has been told; not one act in ten is reported. Go where you will, and you will hear of fresh murders and violence. . . . The civil authority is powerless—the military insufficient in number, while hell has transferred its capital from pandemonium to Jefferson, and the devil is holding high carnival in Gilmer, Tyler, Canton, Quitman, Boston, Marshall, and other places in Texas.

Judge Hardin Hart wrote Governor Pease in September to say that on account of "a regularly organized band which has overrun the country" he could not hold court in Grayson, Fannin, and Hunt counties without a military escort.

Much of this difficulty was attributable to outlaw gangs like those of Ben Bickerstaff and Cullen Baker, but even their activities were often racially and politically inspired, with Negroes and Union men the chief sufferers. Army officers and soldiers reported that most of the population at Sulphur Springs was organized into Ku Klux clubs affiliated with the Democratic party and some of the outlaws called themselves Ku Klux Rangers. At Clarksville a band of young men calling themselves Ku Klux broke up a Negro school and forced the teacher to flee the state.

White Conservatives around Paris at first took advantage of Klan depredations among Negroes by issuing protection papers to those who agree to join the Democratic party. But the marauding reached such proportions that many freedmen fled their homes and jobs, leaving the crops untended. When a body of Klansmen came into town early in September, apparently to disarm more blacks, some of the leading citizens warned them to stop. The freedmen were not misbehaving, they said, and if they needed disarming at a later time the local people would take care of it themselves. Still the raiding continued, and after a sheriff's posse failed to catch the culprits the farmers in one neighborhood banded together to oppose them by force. (Since the Klan had become sacred among Democrats, these men claimed that the raiding was done by an unauthorized group using its name. They carefully denied any idea of opposing the Klan itself.) Even this tactic was ineffective so far as the county as a whole was concerned, and the terror continued at least into November. The Freedmen's Bureau agent, Colonel DeWitt C. Brown, was driven away from his own farm thirty miles from Paris and took refuge in town. There he was subjected to constant threats of assassination by Klansmen or their symphathizers. From where he stood the Klan seemed to be in almost total command.

The Bureau agent at Marshall (like his predecessor in the summer) suspected that the planters themselves were implicated in much of the terrorism. By driving Negroes from their homes just before harvest time the Klan enabled many landowners to collect the crop without having to pay the laborers' share.

Jefferson and Marion County remained the center of Ku Klux terrorism, as the Cincinnati reporter pointed out. A garrison of twenty-six men under Major James Curtis did little to deter violence. Bands of hooded men continued to make noctural depredations on Negroes in the surrounding countryside during September and October as they had for weeks past. "Whipping the freedmen, robbing them of their arms, driving them off plantations, and murdering whole families are of daily, and nightly occurrence," wrote the local Bureau agent at the end of October, "all done by disguised parties whom no one can testify to. The civil authorities never budge an inch to try and discover these midnight marauders and apparently a perfect apathy exists throughout the whole community regarding the general state of society. Nothing but martial law can save this section as it is at present. . . ." Inside town, Republicans hardly dared go outdoors at night, and for several weeks the county judge, who was afraid to go home even in the daytime, slept at the Army post. The local Democratic newspapers, including the *Ultra Ku Klux,* encouraged the terror by vying with one another in the ferocity of their denunciations of Republicans.

Major Curtis confirmed this state of affairs in a report to General Reynolds:

Since my arrival at the Post . . . [in mid-September] I have carefully observed the temper of the people and studied their intentions. I am constrained to say that neither are pacific. The amount of unblushing fraud and outrage perpetrated upon the negroes is hardly to be believed unless witnessed. Citizens who are esteemed respectable do not hesitate to take every unfair advantage. My office is daily visited by large numbers of unfortunates who have had money owing them, which they have been unable to obtain. The moral sense of the community appears blunted and gray headed apologists for such men as Baker and Bickerstaff can be met on all the street corners. . . . The right of franchise in this section is a farce. Numbers of negroes have been killed for daring to be Radicals, and their houses have so often been broken into by their Ku Klux neighbors in search of arms that they are now pretty well defenseless. The civil officers cannot and will not punish these outrages. Cavalry armed with double-barrelled shotguns would soon scour the country and these desperadoes be met on their own ground. They do not fear the arms that the troops now have, for they shoot from behind hedges and fences or at night and then run. No more notice is taken here of the death of a Radical negro than of a mad dog. A democratic negro however, who was shot the other day by another of his stripe, was followed to his grave through the streets of this city by a long procession in carriages, on horseback, and on foot. I saw some of the most aristocratic and respectable white men in this city in the procession.

On the same night that Curtis wrote, the new Grand Officers of the Knights of the Rising Sun were installed in the presence of a crowd of 1,200 or 1,500 persons. "The town was beautifully illuminated," a newspaper reported, "and the Seymour Knights and the Lone Star Club turned out in full uniform, with transparencies and burners, in honor of the occasion." Sworn in as Grand Commander for the ensuing twelve months was Colonel William P. Saufley, who doubled as chairman of the Marion County Democratic executive committee. Following the installation "able and patriotic speeches" were delivered by several notables, including a Democratic Negro.

As usual, the most hated Republican was the one who had the greatest Negro following. This was Captain George W. Smith, a young Union army veteran from New York who had settled in Jefferson as a merchant at the end of the war. His business failed, but the advent of Radical Reconstruction opened the prospect of a successful political career; at the age of twenty-four Smith was elected to the state constitutional convention by the suffrage of the Negro majority around Jefferson. At the convention, according to a perhaps overflattering posthumous account, he was recognized as one of the abler members. "In his daily life he was correct, almost austere. He never drank, smoked, chewed, nor used profane language." However, "he was odious as a negro leader, as a

radical, as a man who could not be cowed, nor scared away." Smith may also have alienated his fellow townspeople by the strenuous efforts he made to collect debts they owed him. Even a few native Republicans like Judge Charles Caldwell, who was scarcely more popular with Conservatives, refused to speak from the same platform with him. As his admirer pointed out, Smith "was ostracized and his life often threatened. But he refused to be scared. He sued some of his debtors and went to live with colored people." One day, as he returned from a session of the convention, his carpet-bag—perhaps symbolically—was stolen, its contents rifled, and a list of them published in a local newspaper.

The beginning of the end for Smith came on the night of October 3, after he and Anderson Wright, a Negro, had spoken at a Republican meeting. As he opened the door of a Negro cabin to enter, Smith was fired upon by four men outside including Colonel Richard P. Crump, one of Jefferson's leading gentry. Smith drew his revolver and returned the fire, wounding two of the assailants and driving them away. He then went to Major Curtis at the Army post. Here Crump, with the chief of police and others, soon arrived bearing a warrant for his arrest on a charge of assault. The attackers' original intention to kill Smith now assumed greater urgency because he and several Negroes present had recognized their assailants. Smith objected strenuously to their efforts to get custody of him, protesting that it was equivalent to signing his death warrant. Nevertheless Curtis turned him over to the civil authorities on their assurance of his safety. Smith was taken off to jail and a small civilian guard was posted around it. The major was uneasy, however, and requested reinforcements from his superior, but they were refused.

The next day there were signs in Jefferson of an assembling of the Knights of the Rising Sun. Hoping to head off a lynching, Curtis dispatched sixteen soldiers (the greater part of his command) to help guard the jail. At 9 P.M., finally, a signal was sounded—a series of strokes on a bell at the place where the Knights held their meetings. About seventy members now mobilized under the command of Colonel Saufley and proceeded to march in formation toward the jail; they were in disguise and many carried torches. The jail building lay in an enclosed yard where at that time four black men were confined for a variety of petty offenses. One of the prisoners was Anderson Wright, and apparently the real reason for their being there was that they had witnessed the previous night's attempt to murder Smith; they may even have been fellow targets at that time. When the Knights reached this enclosure they burst through it with a shout and overpowered the guard, commanded by a young Army lieutenant. The invaders then turned to the Negro prisoners and dragged them into some adjoining woods. Wright and a second man, Cornelius Turner, managed to escape from them, although Wright was wounded; the other two prisoners were shot nearly to pieces. As soon as Major Curtis heard the shooting and firing he came running with his remaining soldiers; but they too were quickly overpowered. Repeatedly the major himself tried to prevent the mob from entering the jail building in which Smith was confined, only to be dragged away from the door each time. They had no trouble unlocking the door, for city marshall Silas Nance, who possessed the key, was one of the conspirators.

At first Smith tried to hold the door shut against their entry. Eventually failing at this, he caught the foremost man, pulled him into the room, and somehow killed him. "It is common talk in Jefferson now," wrote a former Bureau agent some months later, "that Capt. Smith killed the first man who entered—that the Knights of the Rising Sun afterward buried him secretly with their funeral rites, and it was hushed up, he being a man from a distance. It is an established fact that one Gray, a strong man, who ventured into the open door, was so beaten by Capt. Smith that he cried, 'Pull me out! He's killing me!' and he was dragged out backward by the leg." All this took place in such darkness that the Knights could not see their victim. Some of them now went outside and held torches up to the small barred window of Smith's cell. By this light they were able to shoot him four times. "The door was burst open and the crowd surged in upon him as he fell, and then, man after man, as

By 1868 the Ku Klux Klan had become a full fledged terrorist organization, involving community members of all classes and veterans of the Confederate army.

they filed around fired into the dying body. This refinement of barbarity was continued while he writhed and after his limbs had ceased to quiver, that each one might participate in the triumph."

Once the mob had finished its work at the jail it broke up into squads which began patrolling the town and searching for other Republican leaders. County Judge Campbell had anticipated trouble earlier in the evening and taken refuge as usual at Major Curtis' headquarters. Judge Caldwell was hated second only to Smith after his well-publicized report as chairman of the constitutional convention's committee on lawlessness.

Hearing the shooting around the jail, he fled from his home into the woods. In a few moments twenty-five or thirty Knights appeared at the house, looking for him. Some of the party were for killing him, and they spent two hours vainly trying to learn his whereabouts from his fifteen-year-old son, who refused to tell. Another band went to the house of G. H. Slaughter, also a member of the convention, but he too escaped.

The next day the few remaining white Republicans in town were warned by friends of a widely expressed desire to make a "clean sweep" of them. Most of them stayed at the Haywood House hotel the following night under a military guard. Meanwhile the KRS scoured the city looking for dangerous Negroes, including those who knew too much about the preceding events for anyone's safety. When Major Curtis confessed that the only protection he could give the white Republicans was a military escort out of town, most of them decided to leave. At this point some civic leaders, alarmed at the probable effects to the town and themselves of such an exodus under these circumstances, urged them to stay and offered their protection. But the Republicans recalled the pledge to Smith and departed as quickly as they could, some openly and others furtively to avoid ambush.

White Conservatives saw these events—or at least their background and causes—in another light. They regarded Smith as "a dangerous, unprincipled carpet-bagger" who "lived almost entirely with negroes, on terms of perfect equality." Whether there was evidence for it or not, they found it easy to believe further that this "cohabitation" was accompanied by "the most unbridled and groveling licentiousness"; according to one account he walked the streets with Negroes in a state of near-nudity. For at least eighteen months he had thus "outraged the moral sentiment of the city of Jefferson," defying the whites to do anything about it and threatening a race war if they tried. This might have been overlooked if he had not tried repeatedly to precipitate such a collision. As head of the Union League he delivered inflammatory speeches and organized the blacks into armed mobs who committed assaults and robberies and threatened to burn the town. When part of the city did go up in flames earlier in the year Smith was held responsible. Overlooking the well-attested white terrorism which had prevailed in the city and county for months, a Democratic newspaper claimed that all had been peace and quiet during Smith's absence at the constitutional convention. But on his return he resumed his incendiary course and made it necessary for the whites to arm in self-defense.

According to Conservatives the initial shooting affray on the night of October 3 was precipitated by a group of armed Negroes with Smith at their head. They opened fire on Crump and his friends while the latter were on their way to protect a white man whom Smith had threatened to attack. Democrats did not dwell over long on the ensuing lynching, nor did they bother to explain the killing of the Negro prisoners. In fact the affair was made deliberately mysterious and a bit romantic in their telling. According to the Jefferson *Times,* both the soldiers and the civilians on guard at the jail characterized the lynch party as "entirely sober and apparently well disciplined." (One of the party later testified in court that at least some of them had put on their disguises while drinking at a local saloon.) "After the accomplishment of their object," the *Times* continued, "they all retired as quietly and mysteriously as they came—none knowing who they were or from whence they came." (This assertion, it turned out, was more hopeful than factual.)

The *Times* deplored such proceedings in general, it assured its readers, but in this case lynching "had become . . . an unavoidable necessity. The sanctity of home, the peace and safety of society, the prosperity of the country, and the security of life itself demanded the removal of so base a villain." A month later it declared: "Every community in the South will do well to relieve themselves [*sic*] of their surplus Geo. Smiths, and others of like ilk, as Jefferson rid herself of hers. This is not a healthy locality for such incendiaries, and no town in the South should be." Democratic papers made much of Judge Caldwell's refusal to appear publicly with Smith—which was probably inspired by his Negro associations. They claimed that Smith's fellow Republicans were also glad to have him out of the way, and noted that the local citizens had assured them of protection. But there was no mention of the riotous search and the threats upon their lives which produced that offer, nor of their flight from the city anyway.

The Smith affair raises problems of fact and interpretation which appeared in almost every Ku Klux raid across the South. Most were not so fully examined or reported as this, but even here it is impossible to know certainly where the truth lay. Republican and Democratic accounts differed diametrically on almost every particular, and both were colored by considerations of political and personal interest. But enough detailed and impartial evidence survives to sustain the Republican case on most counts. Negro and republican testimony concerning the actual events in October is confirmed by members of the KRS who turned state's evidence when they were later brought to trial. Smith's prior activities and his personal character are less clear. Republicans all agreed later that he was almost puritanical in his moral code and that he was hated because of his unquestioned social associations and political influence with the blacks. He never counseled violence or issues threats to burn the town, they insisted; on the contrary, on the only time he ever headed a Negro crowd was when he brought a number of them to help extinguish the fire which he was falsely accused of starting.

As elsewhere in the South, the logic of some of the charges against Smith is not convincing. Whites had a majority in the city and blacks in the county. Theoretically each could gain by racial-violence, offsetting its minority status. But Conservatives always had the advantage in such confrontations. They were repeatedly guilty of intimidating the freedmen, and in case of an open collision everyone (including Republicans) knew they could win hands down. Democrats were certainly sincere in their personal and political detestation of Smith; almost as certainly they were sincere in their fears of his political activity and what it might lead to. From their viewpoint an open consorter with and leader of Negroes was capable of anything. It was easy therefore to believe the worst and attribute the basest motives without clear evidence. If some Negroes did threaten to burn the town—often this was a threat to retaliate for preceding white terrorism—it was easy to overlook the real cause and attribute the idea to Smith. The next step, involving hypocrisy and deliberate falsehood in some cases, was to charge him with specific expressions and activities which no other source substantiates and which the logic of the situation makes improbable. Men who practiced or condoned terrorism and murder in what they conceived to be a just cause would not shrink from character assassination in the same cause.

Interestingly enough, most of the character assassination—in Smith's case and generally—followed rather than preceded Ku Klux attacks. This did not arise primarily from a feeling of greater freedom or safety once the victim was no longer around to defend himself; some victims, unlike Smith, lived to speak out in their own behalf. Accusations after the fact were intended rather to rationalize and win public approval of the attack once it had occurred; since these raids were the product of at least semi-secret conspiracy there was less need to win public approval beforehand. Sometimes such accusations were partially true, no doubt, and it was never easy for persons at a distance to judge them; often it is no easier now. Democrats tended to believe and Republicans to reject them as a matter of course. The *Daily Austin Republican* was typical of Radical papers in its reaction to Democratic newspaper slurs against Smith after his death: "We have read your lying sheets for the last *eighteen* months, and this is the first time you have made any such charges. . . ." It was surely justified in charging the Democratic editors of Texas with being accessories after the fact in Smith's murder.

The military authorities had done almost nothing to stop KRS terrorism among the Negroes before Smith's murder, and this violence continued for at least two months afterward. Similar conditions prevailed widely, and there were to few troops—especially cavalry—to patrol every law-less county. But the murder of a white man, par-ticularly one of Smith's prominence and in such a fashion, aroused officials to unwonted activity. The Army recalled Major Curtis and sent Colonel H. G. Malloy to Jefferson as provisional mayor with orders to discover and bring to justice the murder-ers of Smith and the two freedmen killed with him. More troops were also sent, amounting ulti-mately to nine companies of infantry and four of cavalry. With their help Malloy arrested four of Jefferson's leading men on December 5. Colonel W. P. Saufley, whom witnesses identified as the or-ganizer of the lynching, would have been a fifth, but he left town the day before on business, a De-mocratic newspaper explained, apparently un-aware that he was wanted. (This business was to take him into the Cherokee Indian Nation and per-haps as far as New York, detaining him so long that the authorities never succeeded in apprehending him.) That night the KRS held an emergency meet-ing and about twenty men left town for parts un-known while others prepared to follow.

General George P. Buell arrived soon afterward as commandant, and under his direction the ar-rests continued for months, reaching thirty-seven by early April. They included by common repute some of the best as well as the worst citizens of Jefferson. Detectives were sent as far as New York to round up suspects who had scattered in all directions. One of the last to leave was General H. P. Mabry, a former judge and a KRS leader who was serving as one of the counsel for the defense. When a soldier revealed that one of the prisoners had turned state's evidence and identified Mabry as a leader in the lynching, he abruptly fled to Canada.

The authorities took great pains to recover Anderson Wright and Cornelius Turner, the Negro survivors of the lynching, whose testimony would be vital in the forthcoming trials. After lo-cating Wright, General Buell sent him with an Army officer to find Turner, who had escaped to New Orleans. They traveled part of the way by steamboat and at one point, when the officer was

momentarily occupied elsewhere, Wright was set upon by four men. He saved himself by jumping overboard and made his way to a nearby Army post, whence he was brought back to Jefferson. Buell then sent a detective after Turner, who eventually was located, and both men later testi-fied at the trial.

The intention of the authorities was to try the suspects before a military commission, as they were virtually sure of acquittal in the civil courts. Defense counsel (who consisted ultimately of eleven lawyers—nearly the whole Jefferson bar) made every effort to have the case transferred; two of them even went to Washington to appeal personally to Secretary of War Schofield, but he refused to interfere. R. W. Loughery, the editor of both the Jefferson *Times* and the *Texas Republi-can* in Marshall, appealed to the court of public opinion. His editorials screamed indignation at the "terrible and revolting ordeal through which a refined, hospitable, and intelligent people are passing, under radical rule," continually subject to the indignity and danger of midnight arrest. He also sent requests to Washington and to Northern newspapers for intercession against Jefferson's military despotism. The prisoners, he said, were subject to brutal and inhuman treatment. Lough-ery's *ex parte* statement of the facts created a mo-mentary ripple but no reversal of policy. In reality the prisoners were treated quite adequately and were confined in two buildings enclosed by a stockade. Buell released a few of them on bond, but refused to do so in most cases for the obvious reason that they would have followed their broth-ers in flight. Although they seem to have been de-nied visitors at first, this rule was lifted and friends regularly brought them extra food and del-icacies. The number of visitors had to be limited, however, because most of the white community regarded them as martyrs and crowded to the prison to show their support.

After many delays the members of the military commission arrived in May and the trial got under way; it continued into September. Although it proved somewhat more effective than the civil courts in punishing Ku Klux criminals, this tribunal was a far cry from the military despotism depicted by its hysterical opponents. The defense counsel presented their case fully and freely. Before long it was obvious that they would produce witnesses to swear alibis for most or all of the defendants. Given a general public conspiracy of this magnitude, and the oaths of KRS members to protect each other, this was easy to do; and given the dependence of the prosecution by contrast on Negro witnesses whose credibility white men (including Army officers) were accustomed to discounting, the tactic was all too effective. The results were mixed. At least fourteen persons arrested at one time or another never went to trial, either for lack of evidence or because they turned state's evidence. Seventeen others were tried and acquitted, apparently in most cases because of sworn statements by friends that they were not present at the time of the lynching. Only six were convicted. Three of these were sentenced to life terms, and three to a term of four years each in the Huntsville penitentiary. General Reynolds refused to accept the acquittal of Colonel Crump and three others, but they were released from custody anyway, and the matter was not raised again. Witnesses who had risked their lives by testifying against the terrorists were given help in leaving the state, while most of the defendants returned to their homes and occupations. The arrests and trials did bring peace to Jefferson, however. The Knights of the Rising Sun rode no more, and the new freedom for Radicals was symbolized in August by the appearance of a Republican newspaper.

Relative tranquillity came to northeast Texas generally during the early part of 1869. Some Republicans attributed this to the election of General Grant, but that event brought no such result to other parts of the South. Both Ben Bickerstaff and Cullen Baker were killed and their gangs dispersed, which certainly helped. The example of military action in Jefferson likely played a part; it was accompanied by an increase of military activity throughout the region as troops were shifted here from the frontier and other portions of the state. Immediately after the Smith lynching in October, General Reynolds ordered all civil and military officials to "arrest, on the spot any person wearing a mask or otherwise disguised." Arrests did increase, but it was probably owing less to this order than to the more efficient concentration of troops. In December the Bureau agent in Jefferson had cavalry (for a change) to send out after men accused of Ku Klux outrages in Upshur County. Between October 1868 and September 1869 fifty-nine cases were tried before military commissions in Texas, chiefly involving murder or aggravated assault; they resulted in twenty-nine convictions. This record was almost breathtaking by comparison with that of the civil courts.

The Texas crime rate remained high after 1868. Organized Ku Klux activity declined markedly, but it continued in sporadic fashion around the state for several years. A new state government was elected in November 1869 and organized early the next year under Republican Governor E. J. Davis. In his first annual message, in April 1870, Davis called attention to the depredations of disguised bands. To cope with them he asked the legislature to create both a state police and a militia, and to invest him with the power of martial law. In June and July the legislature responded affirmatively on each count. The state police consisted of a mounted force of fewer than 200 men under the state adjutant general; in addition, all county sheriffs and their deputies and all local marshals and constables were considered to be part of the state police and subject to its orders. In November 1871 a law against armed and disguised persons followed. Between July 1870 and December 1871 the state police arrested 4,580 persons, 829 of them for murder or attempted murder. Hundreds of other criminals probably fled the state to evade arrest. This activity, coupled with occasional use of the governor's martial law powers in troubled localities, seems to have diminished lawlessness by early 1872. There still remained the usual problems of prosecuting or convicting Ku Klux offenders, however, and very few seem to have been punished legally.

STUDY QUESTIONS

1. Why was Klan terrorism so rampant in Texas? Why didn't the federal government intercede?

2. What was the relationship between the Ku Klux Klan in Texas and the Democratic party?

3. How did well-to-do white planters respond to the Ku Klux Klan?

4. What were the objectives of the Ku Klux Klan in Texas?

5. Who were the White Conservatives? How did they interpret Klan activities?

6. Why did the state government try to curtail Klan activities in the early 1870s? Were these efforts successful?

BIBLIOGRAPHY

The standard work on Reconstruction, one which created two generations of stereotypes by vindicating the South and indicting the North, is William A. Dunning, *Reconstruction, Political and Economic* (1907). The first major dissent from Dunning was W. E. B. DuBois's classic work *Black Reconstruction* (1935). It was not until the social changes of the 1960s, triggered by the civil rights movement, that historians took a new look at the Reconstruction. John Hope Franklin's *Reconstruction After the Civil War* (1961) first questioned the Dunning view, arguing that northern intentions toward the South were humanitarian as well as political. Kenneth Stampp's *The Era of Reconstruction* (1965) carried that argument further, restoring the reputation of "carpetbaggers" and "scalawags," describing the successes of black politicians, and criticizing the Ku Klux Klan. Also see Allen Trelease, *White Terror* (1967); Sarah Wiggins, *The Scalawag in Alabama Politics, 1865–1881* (1977); L. N. Powell, *New Masters: Northern Planters During the Civil War and Reconstruction* (1980); and Paul D. Escott, *Many Excellent People* (1985). For studies of Andrew Johnson, see Howard K. Beale, *The Critical Year: A Study of Andrew Johnson and Reconstruction* (1930), which takes the traditional point of view. A very critical view is Eric McKitrick, *Andrew Johnson and Reconstruction* (1960). Also see Michael Benedict, *The Impeachment of Andrew Johnson* (1973).

DAY OF THE LONGHORNS

Dee Brown

The Texas Longhorn looked slightly unbalanced, as if it were about to fall over. Its body often appeared thin, and its horns stretched out like the curved balancing rod of a high-wire performer. And its face—only another Longhorn or a Texan could love it. Nevertheless, this rugged breed of steer was the focus of the long drives during the dusty, golden age of cowboys.

Ironically, this era of the cowboy was made possible by the westward push of railroad builders. After the Civil War, a three- or four-dollar Texas Longhorn could be sold in the upper Mississippi region for forty dollars. If Texas entrepreneurs could drive the steers to the railheads, they could earn a $100,000 profit from 3,000 head of cattle. And so the drive was on, first to Sedalia, Missouri, and later, as railways extended west, to the Kansas cow towns of Newton, Abilene, Ellsworth, and Dodge City. During the late 1860s and 1870s, over four million cattle survived the heat, dust, Indian attacks, and other problems and reached the Kansas railroads. Dee Brown describes the difficult journey and the Longhorns—and the cowboys who drove them to the railheads.

When Coronado marched northward from Mexico in 1540, searching for the mythical golden cities of Cibola, he brought with his expedition a number of Spanish cattle. These were the first of the breed to enter what is now the United States. Over the next century other Spanish explorers and missionaries followed, most of them bringing at least "a bull and a cow, a stallion and a mare." From these seed stocks, Longhorns and mustangs and cowboys and ranching slowly developed in the Southwest, the Spanish cattle mutating and evolving, the vaquero perfecting his costume and the tools of his trade.

The Longhorns, which also came to be known as Texas cattle, took their name from their wide-spreading horns which sometimes measured up to eight feet across, and there are legends of horn spreads even more extensive. From their mixed ancestry of blacks, browns, reds, duns, slates, and brindles the Longhorns were varicolored, the shadings and combinations of hues so differentiated that, as J. Frank Dobie pointed out, no two of these animals were ever alike in appearance. "For all his heroic stature," said Dobie, "the Texas steer stood with his body tucked up in the flanks, his high shoulder-top sometimes thin enough to split a hail stone, his ribs flat, his length frequently so extended that his back swayed."

Ungraceful though they were, the Longhorns showed more intelligence than domesticated cattle. They were curious, suspicious, fierce, and resourceful. After all, by the mid-nineteenth century they were the survivors of several generations which had lived under wild or semiwild conditions. They possessed unusually keen senses of smell, sight, and hearing; their voices were powerful and penetrating; they could survive extreme heat or cold; they could exist on the sparest of veg-

etation and water; they could outwalk any other breed of cattle. It was this last attribute that brought the Texas Longhorns out of their native habitat and onto the pages of history to create the romantic era of the cowboys, the long drives, and riproaring trail towns of the Great Plains.

The drives began even before Texas became a state. A few enterprising adventurers occasionally would round up a herd out of the brush and drive them overland to Galveston or Shreveport where the animals were sold mainly for their hides and tallow. After the California gold rush of 1849 created a demand for meat, a few daring young Texans drove herds all the way to the Pacific coast. W. H. Snyder put together an outfit that moved out of Texas into New Mexico, and then crossed Colorado, Wyoming, Utah, and Nevada. After two years Snyder finally got his Longhorns to the miners. Captain Jack Cureton of the Texas Rangers followed a southern route across New Mexico and Arizona, dodging Apaches all the way, but from the meat-hungry goldseekers Cureton took a profit of $20,000, a considerable fortune in those days.

In the early 1850s a young English emigrant named Tom Candy Ponting probably established the record for the longest trail drive of Longhorns. Ponting was engaged in the livestock business in Illinois when he learned of the easy availability of Longhorns in Texas. Late in 1852 he and his partner traveled there on horseback, carrying a small bag of gold coins. They had no trouble assembling a herd of 700 bawling Longhorns at nine dollars or less a head. Early in 1853 they headed north for Illinois. It was a rainy spring and Ponting and his partner had to hire Cherokees to help swim the cattle across the Arkansas River. "I sat on my horse every night while we were crossing through the Indian country," said Ponting. "I was so afraid I could not sleep in the tent, but we had no stampede." Missouri was still thinly settled, and there was plenty of vegetation to keep the Longhorns from losing weight. At St. Louis the animals were ferried across the Mississippi, and on July 26, Ponting and his cattle reached Christian County, Illinois.

There through the winter months he fed them on corn, which cost him fifteen cents a bushel.

"Day of the Longhorns" by Dee Brown. This article is reprinted from the January 1975 issue of *American History Illustrated* 9, pp. 4–9, 42–48 with the permission of Cowles History Group, Inc. Copyright *American History Illustrated* magazine.

He sold off a few scrubs to traveling cattle buyers, and then in the spring he cut out the best of the herd and started trail driving again, this time toward the East. At Muncie, Ponting found that railroad cars were available for livestock transport to New York. "We made arrangements and put the cattle on the cars. We unloaded them at Cleveland, letting them jump out on the sand banks. We unloaded them next to Dunkirk, then at Harnesville, and then at Bergen Hill." On July 3, 1854, from Bergen Hill in New Jersey, Ponting ferried the much-traveled Longhorns across the Hudson to the New York cattle market, completing a two-year journey of 1,500 miles on foot and 600 miles by rail. They were the first Texas Longhorns to reach New York City.

"The cattle are rather long-legged though fine-horned, with long taper horns, and something of a wild look," reported the New York *Tribune.* "The expense from Texas to Illinois was about two dollars a head, the owners camping all the way. From Illinois to New York, the expense was seventeen dollars a head." To the New York buyers the Longhorns were worth eighty dollars a head. Tom Ponting had more than doubled his investment.

About this same time another young adventurer from Illinois, Charles Goodnight, was trying to build up his own herd of Longhorns in the Brazos River country. As a young boy Goodnight had journeyed to Texas with his family, riding much of the way bareback. When he was 21, he and his stepbrother went to work for a rancher, keeping watch over 400 skittish Longhorns and branding the calves. Their pay for this work was one-fourth of the calves born during the year. "As the end of the first year's branding resulted in only thirty-two calves for our share," Goodnight recalled afterward, "and as the value was about three dollars per head, we figured out that we had made between us, not counting expenses, ninety-six dollars."

Goodnight and his partner persevered, however, and after four years of hard work they owned a herd of 4,000. Before they could convert many of their animals into cash, however, the Civil War began. Goodnight soon found himself scouting for a company of Confederate mounted riflemen and spent most of the war disputing control of the upper Brazos and Red River country with Comanches and Kiowas instead of with blue-coated Yankees. At the war's end his makeshift uniform was worn out, his Confederate money was worthless, and his Longhorn herd had virtually disappeared. "I suffered great loss," Goodnight said. "The Confederate authorities had taken many of my cattle without paying a cent. Indians had raided our herds and cattle thieves were branding them, to their own benefit without regard to our rights." He was 30 years old and financially destitute.

Almost every other Texan returning from the war found himself in the same situation. When rumors reached the cattle country early in the spring of 1866 that meat was in short supply in the North, hundreds of young Texans began rounding up Longhorns. Huge packing houses were being constructed in Northern cities, and on a 345-acre tract where nine railroads converged, the Chicago Union Stock Yards was opened for business. A Longhorn steer worth five dollars in useless Confederate money in Texas would bring forty dollars in good U.S. currency in the Chicago market.

From the brush country, the plains, and the coastal regions of Texas, mounted drivers turned herd after herd of cattle northward across Indian Territory. Their goal was the nearest railhead, Sedalia, in west-central Missouri. Following approximately the route used by Tom Ponting thirteen years earlier, the trail drivers forded Red River and moved on to Fort Gibson, where they had to cross the more formidable Arkansas. Plagued by unseasonable cold weather, stampedes, and flooded streams, they pushed their Longhorns on into southeastern Kansas.

Here they encountered real trouble. From Baxter Springs northward to Sedalia railhead, the country was being settled by small farmers, many of them recent battlefield enemies of the Texans. The settlers did not want their fences wrecked and their crops trampled, and they used force in stopping the Texans from driving cattle across their properties. By summer's end, over 100,000 stalled cattle were strung out between Baxter

Springs and Sedalia. The grass died or was burned off by defiant farmers. Dishonest cattle buyers from the North bought herds with bad checks. The unsold cattle died or were abandoned, and the great drives of 1866 came to an end. For many of the Texans it had been a financial bust.

A less optimistic folk might have gone home defeated, but not the cattlemen of Texas. By the spring of 1867 many were ready to drive Longhorns north again. And in that year, thanks to an enterprising Yankee stockman, a convenient shipping point was waiting to welcome their coming. At the end of the Civil War, Joseph McCoy of Springfield, Illinois, had started a business of buying livestock for resale to the new packing houses in Chicago. Appalled by the Baxter Springs—Sedalia debacle of 1866, McCoy was determined to find a railroad shipping point somewhere at the end of an open trail from Texas. He studied the maps of new railroads being built westward and chose a town in Kansas—Abilene, near the end of the Kansas Pacific Railroad.

"Abilene in 1867 was a very small, dead place," McCoy admitted. But it met all the requirements for a cattle-shipping town. It was west of the settled farming country; it had a railroad, a river full of water for thirsty steers, and a sea of grass for miles around for holding and fattening livestock at the end of the drives. And nearby was Fort Riley, offering protection from possible Indian raids.

Within sixty days McCoy managed to construct a shipping yard, a barn, an office, and a hotel. From the Kansas Pacific he wheedled railroad ties to build loading pens sturdy enough to hold wild Longhorns. Meanwhile, he had sent messengers southward to inform the cattlemen of Texas that Abilene was "a good safe place to drive to, where they could sell, or ship cattle unmolested to other markets."

Over what soon became known as the Chisholm Trail, thousands of Texas cattle began moving into Abilene. Although the 1867 season got off to a late start and rail shipments did not begin until September, 36,000 Longhorns were marketed that first year. In 1868 the number doubled, and in 1870 the Kansas Pacific could scarcely find enough cars to handle the 300,000 Longhorns sold to Northern packing houses. Abilene in the meantime had grown into a boom town of stores, hotels, saloons, and honkytonks where Texas cowboys celebrated the end of their trail drive and engendered the legends of gunmen, lawmen, shootouts, and exotic dance-hall girls.

One Texas cowman who did not make the long drive north to Abilene was Charles Goodnight. Back in the spring of 1866 when most of his neighbors were driving herds across Indian Territory for the Sedalia railhead, Goodnight was still trying to round up his scattered Longhorns. By the time he was ready to move out, he suspected that there was going to be a glut of cattle in Kansas and Missouri. Instead of heading north, he combined his Longhorns with those of Oliver Loving and they started their herd of 2,000 west toward New Mexico. Cattle were reported to be in great demand there by government agents who bought them for distribution to reservation Indians.

To reach New Mexico, Goodnight and Loving followed the abandoned route of the Butterfield Overland Stage along which waterholes and wells had been dug by the stage company. For this arduous journey, Goodnight constructed what was probably the first chuck-wagon. Obtaining an old military wagon, he rebuilt it with the toughest wood he knew, a wood used by Indians for fashioning their bows—Osage orange or *bois d'arc*. At the rear he built a chuckbox with a hinged lid to which a folding leg was attached so that when it was lowered it formed a cook's work table. Fastened securely in front of the wagon was a convenient spigot running through to a barrel of water. Beneath the driver's seat was a supply of necessary tools such as axes and spades, and below the wagon was a cowhide sling for transporting dry wood or buffalo chips to be used in making cooking fires. A generation of trail drivers would adopt Goodnight's chuck-wagon for long drives and roundups, and variations of it are still used today.

Goodnight's and Loving's first drive to New Mexico was uneventful until they began crossing the lower edge of the Staked Plains, where the water holes had gone dry. For three days the rangy Longhorns became almost unmanageable from thirst, and when they scented the waters of the Pecos they stampeded, piling into the river, some drowning under the onrush of those in the rear. The partners succeeded, however, in driving most of the herd into Fort Sumner, where several thousand Navajos confined in the Bosque Redondo were near starvation.

A government contractor took more than half the Longhorns, paying Goodnight and Loving $12,000 in gold. By the standards of the day they had suddenly become prosperous. While Loving drove the remainder of the cattle to the Colorado mining country, Goodnight returned to Texas to round up another herd of Longhorns.

In the years immediately following the disruptions of the Civil War, thousands of unbranded Longhorns roamed wild in the Texas brush country. The cowboys soon discovered that the easiest way to round up these cattle was to lure them out of the chaparral with tame decoys. James H. Cook, an early trail driver who later became a leading cattleman of the West, described such a wild Longhorn roundup:

"About sunrise we left the corral, taking with us the decoy herd, Longworth leading the way. After traveling a mile or more he led the herd into a dense clump of brush and motioned us to stop driving it. Then, telling two men to stay with the cattle he rode off, signaling the other men and myself to follow him . . . in the brush ahead I caught a glimpse of some cattle. A few minutes later I heard voices singing a peculiar melody without words. The sounds of these voices indicated that the singers were scattered in the form of a circle about the cattle. In a few moments some of the cattle came toward me, and I recognized a few of them as belonging to the herd which we had brought from our camp. In a few seconds more I saw that we had some wild ones, too. They whirled back when they saw me, only to find a rider wherever they might turn. The decoy cattle were fairly quiet, simply milling around through the thicket, and the wild ones were soon thoroughly mingled with them." Cook and the other cowboys now had little difficulty driving the combined tame and wild Longhorns into a corral where they were held until time to start an overland drive to market.

The work of rounding up Longhorns gradually developed into an organized routine directed by a man who came to be known as the range boss. During a roundup, his authority was as ironclad as that of a ship's captain. At the beginning of a "gather" the range boss would assemble an outfit of about twenty cowhands, a horse wrangler to look after the mounts and, most important of all, a camp cook. Roundups began very early in the spring because every cattleman was eager to be the first to hit the trail before the grass overgrazed along the route to Kansas.

On the first morning of a roundup the men would be up before sunrise to eat their breakfasts hurriedly at the chuckwagon; then in the gray light of dawn they would mount their best ponies and gather around the range boss for orders. As soon as he had outlined the limits of the day's roundup, the boss would send his cowhands riding out in various directions to sweep the range. When each rider reached a specified point; he turned back and herded all the cattle within his area back into the camp center.

After a herd was collected, the second operation of a roundup began. This next step was to separate the young stock which were to be branded for return to the range from the mature animals which were to be driven overland to market. "Cutting out" it was fittingly called, and this performance was, and still is, the highest art of the cowboy. Cutting out required a specially trained pony, one that could "turn on a dime," and a rider who had a sharp eye, good muscular reflexes, and who was an artist at handling a lariat. After selecting an animal to be separated from the herd, the rider and his horse would begin a quick-moving game of twisting and turning, of sudden stops and changes of pace.

Roping, the final act of the cutting out process, also required close cooperation between pony and rider. Forming an oval-shaped noose six or seven feet in diameter, the cowboy would spin it over his head with tremendous

The Old Chisholm Trail by Clara McDonald Williamson. Between 1867 and 1887, a total of 5.5 million head of Texas Longhorns were trailed north.

speed. A second before making the throw, he would draw his arm and shoulder back, then shoot his hand forward, aiming the noose sometimes for the animal's head, sometimes for its feet. As the lariat jerked tight, the rider instantly snubbed it around his saddle horn. At the same moment the pony had to be stopped short. The position of the pony at the moment of throw was important; a sudden jerk of a taut lariat could spill both horse and rider.

As soon as the unbranded animal was roped, it was immediately herded or dragged to the nearest bonfire where branding irons were kept heated to an orange red. In Texas, all branding was done in a corral, a legal requirement devised to prevent hasty and illegal branding by rustlers on the open range. The first brands in Texas were usually the initials of the owners, and if two cattlemen had the same initials, a bar or a circle distinguished one from the other. Law required that brands be publicly registered by counties in Texas; other Western states had state brand books. In the early years when ranches were unfenced and land boundaries poorly marked, friction over unbranded cattle caused many a gunfight. To discourage rustlers who could easily change a "C" to an "O," an "F" to an "E," a "V" to a "W," ranchers designed unusual brands, some of the more famous being the Stirrup, Andiron, Scissors, Frying Pan, and Dinner Bell.

As soon as the work of branding was completed, preparations for the trail drive began in earnest. The owner of the cattle was responsible for food and other supplies, but each cowboy assembled the personal gear he would need on the journey. Every item he wore or carried was designed for utility. Tents were seldom taken along, two blankets being considered sufficient shelter from the elements. If the weather was warm, the cowboys shed their coats, and if they wore vests they rarely buttoned them because of the rangeland belief that to do so would bring on a bad cold. Most wore leather chaps to protect their legs from underbrush and weather. They put high heels on their boots to keep their feet from slipping through the stirrups, and they wore heavy leather gloves because the toughest palms could be burned raw by the lariats they used constantly in their work. They paid good money for wide-brimmed hats because they served as roofs against rain, snow, and sun. They used bandannas for ear coverings, as dust masks, as strainers when drinking muddy water, for drying dishes, as bandages, towels, slings for broken arms, to tie hats on in very windy weather, and for countless other purposes.

Getting the average trail herd of about 3,000 cattle underway was as complicated an operation as starting a small army on a march across country. Each rider needed several spare mounts for the long journey, and this herd of horses accompanying a cow column was known as the remuda—from a Spanish word meaning replacement. A trail boss, sixteen to eighteen cowboys, a cook and chuckwagon, and a horse wrangler for the remuda made up the personnel of an average drive.

It was necessary to move slowly at first until the restive Longhorns grew accustomed to daily routines. To keep a herd in order a wise trail boss would search out a huge dominating animal and make it the lead steer. Charles Goodnight had one called Old Blue which he considered so valuable as a leader that after every long drive he brought the animal back to the home ranch. Two or three

quiet days on the trail was usually long enough to calm a herd of Longhorns. After that the cattle would fall into place each morning like infantrymen on the march, each one keeping the same relative position in file as the herd moved along.

Cattleman John Clay left a classic description of an early trail herd in motion: "You see a steer's head and horns silhouetted against the skyline, and then another and another, till you realize it is a herd. On each flank is a horseman. Along come the leaders with a swinging gait, quickening as they smell the waters of the muddy river." The pattern of trail driving soon became as routinized as that of roundups—the trail boss a mile or two out in front, horse herd and chuckwagon following, then the point riders directing the lead steers, and strung along the widening flow of the herd the swing and flank riders, until at the rear came the drag riders in clouds of dust, keeping the weaker cattle moving.

Not many trail drivers had time to keep diaries, that of George Duffield being one of the rare survivors. From it a reader can feel the tensions and weariness, the constant threats of weather, the difficult river crossings, and dangers of stampedes.

MAY 1: Big stampede. Lost 200 head of Cattle.

MAY 2: Spent the day hunting & found but 25 Head. It has been Raining for three days. These are dark days for me.

MAY 3: Day spent in hunting Cattle. Found 23. Hard rain and wind. Lots of trouble.

MAY 8: Rain pouring down in torrents. Ran my horse into a ditch & got my Knee badly sprained—15 miles.

MAY 9: Still dark and gloomy. River up. Everything looks Blue to me.

MAY 14: Swam our cattle & Horses & built Raft & Rafted our provisions & blanket & covers. Lost Most of our Kitchen furniture such as camp Kittles Coffee Pots Cups Plates Canteens &tc &tc.

MAY 17: No Breakfast. Pack & off is the order.

MAY 31: Swimming Cattle is the order. We worked all day in the River & at dusk got the last Beefe over—I am now out of Texas—This day will long be remembered by me—There was one of the our party Drowned today.

George Duffield made his drive along the eastern edge of Indian Territory in 1866. Ten years later the drives were still as wearisome and dangerous, but the trails had shifted much further westward and there had been a swift succession of trail towns. A new railroad, the Sante Fe, pushed sixty-five miles south of Abilene in 1871, and Newton became the main cattle-shipping town. Newton's reign was brief, however; it was replaced by Ellsworth and Wichita. Although the advancing railroad tracks were a boon to cattlemen seeking shorter routes to markets, they also brought settlers west by the thousands. By 1876 the life of the Chisholm Trail was ending and the Western Trail, or Dodge City Trail, had taken its place.

Dodge City was the king of the trail towns, the "cowboy capital," a fabulous town of innumerable legends for a golden decade. The names survive in history: Long Branch Saloon, the Lady Gay, the Dodge Opera House, Delmonico's, Wyatt Earp, Doc Holliday, Boot Hill, Bat Masterson, Clay Allison, Luke Short, and Big Nose Kate. But it was Longhorns and cattlemen that made Dodge City, and it was during Dodge's long reign that the Longhorns came to the end of their day of glory.

One of the men responsible for the change was Charles Goodnight. In the year that Dodge opened as a cow town, 1875, Goodnight found himself financially destitute for the second time in his life. He had made a fortune with Texas cattle, bought a ranch in Colorado, become a banker, and then lost everything in the Panic of 1873. All he had left in 1875 was a small herd of unmarketable Longhorns, and he decided it was time to return to Texas and start all over again.

He chose an unlikely region, the Texas Panhandle, an area long shunned by cattlemen because it was supposed to be a desert. Goodnight, however, recalled the immense herds of buffalo which had roamed there for centuries, and he reasoned that wherever buffalo could thrive so could Longhorns. He found a partner, John Adair, to furnish the capital and drove his Longhorns into the heart of the Panhandle, to the Palo Duro Canyon, where he discovered plenty of water and grass. There he founded the JA Ranch. Soon after starting operations, Goodnight began introducing Herefords and shorthorns, cross-breeding them at first with Longhorns so that his cattle produced more and better beef, yet retained the ability to flourish on the open range and endure long drives to Dodge City.

Other ranchers soon followed his example, and "White Faces" instead of "Longhorns" gradually became the symbol of trail cattle. After a continuing flood of homesteaders, brought west by the proliferating railroads, made it necessary to close the trail to Dodge City, one more overland route—the National Trail to Wyoming and Montana—saw the last treks of the Longhorns.

As the nineteenth century came to an end, so did open range ranching and trail driving. There was no longer any place for rangy Longhorns. Until the day he died, however, Charles Goodnight kept a small herd of them to remind him of the old days. A few specimens survive today in wildlife refuges and on larger ranches as curiosities, or for occasional use in parades and Western movies. But most of these animals are descendants of crossbreds. The day of the genuine Texas Longhorn—with his body tucked up in the flanks, his high shoulder-top thin enough to split a hail stone, his ribs flat, his back swayed, his ability to outwalk any other breed of cattle—now belongs to history.

STUDY QUESTIONS

1. What were the origins of the Texas Longhorns? Why were they so well suited for the long drive?

2. How did the Civil War affect the cattle business?

3. Why did Joseph McCoy choose to drive cattle to Abilene?

4. What was life like on the long drive?

5. Why did the drive end?

BIBLIOGRAPHY

Ray Allen Billington's *The Far Western Frontier* (1963) and *Westward Expansion* (1974) are excellent introductions to the westward movement. Ernest S. Osgood, *The Day of the Cattlemen* (1929) is a classic work on the subject, and Lewis Atherton, *The Cattle Kings* (1961) is a more recent study. Gene M. Gressley, *Bankers and Cattlemen* (1966) deals with Eastern as well as Western interests. Wayne Gard, *The Chisholm Trail* (1954) is an outstanding study of the Long Drive, and J. Frank Dobie's *The Longhorns* (1941) tells the story delightfully well. Robert R. Dykstra, *The Cattle Town* (1968) and Joe B. Frantz and J. E. Choate, *The American Cowboy* (1981) remove the myths that surround their subjects.

Photo Acknowledgments